OLD TESTAMENT STUDIES

Editor
David Reimer

Published under

JOURNAL FOR THE STUDY OF THE OLD TESTAMENT SUPPLEMENT SERIES
406

In Search of Pre-exilic Israel

Proceedings of the Oxford Old Testament Seminar

edited by
John Day

T & T CLARK INTERNATIONAL
A Continuum imprint
LONDON • NEW YORK

Copyright © 2004 T&T Clark International
A Continuum imprint

Published by T&T Clark International
The Tower Building, 11 York Road, London SE1 7NX
15 East 26th Street, Suite 1703, New York, NY 10010

www.tandtclark.com

British Library Cataloguing-in-Publication Data
A catalogue record for this book is available from the British Library

ISBN 0 56708196 6 (hardback)
      0 56708206 7 (paperback)

Typeset by Data Standards Ltd, Frome, Somerset BA11 1RE
Printed on acid-free paper in Great Britain by Antony Rowe Ltd,
Chippenham, Wiltshire.

CONTENTS

PREFACE

This volume consists of seventeen essays which were originally delivered as papers to the Oxford Old Testament seminar between January 2001 and June 2003, and which have subsequently been revised and often expanded. The purpose of this volume is to offer a critique of various aspects of the 'everything is late' school of thought in Old Testament studies that has been fashionable in some circles in recent years, not from any reactionary standpoint but from a thoroughly reasoned, critical point of view. We hope to show that though much of the editing of the Old Testament took place in the exilic and post-exilic periods, we do nevertheless have access to pre-exilic sources of information about ancient Israel greater than some recent scholars have allowed.

I am extremely grateful to all the many distinguished contributors who so readily agreed to participate in this enterprise, some from within Oxford, others from elsewhere in the United Kingdom, and yet others who travelled vast distances from overseas in order to address the Oxford seminar. In particular I am indebted to one of the participants, my colleague Professor John Barton, who facilitated the project by enabling me to take over for such a long period the organization of the deliberations of the seminar which he normally convenes. I also wish to thank T. & T. Clark International for publishing this work, and to express gratitude to all their staff who have been involved with its production. A word of thanks is also due to Dr Duncan Burns, who undertook the laborious task of compiling the Indexes as well as assisting me in other ways.

This is now the second series of published proceedings of the Oxford Old Testament seminar, the first of which appeared under my editorship as *King and Messiah in Israel and the Ancient Near East* (JSOTSup, 270; Sheffield: Sheffield Academic Press, 1996). A third volume, *Temple and Worship in Ancient Israel,* based on an Oxford Old Testament seminar series which ran concurrently with the series on *In Search of Pre-exilic Israel,* will be published shortly after the appearance of the present volume.

John Day

Acknowledgments

Gratitude is expressed to the following for permission to reprint images on pp. 93 and 94.

Fig. 1a, nos. 1, 2, 8, and fig. 1b, nos. 7, 12, 13, courtesy of the Israel Exploration Society.
Fig. 1a, nos. 4, 5, 6, courtesy of the Oriental Institute of the University of Chicago.
Fig. 1a, no. 7, and 1b, nos. 8, 9, 10, 11, printed by permission of the Institute of Archaeology of Tel Aviv University.
Fig. 1b, nos. 3, 4, 5, courtesy of the Hebrew Union College/Nelson Glueck School of Biblical Archaeology.
Fig. 1a, nos. 9, 10, and fig. 1b, nos. 1, 2, courtesy of the Hebrew University of Jerusalem Institute of Archaeology.
Fig. 1a, no. 3, courtesy of the Hebrew University of Jerusalem.
Fig. 1a, no. 11, courtesy of the Palestine Exploration Fund.
Fig. 1b, no. 6, courtesy of Haverford College.

ABBREVIATIONS

AASOR	Annual of the American Schools of Oriental Research
AB	Anchor Bible
ABD	David Noel Freedman, *Anchor Bible Dictionary* (6 vols; New York: Doubleday, 1992)
ABRL	Anchor Bible Reference Library
ADPV	Abhandlungen des deutschen Palästinavereins
AION	*Annali dell'istituto orientale di Napoli*
Alttest. Abhandl.	Alttestamentliche Abhandlungen
AnBib	Analecta biblica
ANET	J.B. Pritchard (ed.), *Ancient Near Eastern Texts Relating to the Old Testament* (Princeton: Princeton University Press, with supplement, 1969, 3rd edn)
Ann.	Annal
AnOr	Analecta orientalia
AOAT	Alter Orient und Altes Testament
AOS	American Oriental Series
ARAB	D.D. Luckenbill, *Ancient Records of Assyria and Babylonia* (2 vols; Chicago: University of Chicago Press, 1926–27)
ASOR	American Schools of Oriental Research
ATD	Das Alte Testament Deutsch
BA	*Biblical Archaeologist*
BAR	British Archaeological Reports
BARev	*Biblical Archaeology Review*
BASOR	*Bulletin of the American Schools of Oriental Research*
BBB	Bonner biblische Beiträge
BDB	Francis Brown, S.R. Driver and Charles A. Briggs, *A Hebrew and English Lexicon of the Old Testament* (Oxford: Clarendon Press, 1907)
BETL	Bibliotheca ephemeridum theologicarum lovaniensium

BHS	*Biblia hebraica stuttgartensia*
Bib	*Biblica*
BibInt	*Biblical Interpretation*
BKAT	Biblischer Kommentar: Altes Testament
BM	British Museum
BO	*Bibliotheca Orientalis*
BR	*Bible Review*
BSOAS	*Bulletin of the School of Oriental and African Studies*
BWANT	Beiträge zur Wissenschaft vom Alten und Neuen Testament
BZAW	Beihefte zur *ZAW*
CAD	Ignace J. Gelb *et al.*, *The Assyrian Dictionary of the Oriental Institute of the University of Chicago* (Chicago: Oriental Institute, 1956–)
CBQ	*Catholic Biblical Quarterly*
ConBOT	Coniectanea biblica, Old Testament
CRAIBL	*Comptes rendus de l'Académie des inscriptions et belles-lettres*
CRINT	Compendia rerum iudaicarum ad Novum Testamentum
DDD	K. van der Toorn, B. Becking and P.W. van der Horst (eds), *Dictionary of Deities and Demons in the Bible* (Leiden: E.J. Brill, and Grand Rapids, MI: W.B. Eerdmans, 1999, 2nd edn)
DJD	Discoveries in the Judaean Desert
Ebib	Etudes bibliques
ET	English Translation
EvT	*Evangelische Theologie*
ExpTim	*Expository Times*
FAT	Forschungen zum Alten Testament
FOTL	The Forms of the Old Testament Literature
FRLANT	Forschungen zur Religion und Literatur des Alten und Neuen Testaments.
FzB	Forschung zur Bibel
GKC	*Gesenius' Hebrew Grammar* (ed. E. Kautzsch, revised and trans. A.E. Cowley; Oxford: Clarendon Press, 1910)
HALOT	L. Koehler, W. Baumgartner, J.J. Stamm *et al.*, *Hebrew and Aramaic Lexicon of the Old Testament* (trans. M.R.J. Richardson; 5 vols; Leiden: E.J. Brill, 1994–2000)
HAR	*Hebrew Annual Review*
HAT	Handbuch zum Alten Testament

HKAT	Göttinger Handkommentar zum Alten Testament
HL	Hammurabi's Laws
HSM	Harvard Semitic Monographs
HSS	Harvard Semitic Studies
HUCA	*Hebrew Union College Annual*
IAA	Israel Antiquities Authority
ICC	International Critical Commentary
IEJ	*Israel Exploration Journal*
Int	*Interpretation*
JANESCU	*Journal of the Ancient Near Eastern Society of Columbia University*
JAOS	*Journal of the American Oriental Society*
JBL	*Journal of Biblical Literature*
JCS	*Journal of Cuneiform Studies*
JEA	*Journal of Egyptian Archaeology*
JJS	*Journal of Jewish Studies*
JNES	*Journal of Near Eastern Studies*
JSOT	*Journal for the Study of the Old Testament*
JSOTSup	*Journal for the Study of the Old Testament, Supplement Series*
JSS	*Journal of Semitic Studies*
JTS	*Journal of Theological Studies*
KAgr	Kuntillet Agrud (Kuntillet ʿAjrud)
KAI	H. Donner and W. Röllig (eds), *Kanaanäische und aramäische Inschriften* (3 vols; Wiesbaden: Otto Harrassowitz, 1962–64; 2002– , 5ᵗʰ edn)
KAT	Kommentar zum Alten Testament
KHAT	Kurzer Hand-Kommentar zum Alten Testament
KTU²	M. Dietrich, O. Loretz, J. Sanmartín, *The Cuneiform Alphabetic Texts from Ugarit, Ras Ibn Hani and Other Places (KTU: Second Enlarged Edition)* (Münster: Ugarit-Verlag, 1995). 2ⁿᵈ edn of M. Dietrich, O. Loretz, J. Sanmartín, *Die keilalphabetischen Texte aus Ugarit* (Neukirchen–Vluyn: Neukirchener Verlag, 1976)
LAPO	Littératures anciennes du Proche-Orient
LCL	Loeb Classical Library
LXX	Septuagint
MA	Middle Assyrian
MAH	Museum siglum of the Musée d'Art et d'Histoire, Geneva
MB	Middle Babylonian
MT	Masoretic Text
NB	Neo-Babylonian

NCB	New Century Bible
NEAEHL	Ephraim Stern (ed.), *The New Encyclopedia of Archaeological Excavations in the Holy Land* (4 vols; Jerusalem: Israel Exploration Society and Carta, and New York: Simon & Schuster, 1993)
NedTTs	*Nederlands theologisch tijdschrift*
NF	Neue Folge
NRSV	New Revised Standard Version
NS	New Series
OB	Old Babylonian
OBO	Orbis biblicus et orientalis
OEANE	Eric M. Meyers (ed.), *The Oxford Encyclopedia of Archaeology in the Near East* (5 vols; New York and Oxford: Oxford University Press, 1997)
OLA	Orientalia lovaniensia analecta
OLZ	*Orientalische Literaturzeitung*
Or	*Orientalia*
OTG	Old Testament Guides
OTL	Old Testament Library
OTS	*Oudtestamentische Studiën*
PBA	*Proceedings of the British Academy*
PEQ	*Palestine Exploration Quarterly*
PJB	*Palästinajahrbuch*
QD	Quaestiones disputatae
RB	*Revue biblique*
RHPR	*Revue d'histoire et de philosophie religieuse*
RS	Ras Shamra
RSO	*Rivista degli studi orientale*
SAAS	State Archives of Assyria Studies
SB	Sources bibliques
SBAB	Stuttgarter biblische Aufsatzbände
SBL	Society of Biblical Literature
SBLDS	Society of Biblical Literature Dissertation Series
SBLMS	Society of Biblical Literature Monograph Series
SBS	Stuttgarter Bibelstudien
SBT	Studies in Biblical Theology
ScrHier	Scripta Hierosolymitana
SEL	*Studi epigrafici e linguistici*
Sem	*Semitica*
SHANE	Studies in the History of the Ancient Near East
SHCANE	Studies in the History and Culture of the Ancient Near East
SJLA	Studies in Judaism in Late Antiquity
SJOT	*Scandinavian Journal of the Old Testament*

SOTSMS	Society for Old Testament Study Monograph Series
STDJ	Studies on the Texts of the Desert of Judah
Str.	Stratum
StudBib	Studia biblica
Summ.	Summary Inscription
TBü	Theologische Bücherei
TCS	Texts from Cuneiform Sources
TDOT	G.J. Botterweck and H. Ringgren (eds), *Theological Dictionary of the Old Testament* (trans. D.E. Green *et al.*; Grand Rapids, MI: W.B. Eerdmans, 1974–)
ThWAT	G.J. Botterweck and H. Ringgren (eds), *Theologisches Wörterbuch zum Alten Testament* (Stuttgart: W. Kohlhammer, 1970–)
TOTC	Tyndale Old Testament Commentaries
TynBul	*Tyndale Bulletin*
TZ	*Theologische Zeitschrift*
UBL	Ugaritisch-biblische Literatur
UCOP	University of Cambridge Oriental Publications
UF	*Ugarit-Forschungen*
VF	*Verkündigung und Forschung*
VT	*Vetus Testamentum*
VTSup	*Vetus Testamentum,* Supplements
WBC	Word Biblical Commentary
WMANT	Wissenschaftliche Monographien zum Alten und Neuen Testament
WO	*Die Welt des Orients*
WSS	N. Avigad and B. Sass, *Corpus of West Semitic Stamp Seals* (Jerusalem: Israel Exploration Society, 1997)
ZAH	*Zeitschrift für Althebraistik*
ZÄS	*Zeitschrift fur ägyptische Sprache*
ZAW	*Zeitschrift für die alttestamentliche Wissenschaft*
ZDPV	*Zeitschrift des deutschen Palästina-Vereins*

LIST OF CONTRIBUTORS

John Barton, Oriel and Laing Professor of the Interpretation of Holy Scripture, University of Oxford, and Fellow of Oriel College, Oxford

Graham Davies, Professor of Old Testament Studies, University of Cambridge, and Fellow and Director of Studies in Theology & Religious Studies of Fitzwilliam College, Cambridge

John Day, Professor of Old Testament Studies, University of Oxford, and Fellow and Tutor of Lady Margaret Hall, Oxford

Katharine J. Dell, Senior Lecturer in Divinity, University of Cambridge, and Fellow, Tutor and Director of Studies in Theology & Religious Studies of St Catharine's College, Cambridge

William G. Dever, formerly Professor of Near Eastern Archaeology and Anthropology, University of Arizona

J.A. Emerton, Emeritus Regius Professor of Hebrew, University of Cambridge, and Fellow of St John's College, Cambridge

Terry Fenton, Senior Lecturer in Biblical Studies, University of Haifa

Anthony J. Frendo, Head of the Department of Arabic and Near Eastern Studies, University of Malta

Walter Houston, Chaplain Fellow in Theology, Mansfield College, Oxford

Gary N. Knoppers, Head of the Department of Classics and Ancient Mediterranean Studies, The Pennsylvania State University

W.G. Lambert, Emeritus Professor of Assyriology, University of Birmingham

André Lemaire, Directeur d'études, Ecole Pratique des Hautes Etudes, Histoire et Philologie, Paris-Sorbonne

Bernard M. Levinson, holder of the Berman Family Chair of Jewish Studies and Hebrew Bible, and Associate Professor of Classical and Near Eastern Studies and of Law, University of Minnesota

B.A. Mastin, formerly Senior Lecturer in Hebrew, University of Wales, Bangor

Ernest Nicholson, Honorary Fellow of Oriel College, Oxford. Formerly Provost of Oriel College, Oxford and previously Oriel Professor of the Interpretation of Holy Scripture, University of Oxford

David J. Reimer, Senior Lecturer in Hebrew and Old Testament Studies, University of Edinburgh

H.G.M. Williamson, Regius Professor of Hebrew, University of Oxford, and Student of Christ Church, Oxford

Chapter 1

CURRENT 'REVISIONISM' AND THE LITERATURE OF THE OLD TESTAMENT

Ernest Nicholson

1. *The Legacy of Hermann Gunkel*

Though the word 'revisionist', defined in *The Oxford English Dictionary* as 'one who advocates or supports revision', implies disapproval and censure of those of whom it is used, there is nothing new in either the principle or the practice of revising received conclusions and opinions. This is so not merely as a result of bringing to bear on the work of earlier generations fresh discoveries or new methods of study, but for its own sake, knowing that no generation is in possession of all truth. This is especially the case in a field of research such as the Hebrew Bible, the complexities and problems of which conspire with the limitations of our own knowledge of such an ancient society to render the task of understanding and interpretation a task that each new generation must freshly undertake. The principle of such a task was well formulated by one of the founders of modern British historiography, Bishop Stubbs (1825–1901), who wrote 'History knows that it can wait for more evidence and review its older verdicts; it offers an endless series of courts of appeal, and is ever ready to re-open closed cases'.[1] The practice of looking again at verdicts and conclusions arrived at by scholars and subjecting them to fresh thought and revision is nothing new in biblical studies. Indeed the modern history of the subject is one of virtually constant revision.

One hundred years ago Old Testament study was entering a new stage of research that was to offer a markedly revised understanding of Israelite origins and history, of the creative stages in the emergence of Israelite religion, as well as of the development of Israelite traditions and institutions and, not least of all, of the history of the literature involving a study of the traditional literary 'types' or 'forms' (*Gattungen*) reflected or employed in the composition of the literature. More than any other scholar it was Hermann Gunkel who pioneered the new methods of

---

1. Cited in J.R. Hale 1967: 58.

research.[2] If nineteenth-century research had shown of the literature of the Old Testament that 'there is more here than meets the eye', the new methods introduced by Gunkel sought to show that 'there is still more, indeed much more here than meets the eye'. Thus in his commentary on Genesis (Gunkel 1901, ET 1997) he sought to penetrate behind the relatively late literary sources of Genesis, which research hitherto had uncovered, to earlier stages in the formation of the stories about the patriarchs and the emergence, still in the pre-literary stage, of 'cycles' of these stories. In his study of creation mythology (Gunkel 1895), he illustrated the possibility of finding much earlier elements of ancient tradition in the literature of the Old Testament, including such a relatively late text as Genesis 1. And where Gunkel led, many followed with results that transformed our knowledge of ancient Israel and the literary remains that have come down to us in the Hebrew Bible.

The new methods and the results they yielded worked a virtual revolution in what scholars believed they could ascertain about early periods of Israelite history and tradition, and about the history of the literature. Thus Albrecht Alt, one of Gunkel's most distinguished pupils, in his influential essay on 'The God of the Fathers' in 1929 (ET 1966) commented that as a result of recent developments in Old Testament study 'the prehistory of Israel now seemed as a whole to grow more important and easier to understand than in the research of the previous generations'.[3] This essay was itself a striking example of what Alt believed to be now possible, since it endeavoured to uncover traces of the nature of the gods worshipped by Israel's ancestors and to compare this cult with the worship of Yahweh by the Israelite tribes of a subsequent time.

Alt had earlier published a study of far-reaching significance in 'The Settlement of the Israelites in Palestine' (Alt 1925, ET 1966). Here he argued that Israelite origins are to be traced to semi-nomadic people who dwelt on the desert fringes of Palestine whence they migrated annually into the sown land in search of summer pastures for their herds. Over a protracted period numerous of these semi-nomadic clans settled permanently in the land where initially they inhabited the sparsely populated areas, especially the hill country, well away from centres of Canaanite population; it was only at a later stage of territorial expansion that conflict took place between them and the indigenous population of the Canaanite city-states.

This understanding of Israelite origins provided the basis for a new understanding of pre-monarchic Israel developed and presented by one of

---

2. On Gunkel and these methods and his writings see Klatt 1969. Douglas Knight's book (1974) remains the best introduction in English to the development of these methods and results achieved.

3. The quotation is from the English translation, Alt 1966: 4.

Alt's most distinguished pupils, Martin Noth, in his celebrated mono-graph *Das System der zwölf Stämme Israels* (Noth 1930). Building upon Alt's findings, Noth argued his well-known theory that pre-monarchical Israel took the form of a twelve-tribe confederation whose worship of Yahweh and sacral institutions and traditions, it was argued, were crucially formative of the future history of Israel and of the peculiar development of Israelite religion. On the analogy of the city-state leagues later attested in Greece and known to the Greeks as 'amphictyonies', Noth described the Israelite confederation as an 'amphictyony', the communal cultic life of which focused upon a central sanctuary recognized by all the tribes. Noth argued that the narrative in Joshua 24 preserves the memory of the founding of the Israelite 'amphictyony' at Shechem under the leadership of Joshua by means of a covenant binding all the tribes to the worship of Yahweh. The narrative also reflects an annually recurring festival celebrating the covenant between Yahweh and the confederation.

Thus, if Gunkel had provided the methods for understanding earlier stages in the history of Israelite traditions and literature, Noth's study now provided the social, religious and cultic context in which their beginnings and initial development could be investigated.

During the post-Second World War period the theory of an early Israelite 'amphictyony' and its institutions commanded widespread acceptance internationally. Popular textbooks such as Noth's *The History of Israel* (1950, ET 1960) as well as Bernhard W. Anderson's *The Living World of the Old Testament* (Anderson 1958) and John Bright's *A History of Israel* (Bright 1960) became staple reading for students and were prescribed as standard texts in courses of biblical studies.

Not least among the reasons for this were the manifold ways in which such an understanding of early Israel offered a key for explaining much else in the study of the Old Testament and of the history of ancient Israel. Thus it was against the background of the history and institutions of the tribal confederation, especially its central cult, that Noth himself endeavoured to trace the formation and development of the Pentateuchal traditions and of their combination to form a Pentateuchal *Grundlage* from Moses to the settlement (Noth 1948, ET 1972). Similarly, though with a different approach from that of Noth, Gerhard von Rad's influential monograph on the Yahwist source in the Hexateuch (von Rad 1938, ET 1966) – itself a landmark in twentieth-century scholarship – also presupposed this understanding of early Israel. One major result of von Rad's monograph was to redate the work of J to the tenth century – a dating that was subsequently widely adopted.

The central role of the covenant in the formation and ordering of the relations between the tribes, and the celebration of an annual covenant renewal festival provided a new *Sitz im Leben* for investigating the origin and peculiar nature of Israelite law. The so-called 'apodeictic' commands were traced to this setting and pointed to a long transmission and development of the sacral law governing the relationship between Israel and Yahweh (see Alt 1934, ET 1966; Noth 1940, ET 1966). The covenant with its laws and sanctions offered also a solution to the basis of the ethical teaching of the great prophets. No longer seen as innovators of a new ethical dimension into Israel's relation with God, the prophets were now understood as standing in the ancient tradition of the covenant, their proclamation of Yahweh's law deriving from the covenant cult, which was still celebrated annually in their day, and their announcement of judgment reflecting the threat of curse if Israel failed to observe the covenant law (see, e.g., Clements 1965). The so-called 'covenant festival' provided the *Sitz im Leben* also for a new approach to the study of the Psalms, the particular literary forms of which had already been freshly illuminated by Gunkel's form-critical analysis. Increasingly the Psalms were now viewed as 'fragments of liturgy' from the cult of the pre-exilic Temple in Jerusalem (see Weiser 1959, ET 1962; Mowinckel 1951, ET 1962).

In these ways the literature of the Old Testament was more and more related closely to the life of the people over many generations, whether in the national cult with its annual festivals, the transmission of sacral law, in the many forms (*Gattungen*) from distinctive settings in life which speakers and writers employed, or in stories reflecting folk literary forms and in the work of accomplished authors.

Though there was much variation in detail among scholars and no lack of controversy on issues such as the background of the patriarchal traditions, the nature of the settlement of the tribes in Palestine, and the early relationship between the Exodus and Sinai traditions, we can speak of a broad consensus on the new understanding of pre-monarchical Israel and its institutions and major traditions, and the possibility this offered for the study of other major issues in Old Testament research and not least of all on the history of the literature of the Old Testament.

2. *Questions Revisited and Reopened*

From the 1960s onwards, however, and with increasing momentum the conclusions which commanded such a consensus of the mid-twentieth century were one by one subjected to fresh critical review and revision. Little has remained intact. A number of studies effectively undermined the credibility of the theory of an early Israelite 'amphictyony' and with it the social and religious context that had provided the background and basis of other widely accepted results of research (see Mayes 1974; de Geus 1976). A new theory of Israelite origins according to which the tribes of Israel emerged from within the population of Canaan was advanced against the hitherto prevailing view of settlement by groups from outside the land. The view was once again argued that in writing a history of pre-exilic Israel one had to begin with the narratives of the reign of David for lack of any firm ground under foot prior to the tenth century (e.g. Soggin 1984). The antiquity of the tradition of a covenant between Israel and Yahweh, so central to the understanding of early Israel as a sacral league of tribes, was compellingly challenged in a detailed study by Lothar Perlitt, who reargued the case for a much later coining of the notion of such a covenant among Deuteronomic circles (Perlitt 1969). A new debate on the supposed antiquity of the patriarchal traditions was opened by substantial studies by John Van Seters and Thomas L. Thompson, who placed the origin of these traditions either in the early first millennium BCE (Thompson 1974) or as late as the exilic period (Van Seters 1975). Concurrently, Alt's influential study 'The God of the Fathers' was critically re-examined.[4] Von Rad's much favoured view of the Yahwist source as a product of a supposed 'Solomonic enlightenment'[5] of the tenth century was challenged in favour of a much later origin, much closer to the period of the Deuteronomistic literature, and a trend set in which places the work of the Yahwist no earlier than the exilic period.[6] Other texts usually considered to be early, for example the so-called 'court history of David' (2 Sam. 9–20; 1 Kgs 1–2), which was widely believed to have been composed not long after the events it narrates, was likewise assigned to a much later, post-exilic author (Van Seters 1983: 277–91).

These reversals of hitherto widely accepted conclusions seemed drastic enough, and the dating of the Yahwist to such a late period, even later than Deuteronomy, as some proposed, was generally viewed as an excessively radical shift. More recently, however, there has come a markedly more extreme phase of revision according to which nothing in the Old Testament or at best only some 'relics' can be assigned to the pre-exilic period. Rather, it is argued, the literature of the Old Testament virtually as a whole was composed no earlier than the Persian period or even as late as the Hellenistic period and was motivated by ideological or 'propagandist' goals. Further, the pre-exilic period as presented in the Old Testament or as reconstructed by historical scholarship is very largely a fiction. Concomitant with this, the composition of the literature of the Old Testament, far from being the deposit of centuries of writers and redactors

---

4. See Diebner 1975; Cross 1973: 3–12. A review of the debate about Alt's conclusions is offered in, for example, Köckert 1988.

5. For a review of the idea of a so-called 'Solomonic Enlightenment' see Barton (1984). Earlier critical assessments of it are, for example, Scott (1955), Noth (1955), and Whybray (1982).

6. H.H. Schmid's lively monograph (1976) and John Van Seters's study of the Patriarchal traditions (Van Seters 1975) were among the first of a number of recent studies arguing for such a late dating of the Yahwist source. For the literature and an assessment see Nicholson 1998.

and reflecting the changing circumstances in the life and history of the nation, has been 'concertinaed' into the work of a body of scribes commissioned to author an official 'national story' on behalf of a community of immigrants who entered and occupied Judah from elsewhere in the Persian Empire and whose ancestry had never been part of the historic population of the land of Israel. We have indeed come a long way not merely from the main results of twentieth-century research but also from those of the nineteenth century.

This new 'revisionism' is primarily associated with scholars such as Philip Davies, Niels Peter Lemche, Thomas L. Thompson, and the late Robert Carroll, who have in common the view that the biblical literature is incorrectly classified as historiography and is best understood as 'ideology'. The term 'ideology' has become ubiquitous in contemporary biblical scholarship, and its use, and the extreme revisionist tendency that has been constructed by means of it, have been the subject of a characteristically incisive review and critique by James Barr (2000), the title of which, *History and Ideology in the Old Testament*, is itself witness to the place that so-called 'ideology criticism' has currently gained. [7] What follows offers support for various critical observations he has made. I have limited myself to the conclusions of two scholars who are in a number of ways the leading protagonists of these new views: Philip Davies, whose lively and provocative advocacy of this new 'revisionism' has attracted widespread attention, and Thomas L. Thompson, whose conclusions would place the composition of the Old Testament as late as the second century BCE (Davies 1995; 1996; Thompson 1998). [8]

3. *'Ancient Israel' and its Literature*

3.1.

According to Davies (1995,[9] esp. ch. 4) we must distinguish between no less than three Israels. Previous scholarship has left us with an 'ancient Israel', which he places between inverted commas, to distinguish it from the biblical Israel and the historical Israel. The last, historical Israel, existed in the northern and central Palestinian highlands between roughly the ninth and the late eighth centuries BCE and has left traces in the soil of Palestine over a couple of centuries. Its existence as an independent state came to an end in the late eighth century when it became a province of the Assyrian empire. It is unlikely that the Judaean state evolved independ-

---

7. For a discussion of the variety of ways in which the word is employed currently in theology and biblical studies see Barr 2000, especially ch. 5.

8. For an incisive critique of Lemche's key position see Barstad (2002).

9. References here are to the 1995 edition which, though described as a reprint of the first edition (1992), has a somewhat different pagination.

ently of the relatively more powerful state of Israel. It may have been 'formed as a secondary state, perhaps in the ninth century, and possibly by the Assyrians' (66). There was no so-called 'united monarchy', as described by the authors of biblical Israel, uniting the people who inhabited the northern highlands with those who inhabited the Judaean hill country. The Davidic–Solomonic 'empire' is a fiction.

Biblical Israel is a 'literary construct' that emerged as a political-cultural product of the Jerusalem 'establishment' based on the Temple there, perhaps also in the court of the Governor, and was the work of schools of state scribes during the Persian Period who sought to provide a cultural, political and ideological identity for the newly formed state of Yehud established by the Persian imperial authorities.

'Ancient Israel' is a 'scholarly creation', an amalgam of biblical Israel and historical Israel. It 'owes nearly everything to Bible reading, nothing to critical reflection, and very little indeed to historical research' (29). That is, the 'literary construct' Israel has been 'exported' by the scholars and 'dumped' into Iron Age Palestine to create a 'history of ancient Israel' (30).

Biblical Israel as a 'literary construct' has drawn in two ways upon historical Israel: in adopting the name Israel and in being described as a state or kingdom. 'Yet the biblical Israel cannot be attributed to that historical Israel, of whose society, culture, and religion what we can discover does not afford any plausible context for the creation of such literature and such constructs ... The "Israel" of the biblical literature is a concept that has *no discernible setting during this time*' (70).

Whence came biblical Israel? Davies argues that we must see in the biblical literature 'the fruits of a process of ideological enterprise which has its roots in the society of Persian period Yehud/Judah' (89). We must conclude 'that the creation of what was in truth a new society, marking a definitive break with what had preceded, was accompanied by – or at least generated – an ideological superstructure which denied its more recent origins, its imperial basis, and instead "indigenized" itself. Its literate class (drawn from those who had come from Babylonia) created an identity continuous with the kingdoms that had previously occupied that area, of which some memory, and probably some archival material, will have remained within Palestine' (84). These immigrants, transported by the Persian imperial authorities from elsewhere in the empire and not necessarily people whose ancestors had once lived in Palestine, wrote into their history an 'Israel' which 'explained their own post-"exilic" society and the rights and privileges of the immigrant élite within that society' (84). The end product of this activity 'formed the major part of what we now know as the biblical literature' (84).

Davies allows that the authors of this literature inherited a certain amount of material from earlier times, pieces of written or of oral literature that must have survived in Palestine, for example stories about kings, warriors and holy men, songs cultic and non-cultic (90). But such 'relics' – he does not specify any examples of these in the Old Testament texts – cannot be ascribed to 'ancient Israel'. They emerge from a society about which we know very little. 'What we cannot do with any of these relics is to carry back with them into their antiquity the social and religious context with which they have been provided by the writers of the biblical literature, who are creating their own literary "Israel"' (91). Rather, we must see such relics as having been 'incorporated and re-formed and re-contextualized' as part of literature that was created for its own ideological purposes by the ruling élite of the newly constituted province of Yehud in the Persian period. There is no necessity 'to assign *any* part of the formation of *any* biblical book to the period of the historical kingdoms of Israel and Judah' (95).

According to Davies, the main ingredients of the biblical 'Israel' as the creation of this new society of Yehud account for what scholars have termed 'the biblical tradition'. Thus the 'exile', the story of transportation out of and a later transportation into Judah, was a central way in which the official scribes turned the historical discontinuity of the newly formed community with the past in the land into continuity. In this respect, 'the exile is the central myth of the biblical account of the past. The immigrants, like the Pilgrim Fathers, had their minority experience come to determine the identity of the majority whose real history was different' (84). This same 'displacement' of the indigenous by the immigrants is manifest in other narratives – those concerning Abraham, the Exodus and conquest – celebrating an original 'Israel' that was brought into the 'promised land' from outside, there to differentiate itself radically and polemically from the indigenous population. Just as the narratives of the 'settlement' of the tribes in Canaan do not describe the Israelites as having displaced the Canaanites, so also for the new community in the Persian period the 'people of the land' are characterized as alien stock, with whom the true 'Israel' is not to mingle its 'holy seed'. 'It is these ... who become in Genesis–Kings transformed into the "Canaanites", of whom much the same is said' (85). Similarly, the relationship between the new province of Yehud and Samaria has its parallel in the narrative in Kings 'in which Israel is presented as a defecting (and defective) branch of the true "Israel" whose religion is focused on Jerusalem' (85). The covenant between Yahweh and 'Israel' so prominent in Genesis–Kings also originated at this time, according to Davies, and lies at the heart of the Ezra–Nehemiah narrative.

It is within the orbit of the Temple and court that we look for the authors of this literature which was the product of a class or body of professional scribes and arose from ideological, economic and political conditions. More specifically, a number of scribal 'schools' must be envisaged as the source of the literature – Davies writes of five such 'schools' – and these 'schools' are sponsored and controlled by the ruling élite. 'These scribes write what their paymasters tell them to, or allow them to, which means generally that they write to safeguard or increase the power and prestige of the monarch or the temple. Their scribal duties cover a wide range of activities, among them the keeping of commercial records (control over the economy), archiving (control and possession of the past, control of the literature class), or history writing (control and possession of the past; matching the claims of neighbouring powers), didactic writing (maintenance of social values among the élite), predictive writing (control over the future)' (103).

3.2.

There are similarities but also significant differences between the view of Davies and that of Thompson. Like Davies, Thompson argues that there is little relationship between so-called 'biblical Israel' and the historical Israel and Judah. We know little about either of these states and little in the Old Testament has come down to us from them. There never was a 'united monarchy' or a 'Davidic empire', and the figures of Saul, David and Solomon are fictitious. The state of Israel in the north lasted barely two centuries until its destruction by the Assyrians in the late eighth century. It was only in the seventh century that Jerusalem became the capital of a small Judaean state, but this endured only into the early sixth century when it was brought to an end by the Babylonians who deported its king and set about restructuring its society.

'Biblical Israel, as an element of tradition and story, such as the Israel of the murmuring stories in the wilderness, or the people of the stories of II Kings who are faithless as their kings are faithless, or the lost Israel, which is the object of prophetic diatribe in Isaiah and Amos, is a theological and literary creation' (Thompson 1998: 78). This Israel is what he calls 'old Israel'. 'It is presented as the polar opposite of an equally theological and literary "new Israel" ...' (78); the biblical tradition and narrative of the 'old Israel' and the 'new Israel' was a result of the success of a long-established tradition of imperial propaganda upon those settled in Palestine by the Persian authorities.

Thompson writes of two great defining story periods that have influenced the Bible's perception of 'old Israel' and formed its description of the past. The period of the 'united monarchy' was a great golden age, centred in the figure of David, the heroic and eponymous ancestor and founder of Jerusalem's House of David. 'This "House of the Beloved" not only evoked the temple as the centre of old Israel's story, it found in the stories about David a fictional representation of Yahweh's eternal rule over his people from Zion, his holy mountain. This was the tradition of Israel past, of Israel lost' (210). He continues: 'The other tradition centres on "exile and return", which is a defining story of a "new Israel". This origin story is equally legendary. Following the legendary motifs of the phoenix, the exile carries us through the death of the old Israel to the resurrection of the new. It is through the motifs of dying and rebirth that the stories take on their substance in the Bible's vision of the past' (210–11). That is, exile is a 'metaphor' for the psychological events from which new beginnings are launched.

Under the rule of the Persians a number of groups and families were transferred from Mesopotamia and resettled in southern Palestine, establishing a new colony in and around Jerusalem, but they were unrelated to the people who had been deported from this area in the early sixth century BCE. Stories about a 'return', as though those now settled in Judah were coming back to the homeland of their ancestors, are unhistorical. Indeed, it is striking that nowhere in the Old Testament is there any narrative about the exile, though we read about going into exile and returning from exile. The absence of such a narrative 'must at least raise for us the question of whether any such historical period of the past is in fact the subject of the traditions we do have' (219). Exile, Thompson suggests, is rather a 'metaphor' that is part of the stories of 'return' than of destruction, and is to be understood as deriving from imperial propaganda.

According to Thompson (1998: 190–96) population resettlement such as was practised by the Assyrians, Babylonians and Persians was backed by extensive political propaganda. Far preferable to the costly use of troops to force compliance of conquered peoples, was to gain the willing acceptance and support of those transported. 'Deportation is described as a "reward" for populations who rebelled against their leaders ... The people are always "restored to their homelands". Such returns involve the "restoration" of "lost" and "forgotten" gods, following long periods of exile' (191). 'The situation', he comments, 'required persuasive interpretation' (192) and he continues: 'Here our texts, from as early as the mid-ninth century, are a great help in deciphering the goals and direction of imperial propaganda. In these texts, deportation is not presented as a punishment, so much as an act undertaken on behalf of the people. It promoted their interests and protected them. It saved them from their former rulers who had oppressed and enslaved them ... [T]he dislocated peoples were encouraged to think of themselves in terms of restoration rather than punitive deportation: as saved from exile by the will of the king. They became returnees to their homelands, reunited with their lost and forgotten gods' (192).

Such political propaganda, when successful, was also mirrored, he argues, by changes in religious world-views, which became increasingly universalist and homogeneous. Indeed, the 'language of political propaganda helped to change and determine the language of religious metaphor. It played a vital role in the development of ideas that become reflected in the Bible as monotheism, restoration, the self-understanding of having been a people who had suffered exile, the restoration of a lost god to his temple, and the role of a messiah or saviour acting to carry out the will of their god. This was language intrinsic to empire' (193–94).

Thompson traces the formation of the literary tradition of 'old Israel' and 'new Israel' to the Hellenistic period, more specifically to the Maccabaean period of the second century BCE. Revival during the Persian period seems to have been slow and prosperity modest at best. He argues that during the early Hellenistic period it was Samaria and not Jerusalem among the highland centres that received settlers from Macedonia, and that Samaria was the dominant town of the hill country at least until the second quarter of the second century BCE when Jerusalem went over to the Maccabaean rebels and supported their successful revolt against Antiochus IV. 'It is during this next century, prior to Pompey's conquest of the region for Rome, that Jerusalem was finally able to establish itself – for the first time in history – as both religious and political centre for nearly the whole of Palestine. Many have found both David and Josiah reflected in the image of John Hyrcanus, one of the Hasmonean kings of this period. Surely our philosopher king Solomon is a Hebrew-speaking Alexander' (207). 'The stories of the golden age of the United Monarchy reflect the fantasy and ambitions of Jerusalem of the Maccabees. The image of this single kingdom ruled from Jerusalem hardly goes back in history any earlier than this period when the drama of the eternal Davidic dynasty and its forty kings first had an audience to play to' (207–208).

3.3.
Early in his book, in a sub-section entitled 'Common Sense and Credulity' Davies (1995: 38–42) accuses Old Testament scholars of being guilty of credulity in their reconstruction of the history of Israel on the basis of the biblical text. He gives as an example the usual treatment of the exilic period. 'Of this period', he writes, 'we *actually* know next to nothing', commenting that 'the idea that the authentic "Israel" was preserved by deportees and replanted in Palestine several decades later by their grandchildren is a fairly suspicious piece of ideology on the part of the biblical writers and even more dubious speculation on the part of biblical scholars. All that the biblical ideology of "exile" proves is that the rulers and writers of the Persian province of Yehud who came (in large measure, at least) from Babylonia claimed that they were the legitimate judges of what was right – that they could rule, legislate, and be priests, because they had brought the ancient law and preserved the authentic priesthood' (41). This is not an argument, however, but simply a reiteration of Davies's own theory: the tradition of a return from exile is declared to be 'a piece of ideology' and this proves Davies's theory.

As for the supposed credulity of biblical scholars, nowhere is it more required than by the claims made by Davies. Thus his theory rests upon speculation about 'scribal schools' in Persian period Jerusalem of which we have no evidence; it holds that deportees from parts of the Persian empire who had no prior relationship with Palestine were persuaded by the imperial authorities that they actually were descendants of people who had once lived there and were thus in reality being brought back to their ancestral homeland. Moreover, these deportees were so convinced by this propaganda or were so much its willing protagonists that they set about 'indigenizing' themselves, adopting the local language, the worship of the local deity, and any scrap of preserved local traditions or literary 'relics' they could lay hold of in order to engage in an elaborate literary exercise of ideological propaganda to persuade the local population that they were the rightful leaders of the nation in this new and God-given period of their history. Davies's suggestion that these deportees readily 'denied' their more recent origins strains both credulity and common sense. Such a 'denial' would have required abandoning their sense of 'roots' in a region, city or township where they were born and where over generations their fathers had lived; it would have entailed also, *ex hypothesi*, adopting a new language, creating a corpus of folk memories to replace their own erstwhile native folklore and ancestral history; they had also to forget or ignore any literature their former society had generated, whilst their ancestral or state god(s) and their traditional sacral and cultic rites and practices had likewise to be put aside in the interests of the endeavour to create a new 'ideological superstructure' for the new state which they now sought to establish and rule. Not for these deportees any weeping in a land far away as they remembered their homeland, or bitter lamentation for what was normally experienced as a grievous fate; no questioning among them of divine justice or, alternatively, a call for penitence for whatever offences against their god(s) had brought such calamity upon them.

Thompson's argument that long-established 'resettlement propaganda' was employed to persuade the deportees that they were now being 'returned' to their ancestral homeland suffers from the same lack of credibility. We are asked to believe that citizens of another city or cities in the empire, who would have belonged to the upper echelons of their society, both socially and intellectually, were persuaded that through the gratitude of the Persian king and his desire to 'reward' them they were not in reality being uprooted from their homeland and deported but 'returned' to the land of their ancestors who had been exiled from it; that the generous and solicitous imperial authorities were not only returning them to their proper land but were also 'restoring' to them the 'lost' and 'forgotten' god(s) of their ancestors following their long period of exile; and we are asked to believe that these deportees were so persuaded by all this as to adopt the culture, religion and such traditions and records of an alien population as were available, not to mention the local language, and set about an extensive programme of propaganda of their own in order to assert and give legitimacy to their claims to appropriate as their own the land into which they had recently been brought and to govern the local indigenous population. It does not seem at all likely that such deportees would have been so credulous or gullible and, indeed, in what surely must be regarded as the understatement of his book, Thompson comments that the 'situation' of the deportees would have 'required persuasive interpretation'!

Granting that there are obscurities and inadequacies about conditions in the exilic period, both in the land itself and in Mesopotamia, and that the information we have about the period is partial and incomplete, James Barr comments (2000: 100–101) that

> it remains that the 'revisionist' picture, according to which bands of unknown people, of whom the only thing certain is that they were not Jews or 'Israel', were formed into a new society by the initiative of the Persian government (!) and provided with a newly created ideology, still under construction in the Greek period, which then identified them with a past people of Israel and made them into 'Jews' with the traditions of Abraham, Moses, and David, cult and temple – such a reconstruction, far from being well evidenced historically, is – a least at present – too absurd to be taken seriously. It rests very little upon evidence, very largely on the conceptions and methods of those who have constructed it. It forms rather a *reductio ad absurdum* of the way in which the narrative traditions referring to earlier times have been handled.

Barr continues:

> Central to this is the emphatic, but unequal, insistence of revisionist historiography on *proof*. Proof for the Davidic and Solomonic empire is not available, and that means that the reports of it are likely to be explicable as ideology from a much later time. But for the highly conjectural suggestions made by the same historians about the exile, the return, the supposed part of the Persian government, and the activity of the literary élite during the Hellenistic period, commonly no such demand for proof is made. Many of these proposals rest not at all upon positive proof. They tend to depend rather on a sort of residual logic: other explanations being without proof, nothing is left except to suppose an explanation through late ideology, fabrications of the literary élite, and other hypotheses. Inequality in the application of the demand for proof is a serious fault.

3.4.

Turning to the case that Davies attempts to make, if much of the literature of the Old Testament is a product of state ideology, the work of 'schools' of officially employed scribes whose task was to provide legitimacy for the

new state of Yehud and its ruling élite, how does the prophetic protest
literature square with this? If, as Davies argues, these 'scribes write what
their paymasters tell them to, or allow them to', how are we to account for
much of the prophetic literature which takes the form of a critique, at
times trenchant critique, of the state? It is unlikely, he asserts, that this
literature comes from ancient social protesters who were also spontaneous
poets (Davies 1995: 118). There are two answers, he believes, though
neither is exclusive of the other: 'One is that there was no serious purpose,
but ... an effort to master a genre (and improve one's scribal "classical
Hebrew" at the same time). Another is that a good deal of genuine social
criticism is imbedded here. If so, it would not be surprising to find it in the
composition of apprentice scribes, or even of graduated scribes. Simply
because scribes work for the government does not mean that they admire
or approve of it' (118). Privileged though these scribes were, this need not
have prevented them from criticizing their own regime. In any event their
criticisms are always expressed in the words of an earlier prophet, so that
no direct criticism of the current authorities is explicit (103). He concludes:
'I do not resist the idea that there is real anger, morality and passion in
this poetry. But I see no reason to attribute it to "prophets" nor to anyone
before the fifth century BCE' (119).

How was the 'message' of these scribal protesters received, however? To
this no answer is given by Davies. Writing of Amos, he comments: 'Even if
we could be confident of the existence of a prophet called Amos who lived
in the mid-eighth century BCE, we could not be confident that he was
speaking in the name of the god Yahweh, or what his social location was,
or what his words were meant to do. For we do not know his society: it is
not the biblical "Israel". For, from a literal, historical point of view, the
words of this Amos are useless for his own time ... The only *point* of such
"prophecies" is as an implied warning to those of a later generation' (118).

We are not told by Davies, however, what the 'implied warning' of
'Amos' to the authorities of Judah in the Persian period might have been.
What was the implied warning of, for example, the oracles against the
nations including Israel and Judah in the first two chapters of the book?
Most commentators agree that the purpose of this series, which reaches its
climax in the indictment of Israel (2.6–8), may be aptly summed up in
some such title as 'The Guiltiest of the Guilty'.[10] Was this the warning
that the scribes of what Davies terms 'the college or school of politics'
intended for the ruling élite of their time, their 'paymasters'? If so, what
might have prompted such a threat? Is the 'new society' and its rulers here
indicted of the crimes mentioned? And whether or not the oracle against
Judah (Amos 2.4–5) is a secondary addition to these oracles, what can its
'implied warning' have been in the context of the 'new society' of Yehud?

---

10.   This is the superscription given by Wolff to these oracles (Wolff 1975, ET 1977).

Further, why would such a late author of this fictitious book have been concerned with such details as the home town of 'Amos'? Why did he choose for this the relatively unimportant town of Tekoa in southern Judah, and why add the detail that the prophet was a sheep breeder and 'dresser of mulberry trees', all of which we must presume, on Davies's view, is fiction? Is the figure of Amaziah – whose name indicates that he was a priest of Yahweh even if, according to Davies, we cannot be sure that Amos spoke in the name of Yahweh (if there ever was an Amos) – also a fiction of a scribe of the Persian period? One is reminded of James Barr's apt comment on the proposed dating of the story of David to the same period: 'I just cannot see that anyone in the Second Temple period, inspired by ideology, would just invent all the material about Abner and Asahel and Ittai the Gittite and Paltiel the son of Laish. Elements of invention, yes, one can see in any story, but the invention of material on such a scale seems entirely unconvincing as a theory' (Barr 2000: 87). The same observation is justified in the case of Davies's view of the book of Amos: is it credible that a scribe of the Second Temple period would have thought it necessary to draw up such details as these?

A more general observation is here in place, which I base upon a perceptive critique by Hans Barstad of some recent radical suggestions about prophecy in the Old Testament (Barstad 1993). He comments that the major problem with recent trends in prophetic research is that 'they tend to be too theoretical and take little or no heed of what is actually *to be found* in the biblical texts, above all lacking any serious attempt to relate the *contents* of the prophetical books to the phenomenon of biblical and ancient Near Eastern prophecy in general' (46). He draws attention, as many have done in the past, to parallels between Israelite prophecy and prophecy as exemplified in other ancient Near Eastern nations from texts such as those from Mari in the early second millennium BCE and texts from later, first millennium periods. As Barstad shows, there are manifestly features in the books bearing the names of Isaiah, Jeremiah, Ezekiel and the minor prophets, and much also in the narratives about prophets in the historical books of the Old Testament, that are also attested in the growing number of prophetical texts from other ancient Near Eastern nations. This places the onus heavily upon Davies to show why, in view of the widespread phenomenon of prophecy in the ancient Near East, what we find in the prophetic literature of the Hebrew Bible is a late literary imitation of this phenomenon, wrought by scribes for some (unspecified) purpose of the state – if not merely to 'master a genre'! – and not related to and arising from the life of a society to which were addressed by prophets from time to time, over many generations and in different social and historical situations, words proclaiming prosperity ('salvation') or calamity ('doom') as well as words of accusation and words of consolation, as in the case of prophecies in other ancient Near

Eastern societies. Why is the prophetic activity displayed in other ancient Near Eastern texts 'genuine', and the same phenomenon in the Hebrew Bible the work, not of prophets reacting to particular social or historical situations in the life of their society, but of professional scribes in pursuit of an agenda prescribed by state 'élite'? In short, it is theory rather than any normal scholarly assessment of the phenomenon of the prophetic literature and its manifold *Gattungen* in the Old Testament, including a comparative study, that governs Davies's conclusions.

3.5.

Similar objections are in place in the case of the view of Thompson (1998: 391) who writes: 'How much longer can we assert that the Jonah of his tale is any more fictional than the Isaiah of his story, or, indeed the Hosea of that fantastic metaphor [the 'marriage' metaphor in Hos. 1–3]? How are Jeremiah's prose sections more historical than Job's? And we must not forget either the Elijah or the Elisha of Kings.' It is difficult to take seriously, however, that an author as late as the Maccabaean period would, for example, have concocted a name such as 'Maher-shalal-hash-baz' in composing an oracle by his fictitious prophet whose activity he places more than six centuries earlier. What possible reason would such an author have had for inventing such names as this and 'Immanuel' and 'Shear-jashub' and relating them to a historical context of so long ago? Why would he have attached such significance to the Syro-Ephraimite coalition of the eighth century BCE and composed a narrative of an encounter between an imaginary figure given the name 'Isaiah' and the Judaean King Ahaz at that time? In what way was this 'theological propaganda', placed historically six centuries earlier, intended to provide legitimacy for Thompson's supposed 'new Israel' of the Hellenistic period? Of Thompson no less than of Davies it may also be asked what 'ideological' or 'propaganda' purpose or significance the oracles in Amos 1–2 served in this supposed new society of Hellenistic Judah?

A telling example of the lengths to which Thompson is prepared to go in arguing his theory is provided by his understanding of Lamentations. Needless to say, *ex hypothesi* these laments and dirges are not to be understood as an outpouring of grief, of divine judgment upon Jerusalem, and of repentance by those who had suffered the destruction of the city and the exile of citizenry in the early sixth century. Thompson regards the story of 'exile and return' as a defining story of a 'new Israel'. This 'origin story' is of course as legendary as that of the beginnings of the 'nation'. 'Following the legendary motifs of the phoenix, the exile carries us through the death of the old Israel to the resurrection of the new. It is through the motifs of dying and rebirth that the stories take on their substance in the Bible's vision of the past' (210–211). That is, exile is a 'metaphor for the psychological events from which new beginnings are launched' (31). Lying at the heart of this 'defining story' of exile and return is the notion of the empty land and an empty Jerusalem. Thus, Thompson argues, the empty Jerusalem of the book of Lamentations is a 'theological Jerusalem', not a historical one; in 'Lamentations the wilderness as godless chaos subject to Yahweh's destruction marks this same Jerusalem of the exile as a wilderness of the soul seeking repentance' (221). 'Exile is Jerusalem as a wasteland; it is the emptiness of the soul; it is to be without God' (222). He continues: 'Jeremiah, in his Lamentations over Jerusalem in exile, like Hosea in his poems about Israel as a prostitute-wife with her bastard children, have Nehemiah's[11] return as their points of departure ... It is the "New Jerusalem" and the Chronicler's "New Israel", that all hold as a central theme' (222).

The point of departure for the composition of Lamentations was the theological requirements of 'new Israel', that is, the supposed immigrant community that was settled by the Persians in Judah, and the need of this community to legitimate its possession of the land and the rights it claimed against the indigenous population of which neither they nor their ancestors were ever part. Unlike the old, 'lost Israel', this 'new Israel' is 'supersessionist'. 'It is Israel saved: a new generation. If we might draw on the overlapping syntax for "return", "turn", and "repent", only those who are among the remnant who have "turned" (in Lamentations "repentance" and, in Ezra/Nehemiah "returned") belong. Only those whom Yahweh has changed in the wilderness, who have again become "his people" can respond with Hosea's children: "You are my God"' (222). 'This is not historiography at all, but a metaphor of pietism ... It is in an Israel redivivus that punishment, destruction and the wilderness of exile all take on meaning within the tradition' (222).

Understood in this way, the poems of Lamentations had for their purpose, as required by Thompson's theory, theological legitimation of the new immigrant community of Judah founded by the Persian imperial authority and claiming to be the 'new Israel'. It is an understanding of these poems, however, that owes more to a midrashic approach to these texts than to serious, modern exegesis. Put differently, the theory has to indulge in an interpretative tour de force to accommodate texts which on any normal reading yield no indication that their author's intention was to contribute to the legitimizing of the state.

3.6.

I return to the gains of literary analysis and form-critical research of previous generations mentioned earlier in this essay. It was one of the most illuminating advances made by this research to have demonstrated

---

11. On Thompson's view, the story of this Jewish leader with his Yahwistic theophoric name and his 'return' from exile to the land of his ancestors are presumably fictitious.

that most of the literature of the Hebrew Bible has demonstrably undergone a more or less complex process of growth and development in reaching its present form. By contrast, on the view of Davies, the literature becomes one-dimensional, so to speak: much of it was composed by scribes at their desks and within the context of so-called 'colleges' or 'schools' of scribes. It did not therefore come from 'an actual life of the people', as James Barr (2000: 99–100) has commented. Instead, according to both Davies and Thompson, there is a monolithic cause of the literature: 'ideology' or a quest for 'theological legitimacy' for the state newly founded in the Persian period. According to Davies, the literature was commissioned by the intellectual élites of this newly founded state and duly delivered by the professional scribes in their employment working in different scribal 'colleges'. That this literature seems to reflect many changing circumstances of a people's long history and the response to these changing circumstances by its religious and theological thinkers and writers, prophets, priests, psalmists and wisdom teachers, is on the analysis of both Davies and Thompson an illusion.

Contrary to such a verdict, however, there is ample evidence of the presence of originally discrete texts within the larger literary complexes of the Hebrew Bible such as the Pentateuch and the Former Prophets, and, indeed, of still earlier stages in the emergence of some of these texts. For example, there remain good grounds for discerning behind the stories of Abraham in Genesis, each with its own distinctive atmosphere, a pre-literary stage of story-telling about this ancestor. We can also discern originally independent ethnological legends about the origin and relationship between different tribes or people, as well as aetiological stories explaining some custom or institution, including cultic legends narrating the foundation of particular sanctuaries, and etymological stories explaining how someone or some place acquired their name. On the other hand, the Joseph narrative (Gen. 37–50) stands out as a skilfully authored story that can be classified as a *Novelle*. The so-called 'court history of David' (2 Sam. 9–20; 1 Kgs 1–2) is usually similarly classified. Different from this genre, however, is the 'cycle' of Elijah-Elisha stories in 1 Kings 17–19, 2 Kings 1–2, which probably had its own pre-history of development before its incorporation in its present, larger context. There are good reasons for believing also that this same 'cycle' comprises two originally separate collections of stories about each of these prophetic figures, and, indeed, behind this earlier stage can be discerned originally discrete individual stories.

Each of the larger prophetic books of Isaiah, Jeremiah and Ezekiel are manifestly also the result of a complex and lengthy history of development, and this is true of most of the books of the so-called 'minor prophets'. Further, the many different forms (*Gattungen*) of speech employed in these books, the different focus of individual oracles or series of oracles, oracles of judgment and oracles of hope or blessing, dirges and laments, vision oracles and records of call-visions, speech forms and formulae derived from different social or state institutions such as the office of royal messenger, parodies, the use of sarcasm and irony, of legal forms, references or allusions to breaches of inherited statutes and moral norms, hymns, evidence of differing audiences or locations for different oracles – all of this is much more plausibly explained as the deposit of the living voice of individual prophets, allowing also of course for subsequent expansion and additions, whether by disciples of these prophets or others, and naturally also for the creative contribution of redactors and scribes.

Many voices from many different times and eras speak to us in this literature, many thinkers, writers, redactors and scribes contributed to its composition, growth, enrichment and the adaptation of what had been handed down to them to meet the changing circumstances of the people for whom over many generations it was addressed. The faith, hopes, promises and the threats this literature contains, its extensive narrative content, its psalms reflecting praise, lament, petition, joy, disaster, hope and faith, its collections of ordinances for worship, which in some important ways differ so strikingly from each other, its instructions for the ordering of the life of the community and nation that presuppose differing historical backgrounds, the rebukes, exhortations, the promises and woes announced by great prophets – from all of this we have learned that this literature is complex in its origins and growth and multiplex in its sources in the life of the people of Israel throughout many centuries. From being regarded as the literary work of a small number of writers, beginning with Moses, we have learned that there is indeed here much more than meets the eye. Attempts to limit the creation of such a literature to a largely scribal activity carried out in the interests of political propaganda or for the purpose of legitimizing a newly founded state of the Persian period or later are in the face of overwhelming evidence to the contrary.

Bibliography

Alt, A.
  1925   *Die Landnahme der Israeliten in Palästina* (Leipzig: Reformationsprogramm der Universität Leipzig). ET 'The Settlement of the Israelites in Palestine', in his *Essays in Old Testament History and Religion* (trans. R.A. Wilson; Oxford: Basil Blackwell, 1966): 133–69.
  1929   *Der Gott der Väter* (BWANT, 3.12; Stuttgart: W. Kohlhammer). ET 'The God of the Fathers', in *Essays in Old Testament History and Religion* (trans. R.A. Wilson; Oxford: Basil Blackwell, 1966): 1–66.
  1934   *Die Ursprünge des israelitischen Rechts* (Berichte über die Verhandlungen der Sächsischen Akademie der Wissenschaften zu Leipzig. Philologisch-historische Klasse, Band 86, Heft 1; Leipzig: S. Hirzel). ET 'The Origins of Israelite

Law', in *Essays in Old Testament History and Religion* (trans. R.A. Wilson; Oxford: Basil Blackwell, 1966): 79–132.

Anderson, B.W.
1958   *The Living World of the Old Testament* (London: Longmans, Green).

Barr, J.
2000   *History and Ideology in the Old Testament: Biblical Studies at the End of a Millennium* (Oxford: Oxford University Press).

Barstad, H.M.
1993   'No Prophets? Recent Developments in Biblical Prophetic Research and Ancient Near Eastern Prophecy', *JSOT* 57: 39–60.
2002   'Is the Hebrew Bible a Hellenistic Book? Or: Niels Peter Lemche, Herodotus, and the Persians', *Transeuphratène* 23: 129–51.

Barton, J.
1984   'Gerhard von Rad on the World-View of Early Israel', *JTS* NS 35: 301–23.

Bright, J.
1960   *A History of Israel* (London: SCM Press).

Clements, R.E.
1965   *Prophecy and Covenant* (SBT, 43; London: SCM Press).

Cross, F.M.
1973   *Canaanite Myth and Hebrew Epic* (Cambridge, MA: Harvard University Press).

Davies, Philip R.
1995   *In Search of 'Ancient Israel'* (JSOTSup, 148; Sheffield: JSOT Press, 2nd edn).
1996   *Scribes and Schools: The Canonization of the Hebrew Scriptures* (Louisville, KY: Westminster John Knox Press).

Diebner, B.
1975   'Die Götter der Väter. Eine Kritik der "Vätergott"-Hypothese Albrecht Alts', *Dielheimer Blätter zum Alten Testament* 9: 21–51.

Geus, C.H.J. de
1976   *The Tribes of Israel* (Studia Semitica Neerlandica, 18; Assen and Amsterdam: Van Gorcum).

Gunkel, H.
1895   *Schöpfung und Chaos in Urzeit und Endzeit: eine religionsgeschichtliche Untersuchung über Gen 1 und Ap Joh 12* (Göttingen: Vandenhoeck & Ruprecht).
1901   *Genesis übersetzt und erklärt* (HKAT, 1.1; Göttingen: Vandenhoeck & Ruprecht). ET *Genesis Translated and Interpreted* (trans. Mark E. Biddle; Macon, GA: Mercer University Press, 1997).

Hale, J.R.
1967   *The Evolution of British Historiography* (London: Macmillan).

Klatt, W.
1969   *Hermann Gunkel: Zu seiner Theologie der Religionsgeschichte und zur Enstehung der formgeschichtlichen Methode* (FRLANT, 100; Göttingen: Vandenhoeck & Ruprecht).

Knight, D.A.
1974   *Rediscovering the Traditions of Israel* (SBLDS, 9; Missoula, MT: SBL [Scholars Press]).

Köckert, M.

1988   *Vätergott und Väterverheissungen: eine Auseinandersetzung mit Albrecht Alt und seinen Erben* (FRLANT, 142; Göttingen: Vandenhoeck & Ruprecht).

Mayes, A.D.H.

1974   *Israel in the Period of the Judges* (SBT, second series, 29; London: SCM Press).

Mendenhall, G.E.

1954   'Covenant Forms in Israelite Tradition', *BA* 17: 50–75.

Mowinckel, S.

1951   *Offersang og sangoffer; salmediktingen i Bibelen* (Oslo: Aschehoug). ET *The Psalms in Israel's Worship* (trans. D.R. Ap-Thomas; 2 vols; Oxford: Basil Blackwell, 1962).

Nicholson, E.W.

1998   *The Pentateuch in the Twentieth Century: The Legacy of Julius Wellhausen* (Oxford: Clarendon Press).

Noth, M.

1930   *Das System der zwölf Stämme Israels* (BWANT, 4.1; Stuttgart: W. Kohlhammer).

1940   *Die Gesetze im Pentateuch (Ihre Voraussetzungen und ihre Sinn)* (Schriften der Königsberger gelehrten Gesellschaft. Geisteswissenschaftliche Klasse, 17. Jahr, Heft 2; Halle [Saale]: Max Niemeyer). ET 'The Laws in the Pentateuch: Their Assumptions and Meaning', in M. Noth, *The Laws in the Pentateuch and Other Essays* (trans. D.R. Ap-Thomas; Edinburgh & London: Oliver & Boyd, 1966): 1–107.

1948   *Überlieferungsgeschichte des Pentateuch* (Stuttgart: W. Kohlhammer). ET *A History of Pentateuchal Traditions* (trans. B.W. Anderson, with Introduction; Englewood Cliffs, NJ; Prentice-Hall, 1972).

1950   *Geschichte Israels* (Göttingen: Vandenhoeck & Ruprecht). ET *The History of Israel* (revised trans. Peter Ackroyd; London: A. & C. Black, 1960, from the 2nd German edn, 1954).

1955   'Die Bewährung von Salomos "göttliche Weisheit"', in M. Noth and D. Winton Thomas (eds), *Wisdom in Israel and in the Ancient Near East: Presented to Professor Harold Henry Rowley* (VTSup, 3; Leiden: E.J. Brill): 225–37.

Perlitt, L.

1969   *Bundestheologie im Alten Testament* (WMANT, 36; Neukirchen–Vluyn: Neukirchener Verlag).

Rad, G. von

1938   *Das formgeschichtliche Problem des Hexateuch* (BWANT, 4th Series, 26; Stuttgart: W. Kohlhammer). ET 'The Form-Critical Problem of the Hexateuch', in *The Form-Critical Problem of the Hexateuch and other Essays* (trans. E.W. Trueman Dicken; Edinburgh 1966: Oliver & Boyd): 1–78.

1958   *Der heilige Krieg im alten Israel* (Göttingen: Vandenhoeck & Ruprecht, 3rd edn). ET *Holy War in Ancient Israel* (trans. and ed. Marva J. Dawn; Grand Rapids, MI: W.B. Eerdmans, 1971).

Schmid, H.H.

1976   *Der sogenannte Jahwist: Beobachtungen und Fragen zur Pentateuchforschung* (Zürich: Theologischer Verlag).

Scott, R.B.Y.
1955   'Solomon and the Beginnings of Wisdom in Israel', in M. Noth and D.
        Winton Thomas (eds), *Wisdom in Israel and in the Ancient Near East:*
        Presented to Professor Harold Henry Rowley (VTSup, 3; Leiden: E.J. Brill):
        262–79.

Soggin, J.A.
1984   *A History of Israel from the Beginnings to the Bar Kochba Revolt*, AD *135*
        (trans. John Bowden; London: SCM Press).

Thompson, T.L.
1974   *The Historicity of the Patriarchal Narratives* (BZAW, 133, Berlin: W. de
        Gruyter).
1998   *The Bible in History: How Writers Create a Past* (London: Jonathan Cape).
        Also published as *The Mythic Past: Biblical Archaeology and the Myth of*
        Israel (New York: Basic books).

Van Seters, J.
1975   *Abraham in History and Tradition* (New Haven and London: Yale University
        Press).
1983   *In Search of History: Historiography in the Ancient World and the Origins of*
        Biblical History (New Haven and London: Yale University Press).

Weippert, M.
1967   *Die Landnahme der israelitischen Stämme in der neueren wissenschaftlichen*
        Diskussion (FRLANT, 92, Göttingen: Vandenhoeck & Ruprecht). ET *The*
        Settlement of the Israelite Tribes in Palestine (trans. J.D. Martin; SBT, 2nd
        series, 21; London: SCM Press, 1971).

Weiser, A.
1959   *Die Psalmen* (ATD. 14/15; Göttingen: Vandenhoeck & Ruprecht, 5th revised
        edn). ET *The Psalms: A Commentary* (trans. Herbert Hartwell; OTL; London:
        SCM Press, 1962).

Whybray, R.N.
1982   'Wisdom Literature in the Reigns of David and Solomon', in T. Ishida,
        Studies in the Period of David and Solomon and Other Essays (Winona Lake,
        IN: Eisenbrauns): 13–26.

Wolff, H.W.
1975   *Dodekapropheten,* II: *Joel und Amos* (BKAT, 14.2; Neukirchen–Vluyn:
        Neukirchener Verlag, 2nd edn). ET *Joel and Amos* (trans. W. Janzen, S.
        Dean McBride and Charles A. Muenchow; Hermeneia; Philadelphia: Fortress
        Press, 1977).

Chapter 2

WAS THERE AN EXODUS?

Graham Davies

Only a generation ago this would have seemed an absurd question to ask.
The patriarchs might be figures of folklore, the conquest of Canaan a
gross exaggeration of the entry of semi-nomads into the land, but there
surely must have been an Exodus! As John Bright put it (1960: 110):

> There can really be little doubt that ancestors of Israel had been slaves
> in Egypt and had escaped in some marvellous way. Almost no one today
> would question it ... Although there is no direct witness in Egyptian
> records to Israel's presence in Egypt, the Biblical tradition a priori
> demands belief: it is not the sort of tradition any people would invent!
> Here is no heroic epic of migration, but the recollection of shameful
> servitude from which only the power of God brought deliverance.

The only questions worth asking about the Exodus were when did it
happen, by what route did the Israelites leave Egypt, and how many of
them were actually there?

But now all this has changed. Everything about the early history of
Israel is in doubt, including the Exodus. N.P. Lemche, summing up his
detailed study of 'the biblical sources and history', writes as follows (1996:
68, 69, 72: my translation):

> In what has preceded it has been shown that the biblical texts which deal
> with the earliest history of Israel (or better its 'pre-' or 'proto-history')
> and with Western Asia and Egypt in the pre-Israelite period were not
> composed as historical sources but must be regarded as literary fictions
> ... A portrayal of this period [sc. the third and second millennia] that
> has a truly historical foundation would show that there is absolutely no
> historical background for what is narrated in the Pentateuch ... There is
> in the Pentateuch practically nothing which can be used by the
> historian. The latter would do better to look around for other sources,
> instead of vainly leafing through the Bible.[1]

---

1. In his detailed discussion of the Exodus and Sinai traditions (1996: 52–68) Lemche
sometimes shows a readiness to allow a very limited historical foundation for them (64–65),
but such a possibility is quickly eliminated. The view taken by Johnstone (1990: ch. 1) is very
similar to Lemche's. Compare also Van Seters 1987: 116, on the figure of Moses: 'The quest
for the historical Moses is a futile exercise. He now belongs only to legend'.

Even William Dever, who has recently emerged as the scourge of the minimalists and is a contributor to this volume, has been if anything even more sceptical about the historicity of the Exodus. In a recent volume of essays he wrote (1997a: 81):

> Not only is there no archaeological evidence for an exodus, there is no need to posit such an event. We can account for Israelite origins, historically and archaeologically, without presuming any Egyptian background. As a Syro-Palestinian archaeologist, I regard the historicity of the Exodus as a dead issue, despite this symposium's raising it again.[2]

It seems as though talk of 'minimalism' only begins with the period of the Judges – prior to that scepticism is in order! As far as the Exodus is concerned, the answer to the question in the title of Dever's recent book, *What did the Biblical Writers Know and When did they Know it?*, seems to be 'nothing' and 'never'![3]

So the question 'Was there an Exodus'?' is indeed a real one and we shall need to consider the relevant evidence carefully. But before we do so, it is worth asking why there has been such a sea change in attitudes to the issue among Old Testament scholars. I think there are two kinds of factor, general and particular. In general, the reassessment of Old Testament history, which flows from the rejection of older hypotheses such as the amphictyony theory, the tendency to date Old Testament literature later and sometimes very much later than in the past, and the greater emphasis placed today on the literary, creative aspects of Old Testament narratives, cannot but have its effects on the study of the Exodus tradition too. But more particularly the latter has been affected by new developments in the study of a closely related issue, the emergence, as it is now fashionable to call it, of Israel in Canaan. This connection is made very clear in another statement by William Dever, for whom this factor is especially influential (1997a: 67; cf. 1997b: 45–48): 'And with new models of indigenous Canaanite origins for early Israel, there is neither place nor need for an

---

2. Dever continues: 'There are, no doubt, theological problems that this negative evidence presents, but I leave such problems to others'. See further Dever 1997a: 67 and 1997b: 45–48.

3. Such views as I have described are not, however, universally held even today: among leading authorities who have recently taken a more or less positive view of the historicity of the Exodus tradition would be R. Albertz (1992: I, 73–85, ET 1994: 44–52), H. Donner (1995: 97–111), A. Malamat (1997) and F. Yurco (1997). In a recent popular book a Cambridge scientist, C.J. Humphreys (2003), has argued that the events of the Exodus story are all scientifically plausible and are to be regarded as historical. He pays scant attention, however, to the history of the tradition and some of his detailed argument is unconvincing. The sites envisaged for the Re(e)d Sea event (the Gulf of Aqaba) and Mount Sinai (the volcano Hala'l-bedr in Saudi Arabia) are also not the most probable from a geographical point of view, as I have shown elsewhere (Davies 1979a; 1979b).

exodus from Egypt'. Dever's point is that if all Israelites were basically Canaanites who made their way up into the hills and built for themselves the Iron Age I village sites that are now so well known, *that* is the story of Israel's origins and there is no need or justification to complicate it by references to an Exodus or related events. This thesis of a Canaanite origin for the Israelites is of course entirely grounded on archaeological evidence, Dever is an archaeologist, and so one can see how it appeals to him. It is not for me to discuss that thesis further here – another chapter in this volume will do that – but I do want, first, to point out the interrelation of the two issues in Dever's and others' minds and, secondly, to question whether they should be so closely tied together. For, in the first place, it is only an extreme version of the 'Canaanite origins' thesis and an extreme version of the 'Exodus origins' tradition that are incompatible with each other: clearly it is impossible for *all* the ancestors of Israel to have come both from the cities of Canaan and from Egypt. More moderate versions of both theories could, however, readily be combined.[4] Secondly, whatever a Syro-Palestinian archaeologist may wish to do, a historian cannot simply ignore the textual evidence (both biblical and non-biblical) that is relevant to an issue, and in this case the textual evidence purports, at least, to give a different view from that which archaeologists now tend to favour (or most of them, anyway).

In addition to a priori arguments like the one I quoted from Bright, historical approaches to the Exodus have based themselves on both direct and indirect evidence, the latter being perhaps better referred to as an argument from analogy (cf. Malamat 1997). The direct evidence consists of the biblical tradition, which of course has its own history, and within which certain elements have been thought to be particularly significant. The argument from analogy is based on a number of Egyptian texts. As well as this material, which is mostly well known, there has in recent years been a fresh suggestion about specific references to Moses in Egyptian

---

4. In fact Dever concedes at one point that 'Elements of this group ['the house of Joseph'] may indeed have originally been slaves in Egypt and made their way to Canaan independently, perhaps making contact on the way with nomadic tribes in southern Transjordan who worshipped a Yahweh deity' (1997b: 46) and that 'the story of the "house of Joseph" became in time the story of "all Israel"' (47). In a more recent book Dever has presented a fuller, while still cautious, account of his views about the origins of the biblical tradition (2003: 229–34): 'Among the principal architects who shaped the biblical overall tradition we assume that there were elements of the House of Joseph. Although a minority, they told their story as the story of all Israel. That would explain how the Exodus/Sinai tradition came into being. Some of these groups probably had come out of Egypt to Canaan, and in a way that upon reflection seemed miraculous to them ... It is not the whole story of Israelite origins, to be sure; but I would suggest that it may rest on some historical foundations, however minimal' (231).

texts, with an associated claim of a very precise date for the Exodus, and attention will need to be given to this as well.

First, then, the biblical evidence, the Exodus tradition. This consists, of course, not only of chs 1–15 of the book of Exodus but of countless references elsewhere in the Old Testament as well. While it would be an exaggeration to say that the Exodus story is mentioned in every part of the Old Testament, the exceptions are fairly few: one thinks of the wisdom literature of the Hebrew canon and certain of the prophets, including perhaps Isaiah of Jerusalem. The impact of the tradition can be seen in worship, law, historical narrative, prophecy and ritual, and it is by no means restricted to one particular period: it is there in pre-exilic, exilic and post-exilic texts. It does seem to have a particularly central place, as far as the majority of the pre-exilic period is concerned, in documents from the northern kingdom of Israel: one thinks of the prophets Hosea and Amos, and certain psalms which are likely to be of north Israelite origin because of their use of the term 'Joseph' for the people (77, 80 and 81),[5] and one might also include here the book of Deuteronomy as a witness largely to traditions handed down in the north, even if the first stage of its actual composition is most likely to be placed in Judah. This all fits in with the statement in 1 Kgs 12.28 that Jeroboam I introduced the golden calves at Bethel and Dan with the words: 'Here are your gods, O Israel, who brought you out of the land of Egypt'. One might well see here an important clue to the history of the Exodus tradition (cf. Loewenstamm 1992: 44–52). In southern tradition it is much more difficult to find definite references to the Exodus before the late seventh century (Deuteronomy, Jeremiah): difficult, but not perhaps impossible. Psalm 114 could be a quite early Judaean psalm, and the Song of Moses in Exod. 15.1–17 (of which more later) is best viewed as a Jerusalem psalm from the early monarchy. In addition, a strong case has been made out for Psalm 78 having its origin in the eighth century or earlier (Day 1986; 1990: 58–59). Much of it is concerned with the story of the Exodus and the subsequent

---

5.   Of course not every psalm where the term 'Joseph' appears is of northern origin, as the case of Ps. 78 shows: v. 67 is part of an outright polemic against the northern kingdom which clearly derives from Jerusalemite circles. But where 'Joseph' is a name for the community which is using the psalm, a northern origin is to be presumed. It is sometimes held that in Ps. 80 (where the tribal names in v. 3, ET 2 point to the north, in addition to the use of the term 'Joseph' in v. 2, ET 1) the references to the cherubim in v. 2 (ET 1) and the extent of the kingdom's influence in v. 12 (ET 11) indicate a Judaean origin (so Day 1990: 35–36). Neither of these factors is decisive, however. The description of Yahweh as 'enthroned upon the cherubim' probably refers to his heavenly throne and is certainly not to be limited to the temple in Jerusalem (Gunkel 1926: 353, 429; cf. Clements 1965: 31–35); and 'the sea' and 'the River' may allude to the extent of northern rule under Omri and Ahab in the ninth century (1 Kgs 16.27) or under Jeroboam in the eighth (2 Kgs 14.25, 28), rather than to the time of David and Solomon.

journey through the wilderness, and the final verses make its Judaean provenance crystal clear. The plagues referred to in vv. 42–51 are precisely those included in the J source of the Pentateuch as commonly identified, which has generally been thought to be from the southern kingdom.[6] There is thus sufficient evidence to show that the Exodus tradition was known in Judah (the references in Amos might be taken to imply this too), though perhaps not as well known there as it was in the north. From the evidence we have it seems not to have been prominent in the traditions of pre-exilic worship at the Jerusalem temple. This may even be implied in Psalm 78, since the Exodus and wilderness traditions are introduced there with specific reference to the Ephraimites (vv. 9–11), who are said not to have been true to the tradition which *they* inherited. If the Exodus tradition is indeed represented in the sacred memories of both kingdoms, then we have good reason to suppose that it goes back at least to the time when they were a united kingdom.

But has it a historical foundation or is it just a wonderful but purely fictitious story? It is not hard, especially nowadays, to find descriptions of the Exodus story as being based on 'ahistorical folk tradition' and 'popular folklore and folk history of the time' (Thompson 1987: 39, 195) and statements like: 'It is generally acknowledged by scholars that the traditions about Israel's sojourn in Egypt and the *exodus* of the Israelites are legendary and epic in nature … There is accordingly no real reason even to attempt to find a historical background for the events of the Exodus' (Lemche 1988: 109). Hugo Gressmann was saying this sort of thing decades ago (1913), and much of it was echoed in Martin Noth's book on the history of traditions in the Pentateuch (1948, ET 1972). It is not my purpose to try to rebut these claims across the board and there is undoubtedly a good deal of truth in them, but they are not the whole truth and much depends on how the key terms are defined. To establish that there was an Exodus it is not necessary to defend the historicity of the whole Exodus story as we have it. Indeed even a fairly limited application of source criticism to Exodus, which would be widely agreed upon even in these confusing times, would distinguish a Priestly account of the Exodus from older source material and so identify elements of the story which are certainly secondary and unhistorical. What I shall therefore do here is to look at a few elements of the tradition which have commonly been thought to provide a historical core to the story, whatever one makes of the rest.[7]

6. This argument depends of course not only on the southern origin of J but on the existence of such a document in pre-exilic times, which is often questioned today. But see the discussion by J.A. Emerton in this volume.

7. For attempts to make more extensive claims about historical elements in the Exodus story see, e.g., Herrmann 1970 (ET 1973), Weimar and Zenger 1975 and Hoffmeier 1997.

First, Exod. 1.11: 'Therefore they (*sc.* the Egyptians) set taskmasters over them (i.e. the Israelites) to oppress them with forced labour. They built supply cities, Pithom and Raamses, for Pharaoh.' Some of the vocabulary of this verse (*missîm, ʿārê miskᵉnôt*) is paralleled in the account of Solomon's reign in Kings (cf.1 Kgs 9.15, 19) and may reflect its time of writing, but the names Pithom and Raamses assuredly do not and both can be convincingly correlated with a second-millennium Egyptian situation. Ramesses was the name of a series of eleven Pharaohs who reigned between about 1300 and 1070, but it was also (with the prefix Per- or Pi-) the name of the dynastic capital in the eastern Nile delta which began to be constructed on the site of the old Hyksos capital of Avaris under Ramesses II and is frequently referred to in texts of his long reign (1279–1212) (see *ANET*, 470–71; summaries in Kitchen 1982: 119–23, and Wente 1992). Of particular interest in the present context are the passages which refer to the great granaries of Pi-Ramesse: it is said to be 'full of food and provisions' and 'its granaries are (so) full of barley and emmer (that) they come near to the sky' (cf. Weimar and Zenger 1975: 118–20).

It is now agreed that Pi-Ramesse (like the earlier Hyksos capital Avaris) was at Qantir/Tell el-Daba and that the Ramesside monuments now at Tanis were taken from Qantir/Tell el-Daba to there when, in the mid-eleventh century, Tanis took over the role of major political centre in the eastern Delta. It is this later pre-eminence of Tanis which is reflected in the biblical references to its Hebrew equivalent Zoan as the site of events associated with the Exodus (Ps. 78.12, 43). Excavations at Tell el-Daba in 1966–69 and from 1975 to the present and at Qantir since 1980 have confirmed these conclusions and brought to light further archaeological evidence of the Hyksos capital and of the New Kingdom structures in the area (cf. Bietak 1979, 1996; Pusch and Knauer 1997; Pusch *et al.* 1999; Dorner 1999). The reference to Raamses by name seems likely to be an early element of the biblical tradition. Doubts raised by D.B. Redford about the omission of the original Pi (or Per) of the name and the spelling of the main element of it (1963: 409–13) were answered by W. Helck (1965: 40–48; cf. Kitchen 1998: 69). The fact that Pi-Ramesse ceased to be a place of any importance in the mid-eleventh century (Helck 1965: 47), even though the memory of Ramesses II himself was maintained for centuries (cf. Kitchen 1982: 227–31; 1998: 81; Bietak 2000: 186) makes it unlikely that it would have first come to the notice of Israelites at the time, say, of the Babylonian exile.

Pithom is a form of the Egyptian expression 'Per-Atum', 'the house/ temple of Atum', Atum being the primordial Egyptian god. His greater cultic centre was at Heliopolis/On (the site is in the north-east suburbs of modern Cairo) and a minority view holds that this ancient city is meant by Pithom here (see Uphill 1968: 292–99). But its ancient name was not Pithom/Per-Atum but On, and the biblical tradition seems to place the later Israelites' sojourn further to the north-east in the Eastern Nile Delta (see below). Possible sites for Pithom have therefore generally been sought in this region, where the worship of Atum is also attested (cf. Goedicke 1987b, Pap. Anastasi VI.51–61 = iv.11-v.5; *ANET*, 259; Galling 1979: 40). The choice has appeared to be between two sites in Wadi Tumilat, a shallow valley extending west from modern Ismailiya: Tell el-Maskhuta and Tell er-Retabeh (for a fuller discussion of the evidence see Bleiberg 1983).

Tell el-Maskhuta is situated 10 miles west of Ismailiya: ancient monuments, some of which proved to be from the time of Ramesses II, were observed there from the late eighteenth century onwards and excavations by E. Naville in 1883 brought to light remains of a temple of Atum, 'storehouses' and structures from the Roman period (Naville 1885, with several plates of inscriptions from the site). Naville proposed that Tell el-Maskhuta was the site of Pithom and has been widely followed in this. But subsequent investigations by J. Clédat and especially the excavations directed by J.S. Holladay (1977–85) have added much new information and made it clear that the site lay unoccupied between a period in the Middle Bronze Age (c. 1750–1625) and the very end of the seventh century (see the full summary in Holladay 1992, with bibliography). There can be no doubt, therefore, that the Ramesside monuments found there were brought secondarily from another site. Evidence from the seventh century and later confirms that at this time Tell el-Maskhuta was known as 'Per-Atum Ṭukw', which would permit the retention of the identification if the reference to Pithom is regarded as a late element of tradition, and a number of scholars have favoured this view.

Tell er-Retabeh, which is less well known, is located 9 miles west of Tell el-Maskhuta. It was first excavated by Flinders Petrie in the early twentieth century: he reported evidence of occupation in the Egyptian Middle Kingdom period and under Ramesses II and Ramesses III (including a temple), but nothing later (Petrie 1906: 28–34; see further Uphill 1968: 299–301; Goedicke 1987a). Further excavations were conducted at the site by H. Goedicke in the late 1970s, with similar results (see summary and references in Hoffmeier 1997: 119–20, with notes). A relief found there by Petrie shows Ramesses II striking an Asiatic before the god Atum, which suggests that Atum was worshipped at the site in the New Kingdom period, perhaps at the temple discovered by Petrie; and an inscription from the site refers to an official (Ramesside?) who was responsible for 'storehouses' (see Uphill 1968: 300).

Prior to Naville's excavations at Tell el-Maskhuta the dominant view was that Pithom was at Tel(l) el Kebir or Tell Abu Suleiman, c. 35 miles west of Ismailiya (e.g. Lepsius 1849: 357; 1883: 45–46). Naville, on the basis of the Ramesside monuments, his other finds, a passage of Herodotus (2.158) and literary evidence relating to the Graeco-Roman toponym Heroopolis, proposed that Tell el-Maskhuta was the site of Pithom and this view has been widely followed (so Helck 1965: 35–40; after him Herrmann, 1970: 26, ET 1973: 26; Weimar and Zenger 1975: 118; Davies 1979a: 79; Schmidt 1988: 36). Even after D.B. Redford's questioning of the antiquity of Pithom as the name of a town (1963: 403–408; severely criticized by Helck 1965: 35–40) and Holladay's demonstration that there was no Ramesside occupation at the site, there is good reason to conclude (see above) that in later periods (from c. 600 onwards) it was known as Per-Atum/Pithom and that it is what Herodotus referred to as Πάτουμον τὴν Ἀραβίην. The key question is whether another site in the vicinity may have been known by that name in earlier times.

The identification of Pithom with Tell er-Retabeh was first proposed by A.H. Gardiner (1918: 267–69; 1933: 127) and was adopted – before the recent debate about the merits of Tell el-Maskhuta – by, e.g., M. Noth (1954: 107 n. 2, ET 1960: 112 n. 2), J. Bright (1960: 111) and J.A. Wilson (in *ANET*, 259 n. 5). Recently it has been supported by H. Goedicke (1987b, with qualifications), M. Dijkstra (1989), F. Yurco (1997: 55 n. 62), J.K. Hoffmeier (1997: 119–21) and K.A. Kitchen (1998: 77–78; for an earlier, oral, statement see Hoffmeier 1997: 131 n. 118). Although there is no explicit evidence that the site was ever known as Pithom, it apparently had a temple of Atum (a Per-Atum) in the Ramesside period and the significance of the site for Ramesses II has been underlined by Goedicke, who has also argued that it is referred to in Pap. Anastasi V.xix.3-xx.6; VI.51–57 (1987b). According to Goedicke (1987a: 13; 1987b: 95–96) and Hoffmeier (1997: 120) the Ramesside monuments at Tell el-Maskhuta could have been brought there from Tell er-Retabeh. Tell er-Retabeh can provide a plausible location for Pithom in the New Kingdom period. If we consider the two names Raamses and Pithom together, it has to be said that they are more likely as a pair to belong to a tradition that originated in the Ramesside period than to a later time. Exodus 1.11 remains an important historical datum for the Exodus tradition.

Secondly and more briefly, there is the reference to Moses' stay in Midian, his marriage to the daughter of a Midianite priest and the tradition that he (and subsequently the 'Exodus group' as a whole) met with Yahweh at a desert mountain in the vicinity. The Midianite connections of Moses are scarcely likely to have been invented,[8] and the association of Yahweh with a mountain to the south of Canaan is both strongly supported and unlikely to have arisen from a population that was solely derived from the Canaanite city-states. Although none of this directly supports the occurrence of the Exodus as such, it does indicate

---

8. The suggestion of J. Van Seters (1994: 29–33) that the episode was based on the story of Hadad in 1 Kgs 11 fails to account for more than the name 'Midian'.

that some influential 'proto-Israelites' were in regions far to the south of Canaan at some point in their history.

Thirdly, it is striking how often in Exodus 1–10 the term 'Hebrew' occurs as an alternative name for the people. Given the relative scarcity of this term in the Old Testament and the existence in both the Exodus tradition and elsewhere of the much more frequent term '(children of) Israel', the occurrences of 'Hebrew' and 'Hebrews' deserve more attention than they have been given. The word appears seven times in the Masoretic text of Exodus 1–2 and then in a series of six passages which mention 'the God of the Hebrews' (Exod. 3.18; 5.3; 7.16; 9.1, 13; 10.3), always in connection with the request to Pharaoh to allow the people to make a pilgrimage into the desert. Whatever their wider background (a point to which we shall return), these expressions look, in the context of the biblical tradition itself, like a special element which is not in conformity with the terminology which elsewhere became normal, and one which might reasonably be regarded, from a traditio-historical point of view, as going back to a stage in the tradition when the now dominant 'Israel' perspective had not yet been imposed upon it. If we accept the historical conclusion that 'Israel' was from the outset an entity that came into being on the soil of Canaan (however that took place), we could well envisage that this 'Hebrew' form of the tradition belonged to an early stage in the history of one of the constituent groups of later Israel, when they were still independent. In the absence of any indication to the contrary it might indeed be an original element of the tradition (so e.g. Koch 1969; Schmid 1969).

Fourthly, we come to the two poems in Exodus 15, the Song of Moses in vv. 1–17 and the Song of Miriam in v. 21. Great antiquity has been claimed for both of them and each bears witness to a catastrophe, attributed to the intervention of Israel's God Yahweh, which befell an Egyptian force to the advantage of 'Yahweh's people' (who are not given a name in the text of either poem). As F.M. Cross noted, the description of the catastrophe has only a little in common with the story of the 'crossing of the Red Sea' in Exodus 14 and elsewhere, a fact which Cross took to indicate the antiquity of the poems (Cross 1973: 121–44, esp. 131–37). Much more widespread emphasis has been placed, in America at least, on the archaic features in the language of the Song of Moses as proving an early date for its composition (see esp. Cross and Freedman 1975: ch. 2; Robertson 1972: 155; Propp 1999: 565 ['premonarchic']). *How* early of course remains a question. If, as seems probable, the imperfect verbs in vv. 14–17 are to be treated as preterites, as in Ugaritic, and so translated in the past; and if 'the mountain of your own possession, the place, O Lord, that you made your abode, the sanctuary, O Lord which your hands have established' in v. 17 is indeed Jerusalem, as seems most likely, the poem cannot have been composed, or at least cannot have been completed, before the tenth century. I say 'or cannot have been completed' because we might envisage that vv. 1–12, which are quite self-contained, existed independently at an earlier date than that (so e.g. Hyatt 1971: 163). But barring that possibility, the combination of archaic language and a reference to the Jerusalem sanctuary points to a date for the poem in the early monarchy period. Much later dates for it have been proposed, especially in Germany, in the late monarchy or even the post-exilic period (for references see Houtman 1996: 242), but they do not seem to me to rest on convincing arguments. The Song of Moses provides, at the latest, evidence of a deliverance from the Egyptians from the early monarchy period.

With the brief Song of Miriam we may be able to push further back. From a form-critical point of view it has been seen as the prototype of the classic narrative form of the hymn of praise (Gunkel and Begrich 1933: 42, ET 1998: 29; Westermann 1977: 66, ET 1981: 89), and from a traditio-historical point of view it was seen by Martin Noth as the oldest surviving statement of the Exodus tradition (1948: 52–53, ET 1972: 50–51; 1959: 96–98, ET 1962: 121–23). As Noth also saw, the figure of Miriam is likely to derive from a genuine historical tradition at an early time (1948: 199–200, ET 1972: 182–83), when perhaps the attribution of such a liturgical piece to a woman was not so unusual (cf. the Song of Deborah in Judg. 5). It would seem likely to be older than the Song of Moses, in which it has been adapted and amplified with much more narrative material, and to go back at least to the Judges period. Noth's hesitation to consider a direct association with the historical event to which it refers is no doubt connected with his well-known view about the absence of Moses from the original Exodus tradition. If, as seems probable, that view is held to be an example of undue scepticism, we might well be justified in regarding this strange little piece as an authentic element of historical memory.

We move now from direct evidence to some indirect evidence or evidence which provides an analogy to some of what the biblical narratives of the Exodus say. Most of this is well known. I drew attention earlier to the fact that in Exodus the Israelites are quite often referred to as 'Hebrews'. In texts of the Egyptian New Kingdom there are numerous references to people called ʿ*pr(w)*, probably vocalized ʿ*apiru*, being in Egypt, though that is apparently not their place of origin: some of the texts refer to ʿ*apiru* being brought as prisoners of war from Palestine (for a listing of the Egyptian texts see Loretz 1984: 35–44). For example, in Amenhotep II's second campaign (second half of the fifteenth century) he claims to have captured, among other groups, 3600 ʿ*apiru* and 15,200 Shasu (Bedouin) (*ANET*, 247). The precise nature of these people is much debated, but further references to them in Palestine appear in the Amarna letters, and they seem best described as 'outsiders' from the point of view of the city-state population of Canaan: the term is one that is used, however, all over the Near East. In Egypt the ʿ*apiru* are generally mentioned as workmen on state projects, in which they were forced to participate with other prisoners of war. A tomb-painting of a royal vizier (Rekhmire) of the mid-fifteenth century shows such prisoners-of-war making bricks (Hoffmeier 1997: fig. 8): some of them are said to have come from the Levant. More specifically two Leiden papyri (nos. 348 and 349), which are dated to the thirteenth century, mention ʿapiru as labourers: the former says 'Give grain rations to the people of the army and to the ʿapiru who are dragging stones for the great pylon of ... Ramses Miamun' (Galling 1979: 35 [D]), while the latter contains a response to a similar command: 'A further matter: [I] have taken note of my lord's message to me saying, "Give grain rations [to] the soldiers and the Apiru(-laborers) who are drawing (water from) the well of Pre of Ramesses II, l.p.h., south of Memphis". Farewell!' (Wente 1990: 124). Apparently ʿapiru and other foreigners also worked in agriculture: Ellen Morris has evidently made a study of Eighteenth Dynasty tomb-paintings from Upper Egypt which show this (see the summary in Hoffmeier 1997: 115).

This evidence might simply be valued, as it often is, as showing that the oppression of the Israelites in Exodus has some general plausibility because of the way in which foreign prisoners of war were utilized in the New Kingdom period. Its significance is sometimes dismissed on the ground that the Israelites entered Egypt of their own accord, seeking food, and were not prisoners of war. Can we be so sure? The historical link between the Exodus story and the Joseph story is not very tight: there is a long gap assumed during which the small family becomes a great people. May not the 'Exodus group' have consisted largely of prisoners of war? There is after all the tantalizing similarity between the words ʿapiru and 'Hebrew'. It is widely recognized that they could be and probably are connected. A connection is sometimes thought to be improbable because, while ʿapiru is a sociological term for a certain kind of person ('outsider'), 'Hebrew' is an ethnic term. But is it so clear that 'Hebrew' in Exodus is an ethnic term? It seems to me quite possible that there too it actually has a *social* meaning and that it can be dissociated from any particular ethnic identity. If so, there is probably more significance than is usually recognized in the coincidence of nomenclature between what seems to be an early stratum of the Exodus tradition and the references to ʿapiru in Egypt in the New Kingdom period. I am not suggesting one-to-one identity between an Exodus-group and any of the ʿapiru mentioned in the Egyptian texts – we are still dealing with an argument from analogy – but that the comparison may make us more confident that the biblical tradition is based on some knowledge of not only labour relations in general but specific nomenclature of the New Kingdom period.[9]

9. For evidence specifically of brickmaking in the New Kingdom see Kitchen 1976.

There are some further texts, often referred to, which also have a contribution to make to the case for seeing some historical content in the Exodus tradition and its precursor in Genesis. There is the so-called 'Report of a Frontier Official' on a papyrus in the British Museum from the end of the thirteenth century, which speaks of 'Shasu (Bedouin) of Edom' being admitted to 'the pools of Per-Atum of Merneptah Hotep-hir-Maat, which are in Tjeku' (Pap. Anastasi VI.51–61 = iv. 11 – v. 5: *ANET*, 259). This has been compared to the arrival of Jacob and his family in a time of famine. Tjeku is located in the modern Wadi Tumilat, in the eastern Delta, and may be the original Egyptian form of the name Succoth, which is the second stage of the Exodus itinerary (Exod. 12.37), and Per-Atum is, as already noted, the native Egyptian form of Pithom. Another papyrus from the same collection contains a report about the pursuit of two slaves who were seeking to escape from the same region into the desert: there is a reference there to 'the enclosure-wall of Tjeku' and a little later to the escapees passing 'the walled place north of the Migdol of Seti Merneptah' (Pap. Anastasi V.xix. 2 – xx. 6: *ANET*, 259). Although of course this is not on the scale of even a minimal view of the Exodus event, it does confirm what one would in any case have expected, that those subjected to slave labour in Egypt would from time to time attempt to escape and even succeed in doing so. In various ways, therefore, it can be claimed that evidence external to the Bible suggests that important elements of the Exodus tradition are realistic and could well reflect genuine memories of life in Egypt in the thirteenth century.

I come, finally, to a recent suggestion that some Egyptian texts may be able to offer confirmation of a much more direct kind for the historicity of at least some elements in the Exodus tradition. The original suggestion seems to have been made by E.A. Knauf (1988: 135–39), but it has been taken up in both a more cautious and a bolder form by A. Malamat and by J.C. de Moor respectively. Malamat limits himself to two Egyptian texts, both of the early twelfth century (1997: 22–25). The first is the Elephantine stele of Sethnakht (c. 1190–1188), which includes an account of how he overcame a coalition of 'the chiefs of Egypt' and a body of 'Asiatics' (*sttw*), to whom they had paid silver and gold, and how this group fled from Egypt and left Sethnakht unopposed (translation of the text in de Moor 1990: 145). Malamat is particularly intrigued by the parallels to two features of the account in Exodus: the borrowing/ extortion of silver and gold from the Egyptians by the Israelites (Exod. 12.35–36; cf. 3.21–22; 11.2) and Pharaoh's fear that the Israelites might ally themselves with his enemies (Exod. 1.10). He seems to waver between seeing these as mere analogies and understanding them as reflections of the same events. Secondly, he refers to a passage that has been known for much longer, from Papyrus Harris I, a document from the next reign, of Ramesses III (c. 1188–1157) (*ANET*, 260; de Moor 1990: 143–44). This speaks of an 'Asiatic' or 'Syrian' (*'3mw*), either named Irsu or more likely described as a usurper, who 'had made the entire land subservient to him' and presided over a time of disorder in which the gods were negelected: 'no offerings were offered up within the temples'. Rather cautiously Malamat writes: 'Some connection with the Asiatics of the Elephantine stele is not altogether implausible and certainly seems intriguing' (1997: 24). He goes on to note the common identification of this 'Asiatic' leader with one Beya, a 'prominent Egyptian official' who was active at just this time, one of whose diplomatic letters turned up in the excavations at Ugarit in the 1980s. That is as far as Malamat wants to go, except that in an Addendum he states clearly that because of the analogies he now dates the Exodus 'or its dominant phase' at precisely the time to which the two Egyptian documents refer, c. 1190. This is not very convincing: the rather dimly perceptible behaviour of these 'Asiatics' does not sound at all like the uprising of slaves described in the book of Exodus, and the only significant feature which the two stories share is that both groups 'escaped' from Egypt. It would take greater similarities to establish any real connection, even of an analogical kind.

It is precisely this that de Moor attempts. He has no hesitation in accepting the identification of Beya with the mysterious 'Asiatic' leader, and he presents more of the evidence for this Beya's attitudes and behaviour (1990: 137–44). De Moor sees him as mocking the official religion of Egypt, while at the same time wielding great power. He argues that this could only have been done with the direct support of the chief wife of the Pharaoh under whom he is first mentioned in texts, Seti II, a faint analogy perhaps with the way that Moses was brought up by Pharaoh's daughter according to ch. 2 of Exodus and maybe, de Moor suggests, more than an analogy. 'Could it be', he says, 'that Beya did not want to bow to the images of the gods of Egypt because his own religion forbade him to do so?' (143). He suggests that the name Beya might mean 'In Yah (is my trust)', comparing a Ugaritic proper name *bil* = 'In El (is my trust)' (149–50 n. 217). In what follows he gradually becomes bolder in the equation of Beya with Moses. Since Beya's Egyptian name began with R'-*mssw* = Ramesses, 'Moses' could be just an abbreviation of it. Although he admits that 'the identification of Beya with Moses has not been proved in any definitive way', he allows himself the statement: '(This means that) if Beya was *not* Moses, there must have existed a different person with an almost identical history in the very same short period' (150–51).

In one sense, by making more of what we know of Beya, de Moor (following Knauf) has made a stronger case than Malamat for seeing traces of the Exodus events in these Egyptian texts. This Semite leader who scorns the Egyptian gods does seem to be exceptional and to share much with Moses' defiance of Egyptian royalty and religion. And while the date implied for the Exodus is somewhat later than that which is usually envisaged (later of course than the Merneptah stele, which refers to Israel being already in Canaan), it is a date which some have championed for other reasons (Rendsburg 1992; Bietak 2000), including the neat fit with the dating of the archaeological evidence of Iron Age I 'highland villages', which many take to be the first Israelite settlements in Canaan.[10] Even so, problems remain. It has been argued by J. Freu that Beya died in the reign of Siptah (c. 1197–1192), which means that he could not have been involved in events under Sethnakht (1988: 396–97). The behaviour of Beya is in some respects very unlike that of the biblical Moses (especially his involvement in the government of Egypt and the internal power struggles of the court), just as the 'Asiatics' of the other Egyptian texts are not very like the Exodus-group in the Old Testament. It is certainly possible to write a fascinating story by combining both sets of evidence, but that does not mean that they originally had anything to do with each other. The date is also a difficulty. Not so much because of the Merneptah stele, because in a more 'fluid' approach to the biblical narrative one could imagine the 'Hebrews' from Egypt arriving in Canaan after other 'proto-Israelites' had already established themselves as a recognizable group, in time to be attacked and defeated by Merneptah. It is Exod. 1.11 which poses a more serious problem, because it does seem to point to the reign of Ramesses II as the most likely time for the Exodus group's oppression and it is awkward to have to separate the 'Exodus' too much from that. Of course on the dating that is now widely favoured Ramesses II died c. 1212, which is only just over twenty years from 1190, so chronology is perhaps not an insuperable problem. But I remain dubious about these theories on the other grounds stated.

This leaves the case for a positive estimate of the historicity of some kind of 'Exodus event' to be made on the basis of the arguments expounded earlier. The tradition is a priori unlikely to have been invented; the biblical evidence is widespread and can be followed back to a respectable antiquity, within at most two hundred years of the supposed event; some elements of it have a particular claim to authenticity; and in various ways what is said corresponds more closely to the realities of New Kingdom Egypt than one would expect from a later wholly fictitious account.

Bibliography

Albertz, R.
1992   *Religionsgeschichte Israels in alttestamentlicher Zeit* (ATD Ergänzungsreihe, 8.1–2; Göttingen: Vandenhoeck & Ruprecht). ET *A History of Israelite Religion in the Old Testament Period* (trans. John Bowden; London: SCM Press, 1994).

---

10. See the chapter by A.J. Frendo in this volume.

Bietak, M.
1979   'Avaris and Pi-Ramesse', *PBA* 65: 225–89 [also published separately].
1996   *Avaris, The Capital of the Hyksos: Recent Excavations at Tell el Dabʿa* (London: British Museum Press).
2000   'Der Aufenthalt "Israels" in Ägypten und der Zeitpunkt der "Landnahme" aus heutiger archäologischer Sicht', *Ägypten und Levante* 10: 179–86.

Bleiberg, E.L.
1983   'The Location of Pithom and Succoth', *Ancient World* 6: 21–27.

Bright, J.
1960   *A History of Israel* (London: SCM Press).

Clements, R.E.
1965   *God and Temple* (Oxford: Basil Blackwell).

Cross, F.M.
1973   *Canaanite Myth and Hebrew Epic* (Cambridge, MA: Harvard University Press).

Cross, F.M., and D.N. Freedman
1975   *Studies in Ancient Yahwistic Poetry* (SBLDS, 21; Missoula, MT: Scholars Press).

Davies, G.I.
1979a *The Way of the Wilderness: A Geographical Study of the Wilderness Itineraries in the Old Testament* (SOTSMS, 5; Cambridge: Cambridge University Press).
1979b 'The Significance of Deuteronomy I.2 for the Location of Mount Horeb', *PEQ* 111: 87–101.

Day, J.
1986   'Pre-Deuteronomic Allusions to the Covenant in Hosea and Psalm lxxviii', *VT* 36: 1–12.
1990   *Psalms* (OTG; Sheffield: JSOT Press).

Dever, W.G.
1997a 'Is there any Archaeological Evidence for the Exodus?', in Frerichs and Lesko 1997: 67–86.
1997b 'Archaeology and the Emergence of Early Israel', in J.R. Bartlett (ed.), *Archaeology and Biblical Interpretation* (London and New York: Routledge), 20–50.
2003   *Who Were the Early Israelites and Where Did They Come From?* (Grand Rapids, MI, and Cambridge: W.B. Eerdmans).

Dijkstra, M.
1989   'Pithom en Raämses', *NedTTs* 43: 89–105.

Donner, H.
1995   *Geschichte des Volkes Israel und seiner Nachbarn in Grundzügen*, I (Göttingen: Vandenhoeck & Ruprecht, 2nd edn).

Dorner, J.
1999   'Die Topographie von Piramesse – Vorbericht', *Ägypten und Levante* 9: 77–83.

Frerichs, E.S., and L.H. Lesko (eds).
1997   *Exodus: The Egyptian Evidence* (Winona Lake, IN: Eisenbrauns).

Freu, J.
1988   'La tablette RS 86.2230 et la phase finale du royaume d'Ugarit', *Syria* 65: 395–98.

Galling, K. (ed.)
1979   *Textbuch zur Geschichte Israels* (Tübingen: J.C.B. Mohr [Paul Siebeck], 3rd edn).
Gardiner, A.H.
1918   'The Delta Residence of the Ramessides', *JEA* 5: 127–38, 179–200, 242–71.
1933   'Tanis and Pi-Raʿmesse: A Retractation', *JEA* 19: 122–28.
Goedicke, H.
1987a   'Ramesses II and the Wadi Tumilat', *Varia Aegyptiaca* 3: 13–24.
1987b   'Papyrus Anastasi VI, 51–61', *Studien zur altägyptischen Kultur* 14: 83–98.
Gressmann, H.
1913   *Mose und seine Zeit* (FRLANT, NF 1; Göttingen: Vandenhoeck & Ruprecht).
Gunkel, H.
1926   *Die Psalmen* (HKAT, 2.2; Göttingen: Vandenhoeck & Ruprecht).
Gunkel, H., and J. Begrich
1933   *Einleitung in die Psalmen: Die Gattungen der religiösen Lyrik Israels* (Göttingen: Vandenhoeck & Ruprecht). ET *Introduction to Psalms: The Genres of the Religious Lyric of Israel* (trans. James D. Nogalski; Macon, GA: Mercer University Press, 1998).
Helck, W.
1965   'Ṯkw und die Ramses-Stadt', *VT* 15: 35–48.
Herrmann, S.
1970   *Israels Aufenthalt in Ägypten* (SBS, 40; Stuttgart: Katholisches Bibelwerk). ET *Israel in Egypt* (trans. Margaret Kohl; SBT, 2nd series, 27; London: SCM Press, 1973).
Hoffmeier, J.K.
1997   *Israel in Egypt: The Evidence for the Authenticity of the Exodus Tradition* (New York and Oxford: Oxford University Press).
Holladay, J.S.
1992   'Maskhuta, Tell el', in *ABD*, IV: 588–92.
Houtman, C.
1996   *Exodus, II: Chapters 7:14–19:25* (Historical Commentary on the Old Testament; Kampen: Kok).
Humphreys, C.J.
2003   *The Miracles of Exodus: A Scientist's Discovery of the Extraordinary Natural Causes of the Biblical Stories* (New York: HarperSan Francisco).
Hyatt, J.P.
1971   *Exodus* (NCB; London: Oliphants).
Johnstone, W.
1990   *Exodus* (OTG; Sheffield: Sheffield Academic Press).
Kitchen, K.A.
1976   'From the Brickfields of Egypt', *TynBul* 27: 137–47.
1982   *Pharaoh Triumphant: The Life and Times of Ramesses II* (Warminster: Aris & Phillips).
1998   'Egyptians and Hebrews from Raʿamses to Jericho', in S. Aḥituv and E.D. Oren (eds), *The Origin of Early Israel – Current Debate* (Beer-Sheva, 12; Beersheva: Ben-Gurion University of the Negev Press), 65–131.

Knauf, E.A.
  1988   *Midian: Untersuchungen zur Geschichte Palästinas und Nordarabiens am Ende des 2. Jahrtausends v. Chr.* (ADPV, 7; Wiesbaden: Otto Harrassowitz).
Koch, K.
  1969   'Die Hebräer vom Auszug aus Ägypten bis zum Grossreich Davids', *VT* 19: 37–81.
Lemche, N.P.
  1988   *Ancient Israel: A New History of Israelite Society* (The Biblical Seminar, 5; Sheffield: JSOT Press)
  1996   *Die Vorgeschichte Israels* (Biblische Enzyklopädie, 1; Stuttgart: W. Kohlhammer).
Lepsius, R.
  1849   *Die Chronologie der Aegypter* (Berlin: Nicolaische Buchhandlung).
  1883   'Über die Lage von Pithom (Sukkoth) und Raëmses (Heroonpolis)', *ZÄS* 21, 41–53.
Loewenstamm, S.E.
  1992   *The Evolution of the Exodus Tradition* (Jerusalem: Magnes Press).
Loretz, O.
  1984   *Habiru-Hebräer: eine sozio-linguistische Studie über die Herkunft des Gentiliziums ʿibrî vom Appellativum ḫabiru* (BZAW, 160; Berlin: W. de Gruyter).
Malamat, A.
  1997   'The Exodus: Egyptian Analogies', in Frerichs and Lesko 1997: 15–26.
de Moor, J.C.
  1990   *The Rise of Yahwism: The Roots of Israelite Monotheism* (BETL, 91; Leuven: Leuven University Press and Peeters).
Naville, E.
  1885   *The Store-City of Pithom and the Route of the Exodus* (London: Trübner and Co.).
Noth, M.
  1948   *Überlieferungsgeschichte des Pentateuch* (Stuttgart: W. Kohlhammer). ET *A History of Pentateuchal Traditions* (trans. B.W. Anderson; Englewood Cliffs, NJ: Prentice–Hall, 1972).
  1954   *Geschichte Israels* (Göttingen: Vandenhoeck & Ruprecht, 2nd edn). ET *The History of Israel* (trans. P.R. Ackroyd; London: A. & C. Black, 2nd edn, 1960).
  1959   *Das zweite Buch Mose, Exodus* (ATD, 5; Göttingen: Vandenhoeck & Ruprecht, 2nd edn). ET *Exodus* (trans. John Bowden; OTL; London: SCM Press, 1962).
Petrie, W.M.F.
  1906   *Hyksos and Israelite Cities* (British School of Archaeology in Egypt, and Egyptian Research Account, 12; London: School of Archaeology, University College, and Bernard Quaritch).
Propp, W.H.C.
  1999   *Exodus 1–18* (AB, 2; New York: Doubleday).
Pusch, E.B., H. Becker and J. Fassbinder
  1999   'Wohnen und Leben: oder Weitere Schritte zu einem Stadtplan der Ramses-

Stadt', *Ägypten und Levante* 9: 155–70 (see also the list of publications for the whole expedition [1980–1997] on pp. 193–95).

Pusch, E.B. and N. Knauer
1997   'Die Grabungen des Pelizaeus-Museums Hildesheim in Qantir/Piramesse 1980–1996', in H. Reyer (ed.), *Hildesheimer Jahrbuch* 69: 395–409.

Redford, D.B.
1963   'Exodus I 11', *VT* 13: 401–18.

Rendsburg, G.A.
1992   'The Date of the Exodus and the Conquest/Settlement: The Case for the 1100s', *VT* 42: 510–27.

Robertson, D.A.
1972   *Linguistic Evidence in Dating Early Hebrew Poetry* (SBLDS, 3; Missoula, MT: SBL).

Schmid, H.
1969   'Jhwh, der Gott der Hebräer', *Judaica* 25: 257–66.

Schmidt, W.H.
1988   *Exodus, I: Exodus 1–6* (BKAT, 2.1; Neukirchen–Vluyn: Neukirchener Verlag).

Thompson, T.L.
1987   *The Origin Tradition of Ancient Israel, I: The Literary Formation of Genesis and Exodus 1–23* (JSOTSup, 55; Sheffield: JSOT Press).

Uphill, E.P.
1968   'Pithom and Raamses: Their Location and Significance', *JNES* 27: 281–316.

Van Seters, J.
1987   'Moses', in M. Eliade (ed.), *Encyclopedia of Religion* (New York: Macmillan), X: 115–21
1994   *The Life of Moses: The Yahwist as Historian in Exodus-Numbers* (Louisville, KY: Westminster John Knox Press).

Weimar, P., and E. Zenger
1975   *Exodus: Geschichte und Geschichten der Befreiung Israels* (SBS, 75; Stuttgart: Katholisches Bibelwerk).

Wente, E.F.
1990   *Letters from Ancient Egypt* (SBL Writings from the Ancient World; Atlanta, GA: Scholars Press).
1992   'Rameses (Place)', in *ABD*, V: 617–18.

Westermann, C.
1977   *Lob und Klage in den Psalmen* (Göttingen: Vandenhoeck & Ruprecht). ET *Praise and Lament in the Psalms* (trans. Keith R. Crim and Richard N. Soulen; Edinburgh: T. & T. Clark, 1981).

Yurco, F.
1997   'Merenptah's Canaanite Campaign and Israel's Origins', in Frerichs and Lesko 1997: 27–55.

Chapter 3

BACK TO BASICS: A HOLISTIC APPROACH TO THE PROBLEM OF THE
EMERGENCE OF ANCIENT ISRAEL

Anthony J. Frendo

In 1971, Roland de Vaux had claimed that 'Le problème de l'installation des Israélites en Canaan et de la formation du système des douze tribus est le plus difficile de toute l'histoire d'Israël' (de Vaux 1971: I, 443).[1] Notwithstanding all the research that has been undertaken since de Vaux had made this statement, the difficulties related to the problem of the emergence of ancient Israel in Canaan have not really been solved. Indeed, it is a commonplace that the overflow of publications regarding this problem are at times more confusing than ever, and that in the process many have opted to undervalue the biblical evidence. It is well known that nowadays in many circles it is virtually taken for granted that ancient Israel never really came from outside Canaan, that it was basically made up of discontented Canaanites, and that the biblical narratives relative to Israel's entry into Canaan are in essence fictional and that they do not reflect pre-exilic historical traditions (see, e.g., Dever 1997; Davies 1992). Such a picture has been maintained not so much by the marshalling of evidence, as by virtue of what can be called the argument 'ad nauseam', which '... might serve, tongue in cheek, as a tag-name for a serious form of error, in which a thesis is sustained by repetition rather than by reasoned proof' (Fischer 1971: 302).

I think that it is high time that we go back to basics, and seriously reconsider the issue of the emergence of ancient Israel in Canaan in the light of all the available evidence without unjustly preferring one type of evidence to another. Thus, the biblical evidence, the archaeological evidence, and other extra-biblical evidence should all be given their due weight. It appears that currently the biblical evidence is being treated as the underdog; consequently, it would be healthy (by way of a methodo-

---

1. ET 1978: II, 476, 'The problem raised by the settlement of the Israelites in Canaan and the growth of the system of the twelve tribes is the most difficult problem in the whole history of Israel'.

logical antidote) to suspend our disbelief (in the historical narratives of the Bible) rather than our judgment.[2] Only after we give a fair hearing to all the witnesses concerned, can we proceed to pronounce a judgment regarding the manner in which Israel appeared on Canaanite soil. Given the current state of research, which often labours under silent assumptions, it is important to underscore the methodological issues involved and to treat them carefully when the evidence is being assessed. Thus, for example, the so-called 'minimalists' endorse one particular assumption which needs to be treated urgently, namely 'that a text's claims must be corroborated before they can be considered historical. This expectation is the opposite of the Western legal tradition of "innocent until proven guilty"'.[3] Indeed, when archaeological evidence is not to be found in support of a claim made by the biblical text, it certainly does not follow that the text is necessarily false. On the contrary, we have to consider carefully what Newman has called the 'preponderance of probability',[4] which when analogically applied to the problem of the emergence of ancient Israel would lead us to assume (until the contrary is proven) that Israel must have somehow (at least partially) come from outside Canaan in view of the multiple texts in the Old Testament which point in this direction. Why should the Old Testament authors have made this up? Should we not try harder to understand our texts in connection with the results of good archaeology, rather than superficially to dismiss the former?

In view of the foregoing considerations, it is clear that a holistic approach (with the necessary methodological underpinnings) is needed in order to try and understand better the problem of the emergence of ancient Israel. A critical assessment of the biblical evidence indicates that on leaving Egypt, the Israelites did not have Canaan as their objective but Kadesh.[5] This explains how they could have picked up their faith in Yahweh from somewhere in the desert; indeed, Yahweh has been described by Herrmann (1964: 72) as a God of mountainous desert land, who is accompanied by volcanic activity, and who is linked to

2.   Very rarely do we hear of a 'suspension of disbelief' (Hallo 1990: 187).

3.   Hoffmeier 1997: 10. Danell (1946: 14) also maintains that a text is innocent until proven guilty. For a succinct and vivid description of this principle, see Newman (1889: 180), who writes: 'Supposing a boy cannot make his answer to some arithmetical or algebraical question tally with the book, need he at once distrust the book?'

4.   Newman 1889: 180 expands on the metaphor mentioned in the previous note when he says that in fact the boy sticks to the *principle* (even though implicitly) 'with which he took up the book, that the book is more likely to be right than he is; and this mere *preponderance of probability* [my italics] is sufficient to make him faithful to his belief in its correctness, till its incorrectness is actually proved'.

5.   Oesterley and Robinson 1937: 142, especially n. 2 where the relevant biblical texts are listed.

nomads and not to an agricultural group. However, the 'mountain of God' could have actually been much closer to Palestine (for example in the mountains of Wadi el-Arabah, where biblical Seir is to be found) than we normally think (Herrmann 1964: 75 n. 3). It is very probable that Yahwism originated with the Kenites (a branch of the Midianites), who via Hobab and Moses passed it on to the Israelites (van der Toorn 1999: 912). Thus, it was somewhere in the desert regions to the south of Edom that the Israelites would have embraced the Yahwistic faith before entering Canaan.[6]

One important qualification needs to be made. The term 'Israel' as applied to the group of people who had been led by Moses and Joshua seems to be an anachronism. Indeed, Israel is likely to have been in Canaan before Joshua arrived. It can be suggested that in Joshua 24, 'Joshua and his house' were Yahweh's worshippers, whilst the people who had worshipped other gods were the Israel whom Joshua and his group met in Canaan. After the covenant which Joshua made at Shechem, Israel promised to worship 'Yahweh Elohe Israel' instead of 'El Elohe Israel' (Gen. 33.20; cf. Danell 1946: 41–42 and references there). It is probable that on entering Canaan the people led by Joshua were considered to be Hebrews; however, 'what they called themselves before migrating we do not know' (Danell 1946: 42). Notwithstanding this, it is important to remember that when referring to the Israelites before the settlement, the Old Testament never uses any of the usual parallel names such as Jacob, Joseph, or Ephraim. The terms employed, besides 'Israel' (which is used anachronistically), are 'people', 'the people', and 'Hebrews'.[7]

Obviously, this leads us into the problem of the meaning of the term 'Hebrews' and of when it was used in the Old Testament. Loretz's important study on the Habiru had led him to conclude that in the Old Testament the term 'Hebrew' indicates a member of the post-exilic Jewish

6. I do not agree with van der Toorn (1999: 913) when he claims that 'it is unlikely' that the Kenites introduced the Israelites to Yahwism outside Palestine; his claim is based on the fact that Kenites and Rechabites dwelt in northern Israel at an early stage, just like the Gibeonites who were related to the Edomites, and on the hypothesis (which he calls a fact) that 'the majority of the Israelites were firmly rooted in Palestine' (van der Toorn 1999: 912). Such arguments beg the question of whether Israel entered Canaan (at least partially) from outside, and in no way do they diminish the likelihood that the Israelites picked up Yahwism from the Kenites in their home territory.

7. Danell 1946: 40 and references there. Danell's observations on the matter are most interesting: 'Though it may seem bold, the question must be asked whether it is conceivable that the immigrants took the name Israel only after entering Canaanite territory. In any case it is remarkable that the name arose traditionally on Canaanite territory and in connection with a migration (cf. Gen 32: 25ff.; 35: 9ff.). Further, it is remarkable that the name Israel, (which even if it were originally the name of a god, came later to designate a cult-unit) contains no reference to Yahweh, who according to tradition was the God of Israel right from Egypt and Sinai' (Danell 1946: 40).

community, and that when referring to the Hebrews in Egypt, the Bible means to talk about the immediate ancestors of Israel and the Jews or of those who are identical with them; in this manner, history and post-exilic Judaism are virtually fused (Loretz 1984: 271, 274). However, not all scholars agree that 'Hebrews' is simply a term being used anachronistically when applied to the progenitors of the people who 'can later be called "Israel", or "the sons of Israel"'; indeed, the Israelites or their ancestors refer to themselves as Hebrews when discussing with foreigners (Rainey 1985: 379). Joseph claims to come from 'the land of the Hebrews' (Gen. 40.15), and the phrase 'the land of Israel' is used with reference to the period after the settlement of the tribes (Rainey 1985: 379). This gentilic use of the word 'Hebrew' in the Bible does not militate against the fact that the term *habiru* (with which it can be etymologically linked) indicates a social group and not an ethnic one.[8] Knight (1993: 273) thinks that 1 Sam. 13.3–4 shows that even in the Bible we can have a similar situation echoing an ancient distinction which was no longer valid later on, showing that the Israelites may be understood as stemming from the larger socioeconomic group of Hebrews and banding 'together in the Canaanite highlands to form a new nation'. In this sense, it is likely that it was a group of people called Hebrews (both in a socioeconomic sense and in a gentilic sense) who had embraced Yahwism under Moses in the desert and brought it with them to Canaan under Joshua's leadership.

It is well known that the biblical texts claim that after wandering in the desert these Hebrews took possession of northern Transjordan under the leadership of Moses, later occupying western Palestine under Joshua's leadership. At times the accounts are concerned with the activities of all the group, whereas at other times 'local conquests and settlements' in western Palestine are dealt with; moreover, some groups are also portrayed as entering Judah from the Kadesh region.[9] It is a commonplace that the biblical narrative regarding the settlement of the Israelite tribes in Canaan contains traditions of a variegated nature. Thus, one tradition represents the conquest of Palestine as a *Blitzkrieg*: Joshua 1–12, Num. 21.21–35 and 32.39–42. A second tradition in Judg. 1.1–2.5 describes the entry of the Hebrew tribes in Canaan as a slow and variegated process. In this case, there is also the theme of the land which remains to be conquered: Josh. 13.1–7 and Judg. 1.1–2.5. Finally, there is a tradition which knows of a peaceful settlement by the Hebrew tribes

8. Loretz 1984: 272, 273. See also McKenzie (1965: 346), who aptly writes with respect to Eber that it probably was 'a fictitious eponymous ancestor invented to explain the existence of a group under a name which had become a gentilic instead of a social designation.'

9. Isserlin 1998: 54. For a good summary of the biblical evidence regarding the 'conquest' of Canaan see Isserlin 1998: 53–54.

(Num. 32.1–38) and of a coexistence with the Canaanites (Judg. 1.21). Judges 5 (generally taken to be a genuine ancient source) should be singled out, in view of the fact that it recalls military operations, which were undertaken by Israelite tribes against the Canaanites, without giving the idea of a *Blitzkrieg* by 'all Israel' occupying the whole territory of Canaan.

Finkelstein and Silberman have underscored the fact that the overall battle plan in the book of Joshua 'fits seventh century realities far better than the situation of the Late Bronze Age', and that the conquest stories too are strongly reminiscent of the seventh century BCE (Finkelstein and Silberman 2001: 93, 283–84). We are reminded that Joshua's figure is used as a metaphor for King Josiah 'the would-be savior of all the people of Israel. Indeed, the American biblical scholar Richard D. Nelson has demonstrated how the figure of Joshua is described in the Deuteronomistic history in terms usually reserved for a king' (Finkelstein and Silberman 2001: 95). However, this does not mean that there was no earlier tradition regarding a historical Joshua. Could we not be simply dealing with a rereading of past traditions which were applied to later contemporary events, with the result of an intertwining of earlier history and its application to later historical circumstances? Is not this a common procedure in the Old Testament? The Joshua narratives could have very well been edited in the seventh century BCE, but this does not mean that the core narratives could not have been composed earlier.[10] Be that as it may, Finkelstein and Silberman themselves accept that there was an original ancient historical tradition lying behind the narratives in Joshua which contains 'folk memories' regarding the conquest of Canaan by the Hebrew tribes.[11] And, as we all know, the mainstream opinion is that the exodus and settlement belong to late thirteenth and early twelfth centuries BCE. Thus, the tradition behind the Old Testament narratives regarding the entry and settlement of the Israelite tribes in Canaan could have developed any time between the twelfth and the seventh centuries BCE.

---

10. The second-millennium Assyrian texts parallel the Joshua narratives as much as, if not in a 'more compelling' way than the Neo-Assyrian texts of the seventh century BCE. See Hoffmeier 1997: 42–43.

11. Thus, Finkelstein and Silberman (2001: 91–92) tell us that such memories 'may offer us highly fragmentary glimpses of the violence, the passion, the euphoria at the destruction of cities and horrible slaughter of their inhabitants that clearly occurred. Such searing experiences are not likely to have been totally forgotten, and indeed, their once-vivid memories, growing progressively vaguer over the centuries, may have become the raw material for a far more elaborate retelling. Thus there is no reason to suppose that the burning of Hazor by battle forces, for example, never took place. But what was in actuality a chaotic series of upheavals caused by many different groups became – many centuries later – a brilliantly crafted saga of territorial conquest under God's blessing and direct command.'

Given such a complicated history of the 'conquest' traditions, it is no wonder that contradictions are found in the narratives we have and that we cannot find a solution to each of them. Thus, for example, the book of Judges lists Megiddo, Beth-shean, Dor and Gezer as not having been captured by the Israelites, whereas in the book of Joshua these cities are listed as captured (Finkelstein and Silberman 2001: 99). The problem of the capture of Ai is notorious. Since 'the question of aetiology is a literary one, not a historical one' (Hess 1996: 158), it cannot be used to solve this problem. Then there is the apparent contradiction between Josh. 13.1–21.42 and 21.43–45. In the former, the nations are presented as 'isolated individuals and groups that must still be uprooted', whereas 'from 21: 43 on the nations are once again (as in chs. 1–12) a combined force' (Hess 1996: 286). This provides a contrast and not a contradiction in that Israel had defeated the nations as a coalition, but it would still have to fight them as the remaining isolated pockets; indeed, 'the coalitions were defeated' (Hess 1996: 286).

Biblical historians are wont to contrast the different conquest traditions mentioned above, especially those in Joshua 6–11 with that in Judges 1. On closer critical analysis, it turns out that we are dealing not so much with a contradiction as with the use of hyperbole alongside more accurate historical statements. This situation is found in Egyptian inscriptions – at times even in one single literary unit, and such a 'precise combination is found in the Joshua narratives'.[12] Hoffmeier singles out a very interesting verse in Joshua 10, namely v. 20 which in one breath seems to be using contradictory language unless one keeps in mind the use of hyperbole.[13] The latter was widely employed in the ancient Near East where the description of enemy defeats was concerned (Hoffmeier 1997: 39, 49 n. 122). Moreover, critical analysis of Joshua 10 does not support the idea 'that the land of Canaan and its principal cities were demolished and devastated by the Israelites' (Hoffmeier 1997: 34). Indeed, the Hebrew verbs used to describe the attack by the Israelites are 'to rush upon/to capture', 'to fight', 'to wound/to smite', and 'to besiege', and as such they do not 'indicate that a city was deliberately set ablaze and destroyed' (Hoffmeier 1997: 34). Early Israel's military tactics were mainly indirect,

12. Hoffmeier 1997: 42. Thutmose III spoke of absolute victories, but so does his son Amenhotep II; the latter could not have done this had his father's victories been so thorough as he claims. Moreover, in his famous stele, Merneptah claims to have decimated whole regions, whilst simultaneously saying that he conquered particular cities such as Ashkelon and Gaza. See Hoffmeier 1997: 41, 42, 50.

13. See Hoffmeier 1997: 41, where he translates the passage in question thus: 'When Joshua and the men of Israel had finished slaying them with *a very great slaughter, until they were wiped out,* and *when the remnant which remained* of them had entered into the fortified cities, all the people returned safe to Joshua at the camp of Makkedah'.

such as secret infiltration and enticement to draw the enemy out into the open. In fact, Joshua reports that the Israelites destroyed only three cities by fire, namely Jericho (6.4), Ai (8.19–20.28), and Hazor (11.11).[14]

Thus, the biblical evidence regarding the emergence of Israel in Canaan seems to be basically describing the entry (partly peacefully and partly militarily, though not in an unusually violent manner) of Hebrew tribes from the desert who brought the Yahwistic faith with them and who settled mainly in the central hills of the country. Early Israel had no memory of the Egyptian armies in the valleys of Canaan simply because it did not form part of the administrative unit of the Egyptian empire, as well as because, living in the hills, it would have had no 'cause to recall participating in the Egyptians' expulsion' (Halpern 1992: 1132). Even if it were to be proven that the deuteronomistic composition regarding the traditions concerning the emergence of early Israel was late, the underlying historicity of these traditions would not be thereby undermined. Finkelstein and Silberman themselves are ready to grant that the lateness of a particular composition does not necessarily imply the non-historicity of the traditions concerned.[15] In this context, it is interesting to note that in the pre-monarchic period 'explicitly Yahwistic personal names are very rare (apart from Joshua only five from the Judges period)' (Day 2000: 17). Does not this tally with the probability that Yahwism was being introduced in Canaan by the incoming Hebrew tribes?

A critical appreciation of the archaeological evidence relevant to the problem of the emergence of Israel in Canaan yields a picture similar to the one just described. Up to about four decades ago, scholars often used to link certain artefacts from the Late Bronze and Early Iron Age strata in Palestine with an insufficiently critical reading of the conquest accounts in the Old Testament. Thus, for example, the collar-rim jar, the four-room house as well as the destruction layers in many sites of Palestine were too hastily linked with the conquest accounts in Joshua.

A fresh critical look at the overall archaeological evidence of the Late Bronze and Early Iron Ages in Palestine is needed. Biblical scholars generally date the emergence of Israel in Canaan to around the beginning of the twelfth century BCE, which in archaeological terms matches the transition from the Late Bronze to the Early Iron Age in Palestine. It is important to note how this transition is reflected in the material culture. Thus, for example, the Early Iron Age pottery continued 'generally in the

14. Hoffmeier 1997: 35, where he interestingly also notes that the Joshua narratives 'are very clear when the Israelites' [*sic*] did in fact burn a city, which *would* leave its mark in the archaeological record'.

15. Finkelstein and Silberman 2001: 255–56 where they uphold the historical accuracy of the Chronicler with respect to the preparations of King Hezekiah in view of the attack on Jerusalem by the Assyrians.

degenerate Late Bronze Age tradition, but wares are now often partly handmade rather than fashioned on a fast wheel' (Dever 2000: 33). As will be shown below, not even the collar-rim jar is an Israelite innovation.

As far as architecture is concerned, the main Iron Age novelty is the use of stone pillars; in the Late Bronze Age there had been only occasional buildings in which rooms were divided by such stone pillars (Fritz 1997: 195). The four-room house is often adduced as another architectural novelty of the Early Iron Age in Palestine. However, we now know that this is not so, for in Palestine itself there is one possible example of such a house from a Late Bronze Age context from Tel Batash, and in Egypt a four-room house dating to about the mid-twelfth century BCE has been unearthed at western Thebes, making it unlikely that this type of house was an Israelite invention.[16]

Plastered water cisterns and agricultural terraces too have often been invoked as an Early Iron Age novelty which can be connected with the emergence of ancient Israel in Palestine. However, this viewpoint can no longer be upheld, since such cisterns had already been used by the Middle Bronze Age and possibly even by the Late Bronze Age people of Canaan; indeed, 'many of the Iron I highland sites are devoid of such water cisterns; apparently, their inhabitants brought water from distant springs and stored it in the typical, large Iron I pithoi . . .' (Finkelstein 1995: 364). As far as the terraces are concerned, we now know that the Early Iron Age settlement process began in areas where no such terraces were needed and that Middle Bronze Age activity has been detected on the western slopes of Canaan where it would have been impossible to have cultivation without terraces. Moreover, it seems plausible that terraces had already appeared during the Early Bronze Age in the hill country of Palestine 'with the first widespread cultivation of olives and grape vines' (Finkelstein 1995: 364) in this region. Indeed, the Early Iron Age plastered water cisterns and agricultural terraces in Palestine now seem to have been the result of settlement in the hill country and not an innovation which made this settlement possible (Finkelstein 1995: 364).

It is notorious how certain archaeological sites in Palestine have been linked in vain with the settlement of the Israelite tribes. Thus, for example, at Jericho between c. 1425 and 1275 BCE there seems to have been only 'a very limited and increasingly impoverished settlement' (which was apparently unwalled) for Joshua and his followers to have conquered any time during this period (Isserlin 1998: 57). Moreover, at Ai and Gibeon there simply was no city during the Late Bronze Age (Isserlin 1998: 5).

---

16. Hoffmeier 1997: 32 who says that 'Since the chances are remote that the Theban house is of Israelite construction, Finkelstein's beflief that this type of house is an Israelite innovation is questionable.'

In recent years, Palestinian archaeologists have been giving great importance to the study of settlement patterns. Indeed, the Early Iron Age settlements in Palestine should not be seen in isolation; on the contrary, they should be viewed within the context of the overall settlement patterns from the Early Bronze right through the Early Iron Age. It is interesting to note that in this period there were two major waves of settlement (in the Middle Bronze and Early Iron Ages), each following a period of crisis (during which people generally passed from sedentary existence to nomadism), namely the Early Bronze–Middle Bronze period and the Late Bronze Age. It has been noted that each wave of population growth started in the east and gradually moved west, and that each one 'is characterized by a roughly similar material culture – pottery, architecture, and village plan – that was probably a result of similar environmental and economic conditions' (Finkelstein and Silberman 2001: 115). In this sense, the emergence of ancient Israel is viewed not as the cause of the demise of Canaanite culture but as its upshot (Finkelstein and Silberman 2001: 118). This view seems to be supported by the fact that in all the three major phases of sedentary existence the same sites were often settled. As far as the Early Iron Age sites are concerned, many of them were established on spots which had been occupied in the Early Bronze I and especially during the Middle Bronze Age. Surveys indicate that out of 254 Early Iron Age sites, 116 had been occupied in the Middle Bronze Age and that the vast majority had been deserted during the Late Bronze Age (Finkelstein 1995: 355). Indeed, the central hill country sites of these three main phases of sedentary existence often seem to share many cultural traits. Thus, for example, the famous Early Iron Age collar-rim jar which has been often diagnosed as being Israelite can already find its parallels in the Middle Bronze Age pithoi from Shiloh. All in all, the Early Iron Age material culture should not be viewed in ethnic terms but rather it should be seen as reflecting ecological background, subsistence economy, and the social framework of the communities involved (Finkelstein 1995: 359).

However, one should also look closely at the Early Iron Age settlements in view of the problem of the emergence of ancient Israel. These settlements are mainly found in Galilee, in the central hill country, in the Negev desert, and in the middle of the east bank of the Jordan River. They are small (ranging from one to two and a half acres) and consist of three main types, namely ring-form settlements (where the houses are arranged in an oval or circle around a central open space), nucleated villages (with individual houses or complexes of buildings randomly built without any defensive perimeter) and farmsteads (single buildings or groups thereof surrounded by a wall) (Fritz 1997: 194). The central hill country settlements are of special importance since this is where it seems that the early Israelites first settled (Isserlin 1998: 61). This area comprises the mountains lying between the Jezreel and Beer-sheba valleys, and it is presumed that the first Israelite settlements occurred on the eastern parts of Ephraim and Manasseh, whence they then spread (Finkelstein 1995: 349; Isserlin 1998: 61). In fact the central hill country is bordered by steppe both to its east and south, and as far as the eastern side of this hilly region is concerned, it should be remembered that it 'was especially convenient for sedentary activity of groups which originated from a pastoral background, since they could continue to practice animal husbandry alongside dry farming' (Finkelstein 1995: 353). The central highland settlements of the Early Iron Age in Canaan consisted of small villages which were uniform and which appeared suddenly without any trace of burning or sudden destruction; interestingly enough, no weapons were retrieved from them, 'although such finds [such as swords or lances] are typical of the cities in the lowlands' (Finkelstein and Silberman 2001: 110). The villagers were self-sufficient, drawing water from nearby springs or from rock-cut plastered cisterns. Few silos, sickle blades, grinding stones, and a large enclosed courtyard, all together indicate that these highland villagers were both growing grain and herding their flocks. Archaeologically speaking, their religion is unknown as no shrines were found (Finkelstein and Silberman 2001: 107–111). Most of these settlements are found in previously uninhabited areas,[17] and it should be underscored that 'settlement pattern is precisely the best historical evidence we are in possession of with respect to the emergence of Israel' (Coote and Whitelam 1987: 18). However, scholars are now generally prone to interpret the evidence of the Early Iron Age highland settlements as an instance of the sedentarization of local Canaanite nomads; indeed, early Israel would have emerged largely from within Canaan itself.[18]

Archaeology seems to corroborate the above-mentioned biblical evidence with respect to the origin of Yahwism. Indeed, two Egyptian texts of the fourteenth and thirteenth centuries BCE indicate that the name Yahweh is connected to a place in southern Transjordan. The fourteenth-century text is inscribed on the columns of Amun's temple at Soleb in Nubia and it twice mentions the 'land of the Shasu of *yhw*'', whereas in a list from Amara west from the time of Ramesses II we find mentioned 'the land of Shasu (of) *yhw*''. It is interesting to note that the list of Ramesses II also speaks of the 'Land of Shasu *s'rr*', where *s'rr* stands for Mount Seir in Edom. In view of this, it is logical to assume that the word *yhw*' is a

17. Finkelstein 1995: 361 notes the difference between the settlements in the northern and southern parts of the hill country: 'Archaeologically speaking, parts of the southern hill country were now inhabited after a long occupational gap, but in northern Samaria there was a significant settlement-demographic continuity from the former period . . .'.

18. Finkelstein and Silberman 2001: 118, for example, claim that 'Most of the people who formed early Israel were local people – the same people whom we see in the highlands throughout the Bronze and Iron Ages. The early Israelites were – irony of ironies – themselves originally Canaanites!'

place name corresponding to *sᶜrr*, and that both refer to an area in Edom. Thus, it follows that most probably *yhwᵓ* is also used as a place name in the inscriptions from Soleb (Herrmann 1967: 213, 216 and references there). Herrmann thinks that the place name *yhwᵓ* could very well also be the name of a God, namely a mountain God; such a hypothesis is most tempting in view of the fact that in antiquity the name of Mount Carmel was also the name of a god.[19] Be that as it may, it is clear that by the ninth century BCE Yahweh is found as the name of a God in West Semitic epigraphy, namely in the Mesha stele (van der Toorn 1999: 911). Moreover, it seems logical to conclude that 'by the 14th century BCE, before the cult of Yahweh had reached Israel, groups of Edomite and Midianite nomads worshipped Yahweh as their god' (van der Toorn 1999: 912). Scholars are now generally agreed that Yahweh was not indigenous to Canaan and that his original homeland lay in Edom or further south among the Midianites.[20]

It is well known that most scholars refer to the famous Merneptah stele (c. 1207 BCE) when examining the emergence of ancient Israel, and that generally they do so in the sense of invoking the earliest non-biblical historical reference to Israel in its period of settling down in Canaan. Indeed, it is generally claimed that in this stele the determinative for the word 'Israel' indicates a non-settled people. However, things are not that clear cut. The stele is a poetic eulogy of Merneptah's victory over the Libyans, and it 'is not historical in the same sense as two other records of that victory' (Wilson 1969: 376). It is in such a context that Merneptah added his 'real or figurative' victory over Asiatic peoples in the last section of the stele where Israel is also mentioned (Wilson 1969: 376). In Merneptah's time it was customary to add lists of conquered people who had actually nothing to do with a particular war. In this case the Pharaoh had actually fought against the Libyans, but he had certainly not conquered Hatti, whilst Ashkelon and Gezer were important for the Egyptians themselves and therefore they could not have been conquered by him (Engel 1979: 379). Israel's name should not even be really linked with Merneptah, for it appears that the section of the stele where Israel is mentioned takes over texts from Ramesses II (Engel 1979: 379). Indeed, Merneptah did not have the opportunity of fighting in Palestine in his first regnal years (Engel 1979: 380 n. 23), except perhaps for a minor punitive raid against Gezer during his first year as king without necessarily having actually conducted the operation himself (Redford 1986: 199).

---

19. Herrmann 1967: 216; note that on 214 n. 13 Herrmann quotes Tacitus (*Histories*, 2.78.3) with respect to Mount Carmel: 'est Iudaeam inter Syriamque Carmelus: ita vocant montem deumque'.

20. 'On present evidence, a southeastern derivation [for Yahweh] seems likely in general terms' (Isserlin 1998: 53).

Despite the essentially unhistorical character of Merneptah's description of his raid in Canaan, the fact remains that an entity called Israel is mentioned alongside places like Gezer and Ashkelon. Who is this Israel? Redford (1986: 199) has pointed out that 'with the possible exception of Gezer, Israel is the only one of the groups or cities of the Merneptah poem which is not depicted and named' in the war reliefs at Karnak. It is also interesting that all the names featuring in these reliefs appear in Merneptah's stele except for the Shasu. This led Redford (1986: 199–200) to conclude that the Shasu of the Karnak reliefs were known as Israelites to the scribe of Merneptah. Although the precise relationship between the Israel of the Merneptah stele and that of the Old Testament remains an open question, Herrmann (1964: 68) believes that the former either refers to the 'House of Joseph' (which means that the latest members of the twelve tribes had already settled in Canaan), or to an older union of tribes in Palestine (for example, those stemming from Leah, namely Reuben, Simeon, Levi, Judah, Issachar and Zebulun). However, at this point it is good to remember that, as was already noted above, at first the Israelites were distinct from the incoming Hebrews who had at some point joined themselves to them.

Many scholars have given much weight to the determinative after the word 'Israel' in the Merneptah stele, which they read as indicating a people and not a land. However, some have always distanced themselves from this position. Thus, for example, Giveon explicity tells us not to attach importance to this determinative; indeed in an Egyptian document which he studied, the determinative for land is used for the Shasu, though they were a people on the move (Giveon 1971: 268 n. 2). This is better understood when we remember that Late-Egyptian scribes were notoriously careless, and that there were 'several blunders of writing' in the Merneptah stele itself.[21] When discussing the determinative of the word 'Israel' in the Merneptah stele, Hoffmeier ends up by rejecting the possibility of interpreting it as referring to a land rather than to a people.[22] This is rather strange and quite imprecise, especially in view of the article which Spiegelberg had published in 1908 and which Engel views

---

21. Wilson 1969: 378 n. 18 is well worth quoting here: 'Determinatives should have meaning, and a contrast between determinatives in the same context should be significant. This stela [Merneptah's] does give the country determinatives to settled peoples like the Rebu, Temeh, Hatti, Ashkelon, etc., and the determinative of people to unlocated groups like the Madjoi, Nau, and Tekten. The argument is good, but not conclusive, because of the notorious carelessness of Late-Egyptian scribes and several blunders of writing in this stela.'

22. Hoffmeier 1997: 30, where he writes: 'Emending the writing of Israel to include the land determinative is superficially plausible, but to build a theory about the origin of Israel based on such a reconstructed text is methodologically ill-advised'.

as not yet having been rebutted by anybody.[23] Indeed, nowhere does Hoffmeier mention this article.[24] But it is precisely this very short article which must be heeded. Spiegelberg finds grammatical difficulties with the commonly accepted translation of the last section of the Merneptah stele where Israel is mentioned. Thus, for example, he mentions the fact that a masculine singular suffix with the word 'seed' does not fit the context. Moreover, Spiegelberg (1908: 404) believes that the scribe left out the sign of a throwing stick after that of a hilly country. His analysis leads him to translate the section where Israel is mentioned as follows: 'Israel – its inhabitants are destroyed; its seed (harvest) does not exist any more' (Spiegelberg 1908: 404). In such a translation, Israel (as expected) has a determinative like the other place names, namely one which consists of the sign of a throwing stick and that of a hilly country, and like Canaan it is described as a singular masculine word (Spiegelberg 1908: 404–405). Spiegelberg's assumption that the scribe must have forgotten the sign for hilly country after that of a throwing stick is more plausible than the usual reading which has to assume that the scribe made orthographic and grammatical mistakes (Engel 1979: 387). Thus, the general opinion that in Merneptah's stele Israel stands for an unsettled people rather than for a land should – to say the least – be viewed simply as one possible hypothesis and not even as the more probable one.[25]

Indeed, Zertal's survey of Manasseh 'leads him to contend that the settlement "explosion" in the hill country begins in the mid-thirteenth century in eastern Manasseh. Thus, settlement was already going on before Merneptah's stele' (Hess 1996: 142 and reference there). This would support the idea that in his stele Merneptah referred to Israel as a land in which there were unruly people who were already settled and who were a force to be reckoned with. Obviously, the people in a region called Israel would have called themselves Israelites. The latter must have been those Israelites who, at some point, were joined by the incoming Hebrews.

One uncommon but important piece of archaeological evidence in connection with the emergence of ancient Israel is pig bones. Finkelstein

---

23. Engel 1979: 386. The situation is still basically the same. Thus, for example, (Hasel 1994) does not seem to tackle all the objections raised by Spiegelberg. He (1994: 51–52) views the determinative with the word Israel as that of a people, and the structure of the last section of the Merneptah stele leads him to conclude that 'Israel is a socioethnic entity within the region of Canaan in the same way in which the three city-states are sociopolitical entities in the same geographical region' (51).

24. Hoffmeier does not mention Spiegelberg's study at all either in his discussion of the Merneptah stele (Hoffmeier 1997: 27–30) or in his endnotes (44–46) when he refers to this discussion.

25. Spiegelberg's position is reinforced in view of his strong affirmation that the Egyptian word *pr.t* can only mean 'seed, harvest, corn, fruit' and not *seed in the sense of descendants*. See Spiegelberg 1908: 404 n. 5 and references there.

and Silberman (2001: 119) remind us that the material culture of the Early Iron Age highland herders and farmers who became the first Israelites 'offers no clear indication of their dialect, religious rituals, costume, or burial practices'. However their villages are in contrast with other regions of Palestine with respect to dietary customs, for in them no pig bones were retrieved right through the period of the monarchy. On the other hand, pig bones are found in the highlands themselves both before and after the Iron Age, as well as during the Iron Age in the coastal Philistine settlements, and (albeit the evidence is sketchier) even among the Ammonites and the Moabites (Finkelstein 1995: 365; Finkelstein and Silberman 2001: 119). Dever too latches on to this type of evidence, viewing it as an ethnic marker of early Israel. He tells us that pig bones, being a 'statistical rarity' in the Early Iron Age hill-country sites and 'often absent altogether or composing only a fraction of a percent – may therefore be an ethnic marker' (Dever 2000: 33).

However, this latter point needs to be qualified in view of various factors. First of all, one should remember that the distribution of pigs is linked to the environment; thus, pigs prefer forest areas and 'in all periods, increased moisture is predictive of swine exploitation' (Hesse 1997: 348). Moreover, the abstinence from pig's meat was a widespread custom in antiquity,[26] and 'the most likely answer is that the prohibition was pre-Israelite in origin and that it was preserved in Israel after its religious origins were forgotten' (de Vaux 1967: 514, ET 1971: 267). Recent research does not seem to allow us to conclude that the simple presence or absence of pig bones in Early Iron Age Israel can be used as an ethnic marker. In the Near East, pigs are generally less abundant (and substantially so) after the beginning of the Middle Bronze Age; there is only one exception, namely amongst the first wave of Philistine settlers in Palestine, but this is 'more likely an example of the worldwide pattern in which immigrants in the first phase of settlement turn to pig husbandry than a reflection of ideology'.[27] Hesse and Wapnish (1997: 253) remind us that various factors can produce similar effects in the archaeological record, and that consequently the presence or absence of pig bones cannot be directly related to a particular social identity.[28] Pig bones can be related to ethnicity, but 'not on a straightforward presence/absence basis' (Hesse

26. This custom was known among the Phoenicians, the Cypriots, the Syrians, the Arabs 'and in fact among all the Semitic peoples, with the exception of the Babylonians, not to mention other peoples even farther away from Israel' (de Vaux 1967: 513, ET 1971: 266).

27. Hesse 1997: 348, where we are also told that pigs reproduce faster than other 'stock' and that they are 'a quick and abundant source of protein' and that 'certainly, in later phases of Philistine settlement, pig husbandry declines abruptly'.

28. Indeed, they explicitly say that 'if the absence of pig bones in an Iron Age archaeological site is taken as diagnostic for the presence of ethnic Israelites, there were a lot more Israelites in the ancient world than we ever suspected' (Hesse and Wapnish 1997: 238).

and Wapnish 1997: 263). Thus, though we do know that the Israelites favoured pig prohibition, not every case of pig prohibition reflected in the absence of pig bones is necessarily indicative of an Israelite presence.

A survey of the general archaeological evidence of the Early Iron Age in comparison with that of the Late Bronze Age in Palestine does not allow us to view any item in the material record as specifically Israelite. However, the foregoing points also show that by 1207 BCE at the latest there was a people settled in an area called Israel strong enough to draw the attention of Pharaoh Merneptah. Moreover, archaeology (like the Old Testament) points to a region to the south-east of Canaan as the birthplace of Yahwism, and above all it also shows a drastic change in settlement patterns at the beginning of the Early Iron Age. Further, although 'archaeological research indicates that the Israelites had settled in Canaan mainly in a peaceful manner', still 'it has not disproved that some military activity had been undertaken at some point' (Frendo 2002: 42).[29] Such historical reminiscences could be echoed in Judges 5 which, as was seen above, deals with limited Israelite military operations against the Canaanites in a circumscribed area of Canaan.

The basic results of the foregoing survey show that what scholars call proto-Israelites were in fact a mixed group of people and that by calling them Hebrews, the Old Testament found 'an early means of distinguishing this new entity from other existing ethnic groups' (Knight 1993: 274). The above-mentioned points also show that the conquest account in Joshua and Judges is in contrast with twentieth-century scholarship and not with other biblical accounts of the settlement of the Israelite tribes in Canaan. Indeed, as Hoffmeier says: '... it appears that the real contradiction was between the model [the conquest model] and the archaeological record, not the record and the narratives of Joshua and Judges. The conquest model has become something of a straw man that ostensibly represented the biblical record, the latter being guilty by association with the former' (Hoffmeier 1997: 36 and references there). Above all it should be noted

---

29. In the article just cited (Frendo 2002) I have drawn attention to Procopius of Caesarea, *History of the Wars of Justinian* 4.10.21–22 (1916: 289), which states: 'They [the Canaanites] also built a fortress in Numidia, where now is the city called Tigisis. In that place are two columns made of white stone near by the great spring, having Phoenician letters cut in them which say in the Phoenician tongue: "We are they who fled from before the face of Joshua, the robber, the son of Nun."' Procopius is generally deemed by scholars to be a reliable source, so the existence of these columns is reasonable, and I have argued in the above-mentioned article that they may possibly provide an authentic Phoenician allusion to Joshua. The date and precise background of these columns is, of course, open to debate, but an even earlier echo of a comparable tradition dating to 234 BCE is found in the Greek original of a Latin inscription quoted in the *Chronicon Paschale* which says: 'The inhabitants of these [islands, the Balearic ones] were Canaanites fleeing from the presence [literally, face] of Joshua the son of Nun' (Dindorf 1832: 102; see also Schröder 1869: 3 n. 2, and Whitby 1996: 328).

that both the biblical and archaeological evidence agree that Yahwism was foreign to Canaan and that it was very likely brought there by the incoming Hebrew tribes (Day 2000: 15 and references there), who basically settled in a peaceful manner but who sometimes did engage in military operations with the indigenous population.

It is a commonplace that the so-called 'minimalists' or 'revisionists' are clamouring for positive archaeological evidence before accepting even the few above-mentioned results based on biblical and archaeological evidence. Indeed, they seek 'to explain the uncertain by pushing it into the unknown. In spite of the emphasis of historians on archaeology, their writings are full of complaints about the lack of information to be gained from that source. Push the biblical sources down to the exile, and here again we have complaints about the lack of information' (Barr 2000: 97). Such an attitude is tantamount to a '*reductio ad absurdum* of the way in which the narrative traditions referring to earlier times have been handled' (Barr 2000: 101). The fact that the biblical texts in question contain ideology does not mean that they are completely bereft of historical information.[30]

One important archaeological datum needs to be underscored, namely that of the registered population explosion in the central hill country of Palestine in the Early Iron Age. Estimates show that the population here in the Late Bronze Age was about 12,000 and that it became 55,000 in the twelfth century BCE and 75,000 two centuries later. Such a population explosion cannot be simply explained by assuming the settlement of small groups of local nomads. On the contrary, the evidence leads us to infer a migration from outside the central highlands.[31] According to Dever, 'there is simply no way that the majority of those who settled in the hill country and came gradually to be known as Israelites could have been resedentarized local nomads, or even for that matter any sort of nomads from western Palestine, much less from Transjordan. The demographic data alone are decisive: there were not enough such nomads to account for the dramatic population growth we have in the 12th century B.C. hill country settlements' (Dever 2003: 176–77). Why not mention at this point the likelihood of a migration (not necessarily on a large scale) from outside Canaan and the Transjordan? This possibility seems to be supported by the consideration that general probabilities are in its favour;

30. As Barr (2000: 82) says: 'Just as historical texts will commonly be ideologically slanted, ideological texts will commonly contain historical material. One could say that this is true of every newspaper every day. Of course the news is slanted: but it would be excessive to suppose that on that account none of the reports have any factual reality at all behind them. If one asks how one identifies the difference between historical realities and reports as they stand, the answer is that this is exactly what the despised historical criticism (of any book or report; …) tries to do'.

31. Dever 2000: 32–33 does not specify whence the migrants would have come, though it seems that he has the lowland Canaanites in mind (see also Dever 2003: 178).

indeed as Isserlin (1998: 62–63) says, 'the belief among Israelites that they were descended from liberated slaves is most unusual – ancient nations tended to claim descent from gods or heroes. The story should then have some factual foundation (some deny this but the analogies to which they refer are not compelling)'.

As far as the above-mentioned *few* and *small-scale* military operations connected with the settlement of the Israelite tribes are concerned, one should also remember that conquests are not always registered in the archaeological record. Thus, Isserlin (1998: 57) reminds us that 'it is, for instance, very difficult to document the Muslim conquest of Palestine archaeologically. Since cultural continuity prevailed then, the continuity which similarly prevailed on both sides of the Jordan during the late thirteenth/early twelfth century may not in itself rule out an Israelite conquest'.

However, at this point it is also important to adduce Judges 4 (in connection with which see also Josh. 11.1 and Ps. 83.10, ET 9) which mentions Jabin, the Canaanite king of Hazor, as well as the excavations at this site which have yielded a mid-second millennium BCE Akkadian inscription incised on a clay tablet referring to a king named Ibni, 'who was apparently part of a dynasty by that name in the 18th–16th centuries B.C.'.[32] It is generally held that Akkadian Ibni is linguistically equivalent to Hebrew Jabin, and thus whoever drew up Josh. 11.1, must have known of an ancient Ibni dynasty at Hazor. There is also strong archaeological evidence that Late Bronze Age Hazor was violently destroyed and that the agents for this destruction could very well have been the Israelites.[33] The archaeological evidence thus 'suggests strongly that the writers of the book of Joshua did not entirely "invent" the story of the fall of Hazor. They had reliable historical sources, oral and/or written. ... And it may turn out that the current archaeological data does [*sic*] indeed support the idea of an "Israelite Conquest" at Hazor' (Dever 2003: 68).

32. Dever 2003: 67. The clay tablet in question (dating from the Old Babylonian Period) actually had the words 'To Ibni-[- - -]' incised in the first line of the inscription, and the scholars who studied it were 'tempted to restore' these words thus: 'To Ibni-Addu', the latter being 'the king of Hazor known from the Mari documents' (Horowitz and Shaffer 1992: 166 and reference there).

33. Dever 2003: 67–68 and references there. Ben-Tor and Rubiato (1999: 38) present good reasons as to why the Israelites were the most likely agents to have destroyed Late Bronze Age Hazor in the thirteenth century BCE; indeed, they specify that 'with what we now know, the "Israel" of the Merneptah Stele seems to be the most likely candidate for the violent destruction of Canaanite Hazor' (Ben-Tor and Rubiato 1999: 39). Obviously, this still leaves open the question as to whether by the time of Hazor's destruction the incoming Hebrews (hailing from outside Canaan), who brought Yahwism with them, had as yet associated themselves with the Israelites of the Merneptah stele, and therefore as to whether there is a direct link or not with the biblical Israelites as those who destroyed the site in the Late Bronze Age.

The aforementioned cultural continuity in Late Bronze–Early Iron Age Canaan is not at odds with the biblical record. Indeed, in Josh. 24.13 we find that after the Israelite tribes have finished their battles and settled down in Canaan, they are told that they now inhabit 'a land on which you have not laboured, and cities which you had not built, and you dwell therein; you eat the fruit of vineyards and oliveyards which you did not plant'.[34]

Various models have been proposed to explain the data relevant to the emergence of ancient Israel.[35] The most common ones are the well-known 'conquest model' and 'the peaceful infiltration model',[36] which are often erroneously set against each other. No single model could do justice to the problem of the emergence of ancient Israel, and very probably each of the models proposed has some truth to it. As shown above, the mainly peaceful entry of the Hebrew tribes in Canaan does not exclude the use of some military force at some point. In fact, 'the biblical texts indicate that in the process of settling down in Canaan, the Israelites did engage militarily with the local inhabitants. This tradition was later indeed embellished and expanded, but the original historical nucleus seems to have lingered not only in the minds of the Israelites but in that of the Canaanites as well' (Frendo 2002: 42). The so-called 'Internal Revolt Hypothesis' posits a revolt by the peasants against their Canaanite overlords towards the end of the Late Bronze Age. This model was originally proposed by Mendenhall and accepted by Gottwald, though the former did not want to be associated with the latter's mainly Marxist sociological approach (Stiebing 1989: 157 and references there). Moreover, Mendenhall had stressed the withdrawal of the peasants mainly in the subjective and political sense, whereas other scholars had underscored the physical and geographical withdrawal of the peasants from their Canaanite masters (Stiebing 1989: 158). The idea of a peasants' revolt has been recently endorsed in essence by Dever, who views the emergence of ancient Israel as a phenomenon to be explained as a peasants' social revolt in the sense of a *withdrawal*, but above all as an 'agrarian land reform' (Dever 2003: 178–80, 187). Indeed, Dever (2003: 187–88) claims that the evidence he marshalled of 'social upheaval, mass

34. Quoted by Hoffmeier (1997: 44), where he adds: 'This suggests that the arrival of the Israelites did not significantly affect the cultural continuity of the Late Bronze Age and may explain why there is no evidence of an intrusion into the land from outsiders, for they became heirs of the material culture of the Canaanites.'

35. For a lucid presentation of these models, see Stiebing 1989: 149–65. For the change in climate in the Eastern Mediterranean, Egypt and the Near East between c. 1300 and 950 BCE see Stiebing 1989: 182–87, and for this change in climate linked to the general historical conditions in the region see Stiebing 1989: 190–94.

36. For a fully-fledged contemporary archaeological presentation of this model, see Finkelstein 1988, where nomads indigenous to Canaan are seen as the primary settlers in the central hill country of Palestine at the beginning of the Iron Age.

migration to the hill country, and the relatively sudden emergence of a distinctive rural lifestyle, is all best explained by positing a social revolution of some kind. And if land and landholding were the bones of contention, then most of those involved were by definition peasants, seeking land reform perhaps more than anything else'. Though a social revolt of an agrarian type could very well account for the emergence of ancient Israel, we do well to remember that it could not have been that widespread in view of the fact that the early Iron Age highland settlements were (as noted above) unfortified. In the case of a large-scale withdrawal/ revolt by the Canaanite peasants, one would have expected them to fortify their early settlements in the hills. Moreover, Dever himself does not exclude the fact that early Israel was made up of various groups of people, which would have included local pastoral nomads and 'even perhaps an "Exodus group" that had been in Egypt among Asiatic slaves in the Delta' (Dever 2003: 182). Thus, we see that 'no model can account for every aspect of ancient life' (Hoffmeier 1990: 86) and that various factors were most probably playing a role in the emergence of ancient Israel.

However, the fact that multiple factors bear on the emergence of ancient Israel in Canaan does not mean that we can indiscriminately adduce more than one cause for this event.[37] We must ask ourselves the blunt question: What really brought about the emergence of ancient Israel? On the basis of the variegated evidence marshalled above, it seems that the Yahwistic faith which the few incoming Hebrew tribes brought with them to Canaan is what transformed the Early Iron Age inhabitants of the hill country of Palestine into a new society as distinct from the Late Bronze Age Canaanites.[38]

37.   Fischer (1971: 175–76) writes about such 'indiscriminate pluralism'. He further says that where various causes are referred to or invoked, a historian should 'carefully weigh one against the other in an integrated and refined interpretation. The result is more useful in its various parts than in the whole, which is shapeless and diffuse' (176).

38.   It is not possible to do justice to Dever's recent book (2003) here, especially in view of the fact of its having been published after this paper was virtually ready for publication. However, when he (Dever 2003: 188) writes: 'Yet to my mind, land reform must have been the driving force behind, and the ultimate goal of, the early Israelite movement. No other scenario really makes sense of what we now know from all sources', he is in fact proposing one possible hypothesis for the emergence of early Israel which does not account for all the data. This is also tantamount to begging the question of early Israel's identity as distinct from Canaanite society. Moreover, elsewhere Dever (107) even mentions 'Izbet Ṣarṭah as one of the Iron I villages which had a substantial surplus of agricultural produce. In doing this, Dever is ignoring what is commonplace knowledge, namely that the *earliest* period at this site (which lasted for at least two hundred years, c. 1200–1000 BCE) indicates little agricultural activity, let alone a surplus of agricultural produce (Finkelstein 1986: 12, 18, 199–200). Besides, Dever did not take into account the fact that 'the number of silos in a particular level does not necessarily reflect the grain storage capacity, since it is possible that they were not all used at the same time' (125).

Such a probability is to be linked with the fact that there exists no known law of coincidence. Thus the above-mentioned hypothesis of Finkelstein whereby he tries to account for the Early Iron Age sedentarization in the hill country of Palestine in terms of a cyclic phenomenon which is known to have happened also in the Early Bronze and Middle Bronze Ages, has to be put alongside the question: Why did early Israel emerge in the Early Iron Age and not in the Early or Middle Bronze Age? The answer lies in the probability that it was only during the transition from the Late Bronze Age to the Early Iron Age that Hebrew tribes who had escaped from bondage in Egypt and wandered in the desert entered Canaan and brought the Yahwistic faith with them into the central hill country there. Indeed, early Israel could have many characteristics which resemble those of the hill country communities of Palestine in other eras. Yet the combination of all its traits together (which constitute its identity) are peculiar to it; this resembles the situation where the experiences which one individual has may be similar to those which another one has, 'although those experiences result each from the combination of its own accidents, and are ultimately traceable each to its own special combination or history'.[39]

In trying to understand how ancient Israel emerged, we are dealing with something concrete and not notional. Hence we do well to aim at reaching the truth about it, though we have to remember that truth in concrete matters cannot be reached by laws, for 'a law is not a fact, but a notion' (Newman 1889: 280). Thus rather than concentrating on models to account for the emergence of ancient Israel in Canaan, it would be better to understand the combination of the various pieces of evidence at hand, for 'to arrive at the fact of any matter, we must eschew generalities, and take things as they stand, with all their circumstances' (Newman 1889: 306). Now when we do this with respect to all the evidence mentioned above, it seems that both long-term and short-term factors must be taken into account. This has been recognized by Finkelstein himself who wrote that 'The emergence of early Israel (and the other "national" entities in the southern Levant) was, therefore, determined by a combination of long-term history and short-term circumstances, and by a balance between local developments and external influences' (Finkelstein 1995: 362). Hence, the alternating cycles of sedentarization and nomadization of groups indigenous to Canaan should be put alongside the probability that

---

39. Newman 1889: 86. Newman (85) explains the fact that there is no known law of coincidence thus: 'if a healthy man has a fever in a healthy place, in a healthy season, we call it an accident, though it be reducible to the coincidence of laws, because there is no known law of their coincidence'.

Hebrew tribes entered the country from outside towards the end of the Late Bronze Age.[40]

Thus, it seems that early Israel was mainly made up of various groups of hill country villagers originally indigenous to Canaan. However, the evidence also indicates that a small group of Hebrews joined these villagers after having been freed from slavery in Egypt and after having picked up Yahwism in the desert areas to the south-east of Canaan. They entered the land (bringing the Yahwistic faith with them) mainly in a peaceful manner, though at times they took part in military attacks. Grant reminds us that Ps. 105.12–13 presents a realistic picture of the Hebrew tribes in Canaan: 'the people were few in the land, strangers in the land of Canaan they wandered'.[41] When the biblical, archaeological, and extra-biblical literary evidence are taken into account, it appears that no single model can do justice to the complex phenomenon of the emergence of ancient Israel in Canaan around 1200 BCE. But what is still important is to make use of both text and artefact in trying to unravel one of the most complex periods in ancient Israelite history.[42]

Bibliography

Barr, J.
   2000   *History and Ideology in the Old Testament: Biblical Studies at the End of a Millennium* (Oxford: Oxford University Press).
Ben-Tor, A., and M.T. Rubiato
   1999   'Excavating Hazor, Part Two: Did the Israelites Destroy the Canaanite City?', *BARev* 25.3: 22–39.
Coote, R.B., and K.W. Whitelam
   1987   *The Emergence of Early Israel in Historical Perspective* (Sheffield: Almond Press).
Danell, G.A.
   1946   *Studies in the Name Israel in the Old Testament* (trans. S. Linton; Uppsala: Appelbergs Boktryckeriaktielbolag).
Davies, P.R.
   1992   *In Search of 'Ancient Israel'* (JSOTSup, 148; Sheffield: JSOT Press).

40. Finkelstein (1995: 362) states: 'short-term local events, foreign interventions and migrations of alien groups also played a significant role in the demographic history of the country'. This is also valid for the Early Iron Age in Canaan.

41. Grant 1997: 53. See also Mitchell 1993: 158 for the fact that even the Deuteronimistic History itself is aware that Israel lived amidst the Canaanites.

42. I would like to thank the editor, Professor John Day, for his critical comments on my first draft, which I appreciated. Thanks are also due to the Academic Work Resources Fund Committee of the University of Malta, which enabled me to attend the Oxford Old Testament Seminar ('In Search of Pre-exilic Israel'), as well as conduct various research visits to the University of Oxford.

Day, J.
    2000   *Yahweh and the Gods and Goddesses of Canaan* (JSOTSup, 265; Sheffield: Sheffield Academic Press).
Dever, W.G.
    1997   'Archaeology and the Emergence of Early Israel', in J.R. Bartlett (ed.), *Archaeology and Biblical Interpretation* (London and New York: Routledge): 20–50.
    2000   'Save us from Postmodern Malarkey', *BARev* 26.2: 28–35, 68–69.
    2003   *Who were the Early Israelites and Where did they Come from?* (Grand Rapids, MI: W.B. Eerdmans).
Dindorf, L. (ed.)
    1832   *Chronicon Paschale* (Bonn: Impensis Ed. Weberi).
Engel, H.
    1979   'Die Siegesstele des Mernephtah: kritischer Überblick über die verschiedenen Versuche historischer Auswertung des Schlussabschnitts', *Bib* 60: 373–99.
Finkelstein, I. (with contributions by V. Hankey *et al.*; manuscript ed. I. Aranne)
    1986   '*Izbet Ṣarṭah: an Early Iron Age Site near Rosh Ha 'ayin, Israel* (BAR International series, 299; Oxford: BAR).
Finkelstein, I.
    1988   *The Archaeology of the Israelite Settlement* (Jerusalem: Israel Exploration Society).
    1995   'The Great Transformation: the "Conquest" of the Highlands [*sic*] Frontiers and the Rise of the Territorial States, in T.E. Levy (ed.), *The Archaeology of Society in the Holy Land* (London: Leicester University Press): 349–65, 585–86.
Finkelstein, I., and N.A. Silberman,
    2001   *The Bible unearthed: Archaeology's New Vision of Ancient Israel and the Origin of its Sacred Texts* (New York: The Free Press).
Fischer, D.H.
    1971   *Historians' Fallacies: Toward a Logic of Historical Thought* (New York: Harper & Row).
Frendo, A.J.
    2002   'Two Long-lost Phoenician Inscriptions and the Emergence of Ancient Israel', *PEQ* 134: 37–43.
Fritz, V.
    1997   'Israelites', in *OEANE*, II: 192–97.
Giveon, R.
    1971   *Les Bédouins Shosu des documents égyptiens* (Leiden: E.J. Brill).
Grant, M.
    1997   *The History of Ancient Israel* (London: Phoenix; originally published in 1984 by Weidenfeld & Nicolson).
Hallo, W.W.
    1990   'The Limits of Skepticism', *JAOS* 110: 187–99.
Halpern, B.
    1992   'Settlement of Canaan', *ABD*, V: 1120–43.
Hasel, M.G.
    1994   '*Israel* in the Merneptah Stela', *BASOR* 296: 45–61.

Herrmann, S.
1964   'Israel in Ägypten', *ZÄS* 91: 63–79.
1967   'Der Name JHW' in den Inschriften von Soleb: Prinzipielle Erwägungen', in
         World Union of Jewish Studies (ed.), *Fourth World Congress of Jewish Studies,*
         Papers, I (Jerusalem: World Union of Jewish Studies): 213–16.
Hess, R.S.
1996   *Joshua: an Introduction* (TOTC; Leicester: Inter-Varsity Press).
Hesse, B.
1997   'Pigs', in *OEANE,* IV: 347–48.
Hesse, B., and P. Wapnish
1997   'Can Pig Remains be Used for Ethnic Diagnosis in the Ancient Near East?', in
         N.A. Silberman and D. Small (eds), *The Archaeology of Israel: Constructing*
         the Past, Interpreting the Present (JSOTSup, 237; Sheffield: Sheffield
         Academic Press): 238–70.
Hoffmeier, J.K.
1990   'Some Thoughts on William G. Dever's "Hyksos", Egyptian Destructions,
         and the end of the Palestinian Middle Bronze Age', *Levant* 22: 83–89.
1997   *Israel in Egypt: Evidence for the Authenticity of the Exodus Tradition* (New
         York and Oxford: Oxford University Press).
Horowitz, W., and A. Shaffer
1992   'A Fragment of a Letter from Hazor', *IEJ* 42: 165–66.
Isserlin, B.S.J.
1998   *The Israelites* (London: Thames & Hudson).
Knight, D.A.
1993   'Hebrews', in B.M. Metzger and M.D. Coogan (eds), *The Oxford Companion*
         to the Bible (New York and Oxford: Oxford University Press): 273–74.
Loretz, O.
1984   *Habiru-Hebräer: eine sozio-linguistische Studie über die Herkunft des*
         Gentiliziums 'ibrî vom Appellativum ḫabiru (BZAW, 160; Berlin: W. de
         Gruyter).
McKenzie, J.L.
1965   *Dictionary of the Bible* (London and Dublin: Geoffrey Chapman).
Mitchell, G.
1993   *Together in the Land: A Reading of the Book of Joshua* (JSOTSup, 134;
         Sheffield: JSOT Press).
Newman, J.H.
1889   *An Essay in Aid of a Grammar of Assent* (London: Longmans, Green & Co.,
         8th edn; new impression 1939).
Oesterley, W.O.E., and T.H. Robinson
1937   *Hebrew Religion: Its Origin and Development* (London: SPCK, and New York:
         Macmillan, 2nd edn).
Procopius [of Caesarea]
1916   *History of the Wars,* II, *Books III and IV* (LCL; with an English translation by
         H.B. Dewing; London and New York: Heinemann and Putnam's Sons).
Rainey, A.F.
1985   'Hebrews', in P.J. Achtemeier (ed.), *Harper's Bible Dictionary* (San Francisco:
         Harper & Row): 378–80.

Redford, D.B.
   1986   'The Ashkelon Relief at Karnak and the Israel Stela', *IEJ* 36: 188–200.
Schröder, P.
   1869   *Die phönizische Sprache: Entwurf einer Grammatik nebst Sprach- und Schriftproben. Mit einem Anhang, enthaltend eine Erklärung der punischen Stellen im Pönulus des Plautus* (Halle: Verlag der Buchhandlung des Waisenhauses). Reprinted Liechtenstein: Saendig Reprint Verlag, Hans R. Wohlwend, 1979.
Spiegelberg, W.
   1908   'Zu der Erwähnung Israels in dem Merneptah-Hymnus', *OLZ* 11: 403–405.
Stiebing, W.H.
   1989   *Out of the Desert? Archaeology and the Exodus/Conquest Narratives* (Buffalo, NY: Prometheus Books).
Toorn, K. van der
   1999   'Yahweh', in K. van der Toorn, B. Becking and P.W. van der Horst (eds), *Dictionary of Deities and Demons in the Bible* (Leiden: E.J. Brill, and Grand Rapids, MI: W.B. Eerdmans, 2nd edn): 910–19.
Vaux, R. de
   1967   *Bible et Orient* (Paris: Cerf). ET *The Bible and the Ancient Near East* (trans. D. McHugh; London: Darton, Longman & Todd, 1971).
   1971–73 *Histoire ancienne d'Israël* (2 vols; Ebib; Paris: Gabalda). ET *The Early History of Israel* (trans. David Smith; 2 vols; London: Darton, Longman & Todd, 1978).
Whitby, L.M.
   1996   'Chronicon Paschale', in S. Hornblower and A. Spawforth (eds), *The Oxford Classical Dictionary* (Oxford and New York: Oxford University Press, 3rd edn): 328–29.
Wilson, J.A.
   1969   'Hymn of Victory of Mer-ne-ptah (The "Israel Stela")', in *ANET*, 376–78.

Chapter 4

HISTORIES AND NON-HISTORIES OF ANCIENT ISRAEL:
THE QUESTION OF THE UNITED MONARCHY

William G. Dever

The 'revisionist' controversy that began just over a decade ago in a small circle of European biblical scholars, principally at Sheffield and Copenhagen, has provoked what I would regard as a historiographical crisis, one that is now spreading even to archaeological circles in both Israel and America. Elsewhere I have dealt with the burgeoning 'revisionist' literature, especially in my recent critique *What did the Biblical Writers Know, and When did they Know it? What Archaeology can Tell us about the Reality of Ancient Israel* (Dever 2001b).

Here I shall comment only on a case study that has become pivotal, because it has to do with an era that would mark the beginnings of a people and nation-state that some 'minimalists' (I would say 'nihilists') would like to erase from history, namely the 'United Monarchy' of ancient Israel.

1. *'Revisionism': The Question of the 'United Monarchy'*

The question today is whether the 'United Monarchy' is simply the centre-piece of an 'Israel' invented by the writers and editors of the Hebrew Bible living in Judah in the Persian or Hellenistic era, and a piece of pious propaganda, or whether the biblical portrait reflects an actual historical era in the Iron Age of Palestine (c. 1200–600 BCE), which however exaggerated can be corroborated to some degree by archaeological and extra-biblical textual remains.

For the biblical 'revisionists' the answer is simple. As Lemche and Thompson (1994: 18)[1] put it, 'King David is no more historical than King Arthur'. They went on to say: 'In the history of Palestine that we have presented, there is no room for a historical United Monarchy... The early period in which the traditions have set their narratives is an imaginary

---

1. Virtually all of the literature, both pro and con, will be found here. A convenient summary of the issues concerning the tenth century, aimed at biblicists, is Knoppers 1997. Add now contra the 'revisionists' Barr 2000; Long, Baker and Wenham 2002.

world of long ago that never existed as such' (1994: 19). It is just such statements that have prompted me to regard the 'revisionists' not as minimalists, but rather as nihilists.

For Israel Finkelstein, the only significant archaeological 'revisionist' thus far, David and Solomon might have existed, but only as chiefs of a small highland patronate in the Judaean hills. Jerusalem did not become the capital of a real state until after the fall of Samaria in 721 BCE; therefore it was 'at best, no more than a typical highland village' (Finkelstein and Silberman 2001: 142).[2]

2. The 'Revisionist' Argument and Its Refutation

The 'revisionist' argument represents the extreme of what Hallo (1990) and others have aptly termed 'creeping scepticism' – scepticism elevated to the level of a method, indeed one so absurd that most mainstream biblical scholars seem inclined to view 'revisionism' as a passing fad. I take their historiographical challenge seriously, however, enough so to undertake a refutation of their arguments. The main arguments, despite some divergences, run as follows.

(1) The Hebrew Bible is 'not about history at all' (Lemche and Thompson 1994: 18), at least a history of the Iron Age in Palestine *or* a 'biblical Israel'. That Bible is rather a tall tale – a phantasmagoria of confused Jews seeking their identity in a second-century Hellenized Palestine. The story is all fiction, a typical 'origin myth'. The fundamental argument for the non-historical character of the Hebrew Bible – i.e. 'too late' – rests entirely on the assertion that its composition (not simply its final redaction) does in fact date to the second century BCE. It is not often noted, however, that there is not a shred of evidence for such a late date.[3]

As numerous expert Hebraists have pointed out, the language of the Deuteronomistic history, our principal biblical source, is not as Davies puts it a *Bildungssprache*, a late archaizing scribal argot, but is genuinely archaic. It is precisely the actual language of the biblical writers, as well as

2. This work has no footnotes and provides little or no documentation for its many sweeping claims. See my review in Dever 2001a. For Finkelstein's latest statement, see 2002. Other recent views see Judah as 'most probably a kingdom, most probably subject to the site of Jerusalem' (Ofer 2001: 27); and Jerusalem as 'a regional administrative centre or as the capital of a small, newly established state', although 'tenth, or more likely the ninth century BCE' (Steiner 2001: 283); or simply assume that the archaeological evidence for the tenth–ninth centuries BCE is still ambiguous (Knauf 2000).

3. The 'revisionists' typically cite Lemche 1993 as their source for a Hellenistic date. Yet the only 'proof' there is a single footnote (1993: 183), asserting without documentation that the historiography of the biblical writers most closely resembles that of the Roman historian Livy. See further n. 4 below; Grabbe 2001.

the hundreds upon hundreds of Iron Age inscriptions that we now have.[4] Furthermore, there is not a single Greek loanword, Greek institution, or Hellenistic idea in the whole of the Tetrateuch and the Deuteronomistic corpus.

We *know* what a 'Greek Bible' would look like; and this is not what we have. If the Hebrew Bible had actually been written in the second century BCE, purporting to describe an 'Israel' centuries earlier in the Iron Age, yet without exhibiting a single anachronism that would give it away, it would be the greatest literary hoax of all time. And the 'revisionists' would be extraordinary geniuses for having exposed the fraud at last.

(2) The second argument is that the population of Judah in the tenth century BCE was too small for it to have constituted a state of any kind. Thompson, for instance, declared in an off-the-record discussion with me, Lemche, and McCarter that according to Finkelstein the population of the entire Judaean hill country in the tenth century BCE was only 'about 2000'. Thus Israel was 'too small' to be a state in the tenth century BCE. I was astounded by that remark; and when I checked the reference later, I found what I knew to be the case. Finkelstein's demographic estimate of 2000 was for the *few villages surrounding Jerusalem* alone. Elsewhere, for the entire country, north and south, he has given a figure of c. 100,000, in accord with the estimates that I and other scholars have suggested (cf. below).[5]

In any case, the 'revisionists' miss the point. In all the comparative literature on 'state formation processes' in the fields of anthropology, sociology, and archaeology (which they never cite), 'states' are not defined by relative size but rather by the degree of *centralization* that is discernible, as I shall show presently.

(3) Third, the 'revisionists' assert that early Israel became a state only in the ninth century BCE, when the Neo-Assyrian texts recognize it as such (cf. below); and that Judah did not become a state with a true capital in Jerusalem before the mid-seventh century BCE.[6] But since they never define what they mean by 'state', their argument is meaningless (as well as their 'statistics' being wrong). I shall return presently to what we may call the archaeological or material 'correlates' of state formation processes – the crucial evidence with which the 'revisionists' cannot or will not deal.

(4) A related argument is that there cannot have been a 'United Monarchy' with Jerusalem as its capital because there is no archaeological evidence for Jerusalem as an urban centre, much less a political capital, in the tenth century BCE.

4. See further Dever 2001b: 273–77, also with reference to Zevit 1995; Hurvitz 1997.
5. See Shanks 1997: 36; and cf. the source, Finkelstein 1996b: 184; cf. also Thompson 1999: 206 for a similar statement. On demography, see further below.
6. Cf., for instance, Thompson 1997: 166, 187, 207. Elsewhere, a Hellenistic date is asserted (Thompson 1999: 190, 207).

Again, this is an argument from silence: the relevant areas of Jerusalem, such as the Temple Mount and the Upper City, have never been excavated at all. The relative scarcity of tenth-century BCE material from the scattered soundings of Kenyon, or even the larger-scale exposures of Shiloh on the spur of the Ophel, means absolutely nothing. As Naʾaman (1996) has pointed out, we *know* from the fourteenth-century BCE Amarna letters that Jerusalem in the Late Bronze Age was already the capital of a large city-state system, and we even know the names of some of its kings. Yet scarcely a Late Bronze Age sherd has been found in any of the archaeological investigations to date. As often observed: 'the absence of evidence is not evidence of absence'. The question of Jerusalem as a capital is still open, despite the dogmatic pronouncements of a number of non-archaeologists.[7]

(5) The one archaeological criterion of centralization and statehood that the 'revisionists' have acknowledged – the existence of monumental architecture such as the city walls, gates, and palaces at Hazor, Megiddo and Gezer – they dismiss. According to them, these are all ninth century in date and are thus evidence of Ahab's reign (if any king's) and not that of a putative Solomon. Initially, being innocent of any archaeological expertise, they simply asserted a ninth century BCE date; but nowadays they are emboldened by the 'low chronology' of Finkelstein, their new authority. Yet as I shall show, Finkelstein's idiosyncratic Iron Age chronology is entirely without supporting evidence, no matter how convenient it may be for 'revisionist' theories. As the social philosopher Eric Hobsbawn once observed: 'there are facts; facts matter; and some facts matter a great deal'. The tenth century BCE is just such a fact.

(6) Another 'revisionist' argument is that a historical 'Israel' cannot have existed before the mid-ninth century BCE because that is when we first encounter the mention of it in the Neo-Assyrian texts (presumably not biased, as the biblical texts must perforce be). Even then, in this view, the texts consistently refer to this political entity not as 'Israel', but as 'the House/dynasty of Omri' (*Bīt Ḥumrī*), or somewhat later as 'the province of Samarina'. Thus Thompson will not even deign to refer to Israel by name but prefers to speak rather of the Iron Age population of southern Syria's marginal fringe.[8] In my view, it is in such bizarre statements that Thompson's real agenda is exposed; and it is ideological, rather than scholarly.

7. Cf. Naʾaman 1996; Cahill 1998, and full references there. In addition, see the more recent works cited in n. 2 above.

8. See, for instance, Thompson 1999: 235–37, 252; and cf. 1997: 183–85. In Thompson 1999: 179–90, the only place where an actual historical sketch of Israel is given, the name 'Israel' is never once mentioned. Similarly, Lemche (1998: 51–55) consistently uses the term 'House of Omri' rather than 'Israel'. He even asserts that 'not a single document from the rich treasures of Assyrian and Babylonian inscriptions ever refers to the kingdom of Israel as Israel' (51). This is simply not true; cf. n. 9 below.

The relevant facts are these. (a) The Neo-Assyrian texts could not possibly have referred to 'Israel' by name before the battle of Qarqar in 853 BCE, when Shalmaneser III advanced westward for the first time and thus met a coalition of western petty states, including Israel. And, despite the 'revisionists'' insistence on some other name ('House of Omri', 'Samarina'), the very first reference we have in the Neo-Assyrian texts specifies 'Ahab, King of *Israel*'.[9] Furthermore, that Israel must have been in existence for some time for Ahab to have attained the status of *primus inter pares* that the Neo-Assyrian texts accord him.

(b) In the Assyrian annals, Ahab is said to have fielded 2000 chariots, more than any other king in the western coalition. And that barely two generations after the death of a Solomon – who never lived. Kingdoms rarely spring into full-blown existence overnight. The ascendancy of Omri and Ahab by the early to mid-ninth century BCE requires us to postulate predecessors who had founded a kingdom somewhat earlier – if not the biblical Solomon, then Solomon by another name.

(7) The Tel Dan inscription discovered in 1993 by Avraham Biran alone should have demolished the 'revisionist' argument, since it mentions both a 'king of Israel' (who can only be Jehoram, c. 849–842 BCE) and a 'House/ dynasty of David'. The attempts of Davies, Lemche, and Thompson to read 'David' as *dwd*, uncle' or 'Beth-david' as a place-name, are a counsel of despair, as pointed out by numerous leading epigraphers.[10] A word-divider is not necessarily expected in a construct relationship in the West Semitic dialects. And the charge that the stele is a modern forgery, planted on the venerable archaeologist Biran, is slanderous, too absurd for words. (If a forger had produced the Dan stele, he would not have given it away but would have sold it for a million dollars.)

(8) Finally, there is an obvious ideological factor in all the 'revisionist' arguments, including Finkelstein's. In the case of the biblicists the bias is transparent, despite their denial. The whole story of a 'biblical Israel' has been invented, not only by the writers of the Hebrew Bible but by modern scholars (especially Christian and Jewish), whose histories of ancient Israel are largely 'rationalistic paraphrases of the bible'.[11] Thus there simply cannot have been a 'United Monarchy', the centrepiece of the tale. As one who has read all of the vast literature, I cannot escape the conclusion that for the 'revisionists' the facts no longer matter, especially

---

9.   Lemche acknowledges this fact, despite his statement quoted in n. 8 above. Yet he argues for restoring the Assyrian name as 'Sirila', a name he says is otherwise unknown (1998: 52). Such distortion of the data is all too typical of revisionism.

10.   For discussion and references, see Dever 2001b: 29, 30; add now Schniedewind 1996.

11.   The phrase 'rational paraphrase' seems to have been coined by Garbini 1988. It is frequently used by 'revisionists' like Lemche (1998: 153–55) and Thompson (1997: 178, 179). Whitelam 1996 throughout is an indictment of virtually all histories of Israel as simply 'rationalistic paraphrases'; cf. my review in Dever 1999.

the crucial archaeological data. They either ignore these facts or distort them in virtually everything they write. Reasoned, well-documented dialogue has given way to escalating rhetoric and near-hysterical personal invective – the last refuge of those who have no evidence. As a single example, in his *In Search of 'Ancient Israel'*, Davies (1992: 24 n. 4) cites the standard archaeological handbook of Mazar (1990), *Archaeology of the Land of the Bible, 10,000–586 B.C.E.*, only once, in a footnote – and that to dismiss it since it does not extend into the Persian-Hellenistic period, Davies's 'biblical world' (1992: 24). Similarly, he has dismissed my use of archaeological data to illuminate Israelite origins as 'irrelevant' (claiming that I have little field experience). I can multiply these instances many times over in the publications of Lemche and Thompson (less blatant in Whitelam's work).[12] The 'revisionists', despite the merits of their initial onslaught on conventional 'positivist' scholarship, have become ideologues. That is a serious charge, one that I have made implying, of course, dishonest scholarship. But it is now substantiated by no less an authority than James Barr, in his recent *History and Ideology in the Old Testament: Biblical Studies at the End of a Millennium*, where he devotes some seventy pages to documenting the 'revisionist' ideology (2000: 82–140).

Finkelstein, the only archaeologist to align himself thus far with the biblical 'revisionists', is much less culpable here. For one thing, most archaeologists, including myself, are 'revisionists' in the proper sense, constantly revising their histories in the light of new discoveries. Indeed, most of us are also 'minimalists' on such topics as a 'Patriarchal era', an 'Exodus and Conquest' or 'Israelite monotheism'. Nevertheless, one suspects that Finkelstein's admitted 'post-Zionist' stance affects his own rewriting of early Israel's existence. The ideological agenda is most obvious in Finkelstein's charge that Amihai Mazar and I, for instance, are really closet 'Bible archaeologists' (despite my well-known campaign against this kind of archaeology for more than thirty years).[13] The ideology is even clearer in Finkelstein's recent book with the journalist Neil Silberman, *The Bible Unearthed: Archaeology's New Vision of Ancient Israel and the Origin of its Sacred Scriptures* (2001).[14] As in many other works influenced by postmodernism's revolt against 'the tyranny of footnotes', Finkelstein and Silberman offer no documentation for their sweeping claims. (The same is true for Thompson's *The Bible in History:*

12. The most egregious example is Thompson 1996, which is so obviously slanderous that I have not deigned to reply.

13. Cf. Finkelstein 1998b; neither Mazar nor I feel compelled to defend ourselves. On the history of 'biblical archaeology' and my critique of it, see most recently Dever 2001b: 55–64, and references there. Thompson's attempt (as 1996) to discredit me as a 'biblical archaeologist' is too absurd to address.

14. See the extensive review in Dever 2001a.

How Writers Create a Past, also published as *The Mythic Past: Biblical Archaeology and the Myth of Israel* [1999], which also has no footnotes.)

3. *'Revisionism' as Ideology*

When one ponders the 'revisionist arguments', one must ask: what is going on here? Elsewhere I have shown in more detail (Dever 1997) that there is no real *evidence* for their case against the United Monarchy of the Hebrew Bible. What we have here is nothing more than 'postmodernist nonsense'. As with deconstructionists and New Literary Critics, 'all readings of texts are political'; everything is about race, class, and gender. There are no truths – except theirs. Of course, the 'revisionists' deny that they are postmodernists; but their ideological agenda, their methodology and their rhetoric betray them. The typical jargon may be missing, but their mindset is the same. Unfortunately, the 'revisionists' do not know that in most social science disciplines, not to mention real intellectual circles, postmodernism is *passé*. And in the hard sciences, postmodernism never had any currency.[15]

Once again we confront the sorry spectacle of 'avant-garde' biblical scholarship belatedly adopting a paradigm that has long been obsolete in its parent disciplines. Fortunately, archaeology never fell prey to postmodernist epistemology (a theory of knowledge according to which there is no knowledge). We *have* facts, 'facts on the ground'. It is not our 'Israel' that has been invented, but theirs.

In the light of the above refutation of all the 'revisionist' arguments, based largely on archaeological facts over which they have no control, I have suggested recently that some of the 'revisionists' are no longer honest scholars, confronting the evidence that we now possess and which all good scholars know, but have become demagogues. Theirs is the Brave New World where facts no longer matter – *Wissenschaft* at last, as Thompson (1995: 698) puts it. If so, would someone please show me the way back to the Renaissance?

4. *The 'Finkelstein Factor'*[16]

4.1. *Is this a Factor or a Fad?*
It is obvious that the biblical 'revisionists' have no independent methods for down-dating the crucial monumental architecture mentioned above from the tenth to the ninth century BCE, thus effectively removing it as

---

15. See the extensive discussion, with full references, in Dever 2001b: 245–66.

16. The epithet here is that of Amy Dockser Marcus, in an article in *The Wall Street Journal*, which she later developed more fully into a semi-popular book (2000). Such sensationalist works do not educate the public; they only titillate.

evidence for a 'United Monarchy'. Not possessing even minimal competence in archaeology or the interpretation of material culture remains, they are totally dependent upon the recent idiosyncratic 'low chronology' of Israel Finkelstein, whom they have embraced with delight (whether he is really a collaborator or not). Thus we need to examine Finkelstein's arguments in support of his 'low chronology' for the Iron Age, first advanced in 1995 and elaborated in several publications since then.[17]

The case hangs on two supposed chronological 'pegs'. (1) The first or upper one would lower the date of the earliest Philistine settlement in Canaan to the late twelfth century BCE, placing the characteristic Philistine Bichrome pottery later still, in the late eleventh–early tenth century BCE. Thus the first post-Philistine or 'Israelite' strata must be pushed down into the mid–late tenth or even the ninth century BCE.

(2) The lower peg is provided by the Assyrian campaigns in the eighth century BCE, but that is not relevant here.

4.2. *Mainstream Scholarship and the Data*
4.2.1. *The ceramic data.* Several leading Israeli archaeologists, such as Amnon Ben-Tor, Amihai Mazar, Shlomo Bunimovitz, and others have pointed out that Finkelstein's entire 'low chronology' rests on an argument from silence.[18] Finkelstein contends that the absence of the predecessor of Bichrome pottery – the Late Mycenaean IIIC:1b or 'Monochrome' ware – in local sites dating to the Egyptian Twentieth Dynasty means that Bichrome ware must have postdated the Egyptian collapse, appearing thus only c. 1135 BCE or later, rather than according to the conventional date c. 1180 BCE or fifty years earlier.

It is noteworthy that this assertion of the absence of Philistine pottery at *non-Philistine* sites is the only fulcrum that Finkelstein has, by means of which he then attempts to force all Iron I ceramic dates down – not simply by fifty years, but by a hundred years or more. Several years ago I pointed out that this argument rests on the false assumption that pottery, which all would agree often constitutes an 'ethnic marker', does not necessarily diffuse beyond recognizable ethnic boundaries. Thus twelfth-century BCE Tel Miqne, biblical Ekron, has turned up massive quantities of Philistine Monochrome pottery, while contemporary Tell Gezer, a Canaanite site only seven miles distant as the crow flies, has not produced a single sherd of this ware (Dever 1998: 48). The distinguished Tel Aviv historian Nadav

---

17.	See Finkelstein 1995; 1996a; 1996b; 1998a; 1998b; 1999; 2001; 2002; also the semi-popular summary in Finkelstein and Silberman 2001: 123–45, 340–46 (which, however, provides no documentation).

18.	Cf. Mazar 1997; 1999; Zarzeki-Poleg 1997; Ben-Tor and Ben-Ami 1998; Bunimovitz and Faust 2001; and especially Bunimovitz and Lederman 2001.

Na'aman, a 'revisionist' of sorts himself, has adduced similar case studies (2000). And more recently, Shlomo Bunimovitz and Zvi Lederman (2001) – Finkelstein's own colleagues at Tel Aviv – have published a devastating critique of his simplistic (and, I would say, functionalist) assumptions, pointing rather to cultural-behaviourial factors that affect ceramic distribution patterns.

Demolishing Finkelstein's supposed late date for the appearance of Philistine Bichrome pottery, based on an argument entirely from silence, leaves him without a leg to stand on for the remainder of his Iron I 'low chronology'. While he continues to present it as a fact, even claiming a growing consensus, there is not a shred of empirical (that is, stratigraphic) evidence to support this chronology. It should not go unnoticed that not a single other ranking Syro-Palestinian archaeologist in the world has come out in print in support of Finkelstein's 'low chronology'. Biblicists beware.

4.2.2. *Carbon dating.* Still more recently, Finkelstein has claimed that C14 analyses now in progress will vindicate his 'low chronology', particularly those from his own site of Megiddo, from Mazar's current excavations at Tel Reḥov in the upper Jordan Valley, and from the coastal site of Dor. All this may seem very 'scientific'. The facts, however, are these.

(1) The dates for the destruction of Str. VIA at Megiddo, which shortly precedes the conventional 'Solomonic' Str. VA/IVB and which Finkelstein down-dates to the Shishak raid c. 925 BCE (cf. below), are published thus far principally in a *Newsletter* that assigns them broadly to the eleventh and early tenth century BCE.[19] That is hardly conclusive, and in fact supports the traditional chronology, if any. Elsewhere, Finkelstein implies that the current excavations have clarified (and of course lowered) the date of the four-entryway city gate. But that is misleading: the gate is there for anyone to see, and it has not been touched since the 1930s.

(2) The Tel Reḥov dates of Mazar are crucial, because there are two distinct destruction layers in early Iron II. The upper one, or general Str. IV, was dated by the University of Arizona laboratory to c. 916–832 BCE and almost certainly reflects the well-known Aramaean incursions around 840 BCE that are attested elsewhere in the north (notably on the Tel Dan stele; cf. above). The middle destruction, that of Str. V, has produced

19. Six of the fifteen samples are said to give eleventh-century dates, while nine fell 'well within the tenth century', Finkelstein, Ussishkin and Halpern 2000; cf. also Finkelstein 1998b: 170. Yet Finkelstein wants to date the massive destruction of Str. VI to 925 BCE. How so? More recently Finkelstein asserts the validity of Megiddo 'low dates', but with no details (2002: 121).

calibrated dates of c. 935–898 BCE and is surely to be attributed to the well-known Shishak campaign noted in 1 Kgs 14.25, 26 and 2 Chron. 12.2–4 – the biblical 'Shishak' being, of course, the Egyptian Pharaoh Shoshenq I of the Twenty-second Dynasty.[20] His victory stele found at Karnak lists Reḥov among some dozens of sites in Palestine that are said to have been destroyed (cf. below). The date of Shishak's Asiatic campaign is now firmly established by Kitchen and others within a year or two of 925 BCE. And, of course, the synchronism with Solomon's death five years earlier (cf. above) has long been noted. Once again, however, the Shishak-Solomon datum, even though it is now buttressed by C14 dates, has been downplayed by Finkelstein and it is routinely ignored by the biblical 'revisionists'. It is inconvenient for their theories.[21]

For the Shishak destructions, I use the term 'datum' advisedly, since contrary to postmodernists, there *are* some empirical facts, not merely 'social constructs'. This datum is critical because it correlates with the stratification of many of the sites mentioned on the stele and thus provides an external, absolute date. But it is also critical because it dates the distinctive hand-burnished pottery found at *other* sites to the late tenth century BCE (cf. below). Yet once again, the 'revisionists' ignore or dismiss the significance of hand-burnishing for establishing a 'Solomonic' horizon. Biblicists can be excused, but Finkelstein cannot be (but see Finkelstein 2002; cf. Mazar 2001: 294; Singer-Avitz 2002: 114–19; and further below).

(3) Finally, on the internet and other places Finkelstein repeatedly asserts that the Dor C14 dates will fully vindicate his 'low chronology'. Yet the following observations are pertinent. (a) These dates are unpublished, known only to a few of us who are privy. (b) Although some of them do seem relatively low, they relate only to the coastal *Phoenician* sites. (c) There is absolutely no way as yet to correlate any of the Dor strata, relatively or absolutely dated, to the complex stratigraphy of the inland Israelite sites.[22]

---

20. Cf. Mazar 1999: 40, 41. Mazar's intuition (1999: 41, 42) that the C14 dates for the middle destruction would prove to be mid–late tenth century BCE was confirmed; see Bruins, van der Plicht, and Mazar 2003. The latter completely discredits Finkelstein's 'low chronology'.

21. Further on the Shishak datum, see Dever 2001b: 134–48; add now Na'aman 1998; Kitchen 2001. Finkelstein (2002) further acknowledges the importance of the Shishak datum, but his idiosyncratic reconstruction, based on very selective citing of the archaeological data, is unimpressive. And, of course, Finkelstein's entire scenario rests on his 'low chronology', now more questionable than ever (see above and n. 20).

22. I have seen these dates due to the courtesy of Ilan Sharon, who is now continuing the excavations at Dor.

5. *Some Further Observations on Ceramic Chronology*

Having pushed early Iron II dates down from the tenth to the ninth (or now even to the eighth century) BCE on the basis of lowering the *floruit* of Philistine Bichrome pottery (cf. above), Finkelstein has now drastically lowered the date of demonstrably Israelite wares accordingly. Thus he argues that the characteristic pottery of Megiddo VA/IVB is not 'Solomonic', but rather mid-ninth century BCE. He compares diagnostic ceramic forms with those of nearby Jezreel, which according to textual (i.e. biblical!) data was founded only c. 875 BCE by Omri.[23] What Finkelstein does not tell the reader is that identical forms such as cooking pots are found in pre-Israelite levels as early as the *eleventh century BCE,* as shown now by Doron Ben-Ami's restudy of the pits and 'squatter occupation' of Hazor XII-XI (2001). The fact is that many ceramic forms have such a long timespan that they are irrelevant for the present chronological argument (see fig. 1a below). They would allow us to move the older 'tenth century BCE' dates up a century as easily as down a century (a fact that Finkelstein tacitly admitted in one of his earliest publications [1996a: 185]). And when Finkelstein tries to project his supposed northern ceramic chronology to Judaean sites like Gezer, he is comparing apples and oranges. As Bunimovitz and Lederman, who are excavating the Judaean site of Beth-shemesh, have recently noted, the tenth–ninth century BCE southern ceramic sequence cannot be directly correlated (2001: 14).

I have long argued that ceramic developments in the south are somewhat slower, not surprisingly. Thus at Gezer, the concave flanged-rim cooking pots do not occur in eleventh or even in tenth century BCE deposits but begin only in the ninth century BCE. The cooking pot rims of our Str. VIII, in the four-entryway Field III gate and elsewhere, are almost exclusively of an elongated *flat*-rim type, which is a direct outgrowth of the simple twelfth–eleventh century BCE rims, and which typologically is the predecessor of the concave variety (cf. fig. 1b:3–5).[24] On the basis of the well-documented southern ceramic sequence, we could just as easily *raise* the date of the Gezer Field III gate as lower it.

Non-specialists should beware of the fact that the ceramic arguments for or against a biblical 'United Monarchy' in the tenth century BCE are exceedingly complex. They are by no means conclusive, tending to either a 'middle' or 'low' chronology; and they are thus far largely confined to northern or Israelite sites such as Hazor, Megiddo, Jezreel, Beth-shean,

---

23. Cf. Finkelstein 1996; 1998a: 215–17; 1998b: 167–73; 1999: 56–59.

24. Cf. Dever, Lance and Wright 1970: pl. 34:11, 12, 19, 27; Gitin 1990: pl. 8:21–25; 9:16–24. See also fig. 1 here.

and Tel Reḥov. To illustrate the problem of the cooking pots alone, I append fig. 1, illustrating Iron Age cookers from the eleventh–ninth century BCE from Hazor, Jezreel, Megiddo, Gezer, and other sites. The strong similarities between eleventh, tenth and ninth-century BCE examples completely negate Finkelstein's arguments for down-dating Hazor X, Megiddo VA/IVB, and Gezer VIII to the ninth century BCE. And the southern examples on fig. 1b demonstrate the slower rate of ceramic evolution in this region.

6. *Archaeology and 'State Formation Processes'*

I have already faulted the 'revisionists' for asserting that there was no Israelite state in the tenth century BCE, without ever specifying what they mean by 'state'. Their failure to cite any of the extensive literature on what anthropologists and archaeologists call 'state formation processes' suggests either ignorance or, at best, disdain for methodological rigour. Neither characterizes serious scholarship.

6.1. *Defining 'States': Centralizaion*
All definitions of statehood in comparative, cross-cultural analyses focus on *centralization* as the essential criterion – the emergence of centralized administrative institutions for decision-making and the distribution of goods and services. Noted authorities such as E.R. Service thus define statehood as 'bureaucratic governance by legal force' (1962: 175); or Marshall Sahlins, 'the State is a society in which there is an official authority, a set of the offices of the society at large, conferring governance over the society at large' (1968: 6).

6.2. *Statehood, Demography, and Urbanization.*
It must be stressed that the emergence of a true state, by universal definition, does not necessarily presuppose a relatively large territory or population, or for that matter even extensive urbanization. Nevertheless, Israel by the tenth century BCE would meet these if they were requirements. In size, ancient Israel west of the Jordan may have had a population of as much as 100,000 (cf. below). That is easily comparable with the acknowledged lowland state of Tikal, with 24,000–40,000 people, or several of the multi-valley Inca states, which ranged from a population of c. 75,000 to 160,000.[25]

Population estimates, while they may be related to land mass, are more difficult to quantify, but recent demographic projections have come a long

25. Cf. Service 1962: 198; and cf. Sanders and Price 1960: 229. For more extensive discussion of the 'archaeological correlates' of statehood in tenth-century BCE Palestine, see Dever 1977; and cf. Holladay 1995.

way. They are based on extensive surface surveys and mapping of sites, supplemented by ethnographically documented family size and density of population in pre-industrial or less complex societies. Although it is never cited by the 'revisionists', a broad consensus has now emerged among Israeli and American archaeologists suggesting the following population figures of early Israel (i.e. in the Iron I and early IIA periods):[26]

Twelfth century BCE = 50,000
Eleventh century BCE = 75,000
Tenth century BCE = 100,000
Ninth–eighth century BCE = 150,000

The first significant point here is that by the tenth century BCE Israel had attained a population easily comparable to that of other entities that no one hesitates to call 'states' (cf. above).

Second, the doubling of population from the initial stages of settlement in the twelfth century BCE (the 'Period of the Judges' or 'Proto-Israelite' horizon) to the tenth century (or 'United Monarchy') is not only impressive, but suggests an evolutionary stage of growth, urbanization, prosperity, stability and ethnic self-consciousness that often (although not necessarily) accompany nascent statehood. To be sure, some of these phenomena are still difficult to document, although there is growing evidence. In the case of urbanization, however, recent studies fully confirm what some of us suggested years ago. Based on extensive Israeli surveys that now enable us to chart changes in settlement type, size, and distribution patterns from Iron I to early Iron II (twelfth–tenth centuries BCE), it is now clear that a dramatic shift from rural settlements to urban centres had taken place by the tenth century BCE. The change was so pervasive that many of the hundreds of small highland villages that were typical (indeed exclusive) for the early settlement horizon were rapidly abandoned, most never to be re-occupied.[27] In their place there developed the relatively few but large population centres that universally character-ize what we call 'urbanization' (sometimes referred to as a 'three-tier' pattern of socio-economic organization).

Elsewhere (Dever 1997: 219) I have tried to illustrate the above development in chart-form, as follows (Table 1).

26. On Iron Age demography, see Shiloh 1980; Stager 1986; Finkelstein 1993; Broshi and Finkelstein 1992; and the synthesis of the data in Dever 1997: 221, 222.

27. This has been contested (by Finkelstein 2002: 124), but it will be fully demonstrated in a forthcoming paper by Avraham Faust, which I have seen through the courtesy of the author, entitled 'Abandonment, Urbanization, Resettlement and the Formation of the Israelite State'.

Rank	Sites, 10th century BCE	Size (acres)	Population	9th century BCE	Source
'Tier 1'	Dan IV	50	5000	III	
Cities	Hazor X-XI	15	1500	VIII-VII	
(22,350 total	Megiddo VA/!VB*	13.5 (15–25)	1300 (500)	IVA	YS
population)	Taanach IIA-B	16	1600	III	
	Beth-shean Upper	10	1000	IV	
	Tell el-Far'ah N. VIIb	15 (?)	1500	VIIc-d	
	Shechem X	13	1300	IX	
	Aphek X_8	15	1500	X_7	
	Gezer IX-VIII	33	3300	VII	
	Jerusalem 14	32	2500	13	YS
	Lachish V	18 (38)	1800 (500)	IV	YS; H
'Tier 2'	Tel Kinrot V-IV	1.25	1250	III	
Towns	Tel Amal III	0.75	75		
	Yoqneam XVI-XIV	10	1000	XIII	
	Tel Qiri VIIA	2.5	2500	VIIB-C	
	Dothan 4 (?)*	10 (15)	1000		YS
	Tel Mevorakh VIII-VII	1.5	150		
	Tel Michal XIV-XIII	0.3	30		
	Tel Qasile IX-VIII	4	400	VII	
	Azekah	14 (?)	1400 (?)		
	Tel Batash IV	6.5	650	III	
	Beth-shemesh IIa	10	1000	IIb	
	Tell el-Ful II		?	?	
	Tell Hama	1	100		
	Tell Mazar XII	?	?		
	Tell Beit Mirsim B_3*	7.5	750 (1300)	A_2	H
	Tell Halif VII		300	VIA	
	Tel Sera' VII		500	VI	
	Beer-sheba VI (V?)*	2.5	250 (600)	(?V) IV	H
	Arad XII		?	XI-X	
'Tier 3'	Tell el-Kheleifeh			II?	
Villages,	Kadesh-Barnea I			2	
Hamlets,	Negev forts				
Camps, etc.					

Table 1. 'Three-tier' hierarchy of major 10th-century BCE sites in Palestine with population estimates. Some coastal and Jordan Valley sites are eliminated since they are probably 'non-Israelite'. YS = Shiloh 1980; H = Herzog 1992.

6.3. *Other Archaeological 'Correlates' of Statehood*

Apart from the evidence we now possess documenting urban development by the tenth century BCE, what other archaeological data are there that would define statehood? I have already introduced centralization as the primary factor, so let me expand the argument with further, specific archaeological data.

6.3.1. *Monumental Architecture, Administrative Centres, and Centralization.* First, I would refer to something that thus far has scarcely been noted. The much-discussed list of Solomon's twelve administrative districts and their centres in 1 Kings 4 can now be partly confirmed by archaeological data as stemming from early and genuinely historical sources, no matter how late the present version in the Deuteronomistic history may have been compiled and edited (Dever 2001b: 138–44). At least half of the identifiable centres have now been partially excavated and can be shown to have had the monumental architecture that most readily identifies centralized planning and administration (i.e. Hazor, Tirzah, Megiddo, Yoqneam, Gezer and Beth-shemesh; cf. below).

Second, the most extensively excavated of these 'Solomonic' adminis-trative centres, and those figuring most prominently in the present controversy over statehood, are, of course, Hazor, Megiddo and Gezer. The pertinent facts concern the existence at these sites of monumental four-entryway city gates, double or 'casemate' defence walls, and large multi-room palaces (Megiddo and Gezer). The similarities are indeed remarkable, as Yadin pointed out long ago, and now extend to such details as chisel-dressed ashlar masonry with mason's marks. Ever since Yadin's (1958) brilliant recognition of Macalister's partially excavated and reburied gate at Gezer (the 'Maccabaean Castle'), biblical scholars and archaeologists have debated the interpretation of the evidence from Hazor, Megiddo and Gezer. I will not review the extensive discussion here, but will simply refute the recent attempts of all the 'revisionists' to rule out the monumental architecture of centralized planning – and thus perforce of statehood – by down-dating it all to the ninth century BCE, or the 'Divided Monarchy' (which even the most extreme sceptics are obliged to recognize).

The arguments for and against a tenth-century BCE date were first aired by Israeli and American archaeologists a few years before the 'revisionist' controversy emerged, or the current 'low chronology' of the Iron Age as a whole emerged.[28] Initially the discussion had to do with issues of comparative stratigraphy, ceramic chronology, and what I have called 'historical dead-reckoning' based on extra-biblical textual sources such as the tenth-century BCE Shishak stele or the well-known ninth-century Aramaean sources (now including the Tel Dan stele). I would insist that such a procedure is still methodologically correct, requiring now only the addition of C14 dates that are becoming increasingly precise (cf. above). That being the case, most of the tedious discussions of the 'revisionists', all of whom are non-specialists (and few of whom are trained historians) over the past decade can safely be ignored. They constitute secondary sources at best and possess no independent authority. Thus I shall dismiss out of hand the opinions of Davies, Lemche, Thompson and others, however apodictic, because they are not supported by a competent analysis of the pertinent data.

28. Cf. the entire issue of *BASOR* 277/278 (1990), with articles by Dever, Finkelstein, Holladay, Stager, Ussishkin, and Wightman.

Among archaeologists, Ussishkin and the now-controversial Finkelstein opted for a ninth-century BCE date for the three city walls and gates as early as 1990. But since these discussions are now somewhat obsolete and have been refuted by myself elsewhere (cf. Dever 1997; 2001b), I shall turn to the most recent restatement of the case for a low date, namely Finkelstein's.

Finkelstein (2001: 340–46) now asserts confidently that the Hazor, Megiddo and Gezer walls and gates are all ninth-century rather than tenth-century BCE in date, but it is noteworthy that thus far he has provided no substantial documentation for this claim. To advance the discussion, it is thus incumbent upon us to look at the empirical evidence from each of these sites.

(a) *Hazor*. Since the earlier discussions, Amnon Ben-Tor has resumed the excavations at Hazor, partly to test Yadin's admittedly positivist conclusion regarding Str. X as 'Solomonic'. Recently Ben-Tor has published a sample of *in situ* pottery from the cobbled street adjoining the inner face of the casemate city-wall and other floors – what archaeologists call 'sealed diagnostic deposits from a living-surface' (Ben-Tor and Ben-Ami 1998). This is the *only* way to date a city wall. What are particularly significant here are some of the Hazor Xa-b cooking pots, of the elongated, concave-rim variety discussed above (Ben-Tor and Ben-Ami 1998: fig. 13). There I noted that Finkelstein wants to down-date them to the ninth century BCE on the basis of parallels with Samaria Building Periods I-II (and now Jezreel). Yet these rims are *identical* to those of Hazor Str. XI, which have recently been persuasively dated to the eleventh century BCE (and which even Finkelstein cannot move later than the tenth century BCE; Ben-Ami 2001: fig. 6). Thus Finkelstein's arguments regarding Hazor (never actually documented) are without any foundation.

(b) *Megiddo*. Finkelstein and Ussishkin themselves recently resumed excavations at Megiddo. There they have revised the dates of the old University of Chicago excavations and also Yadin's 1960 excavations, as follows.

	Conventional chronology	*New 'low chronology'*
Str. VIA	mid–late tenth cent. BCE	mid-tenth cent. BCE
Str. VB	early tenth cent. BCE	late tenth/early ninth cent. BCE
Str. VA/IVB	mid–late tenth cent. BCE (old 'Solomonic')	mid-ninth cent. BCE

The massive destruction of Str. VIA, now better attested than ever, in new areas, may provide our best chronological peg, since it gives a *terminus post quem* for Str. VA/IVB. In a recent *Megiddo Newsletter*, the current excavators invoke C14 dates in support of lowering the date of the destruction of Str. VIA to c. 925 BCE, connecting it rather than Str. VA/

IVB with the Shishak raid. Yet the excavators do not publish these dates fully, suggesting only that they cluster from the eleventh into the tenth century BCE.[29] *Where* is the tenth century? In any case, the margin of error in all C14 dates is too great to rule out the conventional chronology – certainly too great to support Finkelstein's wholesale lowering of all Iron II dates by a hundred years or more.

Elsewhere, Finkelstein has implied that the current excavations have clarified the date of the four-entryway gate of Megiddo Str. VA/IVA, but that is simply not true (cf. above).

Finally, Finkelstein and other Megiddo staff members have recently asserted that the gate (and other associated structures) may even be eighth century BCE in date. The evidence? It consists only of presumed similarities in the dimensions of buildings at Megiddo and Samaria, arguing that both systems of measurements are based on Neo-Assyrian and Egyptian 'Third Intermediate' units of measure, and thus they must be later.[30] But dating the palace and acropolis at Samaria to the eighth century BCE is absurd. All of this suggests to me how desperate some of the 'revisionists' have become.

(c) *Gezer*. Our excavations of the Gezer Field III gateway, casemate wall, and more recently 'Palace 10,000' have been extensively reported elsewhere, and they need not be discussed in detail here, except for the question of their absolute date. Already in *Gezer,* I (Dever, Lance and Wright 1970) and *Gezer,* II (Dever 1974), we presented some of the relevant Str. VIII pottery. Among the diagnostic pottery forms are (1) cooking pots with elongated *flat* rims (above); and (2) exclusively *hand*-burnished wares. This pottery was supplemented by identical wares brought to light in the 1984 and 1990 excavations of 'Palace 10,000', adjoining the Field III upper gate to the west.[31]

The significant facts are these. The flat-rimmed cooking pot rims are typologically and demonstrably earlier than the concave variety, and they could more easily be redated to the eleventh than the tenth century BCE (as noted above with regard to Hazor). Indeed, Finkelstein has never produced any ceramic comparisons that would support a post-tenth-century BCE date for these distinctive cooking pots. In our various Gezer publications, however, we have adduced the ceramic comparanda, all of which support our tenth-century BCE date – especially those in the *south*, where the somewhat slower evolution of diagnostic forms is coming to be recognized.[32]

29. See above and nn. 19, 20.

30. This view was defended in a Staff paper presented at the Annual Meetings of the American Schools of Oriental Research in Denver in November 2001.

31. Cf. Dever 1986; 1990; 1993; 1997; Holladay 1990; 1995.

32. Cf. Dever 1974: 61–63; Gitin 1990: 213.

Second, it is also significant that of the thousands of sherds from the Field III gate and related structures, hand-burnished wares predominate. There are literally only a handful of wheel-burnished sherds, and these are all from the upper, final phase of the first gate. The relevance of these statistics – long since reported, but never discussed by Finkelstein – is that since Albright's day, hand-burnished wares have been regarded as preceding wheel-burnishing typologically and dating to the tenth century BCE.[33]

We now know that these earliest burnished wares are the direct outgrowth of the characteristic red-slipped and *unburnished* wares of the late eleventh–early tenth century BCE, especially well attested in the south at Gezer, Tell Qasile, Beth-shemesh and elsewhere. And even in the north, it is increasingly clear that hand-burnishing, whatever its exact history, is typical of a number of sites of the mid–late tenth century BCE with destruction layers, such as Beth-shean and others that are listed on the campaign itinerary of the Shishak stele, c. 925 BCE. Yet we have seen that the Shishak datum is rarely mentioned by any of the 'revisionists', and even then never taken seriously. Why not? As far as I can tell, the conventional hand-burnish/Shishak/tenth-century BCE correlation still holds up well – indeed is now being corroborated by C14 dates. And I predict that with more evidence, it will prove definitive. Certainly it cannot be ignored, as all the 'revisionists' do.

The point of the foregoing review of the Hazor, Megiddo and Gezer monumental structures is not only to substantiate their tenth-century BCE date, but also to expose the 'revisionists' charge that our method is that of the now-discredited 'biblical archaeology' for what it is: slander. Our methods have always been those of competent archaeologists everywhere: comparative stratigraphy and ceramic chronology, anchored by textual data that can be correlated with destruction layers.

Finkelstein has declared that we have no fixed dates between the Merneptah stele of c. 1210 BCE and those of the Neo-Assyrian texts relating to the late eighth-century BCE destructions in the north. He is simply wrong, and biblicists should not be misled. The dating of the monumental architecture at administrative centres such as Hazor, Megiddo and Gezer to the tenth century BCE is critical, because contrary to the unfounded assertions of Finkelstein and the other 'revisionists', it assigns them to the horizon of the biblical 'United Monarchy' with its capital at Judaean Jerusalem, not the reign of Ahab and later kings of northern Israel.

---

33.   On hand burnishing and its significance, see further Holladay 1990; Dever 1997: 237–43; Zimhoni 1997; Mazar 1999: 38–40; Bunimovitz and Lederman 2001: 138–40; Mazar 2001: 294; Singer-Avitz 2002: 114–19.

6.3.2. *States and 'frontiers'*. Much of the claim of the 'revisionists', Finkelstein included, that there was no early pan-Israelite state focuses on Judah, since they are forced to accept a 'state of Israel' in the north, at least by the mid-ninth century BCE because the Neo-Assyrian inscriptions referring to such an entity commence then (cf. above). The wholesale depreciation of Judah in general, in my judgment, is only another aspect of the anti-biblical bias of the 'revisionists' (the Hebrew Bible being largely a product of the Judaean theocracy). But the minimalization of Judah by the biblical minimalists has been given a powerful momentum by Finkelstein's increasing attempt to provide an archaeological rationale (necessary, of course, because of his own ideological agenda). Put simply, the assertion is that Judah was insignificant and Jerusalem nothing resembling a 'state capital' until after the fall of Samaria in 721 BCE.[34]

For some time now, I have been pointing out that the depreciation of Judah rests on an argument from silence, since most recent excavations in Israel have concentrated on sites in the north, or on the coast, and in the south at Phoenician or Philistine sites. The principal large-scale excavations of tenth–ninth-century BCE Judaean sites in recent years have been at Arad (XII-X), Beer-sheba (VII-IV), Beth-shemesh (IIb-a), Halif (VII-VIB), and Lachish (V-IV). None is fully published; and the crucial tenth–ninth century remains uncertain and in any case disputed.[35] Where does that leave us (not to mention Finkelstein's scenario)?

I have also directed attention to the more recent excavations at Beth-shemesh (by all accounts a Judaean site), now being directed by Finkelstein's own Tel Aviv colleagues, Shlomo Bunimovitz and Zvi Lederman (2001). Their early announcement at professional meetings of evidence of tenth-century BCE 'state-level' archaeological remains affirmed my argument for early Judaean statehood. But Finkelstein (who was, of course privy to this information) has never alluded to the Beth-shemesh data until very recently (2001). Now the co-directors have published the Beth-shemesh evidence more fully, which alone would demolish Finkelstein's 'no Judaean state' hypothesis (Bunimovitz and Lederman 2001).

Bunimovitz and Lederman adduce factual evidence such as a monumental city gate, a palatial administrative structure, and an astonishing rock-hewn water system – all convincingly dated by typical Judaean pottery that by consensus can scarcely be dated later than the mid-tenth century BCE. They conclude that the Beth-shemesh data can be taken as

34. The depreciation of Judah is seen most recently in Finkelstein and Silberman 2001: 152–68; 229–50 – here without documentation; cf. Finkelstein 2001: 111.

35. On the vexed ceramic dating of Arad and Lachish, for instance, see Zimhoni 1997; Singer-Avitz 2002.

support for the Israelite expansion into the Shephelah during the reigns of David and Solomon. But the indisputable fact is that 'Beth Shemesh was turned into a border town in the Sorek Valley with all symbols of centralised power' (2001: 147). In particular, Bunimovitz and Lederman use comparative ceramic analysis to refute Finkelstein's overall 'low chronology' for Judah. As the few specialists know, that chronology, scarcely credible for northern Israel, cannot possibly work for Judah.

Apparently aware of the weaknesses of his argument, Finkelstein has recently (2001) modified his view of Judaean 'statehood' sufficiently to move its inception from the eighth century BCE (mostly the late eighth century, i.e. after the fall of Samaria and the northern kingdom) back to the ninth century BCE. That would seem to be prudent. And there is, in fact, no actual evidence to preclude a tenth-century BCE date, since the Beth-shemesh data are not likely to stand alone in future. 'Frontier sites' like Beth-shemesh do not exist in isolation, or without nascent states with borders of some sorts to defend. Will the 'revisionists' other than Finkelstein respond to these new data? I doubt it: like the Fundamentalists they decry, their minds are made up; do not confuse them with facts.

6.3.3. *Script, language, and literacy.* One of the objections of the 'revisionists' to there having been an Israelite state in the tenth century BCE has always been their contention that 'states' require a fully literate bureaucracy, and there is no evidence even of Hebrew writing that early. That, however, is disingenuous. It should be noted that we now have archaeologically attested evidence of widespread literacy in early Israel, at least of the 'functional' variety, in the ʿIzbet Ṣarṭah abecedary of the twelfth century BCE, corroborating the long-known tenth-century 'Gezer calendar', also a school boy's exercise.[36] These, say the sceptics, are only two bits of evidence. They miss the point. If school boys and others are learning to write, there must have been 'scribal schools' of some sort; and if schools, then at least rudimentary literacy. Only two inscriptions; but they are decisive. And once again, the relative dearth of twelfth–tenth century BCE. Hebrew inscriptions is an argument from silence. If 'revisionists' object that the *literary witness* to the early history of Israel in the texts of the Hebrew Bible is later, that is irrelevant. Few scholars today would date the Deuteronomistic history, our main historical source, any earlier than the late seventh century BCE, with obvious revisions in the exilic and post-exilic periods. Yet some sources, both oral and textual, must be earlier.

---

36. On the question of literacy, see Lemaire 1992; Niditch 1996; Millard 1987; Young 1998; Hess 2002.

4.6.3.4. *Technology.* One of the 'material correlates' of state formation processes concerns technology, in this case ceramic evolution, since pottery is one of our most sensitive media for perceiving cultural contact and cultural change. It is becoming increasingly clear to specialists that the ceramic repertoire of Iron Age Palestine undergoes significant changes not on the Late Bronze Age–early Iron Age (or 'Canaanite/Proto-Israelite') horizon, but rather sometime in the tenth century BCE.[37] What we see is essentially the crystallization of forms that will dominate the ceramic repertoire from the tenth century BCE (Iron IIA) clear through the early sixth century BCE (Iron IIB-C), or in biblical parlance, from the putative 'United Monarchy' through the better-documented 'Divided Monarchy'.

The diagnostic forms that document the continuity include: (1) storejars; (2) kraters (large open, handled bowls); (3) smaller bowls; and (4) especially cooking pots. The expected typological progression from hand to wheel burnish (above) is also relevant. The point is obvious: if the ninth–early sixth century BCE ceramic repertoire is 'Israelite', which not even the most doctrinaire sceptics can deny, then the tenth-century BCE repertoire is even minimally 'proto-Israelite'. 'Revisionists' (except for the unabashed Thompson) never discuss pottery, which is just as well: they are not competent to do so.

6.3.5. *Toward a 'national self-consciousness'?* One of the 'revisionists'' objections to early Israelite statehood is that the very concept of 'nation-state' is a modern construct (sound familiar?) projected in an unwarranted fashion back upon a putative 'ancient Israel'. Thus a nation of 'Israel' in the tenth (or even the ninth–sixth) century BCE is held to be an absurdity. But what *is* a 'nation'? I would argue that the pertinent criteria include: (1) a fundamental sense of 'ethnic identity' or 'peoplehood'; (2) a perception of differentiation from 'others' of similar character, in such aspects as kinship ('consanguinity'), languages, culture, and religion; (3) the presence of recognizable 'ethnic boundaries', however flexible; and (4) a degree of political organization and centralization that embodies shared cultural values. None of these criteria is essentially 'modern'. Is there any *evidence*, however, for such criteria of 'nationhood' in the tenth century BCE that would help to identify an early Israelite state?

The archaeological evidence thus far is admittedly sparse. I have already noted above the evidence for a 'homogeneous' material culture in general through Iron II, as well as the evidence for political centralization and organization. To that I would add the evidence of specific cultural traits such as language. As is well known, the Hebrew language and script develop out of Late Bronze Age Canaanite. But even the scant epigraphic

---

37. Thus, for instance, Mazar 1999: 38–42.

and linguistic evidence that we have suggests that this development is sufficiently advanced that 'biblical Hebrew', i.e. the Hebrew of the Iron Age monarchy, has emerged as a true 'national' language. That is certainly the case by the mid-ninth century BCE at the latest – as it is also in the Aramaean and Phoenician spheres, and even in Moab in Transjordan. And sceptics like the 'revisionists' (who are notoriously inept as Hebraists or epigraphers) conveniently ignore the fact that many experts would still date some of the earliest written portions of the Hebrew Bible (the J materials) to the early monarchical period, and several of the archaic poems in the Pentateuch even earlier, in the twelfth–eleventh century BCE. Biblical Hebrew is not, as Davies asserts, an archaizing scribal argot; it is genuinely archaic.

The question of the name of this gradually evolving nation-state is easily resolved. I have already noted the ninth-century BCE references to 'Israel' and even a 'Dynasty of David' in the Neo-Assyrian texts, the Dan stele, and also the Moabite stone. But these are not, of course, the earliest references to a historical 'Israel', since the well-known 'Victory Stele' of the Egyptian Pharaoh Merneptah – an independent witness securely dated c. 1210 BCE – refers specifically to an ethnic group calling themselves 'the people of Israel' and thus known to Egyptian intelligence by that name. These peoples of Canaan on the Late Bronze/Iron I horizon, now archaeologically well attested in dozens of small agricultural settlements in the highlands, are the authentic progenitors of the later Israelite state, peoples I have designated 'Proto-Israelites'. Yet the 'revisionists' – including even Finkelstein, who literally wrote the book on *The Archaeology of the Israelite Settlement* (1988) – deny their existence as a distinct ethnic group. That these earliest Israelites are not identical to the *biblical* 'Israelites' is true, but irrelevant. They are their direct ancestors, their authentic cultural progenitors.

Upon closer examination, it seems to me that the 'revisionists'' wholesale rejection of the concept of ethnicity (and its archaeological correlates) simply reveals their mistaken equation of ethnicity with *racism* – another of postmodernism's conceits.

7. Conclusion

The hard evidence in early Israel's trajectory toward statehood is not as conclusive as we might like; but neither is it as negligible as sceptics maintain. Well-informed and fair-minded scholars will conclude that what we have by the tenth century BCE is at least a *nascent* state of Israel – evolved far beyond the rural, undifferentiated, inchoate culture of the Iron I 'Proto-Israelites'.

Bibliography

Aharoni, M.

1981 'The Pottery of Strata 12–11 of the Iron Age Citadel at Arad', in B. Mazar (ed.), *Eretz-Israel*, XV (Y. Aharoni Memorial Volume; Jerusalem: Israel Exploration Society and the Institute of Archaeology, Tel Aviv University): 181–204 (Hebrew).

Barr, J.

2000 *History and Ideology in the Old Testament: Biblical Studies at the End of a Millennium* (Oxford: Oxford University Press).

Ben-Ami, D.

2001 'The Iron Age I at Tel Hazor in Light of Renewed Excavations', *IEJ* 51: 148–70.

Ben-Tor, A., and D. Ben-Ami

1998 'Hazor and the Archaeology of the Tenth Century B.C.E.', *IEJ* 48: 1–37.

Broshi, M. and Finkelstein, I.

1992 'The Population of Palestine in Iron Age II', *BASOR* 287: 47–61.

Bruins, H.J., J. van der Plicht and A. Mazar

2003 '^{14}C Dates from Tel Rehov: Iron-Age Chronology, Pharaohs, and Hebrew Kings', *Science* 300 (11 April): 315–18.

Bunimovitz, S., and A. Faust

2001 'Chronological Separation, Geographical Segregation, or Ethnic Demarcation? Ethnography and the Iron Age Low Chronology', *BASOR* 322: 1–10.

Bunimovitz, S., and Z. Lederman

2001 'The Iron Age Fortifications of Tel Beth Shemesh: A 1990–2000 Perspective', *IEJ* 51: 121–47.

Cahill, J.

1998 'It Is There: The Archaeological Evidence Proves It', *BARev* 24.4: 34–41, 63.

Crowfoot, J.W., G.M. Crowfoot and K.M. Kenyon

1957 *The Objects from Samaria* (Samaria-Sebaste – Reports of the Work of the Joint Expedition in 1931–1933 and of the British Expedition in 1935, 3; London: Palestine Exploration Fund).

Davies, P.R.

1992 *In Search of 'Ancient Israel'* (JSOTSup, 148; Sheffield: Sheffield Academic Press).

Dever, W.G.

1986 'Late Bronze and Solomonic Defenses at Gezer: New Evidence', *BASOR* 262: 9–34.

1990 'Of Myths and Methods', *BASOR* 177/178: 121–30.

1993 'Further Evidence on the Date of the Outer Wall at Gezer', *BASOR* 189: 23–54.

1997 'Archaeology and the "Age of Solomon": A Case-Study in Archaeology and Historiography', in L.K. Handy (ed.) *The Age of Solomon: Scholarship at the Turn of the Millennium* (Leiden: E.J. Brill): 217–51.

1998 'Archaeology, Ideology, and the Quest for an "Ancient" or "Biblical" Israel', *Near Eastern Archaeology* 61: 39–52.

1999   'Histories and Nonhistories of Ancient Israel', *BASOR* 316: 89–105.

2001a   'Excavating the Hebrew Bible, or Burying it Again?', *BASOR* 322: 67–77.

2001b   *What did the Biblical Writers Know, and When did they Know it? What Archaeology can Tell us about the Reality of Ancient Israel'* (Grand Rapids, MI: W.B. Eerdmans).

Dever, W.G., H.D. Lance and G.E. Wright

1970   *Gezer*, I: *Preliminary Report of the 1964–66 Season* (Jerusalem: Hebrew Union College Biblical and Archaeological School).

Dever, W.G. (ed.)

1974   *Gezer*, II: *Report of the 1967–70 Seasons in Fields I and II* (Jerusalem: Hebrew Union College /Nelson Glueck School of Biblical Archaeology).

Finkelstein, I.

1993   'Environmental Archaeology and Social History: Demographic and Economic Aspects of the Monarchic Period', in J. Aviram and A. Biran (eds), *Biblical Archaeology Today, 1990: Proceedings of the Second International Congress on Biblical Archaeology, Jerusalem, June–July 1990* (Jerusalem: Israel Exploration Society): 56–66.

1995   'The Date of the Settlement of the Philistines in Canaan', *Tel Aviv* 22: 213–39.

1996a   'The Archaeology of the United Monarchy: An Alternative View', *Levant* 28: 177–87.

1996b   'The Stratigraphy and Chronology of Megiddo and Beth-shan in the 12th–11th Centuries BCE', *Tel Aviv* 23: 170–84.

1998a   'Notes on the Stratigraphy and Chronology of Iron Age Taʿanach', *Tel Aviv* 25: 208–18.

1998b   'Bible Archaeology or Archaeology of Palestine in the Iron Age?', *Levant* 30: 167–73.

1999   'Hazor and the North in the Iron Age: A Low Chronology Perspective', *BASOR* 314: 55–70.

2001   'The Rise of Jerusalem and Judah: The Missing Link', *Levant* 33: 105–15.

2002   'The Campaign of Shoshenq I to Palestine: A Guide to the 10th Century BCE Polity', *ZDPV* 118: 109–35.

Finkelstein, I., D. Ussishkin and B. Halpern

2000   *Revelations from Megiddo: The Newsletter of the Megiddo Expedition* 5 (November).

Finkelstein, I., and N.A. Silberman

2001   *The Bible Unearthed: Archaeology's New Vision of Ancient Israel and the Origin of its Sacred Texts* (New York: The Free Press).

Garbini, G.

1988   *History and Ideology in the Old Testament* (New York: Crossroads).

Gitin, S.

1990   *Gezer*, III: *A Ceramic Typology of the Late Iron II, Persian and Hellenistic Periods at Tell Gezer* (Jerusalem: Hebrew Union College/Nelson Glueck School of Biblical Archaeology).

Grabbe, L.L. (ed.)

2001   *Did Moses Speak Attic? Jewish Historiography and Scripture in the Hellenistic Period* (JSOTSup, 317; Sheffield: Sheffield Academic Press).

Grant, E., and G.E. Wright
    1938   *'Ain Shems Excavations, Part IV: The Pottery* (Haverford: Haverford.
               College).
Hallo, W.W.
    1990   'The Limits of Skepticism', *JAOS* 110: 187–99.
Herzog, Z.
    1984   *Beer-Sheba, II: The Early Iron Age Settlements* (Tel Aviv: Institute of
               Archaeology, Tel Aviv University).
    1992   'Settlement and Fortification Planning in the Iron Age', in A. Kempinski and
               R. Reich (eds), *The Architecture of Ancient Israel from the Prehistoric to the
               Persian Periods* (Jerusalem: Israel Exploration Society): 231–74.
Hess, R.S.
    2002   'Literacy in Iron Age Israel', in V.P. Long, D.W. Baker and G.J. Wenham
               (eds), *Windows into Old Testament History: Evidence, Argument, and the Crisis
               of 'Biblical History'* (Grand Rapids, MI: W.B. Eerdmans): 82–102.
Holladay, J.S.
    1990   'Red Slip, Burnish, and the Solomonic Gateway at Gezer', *BASOR* 277/278:
               23–70.
    1995   'The Kingdoms of Israel and Judah: Political and Economic Centralization in
               the Iron IIA-B (*ca.* 2000–750 BCE)', in T.E. Levey (ed.), *The Archaeology of
               Society in the Holy Land* (London: Leicester University Press): 368–98.
Hurvitz, A.
    1997   'The Historical Quest for "Ancient Israel" and the Linguistic Evidence of the
               Hebrew Bible: Some Methodological Observations', *VT* 47: 301–15.
Kitchen, K.A.
    2001   'The Sheshonqs of Egypt and Palestine', *JAOS* 93: 3–12.
Knauf, E.A.
    2000   'Jerusalem in the Late Bronze and Early Iron Ages: A Proposal', *Tel Aviv* 27:
               75–90.
Knoppers, G.N.
    1997   'The Vanishing Solomon: The Disappearance of the United Monarchy from
               Recent Histories of Israel', *JBL* 116: 19–44.
Lamon, R.S., and G.M. Shipton
    1939   *Megiddo, I: Seasons of 1925–34, Strata I-V* (Chicago: University of Chicago
               Press).
Lemaire, A.
    1992   'Writing and Writing Materials', in *ABD*, VI: 999–1008.
Lemche, N.P.
    1993   'The Old Testament – A Hellenistic Book?', *SJOT* 7: 163–93.
    1998   *The Israelites in History and Tradition* (Louisville, KY: Westminster John
               Knox).
Lemche, N.P., and T.L. Thompson
    1994   'Did Biran Kill David? The Bible in the Light of Archaeology', *JSOT* 64: 3–
               22.
Levine, L. and A. Mazar (eds)
    2001   *Controversy over the Historicity of the Bible* (Jerusalem: Yad Yitzhak Ben Zvi)
               (Hebrew).

Long, V.P.D., D.W. Baker and G.J. Wenham (eds)
2002   *Windows into Old Testament History: Evidence, Argument, and the Crisis of 'Biblical Israel'* (Grand Rapids, MI: W.B. Eerdmans).
Loud, G.
1948   *Megiddo*, II (Chicago: University of Chicago Press).
Marcus, A.D.
2000   *The View from Nebo: How Archaeology is Rewriting the Bible and Reshaping the Middle East* (Boston: Little, Brown & Company).
Mazar, A.
1985   *Excavations at Tell Qasile*, II: *The Philistine Sanctuary: Various Finds, The Pottery, Conclusions, Appendices* (Qedem, 20; Jerusalem: Institute of Archaeology, The Hebrew University of Jerusalem).
1990   *Archaeology of the Land of the Bible, 10,000–586 B.C.E.* (ABRL; Garden City, NY: Doubleday).
1997   'Iron Age Chronology: A Reply to I. Finkelstein', *Levant* 29: 157–67.
1999   'The 1997–1998 Excavations at Tel Reḥov: Preliminary Report', *IEJ* 49: 1–42.
2001   'Beth Shean during the Iron Age II: Stratigraphy, Chronology and Ostraca', in A. Mazar (ed.), *Studies in the Archaeology of the Iron Age in Israel and Jordan* (JSOTSup, 331; Sheffield: Sheffield Academic Press): 289–309.
Millard, A.R.
1987   'The Question of Israelite Literacy', *BR* 3.3: 22–31.
Na'aman, N.
1992   'Israel, Edom and Egypt in the 10th Century B.C.E.', *Tel Aviv* 19: 71–82.
1996   'The Contribution of the Amarna Letters to the Debate on Jerusalem's Political Position in the Tenth Century B.C.E.', *BASOR* 304: 17–27.
1998   'Shishak's Raid to the land of Israel in Light of the Egyptian Inscriptions; the Bible and the Archaeological Data', *Zion* 63: 247–76 (Hebrew).
2000   'The Contribution of Trojan Grey Ware from Lachish and Tel Miqne-Ekron to the Chronology of the Philistine Monochrome Pottery', *BASOR* 317: 1–7.
Niditch, S.
1996   *Oral Word and Written Word: Ancient Israelite Literature* (Louisville, KY: Westminister John Knox).
Ofer, A.
2001   'The Monarchic Period in the Judaean Highland', in A. Mazar (ed.), *Studies in the Archaeology of the Iron Age in Israel and Jordan* (JSOTSup, 331; Sheffield: Sheffield Academic Press): 14–37.
Sahlins, M.D.
1968   *Tribesmen* (Englewood Cliffs: Prentice–Hall).
Sanders, W.T., and B.J. Price (eds)
1960   *Mesoamerica: The Evolution of a Civilization* (New York: Random House).
Schniedewind, W.M.
1996   'Tel Dan Stela: New Light on Aramaic and Jehu's Revolt', *BASOR* 302: 75–90.
Service, E.R.
1962   *Primitive Social Organization: An Evolutionary Perspective* (New York: Random House).

Shanks, H. (ed.)
1997   'Face to Face: Biblical Minimalists Meet Their Challengers', *BARev* 23.4: 26–42, 66.

Shiloh, Y.
1980   'The Population of Iron Age Palestine in the Light of a Sample Analysis of Urban Plans, Areas and Population Density', *BASOR* 239: 25–35.

Singer-Avitz, L.
2002   'Arad: The Iron Age Pottery Assemblages', *Tel Aviv* 29: 110–214.

Stager, L.E.
1986   'The Archaeology of the Family', *BASOR* 260: 1–35.

Steiner, M.
2001   'Jerusalem in the Tenth and Seventh Centuries BCE: From Administrative Town to Commercial City', in A. Mazar (ed.), *Studies in the Archaeology of the Iron Age in Israel and Jordan* (JSOTSup, 331; Sheffield: Sheffield Academic Press).

Stern, E.
1978   *Excavations at Tel Mevorakh (1973–1976)*, I: *From the Iron Age to the Roman Period* (Qedem, 9; Jerusalem: Institute of Archaeology, The Hebrew University of Jerusalem).

Tappy, R.E.
1992   *The Archaeology of Israelite Samaria*, I: *Early Iron Age through the Ninth Century BCE* (Atlanta, GA: Scholars Press).

Thompson, T.L.
1995   'A Neo-Albrightian School in History and Biblical Scholarship?', *JBL* 114: 683–98.
1996   'Historiography of Ancient Palestine and Early Jewish Historiography: W.G Dever and the Not So New Biblical Archaeology', in V. Fritz and P.R. Davies (eds), *The Origin of the Ancient Israelite States* (JSOTSup, 228; Sheffield: Sheffield Academic Press): 26–43.
1997   'Defining History and Ethnicity in the South Levant', in L.L. Grabbe (ed.), *Can a 'History of Israel' be Written?* (JSOTSup, 245; Sheffield: Sheffield Academic Press).
1999   *The Bible as History: How Writers Create a Past* (London: Jonathan Cape). Also published as *The Mythic Past: Biblical Archaeology and the Myth of Israel* (New York: Basic books).

Whitelam, K.W.
1996   *The Invention of Ancient Israel: The Silencing of Palestinian History* (London and New York: Routledge).

Yadin, Y.
1958   'Solomon's City Wall and Gate at Gezer', *IEJ* 8: 8–18.

Yadin, Y. *et al.*
1961   *Hazor*, III-IV: *An Account of the Third and Fourth Seasons of Excavations 1957–8 (Plates)* (Jerusalem: The Hebrew University of Jerusalem).

Young, I.M.
1998   'Israelite Literacy: Interpreting the Evidence, Parts I-II', *VT* 48: 239–53; 408–22.

Zarzeki-Poleg, A.

  1997   'Hazor, Joqneam and Megiddo in the Tenth Century BCE', *Tel Aviv* 24: 258–88.

Zevit, Z.

  1995   Review of P.R. Davies, *In Search of 'Ancient Israel'* (JSOTSup, 148; Sheffield: Sheffield Academic Press, 1992), *Association for Jewish Studies Review* 20: 155.

Zimhoni, O.

  1997a   *Studies in the Iron Age Pottery of Israel: Typological Archaeological and Chronological Aspects* (Tel Aviv: Institute of Archaeology, Tel Aviv University).

  1997b   'Clues from the Enclosure-fills: Pre-Omride Settlement at Tel Jezreel', *Tel Aviv* 24: 83–109.

Sources for Fig. 1a

1. Hazor, Str. XI; Ben-Ami 2001: fig. 6:12.
2. Hazor, Str. X; Ben-Tor and Ben-Ami 1998: fig. 13:1.
3. Hazor, Str. IX; Yadin *et al.* 1961: pl. CCIX:1.
4. Megiddo, Str. VI; Loud 1948: pl. 85:16.
5. Megiddo, Str. V-IV; Lamon and Shipton 1939: pl. 40:19.
6. Megiddo, Str. IV; Lamon and Shipton 1939: pl. 39:11.
7. Jezreel, 'pre-Omride' level; Zimhoni 1997b: fig. 2:6.
8. Tel Rehov, Str. IV; Mazar 1999: fig. 24:8.
9. Tel Mevorakh, Str. VIII; Stern 1978: fig. 20:6.
10. Tel Mevorakh, Str. VII; Stern 1978: fig. 14:2.
11. Samaria, Building Periods I-II: Crowfoot, Crowfoot, and Kenyon 1957: fig. 3.

Sources for Fig. 1b

1. Tell Qasile, Str. X; Mazar 1985: fig. 47:5.
2. Tell Qasile, Str. IX: Mazar 1985: fig. 53:21.
3. Gezer, Str. IX: Gitin 1990: pl. 5:26.
4. Gezer, Str. VIII; Gitin 1990: pl. 7:25.
5. Gezer, Str. VIB; Gitin 1990: pl. 14:3.
6. Beth-shemesh, Str. III; Grant and Wright 1938: pl. LIX:17.
7. Beth-shemesh, Str. IIA; Bunimovitz and Lederman 2001: fig. 11:15.
8. Lachish, Str. V; Zimhoni 1997a: 3:42:6.
9. Lachish Str. IV: Zimhoni 1997a: 3:43:2.
10. Beer-sheba, Str. IX; Herzog 1984: fig. 18:5.
11. Beer-sheba, Str. VII; Herzog 1984: fig. 22:3.
12. Arad, Str. XII; Aharoni 1981: fig. 5:11.
13. Arad, Str. XI; Aharoni 1981: fig. 7:1.

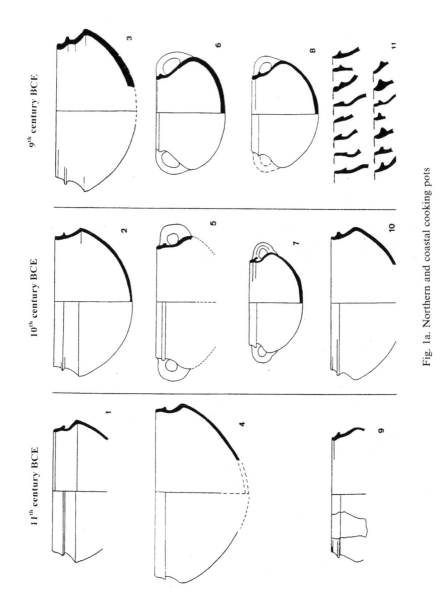

Fig. 1a. Northern and coastal cooking pots

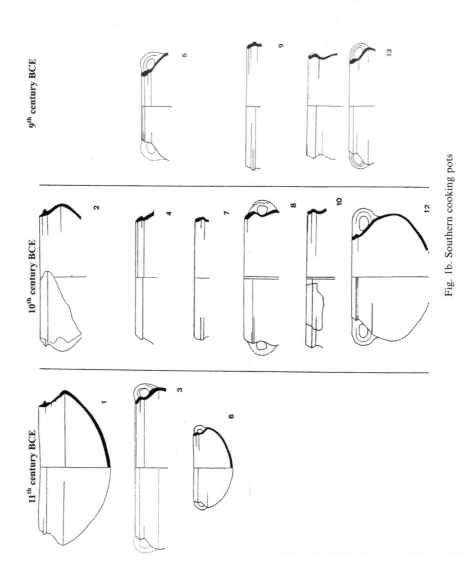

Fig. 1b. Southern cooking pots

Chapter 5

DATING THE 'SUCCESSION NARRATIVE'

John Barton

Thirty years ago it was all so simple. There was definitely a Succession Narrative, consisting of 2 Samuel 9–20 and 1 Kings 1–2, with maybe a few fragmentary extensions back into 2 Samuel; and it was evidently very early, the product of an eyewitness, or at least based on eyewitness testimony, and written at the court of Solomon, probably as Rost (1926) had said *ad maiorem gloriam Salomonis*. For there had been a 'Solomonic Enlightenment', in which Israel had produced the first example of real history-writing in the ancient Near East, perhaps indeed in the world. 'Solomon's New Men', as E.W. Heaton (1974) called them, had invented real historiography, as part of the huge cultural ferment that was the tenth century in Judah, and there was an excitement in studying their work which anyone who was a student at the time will vividly remember. But now the Solomonic Enlightenment has gone the way of many of the other discoveries of Gerhard von Rad. His bold hypothesis in the seminal article 'The Beginnings of History Writing in Ancient Israel' (von Rad 1944, ET 1966) has broken down in three ways.

First, there is a widespread feeling that there probably never was a 'Succession Narrative' in the first place. I placed the expression in inverted commas in my title, and the latest study of the work, by de Pury and Römer, is called *Die sogenannte Thronnachfolgegeschichte*, 'The *So-Called* Narrative of the Succession to David' (de Pury and Römer 2000). An important early opponent of the existence of the Succession Narrative was David Gunn (1978) in his monograph *The Story of King David*, which argued for the integrity of the whole 'David Narrative', of which the stories in 2 Samuel 9–20 are only a part. Rost himself had allowed that some earlier chapters were at least related to the theme of the succession, but Gunn argued that this was not the major theme in chapters 9–20 anyway. As we shall see, some more recent work has been even more sceptical about the integrity of Rost's Succession Narrative, and has argued for these chapters as part of a much larger work: I am thinking here particularly of the recent work of Richard Elliott Friedman (1999), to which we shall return.

Secondly – and this is the central concern of this paper – there are now severe doubts about the date of the material. Wellhausen said of what would come to be called the Succession Narrative 'that in 2 Sam 9–20, 1 Kings 1 and 2 we have a very good historical source requires no proof [*bedarf keines Beweises*] ... it contains great interest in historical detail. From no other period of Israelite history do we have so many historical names' (Wellhausen 1878: 227, my translation; cited in Kaiser 2000: 96) – this latter is an important point that has got lost in subsequent discussion. But in recent times later and later datings have become normal, partly because of the general trend in that direction, but partly because of certain details in the Succession Narrative itself. Gunn, for example, discusses the crux at 2 Sam. 13.18, where the Hebrew has $m^{e\langle}$*īlîm*, arguing that we should follow the usual emendation to *mē*$^{\langle}$*ōlām*, 'thus were the virgin daughters of the king clothed in olden times' (Gunn 1978). But if this is correct, then this verse at least cannot be part of a document contemporary with the events it narrates, though of course the verse could have been added by a later hand.

The extreme case is represented by Van Seters (2000), who thinks that the succession story is the youngest part of the books of Samuel. He argues that its portrayal of David is so sharply at variance with the Deuteronomistic presentation of him as the ideal king who kept the divine laws to perfection, that it is inconceivable that the Deuteronomistic historian would have included the stories about him (especially the Bathsheba episode) in his work; they must have been added later. In his view the Court History (as he prefers to call it) is part of a post-exilic account designed to discredit the monarchy, and to dissuade the people in Yehud from ever seeking to have a king again. 'Dtr could not have known or made use of the Court History ... without committing the most flagrant inconsistencies and producing a totally incoherent history of the monarchy as a whole' (Van Seters 2000: 76). This might draw support from Graeme Auld's work in his important monograph *Kings without Privilege* (Auld 1994), where he argues that Samuel–Kings and Chronicles rest on a common foundation-document, into which the editors of Samuel–Kings have inserted the story of Bathsheba, which was unknown to the editors of Chronicles. Reversing the traditional belief that Chronicles left out an episode the editor found scandalous, this makes it possible to believe that the episode is an anti-monarchic addition which must have been made at quite a late stage in the development of Samuel–Kings. Along these lines one might see the Succession Narrative as a post-exilic text belonging to the kind of novelistic genre represented by Esther, Tobit, and Judith, an example of Larry Wills's 'Jewish novel' (Wills 1990).

A third feature that affects the debate rather more obliquely, and which is certainly present in these late datings, is indeed the shift from von Rad's idea that the Succession Narrative is a kind of rather vivid historiography to the more recent tendency to treat it as prose fiction: in other words there is a question about the genre of the work. This trend can be traced back to the work of Perry and Sternberg in the late 1960s in 'The King through Ironic Eyes' (Perry and Sternberg 1968), which asked purely literary-critical questions about characterization and the implications of narrative style in the work. It has come to a developed form in the work of Robert Alter (1998). One can see from his work that treating the text primarily as literature does not in itself entail a late dating, since he appears to work with a comparatively early one, so far as he is interested in the question at all. But in practice reading 2 Samuel as literature tends to go with treating it as late, or at least later than von Rad thought. No longer is it seen as more or less an eyewitness account; it is a later literary invention whose origins remain obscure, but which has no more claim to historical accuracy than any other of the imaginative accounts in the so-called 'historical' books. Biblical narratives in general, many people today believe, are story rather than history; the liveliness of the narrative does not correlate with a high degree of historical accuracy, in fact rather the reverse. Gunn pointed to the presence of stock themes of folktale in the story of David, which undermine any claim that it rests on accurate historical reminiscence. Thomas Naumann (2000) has recently undertaken a more detailed study of some traditional features, and has shown that the story of David often draws on storytelling conventions – though he thinks it does so in a subversive or ironic way, and I shall return to this point. To summarize: the whole move to reading the Bible as literature has tended to favour later datings, and thus to join hands with scholars who have more ideological reasons for preferring such datings.

Questions of genre in fact lie at the heart of the discussion of the Succession Narrative, and I am going in due course to suggest that they may be the clue to the problem of dating. We should note here, at least, that belief in the very existence of the work depends on a literary decision about genre. Whether we think, with von Rad, that it is a piece of historiography, or (with more recent writers) that it is essentially prose fiction, the separate existence and integrity of the work can be sustained only by arguments about its literary character. The essential issue of perception is that these chapters have a unifying theme, which Rost summed up as 'Who will sit on the throne of David?' The strange gap in the story between the end of 2 Samuel and the beginning of 1 Kings, in which David suddenly grows old, can only be explained if the work is not meant to provide complete coverage of David's reign but is intended to deal with just those incidents that bear on the theme of succession. The thematic unity being attributed to the work may justify its being called a *Novelle*, part of the definition of which is the existence of a single unifying theme.

As we saw, however, even Rost thought that some earlier parts of 2 Samuel related to the same theme, and though the ending in 1 Kings 2 is an obvious cut-off point, the beginning is certainly unclear, even on the view that the succession is the unifying theme. Furthermore it is far from certain that this theme does indeed unify the work and mark it off from the rest of the story of David. The whole Bathsheba episode does establish that Solomon is available to be king in due course, but the great detail of David's murder of Uriah is not necessary to explain the question of the succession. Conversely, the earlier chapters of 2 and even 1 Samuel are relevant to David's attempt not only to be king but to found a dynasty, and as many have noted the tale about the barrenness of Michal (2 Sam. 6.20–23) is as necessary to the succession by Solomon as that of David's relations with Bathsheba. Nor is it at all clear to me that 2 Samuel 9 marks the beginning of a different kind of storytelling from what precedes. I would think, for example, that the story of David and Abigail (1 Sam. 25) exhibits much the same grasp of narrative technique as the Succession Narrative and could easily come from the same pen. Whybray (1968: 7) spoke of the Narrative as 'markedly superior to earlier Israelite saga', but I am not convinced that he was right unless by 'earlier Israelite saga' we mean something like a supposed *Grundlage* underlying the stories of the judges or of Saul; for the present form of many of those stories strikes me as exhibiting much the same narrative skill as the Succession Narrative. I do not think, therefore, that the existence of the Succession Narrative as a separate work can at all be taken as a given.

Still, it may be granted that these chapters of 2 Samuel and 1 Kings are a fine example of Israelite narrative art, whether or not other chapters are too. In dating them a number of factors have to be considered. One is certainly the language, though I doubt if we can get very far with that. The Hebrew is what we think of as classical biblical Hebrew, probably earlier than that in Chronicles or in Ezra–Nehemiah, but not therefore necessarily pre-exilic. (On this see Rooker 1990; Polzin 1976.) I would have problems with Hellenistic datings on linguistic grounds alone, but we do not know enough about the development of Hebrew to be able to discriminate clearly between pre-exilic and fairly early post-exilic writing.

Even though the hypothesis of eyewitness testimony fails for lack of clear evidence, one can still make a case for a dating not too far removed from the events described by noting the many inconsequential pieces of information the narrative contains. Would anyone at a much later period, for example, have invented Chimham, the heir of Barzillai the Gileadite, who is granted the rewards for Barzillai's loyalty to David when Barzillai protests that he is too old to enjoy them himself (2 Sam. 19.32–41, ET 31–40)? Would anyone have invented the complex and long-running feud between Mephibosheth and Ziba, which is unnecessary to the plot (2 Sam. 9.1–13; 16.1–4; 19.25–31, ET 24–30)? Can the contest between Ahithophel and Hushai be made out of whole cloth by a later writer, rather than resting on historical reminiscence (2 Sam. 17.5–14)? Earlier scholars, even if they did not think these stories were actually contemporary with the events they describe, normally supposed that much of the detail derived from real historical information rather than being pure invention, and this still seems to me reasonable. The quality of post-exilic tales does not strike me as being so high that the enormously extended narrative in 2 Samuel, with all the intricacies of its plot, could really have been devised out of nothing in that period. And what we know about the transmission of narrative material over time suggests that successful *oral* transmission over more than a couple of generations is unlikely (see Kirkpatrick 1988), so that at least some *Urform* of the Succession Narrative must have existed soon enough after the events described to have preserved the essential facts. The alternatives seem, in fact, to be either that the Narrative is *pure* fiction – and then it can be almost as late as we like, but sticks out among contemporary works as incomparably better crafted; or else that it is reasonably early, if it contains even a mostly accurate factual record. I do not think that compromise arrangements, in which it is very late yet preserves some historical detail, do justice to its peculiarities.

Among the historical details which are relevant to dating is the fact – which Rost and von Rad both brought out, and which has recently been reiterated by Walter Dietrich (2000) – that the Narrative nowhere even hints at the eventual schism between the northern and southern tribes, in spite of the fact that it contains a good deal of material on the rivalries between them. Dietrich argues that this must mean at least a core version of the Narrative existed before the death of Solomon, though he thinks that it was very much more brief than the version we now have, and concentrated almost entirely on Solomon himself. This is admittedly an argument from silence, but a silence about an event one would have expected to weigh heavily on the mind of any author writing up the history of Israel in a much later period. This argument tends to favour a dating as early as von Rad's.

A further problem that may be relevant is that the *Tendenz* of the Narrative is so hard to fathom. Appraisals have ranged all the way from Rost's *ad maiorem gloriam Salomonis* to Delekat's idea that it systematically undermines the monarchy (Delekat 1967). As de Pury and Römer put it, summarizing the positions of the various contributors to their volume:

> Are we dealing with a decidedly anti-monarchic presentation, tribal or prophetic in origin, which was later reinterpreted or made blander by a redactor (Dietrich, Kaiser)? Or are we dealing with an originally apologetic (Deuteronomistic) portrait of David, which was later changed into a (post-Deuteronomistic) document condemning the Davidic monarchy by the insertion of the Bathsheba episode (McKenzie, and

compare Naumann, though his dating is earlier)? Van Seters even believes that the Succession Narrative can be understood as wholly anti-Davidic and antimessianic, as a rejection of the Deuteronomistic ideology of kingship. For Blum, on the other hand, a generally David- and Solomon-friendly *Tendenz* predominates, despite some negative or apparently negative features (de Pury and Römer 2000: 3, my translation).

Kaiser (2000) even thinks that the Narrative is deliberately ambiguous, which is one way of both having and eating all the available cakes! Surely the correct answer is that we have not succeeded in identifying the *Tendenz*. Perhaps the Narrative was not written with any particular *Tendenz*, but merely to convey the facts in an interesting and compelling way, as is perhaps implied by Gunn's well-known description of it as 'serious entertainment' (Gunn 1978). But the later and/or the more fictitious the work, the more the lack of any overt purpose is a problem, for later Jewish fictional literature on the whole wears its heart on its sleeve. There is much less disagreement about the *Tendenz* of Esther or Judith or Tobit. The very opacity of the story is for me an argument for a reasonably early date.

Recently, however, a new kind of approach has entered the arena, one which subsumes the question of the Succession Narrative into a much larger theory about the origin of Old Testament narrative literature as a whole. I have in mind R.E. Friedman's *The Hidden Book in the Bible* (Friedman 1998). Friedman thinks that the Succession Narrative is simply part of a longer work that goes back not merely further into 2 or even 1 Samuel, but all the way to Genesis 2: in fact, that the Succession Narrative is part of the document we call J, the earliest source (as most scholars still think) in the Pentateuch. In characteristic style, Friedman declares that this is not merely a hypothesis but a 'discovery', the discovery of a 'hidden book' which has been lying there all along, but which no one before has ever noticed. Friedman tells us that he owes his 'eureka!' moment to the suggestion of a literary colleague that J was composed by the same author as the Court History of David. From there he went on to 'discover' that the two documents are in fact linked together, with much of Joshua, Judges, and 1 Samuel coming from the same hand, so that in reality there is only one early historical source in the Bible, not many, and that source is what we have long known as J.

I cannot here go into all Friedman's arguments. Some are linguistic, others stylistic, others again rest on perceptions about *Tendenz* and literary form. It is, however, worth pointing out that his 'discovery' was anticipated some thirty years ago by the German scholar Hannelis Schulte (1972), in her published dissertation *Die Entstehung der Geschichtsschreibung im alten Israel*, which developed an idea she traces back to Gustav Hölscher – not tucked away in an obscure journal but available as a BZAW monograph. So far as I can see, most of Friedman's arguments are there anticipated, though he shows no awareness of Schulte's work and has certainly arrived at his conclusions independently. Schulte maintained that there was one great historical work that united all the narrative material that survives from the tenth century (writing in the early 1970s she simply assumes a Solomonic date for both J and the Succession Narrative). In this work, she claims, the monarchy is presented as the fulfilment both of the purpose of the exodus, and of the promises to the patriarchs. So far as I can see, Schulte's case is in essence identical with that now argued by Friedman.

I concur with H.G.M. Williamson's judgment on the dust-jacket of Friedman's book that the thesis of a single early narrative document lying concealed in Genesis–1 Kings has enormous ramifications, and if it can be sustained will result in the conclusion that we now see, reconstructed and restored, 'the work of the first great prose writer of western civilization'. Friedman helpfully prints out the entire reconstructed document in his own translation, and though every reader must make up his or her own mind, I think it is hard not to feel some persuasive force in his arguments once one has worked through the text as he presents it. If he is right, then of course the dating of the Succession Narrative (which did not actually exist as a separate document) depends on the dating of J as a whole, and this enormously enlarges the range of issues to be settled. Because there are now influential scholars who think that J, too, is post-exilic, one does not automatically produce a pre-exilic date for the Succession Narrative by making it part of J. But the debate will have to be conducted against this wider background, and will not hinge only on the question of when anyone could write a work critical of David, as it has often done in recent times. It will also be necessary to ask when the patriarchal tales were produced, when the career of Moses was written up, and what is the origin of the story of Saul, for all will be relevant to the date of 2 Samuel 9–20, 1 Kings 1–2. So Friedman has made our task considerably harder.

I am not yet convinced by what I would call the Schulte–Friedman hypothesis, but I do think it has succeeded in showing how similar J and the Succession Narrative are. This is a position many scholars would probably concur with, even if they do not take the additional step of regarding them as parts of a single work. It has after all long been thought that the two works come from a similar intellectual milieu: there is nothing novel in that suggestion. It seems to me that, once one has detected the stylistic similarities between J and the Succession Narrative, one can then go on to find a similar style elsewhere in the Old Testament. Take, for example, the extremely laconic character of both works, which tend to refrain from much ethical comment and simply to report incidents, yet in such a way that we are not left in doubt where the author's sympathies lie. This occurs equally in some parts of Judges, for example in the story of Jephthah's daughter:

> Jephthah made a vow to the Lord, and said, 'If you will give the Ammonites into my hand, then whoever comes out of the doors of my house to meet me, when I return victorious from the Ammonites, shall be the Lord's, to be offered up by me as a burnt-offering. So Jephthah crossed over to the Ammonites to fight against them, and the Lord gave them into his hand ... Then Jephthah came to his house in Mizpah; and there was his daughter coming out to meet him with timbrels and with dancing. She was his only child; he had no son and daughter except her. (Judg. 11.30–34)

It is not necessary to postulate common authorship between this text, J, and the Succession Narrative, to note that all belong in a particular tradition of writing narrative prose. Von Rad gave this laconic and rather uncommented style a theological explanation, in terms of a doctrine of the 'hidden hand' of God, concealed beneath an apparently secular narrative (cf. Barton 1984). But it seems to me better to give it a literary or stylistic explanation: this is how classical Hebrew narrative is written, and it influences writers who are not even producing continuous narrative – take, for example, Ezekiel: 'So I spoke to the people in the morning, and at evening my wife died. And on the next day I did as I was commanded' (Ezek. 24.18). Of course there could be a theological reason why narrative texts come out in this way, but I suspect this is probably not the case: the theologies of various Old Testament narrative books differ widely, yet there is often this same style of writing.

The question of the date of the Succession Narrative thus boils down, for me, into the question when in the development of Hebrew literature this particular style of composition established itself, and for how long it lasted. And here it seems to me that there are things that can usefully be said. The post-exilic tales, Esther, Ruth, Jonah, etc., are not written in quite this deadpan style, and Nehemiah certainly did not write in that way. Equally, most of what we call the Deuteronomistic literature feels quite different. But there are materials outside even what Friedman regards as part of 'the hidden book in the Bible' that are in a similar style: parts of the Elijah and Elisha stories, for example. To me it thus seems possible to isolate at least three ways of writing Hebrew narrative. The Succession Narrative belongs to the same category as J and many of the basic stories within the Deuteronomistic history, excluding those sections where the editorial hand of the Deuteronomists themselves can be detected. Alongside these there is a Deuteronomistic style; and, thirdly, there is the style of what Wills calls the Jewish novel.

We can date the last two of these. The Jewish novel is a product of post-exilic times, the Persian era at the earliest; and the Deuteronomistic style is late pre-exilic at the earliest, and had its full flowering during and soon after the Exile. Can we also date what I would call the 'classic' style? It seems to me that it is pre-Deuteronomistic. A famous passage near the end of the Succession Narrative illustrates the point: 1 Kgs 2.1–9, David's last words to Solomon. Most commentators identify the original Succession Narrative material here in vv. 5–9, in which David instructs Solomon to avenge him on his enemies. Verses 1–4 are a Deuteronomistic passage, stressing the importance of keeping the law of Moses. The combination is almost comic. Now Van Seters (2000) argues that the Deuteronomistic portions are the core text, and that a later anti-David writer has added the exhortation to finish off David's opponents. But scarcely anyone, I would predict, is likely to agree with this. Palpably the worldly-wise exhortation is the original text, and the Deuteronomistic admonitions have been added to dilute it, and to fit the model of David as the one after Yahweh's heart: the model king. The text of which the original last words of David are a part is surely, therefore, pre-Deuteronomistic; and that text is the bulk of what we call the Succession Narrative. It seems to me that classical Hebrew narrative is similarly in general pre-Deuteronomistic; and that probably means pre-exilic, though not necessarily dating from very long before the Exile.

We thus arrive at what, in the current debate, has to be called an early dating, though it is not necessarily as early as von Rad thought. My hunch is that this particular prose style was practised over an extended period, and that the works couched in it need not all come from the same century. But the style lasted well into the eighth century at any rate, since the stories of Elijah and Elisha (which cannot be earlier than that) exemplify it as much as does the Succession Narrative. The Narrative could therefore be a product of that century, or even of the seventh. The sometimes mooted idea that this literature reflects a certain renaissance at the court of Hezekiah, whose courtiers are said to have copied out proverbs (Prov. 25.1), is attractive but unprovable.

There is one aspect of what I am calling 'classical' narrative that is brought out very well by Schulte. This is what may be called its ethical flavour. As she observes, in both J and the Succession Narrative the weight falls on custom rather than law: on 'what is not done in Israel', on misdeeds as 'folly'. The Ten Commandments, indeed the law in general, are not mentioned. Of course it was just such an observation that led Wellhausen to conclude that the laws in the Pentateuch were for the most part later than the classical prophets, and belonged to post-exilic Judaism rather than to pre-exilic Yahwism. I see no reason to revise that conclusion. The detailed legislation in the Pentateuch may, as many now think, rest on pre-exilic prototypes, but if so, there is no evidence for it in the stories about the pre-exilic period. In the whole of the Bathsheba episode, for example, no biblical law is ever appealed to: the ethical norms are simply those customary in the society of the day. This was part of the strength of Whybray's argument that the Succession Narrative exemplified Hebrew 'wisdom': its way of thinking reflects a custom- rather than a law-based society (see Whybray 1968).

So far as I can see, the same is true for all 'classical' Hebrew narrative. The concern, even when God is part of the narrative as he often is, is for the way human society functions, and for the natural bonds that bind people together, not for any superstructure of divine law. This is well put by Blum (2000: 37), who writes, 'On the one hand the concern is for the possibilities and necessities of human action, on the other for its gaps, its ambivalence, and its limits, within the horizon of the reality of God' (my translation). At the centre lie concerns for the consequences of human action, not as judged by law, but as evaluated in the light of custom and tradition. This conveys for the later reader the sense that the narrative concerns an archaic period, rather as the Homeric epics do – a time before Israel's national life was ordered by *torah* and regulation, when people acted rather freely yet were subject to fate and divine vengeance. We are dealing with narrative which, especially by the standards being used in biblical scholarship at the moment, is decidedly early.

The date of Israelite narrative has come to be connected with the question of its historicity, but I should like to force the two issues apart. As I have already indicated, I cannot believe that the stories making up what we call the Succession Narrative are pure fiction: they rest on some substratum of historical memory. I think there really was a David who did some of the things related of him, that there really was a Bathsheba, a Barzillai, an Ahithophel. But one might make the same sorts of claim for Homer, or for Greek tragedy: there was an Agamemnon, a Clytemnestra, an Orestes. Real fiction in our sense is probably not to be found in the narrative books of the Bible, which are about famous figures from the past. Only in later times did authors manufacture characters such as Esther or Judith. But that is miles removed from claiming historicity for the stories in a 'hard' sense, and does not justify us in writing a history of Israel à la Bright. Blum (2000: 17) says that the early stories are in intention neither fiction nor non-fiction – such categories being modern ones, alien to these ancient writers. I feel less sure about that: I think that these writers were, in their own minds, genuinely chronicling the past. But whether they got it right is entirely beyond our capabilities to decide, though the presence of a lot of traditional narrative motifs, which were already pointed out by Gunn, might make us veer in a rather sceptical direction.

So: the narrow question of the date of the Succession Narrative opens the door on a vast range of issues in current biblical study. If I opt for a rather early date, that is not because I regard most of these questions as easy to settle, but because I have come to believe that there was a golden age for classical Hebrew narrative, and that it was before the exile. It is the literature of this period that yields to much of the narratological work now being done on the Old Testament; Deuteronomistic narratives and late, conscious fictions are in a different category. Early does not mean reliable, however, and my discussion gets us no closer to deciding what the reign of David was actually like.

Bibliography

Alter, R.
1998   *The David Story: A Translation with Commentary of 1 and 2 Samuel* (New York and London: W.W. Norton).

Auld, A.G.
1994   *Kings without Privilege* (Edinburgh: T. & T. Clark).

Barton, J.
1984   'Gerhard von Rad on the World-View of Early Israel', *JTS* NS 35: 301–23.

Blum, E.
2000   'Ein Anfang der Geschichtsschreibung? Anmerkungen zur sogenannten Thronfolgegeschichte und zum Umgang mit der Geschichte im alten Israel', in de Pury and Römer 2000: 4–37.

Delekat, L.
1967   'Tendenz und Theologie der David–Salomo-Erzählung', in F. Maass (ed.), *Das ferne und nahe Wort: Festschrift Leonhard Rost zur Vollendung seines 70. Lebensjahres am 30. November 1966 gewidmet* (BZAW, 105; Berlin: Alfred Töpelmann, 1967): 26–36.

Dietrich, W.
2000   'Das Ende der Thronfolgegeschichte', in de Pury and Römer 2000: 38–69.

Friedman, R.E.
1998   *The Hidden Book in the Bible* (New York: HarperCollins).

Gunn, D.M.
1978   *The Story of King David: Genre and Interpretation* (JSOTSup, 6; Sheffield: JSOT Press).

Heaton, E.W.
1974   *Solomon's New Men: The Emergence of Israel as a National State* (London: Thames & Hudson).

Kaiser, O.
2000   'Das Verhältnis der Erzählung vom König David zum sogenannten deuteronomistischen Geschichtswerk', in de Pury and Römer 2000: 94–122.

Kirkpatrick, P.G.
1988   *The Old Testament and Folklore Study* (JSOTSup, 62; Sheffield: JSOT Press).

Naumann, T.
2000   'David als exemplarischer König. Der Fall Urijas (2 Sam 11) vor dem Hintergrund altorientalischer Erzähltraditionen', in de Pury and Römer 2000: 136–67.

Perry, M., and M. Sternberg
    1968   'The King through Ironic Eyes', *Hasifrut* 1: 263–92 (Hebrew).
Polzin, R.
    1976   *Late Biblical Hebrew: Towards an Historical Typology of Biblical Hebrew Prose* (HSM, 12, Missoula, MT: Scholars Press.)
Pury, A. de, and T. Römer
    2000   *Die sogenannte Thronnachfolgegeschichte Davids: Neue Einsichten und Anfragen* (OBO, 176; Fribourg: Universitätsverlag; Göttingen: Vandenhoeck & Ruprecht).
Rad, G. von
    1944   'Der Anfang der Geschichtsschreibung im alten Israel', *Archiv für Kulturgeschichte* 32: 1–42. Reprinted in *Gesammelte Studien zum Alten Testament* (Munich: Chr. Kaiser Verlag, 1958): 148–88. ET 'The Beginnings of Historical Writing in Ancient Israel', in *The Problem of the Hexateuch and Other Essays* (trans. E.W. Trueman Dicken; Edinburgh and London: Oliver & Boyd, 1966): 166–204.
Rooker, M.F.
    1990   *Biblical Hebrew in Transition: The Language of the Book of Ezekiel* (JSOTSup, 90; Sheffield: Sheffield Academic Press).
Rost, L.
    1926   *Die Überlieferung von der Thronnachfolge Davids* (BWANT, 3.6; Stuttgart: W. Kohlhammer). ET *The Succession to the Throne of David* (trans. M.D. Rutter and D.M. Gunn, introduction by E. Ball; Historical Texts and Interpreters in Biblical Scholarship, 4; Sheffield: Almond Press, 1982).
Schulte, H.
    1972   *Die Entstehung der Geschichtsschreibung im alten Israel* (BZAW, 128; Berlin: W. de Gruyter).
Van Seters, J.
    2000   'The Court History and DtrH: Conflicting Perspectives on the House of David', in de Pury and Römer 2000: 70–93.
Wellhausen, J. (ed.)
    1878   F. Bleek, *Einleitung in die heilige Schrift* (Berlin, 4th edn).
Whybray, R.N.
    1968   *The Succession Narrative* (SBT, 2nd series, 9; London: SCM Press).
Wills, L.M.
    1990   *The Jewish Novel in the Ancient World* (Ithaca, NY: Cornell University Press).

Chapter 6

THE DATE OF THE YAHWIST

J.A. Emerton

There has never been complete agreement among scholars about the date
of the J, or Yahwistic, document, which has been believed to be the
earliest source, or one of the earliest sources, of the books of Genesis,
Exodus and Numbers. Until recently, it was widely agreed that there was
such a source, which normally used Yahweh as a divine name, in contrast
to E, the Elohistic source, which normally used Elohim. It is convenient to
use the expression 'the Yahwist' to refer to the author, but it is not
intended in the present article to prejudge the question whether one
should think of a single author or of a school of writers.

Various questions arise in an attempt to determine the date of J, and it
is necessary to set some limits to the scope of the discussion, if it is to be
kept within the limits of a single article. Some clarification of the way in
which J is understood below is needed, as are some other presuppositions
of the argument.

1.

First, the following discussion assumes the existence of the J source and,
indeed, also of E. Scholars have not always agreed about the precise
contents of J, especially in passages believed to contain a mixture of J and
E material. In general, I follow the analysis worked out by such scholars
as Julius Wellhausen, S.R. Driver and Martin Noth, and it is usually
satisfactory for the present purpose to ignore differences in the detailed
analysis of the sources. It was once commonly believed that the J source
continued to be used in the book of Joshua, or even in later biblical books.
Without denying the possibility of such continuation, I shall confine my
discussion to the relevant parts of the Pentateuch.

Secondly, questions arise concerning the unity of J. While there is
sufficient continuity of narrative to justify the hypothesis of a single
source, there is much disparate material, and it is widely believed that
Genesis, for instance, contains many short traditions which may earlier
have been transmitted either orally or already in writing. Such traditions

may be regarded as sources used by the Yahwist while compiling his account of the creation and early history of the world, and then the origin and early history of the Israelite people. Further, there have been scholars who have postulated several distinct strands within J, labelled J^1, J^2, etc. Such theories cannot be discussed here, but the opinion may be expressed that the existence of none of these sub-divisions of J has been established with sufficient probability. The possibility remains that the original text of J has been expanded at one time or another. Genesis 15, for example, is probably to be regarded as not an original part of either J or E. Mention needs also to be made of the promises to the patriarchs in the book of Genesis, many of which have long been regarded as later additions. In a discussion of the question, I concluded (Emerton 1982: 32) that the promises of a son to Abraham in 16.11; 18.10, 14, and of the land in 12.7; 28.13, 15 are probably original, but that the others were added to the combined text of JE in the seventh or sixth century. In the present article, I have sought to base no argument about the date of J on any passage whose originality is in serious doubt (apart from Gen. 27.40, which is a special case).

Thirdly, the present article is an examination of the date of J as it is present in the 'classical' theory of the analysis of the text in Pentateuchal criticism, which arranges the sources in the following order: JEDP (though some have thought that E is earlier than J). In the space available in the present article, it is impossible to discuss, for example, the theories of those who would date JE later than D (see, however, the discussion in Nicholson 1998: ch. 5).

Fourthly, since the aim of the present investigation is to find the place of J in the history of Israel, it is appropriate to say something about the reliability of the books of Kings, and their account of the pre-exilic history of the kingdoms of Israel and Judah. I share the widely-held opinion that there were at least two editions of the work. The first was pre-exilic and is probably to be dated in the seventh century during the reign of Josiah. The second edition was exilic but was prepared before the possibility of return from exile became imminent; it is probably to be dated close to 562, the year of the release of Jehoiachin from prison, the last event to be recorded in 2 Kgs 25.27–30. That does not exclude the likelihood that some further additions were made later, but the work was substantially complete by the middle of the sixth century. As far as reliability is concerned, there is reason to think that the authors had access to some reliable information, but some of the sources of information on which they drew (e.g. some prophetic stories) cannot make the same claim to probability.

Fifthly, the present investigation will focus attention primarily on the question whether J is to be dated before the exile or whether an exilic or post-exilic date is more probable, although any evidence for a more precise dating will be welcome.

In 1978, Hermann Vorländer published a book discussing the date of the Jehovist, that is to say, the writer who combined the J and E documents into a single document JE. While his work is not restricted to J, most of what he says is relevant to J. He regards JE as exilic or post-exilic, with a *terminus ad quem* of around 400, but he appears to favour a dating of J and E in the sixth century (368–69, 372). His argument is directed especially against those who favour a date for J in the tenth century, but he also offers arguments against the ninth, eighth and seventh centuries. There have also been other scholars such as J. Van Seters (1975, etc.) and H.H. Schmid (1976) who have argued for a late date for J. Since, however, Vorländer offers so full and systematic an argument against a pre-exilic date, it is convenient to arrange the present article in such a way as to deal in turn with the arguments is each of his three chapters.

2.

Vorländer's first chapter advances an argument from silence. In his opinion, if JE had existed before the exile, there would have been clear references to it in other pre-exilic literature such as the texts ascribed to the prophets who taught in that period. Vorländer claims, however, that no pre-exilic texts show such knowledge. There are indeed, he recognizes, references to some of the people and events that are recorded in JE, but they are to be understood as references to traditions of a different kind (270–83). The traditions were not yet a normative part of Yahwistic religion, since otherwise there would have been creed-like references to it (270).

Vorländer thus recognizes that there are references in pre-exilic literature to people or events mentioned in JE, but he maintains that they are references to a different kind of tradition. The tradition was, he believes, sometimes oral. It was not in the form of a unified document recognized by the nation as a whole, not of a fully-developed, official, creed-like, normative history.

How does Vorländer claim to know that the pre-exilic traditions took the form that he ascribes to them? He states in several places (e.g. 270, 272, 278) that his description is 'offensichtlich', but not every reader will find it self-evident, and he needs to give reasons for his view.

If Vorländer's assumptions about the nature of pre-exilic traditions are not accepted, the question arises whether some of the references to a patriarch or an event may be to a written text, which may be JE. There may even be dependence when the person making the allusion does not follow the original text in every detail. While it can be difficult to prove that a particular reference is to a particular written text rather than to a similar text or to an oral tradition, Vorländer's denial of dependence is sometimes open to question.

J's narrative begins with the creation of the world in Genesis 2–3, but Vorländer does not think that belief in Yahweh as creator is attested in pre-exilic texts (267; cf. 29–44, 48, 267–71). He finds no reference to creation in pre-exilic prophetic or historical texts, except in later additions, and he regards none of the relevant passages in the Psalms as pre-exilic. His dating of some of the Psalms is open to question or even unconvincing. Thus Ps. 93.1 is regarded as post-exilic (40), and Ps. 96.5 as dependent on Deutero-Isaiah ([41] as also [61] is Psalm 47, another Enthronement Psalm, which does not however mention creation; see the arguments in the publications cited by Vorländer in n. 3). Vorländer does not, however, pay due attention to the alternative view that Deutero-Isaiah was dependent on the Enthronement Psalms, and that they are pre-exilic in date, as was argued long ago by Sigmund Mowinckel (1922: 49–50, 195–201), and more recently by John Day (1990: 71–73).

Psalm 89 is an important piece of evidence, for it refers to the creation of the world in vv. 12–13 and 48 (ET 11–12 and 47). Vorländer questions (39) various arguments for a pre-exilic date, and his objections to some of them are cogent. However, one of his claims in unconvincing. He fails to explain the use of the first-person singular in vv. 48 and 51 (ET 47 and 50), which imply that the king is the speaker (and, although the text of v. 48, ET 47 probably needs to be emended, it is likely that the use of the first person should remain). Verses 39–52 (ET 38–51; cf. v. 19, ET 18, if it refers to the king) testify that the Davidic king has been faced by a great disaster, but they also imply that he is still in existence and not beyond the possibility of deliverance. The psalm is therefore most probably to be dated before the Davidic monarchy came to an end in 587 or 586.

Vorländer returns in the last part of his book (358) to the subject of Yahweh as creator. He claims that belief in creation belongs closely together with monotheistic faith, and that the combination of these two beliefs appears for the first time in the message of Deutero-Isaiah, whose monotheism is explicit. The two beliefs are found in JE, which must, Vorländer argues, therefore be dated after Deutero-Isaiah. 'Somit ist dieser Aspekt des jehowistischen Werkes theologiegeschichtlich nur in der exilisch-nachexilischen Epoche anzusiedeln' (358). In view of stories of creation in the literatures of other ancient nations, it is surprising that Vorländer should think it impossible in Israel before the preaching of Deutero-Isaiah. It is no surprise to find references to creation in Psalm 89. Even though the Ugaritic texts do not link Baal's defeat of the sea monster with creation, El is described as *bny bnwt*, 'creator of creatures', literally 'builder of things that have been built'. Indeed, Vorländer recognizes (342) that El is regarded in the Ugaritic texts as the creator. Further, an eighth-century Phoenician text from Karatepe (*KAI* 26.III.18) describes the god

El as 'creator of earth' (cf. Gen. 14.19, 22). Neither the Ugaritic texts nor the Phoenician inscription can be described as monotheistic. There is no reason to deny the likelihood of the J document writing of Yahweh as creator before the exile.

Underlying Vorländer's whole argument in the first chapter of his book is the assumption that, if JE had existed before the exile, there would have been clear allusions to it in pre-exilic literature, and that, if no unambiguous reference to it can be found, then it may be concluded that JE did not yet exist. This assumption is questionable.

It has long been observed – often with surprise – that the books of Kings make no reference to the so-called 'writing prophets' other than Isaiah – and the reference to Jonah in 2 Kgs 14.25 has so little in common with the book of Jonah that this one allusion by the historian is not significant for the present purpose. There is, for example, no reference to Amos or Hosea, Micah the Morashtite, Jeremiah or Ezekiel, although one might have thought that their condemnations of the sins of the people would have been grist to the historian's mill. It seems that, although a mention of them might have been expected by a modern reader, the ancient historian thought otherwise. Vorländer's assumption about the use of JE that would have been made by pre-exilic writers if the document had existed appears to have been mistaken.

Indeed, there is a place in Vorländer's book in which he mentions something that may be held to weaken his own argument: 'Die Sündenfallgeschichte wird im gesamten Alten Testament nirgendwo erwähnt, obwohl sie in der jüdischen und christliche Theologie später eine so grosse Rolle spielt' (269). Vorländer dismisses (270) as 'eine völlig subjektiv-psychologisierende Erklärung' Gunkel's suggestion that ancient Israel was too practical for its activities to be determined by theories about the origin of things. It is striking that the prophets do not mention the story of Adam and Eve and their offence in the garden of Eden, although it would have suited their preaching. Vorländer is speaking, not only of the failure of pre-exilic texts outside the Tetrateuch to mention a particular subject, but the whole Old Testament, whether pre-exilic, exilic or post-exilic. Vorländer obviously cannot deny that the story of Adam and Eve existed in post-exilic times, for it is present in the book of Genesis. The failure of prophets and others to make use of it is not evidence that the story did not exist in the post-exilic period. Why, it may be asked, should the same kind of evidence be used by Vorländer to argue that JE did not exist before the exile?

3.

In his second chapter, Vorländer sets out his criteria for dating JE, and then assesses in turn the arguments for and against a dating of J and of E in the tenth, ninth, eighth and seventh centuries. Some of the arguments against an early date are also relevant to some later periods.

The arguments vary in strength, and there is little point in devoting space to arguments for a pre-exilic date that have little or no force. For example, among the alleged pieces of evidence for dating J in the tenth or ninth centuries are the references to the boundaries of Israel stated in Gen. 15.18 (302, 324). Since, however, Genesis 15 is probably not an original part of J, I agree with Vorländer in questioning its value as evidence for an early dating of J. Other arguments that will not be discussed here are the claim that the reference in Gen. 10.15 to Sidon as the first-born son of Canaan fits only the tenth century, for Vorländer's argument against the theory is convincing (303); and failure to mention Solomon's Temple, or to show the influence of prophecy, seem to be weak arguments against a date in the tenth (315) or ninth (325) century. There are, however, some arguments that need to be discussed. I shall focus attention on them.

Among the arguments for dating J in the tenth century (297) is the claim that this period best fits the peaceful state of affairs that is presupposed (297–98). Consideration is also given by Vorländer to similar arguments for a ninth-century date (322–23) for J and a ninth (328–29) or eighth (331) date for E.

The argument for a peaceful background in the tenth century (297) is that Gen. 21.33; 26.28–29 imply peace with the Philistines, and 31.48–52 peace with the Aramaeans, and that there is no hint of tension between Israelites and the Canaanites. The conflict between the Philistines and Saul (1 Sam. 13–31) and also David (2 Sam. 5.17–25) is over, and the wars against the Aramaeans of Damascus have not yet begun. The tenth century was a period when Assyria, Babylon and Egypt were weak, and Israel could expand peacefully.

Vorländer argues (297–98) that there were also times other than the tenth century when there was peace: the reign of Jehoshaphat over Judah in the ninth century, the reigns of Jeroboam II over Israel and of Uzziah over Judah in the eighth, and of Manasseh over Judah in the seventh. In any case, there are analogies in later literatures of other nations for books describing a peaceful golden age in the past which were, however, written in times of trouble and unrest ('in Zeiten der Not und der Unruhe').

While the reigns of David and Solomon are portrayed in the books of Kings as a time of particular power and splendour for Israel, Vorländer's argument that it was not the only time of peace has force. The important question to ask is, perhaps, not whether JE was written in a time of peace, but whether it is plausible to postulate a date for it in or after the exile, when disaster had struck the people. Is it likely that the disaster would have left no traces in the text? There is evidence in Deuteronomy (29.17–27, ET 18–28; 30.1–10; cf. 4.25–31) of the threat or experience of disaster, and also in the Holiness Code (Lev. 26.14–39). Is JE likely to have been entirely different?

Is it, however, true that J shows no hint of the exile? Vorländer argues in his third chapter (354–58) that the expanded promises to the patriarchs, especially of increase in numbers and possession of the land, come from the exilic period when the future of the nation and its possession of the land were in peril. However, my earlier discussion of the promises (Emerton 1982) suggested a different setting, namely, the time before the exile when the future was threatened, but while the monarchy still existed. Moreover, I argued that the promises (apart from the limited number in the original form of the text) were added after the combination of J and E, and that J therefore existed beforehand. I therefore question whether the promises can be regarded as evidence that J, or even JE, is necessarily exilic.

Whatever else may be said about the J document, it can scarcely be claimed that the past age is portrayed as a golden one as in Vorländer's examples of later non-Israelite texts written in times of disaster. The primaeval story in Genesis 1–11 has its share of human sin, from the eating of the forbidden fruit to the hubris of the builders of the city and tower of Babel, and not everything goes happily. The patriarchs are not without their faults, and their lives are not free from troubles and difficulties. In Egypt the Israelites are subjected to slavery and, even after they have escaped and experienced deliverance at the Red Sea, their years of wandering in the wilderness are times of discomfort and difficulty, as well as of dissatisfaction and rebellion. Nevertheless, the story is one of hope. Israel survives the disasters that are experienced, and there is a spirit of expectation and hope as they approach the land of Canaan. While it is not easy to enter into the mind of an ancient writer, I find it difficult to believe that the writer knew that it would all end in the defeat of the people, the fall of Jerusalem, and then exile from their land.

Another subject discussed by Vorländer in his second chapter is the relationship between Israel and neighbouring peoples and its bearing on the date of J. Those who date J in the tenth century (299–300) (e.g. Wolff 1963: 76–78 = 1964: 348–50, ET 1966: 134–36 = 1975: 43–45) claim that references in J to neighbouring peoples are best understood to imply subjugation by David, as recorded in 2 Samuel 8: Edom (8.13), Moab (8.2), Ammon (8.12), Aram (8.3–11), Amalek (8.12), and the Philistines (8.12), whereas those who favour a date in the ninth century claim that the subjugation of the Canaanites and Edomites in the period of David and Solomon must have been some time in the past when allusion to it is made by J in Gen. 9.25 and 27.40, respectively (323; cf. 301). Vorländer questions the historicity of the narrative in 2 Samuel 8, which he follows Noth (1943: 65, ET 1981: 56) in regarding as the redactional work of the Deuteronomist, and he maintains (301) against a dating in the tenth or ninth century that subjugation in the reign of David is not the only possibility, and he appeals to biblical references to them in exilic and post-exilic texts.

I shall focus attention on verses concerned with Edom, for it is here that Vorländer's case is most open to question (cf. Nicholson 1998: 159–60, 239–40). Before listing relevant exilic and post-exilic references to Edom (300), Vorländer mentions (299) verses in J which are thought by some to be concerned with events in the tenth century. Genesis 25.22–26 tells of the birth of Esau and Jacob and recounts that Jacob was holding his brother's heel, and vv. 29–34 tell how Esau surrendered his birthright to Jacob in exchange for a meal. Isaac's blessing of Jacob says in 27.29 that he will be lord over his brothers, and Isaac tells Esau in v. 37 that he has made Jacob his lord; and his blessing of Esau tells him in v. 40a that he will serve his brother, but v. 40b adds that 'when thou shalt break loose, thou shalt break his yoke from off thy neck'. Genesis 36.31–39 lists the kings of Edom 'before any king ruled over the Israelites'; however, it is disputed whether these verses are to be attributed to J or P or to some other source. Numbers 24.18 says that Edom will be dispossessed, but that Israel will do valiantly (and the preceding verse, which speaks of a star and a sceptre rising out of Jacob, is usually understood to refer to the rise of David).

Genesis 27.40 deserves special comment. As Vorländer observes (299), v. 40b is usually regarded as a later addition. It speaks of the end of Esau's subjection to Jacob, i.e. of Edom's subjection to Israel, and it is thought to do so in the context of a particular historical event. Those who date J in the tenth century think that v. 40b refers to events narrated in 1 Kgs 11.14–22 (e.g. Wolff 1963: 77 = 1964: 349, ET 1966: 135 = 1975: 44–45), which tells how Hadad, an Edomite prince, escaped Joab's massacre of Edomite males and fled to Egypt but was allowed by Pharaoh to return to Edom when David died, and he became an adversary to Solomon. 1 Kings 11.23–24 tells of another of Solomon's adversaries, an adventurer named Rezon who gained control of Damascus and became king there. Verse 25 says that he did as much harm as Hadad and says 'and he reigned over Aram'. Two Hebrew manuscripts, with support from the LXX and the Peshitta, read 'Edom' in place of 'Aram', and some scholars think that the variant reading is correct and that Hadad's return to Edom resulted in his becoming king. On that reading of the text, it appears that, under Hadad as king, the Edomites secured freedom from Israel. Vorländer, however, notes (323) the view that Edom's first successful attempt to achieve independence was in the middle of the ninth century in the reign of Joram of Judah. 2 Kings 8.20–22 tells how Edom revolted against Judah, and v. 21 recounts Joram's unsuccessful attempt to suppress the revolt, and v. 22 says that the result has lasted 'until this day'. It is to this revolt that some scholars (e.g. Gunkel 1910: 314, ET 1997: 306; S.R. Driver 1926: 261) ascribe the addition to the text in Gen. 27.40b. Vorländer mentions (323) another passage which is thought by some who date J in the ninth century to be relevant to Gen. 27.40b: 2 Kgs 14.7, which he dates c. 800. This verse records that Amaziah killed ten thousand Edomites and took possession of Sela and called it Joktheel, 'which is its name to this day'. Although the Edomites were defeated, it is thought by some that the result was the lasting independence of Edom.

Vorländer also mentions (324) the theory that 2 Kgs 16.6 refers to yet another escape from Israelite rule in 735. This verse says that 'Rezin, the king of Aram, restored Elath to Aram' and expelled the people of Judah, and that 'the Aramaeans (*kethibh*) came to Elath and dwelt there until this day'. The text is surprising, since Aram had never possessed Elath before, and it is difficult to see how Rezin can have restored it to Aram. Further, the *qere* says that it was the Edomites, not the Aramaeans, who came to Elath and occupied it. It has also seemed strange that Rezin should thus act on behalf of the Edomites. As a result, it has been conjectured that the two references to Aram in the MT should be read as 'Edom', and that 'Rezin' should be deleted as a mistaken assimilation to the reference to him in the previous verse. However, if the emendation is correct, the verse refers to the Edomites regaining possession of Elath and states that it was the king of Edom who achieved the result. It does not speak of the acquiring of independence by Edom; otherwise, there would have been no king of Edom to reconquer Elath.

In contrast to theories that relate Gen. 27.40b to one or other of the passages listed above, Vorländer maintains that the prophecy of Edom's subjection to Israel fits the exilic and post-exilic situation just as well. In this period, the Edomites sought to occupy the territory of Judah and Israel, and he refers to Ezek. 35.9–10; 36.5; Joel 4.19 (ET 3.19); Obad. 10ff. (in fact, the whole of Obad. 1–16, 21 is about Edom); Ps. 137.7. Other passages to which he refers speak of judgment on Edom: Isa. 11.14; 31.2 (it is not clear why he refers to this verse, and there has perhaps been a misprint or some other mistake); 34; 63.1; Jer. 49.17 (the whole of vv. 7–22 is relevant); Ezek. 25.12ff.; 32.29; Amos 2.1ff. (it is not clear why these verses are thought to be relevant, or why no mention is made of 1.11–12); Ps. 83.7, ET 6; 108.10 (ET 9; v. 11, ET 10 is also relevant as is the parallel passage in Ps. 60.10–11, ET 8–9).

Vorländer's attempt to link Gen. 27.40 with the exilic or post-exilic period is unconvincing. The prophetic passages that he cites tell of the desolation of Edom, not of Edom becoming subject to Israel. Ezekiel 25.14 speaks of Israel playing a part in Yahweh's wreaking vengeance on Edom (cf. Ps. 60.11, ET 9 = 108.11, ET 10, though too much should not be read into this verse and it may not refer to the same historical circumstances), but no mention is made of Israelite occupation of Edom or of Edom having to serve Israel. Nor do the exilic and post-exilic passages cited by Vorländer say anything about Edom breaking the Israelite yoke. The late background postulated by Vorländer seems far less appropriate to Gen. 27.40 than a situation before the exile, when Edom is said to have been subject to Judah but eventually to have gained freedom, whether its liberation is dated in the tenth, the ninth or the eighth century.

There is another objection to Vorländer's theory of an exilic or post-exilic setting for Gen. 27.40. The actions of the Edomites at and after the sack of Jerusalem by the Babylonians led to strong feelings of bitterness, anger and hatred on the part of the Jews. See especially Obadiah 10–12; Ps. 137.7; Amos 1.11; Lam. 4.21–22. Yet there is no trace of such hatred and bitterness in the portrayal of Esau in Genesis. There he is portrayed as a skilful hunter and a man of the open air (Gen. 25.27), and as one who is not very bright and is easily outwitted by his brother. It is understandable that he resents being outwitted and that he plans to kill Jacob once his father is dead (Gen. 27.41), but when Jacob returns after his time with Laban, Esau welcomes him warmly (Gen. 33.4), and he generously declines Jacob's offer of a gift until pressed to do so (Gen. 33.9–11). Then too he is deceived by Jacob, who promises to come along slowly to Esau's home, although he intends to do no such thing but to return to Canaan. There is no suggestion in this narrative that Esau is acting deceitfully, and he does not press his offer to Jacob to leave some of his servants to accompany Jacob and his family and flocks to Seir (Gen. 33.12–16). It is scarcely likely that the portrayal of Esau, the ancestor of the Edomites, reflects a period in which the Jews felt bitterness against the Edomites because of their treacherous behaviour at and after the fall of Jerusalem. The stories about Esau in J and Gen. 27.40a must go back to a time before the exile; and the addition in v. 40b was made after one of the events recorded in 1 and 2 Kings, when Edom regained freedom from Judah.

One of the other neighbouring peoples discussed by Vorländer is the Aramaeans (299–300). He notes that Gen. 24.10 says that Abraham's servant went to Aram-naharaim (where he met Laban, whose sister Rebekah he brought back to Canaan to become Isaac's wife); and Gen. 31.20 tells how Jacob later fled secretly from 'Laban the Aramaean' (cf. v. 24, where the same phrase occurs; some attribute 31.20, 24 to E rather than to J, but that is probably not important for the present discussion). Some who date J in the tenth century relate the story of Laban the Aramaean to the defeat of the Aramaeans in 2 Sam. 8.3–8. Vorländer, however, argues that interest in, and hostility towards, Aram and other neighbouring peoples was not confined to the tenth century but continued into the exilic and post-exilic periods. The only evidence that he gives for Aram is Zech. 9.2 (300). It is, in fact, Zech. 9.1 that mentions Damascus, and 'Adam' later in the verse has been conjecturally emended to 'Aram'. Verses 1–6 tell of disaster coming on a number of peoples who were neighbours of Israel. The date and historical background of this obscure

oracle are uncertain. If the opening verses come from the same period as
v. 13, which mentions Greeks, the passage is unlikely to be earlier than the
fourth century. The point of Vorländer's argument is that the neighbouring peoples were of concern to the Israelites in later periods as well as in
the tenth century. However, it would be a bold conjecture to suppose that
the story of Laban is to be interpreted as an allusion to whatever events lie
behind Zech. 9.1. Moreover, the geographical location of Zech. 9.1–8 does
not suit the stories in Genesis. It is not close to Haran and Aram-
naharaim to the north-east (see Carte 1 in Dion 1997). On the other hand,
it is far from Gilead in the south (see Noth 1941: 50–101 = 1971: 347–90,
esp. 1941: 57–71 = 1971: 354–65). The reason for my mention of Gilead
will appear in the next paragraph.

Genesis 31.44–54 tells of a covenant made between Jacob and Laban,
and attempts have been made to identify its historical background.
Vorländer reasonably questions (300) whether its background is the
alleged subjugation by David of his Aramaean enemies. The story does
not look like an account of a peace treaty at the end of a war between
different states, and it may be suspected that it is a story of a local
boundary between Israelite and Aramaean territories. Vorländer has the
impression (322) that the story is concerned with figures from a distant
past. He also questions (298) whether it is justified to draw from stories
about individuals conclusions about Israel's relations with its neighbours,
and says that one must distinguish between the historical background of a
story and that of the author of the work in which it is recorded. However,
his own theory about the relevance of the story of Laban to Israel's
relations with its neighbours and the relevance of Zech. 9.1 assumes that
there is a connection between stories about Laban and the post-exilic
period. Moreover, Gen. 25.23; 27.29, 40 implies that there is some
relationship between people mentioned in the story of Jacob and what
happened to the peoples who were believed to descend from them. Laban
probably does, in some sense, represent the Aramaeans. Laban is
portrayed as an unpleasant and devious character, but without the degree
of hostility that might have been expected in or after the wars between
Israelites and Aramaeans in the ninth and eighth centuries, but Vorländer
has failed to make a satisfactory case for a connexion with the events
behind Zech. 9.1.

Is it likely that the story of Jacob and Laban was composed in the exilic
or post-exilic period, when the only evidence that Vorländer can adduce is
Zechariah 9? Or is it more likely that it was composed at a relatively early
date, closer in time to the historical background and was preserved in later
times when details no longer fitted the comtemporary situation? The latter
seems more probable, and it is also more in keeping with what Vorländer
himself says about the problem of correlating stories about individuals
and stories about nations.

Before leaving Vorländer's second chapter, mention must be made of the five arguments advanced by him against a tenth-century date for J (320–21; cf. 349–50). First, J speaks in a hostile way of the Pharaoh in the period of the oppression of the Israelites in Egypt and the exodus. Vorländer thinks that such hostility is unlikely in a narrative written in the reign of Solomon, who had friendly contacts with Egypt and married Pharaoh's daughter (1 Kgs 3.1; 7.8; 9.16, 24). It is, he believes, more likely in the exilic and post-exilic period (Ezek. 29–31; Jer. 25.19; 44.30; Joel 4.19, ET 3.19). However, even in the reign of Solomon royal friendship with Egypt (which was perhaps not unqualified; see 1 Kgs 11.17–22, 40; 12.2) may not have obliterated any traditions that may have existed about slavery in Egypt and deliverance at the Red Sea. Vorländer's argument is directed against a tenth-century date for J, but he does not mention that later hostility to Egypt was not restricted to the exilic and post-exilic period. Although he argues that some references to Egypt in Hosea and Amos are secondary, he does not discuss the criticisms of Egypt and of trust in Egypt in the later eighth century in Isa. 20.3–5; 30.2–5, 7. It may also be suspected that there was hostility towards Egypt after the Egyptian incursion into Judah in the seventh century, when Josiah was killed. Second, Vorländer argues that the story of the Tower of Babel in Gen. 11.1–9 points to a knowledge of Babylon that was unlikely in the tenth century. Third, if J had been written in the time of the united monarchy, some reference to Solomon's Temple might have been expected. Fourth, the words 'the Canaanites were then in the land' in Gen. 12.6 (cf. 13.7) do not fit the tenth century, when the Israelites and Canaanites were living side by side. It is perhaps surprising that Vorländer, who regards some verses in Hosea 12 as additions, does not consider the possibility that Gen. 12.6 and 13.7 are secondary; and the text flows well without them. Fifth, Genesis 2–11 show knowledge of Mesopotamia that is unlikely in pre-exilic texts. The second and fifth arguments will be considered below.

4.

Vorländer's third and final chapter sets out further arguments in favour of his dating of JE in the exilic or post-exilic period. The chapter is in two parts: the first presents historical and cultural-historical arguments, and the second theological-historical arguments. Finally, there is a summing up of the whole case that Vorländer has advanced for his dating of JE.

At the beginning of his presentation of the historical and cultural-historical arguments, Vorländer claims (337–47) that there are in the primaeval history and other parts of JE mythological elements, most of which originated in Mesopotamia. Not all his examples of Mesopotamian influence are convincing, but some, such as the story of the flood in the Gilgamesh Epic and elsewhere, are justified and are generally recognized.

The question arises, however, of the period to which the evidence may be dated, and whether it need be dated in the exile or later. Vorländer considers three periods that have been suggested: the fourteenth century, when the Tell el-Amarna letters testify to knowledge of Akkadian and the cuneiform script by scribes in Canaanite cites; the middle of the monarchical period, when the religion of Israel was influenced by Mesopotamian religion, and images of Mesopotamian gods existed in the Jerusalem Temple in the reigns of Manasseh, Amon and Josiah; and the exilic and post-exilic period, when exiled Jews were living in Babylonia. He favours the last of the three. Vorländer's case for a late date is based on arguments advanced by earlier scholars (338–40) and arguments of his own (340–43). I have tried to combine and summarize them as follows.

First, he once again relies on the argument from silence. There is no trace of mythology in general or of creation myths in particular in the pre-exilic prophets: evidence first appears in Ezekiel and later in Deutero-Isaiah, in contrast to prophets like Jeremiah who were never exiles in Mesopotamia. As far as the general argument is concerned, the question arises, as before, whether the pre-exilic prophets had occasion to refer to myths. There is no need to repeat here what was said above about references to Yahweh as creator.

Second, it is claimed (339), that early Babylonian influence was exercised on Canaanite cities in the lowlands, and it is unlikely that the Israelites, who lived in rural and hilly parts, would have come into contact with anything Babylonian before the establishment of the monarchy (339). However, the question is not whether Israelites came into direct contact with anything Babylonian at an early date, but whether they acquired such knowledge from the Canaanites at a later date. Sooner or later, the Israelites came into contact with Canaanites and gained control of Canaanite cities and their culture (I ignore for the present purpose questions that arise about the origin of the Israelites). If Mesopotamian ideas and religion had influenced Canaanites in the fourteenth century, the influence may have been passed on to the Israelites at a later date.

Third, Vorländer agrees (341) with Gunkel's comment (1910: 35, ET 1997: 34) that the mythology used by Ezekiel (Ezek. 28.1–19) is far more mythological in character than that of Genesis 2–3, where the mytho-logical elements have been fully integrated into Yahwistic faith. Genesis 2–3 reflects a later stage of religious development, which implies a process that would have taken some time. The point of Vorländer's argument is presumably that JE must have come some time after Ezekiel (although he later speaks [342–43] of more rapid developments of thought). The argument presupposes that the myth was unknown to Israelites before Ezekiel; but the possibility remains that the process of adaptation was completed long before the time of Ezekiel, and that the prophet made use of an earlier form of the myth, which had not ceased to exist in that form after it had also been adapted to Yahwistic faith in Genesis 2–3.

Fourth, to return to the question of creation myths, it is claimed that they are not attested for the early period (342–43). Although a fragment of an Akkadian tablet of the Babylonian account of the flood has been found at Ugarit, neither it nor creation myths have found an entrance into genuine Ugaritic mythological texts. However, it was seen above that Ugaritic texts refer to El as the creator. If there was such a belief, it is likely that there was some account in Ugaritic mythology of the way in which El acted as creator, and it may well be no more than an accident that no such account has been preserved in the tablets that have survived.

After arguing that JE reflects the influence of Mesopotamian myths and that the influence does not predate the Babylonian exile, Vorländer turns to the influence of Mesopotamian history writing. He argues first that JE has been influenced by such writing and, secondly, that the sixth century was the time when Israelite traditions were committed to writing. The two arguments will now be examined in the reverse order.

Vorländer's discussion (347–49) of the period in which the Israelite tradition was committed to writing is concerned with the motive for such work. In his opinion, the spread of the Aramaic language in Palestine and also in Mesopotamia constituted a threat to the traditions both of the Israelites and of the Assyrians and Babylonians. By the middle of the sixth century Aramaic had completely dominated Mesopotamia, and so the Persian Empire adopted the so-called Imperial Aramaic as an official language. Since the old myths and epics in Sumerian and Akkadian were transmitted largely in oral form, their existence was threatened, and there was a need to commit them to writing (347). Similarly, long before in Old Babylonian times Sumerian tradition had been written down. (It is not clear how Vorländer relates the writing down of Sumerian traditions in the Old Babylonian period to that of the sixth century.) For the Jews there were the further problems of the loss of the archives in Jerusalem, and the deportation of the upper crust of society threatened the continued existence of the nation and its culture. The exiles were unable to carry much with them to Babylonia, and there was a need to collect and write down the traditions that were remembered. Vorländer does not exclude the possibility that some pre-exilic documents had been preserved, but he thinks that committing the traditions to writing on a broader basis began only with the exile. Therefore the Jehovist cannot be dated earlier than the exile (349).

The account given by Vorländer of the situation during the exile is problematic. It is true that the use of Aramaic was spreading and that it became dominant in Mesopotamia. How far, however, it was a threat to the Hebrew language in Judah during the exile, especially in the early years, and how far it was recognized to be a threat and led to attempts to preserve Hebrew traditions in writing, are questions that Vorländer answers by assertions rather than by detailed consideration of the evidence. It is also improbable that much material, including many details, was preserved solely by oral tradition to enable the books of Kings to be written, and all the traditional material that appears in JE and also the pre-exilic psalms. There is evidence from elsewhere that extensive traditions can be memorized and handed down accurately, especially if they also exist in written form, but it may be doubted whether so much tradition – most of it, *ex hypothesi* purely oral – would have been preserved in such detail that it would have been possible to compose and write the books of Kings and JE. It may also be suspected that the transmission of tradition would have been disturbed by the disruption caused by death, uprooting and resettlement in a foreign land. Incidentally, Vorländer does not tell us what he makes of the account in Jeremiah 36 of the prophet having his oracles written down by Baruch, or whether he regards it as historical. It may be observed, however, that it gives no hint that a major need to be met by writing down the oracles was to preserve them from the incursions of a foreign language.

To have taken the postulated oral traditions and to have written them in the form in which they appear in JE or the books of Kings would have required considerable literary skill. Knowledge of the alphabet and practice in writing such documents as the Samarian and Arad ostraca or the Lachish letters are not the same as the ability to write literature. Whence came the necessary literary skill during the exile, with all its disruption, unless it had existed before? If, however, such literary skill existed before the exile, were there not pre-exilic literary texts composed by scribes possessing such skill? Vorländer's theory seems improbable. Further, strong arguments have been advanced for believing that there was a first edition of the books of Kings in the seventh century, and so before the exile, and that the law book that inspired Josiah's reformation was an early edition of Deuteronomy.

Vorländer (345–47) offers several arguments in favour of the view that the influence of Mesopotamian history writing may be discerned in JE. The first is that the primaeval history reflects the influence of the Sumerian King List in structure and content. In both the King List and Genesis 2–9 we find the same order of events: creation, flood and re-establishment of the world. Does Vorländer think any other order would have been possible? In JE, antediluvian people live a long time, and the King List ascribes even longer periods to the reigns of rulers before the flood. Further, there are ten antediluvian patriarchs and ten Sumerian kings. However, the antediluvian patriarchs are not kings, and the J narrative (Gen. 4.17–26) does not ascribe great ages to them. The great ages are found in the P source (Gen. 5.1–28), not in J. It has been argued that the genealogies in J and P go back to a common source, and it has been compared to the tradition in Berossus that there were ten antediluvian kings (see, for example, S.R. Driver 1926: 79–81). As Westermann points out (1974: 474–76, ET 350–51), the number of kings in the Sumerian list varies: it is eight (*ANET*, 265) in the older lists, and ten is found only in one secondary variant. Further, 'the names found in the respective lists themselves [i.e. the Mesopotamian and the Hebrew] have nothing in common' (Speiser 1964: 36). Vorländer's argument thus has an insecure foundation.

Second, it is claimed by Vorländer (345) that the whole conception of JE corresponds to Mesopotamian predecessors. It depends on belief in a divine plan for the world and has a universal perspective. Yet a narrative that begins with creation and tells the story of what happened after it until God's choice of Abraham, the ancestor of the Hebrews, cannot have anything other than a perspective that is in some sense universal. If, as I have argued above, there was an Israelite belief in Yahweh as creator before the exile, then the rest follows from that.

Third, Vorländer refers to an article by Van Seters (1972: 64–81) about references to the Amorites and Hittites in JE, which is said to reflect Mesopotamian usage. According to Van Seters (66–67), in Assyrian royal inscriptions, from 'Tiglath-pileser I (ca. 1100 B.C.) to Shalmaneser III (850 B.C.), the land of Amurru is the region of Syria west of the Upper Euphrates to the Mediterranean'. From the early eighth century it also 'takes in ... Palestine, including Phoenicia, Israel, Moab, Ammon, Edom, and the Philistine cities ... This usage for the settled population of Syria-Palestine ... is not attested later than the seventh century.' Further, by 'the time of Sargon (ca. 720 B.C.)', the words 'Amorite' and 'Hittite' have come to be 'virtually synonymous archaic terms which stand for the indigenous inhabitants of Syrian-Palestine'. A similar, though slightly different view is expressed by de Vaux (1971: I, 30, 132–33, ET 1978: I, 133, 135–36), who also sees in biblical usage the influence of Assyrian terminology.

If the Israelite terminology corresponds to that of the Assyrians, as seems likely, it suggests a date not earlier than the eighth century, and it is compatible with a dating in the exilic or post-exilic period on the assumption that the terminology continued to be used by the Israelites. The biblical references given by Vorländer (344) are Gen. 25.9–10; 26.34; 27.46; Exod. 3.8, 17; 23.20–23; Num. 21.21–35. Of these references, those in Genesis are only to the Hittites, not the Amorites; and it is usually supposed that all the references in Genesis to the Hittites are to be ascribed to P rather than to JE. The only exception is the reference in Gen. 15.20, but that is probably not an original part of J. Standard theories of Pentateuchal analysis regard 'Canaanites' as J's term for the previous inhabitants of Canaan in contrast to the E source, which calls them 'Amorites'; the reference in Gen. 10.16 is thought to be redactional. Similarly, most of the references in Exodus and Numbers are ascribed to E. There are, however, some exceptions: apart from verses that are probably redactional, Exod. 3.8, 17, 13.5 are sometimes ascribed to J (as are the references to the Hittites in Exod. 3.8, 17, 13.5) but they all occur in a chapter in which J and E are combined, and scholars have done their best to separate the two. Yet in a passage in which a redactor has sought to unite the two sources, it is a plausible hypothesis that the anomalous appearance of the Amorites may well be redactional. It may thus be suspected that, though the argument for an eighth-century or later date has a bearing on the age of E, it has less force as an argument for the dating of J.

Fourth, Vorländer notes (344) that the expression 'Fear not' was used in Mesopotamia in the second millennium but that it became common only in the middle of the first. The verses cited by him are Gen. 15.1; 21.17; 26.23–24 (in fact only in the latter verse); 28.13 (wrong reference); 46.1ff. (v. 3), but in all these verses, and other verses in Genesis in which the exhortation appears, it is appropriate to the context. Vorländer would surely not maintain that a narrator could not have recorded an exhortation not to be afraid unless he had obtained the idea from an Akkadian idiom.

Fifth, the way in which, in Numbers 21 for example, the conquest of the land west of the Jordan is described corresponds to records by Assyrian and Babylonian kings of their campaigns. If, however, the biblical narrator had some local knowledge of the land, he would not have needed to depend on Mesopotamian documents for the information.

Sixth, Vorländer asks (345) when and how Israel came into contact with Mesopotamian history writing. It cannot, he thinks, have been through the Canaanites, for obviously ('offensichtlich') history writing in the true sense was unknown. There are royal inscriptions in neighbouring peoples, but they do not testify to a coherent presentation of history; and in Israel not even one royal inscription comparable to the Moabite Stone has been found. Only two peoples in the ancient Near East produced classic history writing: the Mesopotamians and the Hittites. Vorländer even goes so far as to say that a consciousness of past and future cannot be found, and that the world was regarded as static and unchangeable; historical events only upset the eternal order. One wonders how Vorländer can feel so sure about such dogmatic statements about the thinking of a group of ancient peoples.

In 'The Kingdoms of Judah and Israel and Ancient Hebrew History Writing' (Emerton, forthcoming), I have argued that the most probable matrix of Israelite history writing is to be found in some North-West Semitic inscriptions (Moabite, Phoenician and Aramaic) of the ninth to seventh centuries. I am aware that no complete monumental inscription of this kind has yet been found in Israel, but Israelite scribes can scarcely have been unaware of their existence, and the absence of any in Israel may well be accidental. It is, indeed, possible that the inspiration for such inscriptions came from Assyrian royal inscriptions of the ninth century, as Na'aman (1998: 335) suggests, and so, after all, there may have been Mesopotamian influence, but it is not necessary to go down as late as the exilic or post-exilic period to find its result.

Finally, Vorländer's theory of Mesopotamian influence on Israelite history writing raises the question how the influence reached the Jews. Since Vorländer finds Mesopotamian influence in Ezekiel, he presumably dates its beginnings early in the exile. How did the Jews learn about it? Did some scribes already know Akkadian (and also Sumerian?) and its complicated script? If, however, they were thus equipped, how can Vorländer be sure that Mesopotamian influence was not exerted before the exile? If even scribes did not possess such knowledge, how did they acquire it? Did they enrol at Babylonian scribal schools to begin the long and very demanding course? Was it feasible for Jewish exiles to do so? Are we also to suppose that those who went through the laborious process of learning were prepared to borrow wholesale from the religious and historical literature of their conquerors? Is it not more likely that Mesopotamian influence was first exercised on the Canaanite scribes some centuries before, when we know that they studied Akkadian and that there were Mesopotamian religious texts in western libraries?

Vorländer's next argument is that the negative attitude towards Egypt in Exodus, which he regards as unthinkable in the tenth century, is plausible at a much later date. It seems unnecessary to add here to what is said on the subject above.

The story of the tower of Babel in Gen. 11.1–9 is next discussed by Vorländer (350–52), who had already mentioned the passage and its significance earlier (320, 338). The story presupposes that Babylon is a major power, which was not true in the tenth century. It was not until the time of Nabopolassar and Nebuchadnezzar II that Babylon attained that status. Like most scholars, Vorländer assumes that the tower in the story was a ziggurat, indeed the great ziggurat in Babylon (Etemenanki). Vorländer sketches its history. There was a ziggurat in the second millennium, but it was destroyed. It was probably rebuilt by Nebuchadnezzar I (c. 1100) but not completed, and Sennacherib destroyed it in 689. It was rebuilt yet again by Esar-haddon and Ashurbanipal, but it was probably destroyed yet again, at least in part. Nabopolassar and Nebuchadnezzar II, however, built it to its greatest size, and the building inscription records that it was built of burnt brick and asphalt, and the same materials are mentioned in Gen. 11.3. Vorländer concludes that the author of JE was acquainted with the inscription and used it in telling the story. Therefore, in Vorländer's opinion, the story of the Tower of Babel testifies to an exilic or post-exilic date for J.

It is impossible here to discuss the various problems of Gen. 11.1–9. Much has been written about it, and Vorländer's account of the story of the ziggurat in Babylon needs to be brought up to date in the light of the monograph of Uehlinger (1990). Whatever may be thought about the origin of the story, Vorländer's theory is improbable. Even if the Jewish writer had been able to read the inscription, he presumably knew that it was of recent origin. Building work in Babylon had not recently ceased as a result of divine intervention, and a multiplicity of languages had not suddenly appeared and led to a mass migration from Babylon. Moreover, the story is set in ancient times, not in recent history. So far from the story in Gen. 11.1–9 being evidence for an exilic date for J, it tells against it. Even if there was little contact between Babylon and Palestine in the centuries immediately before the exile, the possibility remains of tales brought by travellers, on the basis of which the story arose.

The table of nations in Genesis 10 is believed by Vorländer (352) to contain evidence for his late dating of JE. The absence of any reference to the Hittites tells against a date in the second millennium, but nowhere else is the book concerned with a date before the tenth century. Vorländer ascribes vv. 8–19, 21 and 24–30 to J and the rest to P, and what he says about verses in the latter source need not be discussed here. The reference to Cush in v. 8 is not, he thinks, conceivable before the seventh century, for not until then was there a Cushite ruler of Egypt. This argument makes the questionable assumption that knowledge of the Cushites (Nubians) could not have reached the Israelites from the Egyptians at an earlier date. Moreover, Vorländer does not consider the problematic nature of the reference to Cush here, for it makes him the father of Nimrod, who is associated with Mesopotamia (see vv. 10–12, and also Mic. 5.5, ET 6). Some have therefore supposed that the reference is to a Mesopotamian Kash (the Kassites), not to Cush in Africa. More needs to be said about the South Arabian genealogy (the descendants of Joktan) in vv. 26–30. Vorländer appeals to an article by Winnett (1970: esp. 181–88) for the view that these verses indicate a date in the sixth century, for otherwise J would be older than the native Arabian sources which first come from that century. Vorländer does not explain why the existence of the South Arabian sources must be the *terminus post quem* for the dating of Genesis 10, and why the relevant information could not have been available to J before it was recorded in the South Arabian inscriptions that are now extant. (Incidentally, only a few of the names can be confidently identified with South Arabian sources.) In any case, Winnett's dating is based on the theory that 'the Primeval History, of which the Table of Nations forms an integral part, was composed by a late J writer, J2, who must be dated to the sixth century B.C.' (172), though he adds that it was 'a period for which indigenous Arabian sources in the form of inscriptions are available' (173). The argument for the dating in the sixth century of the Primaeval History was presented in an earlier article (Winnett 1965: esp. 1–5), to which he refers. Winnett appears to ascribe the whole of Genesis 10 to J, but he gives no solid reasons for rejecting the argument of many scholars (including Vorländer, as appears from what was noted above) that it also includes verses from P. Apart from an appeal to the contents of P verses, Winnett's only argument is that references to 'Ur of the Chaldeans' in Gen. 11.28 and 31 'must surely point to a date after the rise of the Chaldean empire in the late seventh century B.C.' (1965: 4). The usual view of scholars is that v. 31 belongs to P, not J, and that in v. 28 J has been assimilated to P, a view that requires more than Winnett's assertions to refute.

The Elephantine papyri are also regarded by Vorländer (353) as evidence for a late date of JE on the ground that they show no knowledge of either the legal or historical parts of the Pentateuch and make no mention of the sabbath. If, he claims, JE had existed in the pre-exilic period, reference would have been expected to the great figures and events of the early history of Israel. Several comments may be made about his argument. First, contrary to what he says, the sabbath is mentioned (see, for example, Porten 1968: 126–27). Second, the exact origin of the Jewish colony at Elephantine, and the date when its members left Palestine, are uncertain. Their religion does not appear to correspond to the standards of the pre-exilic prophets, but the Old Testament itself scarcely leads us to suppose that, even if they were generally known, they were universally practised. The occurrence of names like Anath-yahu and Anath-bethel and other such evidence scarcely favour the view that the Jews at Elephantine were, to use an anachronistic term, 'orthodox'. The fact that their religious practice was such, does not prove that JE did not exist. It must not be assumed that JE was published in the way that a modern book would be published and become generally available. We cannot assume that, if JE had existed, there would have been a copy of it in the library of the temple at Elephantine. It is likely that at least the first edition of Deuteronomy appeared before 621 and that P, or something very like it, existed in the late fifth century, but no knowledge of Deuteronomic or Priestly laws appears in the Elephantine papyri. Third, contrary to what Vorländer says, there seems no reason to suppose that, if JE had been known at Elephantine, reference to the people and events of that early history would have been made in the papyri. Their predominant concern was with practical matters, and Vorländer has not indicated how 'scriptural' references would have been relevant to them. The Elephantine papyri cannot serve as evidence that JE was composed in the exilic or post-exilic period.

5. Conclusions

The present article has been organized to correspond to the steps in the discussion of the date of JE by Vorländer, who presents a thorough and systematic review of the problem and summarizes arguments for and against various dates. He himself argues for a date in the sixth century for the Jehovist and, it seems, one for the Yahwist not long before. My principal conclusions may now be summarized.

1. Vorländer's argument that JE is unlikely to be pre-exilic because there is no clear reference to it in pre-exilic literature is unconvincing. It is certainly difficult, perhaps impossible, to prove dependence, but it is also difficult to prove the opposite. Vorländer's presuppositions about the probability that a pre-exilic writer would have cited JE if he had known it are open to question. Vorländer's description of the nature of pre-exilic traditions is based on assertion rather than argument. His claim that belief in Yahweh as creator is not attested before the exile is probably mistaken; and difficulties for his theory that its origin is associated with monotheism are raised by the fact that some people in the ancient Near East who believed in a creator were polytheists.

2. Vorländer is right to argue that, if JE was written in a time of peace, then the united monarchy is not the only possible time. There were other periods of peace. A more important question, however, is whether it is plausible to postulate a date for JE in the exilic or post-exilic period after the disaster of the fall of Jerusalem and the exile. There is no hint of disaster such as may be found in Deuteronomy and the Holiness Code, and it is not easy to reconcile the atmosphere of JE with the hypothesis that it was written during the exile after a national disaster.

   Further, the portrayal in Genesis of Esau, the ancestor of the Edomites, testifies against an exilic dating, when bitter hatred of the Edomites was occasioned by their behaviour at the time of the Babylonian defeat of the Jews and the sacking of Jerusalem. Nor does Gen. 27.40a and b fit the time of the exile. Similarly, the portrayal of Laban the Aramaean is much less likely during the exile than before it.

3. Vorländer's historical and cultural-historical arguments and his theological-historical arguments for a date in the sixth century are also not persuasive. The presence of Mesopotamian ideas in JE need not presuppose the Babylonian exile, but may owe its origin to mediation through the Canaanites at an earlier date. Nor is it necessary to hold that Israelite history writing owed its origin to the influence of Mesopotamian history writing, and to the fear that the Hebrew language and its traditions were threatened by the exile. Indeed, there is reason to believe that the first edition of the books of Kings was pre-exilic. The story of the tower of Babel in Gen. 11.1–9, which is regarded by Vorländer as evidence for an exilic date, more probably tells against such a date.

4. Winnett's argument that the table of nations in Genesis 10 is shown

by its dependence on South Arabian texts to be exilic, and that J must therefore be exilic, depends on the questionable hypothesis that the chapter is entirely Yahwistic.

5. Contrary to Vorländer's claim, the Elephantine papyri do not testify to an exilic date for J.

6. The case against a pre-exilic date for J is weak, because it fails to provide a satisfactory account of parts of the document. The stories of Jacob's dealings with Esau and Laban testify to a pre-exilic date, and to one that was not too late in the period before the exile. If my hypothesis that the matrix of Israelite history writing was the literary tradition seen in North-West Semitic inscriptions of the ninth-seventh centuries is correct, then the composition of J may plausibly be associated with it. It is difficult to be more precise.[1]

Bibliography

Day, J.
  1990   *Psalms* (OTG; Sheffield: Sheffield Academic Press).
Dion, P.-E.
  1997   *Les araméens à l'âge du fer: histoire politique et structures sociales* (Ebib; NS, 34; Paris: J. Gabalda).
Driver, S.R.
  1913   *An Introduction to the Literature of the Old Testament* (International Theological Library; Edinburgh: T. & T. Clark, 9th edn).
  1926   *The Book of Genesis* (Westminster Commentaries; London: Methuen, 12th edn).
Emerton, J.A.
  1982   'The Origin of the Promise to the Patriarchs in the Older Sources of the Book of Genesis', *VT* 32: 14–32.
  forthcoming   'The Kingdoms of Judah and Israel and Ancient Hebrew History Writing', in S. Fassberg and A. Hurvitz (eds), *Biblical Hebrew in its Northwest Semitic Setting* (Jerusalem: Magnes Press).
Gunkel, H.
  1910   *Genesis übersetzt und erklärt* (HKAT, 1.1; Göttingen: Vandenhoeck & Ruprecht, 3rd edn). ET *Genesis Translated and Interpreted* (trans. Mark E. Biddle; Macon, GA: Mercer University Press, 1997).
Mowinckel, S.
  1922   *Psalmenstudien, II: Das Thronbesteigungsfest Jahwäs und der Ursprung der Eschatologie* (Kristiania: Dybwad).
Na'aman, N.
  1998   'Royal Inscriptions and the Histories of Joash and Ahaz, Kings of Judah', *VT* 48: 333–49.
Nicholson, E.W.
  1998   *The Pentateuch in the Twentieth Century: The Legacy of Julius Wellhausen* (Oxford: Clarendon Press).

1. I am grateful to Professor G.I. Davies for reading an early draft of this article.

Noth, M.

1941 'Das Land Gilead als Siedlungsgebiet israelitischer Sippen', *PJ* 37: 50–101. Reprinted in his *Aufsätze zur biblischen Landes- und Altertumskunde*, I (Neukirchen–Vluyn: Neukirchener Verlag, 1971): 347–90.

1943 *Überlieferungsgeschichtliche Studien* (Halle: Max Niemeyer). ET *The Deuteronomistic History* (trans. J. Doull, J. Barton and M.D. Rutter; JSOTSup, 15; Sheffield: JSOT Press).

Porten, B.

1968 *Archives from Elephantine* (Berkeley, Los Angeles and London: University of California Press).

Schmid, H.H.

1976 *Der sogenannte Jahwist: Beobachtungen und Fragen zur Pentateuchforschung* (Zürich: Theologischer Verlag).

Speiser, E.A.

1964 *Genesis* (AB, 1; Garden City, NY: Doubleday).

Uehlinger, C.

1990 *Weltreich und 'eine Rede': eine neue Deutung der sogenannten Turmbauerzählung (Gen 11,1–9)* (OBO, 101; Freiburg [Switzerland]: Universitätsverlag, and Göttingen: Vandenhoeck & Ruprecht).

Van Seters, J.

1972 'The Terms "Amorite" and "Hittite" in the Old Testament', *VT* 22: 64–81.

1975 *Abraham in History and Tradition* (New Haven and London: Yale University Press).

Vaux, R. de

1971–73 *Histoire ancienne d'Israël* (Ebib; 2 vols; Paris: J. Gabalda). ET *The Early History of Israel* (trans. David Smith; 2 vols; London: Darton, Longman & Todd, 1978).

Vorländer, H.

1978 *Die Entstehungszeit des jehowistischen Geschichtswerkes* (Europäische Hochschulschriften, 23.109; Frankfurt am Main, Bern and Las Vegas: Peter Lang).

Westermann, C.

1974 *Genesis 1–11* (BKAT, 1.1; Neukirchen–Vluyn: Neukirchener Verlag). ET *Genesis 1–11* (trans. John J. Scullion; Minneapolis: Augsburg, and London: SPCK, 1984).

Winnett, F.V.

1965 'Re-examining the Foundations', *JBL* 84: 1–19.

1970 'The Arabian Genealogies in the Book of Genesis', in H.T. Frank and W.L. Reed (eds), *Translating and Understanding the Old Testament: Essays in Honor of Herbert Gordon May* (Nashville and New York: Abingdon Press): 171–96.

Wolff, H.W.

1963 'Das Kerygma des Jahwisten', *EvT* 24: 73–98. Reprinted in *Gesammelte Studien zum Alten Testament* (TBü, 22; Munich: Chr. Kaiser Verlag, 1964): 345–73. ET 'The Kerygma of the Yahwist', *Int* 20 (1966): 131–58. Reprinted in W. Brueggemann and H.W. Wolff, *The Vitality of Old Testament Traditions* (Atlanta, GA: John Knox Press, 1975): 41–66, 132–38.

Chapter 7

WAS THERE A SOCIAL CRISIS IN THE EIGHTH CENTURY?

Walter Houston

1. *The Common View*

Against what historical background should the texts in the prophetic books of Amos, Micah and Isaiah be interpreted which denounce acts of oppression committed against the poor, or simply against peasant landholders?[1] There is a *communis opinio* about this in scholarship, which I cannot do better than give in the words of Rainer Albertz, in his *History of Israelite Religion*. I quote Albertz not because he has something distinctive to say, but precisely because he has not, but says it very well.

> We do not know precisely what concrete factors sparked off the social crisis at a time of economic boom and political stability after the long Aramaean depression in the reign of Jeroboam II (787–47). As similar phenomena can also be noted in the southern kingdom at this time, it is usually assumed that what we have here is a long-term structural development that already has its roots in the social changes introduced by the formation of the state, which came to a head for the first time in the eighth century. The creation of large estates, from the crown downwards, had made holes in the old Israelite order and had forced aside the egalitarian ideal of the period before the state (Micah 2.1f.) A prosperous stratum of large landowners, officials, military and merchants had set themselves above the traditional small farmers intent only on self-sufficiency (Micah 3.1–9; Isa. 1.23; 3.12, 14), and far outstripped them with market-oriented surplus production. This creeping social development became critical in the eighth century when many small farmers – perhaps because of the population growth and the ongoing division of their businesses as they were handed down from generation to generation – were forced to the brink by the tougher economic conditions. They were less and less in a position to cope with

---

1. Minimally defined, these texts are: Isa. 1.21–26; 3.13–15; 5.1–7, 8–10; 10.1–4; Amos 2.6–16; 3.9–15; 4.1–3; 5.10–12; 8.4–7; Mic. 2.1–5, 6–11; 3.1–4, 9–12. Words for 'poor' are not used in the Micah texts, nor in Isa. 5.8.

the normal risks of agricultural production from their own resources, and it became increasingly difficult for them to bear the usual burdens of state taxation and forced labour; they were compelled more and more frequently to resort to loans in order to get by. This put large parts of the farming population under such direct pressure from the economically expanding upper class that on a wide front they were driven to dependence on it and became permanently impoverished. The prophets already typify them as a group of the 'weak' (*dal*), 'poor' (*'ebyōn*) and 'wretched' (*'ānāw/*'anî* [*sic*]). (Albertz 1994: I, 159–60, ET of Albertz 1992: I, 248–49)

But everybody knows all this! Accounts like this appear in every commentary on Amos, and the temptation must be to assume it is true simply by dint of its constant repetition. But serious reasons, though not necessarily conclusive ones, have been put forward for doubting this 'incontrovertible' truth, and it behoves the critical investigator to examine them before accepting the *communis opinio* without further ado.

2. *Counter-arguments*

I would classify these reasons under three heads. First, there are questions concerning the provenance and reliability of the evidence. Are we really dealing with eighth-century texts? Secondly, there are questions about the interpretation of these texts, assuming that we accept them as being what they claim to be. Do they actually support Albertz's account? Thirdly, there is evidence which definitely comes from the eighth century and may be held actually to disprove that account.

2.1. *Are these Eighth-Century Texts?*
I begin with questions about the date and reliability of the evidence, the questions with which this volume is generally concerned. The only textual evidence which Albertz cites from the eighth century is the prophetic texts I have already alluded to. He also refers to 2 Kgs 4.1, from an account whose final composition is not earlier than the sixth century about an event set in the ninth, or possibly the very early eighth century; Nehemiah 5, which is set and presumably composed in the fifth century; and Exodus 21, which it is not possible to date precisely. The only piece of archaeological evidence he cites – the only piece anyone cites – is de Vaux's preliminary report on discoveries now half a century ago at Tell el-Far‘ah North, identified as Tirzah (de Vaux 1955). This is so well known that I do not need to detail it. The remains certainly date from the eighth century, but whether de Vaux's interpretation is correct is another matter, which will occupy us later.

Obviously, Albertz will not be untypical in this. Almost the only texts in the Old Testament which even purport to be of eighth-century date are the prophets Isaiah, Hosea, Amos and Micah, so they are the only biblical texts which could be cited to prove a social crisis in the eighth century. That events of this kind happened there can be very little doubt. They are happening to this day in various parts of the world. But by far the most coherent account of them in the Old Testament is Neh. 5.2–5. If this text does not prove that a social crisis of this kind happened in the *fifth* century, I do not know the meaning of historical evidence. But to support the hypothesis that such events happened also in the eighth century, we are reliant on the prophetic texts noted above in n. 1 plus the Tell el-Far'ah evidence.

But as we know very well, the idea that we can quote an 'eighth-century' prophetic text as evidence for the eighth century is now looking distinctly dodgy. The older picture of the prophetic collections has given place to a thoroughgoing redactional approach, which views each of the collections as the work of creative editors working in the Second Temple era and reducing to order a mass of material, with varied points of view, originating at times spread out over anything from one to three centuries. (Collins 1993 gives a useful overview.)

Redaction critics are not necessarily 'minimalists'. Many remain bizarrely confident that they can identify the precise date and origin of every verse. But they tend not to agree with each other. Other scholars have drawn the obvious conclusion, and deny that we can know anything for certain about the origins of anything in the prophetic books, and particularly nothing very much about their date or social background, a point made emphatically by Robert Carroll, when asked to write on just that topic (Carroll 1989). Carroll's position is well known (see also Carroll 1981; 1986); and the most recent commentary in English on Amos (Coggins 2000), deals with Amos in a very similar way; he treats it as a book of the fifth century, and without denying that parts of it might come from a historical prophet Amos in the eighth, refuses to identify these definitely.

The practical effects of such scepticism operating on texts dissolved by the acids of redaction criticism may be observed on one of the texts relevant to this inquiry. Micah 2.1–2 is a powerful condemnation of landgrabbers who might be supposed to be operating at the time of Ahaz and Hezekiah, when Micah is dated according to Mic. 1.1. However, it has long been observed, for example by Jörg Jeremias (1971: 333–35, 349–51), that the oracle of judgment which follows scarcely fits the condemnation which precedes it, and suggests the presence of redactional work. It is announced against 'this whole clan' (or family, or however one wishes to translate *mišpāḥâ*); but in any case it seems to mean the whole nation, as in Amos 3.1, as is confirmed by 'the land of my people' in v. 4: not the evildoers themselves, as would be appropriate. Further the expressions 'on that day' in v. 4 and 'that will be an evil time' in v. 3 suggest that there will be a long gap between the crime and the punishment – also unexpected in a prophetic announcement of divine punishment. By these manipulations the editors of the text make it an announcement by Micah of the exile of Judah in the sixth century. Ehud Ben Zvi adds to this the point that vv. 1–2 are formulated in a quite general way concerning agrarian abuses which occur in every age and have nothing particular to link them to the eighth century. In his view this is deliberate: the words are intended by the text's authors to be capable of multiple application, and are not intended primarily to reproduce Micah's exact words to the eighth-century oppressors (Ben Zvi 1999: 89).

But the real difference between Jeremias in 1971 and Ben Zvi in 1999 is that whereas Jeremias postulated an eighth-century text for the exilic redactors to work on, and probably thought that this could be used to study eighth-century history, Ben Zvi (1999: 99) places the social history of eighth-century Judah among those things 'which cannot be learned from this text'. Among other reasons, including those already mentioned, one notes his points that 'the need to explain Judah's calamity in terms of the wrongdoing in the monarchic period creates by necessity an image of a sinful "Israel" in the text'; and that 'the reconstruction of the history of eighth-century Judah... was not a concern of those who shaped the text, nor of those for whom it was shaped'.

And inevitably one must add to these points the fact I have already alluded to that the best securely-dated textual evidence for such a social crisis comes from the fifth century. The shapers, to use Ben Zvi's word, of the texts of the prophets could well have been influenced by events much closer to their own times than the eighth century. Can one be certain that they had any eighth-century material before them on this subject at all?

2.2. *Interpreting the Evidence*

But supposing for the moment that they did, does it actually mean what it has been taken to mean in accounts such as Albertz's? S. Bendor argues in his account of Israelite social structure (Bendor 1996) that the structure based on the *bêt ʾāb* as the pivotal land-holding entity, which he takes to be the extended family of three or four nuclear families, remained intact down to the end of the monarchy and despite pressures from the state and from creditors the *bêt ʾāb* generally retained control of its land. We shall look in a moment at the positive evidence he alleges for this. But Bendor is by no means a minimalist, quite the contrary, so he must deal with the evidence which appears to go against his view which he takes to be from the monarchic period.

First, one must understand that he does not see the Israelite village or *mišpāḥâ*, or the *bêt ʾāb* within it, apart from any outside pressures, as an idyllic egalitarian commune. The village was run by the heads of *bātê*

ʾābōt, the zᵉqēnim or elders, who were men of power over their own families and collectively over the village as a whole. There were stronger and weaker, richer and poorer families, and within the bêt ʾāb there were stronger and weaker elements. Some heads of nuclear families had their own plots within the land of the bêt ʾāb, some did not, and weakest of all were the widow and her fatherless children, who had no male to stand up for them, and the gēr who sought refuge in a bêt ʾāb but had no secure footing within it.

To take first the two texts which speak of the taking over of land, Isa. 5.8 and Mic. 2.1–2, which have generally been taken to refer to the formation of latifundia through foreclosure on mortgages; on Mic. 2.1–2 he argues that 'wealthy men of Jerusalem are not needed in order for the fields of Moresheth... to be seized'. 'The events take place within the mišpaḥa ... its strongman (the head of the beit ʾab or the elder of the mišpaḥa or ʿir)' is the culprit. 'Within the mišpaḥa, he does not even require a corrupt court or an actual sale, but because of his power, he can do it in the daylight' (Bendor 1996: 249). In Isa. 5.8 he interprets 'land' (ʾereṣ) as the territory of a village or mišpāḥâ, and the culprits again as the strongmen of the village, who force out the weaker elements and take over their land (252–53). Turning to Amos, on 2.6 he argues that the *seller* of the righteous poor cannot be the creditor, but must be the head of the bêt ʾāb who sells for debt a member of the family who *has rights* (ṣaddîq, mistranslated 'righteous', Bendor 1996: 131–32) in the family land; 8.6 on the other hand denounces the one who buys him (245–48). Elsewhere (232) he refers appositely to Isa. 50.1, where someone is sold to, not by, a creditor. In Isa. 3.13–15 Bendor (257–58) points out that while 'elders' always refers to local leaders, heads of kinship units, śārîm (NRSV 'princes') does not necessarily refer to royal officials as is usually assumed, but can mean 'chiefs' or 'leaders' in general, or of local kinship groups in particular (Job 29.9; Ezra 8.29). He would see the verses as accusing powerful local leaders, powerful through their position in the kinship units, of oppressing the poor of their own locality.

Bendor has, it is clear, given a decidedly different account of matters. For him there is no social crisis in the late monarchy. The social injustices which are denounced by the prophets are a result of the confluence of pressures from the state (and external forces like Assyria) with tensions in the local communities, and the latter had existed and led to inequalities and injustices even before the emergence of the state. This is a reminder that even if we can validate the eighth-century origin of these texts, their interpretation is a precarious matter, and the very worst approach is to assume that the traditional interpretation must be right just because it is so widely assumed.

Moreover, the archaeological evidence from Tell el-Farʿah not only may be but almost certainly has been misinterpreted. The full publication of the excavations, by Chambon in 1984, suggests, at least in Fleischer's interpretation, that de Vaux's conclusions were too hasty, and the significance of the finds much more ambiguous than he suggested (Chambon 1984: 39–44; cf. Fleischer 1989: 393–94). Although Chambon still describes the houses respectively as 'les maisons patriciennes' and 'les maisons pauvres', two of the three so-called 'poor' houses are in fact almost as large as the 'patrician' ones; the main difference is in the quality of construction, in which the poor houses continue an earlier tradition of rubble construction and are without foundations, while the patrician ones have two- or three-course foundations and use stones fitted carefully, with hewn stone on the corners. But the three poor houses are an isolated block, they do not constitute a quarter; and though there can be no question that the inhabitants were poorer, there is no way of knowing, as Fleischer points out, what their position in the town was.

2.3. *Counter-evidence*

Bendor's one real positive piece of evidence for his sanguine view is in a couple of verses, 2 Kgs 15.19–20, which states that King Menahem of Israel paid for the tribute of 1000 talents of silver which he had to pay to the king of Assyria, Tiglath-pileser III, here called by his Babylonian throne name Pul, by levying a poll tax of 50 shekels on each *gibbōr ḥayil*. This expression is often taken to mean 'man of wealth', as in the NRSV. But at 3000 shekels to the talent the text implies that there were 60,000 such men in the kingdom: they are hardly wealthy men, therefore, and Bendor plausibly argues (226) that these are the heads of each *bêt ʾāb*, however poor, and that their number is evidence of the health of the social system: Israel is still a society of independent families working their own land and paying their own taxes.

When we come to assess all these arguments we shall see reason to doubt whether this one short text will bear the weight that Bendor wishes to place on it. However, there are more substantial arguments, especially those drawn from the archaeological evidence.

Already twenty years ago de Geus (1982: 53–54) was pointing out that the apparent evidence from Tell el-Farʿah was unique; at Tell es-Sebaʿ Level 2 is contemporary with de Vaux's Level 2 at Tell el-Farʿah, and it consists of housing uniform in size. Fleischer surveys the available evidence in 1989 with the same conclusion (Fleischer 1989: 394–401). We have now a most valuable survey article by John S. Holladay on Israel and Judah down to 750, though in fact on this particular issue taking the story down to the end of the kingdoms. Holladay comes to the same conclusion on a much broader front.

> The pattern of residence in four- and three-roomed houses clearly designed to house livestock, process crops and store agricultural

> produce on a family-by-family basis (as opposed to redistributive
> mechanisms involving communal store facilities) is... unvarying from
> Early Israel down through the late eighth-century highland and
> Shephelah materials... As far as we... know similar residence patterns
> continued, though less well documented in terms of excavated remains,
> on down to the final destruction of the Judaean state in 586–582 BCE.
> (Holladay 1998: 392)

Further, 'no residence from Iron II Palestine outstrips the average "four-room house" by much more than a factor of two, or three at the outside'. Where we find smaller houses, they are often squeezed into the courtyard space of larger ones, and Holladay supposes that these would be explained within the *bêt 'āb* structure as space found for a house for a son or younger brother on family land within an increasingly crowded fortified village. There is no evidence of one- or two-room hovels or of workers' barracks. Holladay lays stress on the function of these houses as not just residences but, even more, as storehouses, with a capacity in each of more than 15 cubic metres (530 cu. ft.). The total storage capacity of a village of 100 houses would be '3.75 times as much as the estimated capacity of the Area G Silo at Hazor and 3.33 times as much as Storage Pit 1414 at Megiddo, the two largest store facilities yet demonstrated for ancient Israel' (393).

What this means, in Holladay's words, is that Israel was 'emphatically not a "redistributive economy"', that is one in which all surpluses are controlled by the central power and redistributed to its functionaries and supporters – or even to the population as a whole, though, *pace* Holladay, I do not think anyone has suggested that Israel was a redistributive economy in that extreme sense. It is the peasant houses just described which were 'the "Storehouses of Israel"' (Holladay 1998: 393), not any government facilities. However, Holladay is quite ready to admit the pressure of debts, tithes and taxes on the peasant household, and indeed even mounts an argument (389–91) for increased agricultural specialization, which would be a sign of control over the economy, or of individual farmers, at a level above the peasant family or village: D.C. Hopkins has stressed the importance of diversity as a risk-spreading technique for the highland peasant (Hopkins 1985: 213–61). For our own purposes, we may state the conclusion rather differently: there is no archaeological evidence for any elements of the rural population living in abject poverty, and particularly no evidence for any dramatic change in the conditions of life during the eighth century or at any other period prior to the final downfall of the respective kingdoms.

3. *Responses*

I shall take the arguments we have reviewed in reverse order, so we begin with the archaeology.

3.1. *Responses to the Counter-evidence*

It is important to be clear about what Holladay's argument shows and what it does not show. It shows that Israelite peasants continued to build their houses in a traditional style and had the resources to do so to the traditional standard, with their 15 cu. m. of storage space. Excavators can show or estimate the amount of storage space in a house. They cannot show how much of that space was used in any given year. We can tell how much wealth the family was hoping for; we cannot tell how far reality fell short of their expectations.

Moreover, it is not always possible for archaeology to reveal the social relationships subsisting between the inhabitants of these houses. It is not possible to tell how many adjacent houses, or possibly non-adjacent ones, may have belonged to a single *bêt 'āb*, so that the relative strength of one *bêt 'āb* against another cannot be estimated, nor how that may have changed over time. A peasant might lose his children to creditors, as in Nehemiah 5, and still be living in the same house; he might go on to lose his land, work it as a debt-slave, and hand over a substantial part of the harvest to his lord. He would still need some of that storage space for what was left. There are many forms of dependency which do not require the existence of one- or two-room hovels or workers' barracks.

Further, in any crisis of the kind hypothesized there is always a proportion of the poor who fall beyond dependency into destitution, who become what Gerhard Lenski, in his classic study of social stratification, calls 'expendables', 'ranging from petty criminals and outlaws to beggars and underemployed itinerant workers' (Lenski 1966: 281). And such people leave no trace of their existence which archaeology can uncover.

Holladay does also note the existence, alongside the traditional villages, of places dominated by a single household, such as ʿIzbet Ṣarṭah, stratum 2. He suggests that this might be a land grant to a palace retainer (Holladay 1998: 391; see Finkelstein 1986: 12–14, 201[2]). Moreover, in all the general statements he makes about settlement characteristics and residence size, he excepts the capitals and government centres, places such as Samaria, Jerusalem, Lachish or Megiddo. Thus Holladay is not to be read as saying that monarchic Israel and Judah remained relatively equal societies. He is only saying that the village communities were relatively equal societies. The ruling classes resident in the capitals and other major

---

2. However, this is much earlier than the eighth century: its excavator, Finkelstein, dates it to the tenth century.

centres quite certainly lived on a much grander scale, and some at least of their wealth will have been extracted from the villages.

Moreover, in all the statements he makes about retention of produce in the houses of the people, he excepts taxes, tithes and debt services. Thus the materials are there in his own article for a conclusion rather different from his repudiation of the idea of a redistributive economy. This conclusion is secure only against an extreme form of redistribution, virtually caricatured by Holladay, in which the individual household retains nothing and waits for state handouts. As I have said, no one has suggested this. There is no question that redistribution was practised in monarchical Israel and Judah. If they were states, they redistributed; that is what states do. And incidentally, the evidence is there in Holladay's article to conclusively disprove the idea that Israel and Judah only became states in the ninth and eighth centuries respectively. What is in question is whether state exactions, as well as the impact of the credit system, increased to such an extent as to compromise the independence and viability of peasant households, as happened in Nehemiah's time.

It is not clear to me that that question is settled by the evidence surveyed by Holladay, and from Judah in the late eighth century there is other evidence which suggests a positive answer. One is the appearance of standardized shekel weights (Hopkins 1996: 138). This implies an increase in monetary transactions as opposed to barter, and probably in the number of exchange transactions overall. The increased monetization of the economy is not good news for subsistence peasants. Whatever payments they must make to the outside world, taxes, loan repayments, payment for goods, are assessed in monetary units mostly after the harvest when the prices of their produce are at their lowest, while loans that they take out are necessarily made when prices are high.

Another is the well-known prevalence of jar handles inscribed *lmlk*. These finds are confined to late eighth-century contexts. While there are in detail a number of interpretations of this phenomenon, it is unquestionable that it shows that the crown was disposing of large quantities of oil or wine or both, either as taxes or from its own estates; and the four localities also referred to on the handles appear to be central collection points for the produce. (The most recent discussion is in Fox 2000: 216–35.) This may well be an exceptional measure at the time of Hezekiah's revolt against Assyria, but it illustrates the resources which the crown could command.

This is one of a number of signs of increased specialization in agriculture, surveyed by Hopkins (1983), including scores of wine and oil presses, and the isolated farmsteads surveyed by Zwickel (1994) in parts of the Shephelah and the fringes of the Judaean wilderness dating from the late eighth century, which he interprets as estate farmsteads for the royal domains. Hopkins ascribes the ventures into this specialization to the royal estates, obviously, to royal retainers using their land grants profitably, and to wealthier farmers who could afford the investment required and the increased risk involved. He also notes that village pasture land on the steep hillsides usable for these fruit crops would have been sequestered for this purpose, thus damaging the peasants' ability to spread their own risk (Hopkins 1996: 133–34).

There seems to be enough evidence to enable us to say that there were latifundia in some areas. But the buildings surveyed by Zwickel are in relatively marginal areas. We can say with reasonable assurance on the basis of the evidence of the villages that village land was never converted into latifundia in the proper sense, the sense the word bears in Roman history, of large tracts worked by slaves, without free peasant inhabitants. That does not mean that the Isaiah and Micah texts on the subject are worthless, but we should be careful how we interpret them. The evidence does not exclude estates being built up out of the former holdings of free peasants who continued to work the land in a state of dependency.

We now turn to Bendor's interpretation of 2 Kgs 15.19–20. This text gives the appearance of being an archival note and therefore has a prima facie claim to reliability. But it does need testing. To support its plausibility, Bendor (1996: 225, following Montgomery 1951: 451) points to an inscription by an earlier Assyrian king, Adad-nirāri III, reporting his exaction of 2300 talents of silver and 20 of gold from the king of Damascus. But the 1000 talents is not the only figure which has to be tested for plausibility. In the first place, it is hardly plausible that such a round figure as 50 shekels should bring in exactly the three million shekels required, or that Menahem had a precise enough knowledge of his tax base to know that it would. Hence the figure of 60,000 derived from the data can scarcely be relied on. It could be somewhere close to the truth, but it might be wildly out.

The latest estimate of the population of Palestine in the monarchical period, by Broshi and Finkelstein, suggests a figure for the kingdom of Israel of about 350,000 (Broshi and Finkelstein 1992: 54). This is for the total population of the entire area at any time claimed by the kingdom, and we cannot be certain that Menahem controlled the whole of it. If, therefore, the figure of 60,000, or anything near it, is correct, they could not be heads of *bātê ʾābôt*, but heads of nuclear families. Even then it is rather on the high side, considering that the population figure includes slaves, paupers, *gērîm*, and royal and official families which were probably both large and exempt. But the smaller the units from which the tax was taken, the less likely it becomes that they could have paid it.

The 50 shekels is the most difficult figure to test. It is unlikely that the text should be understood literally, that every man had to stump up 50 shekels in silver (about 565 grams). Rather, although the tax was denominated in silver, it would have actually been paid in kind, in agricultural produce. What proportion of a nuclear family's annual requirements might this represent? To answer that, we need to know the exchange rate, the standard price of staple commodities. The only evidence I know of is the story in 2 Kings 7 of the siege of Samaria and the prophecy by Elisha that 'by tomorrow wheat flour will be sold for one shekel the $s^{e^{\cdot}}\hat{a}$ and barley at a shekel for two'. One might assume these prices represent a minimum for a time of plenty. They are, at least the first is, for flour, not for the raw produce, which makes a reliable estimate difficult. The annual dietary requirement for an adult subsisting mainly on bread is between 200 and 300 kg of wheat, which unmilled would fill about 17 to 25 $s^{e^{\cdot}}\hat{o}t$. However, one must remember that the total produce of a working rural family went to feed their animals as well as themselves: Holladay (1998: 387) quotes a minimum figure of 1800 kg of wheat and 1080 kg of barley for a family of five, based on research on peasant agriculture in modern Iran where the conditions are comparable. But even so we can safely say that 50 shekels would represent a substantial proportion of their requirements, if paid in grain, and this would be on top of existing taxes and other exactions. Because of the higher value of olive oil and wine than grain it would be easier to pay in these kinds, provided that the family had sufficient available. But all things considered it seems more likely that a tax at such a rate would have been levied on *bêt 'āb* heads than on householders.

But there cannot have been more than about 20,000 of those at the very most. The text is therefore unlikely to be correct in the implication that the entire tribute was laid off on the *gibbōrê ḥayil*. Menahem may have raised a million shekels or so from this tax, and found the rest in some other way. The text therefore does not give us reliable statistical information about the social structure of the kingdom of Israel in its last years. But I think we can say that, whatever the precise numbers, it would appear, assuming only that the figures of 1000 talents and 50 shekels are correct, that there was still a reasonably large peasant body subsisting in juridical independence and some way above destitution, such that the state could have some prospects of obtaining a return on an extraordinary tax. Anything more than this is speculation.

3.2. *Response to Bendor's Interpretation of the Texts*

What are we then to make of Bendor's interpretation of the prophetic texts? He has made a plausible case, and taken on its own it is hard to refute it. However, he has not dealt with all the evidence. The book of Amos contains a great deal more on this subject than the two texts that he deals with, and apart from 2.6–8, whose addressees are unclear, most of it is clearly directed at groups who live in the capital city or are otherwise obviously wealthy or associated with the ruling class. Thus 3.9, 'Assemble yourselves on Mount Samaria... what oppressions are in its midst...

those who store up violence and robbery in their strongholds'; 4.1, 'you cows of Bashan who are on Mount Samaria...'; 5.11, 'because you exact taxes from the poor and take from them levies of grain'.[3] Whether the exactions attacked here are taxes, rent, tithes or loan repayments, they must be exacted by those who have acquired, legitimately or not, a title to them: tax collectors, landlords, priests or creditors; and they can also determine by their corruptly used power the outcome of legal cases (v. 12b). The people denounced in 8.4–5, generally referred to as merchants, are certainly not members of the village community, and Marlene Fendler and Rainer Kessler have made a good case that they are actually the same class of people as are addressed elsewhere, large landowners selling, or Kessler would suggest lending, their grain to those with insufficient supply of their own (Fendler 1973: 50; Kessler 1989).

Again, while the texts in Micah 2 are filled with difficulties and could be interpreted the way Bendor suggests, Micah 3 is quite unambiguous in addressing 'you heads of Jacob and rulers of the house of Israel' (v. 1, and v. 9 is similar). This chapter in plain and furious terms accuses the rulers of Judah of exploiting their people for their own gain, and other élite groups of corruption.

Finally, in Isaiah, even if Bendor's suggestion were to be accepted about 3.14 and 5.8, both texts stand in contexts which are concerned with the rich or with issues of government. This is particularly clear in ch. 5, the better articulated of the two contexts, where 5.8–10 is the first of a series of woes of which several are unambiguously directed at the ruling class.

The conclusion must be that the social criticism in these three prophets is clearly addressed to ruling groups or groups associated with the ruling class in most of the contexts concerned with the issue. This makes it less likely that in the few texts reinterpreted by Bendor a different set of culprits is in view. They thus represent a protest against exploitation by these groups, at a level regarded by the speakers in the text as unacceptable. One must remember that in most societies where there are differences of wealth associated with leadership in the community, the community will bear without complaint exactions that do not exceed traditional levels and that are clearly balanced by benefits received. But when the ruling élite breaks this unwritten compact and threatens to drive its subjects beyond their normal poverty into destitution, or to undermine their ability to maintain their traditional honour and independence, then complaint and perhaps rebellion will break out. These prophetic texts demonstrate that that point had been reached, and if that is how we define

---

3. The word *bôšas^{e}kem* in 5.11, translated 'you trample' in NRSV, is now widely interpreted (repointed *boš^{e}kem*) as 'you exact taxes', on the basis of an Akkadian verb. S.M. Paul discusses this and other suggestions for its interpretation (Paul 1991: 172–73), and that just mentioned and adopted above certainly seems the most convincing.

a social crisis, and it seems a reasonable definition, then they bear witness to a social crisis. They cannot, however, show on their own that a major transfer of resources had already taken place, resulting in the reduction of the peasant masses in general to dependency or destitution; and the other evidence we have reviewed is rather against that supposition.

3.3. *Reviewing the Setting of the Prophetic Texts*

But we have yet to show that these texts date from the eighth century. We must bear in mind Ben Zvi's most persuasive objections, which can easily be extended beyond the texts of Micah that he studies: that the primary object of the editors was not to reproduce eighth-century prophetic speeches, and that it is unlikely that in the transition from the oral to the written medium they would be reproduced accurately; that it was necessary for them to create an image of a sinful Israel; and that they were not themselves interested in reconstructing eighth-century history.

These objections concentrate on the motives and methods of the editors of the texts, and I judge them persuasive in themselves. It is not, I think, possible to argue successfully that the texts are precisely what they claim to be, that is, respectively 'the vision of Isaiah the son of Amoz which he saw concerning Judah and Jerusalem'; 'the words of Amos which he saw concerning Israel'; and 'the word of the Lord which came to Micah of Moresheth which he saw concerning Samaria and Jerusalem'. The redaction critics have done their work, and it cannot be undone. However, we may reasonably assume that the editors used material which they believed to represent the words of the prophets under whose name they were writing. Whether they really did has to be shown in each case. Are there features in these texts or their contexts which betray an eighth-century origin and which are unlikely to be the contribution of the editors?

Other contributions to this seminar series have addressed this question on a broader front in respect of Isaiah and Amos. Hans Barstad (whose contribution is not included in this volume) argued that the oracles against the nations as a series address a situation which could not have recurred after the eighth century. Damascus was stripped of its independence in 732 BCE, and Israel ten years later. Most of the other states in the series continued to exist in one form or another, but the fact that the series begins with Damascus and ends with Israel is significant. The geopolitical viewpoint of the creator of the series is an eighth-century one. 'Israel', we should note, in Amos normally means the kingdom of Israel. The editors were aware of this; that is why when they wished to include Judah they specifically said so, as in the awkward addition to Amos 3.1: 'against the whole family which I brought up from the land of Egypt'.

These are large-scale features of the text which may be thought to have little direct relevance to the texts we are concerned with. But first of all, the accusation against Israel in Amos 2.6–8 is an integral part of the oracles against the nations series, which we have identified as being of eighth-century origin, and its main elements cannot be later than the composition of the series, although it may contain additions. Secondly, some of the other accusations later in the book are addressed, as we have already seen, to the inhabitants of Samaria: in fact it is precisely the accusations of social injustice in Amos where the connection with Samaria is most deeply embedded. The references to Samaria in the book occur at Amos 3.9, 12; 4.1; 6.1; and 8.14. Only the last of these seems to have no relevance to this issue; Amos 3.9 and 4.1 introduce accusations of oppressive conduct, and Amos 6.1 an accusation of the complacent enjoyment of luxury; Amos 3.12 is in an oracle of judgement. Amos 3.9–11 is an oracle against the city of Samaria itself, 'and the tumults and oppressions within it', and the 'cows of Bashan' oracle is also closely tied up with the city. Amos 6.1 creates a problem with its parallel mention of Zion, which, as Wolff emphasizes (1975: 314–15, ET 1977: 269–70), is contrary to the book's practice elsewhere; yet it makes a far more convincing text than any of the proposed emendations (see Paul 1991: 199 n. 2). But even if we supposed the entire oracle, Amos 6.1–7, to be subsequent to Amos (Wolff sees only *haššaʾᵃnannîm bᵉṣiyyōn* 'at ease in Zion' as secondary), it is still anchored in the pre-722 world, like all these oracles, by its reference to Samaria. Samaria ceased to be the seat of the ruling class of the state of Israel in that year. The references to it in Amos, if they do not bear witness to the composition of these texts before its fall, can only be explained as an elaborate fiction, which I do not choose to regard as a probable explanation of the emergence of prophetic literature.

The book of Isaiah of course includes many references to eighth-century history with every appearance of contemporaneity, but they are probably of limited use for validating the eighth-century origin of the texts we are concerned with, for most of them are in the so-called *Denkschrift*, Isa. 6.1–9.6 (ET 7), or in later parts of the book, whereas the denunciations of oppression occur in Isaiah 3, 5 and 10. However, a line of approach similar to the one we took with Amos may work. The careful reader of Isaiah 1–12 will be struck by the rarity with which the name 'Israel' is used compared with later prophets, including of course Isaiah 40–55, except in the divine name 'The Holy One of Israel' (*qᵉdōš yiśrāʾēl*); similarly in *ʾᵃbîr yiśrāʾēl* (Isa. 1.24) and *ʾōr yiśrāʾēl* (Isa. 10.17). 'Israel' is used as the name of the northern kingdom in Isa. 9.7, 11 and 13 (ET 8, 12 and 14). Isaiah 10.22 and 11.16 are generally regarded as secondary, even by Wildberger (1980: 413–14, 466–67, ET 1991: 435–36, 489–90). That leaves four examples. In Isa. 1.3, 'Israel does not know, my people does not consider', and Isa. 8.18, 'signs and portents in Israel', the whole nation is surely in view, as it obviously is in the phrase 'the two houses of Israel' in Isa. 8.14, and in the divine titles. The remaining text is Isa. 5.7, 'the vineyard of

YHWH of hosts is the house of Israel, and the men of Judah are his pleasant planting'. Isaiah's usage elsewhere should now convince us that the parallelism here does not imply that 'Israel' is being used as a synonym for Judah, as so often happens in later prophets, but rather probably refers to the northern kingdom, as in Isaiah 9, or at least includes it, as in Isa. 8.14. On this point I disagree with Wildberger (1980: 171–72, ET 1991: 184). Gray seems in two minds about it (Gray 1912: 87), and other commentators I have consulted do not refer to the problem. I would thus argue that the usage of this national name mainly reflects the pre-722 political situation.

But 5.7 of course is the central text for Isaiah's social message. It does not refer to evil doings in general. The pairing of *mišpāṭ* and *ṣᵉdāqâ*, as a hendiadys in prose or in parallelism in verse, is a standard expression for what we call social justice (Weinfeld 1995: 25–44[4]). It is what kings are expected to provide for the poor of their kingdoms: see for example Psalm 72 or Jer. 22.15. And this is what was missing in the vineyard of Israel–Judah. Editorially, the parable of the vineyard has been placed next to the woes, which specify this lack in detail, and the first of these is the accusation against those who accumulate land. Naturally we cannot argue from this juxtaposition that because Isa. 5.7 can be traced to the eighth century Isa. 5.8 must also be of that date. But I have shown, I believe, that the early chapters of Isaiah contain material with a social concern dating from that century, and that is perhaps all that can be asked.

The same may be true of Micah. The text here does use 'Israel' in a way I have suggested Isaiah does not, in referring to the Jerusalem governing circles as 'chiefs of the house of Israel' (Mic. 3.1, 9). But there is an oracle against Samaria (Mic. 1.5–7), and Mic. 3.12 is quoted by the elders in Jer. 26.18. Here we touch on an issue mentioned by Williamson in this volume in connection with Isaiah. It will hardly cut any ice with the minimalists, since if the Jeremiah account is itself from the Second Temple period, the prophecy that it quotes could be so also, presumably. But any possible account of literary history which made the Micah text post-exilic would be so strained and convoluted as to be untenable. The minimum conclusion from Jer. 26.18 is that the traditionists who wrote the story, probably in the sixth century, had a text of Micah at their disposal which they understood to be of Hezekian date. And it surely must be earlier than the fall of the city, from the argument from unfulfilled prophecy. It is not true (yet) that Jerusalem ever became a ploughed field or a wooded height (Mic. 3.12). Thus the prophecy is formulated in a way that would not

---

4. But Miranda had already pointed this out long before (1977: 93, with all the Old Testament passages listed at 107 nn. 35, 36), referring in his turn to earlier, unnamed, exegetes.

naturally have occurred to anyone familiar with Jerusalem's condition after its fall.

We may add that Ben Zvi's argument apropos of Mic. 2.1–5 may be countered by another of Williamson's arguments about Isaiah. Where redactional activity is demonstrated by a change in the point of view within a passage, there must be a diachronic process. The presupposition of the addition, if it is one, of 'on that day...' in v. 4 is that the nucleus of the text dates from before the fall of Jerusalem.

We conclude therefore that the books of Isaiah, Amos and Micah contain material dating ultimately to the eighth century which bears witness to a marked deterioration in social conditions and relationships in the latter half of that century at the latest.

4. *Why the Eighth Century?*

However, this deterioration was not severe enough, or more likely not continued long enough owing to the annihilation of the kingdom of Israel and the catastrophic curtailment of the territory of Judah, to leave any direct material evidence. Hence we should try to support this conclusion by asking whether there are any discoverable reasons why such a deterioration might have occurred just at this time.

There are in fact more than one. We can suggest both internal and external pressures working in combination. Fleischer (1989: 370–85) suggests that an important factor was overpopulation resulting in people trying to squeeze a living from smaller and smaller patches of land, which would, of course, make them more vulnerable to exactions. Traditional ways of dealing with this problem would include forming new settlements within the land, expanding into new land, particularly across the Jordan, emigration, enlisting as mercenaries with foreign armies, or indeed the army of Israel, and drifting to the cities in the usually vain hope of bettering oneself. Some of these avenues always remained open; but others closed down over time, and it is particularly relevant to observe that the expansion southwards of the Aramaean kingdom of Damascus in the late ninth century cut off much of the land available for settlement. Jeroboam's reconquest of this area should have eased the situation. But contrary to the view expressed by Albertz (see above) and endlessly recycled in introductions to Amos, this reign shows no evidence of increased prosperity. De Geus points out that there is no evidence of new monumental building in Israel or Judah after the end of the ninth century, and there is continued stagnation in pottery styles down to the end of the kingdoms (1982: 54–55). Far more recently, a state of stagnation or decline in the eighth century has been confirmed for Hazor by its excavator (Amnon Ben-Tor, orally, about 1998). Despite Fleischer's suggestion (1989: 400) that there was no particular further need for monumental building, none of this suggests a burgeoning economy. It is easy to see why the economy might be in decline. The rise of Assyrian power in the west explains almost everything, as de Geus suggests (1982: 55–56). It demanded both higher expenditure on defence and, as under Menahem, an outflow of precious metal and other valuables in tribute. Micah 2.1–2 may reflect specific confiscatory measures taken by Hezekiah's government to prepare for war against Assyria (Wolff 1982: 44, ET 1990: 74–75). The resources had to be extracted from the only ultimate source of wealth in an agrarian commonwealth, the wretched cultivators of the soil.

This scenario accounts far more convincingly for their increased exploitation than the standard picture of burgeoning prosperity. There is one quite general theoretical reason for this. As Lenski shows (1966: 266–71), ruling classes in agrarian societies always aim to secure the whole of the agricultural surplus, that is, what is left after the cultivators have met their basic needs. Hence an increase in the level of exploitation would need to be induced by specific factors such as a rise in external demands made upon the ruling class, and therefore would not necessarily lead to a rise in the net income of the latter.

But there may also be a quite specific reason, peculiar to this time and area. It is quite possible, as Holladay suggests with detailed evidence in support (1998: 383–86), that the kingdoms for some time met their expenses to some or a large extent by tolls on the transit trade through Palestine. But towards the end of the ninth century in Israel, rather later in Judah, first pressure from Damascus and then the Assyrians' seizure of control over the trade would have led to declining revenues from this source. At the same time, it became necessary to start paying tribute to Assyria. The only remaining source of finance was agricultural production, and taxes levied on it must have started to increase at this point, quite apart from extraordinary taxes like Menahem's poll tax. The more prosperous families would have been able to deal with the threat by specializing in higher value crops, especially oil, as we have seen. The less prosperous ones were faced with a serious and sometimes desperate situation which they could only deal with through the suicidal course of going into debt to their patrons, whether these were the heads of their own village or city-based landowners or officials. The failure of many of these to deal justly or humanely with those who had thus placed themselves in their power led to the protests which received permanent expression in the texts we have been studying.

We thus reach the conclusion that the eighth century in Israel and Judah offered the right conditions for the development of economic pressure on the peasantry sufficiently severe to be seen as unjust and denounced on that ground by texts in Isaiah, Amos and Micah, some of which can be linked to that century. Such conditions certainly recurred on more than one later occasion, and were perhaps even more severe in the fifth century; hence we cannot date any specific text in these books to the eighth century simply on the grounds of its subject matter. But there *was* a social crisis in the eighth century.

Bibliography

Albertz, Rainer
   1992   *Religionsgeschichte Israels in alttestamentlicher Zeit* (Grundrisse zum Alten Testament, 8; 2 vols; Göttingen: Vandenhoeck & Ruprecht). ET *A History of Israelite Religion in the Old Testament Period* (trans. John Bowden; 2 vols; London: SCM Press, 1994).

Bendor, S.
   1996   *The Social Structure in Ancient Israel* (Jerusalem Biblical Studies, 7; Jerusalem: Simor).

Ben Zvi, Ehud
   1999   'Wrongdoers, Wrongdoing and Righting Wrongs in Micah 2', *BibInt* 7: 87–100.

Broshi, Magen, and Israel Finkelstein
   1992   'The Population of Israel in Iron Age II', *BASOR* 287: 47–60.

Carroll, Robert P.
   1981   *From Chaos to Covenant: Uses of Prophecy in the Book of Jeremiah* (London: SCM Press).
   1986   *Jeremiah: A Commentary* (OTL; London: SCM Press).
   1989   'Prophecy and Society', in R.E. Clements (ed.), *The World of Ancient Israel: Sociological, Anthropological and Political Perspectives* (Cambridge: Cambridge University Press): 203–26.

Chambon, Alain
   1984   *Tell el-Farʿah, I: L'âge du fer* (Paris: Editions Recherche sur les Civilisations).

Coggins, Richard J.
   2000   *Joel and Amos* (NCB; Sheffield: Sheffield Academic Press).

Collins, Terence
   1993   *The Mantle of Elijah: the Redaction Criticism of the Prophetical Books* (The Biblical Seminar, 20; Sheffield: JSOT Press).

Fendler, Marlene
   1973   'Zur Sozialkritik des Amos', *EvT* 33: 32–53.

Finkelstein, Israel (ed.)
   1986   *ʿIzbet Ṣarṭah: An Early Iron Age Site near Rosh Haʿayin, Israel* (BAR International Series, 229; Oxford: BAR).

Fleischer, Gunther
   1989   *Von Menschenverkäufern, Baschankühen, und Rechtsverkehrern* (BBB, 74; Frankfurt: Athenäum).

Fox, Nili Sacher
   2000   *In the Service of the King: Officialdom in Ancient Israel and Judah* (Monographs of the Hebrew Union College, 23; Cincinnati: Hebrew Union College Press)

Geus, C.H.J. de
	1982	'Die Gesellschaftskritik der Propheten und die Archäologie', *ZDPV* 98: 50–57.
Gray, G. Buchanan
	1912	*A Critical and Exegetical Commentary on Isaiah 1–27* (ICC; Edinburgh: T. & T. Clark).
Holladay, John S.
	1998 [1995]	'The Kingdoms of Israel and Judah: Political and Economic Centralization in the Iron IIA-B (ca. 1000–750 BCE)', in T.E. Levy (ed.), *The Archaeology of Society in the Holy Land* (London: Leicester University Press): 368–98.
Hopkins, David C.
	1983	'The Dynamics of Agriculture in Monarchical Israel', in *SBL 1983 Seminar Papers*: 177–202.
	1985	*The Highlands of Canaan: Agricultural Life in the Early Iron Age* (Social World of Biblical Antiquity, 3; Sheffield: Almond Press).
	1996	'Bare Bones: Putting Flesh on the Economics of Ancient Israel', in V. Fritz and P.R. Davies (eds), *The Origins of the Ancient Israelite States* (JSOTSup, 228; Sheffield: Sheffield Academic Press): 121–39.
Jeremias, Jörg
	1971	'Die Deutung der Gerichtsworte Michas in der Exilszeit', *ZAW* 83: 330–54.
Kessler, Rainer
	1989	'Die angeblichen Kornhändler von Amos VIII 4–7', *VT* 29: 13–22.
Lenski, Gerhard E.
	1966	*Power and Privilege: A Theory of Social Stratification* (New York: McGraw-Hill)
Miranda, José Porfirio
	1977	*Marx and the Bible: A critique of the Philosophy of Oppression* (trans. J. Eagleson; London: SCM Press). Originally published as *Marx y la biblia, Critica a la filosofia de la opresión* (Salamanca: Ediciones Sigueme, 1971).
Montgomery, James A.
	1951	*A Critical and Exegetical Commentary on the Books of Kings* (ICC; Edinburgh: T. & T. Clark).
Paul, Shalom M.
	1991	*Amos: A Commentary on the Book of Amos* (Hermeneia; Minneapolis: Fortress Press).
Vaux, Roland de
	1955	'Les fouilles de Tell el-Fâr'ah près Naplouse – Cinquième campagne', *RB* 62: 541–89.
Weinfeld, Moshe
	1995	*Social Justice in Ancient Israel and in the Ancient Near East* (Jerusalem: Magnes Press).
Wildberger, Hans
	1980	*Jesaja 1–12* (BKAT, 10.1; Neukirchen–Vluyn: Neukirchener Verlag, 2nd edn.). ET *Isaiah 1–12: A Commentary* (trans. T.H. Trapp; Minneapolis: Fortress Press, 1991).
Wolff, Hans Walter
	1975	*Dodekapropheton*, II: *Joel und Amos* (BKAT, 14.2; Neukirchen–Vluyn:

Neukirchener Verlag, 2nd edn.). ET *Joel and Amos* (trans. Waldemar Janzen *et al.*; Hermeneia; Philadelphia: Fortress Press, 1977).

1982   *Dodekapropheton,* IV: *Micha* (BKAT, 14.4, Neukirchen–Vluyn: Neukirchener Verlag). ET *Micah: A Commentary* (trans. Gary Stansell; Minneapolis: Augsburg, 1990).

Zwickel, Wolfgang
1994   'Wirtschaftliche Grundlagen in Zentraljuda gegen Ende des 8.Jh.s aus archäologischer Sicht', *UF* 26: 557–92.

Chapter 8

IN SEARCH OF POST-EXILIC ISRAEL:
SAMARIA AFTER THE FALL OF THE NORTHERN KINGDOM*

Gary N. Knoppers

The opening narrative of 2 Kings 17 presents the fall of the kingdom of
Israel briefly, but with a sense of finality. After Israel's last king Hoshea
had broken his pact with Assyria by withholding tribute and sending
emissaries to the king of Egypt, the Assyrian king captured Hoshea and
put him in prison. The Assyrian monarch later moved against the heart of
the Israelite state itself.

> The Assyrian king came up against the whole land and came up against
> Samaria, besieging it for three years. In the ninth year of Hoshea's reign,
> the Assyrian king captured Samaria and exiled Israel to Assyria. He
> settled them in Halah, by the [River] Habur, (by) the River Gozan, and
> (among) the cities of the Medes. (2 Kgs 17.5–6)

With the blanket statement, 'the Assyrian king captured Samaria and
exiled Israel to Assyria', the author concludes the coverage of the northern
kingdom. If the chapter's opening narrative depicts watershed events
laconically, the following Deuteronomistic commentary is anything but
laconic. Its denunciations of the northern kingdom are specific and greatly
detailed, tracing the demise of the northern realm to the repeated failure
of its monarchs and people to depart from the influential cultic policies
established by their founding king – Jeroboam I – centuries earlier (2 Kgs
17.7–23). The text goes on to speak of the Assyrian-sponsored importation of new settlers, drawn from other sections of the Assyrian empire,
into the territories once occupied by northern Israel (2 Kgs 17.24–41). The
result is a land completely transformed – depleted of Israelites and filled
with foreign immigrants.

Although most scholars recognize the accusations levelled at the
Israelites in 2 Kgs 17.7–41 as Deuteronomistic propaganda, many have
nonetheless agreed with the basic picture the passage presents of a radical

* I would like to thank John Harvey for his helpful comments on an earlier draft of this
paper.

metamorphosis in the land. In this reconstruction, the defeat, destruction, and dislocation associated with the Assyrian western campaigns were nothing short of catastrophic. What occurred after the fall of Israel marked both an end and a new beginning. The ruin of the kingdom coupled with the deportation of its people brought northern Israel to a tragic end. The division of the former kingdom into a number of different Assyrian provinces coupled with the importation of peoples from other lands profoundly changed the land's ethnic and political character (e.g. Orlinsky 1960: 86–87; Donner 1977: 434; 1986: 311–16; Bright 1981: 275–76; Herrmann 1981: 250–52; Ahlström 1993: 665–80; Kuhrt 1995: II, 468–69). However much it is recognized to be tendentious, the Deuteronomistic version of events has held sway over a range of early and modern interpreters. Some early Jewish texts speak of the Samaritans as Cutheans, that is, as descendants of the foreign colonists who settled in the territories vacated by the banished Israelites.[1] The Deuteronomistic interpretation of Israel's fall has also influenced modern scholarship. In accordance with the picture presented in Kings, most modern histories of ancient Israel terminate their coverage of northern Israel with the Assyrian exile. The late eighth century BCE marks the terminus of attention paid to the history of Samaria until the Persian period, when the interaction of Nehemiah and others in Yehud with leading figures in Samaria, such as Sanballat, rekindles an interest among scholars in north–south relations.

The ruin of Israel is one topic that binds older historical-critical studies to newer interpretations championed by a variety of revisionist scholars. In their arguments against the existence of the united monarchy of the tenth century, revisionist scholars contend that archaeological finds and epigraphic evidence only allow one to say that an Israelite state existed for less than a couple of hundred years, from some time in the ninth century to the late eighth century (Knoppers 1997). A much smaller Judahite state, centred around Jerusalem, may be attested from the seventh until the early sixth centuries. In this theory, Israel as a twelve-tribe federation never existed. There never was a united kingdom of Saul, David, or Solomon. Such notions are the fanciful product of Judaean scribes working in the Persian or Hellenistic periods.[2] What one can say on the basis of the material remains is that both states – the House of Omri in the

---

1. Hjelm (2000: 104–238) provides references and a detailed overview of recent discussions.

2. The Israel of the tribal league and the Israel of the united monarchy are fictions promoted by a Judaean élite to buttress their own positions during a much later era. All of the books of the Hebrew Bible were written during this time (the Achaemenid and Hellenistic periods) and address contemporary issues in theological and mythical terms. As such, they cannot be relied upon to present any kind of accurate picture of times past. For further discussion, see Knoppers (1997: 27–33).

north and the House of David in the south – ended violently in destruction and deportations. The demise of each of these states was so ruinous that one cannot speak of any meaningful continuity from a so-called pre-exilic period to a later so-called post-exilic period (Lemche 1998: 84–85; Thompson 1992: 401–23; 1999: 210–25, 254–56). Even though these scholars focus most of their attention on the end of the monarchic period in Judah, rather than that of Israel, they raise a number of legitimate questions about the use of an ideologically laden term such as exile, the long-term effects of the many deportations carried out in the history of the ancient Near East, and the difficulties in defining ethnic identity (Carroll 2001; Davies 1992; 2001; Grabbe 2001; Thompson 1997; 2001). In the view of Carroll (2001: 69–79) and Davies (2001: 132–38), the very use of terms such as the 'pre-exilic period' and the 'post-exilic period' privileges the mythical world created by later biblical writers and is to be eschewed.

The strange and unusual convergence of opinion on the Assyrian invasions and deportations becomes all the more remarkable when one considers the growing divergence of opinion on the nature and extent of the Babylonian deportations. Some commentators, including some revisionists, have questioned 'the myth of the empty land', the notion that the Babylonian campaigns of Nebuchadnezzar were so severe that they resulted in a Judah completely bereft of Judahites.[3] The reasons for interrogating the empty land hypothesis vary. Some argue their case on the basis of a critical reading of the biblical sources. Others also make their case on the basis of studies of the archaeological remains. The latter have contended for some continuity of inhabitation in certain sectors of Judah, including Jerusalem, and especially in the hill country of Benjamin (e.g. Blenkinsopp 1998; 2002; 2003; Lipschits 1998; 1999). Whatever one makes of the questions raised about the nature and extent of the Babylonian deportations, it is surprising that more criticism has not been directed against older notions about the nature and extent of the Assyrian exile. Was there no post-exilic Israel?

In spite of the broad consensus about the effects of Israel's demise, one may question whether such a consensus is warranted. One may begin with the picture presented of the fall of the northern kingdom in the Deuteronomistic writing. If this text and others in Kings are theological reflections to be dated to later times, to what extent can one rely on these texts for reconstructing detailed events in the eighth century? Presenting both the Assyrian exile of the late eighth century and the Judahite exile of the early sixth century as completely devastating events creates, ironically,

---

3. See Carroll (1992: 79–93); Berquist (1995); Whitelam (1996); Barstad (1996; 1997). For further references and discussion, see Knoppers (1999).

a direct parallel between them. Over the course of less than two hundred years, all of the Israelite tribes were forced to exit the land. But should the Assyrian campaigns and the Babylonian campaigns be viewed as parallel? Were there not important differences between them? In the last three decades much archaeological work has been carried out in Syria–Palestine. Does this attention to the material remains confirm a cataclysmic end for the northern tribes? What does one make of the testimony of the Samaritans themselves? In their literature, they avow Israelite status as descendants of the tribes of Joseph (Dexinger 1992; Hjelm 2000: 76–103). These Samaritan documents date to much later times, but what should one make of the Samaritan claims?

In this essay I would like to revisit the archaeological and epigraphic evidence relating to the demise of the northern kingdom. As we shall see, much of this evidence has been marshalled in favour of a maximalist interpretation of Israel's demise, but there is some question, in my judgment, whether it should be. I will also give some attention to a minority opinion as to what the material evidence may say or may not say about the extent of the Israelite deportations. For the sake of convenience, I will label this minority position as the minimalist hypothesis. In this view, the upheaval caused by the Assyrian conquests was temporary and localized to major urban centres. The Assyrian exile purportedly affected only a small portion of society – the élite.

My concern in what follows is not with specific matters such as whether Shalmaneser V or Sargon II was primarily responsible for the capture of Samaria. Rather, my interest lies with the nature, goals and results of the Assyrian campaigns. To what extent should one speak of total discontinuity and to what extent should one speak about continuity? By examining both the maximalist and the minimalist theories in greater detail, one can explore what sort of evidence is mustered for each position and test each theory's relative strengths and weaknesses. Having summarized the two theories, I will evaluate each position and bring to the fore some additional material evidence not covered by either theory. To anticipate my conclusions, I think that both the maximalists and the minimalists have overstated their case.

1. *The Maximalist Case*

To assert that a people was forced to leave its land for a variety of foreign destinations only to be replaced in that land by a variety of foreign peoples, who were themselves forced to leave their lands, is a tremendous claim to make. But the maximalist theory, positing a major case of population exchange, is more than a paraphrase of the text of Kings. The theory involves Assyrian written sources, Assyrian reliefs, the Babylonian Chronicle, and various sorts of archaeological evidence. Assuming a strong link between statehood and ethnic identity, commentators speak of a series of devastating blows to the infrastructure of the Israelite state. For the sake of convenience, we may trace four major events that are said to have cumulatively sealed Israel's demise.

The first major event was the western campaign of Tiglath-pileser III (744–727 BCE) in 733–732 BCE that resulted in the defeat of the House of Omri, the loss of territory, and the destruction of many towns in the Galilee, the northern Transjordan, and the northern coastal region (2 Kgs 15.19, 29; 16.5–9; cf. 1 Chron. 5.6, 25–26). The Assyrian king boasts, 'The land of the house of Omri [. . .its] auxiliary army [. . .] all of its people [. . .] I carried off [to] Assyria' (Tadmor 1994, Summ. 4.15'b-17'a). According to 2 Kgs 15.29, Tiglath-pileser III destroyed a series of sites in upper Galilee: Ijon, Abel Beth-Maachah, Janoah, Kedesh and Hazor.[4] The annals of Tiglath-pileser speak of the conquest of towns in lower Galilee: Ḥinatuna, Yatbite, Aruma and Marum.[5] Another Assyrian source relevant to the reign of Tiglath-pileser may allude to the conquest of the towns of Gilead and Abel Shitim, but both of these readings are contested.[6] Stern (2001: 7) speaks of a 'generalized destruction to all settlements'. His recent work (2001: 7, 9, 50) lists the following sites as razed during this time: Dan, Hazor, Chinnereth, Beth-saida, Tel Hadar, ʿEn Gev, Beth-shean, Kedesh, Megiddo, Jokneam, Qiri, Akko, Keisan, Shiqmona and Dor.[7] Some settlements were purportedly abandoned and did not recover for many years: Beth-saida, Tel Hadar, Kedesh, Beth-shean and ʿEn Gev (Stern 2001: 7).

Conquest in war is one thing, but enforced population displacement is quite another. A second blow to the Israelite state came in the form of unidirectional extraditions enforced by Tiglath-pileser III, who practised 'deportation on an unprecedented scale' (Cogan and Tadmor 1988: 177). The authors of 2 Kgs 15.29 claim that 'he took. . .Galilee, Gilead, and all

---

4.   There is reason to believe that by the time the Assyrian king reached these sites, they had already long passed from Israelite to Aramaean control (Miller and Hayes 1986: 337–39; Naʾaman 1995a). The biblical text is somewhat ambiguous at this point, but it seems evident that the author regarded the conquest of these sites as one indication of Israel's ongoing decline.

5.   Cf. Josh. 11.1, 5; 19.14; 2 Kgs 21.19; 23.26. Some of the names in the annals are uncertain due to the fragmentary condition of the inscriptions (Tadmor 1994, Ann. 18.3'-13'; 24.3'-10'; Naʾaman 1995b).

6.   Probably one of Tiglath-pileser III's Summary Inscriptions (Younger 2000b: 288). On the reading, 'the city of Gil[ead]', see Tadmor (1994, Summ. 9.3'). Regarding the fragmentary 'Abil [. . .]', Tadmor argues for restoring Abel-Shitim, rather than Abel Beit-Maachah (1994, Summ. 4.6'). For another view (Abila), see Oded (1997: 110).

7.   Whether all of the sites should appear in this list is another matter. See further below. Perhaps to be added to his list are Khirbet Marjameh, Tell er-Rumeith (= Ramoth-gilead), and Tell Reḥob.

of the land of Naphtali and exiled them to Assyria'.[8] The annals of this Assyrian king mention the mass deportation of 13,520 prisoners taken from the towns of lower Galilee (Tadmor 1994, Ann. 24.13'). This disastrous scenario, drawn mostly from written sources, may be supplemented by recourse to studies of the material remains. The swath of Assyrian destruction was particularly severe in the regions of Galilee and the northern Transjordan. Gal has conducted a decade-long survey of the lower Galilee region (Gal 1992). Based on his field survey and his study of individual sites, he concludes that the peak occupation of this region occurred in the tenth century BCE and that a large gap in occupation began in the late eighth century. The destruction of Ḥurvat Rosh Zayit and Tel Gath-Ḥepher has been dated to the early or mid-ninth century (Gal 1992: 36–53; Gal and Alexandre 2000: 198–201). The lower Galilee was practically abandoned. Tel Qarney Ḥiṭṭin and Tel Ḥannathon were destroyed at this time.[9] Stern (2001: 7, 46–47) has spoken of a similar occupation gap for sites in upper Galilee (e.g. Tel Chinnereth, ʿEn Gev, Tel Hadar).[10] Nevertheless, one of these sites – Tel Chinnereth – witnesses some rebuilding and resettlement during the Iron II period.[11] If Tiglath-pileser III (745–727 BCE) did indeed deport 13,520 prisoners from northern Palestine, this may have represented much of the eighth-century population of the region. Gal's survey (1992: 109) of the region intimates that less than 18,000 people resided here during the early eighth century BCE. The figure of Broshi and Finkelstein (1992: 50) for Lower Galilee is higher: 22,500. Unfortunately, the demographic estimates based on archaeological surveys are only guesses, so it is impossible to be sure about how many people were left behind. What one can say, based on archaeological studies, is that the Assyrian campaigns caused devastation and severe depopulation in the region.

8.   I speak of authors, because it is likely that 'Galilee' and 'Gilead' are later additions to the text (Würthwein 1984: 383; Cogan and Tadmor 1988: 174). For a different view, see Galil (2000).

9.   Tel Mador (Khirbet Abu Mudawer ʾIʿblin) is sometimes mentioned in this context. The site was destroyed and not reoccupied until the Persian period (mid-sixth to mid-fifth century). The remains suggest that new settlers stemming from the west, most likely the Phoenician coastal plain, began to occupy these rural areas. But the excavator estimates the time of abandonment as the mid-ninth century, not the late eighth century (Gal 1992: 41).

10.   At Hazor, Stratum IV (late eighth century) represents an unfortified settlement, while Strata III-I represent a series of Assyrian (citadel and palace), Persian, and Hellenistic citadels (Yadin 1993; Ben-Tor 1993a; Negev and Gibson 2001: 222–23).

11.   After the late eighth century destruction of Tel Chinnereth, part of the town (in the north-west corner) was rebuilt (Stratum I). The site was abandoned c. 700 BCE (Fritz 1993). There is some confusion in scholarly references to Tel Chinnereth. This site is also spoken of as Kinneret(h). For the sake of clarity, I am referring to the site as Chinnereth (Tell el-ʿOreimeh), on the western shore of the Sea of Galilee. In speaking of Kinneret(h), some scholars mean a very small archaeological site near Kibbutz Kinneret (Mazar 1993).

The third major blow to Israel was the capture of Samaria itself, presumably by Shalmaneser V (727–722/721 BCE) in 722/721 BCE after a two- or three-year siege (2 Kgs 17.1–5; 18.10).[12] Shalmaneser died in 722/721 BCE, but in 720 BCE a new insurrection occurred involving the cities of Hamath, Arpad, Ṣimirra, Damascus, Ḫatarikka, and Samaria and the new Assyrian king Sargon II marched west to end it (Tadmor 1958; Timm 1989–90; Fuchs 1994, 2.3: 23–24; Younger 1999: 71–73). Sargon apparently recaptured Samaria and he (or his predecessor Shalmaneser) conquered a number of major sites.[13] Sargon also implemented, over the course of years, a series of bidirectional deportations. This policy of forced population exchange, occurring over the course of Sargon's reign (722/21–705 BCE), represented a fourth blow to the former northern kingdom (Na'aman and Zadok 1988). In Nimrud Prisms D & E, we read:

> 4.25–41. [The inhabitants of Sa]merina, who agreed [and plotted] with a king [hostile to] me, not to render service and not to bring tribute [to Ashur] and who did battle, I fought against them with the might of the great gods, my lords. I counted 27,280 people as spoil, together with their chariots, and (the) gods in which they trusted. I formed a unit with 200 of [their] chariots for my royal force. I settled the rest of them in the midst of Assyria. (Gadd 1954: 79–80, pls. xlv-xlvi)[14]

This text is interesting not only because it speaks of triumph and the capture of a very large number of prisoners, but also because it speaks of the integration of a Samarian chariot contingent into the army of the conqueror (Dalley 1985). I will return to this matter later.

The interventions of Sargon II represented the undoing of the northern kingdom, because his deportation of Israel's inhabitants and the import of foreign peoples, drawn from other sectors of the Assyrian empire, is said to have resulted in a comprehensive demographic and religious transformation (2 Kgs 17.5b-41; 18.9–12; 18.31–32//Isa. 36.16–17). The book of Kings mentions that each of the peoples entering the land brought along its own gods and cultic customs (2 Kgs 17.24–41). This picture of intrusive foreign religious elements has proved influential. In the words of Mitchell (1991: 344): 'The religious pollution of Israel symbolizes, perhaps more than anything else, its final fall'.

---

12. There are no inscriptions surviving from his reign. The Babylonian Chronicle (I 1.27–28) may allude to a two-year siege resulting in the taking of Samaria, but the city itself is not explicitly mentioned (Grayson 1975: 73). 2 Kgs 17.5 mentions a three-year siege.

13. The text of 2 Kgs 17.5–6 is ambiguous when it speaks of the Assyrian king's capture of Samaria. 2 Kgs 17.5 and 6a may telescope two discrete events (Cogan and Tadmor 1988: 200). Cogan and Tadmor think that the capture of Samaria is to be credited to Shalmaneser, while the exile is to be credited to Sargon II. Younger (1999) provides a helpful summary of opinion.

14. My translation basically follows that of Younger (2000a: 295).

This portrait of widespread destruction and upheaval in service to the maximalist hypothesis, drawn mostly from written sources, has been supplemented by recourse to studies of the material remains. Scholars have pointed to the Assyrian conquests to explain late eighth-century destruction layers at many sites (e.g. Mazar 1990: 544-47; Stern 2001: 3-41). According to Stern (2001: 7-9, 49-50), the 'total destruction' of the region of Samaria is reflected in excavations and surveys conducted at Taanach, Dothan, the city of Samaria, Tell el-Farʿah (north), Gezer, Shechem, and Bethel. Looking further afield within the Levant, Assyrian reliefs depict the conquest of Ashtaroth, Ekron, Gibbethon, Gezer, Lachish, and Raphia (Mazar 1990: 432, 445; Franklin 1994). Creating lists of sites serves more than archival purposes. In service to the maximalist hypothesis, the compilations of destroyed or abandoned settlements demonstrate a larger point, namely that the Assyrian campaigns were thoroughgoing and ruinous to Israel's infrastructure. The long process of repopulation begins under Sargon II and is said to continue under Sennacherib, Esarhaddon, and Ashurbanipal.[15]

In brief, the archaeological evidence is cited to show that the Assyrians created havoc within the Levant. To be sure, those holding to the maximalist theory would not claim that all Israelites exited the land. All acknowledge that some Israelites survived the Assyrian onslaughts, but they claim that the population exchanges sponsored by the Assyrians were so massive and thorough as to alter the character of the local population: 'It seems that as a result of this bi-directional movement of the deportees, great changes occurred in the ethnic composition of the population during the Assyrian domination of Megiddo and Samaria' (Stern 2001: 43). There are thus two essential components in the maximalist line of interpretation. One is the pervasive damage caused by the invasions of Tiglath-pileser III, Shalmaneser V, and Sargon II, while the second is the transformative effects of the Assyrian unidirectional and bidirectional deportations. One of the two components would not be enough by itself to sustain the thesis. Indeed, the argument is cumulative in its application. The damage done resulted from the actions of more than one king. The effect of Assyrian foreign policies over the course of a few generations was to refashion the demographic, ethnic, and religious landscape of Israel.

Information about the post-720 BCE phase of Samarian history is not easy to come by, but scholars have pointed to some bits of evidence to buttress their claim for fundamental discontinuity. In the context of the Assyrian campaigns, the former northern kingdom was divided into a number of different administrative districts. Two of the regional capitals were located in Megiddo and Samaria. Some have contended for the

---

15. The book of Ezra alludes to Assyrian-sponsored immigrations during the reigns of Esarhaddon (ʾēsar ḥaddōn; Ezra 4.2) and Ashurbanipal (ʾosnappar; Ezra 4.10).

existence of other administrative districts in Dor and Gilead.[16] Whatever the case, the larger maximalist argument is that the dismantling of the northern kingdom and its replacement by a system of Assyrian provinces were counter-productive to the survival of distinctive Israelite elements within the land. As an Assyrian province, Samaria's territorial reach extended over only a fraction of the former northern kingdom.

Assyrian influence is reflected in Assyrian-type palaces, residencies, inscriptions, seals, pottery, and metal artefacts (Barkay 1992: 351–53; Stern 2001: 9). The import of settlers, specifically Arabian settlers, is mentioned in Assyrian records (Tadmor 1983: 5; Younger 1998: 226–27). There may be some evidence that the very understanding of who a Samarian was could vary, depending on the situation. In this context, the publication of some non-literary Assyrian documents from Samaria and Gezer may be relevant. In these texts, written during the post-720 BCE period in Akkadian and Aramaic, 'Samarian' can carry more than one connotation (Eph'al 1991: 41). When taken together, the material and literary remains seem to constitute a large set of data to support the maximalist case.

2. *The Minimalist Case*

The number of scholars holding the minimalist position on the Assyrian deportations is few, but their arguments merit closer attention than they have received. Much of their case has been made by citing literary, chiefly biblical, evidence. Some attention has also been given to the archaeological and epigraphic evidence, but most of this attention has been negative. In this minority view, the damage caused by the Assyrian invasions was of limited duration and concentrated at major urban centres. The works of two scholars, Richard Coggins (1975) and Nathan Schur (1989), will be taken as illustrative of this position.

One aspect of the theory involves taking issue with the Assyrian versions of western conquest. The number of 27,280 (or 27,290) northern exiles during the time of Sargon II is said to be an exaggeration, an example of literary hyperbole (Schur 1989: 20). In the minimalist view, the countryside was largely left untouched by the Assyrian invasions and 'the overwhelming majority of the population' remained in the land (Coggins 1975: 18; Schur 1989: 21). Demographically speaking, the Assyrian exile primarily affected the élite of society (Schur 1989: 20). In the opinion of Coggins (1975: 17), the group of northern exiles only amounted to somewhere between 3–4 per cent of the total population. Hence, the

16. Nevertheless, a number of scholars have argued against Gilead constituting a separate province (Younger 1998: 205). Stern (1994: 131–45) argues for Dor's provincial status, but Machinist (1992: 71–72) is doubtful.

effects of the Assyrian conquests for Israel's populace at large were hardly as revolutionary as one would make out from the biblical and Assyrian accounts.

The importation of foreign settlers by Sargon II is not denied, but is said to be concentrated in the city of Samaria itself (Schur 1989: 21–23). In Schur's treatment, this datum mitigates the prospect of a demographic transformation in the region as a whole, because the foreign immigrants are said to be located primarily in one location. Coggins (1975: 18–20) offers, however, a more nuanced view. While not arguing that the foreign settlers were all confined to one area, he disputes the notion that the foreign settlers mixed with native Israelites to form a new amalgam and syncretistic religion.[17] In his view, Yahwists were able to conduct an independent religious life within Samaria.

Scholars in the minimalist camp have focused much of their attention on the testimony provided by a variety of different biblical authors. The account of the northern exile in Kings is said to be partisan, a clear case of special pleading written by Judahite authors eager to denounce the northern kingdom and its many failings. If the account of the northern exile in Kings is judged to be biased and tendentious, other biblical texts are judged to be germane to the larger discussion. One is the testimony provided by the author of Chronicles, who posits continuous inhabitation of the land by remnants of the northern tribes, in spite of the Assyrian exile (Meyers 1965: 176; Coggins 1975: 19–22).[18] Another is the testimony provided by the major prophets, all but ignored by those holding a maximalist interpretation. As Coggins (1975: 28–37; cf. Schur 1989: 23) points out, these prophetic texts all stem from Judah, but they continue to speak of Israel as a larger tribal entity. Prophets living in the early sixth century, such as Jeremiah and Ezekiel, repeatedly refer to specific northern Israelite sodalities. They make no mention of strange peoples as having displaced the original Israelite tribes in the north. They may express sorrow over the fate of Israel and denounce its shortcomings, but they do not speak of the Israelites as having all departed the land, become contaminated by alien blood, or come to naught. On the contrary, some prophetic writers express aspirations for the reunification of north and south. The argument is that the prophets would not express sentiments expressing a desire for reunification if a whole series of tribes had already been eliminated and no longer existed.

To sum up, the minimalist theory holds that the long-term effects of the Assyrian invasions were not nearly as radical as the biblical and Assyrian writings might suggest. The Assyrian policy of forced population

17. The view of Coggins was anticipated, in some respects, by Alt (1953: 250–75).

18. This is a major subject in and of itself. See Japhet (1989); Williamson (1977); Cogan (1988); Willi (1995).

exchange directly affected Israel's élite. In spite of military damage and political upheaval, the vast majority of Israelites continued to live within their territories and practise their traditional religion. The presence of Assyrian-sponsored colonists is not denied, but the arrival of these newcomers is said to have had little or no effect on the lives of average Israelites.

3. *A Via Media*

In presenting my own position, I will be taking issue with some aspects of both the maximalist and the minimalist theories. It may be helpful to begin with some remarks about the minimalist hypothesis. The Deuteronomistic commentary on the fall of the northern realm reveals much about what a series of biblical writers thought about the fate of the northern tribes, but the presuppositions and aims of these writers warrant very close scrutiny (Coggins 1975: 13; Schur 1989: 20–21).[19] The cessation of coverage for the northern tribes in Kings following the collapse of the northern realm reflects a literary and theological decision on the part of the biblical authors and, as such, cannot do justice to the actual situation in the north following the Assyrian campaigns. Hence, the minimalist scholars are right to press the issue about the nature of the theological writing one finds in 2 Kings 17.

Similarly, the points made by Coggins about the prophetic texts in the Hebrew Bible are well taken. If the writers of these works thought that the northern tribes were defunct and no longer had any tangible presence in the land, they do not say so. Because these points are well formulated, they require no more discussion here. Similarly, Coggins' brief discussion of the Chronicler's work is on the mark.[20] His writing, often neglected in this context, presumes that a remnant of the northern tribes survived the Assyrian onslaughts and remained in the land. These northern Israelites retained familiarity with their own traditions and maintained their long-established tribal structure.[21]

Some of the arguments made about the Assyrian materials are, however, weak. It is too strong a generalization to say that the Assyrian exile affected only the élite, a tiny portion (3–4 per cent) of the total population. The Assyrian policies of population exchange affected more than the upper crusts of subject societies. Under Shalmaneser III, Tiglath-

---

19.   Coggins (1975: 14–15) also stresses that neither the authors of 2 Kgs 17.7–23 nor the authors of 2 Kgs 17.24–41 evince any anti-Samaritan bias, even though the former lambaste the northern kingdom and the latter decry the revitalization of the Bethel cultus. I am not as confident as Coggins is that one can maintain the distinction.

20.   By the Chronicler, I mean the author of the book of Chronicles.

21.   I plan to develop these points in a future study.

pileser III, Sargon II, and Sennacherib, the Assyrians claim to have deported hundreds of thousands of people (Oded 1979: 20). Whole communities were dislocated (Oded 1995: 209–12). Assertions about displacement affecting only a slight part of the population are predicated on inflated and outmoded population estimates for the northern kingdom in the eighth century. De Vaux (1958: I, 104, ET 1965: 66), for example, spoke of there being 800,000 Israelites in the land during the eighth century. More recent estimates, informed by the results of archaeological site surveys, have drastically reduced such high numbers (e.g. Broshi and Finkelstein 1992: 47–60; Naʾaman 1993). The assertion of Sargon II that he made Samaria more populous than it was before, if this is what he claims, may be a hyperbole.[22] With one possible exception, the Assyrians do not seem to have undertaken any major construction at the site (Tappy 2001: 571–79). Nevertheless, there do not seem to be any convincing reasons to suggest that the Sargonic figure of 27,280 (or 27,290) prisoners from Samaria is a great exaggeration.[23] Nor is there any clear evidence that the foreign exiles brought into Samaria were confined to the city itself.

One wonders whether the scholars holding to the minimalist position have substantially underestimated the impact of the Assyrian campaigns on the southern Levant. Given the congruence of some of the archaeological findings with the epigraphic and biblical evidence concerning the Assyrian campaigns in the late eighth century, the time in which Tiglath-pileser III, Shalmaneser V and Sargon II achieved a series of impressive victories, those holding the maximalist interpretation are justified in a number of their claims.

Where the maximalist case may be genuinely faulted lies not so much in the evidence that is cited as in the assumptions it makes and how it employs material evidence in support of sweeping, generalized conclusions. Archaeologically, the approach is fundamentally 'tell-centred' and oriented toward the Israelite kingdom as a whole. Presuming close linkages between state and people, politics and cult, centre and periphery, scholars collect sites showing destruction layers and cite the total as proof for the cataclysmic end of northern Israel's existence in the land. One may question, however, whether scholars should either assume or assert such

---

22. The text of Nimrud Prisms D & E can be read in more than one way (cf. the annals of Sargon II; Fuchs 1994, 2.3: 10–16). I am following Dalley (1985: 36), who reads a hendiadys, *uttir…ušēšib*. Hence, she reads the verbs (*w*) *atāru*, 'to increase' (in number or size) and (*w*)*ašābu*, 'to settle, reside', rather than *tāru*, 'to return, restore' and *ewû* (*emû*), 'to become'. In older treatments (e.g. Tadmor 1958: 34), one finds the translation, 'I made it greater than before'. For further discussion, see Fuchs (1994, 2.3.3), who prefers the older reading, and Younger (2000a: 295–96), who follows Dalley.

23. The recent study of De Odorico (1995: 52, 70, 86) suggests that the number is authentic (contra Gray 1974: 644–45). The total probably includes deportees from both the city and the surrounding district (Naʾaman 1993: 106–108; Younger 1998: 218–19).

close linkages. In spite of the attention given to matters of epigraphy and archaeology, there is no clear evidence that the dismantling of the northern kingdom and its replacement by a system of Assyrian provinces were intrinsically destructive to the survival of native cultures. Such a proposition effectively equates a centralized political authority with the cultural and demographic realities of all the geographic areas it claims to control. In a rural society the state should be seen as one institution among others that seeks to impose its authority upon those whom it considers to be its subjects. How effective or ineffective such control may be depends on the economic, political, and military power of the state, how well it communicates its policies, and how well it can defend its interests in the hinterland. Human culture is a larger, much more complex, and enduring phenomenon than any one political institution can represent.

In this context, there is no compelling evidence that the Assyrians systematically imposed their own religious practices on subject peoples.[24] For the most part, as long as subject peoples remained loyal to the Assyrian crown and paid their tribute and taxes, the Assyrian authorities did not interfere with local customs and practices (Cogan 1993; Day 2000: 232–33). Even the authors of 2 Kings 17 do not claim that the Assyrian authorities imposed their own culture and religion upon subject peoples. On the contrary, the author of 2 Kgs 17.24–32 presents an unnamed Assyrian monarch as working to ensure a revival of traditional religion at Bethel following the arrival of state-sponsored Assyrian colonists. Whatever one makes of this odd passage, it is clear that the author did not view the Assyrian crown as demanding that local populations abandon their customs and religious practices.

There is, moreover, other archaeological, literary, and epigraphic evidence that is not brought to bear in addressing the larger historical questions. To begin with, some archaeological field surveys are not given significant attention. To be sure, the data provided by these surveys cannot be considered in isolation from the material evidence pertaining to the history of individual tells, but the surveys are relevant in testing claims of significant depopulation, especially in discerning the number and size of settlements in a given region during a particular era. We will return to this matter in more detail later. Second, closer attention must be given to the individual regions within Israel that were affected by the Assyrian campaigns. There are, as we have seen, cases in which archaeological excavations and site surveys indicate fundamental disruption of settlement and great depopulation. The areas of Galilee and northern Transjordan stand out in this respect. But questions may be raised whether this pattern

---

24. So McKay (1973), Cogan (1974), and Dalley (1985: 41–42). Spieckermann (1982: 212–21) argues the opposite view

holds true for all regions within Israel. In speaking of severe depopulation, long occupation gaps, and site abandonment, one must inquire as to the precise geographic area or location addressed by the claim. The part should not be taken for the whole.

In this context, it may be best to decouple the western campaigns and unidirectional deportation policies of Tiglath-pileser III from those of his immediate successors. The damage done in Galilee by Tiglath-pileser III was not commensurate with the damage done in the hill country of Samaria by Shalmaneser V and Sargon II. This becomes evident, when one revisits the list of sites razed by the Assyrians. In service to the maximalist hypothesis, the documenatation of destruction is extremely important, because such evidence contributes to a larger picture of devastation and displacement. But the location of these sites should be kept in mind. Those sites with evidence for both conflagration and abandonment (or conflagration and a long occupation gap) include Beth-saida, Tel Hadar, Tel Qarney Ḥiṭṭin, Tel Ḥannathon, Beth-shean, Kedesh, and ʿEn Gev.[25] At least two of these are disputed. Beth-saida in Area A (Southern Section, Level 5) shows clear evidence of a destruction dated by the excavators to the late eighth century BCE, but the site was not abandoned.[26] Similarly, Beth-shean shows a partial, albeit temporary, restoration in the years following the Assyrian conquest (Mazar 1993). All of these sites are situated in Galilee, the northern Transjordan, and the northern coastal region at some distance from Samaria itself.

Third, in assessing the damage caused by the Assyrians, it is important to pay close attention not only to razed and abandoned settlements, but also to razed and restored settlements. Sites that evince both destruction and restoration include Akko, Beth-saida, Bethel,[27] Beth-shean, Dan, Dor, Dothan, Gezer, Shiqmona, Tell el-Farʿah north (= Tirzah;

25.   The list differs somewhat from the tabulation of sites provided by Stern (2001: 7, 9, 46–51). On Tel Mador, Tel Chinnereth, and Hazor, see above.

26.   In his report on Beth-saida (et-Tell), located 2 km north of the Sea of Galilee, the excavator stresses that this was a substantial two-tiered Iron II walled settlement with a gateway. Level 4 represents the period covering the time after the Assyrian conquest to the end of the Babylonian period (732–540 BCE). The site, although reduced in occupation, was not abandoned at the end of the Iron Age (Arav 1997; 1999: II, 15, 25–31, 84, 102–104).

27.   There is much that remains unclear about the stratigraphy of Bethel in the Iron II period. According to the excavator, the main evidence for Bethel's destruction in the late eighth century BCE is the absence of pottery finds from after this time (Kelso 1968, §§145, 150, 206). The site was reoccupied in the seventh century, perhaps toward the end of the Assyrian period (Kelso 1968, §§143, 150). Both the southern town wall and a tower underwent reconstruction during the seventh century (Kelso 1968, §§42, 47). The town suffered a major destruction in the mid- to late sixth century BCE. No destruction layers were found dating to the seventh or early sixth centuries BCE. Dever (1997: 300–301) provides a critique of Kelso's report.

Chambon 1984), Shechem[28] and Tel Keisan.[29] The evidence from these sites presents some problems for the maximalist hypothesis, because it does not comport well with notions of complete dislocation. To be sure, most of these sites were not rebuilt to their earlier size, but the settlement continuity is itself important, suggesting that some of the residents at these locations were not permanently uprooted.

Fourth, even granting the validity of the 'tell-centred' nature of traditional archaeology, there are some sites that show continuity in material culture throughout the eighth century. It has to be conceded, however, that such sites are few in number and most are small: Tel Esur, Khirbet el-Hammam, Tel Qiri, and Taanach. Ceramic remains suggest that Tel Esur (Tell el-Asawir), situated at the southern entrance to the Megiddo pass, was continuously inhabited from the ninth cenury up to and including the Byzantine period (Dothan 1993a: 426–28). Similarly, Khirbet el-Hammam, a fortified town in the north-western Samarian hills, seems to have been continuously inhabited from the eleventh-tenth century to the second/early first century BCE (Zertal 1993: 563–65). Tel Qiri, 2 km south of Tel Jokneam, was an unfortified agricultural village in the Jezreel Valley. In the Iron Age, the site was continuously occupied, except for a slight disruption between Strata VIII and VII (Ben-Tor 1987; 1993b; 1997). Taanach, a fortified town at the southern end of Jezreel Valley, exhibits limited Iron II remains. Its occupation continued into the fifth century BCE (Glock 1993; 1997). The residents in these settlements may have temporarily abandoned their sites, only offered nominal resistance to the invading Assyrians, or peacefully surrendered. Fifth, there are sites that experienced only limited or very limited destruction. One example is Megiddo and another is Samaria itself. In constructing their buildings at Megiddo (Stratum III), the Assyrians built over and reused sections of the earlier eighth-century Stratum IVA (Chicago).[30] The Assyrians used the same 'inside-outside' wall evident in Stratum IVA for their own defences. To be sure, there is some evidence of an internal, probably controlled, destruction by fire in the domestic quarters at the site in the late eighth century, which formed the basis for Assyrian rebuilding activities (Joffe, Cline and Lipschits 2000: 143–50; Halpern 2000: 561–69; Finkelstein and Ussishkin 2000: 597–600). But there is no clear evidence that the forces of Tiglath-pileser III, Shalmaneser V or Sargon II destroyed the city of Megiddo, even though the Assyrians took over the

28.   The remains from Stratum VI at Shechem indicate a partial resettlement of this site in the seventh century (Campbell 1993: 1345–54; 1991).

29.   In addition, Tell Hadid (near Gezer) witnesses the construction of what appears to be an unfortified Assyrian administrative centre in the seventh century (Stern 2001: 16, 21).

30.   Three phases in Assyrian construction can be discerned at the site: Levels H-3, H-2, and H-1 (all Stratum III; Joffe, Cline and Lipschits 2000).

location (Peersmann 2000: 526–27). The defenders may have simply surrendered the site.

The site of Samaria exhibits several Iron Age layers. If, as estimated, the area of Iron II Samaria was approximately seventy hectares, Samaria was larger than Jerusalem in the same period (Avigad 1993: 1302).[31] A layer of ashes has been attributed to the Assyrian conquest, but neither Shalmaneser nor Sargon seems to have destroyed the city's fortifications, which continued to be used. In Tappy's recent study of Kenyon's excavation notes, he points out that there are relatively few traces of Assyrian destruction (Tappy 2001: 351–441; so also Na'aman 1990: 209; Dalley 1985: 31–48). There are some Assyrian remains, but there is no evidence of a major razing of the site dating to this time. Moreover, some of the ceramic evidence cited by Kenyon in favour of Assyrian destruction in the late eighth century actually dates to several different periods. Tappy (2001: 440) comments: 'I have not encountered a blanket of destruction debris across the B[uilding] P[eriod] V remains at the site; rather, diverse layers dating from many time periods and extending as late as the Late Roman period have emerged'. In other words, Samaria lacks a coherent destruction level that dates to the time of Tiglath-pileser III, Shalmaneser V and Sargon II. Some new types of pottery appear at the site (Kenyon 1957: 97–98). There are also Assyrian remains, including a fragment of a stele attributed to Sargon II, but these Assyrian material remains are not abundant (Tappy 2001: 572). There is a fundamental material continuity in the Iron II period at Samaria, in spite of whatever political discontinuity the Assyrians may have introduced. The walls at the site continue in use for a long period of time and the city itself survives into the Babylonian and Persian periods (Crowfoot 1957: 3–5). Such evidence of continuing inhabitation belies two critical claims in the maximalist hypothesis, namely that the Assyrians caused generalized destruction to all settlements and that they deported the inhabitants of these communities. One wonders whether much of the newer archaeological evidence that has been unearthed over the past three decades has been forced into the service of upholding an older interpretative paradigm.

In this context, it is relevant to pay close attention to what Assyrian and Babylonian scribes claim (and do not claim) about the taking of the city of Samaria. The Babylonian Chronicle speaks of Shalmaneser V as having 'broken' the city.[32] As for Sargon II, he claims to have 'besieged and

31. Zertal (2001: 49) speculates that its population was around 17,000 people. The estimate of Broshi and Finkelstein (1992: 51) would seem to be much higher, even though they estimate Samaria's area as sixty hectares.

32. The precise translation of *ḫepû* in this context (Babylonian Chronicle I 1.28) is in dispute (Grayson 1975: 73). I am following Becking (1992: 25), Dalley (1985: 33), and Younger (1999: 464–68) in taking the basic meaning as 'to break' or 'to ruin'. Na'aman (1990: 211) takes the sense of *ḫepû*, in this context, to indicate pacification. Cf. *CAD Ḫ*: 173.

conquered' Samaria (Fuchs 1994, 2.4: 23–27). The Assyrian and Babylonian scribes do not assert that Shalmaneser and Sargon razed the city, thus decimating it. The Mesopotamian sources speak of siege and conquest, not of devastation. Similarly, the biblical author speaks of the unnamed Assyrian monarch as capturing (*lākad*) the city (2 Kgs 17.6). It is true that Sargon claims to have taken tens of thousands of Samarians as prisoners, but Sargon also boasts that the annual tax and tribute remained the same as in the time of his predecessor (Fuchs 1994, 2.4: 27). The latter would be impossible if the land's infrastructure had been thoroughly ruined. Dalley observes that Sargon II never claims to have taken any booty from Samaria, aside from its people and its gods (Dalley 1985: 34–35).

One may also ask whether a scorched-earth policy would be in keeping with the strategic goals of Assyria's imperial policy. There are economic consequences to dismantling local infrastructure and implementing an imperial policy of destruction. To lay waste to lands means denuding those territories of people who could bring income to the imperial treasury (Diakonoff 1991). Sargon II claims to have received as much tribute, on an annual basis, from Samaria after its fall as before its fall. Samaria was made into a provincial capital. This would be most unlikely if Sargon's geopolitical and military aims in dealing with Samaria were simply punitive in nature. The king's assertion that he absorbed a contingent of two hundred chariots from Samaria into his forces suggests that he did not relegate Samaria to a pariah status during his time.

Returning to the subject of archaeological site surveys, we have seen that these have been cited in one case (Galilee) as confirming the radical effects of the Assyrian deportations during the eighth century. The results of surveys conducted in the hill country of Ephraim and Manasseh show, however, less revolutionary results. In the hills of Manasseh surveys conducted by Zertal (1990), the Iron II period marks the peak of settlement. Only the Byzantine era is more populous. The number of sites during the Iron II period, defined by Zertal as the tenth to the late eighth centuries, is more than double the number of sites attested during the Iron I period. There is a steep decline during the Iron III period, especially in the eastern valleys, before the area experiences a strong recovery during the Persian period.[33] The number of sites in the Iron III period is approximately 40 per cent the number of those that existed during the Iron II period.[34] Faust points to a large number of farmsteads, as well as

33. The Persian era represents the time in which the northern region of Samaria is the most densely populated (247 sites) of all periods.

34. The Iron II period features 238 sites, compared with 95 sites during the Iron III period (Zertal 1990: 11–16; 1993: 1311–12). These statistics are being revised upward as Zertal continues his studies (2001: 41–44).

some hamlets and villages, that have been excavated in the Samaria highlands (Faust 2003). Almost all of these Iron Age rural sites exhibit continuity into the Persian period. Zertal (2001: 44) estimates that the number of prisoners taken as booty by Sargon II (27,290) might have represented about one third of the state's total population. If the higher estimate of Broshi and Finkelstein (1992: 50–51) for Samaria's population in the eighth century is closer to the mark, the number of prisoners taken as booty by Sargon II might have represented about one quarter of the (reduced) state's total population.[35]

The Iron II period witnessed a major increase of settlements in western Samaria. In the subsequent period, there seems to be a decline (Dar 1986; 1992; 1993). Faust (2003) observes that most Iron Age rural sites excavated in the Samarian foothills, that is, the westernmost slopes of Samaria (above the alluvial valley), did not continue to exist during the Persian period. The date of their destruction/abandonment is not entirely clear, but seems to be earlier than the sixth century, the time in which many rural sites were abandoned in Judah. In his survey of the hills of southern Samaria, Finkelstein also points to the Iron II period, defined by him as the tenth to the early sixth centuries, as a time of unprecedented level of settlement, with the northern area being the most intensively settled (Finkelstein 1988–89; Finkelstein, Lederman and Bunimovitz 1997; Watkins 1997). During the Iron II era, the eighth century marks the peak of occupation. Only the Bethel plateau showed a decrease in sites during the Iron II period. Compared with the Iron II period, the Persian period witnesses a sharp decline in the number of sites. The number of sites in the Achaemenid period (90) is approximately 47 per cent the number of those that existed during the Iron II period (190). During this time of decline there is a shift in settlement toward the western coastal plain.[36]

In brief, site surveys and salvage excavations confirm the late eighth century as a time of real decline in the settlement of certain parts of the Samaria hill country. By the same token, the archaeological remains point to significant continuity in settlement. In this respect, one has to distinguish the results of the archaeological work in Galilee and the northern Transjordan from the results of the archaeological work undertaken in the hills of Manasseh and Ephraim. The former shows severe depopulation with only nominal reinvestment of resources by the Assyrians.[37] The latter shows mixed results, both discontinuity and

35. The estimate (102,500) only includes the areas of Mt Gilboa, Mt Carmel, northern Samaria, and southern Samaria. It does not include any part of Galilee, the Huleh Valley, or the Jordan Valley.

36. A recovery occurs in the Hellenistic period (Finkelstein 1993).

37. Much of their economic effort was probably expended on areas to the south and south-west of the province of Magiddu (Finkelstein and Ussishkin 2000: 602; Stern 2001: 46–51).

continuity. Assuming, for the sake of argument, that Sargon did capture 27,290 prisoners, this figure can only represent a minority of Israel's population in the late eighth century BCE.

To this line of argumentation, an objection may be made. The site surveys showing significant continuity of inhabitation may be mislead-ing, because one has to take into account the bidirectional nature of the Assyrian deportations during the time of Sargon II. If, for example, the reign of Sargon II witnessed both Israelite deportations to various areas in the Assyrian empire and importations of many exiles from elsewhere into the former northern kingdom, the degree of settlement continuity evinced by site surveys may mask the true degree of population exchange in this area. If a two-way deportation occurred, the continuity reflected in settlement surveys might mask the true degree to which the Assyrian campaigns negatively affected the Israelite population.

Three points may be made in response to this possible objection. First, we do not know how many foreigners were transported to Samaria by Sargon II and other Assyrian monarchs. There is no reason to doubt that Sargon II drew such settlers from different geographic areas, but it is unclear how many he imported into the region. This is a critical consideration in assessing the extent of cultural change introduced by the Assyrians. Second, the Assyrian records present a complex picture of the aftermath of Samaria's conquest. On the one hand, they speak of siege, victory, and deportation. On the other hand, the texts speak of maintaining an equal amount of tax and tribute from Samaria and of the integration of a Samarian chariot contingent into Sargon's army. In short, Sargon's royal inscriptions indicate conquest and integration, rather than utter devastation.

Third, if Sargon brought in vast numbers of immigrants into the former northern kingdom, one would expect to find confirmation of this enormous population exchange in the material record. But local pottery traditions continued. Even though the former Aramaean and Israelite territories were transformed into a system of Assyrian provinces, local pottery types changed only minimally (Amiran 1970: 191–92). The importance of this point should not be underestimated. In Syria, Iron Age pottery types remained almost unchanged until the mid-seventh century BCE (Lehmann 1998). Assyrian hegemony did not result in large amounts of Mespotamian pottery being shipped into areas west of the Euphrates. This is not to deny the possibility that some new pottery types were introduced by Assyrian-sponsored immigrants. For instance, Zertal (1989) has called attention to what he deems to be a new 'Cuthean' style pottery in the hills of Samaria. Whatever the case, any influence exerted by incoming immigrants seems to have been quite limited. There is no evidence that the traditional culture in the hill country of Ephraim and

Manasseh was suddenly displaced by a single foreign culture or by a variety of foreign cultures. Stern (2001: 45) comments:

> It seems, however, that this major change in the region's population [following the Assyrian conquest] left but a modest mark in the archaeological record. Almost nothing has been uncovered that can be attributed to the countries of the different groups of deportees, who are said to come from the Iranian plateau or Elam. Even in the capital cities of the two Assyrian provinces, only a handful of finds can be attributed to them.[38]

Especially in rural areas, the basic pottery repertoire (e.g. cooking pots, storage jars, amphorae) changed little in the eighth century.

In discussing the material remains and their possible relationship to different historical reconstructions, consideration of larger geopolitical factors is pertinent. During the reigns of Sargon and his successors, the expansion of Assyrian control in Syria, Lebanon, and Israel encouraged the development of more trade with the Phoenician cities, Cyprus, Arabia, Egypt, and various sites in the west. By defeating the Aramaean and Israelite states and reducing other states, such as Judah, to client status, the Assyrians enlarged their markets for trade. The selective use of forced population movements served a variety of imperial purposes: conscription into the armed forces, weakening or stabilizing local regions (depending on the situation), staving off desolation, providing labour in needed areas, enforcing state control over newly conquered peoples, maintaining psychological control over previously rebellious states, integrating far-off regions into the Assyrian empire, preventing impoverishment, and securing the western border of the Assyrian empire over against the Philistines and the Egyptians (Oded 1979: 33–68; Younger 1998: 225–27; Thompson 2001: 102–103).

There is no doubt that Tiglath-pileser III and Sargon II both employed such deportations of northern Israelites to their advantage in conquering the land of the House of Omri. The question is how many foreign exiles Sargon II imported into the highlands of Samaria. Two considerations suggest that the numbers of such foreign immigrants were not high. First, as we have seen, the archaeological remains point to both significant depopulation and to the relative lack of cultural indicators for deportees stemming from the Iranian plateau or from Elam. Second, a significant disparity in the number of exiles in two-way deportations involving Israelites and peoples from other lands would be broadly consistent with Assyrian imperial policy. The Assyrian authorities typically sent far more people from the periphery toward the urban centres of their empire, than

---

38. Stern concedes that 'this is difficult to understand' (2001: 45); but, at this point, he prefers to follow the 'historical sources' rather than to question some of their claims.

vice versa (Oded 1979: 27–32). Such a great imbalance in population transfers enabled a succession of Assyrian monarchs to build up the main urban centres at the core of their empire (Oded 1979: 28, 60–62; 2000: 91–103). This means that of those who resided in the districts of Samerina and Magiddu – Israelites, Assyrians, and immigrants – the clear majority were Israelites.

4. *Conclusions*

We have seen that both of the two traditional positions on the Assyrian exile are at some variance with the material evidence. Study of the archaeological remains suggests a more complex situation. In the regions of Galilee and the northern Transjordan, the Assyrian invasions caused widespread devastation. It is within these areas that one finds many sites both destroyed and abandoned. Other locations evince long occupation gaps. Site surveys indicate a process of extreme depopulation in the late eighth century. Historically, one may associate this devastation with the western campaigns of Tiglath-pileser in 734–732 BCE, which eliminated the kingdom of Damascus, greatly reduced the size of the Israelite state, and led to mass deportations.

Analysis of the material remains from the hill country of Ephraim and Manasseh suggests a mixed picture. Some sites were either destroyed and abandoned during the late eighth century or evince long occupation gaps. A few locations, showing no traces of destruction, evince continuity in occupation. Other sites including Megiddo and Samaria itself, show only limited or minimal signs of destruction. Yet other sites evince destruction and some rebuilding. Archaeological surveys indicate a process of significant depopulation in the late eighth century. Historically, one may associate these developments with the western campaigns of Shalmaneser V and Sargon II, which overthrew the Israelite state and transformed Samaria into an Assyrian province.

The results of our investigation are at odds with the presentations found in some standard histories. What one finds in the hills of Samaria is not so much the replacement of one local population by a foreign population, but rather the diminution of the local population. Wholesale abandonment does not occur as in parts of Galilee and Gilead, but significant depopulation does occur. Among the causes of such a decline, one may list death by war, disease, and starvation, forced deportations to other lands, and migrations to other areas, including south to Judah (Broshi 1974; Ofer 1993a; 1993b; 1994: 105–106). Some Israelites were deported to other locations in the Assyrian empire, but others survived the Assyrian onslaughts and remained in the land. There is no reason to deny the arrival of state-sponsored immigrants in the hills of Samaria as both the Assyrian royal inscriptions and the authors of Kings maintain. But the numbers of such foreign transplants do not appear to be high. Whatever exiles from foreign states were forcibly imported into the Samarian highlands, most seem to have been absorbed into the local population.

An enduring, but significantly reduced, Israelite presence in the land would explain three major features of the material remains. First, it explains why there is a continuity in material culture in both the city of Samaria and in the Samarian highlands, in spite of the Assyrian invasions and conquest. Such a continuity would be unlikely, if not impossible, were there either an empty land or a land filled with foreign émigrés. Second, it clarifies what features of a foreign presence do appear in the material record. There are indications of Assyrian presence in Samaria, but such signs of foreign occupation coexist with signs of indigenous material culture. Neither the Assyrians themselves nor the immigrants they sponsored arrived in sufficient numbers to replace the Israelites. Third, the Assyrian selectivity in dealing with the House of Omri – destroying some sites while minimizing the damage to others, deporting some Israelites while leaving others in the land, establishing an imperial presence while having indigenous residents carry on their work – explains why the region of Samaria made a swifter recovery after the Assyrian campaigns than Judah did after the Babylonian invasions in the early sixth century BCE (Stern 2001: 49–51).[39] Much of the area grew and prospered during the seventh century BCE.

The Babylonians under Nebuchadnezzar took a much more devastating approach to dealing with rebellions in the southern Levant than Shalmaneser V and Sargon II did. One does not have to embrace the myth of the empty land to acknowledge that the Babylonians inflicted tremendous damage on the economic infrastructure of various Phoenician city-states and to Judah, as well. Excavations in Jerusalem indicate that the Babylonian forces did massive injury to the city's fortifications and major buildings (Lipschits 2001). The contrast with the relatively lenient treatment given centuries earlier to the city of Samaria is striking. Both the Assyrians and the Babylonians were punitive, but the Assyrians were much more interested in deploying the resources of their far-flung empire toward exploiting the possibilities for trade and commerce than were the Babylonians.

Examination of the material remains from the hills of Samaria illumines a later development in the history of this area. The survival of a substantial number of Israelites following the Assyrian campaigns helps to explain the existence of a Yahwistic Samarian community in the Persian

---

39. Stern (2001: 43) attributes this recovery in Samaria to two factors: (1) the smaller degree of damage done in this region in comparison to that done in Galilee; (2) the repopulation of the region by foreign immigrants, anticipated by the Assyrians with careful planning, which brought new growth and prosperity.

period. One of the governors of Samaria – Sanballat – features prominently as an adversary of Nehemiah (2.10, 19; 3.33; 4.1; 6.1–14; 13.28), but extrabiblical documentation reveals that two of his sons had Yahwistic names (Delaiah and Shelemiah; Porten and Yardeni 1986, A4.7: 29; 4.8.28; 4.9.1). Of the many personal names (sellers, buyers, slaves) found within the fourth-century Samaria papyri, the 'vast majority' are Yahwistic (Gropp 1992: 931–32; 2001: 5–7; Eph'al 1998: 110–11; Lemaire 2001: 104–107). Very few are Babylonian or Persian. Recent archaeological studies indicate that the Persian province of Samaria was larger, far more populous, and more wealthy than was Yehud (Zertal 1990: 9–30; 1999). When the Jewish community at Elephantine wished to rebuild their temple in the late fifth century, they lobbied the authorities in both Jerusalem and Samaria for their support (Grelot 1972, §§102–103; Porten 1968: 284–98; Porten and Yardeni 1986, A4.5–10). Certainly, the Jews of Elephantine must have felt some affinity with the community of Samaria or they would not have written to the Samarian leadership to ask for their assistance.

The question thus arises as to the origins of these Yahwistic Samarians. This brings us back to the text of 2 Kings 17. The author of 2 Kgs 17.24– 32 presents an unnamed Assyrian monarch as working to ensure a revival of traditional religion at Bethel after lions had been devouring state-sponsored immigrants. One implication of this highly unusual story is that the Samarians were descendants of Assyrian-sponsored colonists.[40] There is no reason to doubt that many of the settlers adopted the customs of their new land and assimilated into the local population, but one need not resort to such a convoluted scenario as the major means to explain the continuation and development of Yahwism in the north. A less laboured and more historically plausible explanation would be to see the Yahwistic Samarians of the Persian period as descendants of the Israelites who used to have their own kingdom centred in Samaria centuries earlier.

Bibliography

Ahlström, G.W.
    1993   *The History of Ancient Palestine from the Palaeolithic Period to Alexander's Conquest* (JSOTSup, 146; Sheffield: JSOT Press).
Alt, A.
    1953   'Die Heimat des Deuteronomiums', in his *Kleine Schriften zur Geschichte des Volkes Israel*, II (Munich: Beck): 250–75.

40. But in their renewal of the Bethel cultus, these immigrants replicate the exact steps taken by Jeroboam I to invest this cultus centuries earlier. In this manner, they perpetuate Israel's state religion in all of its essential features. The treatment of the Samarians in 2 Kgs 17 is a subject in and of itself. See provisionally, Knoppers (1994: II, 64–70).

Amiran, R.
1970   *Ancient Pottery of the Holy Land* (Jerusalem: Israel Exploration Society).
Arav, R.
1997   'Bethsaida', in *OEANE*, I: 302–05.
1999   'Bethsaida Excavations: Preliminary Report, 1994–96', in R. Arav and R. Freund (eds), *Bethsaida: A City by the Shore of the Sea of Galilee*, II (Kirksville, MO: Truman State University Press): 1–110.
Avigad, N.
1993   'Samaria', in *NEAEHL*, IV: 1300–10.
Barkay, G.
1992   'The Iron Age II-III', in A. Ben-Tor (ed.), *The Archaeology of Ancient Israel* (New Haven: Yale University Press): 302–73.
Barstad, H.M.
1996   *The Myth of the Empty Land* (Symbolae Osloenses Fasc. Suppl., 28; Oslo: Scandinavian University Press).
1997   *The Babylonian Captivity of the Book of Isaiah* (Instituttet for sammenlignende kulturforskning B/CII; Oslo: Novus).
Becking, B.
1992   *The Fall of Samaria: An Historical and Archaeological Study* (SHANE, 2; Leiden: E.J. Brill).
Ben-Tor, A.
1987   *Tell Qiri, a Village in the Jezreel Valley: Report of the Archaeological Excavations, 1975–78* (Qedem, 24; Jerusalem: Institute of Archaeology, the Hebrew University).
1993a   'Hazor: Fifth Season of Excavations', in *NEAEHL*, II: 604–606.
1993b   'Tell Qiri', in *NEAEHL*, IV: 1228–29.
1997   'Tel Qiri', in *OEANE*, IV: 387–89.
Berquist, J.L.
1995   *Judaism in Persia's Shadow* (Minneapolis: Fortress Press).
Blenkinsopp, J.
1998   'The Judaean Priesthood during the Neo-Babylonian and Achaemenid Periods: A Hypothetical Reconstruction', *CBQ* 60: 25–43.
2002   'The Bible, Archaeology and Politics; or The Empty Land Revisited', *JSOT* 27: 169–87.
2003   'Bethel in the Neo-Babylonian Period', in O. Lipschits and J. Blenkinsopp (eds), *Judah and the Judeans in the Neo-Babylonian Period* (Winona Lake, IN: Eisenbrauns): 93–107.
Bright, J.
1981   *A History of Israel* (Philadelphia: Westminster Press, 3rd edn).
Broshi, M.
1974   'The Expansion of Jerusalem in the Reign of Hezekiah and Manasseh', *IEJ* 24: 21–26.
Broshi, M., and I. Finkelstein
1992   'The Population of Palestine in Iron Age II', *BASOR* 287: 47–60.
Campbell, E.F.
1991   *Shechem*, II: *Portrait of a Hill Country Vale* (Atlanta, GA: Scholars Press).
1993   'Shechem (Tell Balâtah)', in *NEAEHL*, IV: 1345–54.

Carroll, R.P.
1992   'The Myth of the Empty Land', *Semeia* 59: 79–93.
2001   'Exile! What Exile? Deportation and the Discourses of Diaspora', in L.L. Grabbe (ed.), *Leading Captivity Captive: 'The Exile' as History and Ideology* (JSOTSup, 278; Sheffield: Sheffield Academic Press): 63–79.

Chambon, A.
1984   *Tell el-Far'ah*, I: *L'âge du fer* (Paris: Editions Recherche sur les Civilisations).

Cogan, M.
1974   *Imperialism and Religion: Assyria, Judah and Israel in the Eighth and Seventh Centuries BCE* (SBLMS, 19; Missoula, MT: Scholars Press).
1988   '"For We Like You, Worship Your God": Three Biblical Portrayals of Samaritan Origins', *VT* 38: 286–92.
1993   'Judah under Assyrian Hegemony: A Reexamination of Imperialism and Religion', *JBL* 112: 403–14.

Cogan, M., and H. Tadmor
1988   *II Kings: A New Translation with Introduction and Commentary* (AB, 11; Garden City, NY: Doubleday).

Coggins, R.J.
1975   *Samaritans and Jews: The Origins of Samaritanism Reconsidered* (Atlanta, GA: John Knox Press).

Crowfoot, J.W.
1957   'Introduction', in J.W. Crowfoot, G.M. Crowfoot and K.M. Kenyon (eds), *The Objects from Samaria* (Samaria-Sebaste – Reports of the Work of the Joint Expedition in 1931–33 and of the British Expedition in 1935, 3; London: Palestine Exploration Fund): 1–8.

Dalley, S.
1985   'Foreign Chariotry and Cavalry in the Armies of Tiglath-pileser III and Sargon II', *Iraq* 47: 31–48.

Dar, S.
1986   *Landscape and Pattern: An Archaeological Survey of Samaria 800 BCE–636 CE* (BAR International Series 308[i]; Oxford: BAR).
1992   'Samaria (Archaeology of the Region)', in *ABD*, V: 926–31.
1993   'The Survey of Western Samaria', in *NEAEHL*, IV: 1314–16.

Davies, P.R.
1992   *Scribes and Schools: The Canonization of the Hebrew Scriptures. Library of Ancient Israel* (Louisville, KY: Westminster John Knox Press).
2001   'Exile? What Exile? Whose Exile?', in L.L. Grabbe (ed.), *Leading Captivity Captive: 'The Exile' as History and Ideology* (JSOTSup, 278; Sheffield: Sheffield Academic Press): 128–38.

Day, J.
2000   *Yahweh and the Gods and Goddesses of Canaan* (JSOTSup, 265; Sheffield: Sheffield Academic Press).

De Odorico, M.
1995   *The Use of Numbers and Quantifications in the Assyrian Royal Inscriptions* (SAAS, 3; Helsinki: Neo-Assyrian Text Corpus Project).

Dever, W.G.
1997   'Bethel', in *OEANE*, I: 300–301.

Dexinger, F.
1992   'Der Ursprung der Samaritaner im Spiegel der frühen Quellen', in F. Dexinger
         and R. Pummer (eds), *Die Samaritaner* (Wege der Forschung, 604; Darmstadt:
         Wissenschaftliche Buchgesellschaft): 76–103.

Diakonoff, I.M.
1991   ערי מדי: The Cities of the Medes', in M. Cogan and I. Eph'al (eds), *Ah,
         Assyria: Studies in Assyrian History and Ancient Near Eastern Historiography
         Presented to Hayim Tadmor* (ScrHier, 33; Jerusalem: Magnes Press): 13–20.

Donner, H.
1977   'The Separate States of Israel and Judah', in J.H. Hayes and J.M. Miller (eds),
         Israelite and Judean History (London: SCM Press): 381–434.

1986   *Geschichte des Volkes Israel und seiner Nachbarn in Grundzügen, II: Von der
         Königszeit bis zu Alexander dem Grossen mit einem Ausblick auf die Geschichte
         des Judentums bis Bar Kochba* (Grundrisse zum Alten Testament, 4.2;
         Göttingen: Vandenhoeck & Ruprecht).

Dothan, M.
1993   'Tel Esur', in *NEAEHL*, II: 426–28.

Eph'al, I.
1991   ' "The Samarian(s)" in the Assyrian Sources', in M. Cogan and I. Eph'al (eds),
         *Ah, Assyria: Studies in Assyrian history and Ancient Near Eastern
         Historiography Presented to Hayim Tadmor* (ScrHier, 33; Jerusalem: Magnes
         Press): 36–45.

1998   'Changes in Palestine during the Persian Period in Light of Epigraphic
         Sources', *IEJ* 48: 106–19.

Faust, A.
2003   'Judah in the Sixth Century B.C.E.: A Rural Perspective', *PEQ* 135: 37–53.

Finkelstein, I.
1988–89 'The Land of Ephraim Survey, 1980–1987: Preliminary Report', *Tel Aviv* 15–
         16: 117–83.

1993   'Southern Samarian Hills Survey', in *NEAEHL*, IV: 1313–14.

Finkelstein, I., Z. Lederman and S. Bunimovitz
1997   *Highlands of Many Cultures: The Southern Samaria Survey* (2 vols; Tel Aviv:
         Institute of Archaeology of Tel Aviv Publications Section).

Finkelstein, I., and D. Ussishkin
2000   'Archaeological and Historical Conclusions', in I. Finkelstein, D. Ussishkin
         and B. Halpern (eds), *Megiddo, III: Seasons 1992–96* (Tel Aviv: Institute of
         Archaeology), II: 576–605.

Franklin, N.
1994   'The Room V Reliefs at Dur-Sharrukin and Sargon II's Western Campaigns',
         Tel Aviv 21: 255–75.

Fritz, V.
1993   'Tel Chinnereth', in *NEAEHL*, I: 299–301.

Fuchs, A.
1994   *Die Inschriften Sargons II. aus Khorsabad* (Göttingen: Cuvillier).

Gadd, C.J.
1954   'Inscribed Prisms of Sargon II from Nimrud', *Iraq* 16: 173–201.

Gal, G., and Y. Alexandre
    2000   Ḥorbat Rosh Zayit: *An Iron Age Storage Fort and Village* (IAA Reports, 8; Jerusalem: Israel Exploration Society).

Gal, Z.
    1992   *Lower Galilee During the Iron Age* (ASOR Dissertation Series, 8; Winona Lake, IN: Eisenbrauns).

Galil, G.
    2000   'A New Look at the Inscriptions of Tiglath-pileser III', *Bib* 81: 511–20.

Glock, A.E.
    1993   'Taanach', in *NEAEHL*, IV: 1428–33.
    1997   'Taanach', in *OEANE*, V: 149.

Grabbe, L.L.
    2001   ' "The Exile" under the Theodolite: Historiography as Triangulation', in L.L. Grabbe (ed.), *Leading Captivity Captive: 'The Exile' as History and Ideology* (JSOTSup, 278; Sheffield: Sheffield Academic Press): 80–100.

Gray, J.
    1974   *I and II Kings* (OTL; Philadelphia: Westminster Press, 3rd edn).

Grayson, A.K.
    1975   *Assyrian and Babylonian Chronicles* (TCS, 5; Locust Valley: Augustin). Reprinted Winona Lake, IN: Eisenbrauns, 2000.

Grelot, P.
    1972   *Documents araméens d'Egypte* (LAPO, 5; Paris: Editions du Cerf).

Gropp, D.M.
    1992   'Samaria (Papyri)', in *ABD*, V: 931–32.
    2001   Wadi Daliyeh, II: The Samaria Papyri from Wadi Daliyeh (DJD, 28; Oxford: Clarendon Press).

Halpern, B.
    2000   'Centre and Sentry: Megiddo's Role in Transit, Administration and Trade', in I. Finkelstein, D. Ussishkin and B. Halpern (eds), *Megiddo*, III: *Seasons 1992–96* (Tel Aviv: Institute of Archaeology), II: 535–75.

Herrmann, S.
    1981   *A History of Israel in Old Testament Times* (trans. John Bowden; Philadelphia: Fortress Press).

Hjelm, I.
    2000   *The Samaritans and Early Judaism: A Literary Analysis* (JSOTSup, 303; Sheffield: Sheffield Academic Press).

Japhet, S.
    1989   *The Ideology of the Book of Chronicles and its Place in Biblical Thought* (Beiträge zur Erforschung des Alten Testaments, 9; Frankfurt am Main: Peter Lang).

Joffe, A.H., E.H. Cline and O. Lipschits
    2000   'Area H', in I. Finkelstein, D. Ussishkin and B. Halpern (eds), *Megiddo*, III: *Seasons 1992–96* (Tel Aviv: Institute of Archaeology), II: 140–60.

Kelso, J.L.
    1968   *The Excavation of Bethel (1934–60)* (AASOR, 39; Cambridge, MA: ASOR).

Kenyon, K.M.
    1957   'Israelite Pottery, 1: Stratified Groups', in J.W. Crowfoot, G.M. Crowfoot

and K.M. Kenyon (eds), *The Objects from Samaria* (Samaria-Sebaste –
Reports of the Work of the Joint Expedition in 1931–33 and of the British
Expedition in 1935, 3; London: Palestine Exploration Fund): 94–133.

Knoppers, G.N.
1994   *Two Nations Under God: The Deuteronomistic History of Solomon and the
         Dual Monarchies* (HSM, 54; Atlanta, GA: Scholars Press).
1997   'The Vanishing Solomon: The Disappearance of the United Monarchy from
         Recent Histories of Ancient Israel', *JBL* 116: 19–44.
1999   'The History of the Monarchy: Developments and Detours', in D.W. Baker
         and B.T. Arnold (eds), *The Face of Old Testament Studies* (Grand Rapids, MI:
         Baker Book House): 207–35.

Kuhrt, A.
1995   *The Ancient Near East c. 3000–330 BC* (2 vols; London: Routledge).

Lehmann, G.
1998   'Trends in Local Pottery Development of the Late Iron Age and Persian
         Period in Syria and Lebanon, ca. 700 to 300 BC', *BASOR* 311: 7–37.

Lemaire, A.
2001   'Epigraphie et religion en Palestine à l'époque achéménide', *Transeuphratène*
         22: 97–113.

Lemche, N.P.
1998   *The Israelites in History and Tradition* (London: SPCK).

Lipschits, O.
1998   'Nebuchadrezzar's Policy in "Ḥattu-Land" and the Fate of the Kingdom of
         Judah', *UF* 30: 467–87.
1999   'The History of the Benjamin Region under Babylonian Rule', *Tel Aviv* 26:
         155–90.
2001   'Judah, Jerusalem, and the Temple 586–539 B.C.', *Transeuphratène* 22: 129–42.
2003   'Demographic Changes in Judah between the Seventh and the Fifth Centuries
         B.C.E.', in O. Lipschits and J. Blenkinsopp (eds), *Judah and the Judeans in the
         Neo-Babylonian Period* (Winona Lake, IN: Eisenbrauns): 323–76.

McKay, J.W.
1973   *Religion in Judah under the Assyrians 732–609 B.C.* (SBT, 2nd series, 26;
         Naperville, IL: Allenson).

Machinist, P.
1992   'Palestine, Administration of (Assyro-Babylonian)', in *ABD*, V: 69–81.

Mazar, A.
1990   *Archaeology of the Land of the Bible 10,000–586 B.C.E.* (ABRL; Garden City,
         NY: Doubleday).
1993   'Beth-Shean', in *NEAEHL*, I: 214–23.

Mazar, B.
1993   'Kinneret', in *NEAEHL*, II: 872–73.

Meyers, J.M.
1965   *II Chronicles* (AB, 13; Garden City, NY: Doubleday).

Miller, J.M., and J.H. Hayes
1986   *A History of Ancient Israel and Judah* (Philadelphia: Westminster Press).

Mitchell, T.C.
1991   'Israel and Judah from the Coming of the Assyrian Domination until the Fall

of Samaria, and the Struggle for Independence in Judah (c. 750–700 B.C.)', in J. Boardman *et al.* (eds), *The Cambridge Ancient History*, III.2: *The Assyrian and Babylonian Empires and Other States of the Near East, from the Eighth to the Sixth Centuries BC* (Cambridge: Cambridge University Press, 2nd edn): 322–70.

Na'aman, N.

1990   'The Historical Background to the Conquest of Samaria (720 BC)', *Bib* 71: 206–25.

1993   'Population Changes following the Assyrian Deportations', *Tel Aviv* 20: 104–24.

1995a   'Rezin of Damascus and the Land of Gilead', *ZDPV* 111: 105–17.

1995b   'Tiglath-pileser III's Campaigns against Tyre and Israel (734–732 B.C.E.)', *Tel Aviv* 22: 271–77.

Na'aman, N., and R. Zadok

1988   'Sargon II's Deportations to Israel and Philistia', *JCS* 40: 36–46.

Negev, A. and S. Gibson

2001   *Archaeological Encyclopedia of the Holy Land* (New York: Continuum, rev. edn).

Oded, B.

1979   *Mass Deportations and Deportees in the Neo-Assyrian Empire* (Wiesbaden: Reichert).

1995   'Observations on the Israelite/Judaean Exiles in Mesopotamia during the Eighth–Sixth Centuries BCE', in K. van Lerberghe and A. Schoors (eds), *Immigration and Emigration within the Ancient Near East: Festschrift E. Lipiński* (OLA, 65; Leuven: Peeters/Departement Oriëntalistiek): 205–12.

1997   'The Inscriptions of Tiglath-pileser III: Review Article', *IEJ* 47: 110–11.

2000   'The Settlements of the Israelite and the Judean Exiles in Mesopotamia in the 8th–6th Centuries BCE', in G. Galil and M. Weinfeld (eds), *Studies in Historical Geography and Biblical Historiography Presented to Zecharia Kallai* (VTSup, 81; Leiden: E.J. Brill): 91–103.

Ofer, A.

1993a   'The Highland of Judah during the Biblical Period' (PhD dissertation, Tel Aviv University) (Hebrew).

1993b   'Judean Hills Survey', in *NEAEHL*, III: 814–16.

1994   ' "All the Hill Country of Judah": From a Settlement Fringe to a Prosperous Monarchy', in I. Finkelstein and N. Na'aman (eds), *From Nomadism to Monarchy* (Jerusalem: Israel Exploration Society): 92–121.

Orlinsky, H.M.

1960   *Ancient Israel* (Ithaca, NY: Cornell University Press, 2nd edn).

Peersmann, J.

2000   'Assyrian Magiddu: The Town Planning of Stratum III', in I. Finkelstein, D. Ussishkin and B. Halpern (eds), *Megiddo, III: Seasons 1992–96* (Tel Aviv: Institute of Archaeology), II: 524–34.

Porten, B.

1968   *Archives from Elephantine* (Berkeley: University of California Press).

Porten, B., and A. Yardeni

1986   *Textbook of Aramaic Documents from Ancient Egypt: Newly Copied, Edited* and *Translated into Hebrew and English*, I: *Letters* (Jerusalem: The Hebrew University, Department of the History of the Jewish People).

Schur, N.
1989   *History of the Samaritans* (Beiträge zur Erforschung des Alten Testaments, 18; Frankfurt am Main: Peter Lang).

Spieckermann, H.
1982   *Juda unter Assur in der Sargonidenzeit* (FRLANT, 129; Göttingen: Vandenhoeck & Ruprecht).

Stern, E.
1994   *Dor: Ruler of the Seas* (Jerusalem: Israel Exploration Society).
2001   *Archaeology of the Land of the Bible*, II: *The Assyrian, Babylonian, and Persian Periods* 732–332 BCE (ABRL; New York: Doubleday).

Tadmor, H.
1958   'The Campaigns of Sargon II of Assur: A Chronological–Historical Study', *JCS* 12: 22–40, 77–100.
1983   'Some Aspects of the History of Samaria during the Biblical Period', *Jerusalem Cathedra* 3: 1–11.
1994   *The Inscriptions of Tiglath-pileser III King of Assyria* (Jerusalem: Israel Academy of Sciences and Humanities).

Tappy, R.E.
2001   *The Archaeology of Israelite Samaria*, I: *The Eighth Century BCE* (HSS, 50; Winona Lake, IN: Eisenbrauns).

Thompson, T.L.
1992   *Early History of the Israelite People: From the Written and Archaeological Sources* (SHANE, 4; Leiden: E.J. Brill).
1997   'Defining History and Ethnicity in the South Levant', in L.L. Grabbe (ed.), *Can a 'History of Israel' be Written?* (JSOTSup, 245; Sheffield: Sheffield Academic Press): 166–87.
1999   *The Mythic Past: Biblical Archaeology and the Myth of Israel* (New York: Basic books). Also published as *The Bible in History: How Writers Create a Past* (London: Jonathan Cape, 1999).
2001   'The Exile in History and Myth: A Response to Hans Barstad', in L.L. Grabbe (ed.), *Leading Captivity Captive: 'The Exile' as History and Ideology* (JSOTSup, 278; Sheffield: Sheffield Academic Press): 101–18.

Timm, S.
1989–90 'Die Eroberung Israels (Samarias) 722 v. Chr. aus assyrisch-babylonischer Sicht', *WO* 20/21: 62–82.

Vaux, R. de
1958–60 *Les Institutions de l'Ancien Testament* (2 vols; Paris: Cerf). ET *Ancient Israel: Its Life and Institutions* (trans. J. McHugh; 2 vols; New York: McGraw-Hill, 2nd edn, 1965).

Watkins, L.
1997   'Survey of Southern Samaria', in *OEANE*, V: 66–68.

Whitelam, K.W.
1996   *The Invention of Ancient Israel* (London: Routledge).

Willi, T.
    1995	*Juda – Jehud – Israel: Studien zum Selbstverständnis des Judentums in persischer Zeit* (FAT, 12; Tübingen: J.C.B. Mohr).
Williamson, H.G.M.
    1977	*Israel in the Books of Chronicles* (Cambridge: Cambridge University Press).
Würthwein, E.
    1984	*Die Bücher der Könige: 1 Kön. 17–2 Kön. 25* (ATD, 11.2; Göttingen: Vandenhoeck & Ruprecht).
Yadin, Y.
    1993	'Hazor', in *NEAEHL*, II: 594–603.
Younger, K.L.
    1998	'The Deportations of the Israelites', *JBL* 117: 201–27.
    1999	'The Fall of Samaria in the Light of Recent Research', *CBQ* 61: 461–82.
    2000a	'Sargon II: Nimrud Prisms D & E (2.118D)', in W.W. Hallo and K.L. Younger (eds), *The Context of Scripture*, III: *Monumental Inscriptions from the Biblical World* (Leiden: E.J. Brill): 295–96.
    2000b	'Tiglath-pileser III: Summary Inscription 4 (2.117C)', in W.W. Hallo and K.L. Younger (eds), *The Context of Scripture*, III: *Monumental Inscriptions from the Biblical World* (Leiden: E.J. Brill): 287–88
Zertal, A.
    1989	'The Wedge-Shaped Decorated Bowl and the Origin of the Samaritans', *BASOR* 276: 77–84.
    1990	'The Pahwah of Samaria (Northern Israel) during the Persian Period: Types of Settlement, Economy, History and New Discoveries', *Transeuphratène* 3: 9–30.
    1993a	'Khirbet el-Ḥammam', in *NEAEHL*, II: 563–65.
    1993b	'The Mount Manasseh (Northern Samarian Hills) Survey', in *NEAEHL*, III: 1311–12.
    1999	'The Province of Samaria During the Persian and Hellenistic Periods', in Y. Avishur and R. Deutsch (eds), *Michael: Historical, Epigraphical and Biblical Studies in Honor of Professor Michael Heltzer* (Tel Aviv: Archaeological Centre Publications): 75*-98* (Hebrew).
    2001	'The Heart of the Monarchy: Pattern of Settlement and Historical Considerations of the Israelite Kingdom of Samaria', in A. Mazar (ed.), *Studies in the Archaeology of the Iron Age in Israel and Jordan* (JSOTSup, 331; Sheffield: Sheffield Academic Press): 38–64.

Chapter 9

IN SEARCH OF THE PRE-EXILIC ISAIAH

H.G.M. Williamson

A recent review of a monograph on Sennacherib's campaign to Judah in 701 BCE as presented in the book of Isaiah accepts that the author has made some telling points against those who would date all the material late, particularly in connection with the passages which have a parallel in the books of Kings. It then maintains that as regards the relevant oracular material in Isaiah, scholars are more likely to be persuaded or not by their preconceptions. Rudman concludes his review with the words, 'Intelligent waverers may, as they have always done, go either way' (Rudman 2001: 229).

While this may initially sound like a counsel of despair and is hardly an accurate description of the whole history of study of the book of Isaiah, it is nevertheless a reasonable assessment of the point which current discussion has reached. While mainstream scholarship in the nineteenth century came to agree that nothing following ch. 39 could be attributed to the eighth-century Isaiah,[1] the twentieth century followed in the footsteps of Duhm (1892) in finding a considerable amount of later material in chs 1–39 as well. This concerned both some substantial blocks of material, such as chs 24–27 and 34–35, and a considerable number of smaller additions interspersed with what were generally regarded as genuinely Isaianic sayings. On some of these, such as 4.2–6 and ch. 12, there would be little disagreement, while others, such as 8.23–9.6 (ET 9.1–7) or 11.1–9, have continued to be disputed. The basic method adopted in these discussions reached its climax in the great commentary of Wildberger (1972–82), who assumed Isaianic authorship unless the contrary could be demonstrated. The tag that 'nothing precludes authorship by Isaiah' was held to be sufficient to conclude that Isaiah was in fact the author.

---

1. The acceptance of this view even by the conservative Franz Delitzsch in the fourth edition of his commentary (1889) is perhaps the most telling confirmation of this point; cf. Driver 1889–90.

Although this assumption is still held by the majority of recent writers, it has been challenged along two lines. On the one hand, the factors which might be thought to preclude Isaianic authorship have increased considerably in the opinion of some, such as Werner (1986, 1988) and to a lesser extent Vermeylen (1977), with the consequence that the amount of admittedly early material with which other more contentious passages might be compared in order to argue they too are early has diminished. This line of argument then has a tendency to snowball (cf. Hardmeier 1986). As the initial props for a conservative dating are successively whittled away, so less and less can be securely regarded as original.

On the other hand, a more radical approach was adopted, as is well known, by Kaiser (1973, 1981), who not only indicated how much of Isaiah could be reasonably read as reflecting the concerns of the much later post-exilic community, but also effectively shifted the ground of the debate away from an assumption of authorship by Isaiah unless the contrary could be proved to a situation where Isaiah could not be held responsible for anything unless there were compelling grounds to establish that no alternative was possible. While such a radical departure from the standard scholarly agenda was met initially with almost total scepticism, there are more recent signs that others are being attracted to this approach. The monograph of Becker (1997) is only the most significant representative of this trend. Both scholars, it is true, still attribute a small handful of verses to Isaiah, though they are not in agreement as to which verses those are.

Whether or not one agrees with the results of these newer studies, they certainly raise an interesting question in the context of the present volume. How can one prove that anything comes from the eighth rather than, say, the fifth century BCE? And even if one can establish with some degree of probability that a passage was of pre-exilic origin, how can we tell if it was written by Isaiah or by some other contemporary or by a somewhat later, but still pre-exilic, disciple or redactor?[2] After all, it is well over a century since de Lagarde (1877: 142) advanced his rather neglected theory that Isaiah 1–39 was a post-exilic anthology of pre-exilic oracles and sayings, any or none of which might have been authored by someone called Isaiah.

The answer to these questions is, of course, that in the case of texts which are demonstrably more than 2000 years old, nothing can be 'proved', with the result that no remarks of mine or anyone else's will be able to alter the opinion of somebody who persists in the (equally

---

2.   This latter question arises in particular in the wake of Barth's influential theory (1977) of a significant Josianic redaction, though of course that in itself presupposes the existence of earlier material in the first place.

unprovable) assumption that nothing in the book of Isaiah was committed to writing before the post-exilic period. Nevertheless, some points can be reasonably held to be infinitely more probable than others, and what the recent late-daters have obliged us to do for the first time is to set about establishing such a probability, if it can be done, on positive grounds for at least a minimum amount of material rather than the previous approach of assuming an early date unless that could be shown to be untenable. Arguments against claims for a late date – the traditional procedure in conservative apologetic – will no longer suffice. The current situation demands the adoption of a whole new agenda.

In the nature of the case, it is likely that the amount of material which is amenable to such anaysis will be relatively small. As a result, were one to restrict one's portrayal of 'the historical Isaiah' to this material, it is probable that a highly distorted picture would emerge. I am reminded of the procedure adopted in my undergraduate days by those who were seeking the *ipsissima verba* of Jesus (whether it is still followed by New Testament scholars I do not know). I was taught that any saying of Jesus for which a parallel could be found in earlier writings, such as the Old Testament, or in early Christian literature, or in later writings for which dependence on an early tradition might be posited, as with the targums, or in contemporary writings of whatever origin (not necessarily Jewish) should be discounted. Any saying which came into any of these categories might in theory have been wrongly ascribed to Jesus by his later followers. The only sayings which could pass this test, therefore, were those which were unique and preferably in blatant contradiction both with Jesus's Jewish environment and with the ethos of the early Christian community which claimed to follow him. While such a minimum core was indeed deemed to survive, the portrayal of the Jesus which emerged from them was one which hardly seemed historically credible precisely because it insisted on detaching Jesus from his historical environment. We appear to be caught in a similar bind with regard to the historical Isaiah. But we have to start somewhere, and provided we recognize that it is only the start of the story, and not the whole story, there is no harm in it.[3]

There are, in fact, a number of methods which may be deployed in this search for pre-exilic material in Isaiah, as I shall try to illustrate in the remainder of this paper. Even if they are successful, it has to be admitted

---

3. For an attempt to summarize historical information from Isa. 1–39 on the basis of conventional literary-critical conclusions, see Schoors 1997. While there is much here with which personally I should agree, it is clear that it rests throughout on critical judgments which, in the nature of the case, will not be universally shared.

at the outset that, applying this minimalist approach consistently, it cannot be demonstrated that Isaiah himself wrote any of them. However, in order to avoid more pedantry than I have already indulged in, I shall not pursue the detail of that particular line of inquiry further, since it is in any case a secondary task within the guidelines of this volume.

For some unknown reason, different lines of argument appeal with greater force to one student than to another, so I can only hope that one or another of the methods illustrated here will be found convincing by different readers. The one which I instinctively find most compelling is that where the account of a purportedly early event for which there is no other direct evidence in the biblical text is corroborated by some contemporary external source which could not, in all probability, have been known to a later biblical writer. The parade example here is the invasion of Palestine by the Pharaoh Shishak, as mentioned in 1 Kgs 14.25. An account of this campaign by Shishak (or rather, Shoshenq) survives on a pylon of the Egyptian temple at Karnak (ancient Thebes).[4] Now it might be considered that a post-exilic Jerusalem resident went on holiday to Egypt and read, or more likely had read to him, the text of this inscription, and made up the account in Kings on the strength of it, but it seems improbable. I consider it not unreasonable to conclude that an account of Shishak's invasion was preserved in Judah and came to be incorporated into the Deuteronomistic history. That is not to deny that it may have been garbled from a historical point of view, nor that it has been given a heavily theological slant by the later writer, but that some record survived from near the time of the event seems to me as certain as anything can be in this type of inquiry (cf. Na'aman 1992 and especially 1996: 170–73). The question then is whether there are any similar examples in the first part of Isaiah.

The first example which comes to mind is, of course, the narrative account of Sennacherib's invasion in chs 36–37. However much allowance is made for theological elaboration by the biblical writer, the coincidences with Sennacherib's own famous accounts (and, to the extent that they are relevant, the results of the excavations at Lachish; cf. Ussishkin 1982) are so striking that even the most sceptical of recent scholars (e.g. Davies 1992: 32–35) have admitted that there is some historical recollection here which goes back to the events in question. Unfortunately, however, this example does not meet our criteria, since the account is parallel with that

---

4. For a translation, references and discussion, see conveniently Kitchen 1973: 293–300 and 432–47. Kitchen himself places great confidence in the biblical accounts. Whether justified or not, it is clear that in the context of the present exercise there is a danger here of circular argument. That does not, however, affect the main point argued above.

in 2 Kings 18–19, and probably dependent upon it.[5] Isaianic authorship is highly unlikely, therefore.

Initially more promising is the account in ch. 20, which talks about Isaiah going naked and barefoot in Jerusalem for three years. The account begins by setting the scene in these words: 'In the year that the commander-in-chief, who was sent by King Sargon of Assyria, came to Ashdod and fought against it and took it ...'. Without going into detail,[6] it is noteworthy that this account has no parallel elsewhere in the Hebrew Bible, and indeed that this is the only explicit reference to Sargon at all. Yet the narrative coincides so closely with Sargon's own account of the affair[7] and with fragments of an Assyrian victory stele found at Ashdod itself (Tadmor 1967) that it is impossible to doubt that a contemporary report underlies this part, at least, of the chapter.

Further inspection raises problems for our particular purpose, however. This has less to do with the unevennesses in the chapter which suggest that in its present form it is the result of later reflection on the course of the event (real though these are) as with the whole genre and style of the chapter. It is a third-person account of Isaiah's involvement in the affair and stylistically it displays many characteristics of Deuteronomistic-type historiographical narrative (these are most cogently summarized by Blenkinsopp 2000a: 321–22 and 2000b). This at once puts the chapter in the same category of writing as chs 36–39, even though it has no parallel in Kings, and with others I have argued elsewhere that the first part of ch. 7 is also closely related in a variety of ways with these chapters (Williamson 1998: 86–90). I am thus strengthened in my opinion that there once existed a (loosely) Deuteronomistic series of narratives about Isaiah's involvement in some of the major national affairs of his time and that, for whatever reason, only part of these found their way into Kings, while others were also incorporated into the book of Isaiah.

The upshot of this analysis is that, as with chs 36–39, there is evidence in Isaiah for solid historical memory in parts of Isaiah and that this rests ultimately on pre-exilic annals or accounts. The latter cannot be attributed to Isaiah himself, however, even though they show awareness of some of his characteristic interests and style, suggestive of a later sympathetic imitator. Whatever their original purpose, it is likely that they were included in the book, not necessarily all at the same time, in order

5. I sought to defend this conclusion, with reference to some alternative proposals, in Williamson 1994: 189–211. The objections to my arguments voiced by Vermeylen (1997) have in turn been examined and rejected by Gonçalves (1999).

6. For which see Wildberger (1978: 752–53, ET 1997: 289–90); Blenkinsopp (2000a: 322); see too Halpern (2000: 548).

7. See conveniently *ANET*, 286–87; for a full presentation, with reference to all previous editions, see Fuchs (1998), with a particular discussion of the chronology of the campaign on pp. 124–31.

primarily to serve the interests of later redactional concerns, which cannot be pursued here in detail.

A final example within this first methodological category[8] comes in ch. 22, which is generally agreed to refer to Isaiah's response to the events of 701.[9] Included within the first half of the chapter is an account of the measures which had been taken in preparation for the rebellion, with reference to weapons, water supply and fortification. In particular, v. 10 states that 'You counted the houses of Jerusalem, and you broke down the houses to fortify the wall'.[10] Excavations on the western hill of ancient Jerusalem have unearthed extensive remains of a substantial wall which cut through modest eighth-century houses, and this has been securely associated with Hezekiah's defensive measures at this time (Avigad 1970). Given the extent of the later Babylonian destruction of the city, it seems unlikely that this point of detail would have been known to a post-exilic writer.[11] The particular significance of this note, brief though it is, is that, unlike the previous examples we have considered, it comes within a purported saying of Isaiah himself.[12]

This conclusion, which personally I find convincing, can be got round in one of two ways. First, many commentators hold that vv. 8b-11, or alternatively 9b-11a, are a later addition to their present context (for full

8.   There are no doubt other examples which might be mentioned, but as already stressed my purpose in this paper is to discuss method rather than to attempt to collect every example of eighth-century material in Isaiah. Thus, for example, John Day, the editor of this volume, has suggested that ch. 18 is likely to include early material, since this is an oracle against Kush (Nubia), and in the time of Isaiah the Nubian 25th dynasty was ruling Egypt, which would explain why Nubia is given prominence here. He has also observed that the oracle against Damascus (Isa. 17) is best dated before 732 BCE, when Damascus fell. Independently, similar comments have been put to me by M.J. de Jong of Leiden, with regard (again) to Kush and also (most strongly, in his opinion) to Ephraim and Samaria.

9.   Earlier dates have occasionally been proposed, but have never attracted significant support; see, for instance, Procksch (1930: 276–77); Vermeylen (1977: 324); Hayes and Irvine (1987: 277). Gallagher (1999: 60–74) has recently proposed the slightly earlier date of 704 BCE.

10.   Strangely, Wildberger (1978: 823, ET 1997: 369) asserts that 'לבצר החומה hardly means "strengthen the wall", but rather "make it hard to get by"'. Although the piel of בצר occurs nowhere else, other forms of the verb are used a number of times with 'city' or 'wall' with the meaning 'fortify' (see especially 2.15 for a close Isaianic parallel), so that Wildberger's objection and his alternative exegesis seem perverse.

11.   In addition, v. 9b, 'you collected the waters of the lower pool', is usually associated with the construction of Hezekiah's tunnel. While this is reasonable, it is clear from other sources (e.g. 2 Chron. 32.30) that independent knowledge of this survived into the post-exilic period. In terms of the minimalist method being pursued here, this example should therefore be discounted, even though it is entirely reasonable in fact to see this as a further contemporary note.

12.   Willis (1993) has sought to reach a similar conclusion with regard to the second half of the chapter as well. While plausible in their own terms, his arguments do not, however, meet the criteria adopted for the present discussion.

documentation, see Gonçalves 1986: 236–37). The issue is complicated, and no discussion here would settle it to everyone's satisfaction; stout defenders of the passage's unity can equally easily be cited (e.g. Childs 1967: 22–27; Wildberger 1978: 809–11, ET 1997: 353–56; Emerton 1980; Gonçalves 1986: 235–40; Sweeney 1996: 288–302; Gallagher 1999: 60–74). But this whole line of attack is not particularly damaging to our case, since, as Donner (1964: 128), who thinks that 9b-11a has been added later, points out, the source from which the added material was drawn must have been well informed. In other words, it would still faithfully reflect pre-exilic conditions.

More seriously, however, Jer. 33.4 indicates that comparable measures were taken in preparation for the later Babylonian siege: '. . . concerning the houses of this city and the houses of the kings of Judah that were torn down to make a defence against the siege-ramps and before the sword'. This, together with conclusions drawn from an assumption that a later addition to a text must reflect later circumstances, has therefore enabled commentators to conclude that we have a recollection of events long after Isaiah's time. While I do not myself regard this as a necessary conclusion, it has to be conceded that, to cite Rudman once again, 'intelligent waverers may, as they have always done, go either way'.

I summarize the results of applying this first method, therefore, by concluding that there is good evidence for finding solid, pre-exilic historical memory at several points in Isaiah 1–39, but that association with Isaiah's own authorship is as yet not firmly established. In the case of chs 7, 20 and 36–39, those memories are incorporated now into material which shows much evidence of later reflection, so that it is not what one might call pristine, while ch. 22 is theoretically open to alternative explanation. Despite this minimal conclusion, it establishes one very important point, namely that somehow pre-exilic material, including the details of names and events, could and did survive the fall of Jerusalem and the exile. While the circumstances in which this happened remain unknown, it is helpful as we proceed not to be troubled by the a priori argument that nothing could have survived in writing.

A second method which may be illustrated here with two examples is that which looks for the reflection in positive terms of beliefs and practices which came to be changed and even condemned in the post-exilic period. While not completely watertight, this method assumes that it is highly improbable that a later writer would have ascribed words to Isaiah, whom *ex hypothesi* he admired, which could have been rapidly turned by opponents to discredit him. The rewriting of parts of Samuel–Kings by the Chronicler illustrates well how later sensitivities were in fact allowed to influence the presentation of the pre-exilic past. While it is reasonable to accept that some examples of what were later regarded as unacceptable practice 'slipped through the net' of the reviser, it is less plausible to hold that such descriptions were introduced in the later period from scratch.

The first example in Isaiah derives from the list of the leaders of society in 3.2–3. Here, alongside such dignitaries as the military leader, judge, prophet and elder, we find the diviner (קֹסֵם), one skilled in magic practices (חֲכַם חֲרָשִׁים)[13] and the expert in charms (נְבוֹן לַחַשׁ).[14] In the pre-exilic period this causes no difficulty, for recent studies have emphasized the extent to which magical practices (however defined in detail) were accepted in ancient Israel and Judah (see, for instance, Cryer 1994; Grabbe 1995: 119–51; Jeffers 1996; Laato 1996: 198–203). In some of the legal corpora, however, such practices are explicitly condemned (e.g. Lev. 19.26, 31; 20.27; Deut. 18.9–14, with specific reference to קֹסֵם), and they are cited as part of the cause for the loss of both the northern (2 Kgs 17.17) and by implication the southern (2 Kgs 21.6) kingdoms. It is thus not surprising that in the post-exilic period such practices came to be viewed as inherently wrong. Their occurrence in Isa. 3.2–3 alongside other respected leaders is thus strong *prima facie* evidence for the pre-exilic origin of this passage (see especially Deck 1991: 150–51).

Once again, a few scholars, such as Gray (1912: 63) and Porath (1994: 36–37), have proposed that the list as a whole is a later addition. If correct,

13. LXX, Pesh (which also avoids a magical association for נְבוֹן לַחַשׁ following by rendering 'one who undertands counsel') and Vg all take this as a reference to skilled builders or craftsmen, which would normally be vocalized חֲרָשִׁים. Delitzsch (1889: 83), followed by Kissane (1941: 37–38) and Auvray (1972: 60), defends this sense even for the Masoretic pointing by appeal to 1 Chron. 4.14 and Neh. 11.35, but in each case this occurs in a place name (and the further use in 1 Chron. 4.14 is clearly dependent upon this), which is not, perhaps, sufficient to establish this as a standard alternative. Nor does Delitzsch's further argument that such skilled artisans were included among the leading citizens who were taken into exile in Babylon (2 Kgs 24; Jer. 24.1; 29.1) demonstrate that they would have been included in a list of those who were regarded by the Judaean society itself as having some kind of authority. Rather, in view of the parallel with the following phrase, there is much to be said for the widely accepted alternative opinion which sees here a *hapax legomenon*, חֶרֶשׁ, 'magic, sorcery'. This has cognates in several Semitic languages, including Ugaritic and some Aramaic dialects (cf. Jeffers 1996: 49–51). There is room for discussion about whether ultimately this is etymologically a separate root or a particular extension from the sense of craftsmanship, but for practical purposes it clearly functioned as a separate verb and noun by the time from which we have textual evidence.

14. The second term, לַחַשׁ, derives from a verb meaning 'to whisper', with cognates in Akkadian, Ugaritic, Aramaic and Phoenician. It is true that in some contexts this has the developed sense of snake-charming (cf. Jer. 8.17; Ps. 58.6, ET 5; Eccl. 10.11), but that is always made explicit by the context; it is not the case that such a meaning inheres in the word itself (cf. Jeffers 1996: 70–74). There is therefore no justification for reading that sense into it in a passage such as the present one (contra Porath 1994: 78). That such practices were not regarded as inherently malicious may be supported by the use of לַחַשׁ in proper names (assuming that the same root is in question): לַחַשׁ occurs on a pre-exilic seal (cf. Davies 1991: 153) and הַלּוֹחֵשׁ at Neh. 3.12 and 10.25.

this would mean that the passage could not be attributed to Isaiah, though it would still be pre-exilic. In fact, the argument is weak. The list interprets the image of v. 1, 'staff and stay', in line with the following elaboration in vv. 4–7, so that it is difficult not to retain it as part of the original form of the oracle.

Kaiser (1981: 77 and 80, ET 1983: 68 and 71), closely followed in this respect by Becker (1997: 162–69), seeks two ways round this evident difficulty for his view that the whole passage is post-exilic, but neither is in the least convincing. First, he classes the absence of a reference to the king in the list as a 'decisive indication' of its late date. It is nothing of the sort, for in that case the absence of priests from the list would be even more remarkable. Clearly at the very least the list is intended to be representative rather than comprehensive. Why the author chose not to include the king can only be the subject of speculation. I suggest that the reason is that, unlike those who are included, the king was single and unique, not one of a class to which any of the people might in principle aspire. He was thus in a different category from those who are listed. The same argument, *mutatis mutandis*, could explain the absence of priests as well, given their hereditary status. Further, as the following verses suggest, the leadership listed here as a whole is suggestive of local rather than state officials. The failure to mention the king can thus tell us nothing about the date of the list.

Secondly, Kaiser advances a metrical argument for making some deletions from the list. 'If we assume that the metre is the *qinah* or funeral dirge, then 2b and 3b, which do not fit, must be seen as disruptions.' And what are these disruptions? – precisely the terms which refer to divination and magic (together with the prophet). This seems to me to be too convenient by half! In the first place, the later it is thought that such people were added to a list of the leaders of society, the more implausible the proposal becomes. Secondly, given the ease with which lists can be grouped, why should it be just these titles rather than some of the others which are deleted to restore the desired metre? And thirdly, what is the reason for assuming that the metre must be the *qinah* in the first place? In my own analysis, I divide the list of leaders into pairs for the most part (with partial support from the presence or absence of the conjunction) with the exception that the final group is expanded to a triplet, a device which can be paralleled many times as a way of marking the close of a section within or at the end of a poetic unit. Arguments from metre in ancient Hebrew poetry are seldom convincing without additional support, and in this case Kaiser's argument seems more than usually weak.

I conclude, therefore, that the presence of diviners and magicians in 3.2–3 is a strong piece of evidence in favour of their pre-exilic, and probably Isaianic, origin.

The second example of this method relates to the attack on cultic abuse in 1.11–15. Although the precise function of this polemic has been debated (cf. Williamson 2002), it stands to reason that it must correspond accurately with what the people were actually doing in the cult and that they must have considered it to be legitimate; otherwise the polemic would be ineffective. Since we know a good deal about the history of the official cult in ancient Israel, it should be possible, in view of the abundance of references in this passage, to pinpoint where it stands in terms of that development. I believe it is possible to show that, taken as a whole, it must be pre-exilic, even though I fully accept that it could have been understood in a developed or altered sense in the context of the restored Second Temple, which I take to be the setting of the chapter's final redactor.

The most obvious example, with a textual reflex, is the re-reading of an orginally qal לִרְאוֹת פָּנָי, 'to see my face', to a niphal (with syncopated ה) לְרָאוֹת פָּנָי, 'to appear before me', in v. 12 (cf. Barthélemy 1986: 3–5). While the original reading need not imply the presence of an image of God in the pre-exilic temple (see recently Naʾaman 1999), its implication that lay worshippers had access to the heart of the sanctuary was more than could be accepted in later times; comparable considerations will have determined the Chronicler's rewriting of 2 Kgs 11.4–20 at 2 Chron. 23.1–21 (see Williamson 1982: 315–18). Similarly, some of the terminology used in this passage does not coincide with the later Priestly legislation for sacrifice: עתודים (v. 11), for instance, do not appear in the primary legislation (Lev. 1–7), though they do occur frequently in the descriptive passage in Num. 7.10–88, and still more strikingly מריאים are nowhere mentioned in legislative texts, but conversely they are used in association with sacrificial animals only in passages which reflect pre-exilic practice (2 Sam. 6.13; 1 Kgs 1.9, 19, 25; Ezek. 39.18; Amos 5.22). Several other terms developed more specific meanings with the passage of time, and so could easily be reapplied to the new circumstances, even though in the present context they suit the earlier usage better: מנחה (v. 13), for instance, is most easily understood here as carrying its earlier general sense of 'gift' when seeking favour from a superior (and so can be appropriately qualified by שוא: it will not attain what the worshipper intended), but will have been readily applied later to the cereal-offering of Leviticus 2; מקרא (v. 13) looks like an early general term for a religious gathering which was later specified in P as a מקרא קדש with tighter regulations; and עצרה (v. 13), a certainly pre-exilic term (cf. 1 Kgs 10.20), will have been associated with the later עצרת, the calendrical term for specific days when work ceased for a particularly solemn ceremony.[15]

---

15. Whether in addition Sabbath (v. 13) developed from a monthly to a weekly occasion and whether the cultic use of incense (v. 13) changed as opposed to being merely more tightly regulated remain disputed matters, and so should not be drawn in as evidence at this point.

It may be worth noting in passing that this process was continued even further in the Septuagint, where קְרֹא מִקְרָא became 'the great day' (i.e. the Day of Atonement).[16] This, together with reflection on Joel 1.14 and 2.15, could well have influenced the translator to introduce a reference to fasting in the next clause. If so, the evidence for emending אָוֶן to צוֹם, as often proposed, is greatly reduced,[17] and the view that the passage is a specific rather than a categorical condemnation of the cult is strengthened.

The cumulative force of all these details makes it overwhelmingly probable that this passage reflects aspects of the pre-exilic cult, and that however much it may have been possible to reapply them to later circumstances it could never have served its purpose if it had been written from scratch in this form at that later time.

If these two examples of the second method in search of the pre-exilic Isaiah are sound, then they mark an important advance on the first in that they both relate to prophetic sayings rather than the record of events. Neither is explicitly ascribed to Isaiah, but I do not know of a stronger candidate for authorship.

The third method is both more slippery in terms of detail but equally more far-reaching in terms of its cumulative effect. I refer to the use of quotations and allusions by later writers, a subject which is attracting a great deal of attention at the present time. If it can be demonstrated that one author is dependent in literary terms upon another, and if the date of the dependent author can be determined, then that establishes a *terminus ad quem* for the earlier author.

I have no wish to underestimate the force of those two 'ifs', especially in the present context, where we are looking for a secure basis on which to build rather than adding further suggestions and speculations to an already disputed field. At the same time, space limitations must be respected! So far as the broad issues of method are concerned, therefore, I must content myself with referring to the full recent discussion by Schultz (1999; see too van Ruiten 1997), who as it happens draws many of his main examples from the book of Isaiah. While an important part of his work is to draw attention to the importance of the study of citations for purposes other than the diachronic, his cautionary remarks on the latter should be carefully heeded.

For this reason, I am inclined not to put too much weight upon Wendel's 1995 study of the echoes of Isaiah in Jeremiah (see too the

16. Cf. Ziegler (1934: 106), and especially Seeligmann (1948: 102–103). It should further be noted that the LXX's rendering of עֲצָרָה following (ἀργία, 'idleness, rest, leisure') is also distinctive, being attested nowhere else either for this word or for the closely related עֲצֶרֶת.

17. Koenig's attempt (1982: 414–24) at a compromise, explaining the change on the basis that there was a homonymous root צוֹם which meant 'injustice' (cf. Arabic *ḍwm*), for which אָוֶן was then substituted, is desperate.

briefer discussion in Holladay 1989: 47–50). Although a considerable number of passages which are usually attributed to Isaiah are compared with an even larger number in Jeremiah, so that in principle the study could provide the kind of evidence for which we are looking, and although the discussion is careful, with attention to differences as well as similarities, it is difficult to escape the impression that those who do not already share Wendel's basic critical standpoint (which is perfectly mainstream in other respects) would be persuaded either that the allusions are real, rather then stemming from a shared culture, or that the direction of dependence is necessarily from Isaiah to Jeremiah (for the latter, see explicitly Becker 1997: 267). Thus, while Wendel's study is valuable once the overall diachronic framework has been established, it is not likely to be probative in establishing that framework in the first place.

Instead, I suggest that a more persuasive approach can be adopted by the evidence for allusions and citations within the book of Isaiah itself. In the first place, it is a priori more likely that in a single work the allusions and citations will be conscious and literary, and this is reinforced by the universal agreement that some citations are so close and extensive that direct influence is beyond doubt, even if the direction of the citation is disputed; the parallel between 11.6–9 and 65.25 is a good case in point (cf. van Ruiten 1992; Schultz 1999: 240–56). Secondly, there are instances where there are multiple allusions which manifest a clear development of theme, so that it is possible to establish some kind of diachronic typological framework. And thirdly, while the composition of the book probably spanned several centuries, the basic stratum of Deutero-Isaiah (even allowing for radical redactional theories in its development) gives us an agreed date at the end of the exilic period which should be sufficient to link relative to absolute chronology.

My own previous attempt to study some of these allusions and citations (1994: 37–93 *et passim*) was, of course, predicated on the kind of critical assumptions and conclusions which for the purposes of the present discussion I maintain are inadequate. Nevertheless, there are some examples which I believe pass even the more rigorous test which we are now adopting.

A familiar case in point, to give just one example by way of illustration, would be the much studied theme of seeing and hearing, knowing and understanding, the blind and the deaf. The number of passages which take up this theme is astonishing, and the criss-crossing of the related vocabulary, some of it very rare, such as the root שׁעע, is impressive. Clements already drew attention to part of this material (1985; see too Rendtorff 1989; Aitken 1993), in my previous study I sought to add further evidence in support (1994: 46–51), and at least one detailed further analysis has appeared since (McLaughlin 1994). It is therefore not necessary to set out the data in full again here.

In a subsequent but related essay, Clements (1988) refined his initial findings to demonstrate that there is a development in this theme (partly, he suggests, by influence from 2 Sam. 5.6–10) whereby metaphorical blindness and deafness becomes literal, and its reversal becomes physical healing. If Isa. 6.9–10 marks the initiation of the theme, 35.5–6 brings it to its culmination, and some other passages can be put midway between the two, including several in Deutero-Isaiah. The important conclusion for our present purposes is that 6.9–10 stands at, or at the very least near to, the beginning of this process. That it is presupposed by the exilic Isaiah is strongly suggested by the fact that the latter uses its language to comment on the reversal of judgment: that the reversal goes in the opposite direction is highly implausible and has not, so far as I am aware, ever been proposed. While this line of argument cannot get us back directly to an eighth-century Isaiah, it at the least points towards a pre-exilic origin for this saying, and thus is fully compatible with Isaianic authorship.

Becker is aware of the force of this argument, especially as he is in full agreement with the nature of the literary allusions here.[18] Unlike Kaiser,[19] he accepts that part of Isaiah 6 derives from the eighth-century prophet, but finds his authentic words only in the first eight verses; it is this (together with a few verses in ch. 8) which enables him to advance his radical suggestion that the historical Isaiah was a prophet exclusively of weal. Whereas many commentators have argued that the last two verses of the chapter are a later addition, Becker extends this backwards to include vv. 9–11 as well. And since this is the first major literary-critical break which he makes in the text, it is clearly crucial for the remainder of his thesis, which depends and builds upon this initial observation. How, then, does he seek to overcome the problem raised by the apparent dependence of Deutero-Isaiah upon these disputed verses?

His argument is simple: with reference to several recent redaction-critical studies of Deutero-Isaiah, he declares all the passages which refer to this theme to belong to later layers of that text. 'Das gilt vor allem (aber nicht nur!) für die Rede in 42,18ff.' There is thus plenty of time for a post-

---

18. Becker 1997: 76–78. He refers to the following texts in association with this theme: 1.3; 29.9–10, 18, 24; 32.3–4; 41.20; 42.7, 18–20; 43.8; 44.18; 63.17.

19. Kaiser's argument for the post-exilic date of the whole of Isa. 6 (a conclusion which in private conversation he tells me he would now wish to revise) is of a much less specific kind than Becker's, and so is less susceptible to detailed examination. For a cautious response to some of his main points, see Barthel 1997: esp. 79–82. I have myself commented on Kaiser's conclusions (as well as those of Whitley 1959) in 1994: 30–37. The lack of rigorous method in the work of Gosse (1992) makes it similarly difficult to interact with his attempt to demonstrate the late date of Isa. 6.

exilic version of Isaiah 6 to have arisen before the dependent passages in Deutero-Isaiah.[20]

In his footnote to justify this conclusion, he refers to four redaction-critical studies and summarizes which of the relevant verses they regard as secondary as follows: Hermisson (1989, with a summary table on p. 311), 42.18–20 and 44.18; Kratz (1991, with a summary table on p. 217), 42.18ff.; 43.8; 44.18; 42.7; Schmitt (1992), 42.18ff.; 43.8; van Oorschot (1993, with a summary table on p. 345), 42.18ff.; 44.18. This, of course, explains the 'vor allem … 42,18ff.', since it is, in fact, the only passage on which all four are agreed, and that is hardly surprising; even among those who broadly defend the unity of Deutero-Isaiah, strong doubts have been expressed about this particular passage. 44.18 would also be regarded as secondary by many, since it comes in one of the anti-idol polemic passages.

Even if, however, in this strictly *ad hominem* argument we concede this point, two severe problems remain for Becker. First, among the very passages which he himself has just agreed relate to this theme, 41.20 is agreed by all to belong to the primary layer, and the same is true of some other verses which he chooses not to mention, such as 42.16 and 43.10 (and possibly 40.21). In addition, however, his procedure of lumping the conclusions of all these redaction critics together is questionable, for each arrives at his conclusions by a presumably self-consistent method, so that it is mistaken to pick and choose from their results to suit some alternative purpose. 43.8 is a good example of this issue. Kratz (who appears to have exerted the greatest influence on Becker) declares the verse secondary for the simple reason that he regards it as dependent upon 42.18 (1991: 65 and 140). Van Oorschot (1993: 33–38), on the other hand, makes a strong case for seeing 43.8 as integral to the rhetoric in 43.8–13, and so by no means to be deleted. Rather, using precisely the form of argument which Becker himself regularly employs elsewhere in his monograph, he maintains that 42.18 obviously *voraussetzt* the occurrence in 43.8 (1993: 210). On either or both counts, therefore, I conclude that Becker has failed to circumvent the problem for his position posed by the apparent allusions to 6.9–10 in Deutero-Isaiah.

It is not possible in the present context to pursue other examples of this sort. While I agree that to those who take a contrary view on a priori grounds it will always be possible to advance some objection to one or

20. He takes a similar line with regard to the arguments which several scholars have advanced to show that Isa. 40.1–8(11) is dependent in many ways upon Isa. 6. While he accepts the force of these arguments, he maintains that they all relate to 40.3aα, 6–8, which several studies have suggested may have been added later; indeed, they may have been added in dependence on Isa. 6 precisely to transform the opening of ch. 40 into something of a 'call-narrative'.

another aspect of this method, I believe that for most scholars the network of correspondences which can be built up between the various parts of the book of Isaiah along these lines points firmly towards the conclusion that some are anchored in the pre-Deutero-Isaianic, and thus almost certainly the pre-exilic, period.

My fourth principal line of argument cannot, perhaps, quite be labelled a method, but it seeks to reflect rather on the consequences of the most familiar of all methods in critical biblical scholarship, that of historical literary analysis. This approach, though being used in defence of a pre-exilic Isaiah, is thus paradoxically not available to ultra-conservative scholars. For them, however, everything in Isaiah 1–39 derives from Isaiah in any case, so they may not feel its loss too acutely. For the remainder, such a unitary view of authorship is contradicted by the many tensions and signs of literary, historical and ideological unevenness which they uncover by a careful reading of the text which seeks to do justice to it in all its dimensions. I share this latter view along with those who use the method in part to argue that virtually the whole of the work comes from the post-exilic period.

Unlike these latter scholars, however, it seems to me that the historical depth which is thereby shown to lie behind the present form of the text, especially when that is related to the likely causes which triggered the later growth, points rather firmly to a pre-exilic origin for the whole process. Unless the reflections which literary criticism has shown to be developments of the original core are understood as looking back on something said previously through the prism of exile and restoration, then the *raison d'être* for the whole procedure seems to disappear without a satisfactory alternative explanation.

The generally agreed growth of ch. 6 once again furnishes a clear example, and it serves the present purpose well as the stages in that growth which are of concern to us for this argument are shared also by Kaiser and Becker. We are therefore all singing from the same hymn-sheet, at least to start with.

First, the final clause of the chapter is an added gloss. Although vv. 12–13a seem certainly to have been originally entirely negative about the future,[21] the gloss has exploited the potential inherent in the notion of a felled tree that there will be renewed growth from the stump (cf. Job 14.7–9), and it identifies this with the 'holy seed'. This phrase is found elsewhere only at Ezra 9.2, where it is the result of a sophisticated piece of midrash (cf. Williamson 1985: 131–32; more generally, Milgrom 1976: 16–35 and 71–73; Fishbane 1985: 114–23). As commentators have generally agreed on other grounds, therefore, this gloss must be post-exilic, a testimony to

---

21. See the full summary and discussion of the textual and linguistic difficulties by Emerton (1982).

the ways in which ancient exegetes sought to connect the reconstituted community of their day with the earlier destroyed and exiled nation.

Verses 12–13a themselves, however, are frequently thought to have been added to the core of ch. 6. Although the case is not completely certain (cf. Gray 1912: 111), I regard it as very probable and am certainly content to accept it here in the interests of close engagement with Kaiser and Becker. The main point which the verses add to the already gloomy v. 11 is that (with a switch to third-person speech about God) not only will the land be laid waste 'without inhabitant' but many will be removed from it, and even those who remain will be destroyed (and there is the second difficulty: who are these who survive the total devastation of v. 11?). This looks very like a comment on the destruction of Judah in the light of the Babylonian exile; Isaiah had predicted defeat in the land, and a (presumably exilic) commentator has added an observation about how this was fulfilled in the events of 598 and 587 BCE.[22] Kaiser (1981: 134, ET 1983: 133) agrees: 'The hand which added v. 12 felt the lack of a clear reference to the deportation of the people', and so does Becker (1997: 64–65): 'V. 12–13bα hat offenbar die Aufgabe, die eher allgemeinen Anschauungen von v. 11 über die Verwüstung des Landes im Sinne einer totalen Deportation genauer zu fassen'.

The question which this raises is what conceivable purpose could be served by this addition if the core text were already post-exilic? The attempt to clarify that the earlier prophecy had been fulfilled in the events surrounding the exile makes sense only on the presupposition that the core text preceded this and needed such clarification. That a reference to the exile was added in the post-exilic period to a text which, *ex hypothesi*, was already written after the event and when no such clarification was required, and when, moreover, the judgment of exile was already a thing of the past, beggars belief.

Again for reasons of space, I limit myself to this one example of what I have called the historical depth in the literature which makes up Isaiah 1–39. Many other examples of additions which clarify how Isaiah's pronouncements were fulfilled in the events of the Babylonian destruction and deportation have been proposed (see especially Clements 1980), and a careful discussion of each would be required. Other arguments of a similar nature might be mounted in terms of the evident dislocations of material during the course of the book's growth (the current setting of 5.25–29 +

22. So the majority; see, for instance, the recent cautious summary by Barthel (1997: 75–77). The main alternative is to agree that the verses have been added to the core of the chapter, but at a much earlier time, and so perhaps by Isaiah himself, in reflection on some other disaster, such as the fall of the northern kingdom or the events of 701 BCE; see, for instance, Wildberger (1980: 257–58, ET 1991: 274–75), Nielsen (1989: 144–58), and Sweeney (1996: 138–39). Of course, my main point argued above would hold a fortiori were this minority view to be correct.

30 is only the best known example), whereby material which once served one purpose has now been reused redactionally, sometimes rather awkwardly, to serve another purpose altogether (for some examples, see Williamson 1995 and 1997). I maintain that, even limiting ourselves to the core of widely agreed examples, this has the effect of shifting a considerable body of oracular material into the pre-exilic, and probably Isaianic, period.

My fifth and final method is similar to the second, but relates to a different topic. There, I argued from the historical development of beliefs and practices, while on this occasion I do much the same with regard to what, for want of a better term, I will call ideology.

The most compelling example of which I am aware in this regard relates to the evaluation of the reign, and indeed the character, of Hezekiah. To put the matter at its simplest, there seems to be a simple, linear development in which his reign comes to be held in ever higher esteem with the passage of time (cf. Ackroyd 1984). In the so-called Isaiah-legends which lie behind 2 Kgs 18.13–20.19; Isaiah 36–39, he is already judged in a positive way overall, though some points of criticism are noted. The Deuteronomistic editor who has included this material in his wider history adds material which is even more laudatory (2 Kgs 18.1–8): 'He did what was right in the sight of the Lord ... He removed the high places ... He trusted in the Lord ... so that there was no one like him among all the kings of Judah after him, or among those who were before him[23] ... The Lord was with him; wherever he went he prospered', and so on. The Chronicler, if anything, takes this still further by the addition of three chapters' worth of cultic reform and ceremonial (2 Chron. 29–31) prior to his summary of the material found already in Kings (2 Chron. 32), so that in the Chronicler's scheme Hezekiah surpasses even Josiah as the greatest of the kings of Judah. This is maintained also by Ben Sira, who again devotes more space to Hezekiah than Josiah (Ecclus 48.17–25), and *inter alia* adds for good measure that Hezekiah 'did what was pleasing to the Lord, ... as he was instructed by Isaiah' (v. 22). And finally, of course, as Hezekiah came to be associated with Immanuel and the child of Isa. 9.5 (ET 6), so in later Jewish tradition he was invested with messianic significance.

In view of this escalation of commendation, and the lack of criticism of Hezekiah in the later writings, it seems clear that the severely critical tone of a number of Isaiah's oracles relating to his policy in the run-up to his rebellion against Assyria in 701 BCE is unlikely to have been invented in the post-exilic period. Not only would such a move run counter to the prevailing ideological ethos of the time, but it is difficult to see what could have triggered such a radically revisionist agenda, and one which, so far as

---

23. For the significance of this formula, see Knoppers (1992).

we can tell, has left no other trace in our extant literature. It is true that Hezekiah is not mentioned by name in the relevant oracles,[24] but as the leader of the anti-Assyrian coalition, to say nothing of his position as king of Judah, it can hardly be denied that he is included among those whom Isaiah castigates. As is well known, even Kaiser accepts that the opening oracles in chs 30 and 31 derive ultimately from Isaiah himself, though on somewhat different grounds (in addition to his commentary, see Kaiser 1989).

It is a bold move by Becker (1997: 212–19 and 245–63), therefore, to challenge this consensus. In his opinion, these oracles (as well as some others earlier in the book) do not precede the narratives in chs 36–39 but rather were written in dependence upon them and were added to pave the way for their incorporation into the book of Isaiah. They opened up the possibility of reading the 'historical' narratives about Assyria in terms of any other world power by which the Jewish people might have been threatened. Since he thinks that 30.1–5 is based upon 31.1–3, it is the latter text which is perhaps the most important one to consider in relation to his hypothesis.

Becker's proposal comes towards the end of his monograph, and so is able naturally to take many of his earlier positions for granted and indeed to build upon them. In a full analysis, it would be unfair to treat his discussion of this passage in isolation from other aspects of his presentation. Clearly, that is not possible in the present context, although some of my previous remarks will have made clear that I am unable to follow him in a number of respects.

I limit myself here, therefore, to two observations only. First, an initial difficulty about arguing that 31.1–3 (and related material) is dependent upon chs 36–39 and intended to prepare the way for it is that, as many scholars have observed, the depiction of the prophet and of his advice to Hezekiah at this time is distinctly at odds, to say the least, with what we find in these prophetic oracles. I am at a loss to understand how anyone, working on the basis of the narratives, could have come up with the idea that Isaiah spoke in the way represented in 31.1–3. And, for reasons we have seen, the later this activity is dated, the more difficult the supposition becomes, given the way that Hezekiah's role in the affair came to be ever more highly praised.

The second observation is simply to direct attention to a careful study of Isa. 31.1–3 by Höffken (2000). Having already published a commentary on this material in 1993, he was apparently goaded by Becker's book in particular[25] to lay out his literary analysis in more technical detail. The

24.   Blenkinsopp (2000b: 21) nevertheless observes that the 3rd person masculine singular suffix at 30.4 ('his messengers') is probably a reference to Hezekiah.

25.   He also interacts with the intervening publications of Deck (1991) and Wong (1996).

most important conclusion he reaches for our purposes is that (along with v. 2, as many commentators agree) the middle line of v. 1 is no part of the original saying. His arguments cannot be summarized here, but it has to be said that they seem cogent, and it is of course a strength that they were worked out independently and in advance of the more recent discussion, and that Deck too had reached broadly similar conclusions, again completely independently, so far as I can tell. Now, the importance of this conclusion is that of the four verbal connections which Becker cites (1997: 257 n. 157) to demonstrate that 31.1–3 is dependent upon ch. 36, three[26] come in this one line alone. If Höffken's conclusions are sound, then Becker's case for dependence is seriously weakened.[27]

I conclude, therefore, that the consensus which ascribes parts, at least, of these anti-coalition oracles to the time of Isaiah remains overwhelmingly probable.

Before summing up, I should perhaps offer a word of explanation as to why I have not introduced a sixth method into this discussion, namely that of style and language. In broad terms, I am in agreement that it is possible to draw typological distinctions at both the syntactic and the lexical levels between pre- and post-exilic Hebrew,[28] though the latter should not be applied to the years immediately following the first return from Babylon. Further, there are some features which seem to have survived from an even earlier form of the language. There is thus a development in the language, reflected in our texts, which speaks strongly in favour of some of the material coming from the pre-exilic period. The difficulty comes when we seek to apply this general conclusion to a particular text. In the nature of the case, it is far easier to demonstrate that a text must be late, because it displays late features, than to argue that a text must be early because it does not. Those who are not already persuaded that there is pre-exilic material in Isaiah can always claim that later imitation, or even deliberate archaizing, accounts for the data. Similarly, although there are some stylistic features in Isaiah 1–39 which scholars have conventionally ascribed to the literary genius of Isaiah, and although differences in style can certainly be detected within these chapters, which suggest that different hands have been at work, one of which could then be identified with Isaiah, it is obvious that these features can equally well be ascribed to other, possibly later, writers. In the

26. The exception is 'horses', 31.1a and 36.8.

27. I am, of course, aware that I earlier criticized Becker himself for using just this kind of argument, but at least that reassures me that he would be sympathetic to this attempt. The difference, of course, is that there he used it only partially and eclectically.

28. See the summary of Hurvitz's many studies of this topic in 1997; see too Polzin (1976).

minimalist method adopted for the purposes of the present exercise, therefore, I do not think that language can help us very much.

To sum up, then, I have sought to describe and illustrate five methods which may be held to point to the pre-exilic date of some of the material in the first part of Isaiah. The first one did not relate directly to authorship, but was helpful in giving us the clearest indication that written material from that period can and did survive into the post-exilic period. The other four, in various ways, were all indicative of passages which have traditionally been ascribed to the eighth-century prophet, and they have related to both the earlier and the later periods of Isaiah's ministry as usually understood. While I have discussed only a limited number of specific examples, the third and fourth methods, at least, are certainly capable of being applied to a wider range of texts, so that from them something of a portrayal of the prophet may be developed, even if, for the reasons I have already given, this may be only partial, and hence distorted.

To return to Rudman's assessment from which I started out, it is a matter of simple observation that 'waverers may ... go either way'. Whether, however, in the light of all the evidence it is 'intelligent' for them to do so is another question.

Bibliography

Ackroyd, P.R.

1984 'The Biblical Interpretation of the Reigns of Ahaz and Hezekiah', in W.B. Barrick and J.R. Spencer (eds), *In the Shelter of Elyon: Essays on Ancient Palestinian Life and Literature in Honor of G.W. Ahlström* (JSOTSup, 31; Sheffield: JSOT Press): 247–59. Reprinted in P.R. Ackroyd, *Studies in the Religious Tradition of the Old Testament* (London: SCM Press, 1987): 181–92.

Aitken, K.T.

1993 'Hearing and Seeing: Metamorphoses of a Motif in Isaiah 1–39', in P.R. Davies and D.J.A. Clines (eds), *Among the Prophets: Language, Image and Structure in the Prophetic Writings* (JSOTSup, 144; Sheffield: Sheffield Academic Press): 12–41.

Auvray, P.

1972 *Isaïe 1–39* (SB; Paris: J. Gabalda).

Avigad, N.

1970 'Excavations in the Jewish Quarter of the Old City of Jerusalem, 1970 (Second Preliminary Report)', *IEJ* 20: 129–40.

Barth, H.

1977 *Die Jesaja-Worte in der Josiazeit: Israel und Assur als Thema einer produktiven Neuinterpretation der Jesajaüberlieferung* (WMANT, 48; Neukirchen–Vluyn: Neukirchener Verlag).

Barthel, J.

1997 *Prophetenwort und Geschichte: Die Jesajaüberlieferung in Jes 6–8 und 28–31* (FAT, 19; Tübingen: Mohr Siebeck).

Barthélemy, D.
1986   *Critique textuelle de l'Ancien Testament*, II: *Isaïe, Jérémie, Lamentations* (OBO, 50.2; Freiburg: Editions Universitaires, and Göttingen: Vandenhoeck & Ruprecht).

Becker, U.
1997   *Jesaja – von der Botschaft zum Buch* (FRLANT, 178; Göttingen: Vandenhoeck & Ruprecht).

Blenkinsopp, J.
2000a   *Isaiah 1–39: A New Translation with Introduction and Commentary* (AB, 19; New York: Doubleday).
2000b   'The Prophetic Biography of Isaiah', in E. Blum (ed.), *Mincha: Festgabe für Rolf Rendtorff zum 75. Geburtstag* (Neukirchen–Vluyn: Neukirchener Verlag): 13–26.

Childs, B.S.
1967   *Isaiah and the Assyrian Crisis* (SBT, NS 3; London: SCM Press).

Clements, R.E.
1980   'The Prophecies of Isaiah and the Fall of Jerusalem in 587 B.C.', *VT* 30: 421–36.
1985   'Beyond Tradition-History: Deutero-Isaianic Development of First Isaiah's Themes', *JSOT* 31: 95–113. Reprinted in R.E. Clements, *Old Testament Prophecy: From Oracles to Canon* (Louisville, KY: Westminster John Knox, 1996): 78–92.
1988   'Patterns in the Prophetic Canon: Healing the Blind and the Lame', in G.M. Tucker, D.L. Petersen and R.R. Wilson (eds), *Canon, Theology, and Old Testament Interpretation: Essays in Honor of Brevard S. Childs* (Philadelphia: Fortress Press): 189–200.

Cryer, F.
1994   *Divination in Ancient Israel and its Near Eastern Environment: A Socio-Historical Investigation* (JSOTSup, 142; Sheffield: Sheffield Academic Press).

Davies, G.I.
1991   *Ancient Hebrew Inscriptions: Corpus and Concordance* (Cambridge: Cambridge University Press).

Davies, P.R.
1992   *In Search of 'Ancient Israel'* (JSOTSup, 148; Sheffield: Sheffield Academic Press).

Deck, S.
1991   *Die Gerichtsbotschaft Jesajas: Charakter und Begründung* (FzB, 67; Würzburg: Echter Verlag).

Delitzsch, F.
1889   *Commentar über das Buch Jesaia* (Leipzig: Dörffling & Franke, 4th edn).

Donner, H.
1964   *Israel unter den Völkern: Die Stellung der klassischen Propheten des 8. Jahrhunderts v. Chr. zur Aussenpolitik der Könige von Israel und Juda* (VTSup, 11; Leiden: E.J. Brill).

Driver, S.R.
1889–90 'Professor Franz Delitzsch', *ExpTim* 1: 197–201.

Duhm, B.
1892   *Das Buch Jesaia* (HKAT, 3.1; Göttingen: Vandenhoeck & Ruprecht).

Emerton, J.A.
1980   'Notes on the Text and Translation of Isaiah xxii 8–11 and lxv 5', *VT* 30: 437–51.
1982   'The Translation and Interpretation of Isaiah vi. 13', in J.A. Emerton and S.C. Reif (eds), *Interpreting the Hebrew Bible: Essays in Honour of E.I.J. Rosenthal* (UCOP, 32; Cambridge: Cambridge University Press): 85–118.

Fishbane, M.
1985   *Biblical Interpretation in Ancient Israel* (Oxford: Clarendon Press).

Fuchs, A.
1998   *Die Annalen des Jahres 711 v. Chr.* (SAAS, 8; Helsinki: The Neo-Assyrian Text Corpus Project).

Gallagher, W.R.
1999   *Sennacherib's Campaign to Judah: New Studies* (SHCANE, 18; Leiden: E.J. Brill).

Gonçalves, F.J.
1986   *L'expédition de Sennachérib en Palestine dans la littérature hébraïque ancienne* (Ebib, NS 7; Paris: Gabalda).
1999   '2 Rois 18,13–20,19 par. Isaïe 36–39: Encore une fois, lequel des deux livres fut le premier?', in J.-M. Auwers and A. Wénin (eds), *Lectures et relectures de la Bible: Festschrift P.-M. Bogaert* (BETL, 144; Leuven: University Press and Peeters): 27–55.

Gosse, B.
1992   'Isaïe vi et la tradition isaïenne', *VT* 42: 340–49.

Grabbe, L.L.
1995   *Priests, Prophets, Diviners, Sages: A Socio-Historical Study of Religious Specialists in Ancient Israel* (Valley Forge, PA: Trinity Press International).

Gray, G.B.
1912   *A Critical and Exegetical Commentary on the Book of Isaiah I–XXVII* (ICC; Edinburgh: T. & T. Clark).

Halpern, B.
2000   'The State of Israelite History', in G.N. Knoppers and J.G. McConville (eds), *Reconsidering Israel and Judah: Recent Studies on the Deuteronomistic History* (Winona Lake, IN: Eisenbrauns): 540–65.

Hardmeier, C.
1986   'Jesajaforschung im Umbruch', *VF* 31: 3–31.

Hayes, J.H., and S.A. Irvine
1987   *Isaiah, the Eighth-Century Prophet: His Times and his Preaching* (Nashville: Abingdon Press).

Hermisson, H.-J.
1989   'Einheit und Komplexität Deuterojesajas: Probleme der Redaktionsgeschichte von Jes 40–55', in J. Vermeylen (ed.), *The Book of Isaiah* (BETL, 81; Leuven: University Press and Peeters): 287–312. Reprinted in *Studien zu Prophetie und Weisheit* (FAT, 23; Tübingen: Mohr Siebeck, 1998): 132–57.

Höffken, P.
2000   'Bemerkungen zu Jesaja 31,1–3', *ZAW* 112: 230–38.

Holladay, W.L.
  1989   *Jeremiah*, II: *A Commentary on the Book of the Prophet Jeremiah, Chapters 26–52* (Hermeneia; Minneapolis: Fortress Press).

Hurvitz, A.
  1997   'The Historical Quest for "Ancient Israel" and the Linguistic Evidence of the Hebrew Bible: Some Methodological Observations', *VT* 47: 301–15.

Jeffers, A.
  1996   *Magic and Divination in Ancient Palestine and Syria* (SHCANE, 8; Leiden: E.J. Brill).

Kaiser, O.
  1973   *Der Prophet Jesaja: Kapitel 13–39* (ATD, 18; Göttingen: Vandenhoeck & Ruprecht). ET *Isaiah 13–39: A Commentary* (OTL; London: SCM Press, 1974).
  1981   *Das Buch des Propheten Jesaja: Kapitel 1–12* (ATD, 17; Göttingen: Vandenhoeck & Ruprecht, 5th edn). ET *Isaiah 1–12: A Commentary* (OTL; London: SCM Press, 1983).
  1989   'Literarkritik und Tendenzkritik: Überlegungen zur Methode der Jesajaexegese', in J. Vermeylen (ed.), *The Book of Isaiah* (BETL, 81; Leuven: University Press and Peeters): 55–71.

Kissane, E.J.
  1941   *The Book of Isaiah*, I (Dublin: Richview).

Kitchen, K.A.
  1973   *The Third Intermediate Period in Egypt (1100–650 B.C.)* (Warminster: Aris & Phillips).

Knoppers, G.N.
  1992   'There was None like Him: Incomparability in the Book of Kings', *CBQ* 54: 418–25.

Koenig, J.
  1982   *L'herméneutique analogique du judaïsme antique d'après les témoins textuels d'Isaïe* (VTSup, 33; Leiden: E.J. Brill).

Kratz, R.G.
  1991   *Kyros im Deuterojesaja-Buch: Redaktionsgeschichtliche Untersuchungen zu Entstehung und Theologie von Jes 40–55* (FAT, 1; Tübingen: J.C.B. Mohr [Paul Siebeck]).

Laato, A.
  1996   *History and Ideology in the Old Testament Prophetic Literature: A Semiotic Approach to the Reconstruction of the Proclamation of the Historical Prophets* (ConBOT, 41; Stockholm: Almqvist & Wiksell International, 1996).

Lagarde, P. de
  1877   *Symmicta*, i (Göttingen: Dietrich).

McLaughlin, J.L.
  1994   'Their Hearts *Were* Hardened: The Use of Isaiah 6,9–10 in the Book of Isaiah', *Bib* 75: 1–25.

Milgrom, J.
  1976   *Cult and Conscience* (SJLA, 18; Leiden: E.J. Brill).

Na'aman, N.
  1992   'Israel, Edom and Egypt in the 10th Century B.C.E.', *Tel Aviv* 19: 71–93.

1996   'Sources and Composition in the History of David', in V. Fritz and P.R. Davies (eds), *The Origins of the Ancient Israelite States* (JSOTSup, 228; Sheffield: Sheffield Academic Press): 170–86.

1999   'No Anthropomorphic Graven Image: Notes on the Assumed Anthropomorphic Cult Statues in the Temples of YHWH in the Pre-Exilic Period', *UF* 31: 391–415.

Nielsen, K.

1989   *There is Hope for a Tree: The Tree as Metaphor in Isaiah* (JSOTSup, 65; Sheffield: JSOT Press).

Oorschot, J. van

1993   *Von Babel zum Zion: Eine literarkritische und redaktionsgeschichtliche Untersuchung* (BZAW, 206; Berlin and New York: W. de Gruyter).

Polzin, R.

1976   *Late Biblical Hebrew: Toward an Historical Typology of Biblical Hebrew Prose* (HSM, 12; Missoula, MT: Scholars Press).

Porath, R.

1994   *Die Sozialkritik im Jesajabuch: Redaktionsgeschichtliche Analyse* (Frankfurt am Main: Peter Lang).

Procksch, O.

1930   *Jesaia*, I (KAT, 9; Leipzig: Deichert).

Rendtorff, R.

1989   'Jesaja 6 im Rahmen der Komposition des Jesajabuches', in J. Vermeylen (ed.), *The Book of Isaiah* (BETL, 81; Leuven: University Press and Peeters): 73–82. ET 'Isaiah 6 in the Framework of the Composition of the Book', in R. Rendtorff, *Canon and Theology: Overtures to an Old Testament Theology* (Edinburgh: T. & T. Clark, 1994): 170–80.

Rudman, D.

2001   Review of Gallagher (1999), in *BO* 58: cols 227–29.

Ruiten, J.T.A.G.M. van

1992   'The Intertextual Relationship between Isaiah 65,25 and Isaiah 11,6–9', in F. García Martínez, A. Hilhorst and C.J. Labuschagne (eds), *The Scriptures and the Scrolls: Studies in Honour of A.S. van der Woude on the Occasion of his 65th Birthday* (VTSup, 49; Leiden: E.J. Brill): 31–42.

1997   '"His Master's Voice"? The Supposed Influence of the Book of Isaiah in the Book of Habakkuk', in J. van Ruiten and M. Vervenne (eds), *Studies in the Book of Isaiah: Festschrift Willem A.M. Beuken* (BETL, 132; Leuven: University Press and Peeters): 397–411.

Schmitt, H.-C.

1992   'Erlösung und Gericht: Jes 43,1–7 und sein literarischer und theologischer Kontext', in J. Hausmann and H.-J. Zobel (eds), *Alttestamentlicher Glaube und biblische Theologie: Festschrift Horst Dietrich Preuss zum 65. Geburtstag* (Stuttgart: W. Kohlhammer): 120–31.

Schoors, A.

1997   'Historical Information in Isaiah 1–39', in J. van Ruiten and M. Vervenne (eds.), *Studies in the Book of Isaiah: Festschrift Willem A.M. Beuken* (BETL, 132; Leuven: University Press and Peeters): 75–93.

Schultz, R.L.
    1999   *The Search for Quotation: Verbal Parallels in the Prophets* (JSOTSup, 180; Sheffield: Sheffield Academic Press).

Seeligmann, I.L.
    1948   *The Septuagint Version of Isaiah* (Leiden: E.J. Brill).

Sweeney, M.A.
    1996   *Isaiah 1–39, with an Introduction to Prophetic Literature* (FOTL, 16; Grand Rapids, MI: Eerdmans).

Tadmor, H.
    1967   'Fragments of a Stele of Sargon II from the Excavations of Ashdod', *Eretz-Israel* 8: 241–45 (Hebrew).

Ussishkin, D.
    1982   *The Conquest of Lachish by Sennacherib* (Tel Aviv: The Institute of Archaeology of Tel Aviv University).

Vermeylen, J.
    1977   *Du prophète Isaïe à l'apocalyptique: Isaïe, I–XXV, miroir d'un demi-millénaire d'expérience religieuse en Israël*, I (Ebib; Paris: J. Gabalda).
    1997   'Hypothèses sur l'origine d'Isaïe 36–39', in J. van Ruiten and M. Vervenne (eds), *Studies in the Book of Isaiah: Festschrift Willem A.M. Beuken* (BETL, 132; Leuven: University Press and Peeters): 95–118.

Wendel, U.
    1995   *Jesaja und Jeremia: Worte, Motive und Einsichten Jesajas in der Verkündigung Jeremias* (Biblisch-Theologische Studien, 25; Neukirchen–Vluyn: Neukirchener Verlag).

Werner, W.
    1986   *Eschatologische Texte in Jesaja 1–39: Messias, Heiliger Rest, Völker* (FzB, 46; Würzburg: Echter Verlag).
    1988   *Studien zur alttestamentlichen Vorstellung vom Plan Jahwes* (BZAW, 173; Berlin and New York: W. de Gruyter).

Whitley, C.F.
    1959   'The Call and Mission of Isaiah', *JNES* 18: 38–48.

Wildberger, H.
  1972–82 *Jesaja 1–12, 13–27, 28–39* (3 vols; BKAT, 10; Neukirchen–Vluyn: Neukirchener Verlag). ET *Isaiah 1–12, 13–27, 28–39* (trans. T.H. Trapp; 3 vols; Minneapolis: Fortress Press, 1991–2002).

Williamson, H.G.M.
    1982   *1 and 2 Chronicles* (NCB; Grand Rapids: Eerdmans, and London: Marshall, Morgan & Scott).
    1985   *Ezra, Nehemiah* (WBC, 16; Waco, TX: Word Books).
    1994   *The Book Called Isaiah: Deutero-Isaiah's Role in Composition and Redaction* (Oxford: Clarendon Press).
    1995   'Isaiah xi 11–16 and the Redaction of Isaiah i–xii', in J.A. Emerton (ed.), *Congress Volume: Paris 1992* (VTSup, 61; Leiden: E.J. Brill): 343–57.
    1997   'Relocating Isaiah 1:2–9', in C.C. Broyles and C.A. Evans (eds), *Writing and Reading the Scroll of Isaiah: Studies of an Interpretive Tradition*, I (VTSup, 70.1; Leiden: E.J. Brill): 263–77.

1998   *Variations on a Theme: King, Messiah and Servant in the Book of Isaiah*
         (Carlisle: Paternoster Press).

2002   'Biblical Criticism and Hermeneutics in Isaiah 1:10–17', in C. Bultmann, W.
         Dietrich and C. Levin (eds), *Vergegenwärtigung des Alten Testaments:
         Beiträge zur biblischen Hermeneutik. Festschrift für Rudolf Smend zum 70.
         Geburtstag* (Göttingen: Vandenhoeck & Ruprecht): 82–96.

Willis, J.T.

1993   'Historical Issues in Isaiah 22,15–25', *Bib* 74: 60–70.

Wong, G.C.I.

1996   'Isaiah's Opposition to Egypt in Isaiah xxxi 1–3', *VT* 46: 392- 401.

Ziegler, J.

1934   *Untersuchungen zur Septuaginta des Buches Isaias* (Alttest. Abhandl., 12.3;
         Münster: Aschendorf).

Chapter 10

JEREMIAH BEFORE THE EXILE?

David J. Reimer

1. *Introduction*

The search for 'pre-exilic Jeremiah' is complicated by a number of factors, some of which it shares with any biblical book, some of which are unique to it. In general, the task of bringing positive proof that some text from antiquity is contemporary with the events it recounts, but which is known only from manuscripts some centuries later, is going to be very difficult in any case. Add to this the observation that Jeremiah stands at the cusp of the period under question ('pre-exilic'), and the historical judgments are even more fine (more fine than for texts dated significantly earlier, I mean). Aside from such general problems, there lurk for Jeremiah three intertwined literary puzzles. First is the well-known discrepancy between the forms of the book reflected in the Masoretic Text and the Septuagint – the latter significantly shorter and differently arranged compared to the former – so not just one, but two quite different editions of the book from antiquity. The second puzzle has to do with the prominence of language many describe as 'Deuteronomistic'.[1] Finally, there is the well-known distinction between the prose and poetry of the book and the problem of their relationship which further complicates our efforts to achieve clarity regarding the historical nature of the traditions contained in the Jeremiah scroll.

Given the amount of historical notice and narrative in Jeremiah's book, it is not surprising that many scholars have thought it to be the most historical of the prophetic scrolls, yielding the most information about the prophet's own life and circumstances. Such factors gave rise to works in the 1920s by John Skinner (1926) and Adam Welch (1928) that have been characterized as 'biographical' in their approach (Carroll 1981: 5–7). In spite of the trend towards historical scepticism in the latter decades of the twentieth century, Robert Carroll proved himself a true prophet when he predicted that 'Books will continue to be written about Jeremiah following

---

1. Recently reassessed in Sharp 2003.

the Skinnerian approach' (1981: 7); the title of Klaus Seybold's 1993 volume (*Der Prophet Jeremia: Leben und Werk*) is virtually a conflation of those of Skinner and Welch! As Carroll allowed, even the older works among these were neither uncritical nor credulous in their approach to Jeremiah's life and times. Welch, for example, apologized to his readers for the time he would spend on questions of 'authenticity'. 'The discussion will seem tedious to many', he remarked (1928: v). This was necessary since the traditions contained in the book had passed through many hands, and 'they did not leave the records untouched' (1928: vi).

Others, having made a similar observation, have drawn the conclusion that the records are too sullied to have any historical value, at least not as evidence for the events they purport to narrate. Robert Carroll's significant work on Jeremiah placed large question marks over the central figures of the book, notably Jeremiah and Baruch – both, he argued, constructs (perhaps even the creations) of the Deuteronomists, designed to bear a heavy load of ideological freight. 'The "historical" Jeremiah may still be there hidden by or weighed down under the additions and interpretations of countless editors, transformed beyond recognition, so that we cannot now rediscover him with any assurance' (Carroll 1986: 64). In this essay, I will not make any attempt to identify certain passages as attributable to the 'historical Jeremiah', for such a move adds unnecessary complication. I do not wish to confuse the effort to identify Jeremiah's own words with the quest for and exploration of pre-exilic (or, at least, contemporary with the 'historical Jeremiah') elements within the book that bears his name.

In the effort to find history in the Jeremiah traditions, analogies have been drawn with the 'quest for the historical Jesus', and Jobling has explored the analogy more fully than most (1984: 291–94). In replying to Schottroff's (1970) claim that prophetic texts should be initially assumed by exegetes to be secondary, Jobling writes: 'It is one thing to doubt the authenticity of the Jeremianic prose, even of this or that poetic oracle. It is quite another to assume that we know nothing of the historical Jeremiah until there appears compelling proof that we do have such knowledge!' (1984: 289). As I will try to show, such an overly-sceptical approach is not warranted. Evidence suggests that the connection between 'biblical Judah' and 'historical Judah' within the Jeremiah scroll is closer than some recent scholarship might have us believe. I will attempt, then, to follow the guidelines for good practice set out by Philip Davies: 'in a well-ordered and critical discipline we might expect a good deal of biblical scholarship to concern itself with discovering how, and then how far, one might set about recovering history from the literature' (Davies 1992: 25). 'How' this might be done requires first an examination of relevant material evidence from antiquity. This has the potential to provide our strongest line of argument. Evidence from within Jeremiah also requires consideration, and is grouped into three difference categories, below: (1) passages seeming to require a given historical context; (2) historical 'mistakes' may suggest a given date for some passages; finally, (3) the possible contribution of literary criticism in discerning earlier or later passages will be assessed.

2. *External Evidence*

Continuity between the biblical narrative and its ostensible historical setting on the one hand, and contemporary historical evidence on the other, can be readily seen. Judging the strength of that continuity is a different matter. But first, what is the nature of the connection?

2.1. *Babylonian Records*

Contemporary records of Babylonian incursions west into Syria–Palestine towards Egypt are well known and much discussed. Evidence from the Babylonian side was substantially strengthened with Wiseman's 1956 publication of the *Chronicles of Chaldaean Kings (626–556 B.C.) in the British Museum*, and the tablet BM 21946 in particular.[2] Covering an approximately twelve-year period, this tablet recites Nabopolassar's and Nebuchadnezzar's western campaigns in the early years of his reign. The entry for 'Year 17' (609)[3] records the encounter of the Assyrian, Egyptian, and Babylonian armies at Harran. For Nebuchadnezzar's first regnal year (604) the Chronicle relates how he marched to Hatti and received the tribute of 'all the kings of Hatti', and then captured, plundered and razed the city of Ashkelon (? the name is broken), taking its king captive. Then, in the seventh year (598): 'In the month of Kislev, the king of Babylonia mobilized his troops and marched to Hatti. He encamped against the city of Judah, and on the second of Adar, he captured the city and he seized (its) king. A king of his choice, he appointed there; he to[ok] its heavy tribute and carried it off to Babylon' (Cogan and Tadmor 1988: 340).

The significance of these passages for Jeremiah has long been noted.[4] Wiseman makes the connection between the fall of the city usually identified as Ashkelon in Nebuchadnezzar's first year with the national fast proclaimed and recorded in Jer. 36.9 (Wiseman 1985: 23; further on Jer. 36 below). Likewise the brief account of the fall of the 'city of Judah' in Nebuchadnezzar's seventh year tallies well with the fuller biblical

---

2. In Cogan and Tadmor (1988: 339–40), conveniently also *ANET*, 563–64 (translated by A.L. Oppenheim); cf. also Freedman 1975 (originally published in 1956) and further the discussion in Wiseman 1985 and Porten 1981. For a more up-to-date edition of the Babylonian Chronicle, see Grayson 1975.

3. The chronology for this period is fairly secure, although inevitably not without complications at the level of detail; discussed in Hughes 1990: 222–32.

4. A recent reassessment of these movements, noting connections to Jeremiah, is found in Vanderhooft 2003.

accounts of this event, and certainly also with the terse notice in Jer. 37.1 that relates Zedekiah's accession to the throne at the expense of 'Coniah's' deposition by Nebuchadnezzar. While in none of these cases do we have direct evidence for Jeremiah, they do provide close to contemporary extrabiblical evidence for events that the book of Jeremiah narrates or uses as settings for its oracles. This does not guarantee that the relevant Jeremiah passages are pre-exilic, but it does suggest that at these points it preserves reliable memories.[5]

2.2. Lachish Ostraca

Closer to 'home', there are of course the Lachish ostraca. Although there remain problems in interpreting the archaeology of Lachish (Tell ed-Duweir), there is widespread agreement that the cache of ostraca found in a guardroom in the city gate is related to the time of the Babylonian incursions of the early sixth century. These letters give some insight into the tense atmosphere present during this phase. In particular, the signal fires of Ostracon 4 have been related to Jer. 6.1 ('...raise a [smoke] signal [*mś'ṯ*] on Beth-hakkerem'), although this is only a very general connection. According to Z.B. Begin (2002), a more precise connection between Ostracon 4 and Jeremiah is found at Jer. 34.7: '...the army of the king of Babylon was fighting against Jerusalem and against all the cities of Judah that were left, Lachish and Azekah; for these were the only fortified cities of Judah that remained'. Ostracon 4 reports that the writer 'cannot see Azekah', and thus must look to Lachish for signals. One early interpretation of the letter understood this to mean that Azekah had fallen – on the face of it contradicting the claim of Jer. 34.7 (Begin 2002: 167–68), although the letter and the notice Jeremiah may be reconciled by supposing they represent different stages of the Babylonian campaign (e.g. *KAI*, II, 195–96) or that the letter writer simply had bad weather (thus Gibson 1971: 43). Begin's own argument – that the letter was written from Maresha, a site about 5 km north-east of Lachish but 12 km south of Azekah – avoids the problem of a fallen Azekah, since the issue turns on lines-of-sight rather than the extent of Babylonian conquest. However, in any case Jer. 34.7 and Lachish 4 remain intimately connected in historical terms.

More tantalizing still is the reference to 'the prophet' in Ostracon 3 (and possibly also 16 where the context is broken but a *-yahu* name is found). The urge to identify the prophet proved too strong for some to resist, with Uriah (cf. Jer. 26.20) and Jeremiah himself both being canvassed as candidates; equally quickly other scholars dashed hopes that the prophet

---

5. This point is noteworthy given the rapidity with which the Neo-Babylonian empire was forgotten in antiquity, at least among the Hellenistic historians, a point discussed by Calmeyer 1987: 18–20. Clearly, Babylon itself was never forgotten in the biblical tradition.

could ever be positively identified (Thomas 1958). The comments of Pardee (1982: 78) are worth noting:

> If the dating in summer 589 B.C. is correct, [the ostraca] give some glimpse into preparations taking place in Judah shortly before the Babylonian invasion which eventually led to the destruction of Judah as an independent state. Finally, whatever the precise relationship of these letters to Jeremiah may have been, their general contributions to our knowledge of that prophet's time is precious enough.

2.3. *Bullae*

One futher body of contemporary documentary evidence remains to be identified: these are the dozens of clay bullae which have appeared since the mid-1970s. If the evidence considered thus far must remain useful only at the general level in providing 'continuity' between the Bible and the extrabiblical historical record, the bullae provide specific connections between Jeremiah and the archaeological record. (Bullae are stamp impressions in clay, about the size of a thumb-nail.) Usually, given the friable nature of clay, they would have disintegrated over time. These bullae, however, were baked in the conflagrations of city destruction and have been preserved. Usually they bear names with patronymics, sometimes name and title, and rarely they have name, patronymic and title. Only a few have pictorial motifs. Unfortunately, the large assemblage of those which came to light in the mid-1970s simply appeared piecemeal on the antiquities market, and to this day their original provenance remains unkown. They were not discovered in a controlled archaeological setting, and the attendant evidence which is so important for dating and interpretation is thus lacking (Avigad 1978a, 1986).[6] Fortunately, another group of bullae were found in August 1982 in the course of a scientific dig in Jerusalem; they have recently been fully published, although preliminary publications have been available for some time (Shiloh and Tarler 1986; Shoham 2000).

The Jerusalem bullae, then, give us a secure starting point. They were found in a house in area 'G', 'along the eastern crest of the City of David spur' (Shoham 2000: 30) and belonging to stratum 10, which is dated to the late seventh and early sixth centuries. The bulla which has greatest interest from this assemblage bears the excavation number B2.G11601; it reads: *lgmryhw [b]n špn*, '[Belonging] to Gemaryahu son of Shaphan'. This makes it one of the few – only three or at most four – bullae which contain a name matching that of a biblical character, and linking that

---

6. In a private communication, Dr Stephanie Dalley (28 May 2002) has reminded me that unprovenanced seal impressions must be treated with caution, since the possibility of forgery cannot confidently be discounted. Given the recent furore over the 'James ossuary' and some other inscriptions widely noted in the mass media, her words should be borne in mind in the course of the discussion which follows.

character to the owner of the seal.[7] Gemariah ben Shaphan appears in Jeremiah 36, the story of Jeremiah's scroll, read out by Baruch and subsequently burned by Jehoiakim, purportedly in 605/4. The identification of this character with the owner of the seal which produced this bulla was quickly made by Shiloh (Shiloh and Tarler 1986), and immediately challenged by Avigad (1986: 129 n. 164). The debate between them turns on the official status of Gemariah: if he was a scribe, as Jer. 36.10 implies, then it would be odd that his title does not appear on his seal, or so Avigad claimed. There are a series of complex 'ifs' which enter into the debate, but Dearman's conclusion, having rehearsed the debate, seems sound: 'To find a *bulla* with the exact name and patronym of Gemariah, discovered in the city where he worked and confidently dated to the period in which he lived, it is reason enough to identify seal owner and biblical figure' (1990: 413 n. 24).

From this bulla coming from an identified provenance, we turn to three other Judaean bullae which came to light through the antiquities market, provenance unknown. Two were part of the same assemblage, published in Avigad 1986 (cf. 1978), as nos 8 and 9:

8: *lyrḥm'l bn hmlk* – '(Belonging) to Yeraḥme'el, son of the king'
9: *lbrkyhw bn nryhw hspr* – '(Belonging) to Berekyahu son of Neriyahu the scribe'

Commenting on these, Avigad notes that the collocation of them is important, given the connection of both names with the story of Jeremiah 36, already cited above regarding Gemariah. 'Jerahmeel, son of the king' appears in Jer. 36.26 as agent of the royal instructions to seize Jeremiah and Baruch because of the scroll they had produced. (The name 'Jerahmeel' appears otherwise only among the clan heads in the genealogies of Chronicles.) It is, of course, the name in Bulla 9 which is the more familiar: it appears in the same arrangement (with 'Baruch' in a shortened form: *bārûk ben-nēriyāhû hassōpēr*) in Jer. 36.32;[8] 'Baruch son of Neriah' appears 9 times in Jeremiah (32.12, 16; 36.4, 8, 14, 32; 43.3, 6; 45.1; 'Baruch' without patronymic appears another 39 times). Avigad had no hestitation in identifying the owner of this seal with the biblical Baruch (Avigad 1978: 53), despite the fact that 'Baruch' is a common biblical name (Avigad 1986: 29).

Much has been made of the fine literary character of Jeremiah 36, and this, for some, militates against its being taken seriously as a historical

7.   Individually, many of the names are of course found in the Bible, but not when the patronymic is taken into account. Cf. Avigad 1986: 116.

8.   This full parallel exists only in the MT; the LXX is much shorter at this point (43.32): καὶ ἔλαβεν Βαρουχ χαρτίον ἕτερον..., making no mention in the first instance of Jeremiah (MT 36.32).

record. Carroll calls it a 'brilliant story' (1981: 152; cf. 1986: 666) which is theologically shaped (1981: 153). 'Baruch' is regarded as a 'Deuteronomistic creation' who bears the weight of tradition that the deuteronomists wish him to carry (1981: 151), a conclusion Carroll did not see fit to return to in his later commentary.[9] But, as Dearman concludes after his extensive study of Jeremiah 36 and the related extrabiblical evidence, 'the point is that not only are there several external agreements between inscriptions and officials in specific instances, but the portraits of their activities are also consistent with the cultural record. It is likely, therefore, that behind the literary portraits of the scribal officials stand real individuals, who were primarily responsible for the contents and the shape of the Jeremiah scroll' (Dearman 1990: 418). While this does not lead to the conclusion that Jeremiah 36, say, is pre-exilic or exactly contemporary with the events it narrates, the continuity with the extrabiblical evidence gives strong support to those regarding it as not only 'theological' and 'literary', but 'historical' as well.

Another bulla deserves notice, although discussion about it is scarce. Avigad, oddly, appears to have forgotten about it when tabulating the number of bullae which can be identified with biblical characters (Avigad 1987: 202), although he mentions it in his preliminary publication of the Baruch and Jerahmeel bullae (1978a: 56) and it was published the same year (1978b). It bears the name *lśryw nryhw* – '(Belonging) to Seriah (son of) Neriyahu', another character involved in the Jeremiah story. In Jer. 51.59–64, 'Seraiah the son of Neriah, son of Mahseiah' (i.e. the same patronymics going back two generations as Baruch), is in royal service en route to Babylon. He takes with him a *sēper* bearing oracles against Babylon which, having been read out over that city, is to be thrown into the Euphrates as a symbolic action. Just as in the case of the previous three bullae providing a link to Jeremiah 36, so this bulla provides a link to a lower-profile episode, which is dated in the Bible to 594 during the reign of Zedekiah.[10]

---

9.   How influential Carroll's viewpoint has become is evidenced in Brueggemann's article 'The Baruch Connection' in which, despite admitting his conviction that 'Dearman's case for "historicity" is a compelling one' (1994: 407; cf. Dearman 1990), Brueggemann nonetheless regards this as unimportant for his purpose. Thus, a few pages later he speaks of 'Baruch', with quotation marks: 'Note that I allow for the role of Baruch to be fictive, following Carroll' (1994: 410). If Dearman's case was compelling, it appears Carroll's was still the more persuasive.

10.   There are also two 'Gedaliah' bullae: *lgdlyhw bn hmlk* ('[Belonging] to Gedaliah, servant of the king'), and in an earlier find from Lachish, *lgdlyhw 'šr 'l hbyt* ('[Belonging] to Gedaliah who is over the house'). Attempts to identify either of these with Gedaliah ben Ahikam ben Shaphan, governor of Judah post-587 remain speculative. See Avigad 1986: 25; Becking 1997.

Finally, we may consider Jer. 40.14. Johanan ben Kareah 'and all the leaders of the forces in the open country' (40.13) come to Gedaliah, recently installed governor of Judah, with the report: ' "Do you know that Baalis *[baˁᵃlîs]* the king of the Ammonites has sent Ishmael the son of Nethaniah to take your life?" But Gedaliah the son of Ahikam would not believe them.' The Ammonite king named in this verse was unknown apart from this reference until 1984 when excavators at Tell el-ˁUmeiri (i.e. in Ammonite territory) discovered a decorated seal impression[11] dated to roughly 600 bearing the inscription *lmlkmʾwr ˁbd bˁlyšˁ* '(Belonging) to Milkomʾur, servant of Baˁalisha'. The impulse to connect the master named in the seal with the biblical Ammonite king Baalis is very strong and has been widely accepted. It is not without difficulties (enumerated by Becking 1997: 80–82; Geraty 1992), chiefly to do with the orthography of the name and the absence of royal identification for it in the seal.[12] However, as Becking notes (1997: 82), the differences of orthography are readily accounted for, and considerations in favour of identifying the master of the seal with Baalis of Jer. 40.14 are quite strong. So, not perhaps conclusive proof, but again an indication that there is demonstrable continuity between Jeremiah's stories and history.

3. *Internal Evidence*

3.1. *Historical Settings*

Even without external evidence as corroboration, some texts by their very nature demand a pre-exilic setting. Others fit best within the window of a given cultural context which we catch a glimpse of through the archaeological record.

Since we are concerned in this paper with 'pre-exilic' rather than 'authentic' words of the prophet, an important pair of texts from Jeremiah call for attention: the versions of the 'Temple Sermon' recorded in Jeremiah 7 and 26. The differences between the two are immediately obvious (cf. Holt 1986). Jeremiah 7 records an extended oracle against trust in the Temple, with only the bare minimum of narrative setting (not even a hint of a date), but laced through with 'Deuteronomistic' phrases and themes. Jeremiah 26, on the other hand, contains only an abbreviated sermon, but has full and dramatic narrative development, including a setting at the beginning of Jehoiakim's reign in 609. The two accounts share the divine directive to deliver an oracle in the Temple environs (*šˁr*

---

11. Apparently neither a docket, nor a bulla, but a shaped and fired clay piece; Herr (1985: 169) speculates it might have been a jug stopper.

12. On spelling: the name in Hebrew uses *samek* rather than *šin* and lacks the *ˁayin* of the Ammonite version. Younker (1985: 174) argues that the pictorial motif – 'a four-winged flying scarab beetle pushing a solar ball, flanked on both sides by what appear to be standards, each surmounted by a lunar crescent' – is royal.

'gate' in 7.2, *hṣr* 'court' in 26.2), so that everyone coming to worship would hear that they must live in justice and fidelity or the Temple would be made like Shiloh. Jeremiah 7.4 records the dramatic saying: 'Do not trust in these deceptive words: "This is the Temple of the Lord, the Temple of the Lord, the Temple of the Lord."' It is widely agreed that both accounts refer to the same event, but that both accounts have been subject to elaboration along quite different lines and with differing intentions.[13]

Our previous discussion has demonstrated that the narratives of Jeremiah contain historically plausible, and even reliable details. My concern here is not to carry out detailed redactional work on Jeremiah 7 and 26; rather to suggest that, like Jeremiah 36 (and by implication 51.59–64), the 'Temple Sermon' demands a pre-exilic setting, even if it was subsequently elaborated in different ways. Carroll argues that the Second Temple period was one of '*contested* temple projects' (1994: 49, italics original) and that references to Temples in late biblical texts have significance symbolically rather than historically, or structurally (that is, you could not build one, based on the descriptions we have [1994: 47]). The positive point he makes is an important one, though, as all the texts he cites in relation to the Second Temple (including Haggai–Zechariah–Malachi, '[t]he one group of prophetic texts that might be regarded as being indisputably the product of the second temple period' [Carroll 1994: 41]) regard the Temple as having a high degree of importance. The immediate task for the communities of Haggai–Zechariah is to build the Temple – whatever it might have looked like (not much, according to Ezra 3.12–13!).

Such a development suggests that later traditionists would have had trouble in constructing a sermon like the one of Jeremiah's which lies behind the two 'Temple Sermon' passages. In either version, the sermon has two related points: (1) God demands ethical behaviour and religious devotion; (2) the result of ignoring these requirements was the destruction of the Temple. While ch. 7 draws out the 'deceptive words' which imply that the Temple had taken on the nature fail-safe protection, and ch. 26 lays the emphasis more on impending destruction, the 'text' found at the root of these applications could not be part of the 'symbolic world' of the Second Temple period. The formulation of Jer. 7.4 would be especially startling, as in 'symbolic' terms, the Temple takes on a treacherous character with potential to deceive the faithful. In the post-exilic period, recovery of the Temple was itself part and parcel of a just society and faithful observance. Jeremiah's Temple Sermon could only be a pre-exilic homily.

A second example can be dealt with more briefly. In a similar fashion, though coming from a slightly later period, the oracles against Babylon

---

13. Cf. in addition to the commentaries: Holt 1986, Kang 1996, and Sharp 2003: 44–62.

(Jer. 50–51) might plausibly be thought to predate 539. Their strident call for a violent end to Babylon's hegemony sits uneasily in the Persian period, after the peaceful capitulation of Babylon to Cyrus. There is, further, the possibility that they require a date prior to roughly 550, given the implication of Jer. 51.11 and 28 that the 'kings of the Medes' oppose Babylon. Frye (1984: 82) notes that dates for the conquest of the Medes by Cyrus are a bit vague,[14] but cites clear evidence for the threat felt in Babylon by the Median tribes, even finding here impetus for the anti-Babylonian oracles of Isaiah and Jeremiah.

Reference to certain religious practices within Jeremiah may also most plausibly be linked to pre-exilic settings.[15] The intriguing references to the 'Queen of heaven' (Jer. 7.18; 44.17–19, 25) have been widely studied, and several plausible suggestions have been made for the identity of the 'Queen'.[16] Whatever the exact identification might be, the admission – indeed, claim – of the Jeremiah tradition that worship of the Queen was widespread and ancestral (44.17, 21) may be exilic but could hardly be later than that. Carroll's argument, that this is a reflection of a deuteronomistic construction of reality in consonance with its picture of Josianic reform (1986: 735–37), sits uneasily with the deuteronom(ist)ic presentation of exclusive Yahweh worship since the days of Moses (e.g. Deut. 4; 13; 1 Kgs 8.60). Something similar might be claimed for solar worship in Jeremiah. In his exhaustive study of sun worship in ancient Israel, Taylor examines Jer. 8.1–3 which condemns the élite of Judaean society who have revered 'the sun and the moon and all the host of heaven' (Taylor 1993: 197–200). Horse figurines with solar discs, prevalent in pre-exilic contexts but not later, provide archaeological evidence for some form of solar worship in Israel and Judah prior to 587 (cf. Taylor 1993: 58–66; Day 2000: 153), though interpretation of this evidence has problems of its own. They are, however, sometimes linked to 2 Kgs 23.11 which gives an account of a removal of horses dedicated to the sun during Josiah's reforms. While again falling short of conclusive 'proof', such clusters of evidence point to the likelihood of a pre-exilic setting for Jer. 8.1–3, or at least of its language having its roots in the pre-exilic period.

14.   Akkadian sources cited by Frye date the fall of the Medes to 550–549 BCE (Frye 1984: 84).

15.   I am indebted to Professor Susan Ackerman for drawing my attention to the significance of material remains and religious practice for my essay on Jeremiah. In addition to the evidence discussed in this paragraph, Professor Ackerman makes further tentative suggestions concerning other archaeological data pertaining to religious practices in pre-exilic Judah; I regret that I am unable to explore them further here.

16.   Day 2000: 144–50 after discussion opts for Astarte, cautiously open to Ackerman's suggestion of a syncretistic Astarte-Ishtar figure (2000: 150).

3.2. *Historical 'Mistakes'*

A text written after the event, or substantially reshaped after the event, might be expected to get things 'right': events, fates of individuals, and so on, should conform to those known outcomes. Where there is a failure for text and 'outcome' to coincide, it is reasonable to think that the text was, in fact, composed before the outcome of the event was known, or before the ultimate fate of a given character was determined.

Two problems arise in this connection with the oracles against the kings contained in Jeremiah 22. The first, and perhaps lesser, problem has to do with the fate of Jehoiakim. Jeremiah 22.18–19 denounce Jehoiakim, predicting for him an ignominious and violent end. Note v. 19 in particular: 'With the burial of an ass he shall be buried, dragged and cast forth beyond the gates of Jerusalem', a prediction elaborated further in 36.30 ('his dead body shall be cast out to the heat by day and the frost by night'), forming part of the conclusion to the story we have already considered above. The problem here is that according to 2 Kgs 24.6, Jehoiakim 'slept with his fathers', i.e. was buried in a royal tomb. Commentators since the time of Jerome have struggled to reconcile these texts. The simplest solution is to suppose that the predictions in Jeremiah are just that – predictions, thus predating Jehoiakim's death. Giving such prophecies after the event is nonsensical. Some have suggested that the grave was desecrated in the course of the Babylonian conquest (e.g. Rudolph 1968: 141) and that this accounts for the divergent traditions; Lipschits argues that the solution is to be found through literary rather than historical means (2002: 10–11/ para. 3.2.10–11).[17] As McKane notes, even Duhm – prepared to excise so much of Jeremiah – finds greater explanatory power in taking this as a sign of the text's 'earliness' rather than in thinking that it must, somehow, have come true (McKane 1986: 534).

Similarly, problems arise with the curse levelled at 'Coniah' (= Jehoiachin) in 22.24–30. The passage begins with a prose denunciation: Jehoiachin is torn off as Yahweh's signet ring, and cast into exile where he will die. This passage forms one half of one of the 'textbook' examples of inner-biblical interpretation, with its counterpart in Hag. 2.23 picking up the language of the 'ring' now grasped and approved by Yahweh: 'I will take you, O Zerubbabel my servant, the son of Shealtiel, says the Lord, and make you like a signet ring; for I have chosen you, says the Lord of hosts.' Clearly there is an issue of interest here for biblical theologians, but the point for this essay is encountered in Jer. 22.30, at the conclusion of the pericope: 'Write this man down as childless, a man who shall not

---

17. Lipschits considers many sides to the problem, but his contention that the writer of Kings omitted the full details of Jehoiakim's burial in part to avoid contradiction with Jeremiah's curse fails to convince, since 2 Kgs 24.6 stands necessarily in tension with the curse(s) in any case; cf. Lipschits 2002: 11/para 3.2.11.

succeed in his days; for none of his offspring shall succeed in sitting on the throne of David, and ruling again in Judah'. The interpretative issues here are somewhat tangled, but there is a body of interpretation which sees a problem in the prediction of being 'childless', for as the Weidner tablet records, Jehoiachin was given rations in captivity for himself and five sons (cf. Wiseman 1985: 81). However, it is possible to take the two features of the larger curse together: it was itself used as a starting point for the Haggai prophecy, and so had passed already into the tradition by that time; and closer to the time of the events themselves, Jehoiachin was not childless in captivity, and one of his offspring seemed destined to rule after him (Zerubbabel). Again, it is not necessary here to deal with all the rough edges to make the broad point that this text is more easily explained as coming before the events than after them. (With the fate of Jehoiachin we have reached, of course, the very remote edge of the 'pre-exilic' period. It is the historical dynamic of this text – which has of course other dimensions – which I wish to align with passages more clearly within the pre-exilic period.)

3.3. *Any Role for Literary Criticism? (Jeremiah 30–31)*
Even some of those who reject most forcefully the dating of biblical texts to the pre-Persian period grant that there is some merit in 'literary' or 'historical criticism', that is, an appreciation that texts changed over time, the boundary between author, editor, and copyist being even more fluid in the ancient world than it is in the modern world. Further, they allow that there are in the Bible relics of an earlier age (cf. Davies 1992: 95) even if, as they contend, these relics are too fragmentary and isolated to allow access to the world from which they derive. Together, this suggests that there remains a role for historical criticism in performing a sort of literary archaeology, even if it is more fraught than the kind that deals with dirt. That is, strands of texts may be disentangled, and the strands identified as relatively prior or later and may point to a pre-exilic setting for the earliest layer.

This may well be the case in many passages in Jeremiah, but one shall suffice as an example for now. The 'Book of Consolation' in Jeremiah 30–33 contains some of the most striking and famous passages in the book. One of its striking features is the degree to which Jeremiah 30–31 holds out restoration for both 'Israel' and 'Judah', with the emphasis falling on the former rather than the latter. Although the older view that this combination reflected a post-exilic, idealized Israel and thus was evidence for the late dating of the passage has not been wholly abandoned, there is now a growing body of scholarship that finds in this passage rather indications of a very early tradition of Jeremiah's preaching which reaches back beyond even Jehoiakim to the time of Josiah.

This suggestion has long been debated. Rudolph, following the lead of earlier scholars, suggested that Jeremiah 30–31 should be dated between the fall of Nineveh and the death of Josiah (Rudolph 1968: 189); he labels this passage 'Heilsweissagung für das Nordreich'. To Lohfink, the issue initially appears clouded, for the earliest dated oracle of Jeremiah's is the Temple Sermon (Jer. 26.1) – dated to *Jehoiakim*'s succession year. His search to probe into Jeremiah's earlier work takes him to Jeremiah 30–31 (Lohfink 1981). In spite of Duhm's claim that Jeremiah 30–31 was 'eine sehr späte, auf jeden Fall nachexilische Schrift' (Lohfink 1981: 352), Lohfink himself follows the majority of commentators in finding a Jeremianic core which was subsequently elaborated. Noting that Jeremiah's typical style is to use brief, but related units, and without 'Deuteronomistic' influences, he thus identifies seven units having an original unity: 30.5–7, 12–15, 18–21; 31.2–6, 15–17, 18–20, 21–22 (1981: 357). Their unity resides essentially in the fact that they all address Israel/ Ephraim with a consistent theme: Yahweh's care for the distressed Israel.[18]

Sweeney followed Lohfink's general line of interpretation, but revised significantly judgments concerning the nature of the redactional activity in the text (1996, and again in 2001: 225–33). Sweeney sets out on his careful critical analysis noting that 'an analysis of the major features of the structure of these chapters provides the criteria for reconstructing an earlier form of the text that calls for the restoration of the former northern kingdom of Israel to Judah and Davidic rule'. He goes on to draw out the implication: 'In so far as this concern was a primary feature of King Josiah's program of national restoration and religious reform, it demonstrates that the prophet Jeremiah was a supporter of Josiah's reform during the early stages of his prophetic career' (Sweeney 1996: 572). Sweeney observes that the materials which treat the restoration of Israel and Judah together at both ends of the passage are found with formula *hinnēh yāmîm bā'îm*, suggesting to Sweeney the presence of 'later supplementary materials' (1996: 578), while different formulae are used in the Israel-alone material. With these and other considerations in mind, Sweeney argues that Jer. 30.1–4; 31.27–34 and 31.38–40 should be regarded as redactional, 'clarifying' the meaning of 30.12–17 and 31.23–25 (Zion/Judah passages, but the former only as a result of later textual activity, and the latter actually referring to a united Israel). As a result, Sweeney finds an older layer in 30.5–31.26 and 31.35–37 – larger and more continuous than Lohfink's analysis – which yields a 'relatively coherent

18. Huwyler employs similar methods and reasoning in his analysis of the oracles against foreign nations in Jer. 46–49: e.g. the first Egypt oracle dated to 605 (1997: 100–106), or the oracle against Ammon (49.3–5) which Huwyler argues has at least a *terminus ad quem* of 582 though does not date this oracle with the same confidence as the Egypt oracle (1997: 206–207).

text with a consistent message concerning the restoration of the downfallen northern kingdom', and a subsequent 'reunification of the northern kingdom of Israel with Judah and its return to the rule of the Davidic dynasty' (Sweeney 1996: 580).

Such reconstructions are, naturally, subject to debate, refinement and even possible rejection! But the convergent lines described in the work of Lohfink and Sweeney point persuasively to Jeremianic material which goes back to the period at least preceding Josiah's death in 609.

4. *Conclusions*

Noting the Lachish ostraca and the Babylonian text referring to Jehoiachin's rations, Davies admits that 'the biblical Israel shares characters and events with the historical populations of Palestine', but these are related only in the same way that Shakespeare and Julius Caesar, or Malory and King Arthur are: 'authentic geographical settings and genuine chronological settings do not of themselves guarantee historicity of anything' (1992: 33). Caution worth heeding – but if they guarantee nothing, they are at least indicative of something. It strikes me that the nature of the connection between extrabiblical evidence and Jeremiah suggests that Davies's analogies are not well chosen. It is not simply a case of old memories (or even sources) being elaborated, let alone fabricated, but of old memories (or even sources) being preserved.

As Herrmann observes, 'it is hardly the case that the desire for recorded historical precision alone has preserved for us names and facts' (1984: 310). Nonetheless, the selection of materials assembled here tilts the balance of probability towards a closer connection between 'event' and text than some have allowed. This is not to suggest that 'ideology' or 'theology' is absent from the biblical text – far from it. It does, however, imply that the gap between event and text is not impossibly large. Even more, it renders the claim that certain named characters were creations of later ideologues highly suspect and in some cases misleading.

Recent debates about history in the Hebrew Bible have sometimes generated more heat than light. Inevitably, disagreements will persist, and not only about what counts as evidence and what is an assumption. The end result, this study suggests, should not be the divorce of Bible and history, but a more careful and ultimately more fruitful ongoing relationship between them.[19]

---

19. This paper was read both in the course of the Oxford Seminar series, and also in the senior Biblical Studies seminar in Edinburgh. I am grateful to conversation partners on both occasions for helpful discussion; particular contributions have been noted above. I am (again!) indebted to Professor John Day for stimulating discussion, fruitful suggestions, and sharp editing. Of course, I am solely responsible for the shortcomings that remain.

Bibliography

Ahlström, G.W.
1993   *The History of Ancient Palestine from the Palaeolithic Period to Alexander's Conquest* (JSOTSup, 146; Sheffield: Sheffield Academic Press).

Avigad, N.
1978a   'Baruch the Scribe and Jerahmeel the King's Son', *IEJ* 28: 52–56 + Pl. xv.
1978b   'The Seal of Seraiah (Son of) Neriah', *Eretz-Israel* 14: 86–87, 125* + Pl. I.3 (Hebrew).
1986   *Hebrew Bullae from the Time of Jeremiah: Remnants of a Burnt Archive* (Jerusalem: Israel Exploration Society).
1987   'The Contribution of Hebrew Seals to an Understanding of Israelite Religion and Society', in P.D. Miller, P.D. Hanson and S.D. McBride (eds), *Ancient Israelite Religion: Essays in Honor of Frank Moore Cross* (Philadelphia: Fortress Press): 195–208.

Becking, B.
1997   'Inscribed Seals as Evidence for Biblical Israel? Jeremiah 40.7–41.15 *par example*', in L. Grabbe (ed.), *Can a 'History of Israel' be Written?* (JSOTSup, 245; Sheffield: Sheffield Academic Press): 65–83.

Begin, Z.B.
2002   'Does Lachish Letter 4 Contradict Jeremiah xxxiv 7?', *VT* 52: 166–74.

Brueggemann, W.
1994   'The Baruch Connection: Reflections on Jeremiah 43:1–7', *JBL* 113: 405–20.

Calmeyer, P.
1987   'Greek Historiography and Achaemenid Reliefs', in H. Sancisi-Weerdenburgh and A. Kuhrt (eds), *Achaemenid History, II: The Greek Sources* (Leiden: E. J. Brill): 11–26.

Carroll, R.P.
1981   *From Chaos to Covenant: Uses of Prophecy in the Book of Jeremiah* (London: SCM Press).
1986   *Jeremiah: A Commentary* (OTL; London: SCM Press).
1994   'So What do we *Know* about the Temple? The Temple in the Prophets', in T. C. Eskenazi and K. H. Richards (eds), *Second Temple Studies, II: Temple and Community in the Persian Period* (JSOTSup, 175; Sheffield: JSOT Press): 34–51.

Cazelles, H.
1981   'La vie de Jérémie dans son contexte national et international', in P.-M. Bogaert (ed.), *Le livre de Jérémie: le prophète et son milieu, les oracles et leur transmission* (BETL, 54; Leuven: Leuven University Press): 21–39.

Cogan, M., and H. Tadmor (eds)
1988   *II Kings: A New Translation with Introduction and Commentary* (AB, 11; Garden City, NY: Doubleday).

Davies, P.R.
1992   *In Search of 'Ancient Israel'* (JSOTSup, 148; Sheffield: Sheffield Academic Press).

Day, J.
2000   *Yahweh and the Gods and Goddesses of Canaan* (JSOTSup, 265; Sheffield: JSOT Press).

Dearman, J.A.
    1990   'My Servants the Scribes: Composition and Context in Jeremiah', *JBL* 109: 403–21.

Freedman, D.N.
    1975   'The Babylonian Chronicle', in G.E. Wright and D.N. Freedman (eds), *The Biblical Archaeologist Reader,* I (Missoula, MT: Scholars Press): 113–27. Originally published in *BA* 19 (1956): 50–60.

Frye, R.N.
    1984   *The History of Ancient Iran* (Munich: Beck).

Geraty, L.T.
    1992   'Baalis (Person)', in *ABD*, I: 556–57.

Gibson, J.C.L.
    1971   *Textbook of Syrian Semitic Inscriptions,* I: *Hebrew and Moabite Inscriptions* (Oxford: Clarendon Press).

Grayson, A.K.
    1975   *Assyrian and Babylonian Chronicles* (TCS, 5; Locust Valley, NY: J.J. Augustin).

Herr, L.G.
    1985   'The Servant of Baalis', *BA* 48: 169–72.

Herrmann, S.
    1981   'Jeremia – der Prophet und die Verfasser der Buches Jeremia', in P.-M. Bogaert (ed.), *Le livre de Jérémie: le prophète et son milieu, les oracles et leur transmission* (BETL, 54; Leuven: Leuven University Press): 197–214.
    1984   'Overcoming the Israelite Crisis: Remarks on the Interpretation of the Book of Jeremiah', in L.G. Perdue and B.W. Kovacs (eds), *A Prophet to the Nations: Essays in Jeremiah Studies* (Winona Lake, IN: Eisenbrauns): 299–311.

Holt, E.K.
    1986   'Jeremiah's Temple Sermon and the Deuteronomists: An Investigation of the Redactional Relationship Between Jeremiah 7 and 26', *JSOT* 36: 73–87.

Hughes, J.
    1990   *Secrets of the Times: Myth and History in Biblical Chronology* (JSOTSup, 66; Sheffield: Sheffield Academic Press).

Huwyler, B.
    1997   *Jeremia und die Völker: Untersuchungen zu den Völkersprüchen in Jeremia 46–49* (FAT, 20; Tübingen: Mohr Siebeck).

Jobling, D.
    1984   'The Quest of the Historical Jeremiah: Hermeneutical Implications of Recent Literature', in L.G. Perdue and B.W. Kovacs (eds), *A Prophet to the Nations: Essays in Jeremiah Studies* (Winona Lake, IN: Eisenbrauns): 285–97

Kang, S.-M.
    1996   'The Authentic Sermon of Jeremiah in Jeremiah 7:1–20', in M.V. Fox *et al.* (eds), *Texts, Temples, and Traditions: A Tribute to Menahem Haran* (Winona Lake, IN: Eisenbrauns): 147–62.

King, P.J.
    1993   *Jeremiah: An Archaeological Companion* (Louisville, KY: Westminster John Knox Press).

Lipschits, O.
2002   '"Jehoiakim Slept with his Fathers" (II Kings 24:6) – did he?', *Journal of Hebrew Scriptures* 4.1: 1–33.

Lohfink, N.
1981   'Der junge Jeremia als Propogandist und Poet: Zum Grundstock von Jer 30–31', in P.-M. Bogaert (ed.), *Le livre de Jérémie: le prophète et son milieu, les oracles et leur transmission* (BETL, 54; Leuven: Leuven University Press): 351–68.

McKane, W.
1986–96 *A Critical and Exegetical Commentary on Jeremiah* (ICC; 2 vols; Edinburgh: T. & T. Clark).

Pardee, D.
1982   *Handbook of Ancient Hebrew Letters: A Study Edition* (Chico, CA: Scholars Press).

Porten, B.
1981   'The Identity of King Adon', *BA* 44: 36–52.

Rudolph, W.
1968   *Jeremia* (HAT, 12; Tübingen: J.C.B. Mohr [Paul Siebeck], 3rd edn).

Schottroff, W.
1970   'Jeremia 2,1–3: Erwägungen zur Methode der Prophetenexegese', in F. Crüsemann, R. Kessler und L. Schottroff (eds), *Gerechtigkeit lernen: Beiträge zur biblischen Sozialgeschichte.* (TBü, Altes Testament, 94; Gütersloh: Chr. Kaiser and Gütersloher Verlagshaus): 272–304.

Seybold, K.
1993   *Der Prophet Jeremia: Leben und Werk* (Stuttgart: W. Kohlhammer).

Sharp, C.J.
2003   *Prophecy and Ideology in Jeremiah: Struggles for Authenticity in the Deutero-Jeremianic Prose* (London: T. & T. Clark).

Shiloh, Y., and D. Tarler
1986   'Bullae from the City of David: A Hoard of Seal Impressions from the Israelite Period', *BA* 44: 196–209.

Shoham, Y.
2000   'Hebrew Bullae', in *Excavations at the City of David 1978–1985 Directed by Yigal Shiloh,* VI: *Inscriptions* (Qedem, 41; Jerusalem: Institute of Archaeology, Hebrew University): 29–57.

Skinner, J.
1926   *Prophecy & Religion: Studies in the Life of Jeremiah* (Cambridge: Cambridge University Press).

Sweeney, M.A.
1996   'Jeremiah 30–31 and King Josiah's Program of National Restoration and Religious Reform', *ZAW* 108: 569–83.
2001   *King Josiah of Judah: The Lost Messiah of Israel* (New York: Oxford University Press).

Taylor, J.G.
1993   *Yahweh and the Sun: Biblical and Archaeological Evidence for Sun Worship in Ancient Israel* (JSOTSup, 111; Sheffield: JSOT Press)

Thomas, D.W.
    1958   'Again "The Prophet" in the Lachish Ostraca', in J. Hempel and L. Rost (eds),
            *Von Ugarit nach Qumran: Beiträge zur alttestamentlichen und altorientalischen
            Forschung Otto Eissfeldt zum 1. September dargebracht* (BZAW, 77; Berlin:
            Alfred Töpelmann): 244–49.

Vanderhooft, D.
    2003   'Babylonian Strategies of Imperial Control in the West: Royal Practice and
            Rhetoric', in O. Lipschits and J. Blenkinsopp (eds), *Judah and the Judeans in
            the Neo-Babylonian Period* (Winona Lake, IN: Eisenbrauns): 235–62.

Welch, A.C.
    1928   *Jeremiah: His Time and His Work* (London: Oxford University Press).

Wiseman, D.J.
    1956   *Chronicles of Chaldaean Kings (626–556 B.C.) in the British Museum* (London:
            The Trustees of the British Museum).
    1985   *Nebuchadrezzar and Babylon* (The Schweich Lectures of the British Academy,
            1983; Oxford: The British Academy and Oxford University Press).

Younker, R.W.
    1985   'Israel, Judah, and Ammon and the Motifs on the Baalis Seal from Tell el-
            'Umeiri', *BA* 48: 173–80.

Chapter 11

How many Pre-exilic Psalms are there?

John Day

It has been a commonplace over the years for scholars to state that the dating of the Psalms is notoriously difficult. As evidence of the great diversity of datings the Psalms have received it is instructive to note that whereas a century ago, a scholar like B. Duhm (1899: xix, 2nd edn, 1922: xx-xxi) could regard Psalm 137 (which reflects the experience of the exile) as the earliest psalm in the Psalter, half a century later I. Engnell (1943 [1967]: 176 n. 2) could regard it as the latest in the book of Psalms. So whereas at one extreme the Psalms have been regarded as almost entirely post-exilic, at the other extreme they have been regarded as almost entirely pre-exilic! For the most part, however, mainline scholarship in recent generations has tended to accept that there are in fact both pre- and post-exilic psalms (though there has been much variation in detail about the precise distribution and proportion of pre- and post-exilic psalms), and that is the viewpoint which I shall be defending in this paper. Although precise dating is usually impossible, I would maintain that with a certain number (though far from all) of the Psalms we can at least establish a general probability as to whether they are pre- or post-exilic. In arguing for this position I shall attempt to controvert the 'everything is late' school of thought, which has asserted itself in some recent work on the Psalms, just as it has in many other areas of Old Testament study. As will be seen, however, the scholars who have ventured into print to defend a late date for all or most of the Psalms are not the usual suspects! In approaching this subject the largest part of this essay will be taken up with seeking criteria for regarding certain psalms as pre-exilic; I shall then go on to consider criteria for exilic psalms and finally consider which psalms are likely to be post-exilic, before going on to formulate some general conclusions.

1. *Evidence for Pre-exilic Psalms*

1.1. *Royal Psalms*
Traditionally, of course, much of the Psalter was regarded as royal inasmuch as many of the Psalms were believed to have been written by

David. Since the rise of modern biblical criticism, however, this view has generally been rejected, since so many of the psalms in question are insufficiently specific as to suggest Davidic authorship or reference (but cf. Goulder 1990). However, since the time of Gunkel (1926; cf. Gunkel and Begrich 1928–33, ET 1998) the following psalms have typically been regarded as royal in the sense of relating to kings of the Davidic monarchy and have accordingly been regarded as pre-exilic (or sometimes in the case of Psalm 89, exilic): Psalms 2, 18, 20, 21, 45, 72, 89, 101, 110, 132 and 144.1–11. (Ps. 144.12–15 is rightly seen as a later addition, as it contains late language as well as distinctive content.) Nevertheless, there has always been a minority of scholars who have rejected the notion that these are pre-exilic Royal Psalms. Three main alternative explanations have been proposed. First, some have seen them as Maccabaean/Hasmonaean Royal Psalms from the second/first century BCE. This view is not much held nowadays but was common a hundred years ago, though it has been revived fairly recently by the Italian scholar M. Treves (1988), who attributes virtually the whole Psalter to the period between 170 and 103 BCE. Against this understanding of the Royal Psalms stand the following points. First, some of the Royal Psalms imply a king of the Davidic line, which the Maccabees/Hasmonaeans could not claim to be (Pss 18.51, ET 50; 89.21, 36, 50, ET 20, 35, 49; 132.1. 10, 11, 17; 144.10). Secondly, the Hebrew is classical and does not show signs of the gradual transformation into the later Mishnaic Hebrew which we might expect at such a late date; indeed, the textual obscurities in Psalm 110 are suggestive of an ancient, not a late origin (note especially v. 3).[1] Thirdly, Ps. 132.8 presupposes the

---

1.   Apart from Treves (1965; 1988), Ps. 110 has been seen as relating specifically to Simon Maccabaeus by other occasional scholars in recent years (cf. Gerleman 1981; Donner 1991; Astour 1992: 685). However, it is most improbable that there are any Maccabaean psalms in the Psalter and, as has been noted, Ps. 110 bears signs of antiquity (cf. further Hardy 1945), and it seems most natural in the light of v. 4's attribution to the king of a priesthood after the order of the pre-Israelite, Jebusite ruler Melchizedek (cf. Gen. 14.18–20) to suppose that this is a very early psalm, perhaps even Davidic, fusing the Israelite and Jebusite royal ideologies. That the title 'high priest of God Most High' (i.e. El-Elyon) should later be appropriated by the Hasmonaean kings (cf. Josephus, *Ant.* 16.163; *Ass. Mos.* 6.1) from Gen. 14.18 is entirely understandable, since taken with Ps. 110.4 this could be used to justify their non-Zadokite status. Moreover, the old view that Ps. 110 contains an acrostic relating to Simon Maccabaeus, revived by Treves and some others, has been thoroughly refuted by Bowker 1967. (See Lindars 1967 for a similar refutation of the old view, revived by Treves, that Ps. 2 contains an acrostic relating to Alexander Jannaeus.)

It has also occasionally been suggested that Ps. 110 pertained to a high priest of the Persian period (cf. Schreiner 1977, who relates it to Joshua, the high priest contemporary with Zerubbabel). However, it may be noted that it was important for the post-exilic high priests (like the priests generally) to be of Aaronic descent, which Melchizedek, to whom the figure of the psalm is related (Ps. 110.4), could not claim to be. Moreover, the warlike lanuage is more suggestive of a king than one who was simply a high priest, and Melchizedek was a king as well as a priest according to Gen. 14.18, so the one after his order in Ps. 110.4 ought to be likewise.

existence of the Ark of the Covenant, which was no longer the case after 586 BCE. Fourthly, converging pieces of evidence suggest that the Masoretic Psalter was already completed well before this time (even if at Qumran there were still variations in the order of the last two books of the Psalms) – compare the fact that 1 Chron. 16.35–36 (surely no later than 300 BCE) already cites Ps. 106.47–48 complete with the concluding editorial doxology at the end of book 4 of the Psalter, suggesting that the division into books had already occurred, at least up to this point. Further, the Septuagint already contains all the Masoretic Psalms (can this really be dated later than the second century BCE?), and Qumran Psalm manuscripts go back to the second and first centuries BCE. Among the very earliest is one containing the Royal Psalm 89, 4QPs89, dating from either the second or first century BCE (cf. Flint 1997: 38).

A second alternative view maintained by some scholars envisages the Royal Psalms as post-exilic eschatological messianic psalms. Seeing them as eschatological was, of course, a common viewpoint in the pre-critical period, and the New Testament builds on this understanding (which had grown up in Second Temple Judaism) when it applied them to Christ. In recent years this view has been followed by scholars such as R. Tournay (1988, ET 1991) and E. Gerstenberger (1988; 2001). Against this viewpoint, however, stands the fact that in the Royal Psalms the king is constantly referred to as one who is already alive and reigning, rather than one whose arrival is expected in the future.

A third alternative view maintains that the Royal Psalms are post-exilic psalms in which the 'king' is merely a collective symbol for the nation. This view was held by a few nineteenth-century scholars but has been revived more recently by J. Becker (1977, ET 1980) and O. Loretz (1988a), though these two scholars often see authentic pre-exilic royal material underlying them. Against this view, however, it has to be stated that it conflicts with the plain meaning of these psalms as relating to real individual kings; nothing in them implies that the 'king' is merely a collective symbol for the nation. It is therefore not surprising that this view has had little following. Accordingly, in the light of the above discussion, we should continue to maintain that the Psalter contains a number of pre-exilic Royal Psalms pertaining to the Davidic kings.[2]

---

2. Although I have never seen it argued in print, a fourth alternative might be to envisage the king in the Royal Psalms as on occasion a Persian monarch. I gather from conversation with my colleague Walter Houston that P.R. Davies considers this a possible interpretation of Ps. 72; this is the source of the suggestion alluded to in Houston 1999: 344 n. 3, though Houston himself appears to prefer on balance the traditional pre-exilic Judaean king interpretation. I can see how one might argue that the Persians receive a good press within the Old Testament and note that Deutero-Isaiah could even speak of Cyrus as $m^e\check{s}\hat{i}h\hat{o}$ 'his (Yahweh's) anointed' (Isa. 45.1). However, against such a view of Royal Psalms like Ps. 72 I

A number of scholars, especially Scandinavian and British, e.g. H. Birkeland (1933; 1955), the later Mowinckel (1951, ET 1962), J.H. Eaton (1976, 2nd edn, 1986), S.J.L. Croft (1987) and M.D. Goulder (1990), have attempted to increase considerably the number of psalms to be regarded as royal, especially by including in this category many of the Individual Laments. If this view were to be accepted the number of pre-exilic psalms would accordingly also be greatly increased. However, I have shown elsewhere (Day 1990: 21–25) that this is unjustified, and only a few additional psalms are conceivably royal, but even they are uncertain. Thus, we find in the Individual Lament Psalms that the psalmist tends to stand alone rather than appearing to be the leader or representative of a group, which we should expect if the subject was a king. Again, when we come to examine the allegedly warlike language which is claimed to indicate that the psalmist is a king battling against foreign enemies, quite often we find that the psalmist is actually speaking of verbal rather than actual violence (cf. Pss 57.5, ET 4; 64.4, ET 3; 140.4, 10, ET 3, 9), making a royal interpretation much less likely. Finally, it should be noted that already before the exile Jeremiah's confessions make use of the Individual Lament form (Jer. 11.18–12.6; 15.10–21; 17.14–18; 18.18–23; 20.7–18),[3] showing that it could be used by private citizens as much as kings. Jeremiah 15.20 declares, 'they will fight against you, but they shall not prevail over you', words which would have been confidently applied to the king by some scholars if they had occurred in a psalm! We need to make allowance for metaphorical language. Having said all that, however, it is true that there are a few Individual Lament Psalms where the enemies are explicitly stated to be foreign nations (cf. Pss 56.8, ET 7; 59.6, 9, ET 5, 8),[4]

would note that (i) there is nothing positive to support such a view; (ii) the words of Ps. 72.8, 'May he have dominion from sea to sea, and from the River to the ends of the earth' are applied to the Davidic messiah in Zech. 9.10, suggesting that they had their origin in language applied to the Davidic monarch; (iii) those Royal Psalms which give further information as to the identity of the ruler indicate an Israelite king, since he is associated with David (Pss 18.51, ET 50; 89.21, 36, 50, ET 20, 35, 49; 132.1, 10, 11, 17; 144.10) and rules from Zion (Pss 2.6; 20.3, ET 2; 110.2; 132.13, 17), so one would most naturally assume the same for other Royal Psalms like Ps. 72 which share the same basic ideology. The fact that David and Zion are not explicitly mentioned in Ps. 72 is probably accidental, this background here being taken for granted.

3. I am not convinced by the attempt of R.P. Carroll (1981: 107–35) to claim that Jeremiah's laments (or confessions) are really collective laments of the exiles. If this were really the case, it is amazing that they contain only the 'I' form and never the 'we' form from beginning to end. One would have expected at least some first-person plural forms if Carroll's view were correct, so as to clarify that the 'I' is a collective 'I'.

4. Foreign nations are explicitly cited as the enemy in another Individual Lament, Ps. 9.6, 9, 16, 18, 20 (ET 5, 8, 15, 17, 19) and 10.16, and I previously considered this to be conceivably a pre-exilic Royal Psalm (Day 1990: 23, 94). However, on balance, I am now inclined to see this as post-exilic because of its acrostic nature (cf. below on acrostic psalms).

so I would leave open the possibility that the subject might be the king here, though even this is uncertain, since conceivably other individuals could identify themselves with the fate of the nation.

Nevertheless, in addition to the actual Royal Psalms, there are a few other probably non-Royal Psalms which also make reference to the king in passing. These include Ps. 28.8, 'The Lord is the strength of his people, he is the saving refuge of his anointed ($m^e\check{s}\hat{\imath}h\hat{o}$)', Ps. 61.7–8 (ET 6–7), 'Prolong the life of the king; may his years endure to all generations! May he be enthroned for ever before God; bid steadfast love and faithfulness watch over him!', Ps. 63.12 (ET 11), 'But the king shall rejoice in God; all who swear by him shall glory', and Ps. 84.10 (ET 9), 'Behold our shield, O God; look upon the face of your anointed ($m^e\check{s}\hat{\imath}hek\bar{a}$)'. These psalms are therefore also likely to be pre-exilic. It is also possible that Ps. 80.18 (ET 17) is alluding to the king when it declares, 'Let your hand be upon the man of your right hand, the son of man whom you have made strong for yourself!', since according to Ps. 110.1 it is the king who sits at the Lord's right hand. The fact that three of these psalms, Psalms 28, 61 and 63, are Individual Lament Psalms is particularly significant, since this type of psalm – the most common in the Psalter – is usually amongst the most difficult to date. It is therefore possible that some other Individual Laments for which no clear date indicators exist might also be pre-exilic in origin.

1.2. *Inviolability of Zion Psalms*
Within the Psalter three of the so-called Zion Psalms present belief in the inviolability of Zion, namely Psalms 46, 48 and 76. In these psalms foreign nations are depicted coming up to attack Jerusalem but Yahweh intervenes to defeat them. Such confidence in the inviolability of Zion is far more natural before 586 BCE than after it when Zion had actually been captured.[5] Those who reject this view (e.g. Wanke 1966), seeing these psalms as post-exilic, presume that they simply depict a future eschatological conflict, such as we find in Joel 4 (ET 3) and Zechariah 12, 14. However, against this stands the crucial point that, unlike these late prophetic passages, the verbs used with regard to the conflict in these psalms are mostly not in the future tense; often the past tense is used, as is consistently the case throughout Psalm 48. It is thus much more likely that the prophetic passages reflect a later eschatological projection of the ideas found in these Zion Psalms, just as the future messianic hope found in the

---

5. The theme of the inviolability of Zion has often been traced back even earlier to the pre-Israelite Jebusite inhabitants of Jerusalem, e.g. by J.H. Hayes 1963, as these psalms appear to contain various Canaanite mythological motifs. This view has been opposed by J.J.M. Roberts (1972, reprinted 2002) but defended by the present writer (Day 1985: 125–38).

prophets and elsewhere similarly reflects an eschatologization of the ideas found in the Royal Psalms discussed above. It should also be noted that the prophet Isaiah in the eighth century BCE already appears to have been familiar with the inviolability of Zion tradition, applying it to the Syro–Ephraimite and Assyrian crises of his time (Isa. 8.9–10; 10.27b-34; 14.24-27; 17.12–14; 29.1–8; 30.27–33; 31.1–9). It is difficult to dismiss all the references to the deliverance of Zion within these verses as later accretions to the Isaianic tradition from the time of Josiah (contra Barth 1977 and Clements 1980a; 1980b).[6] If Isaiah could be inspired by psalms like Psalm 46 in the context of the Syro–Ephraimite crisis when Zion was under siege, as is suggested by his use of the sign-name Immanuel, 'God is with us' in Isa. 7.14 (echoed in Isa. 8.10; cf. Ps. 46.8, 12, ET 7, 11, 'the Lord of hosts is with us', which Clements 1980b: 88 himself compares), then the same seems entirely natural in the context of the Assyrian crisis of 701 BCE.[7] However, when we do encounter later anti-Assyrian prophetic passages from the time of Josiah, when Assyria was on its last legs, we find that they envisage the fall of Nineveh (Zeph. 2.13–15; Nahum), something never mentioned in any of these Isaianic passages.

It was sometimes supposed in the past that the psalms envisaging the inviolability of Zion were written in response to the events of 701 BCE (e.g. Kirkpatrick 1902: 253–54, 262, 449, 453), but it has long been generally recognized that the details of the psalms do not support this. Rather Isaiah has particularized the tradition in order to relate it to the events of his own time, though as J.H. Hayes (1963: 425–26) noted, for Isaiah deliverance for Zion was not automatic but required the response of faith in Yahweh.[8] In addition to Isaiah, it should not be overlooked that another eighth-century prophet, Micah, in what very much appears to be an authentic passage, also seems to show awareness of the inviolability of Zion tradition. He refers in Mic. 3.11 to the leaders of Judah, declaring of them, 'yet they lean upon the Lord and say, "Is not the Lord in the midst of us? No evil shall come upon us"'. It is striking

6. Not that Clements denies the early origin of Pss 46, 48 and 76. Rather, he does not envisage these psalms as implying a full-blown doctrine of the inviolability of Zion, a notion which he believes arose only in the Josianic era after reflection on the events of 701 BCE.

7. In connection with the Syro–Ephraimite crisis I would further add that I agree with Clements (1980b: 83) that the name Shear-jashub in Isa. 7.3, lit. 'a remnant will return', makes good sense in the context as referring to a remnant of the enemy (Syrians and Israelites) attacking Jerusalem, and I have suggested that this could be seen against the background of another of the Zion Psalms, Ps. 76.11 (ET 10), if we follow the rendering of J.A. Emerton (1974), 'you restrain the remnant of wrath'. Interestingly, Syria is spoken of as a remnant in Isa. 17.3. See Day 1981.

8. However, in emphasizing the importance of trust in Yahweh J.W. Olley (1999) goes too far in completely dissociating the preaching of First Isaiah from the theme of the inviolability of Zion found in certain psalms.

that this comes immediately before Micah's ringing declaration of doom on Zion, 'Therefore because of you Zion shall be ploughed as a field; Jerusalem shall become a heap of ruins, and the mountain of the house a wooded height' (Mic. 3.12).[9] Since this prophecy was not immediately fulfilled (cf. Jer. 26.18-19) it bears the stamp of authenticity, and the same should be true of the immediately preceding verse, Mic. 3.11. It was presumably a misplaced belief in Zion's inviolability which also lies behind the popular view criticized in Jer. 7.4, where the prophet says, 'Do not trust in these deceptive words: "This is the Temple of the Lord, the Temple of the Lord, the Temple of the Lord"'. Finally, it should be noted that the book of Lamentations, generally and surely rightly dated to the immediate aftermath of the fall of Jerusalem in 586 BCE,[10] actually quotes from one of the Zion Psalms, in Lam. 2.15. This verse cites mockers as saying of Jerusalem, 'Is this the city which was called the perfection of beauty, the joy of all the earth?' The expression 'the joy of all the earth' is used of Zion elsewhere in the Old Testament only in Ps. 48.3 (ET 2), and its quotation by the mockers in Lam. 2.15 is all the more telling since this psalm speaks of Zion's alleged inviolability, something which we know the writer of Lamentations was conscious of (Lam. 4.12).[11]

1.3. *References to the Ark of the Covenant*

As is well known, the presence of the Ark of the Covenant in the Jerusalem Temple was confined to the pre-exilic period (probably being destroyed in 586 BCE); there is unanimity that there was no Ark in the Second Temple. Consequently, any allusions to the Ark in the Psalms as a present reality imply a pre-exilic date. The most explicit reference to the Ark is in Ps. 132.8, 'Arise, O Lord, and go to your resting place, you and the Ark of your might' (cf. vv. 6-7). Psalm 132 appears to represent

9. I am most grateful to Professor H.G.M. Williamson for alerting me to the relevance of Mic. 3.11. I must further thank him for his kindness in reading an earlier draft of this article and for making numerous suggestions for its improvement.

10. I am not persuaded by the view of I. Provan (1991) that it is impossible to tie the context of Lamentations too specifically to the exile. Since the events described can refer only to those of 586 BCE and since the intensity of emotion and sense of despair surrounding the fall of Jerusalem is so great, I find it difficult (along with the majority of commentators) to believe that the book of Lamentations might have been compiled only after the restoration of the Jerusalem Temple was an accomplished fact. Although O. Kaiser (1981) formerly dated Lamentations in the post-exilic period, he has since abandoned this view (so C. Westermann 1993: 57, ET 1994: 55).

11. As will be noted later, 'the perfection of beauty' with regard to Zion likewise appears to be a quotation from Ps. 50.2. The importance of the Zion tradition in the Psalms as a background for Lam. 2.15 and the book of Lamentations more generally is especially highlighted by Albrektson 1963: 219-30.

a liturgical re-enactment of 2 Samuel 6 and 7, which describe respectively the ascent of the Ark to Jerusalem (signifying God's presence there) and God's promise to David of an eternal dynasty. In 2 Sam. 6.14 the ascent of the Ark is described as follows: 'So David and all the house of Israel brought up the Ark of the Lord with shouting, and with the sound of the ram's horn'. Identical language is used of the divine ascent in Ps. 47.6 (ET 5), which declares, 'God has gone up with a shout, the Lord with the sound of a ram's horn'. It seems very likely that Psalm 47 is likewise referring to the ascent of the Ark. This is further supported by the fact that Psalm 47 is an Enthronement Psalm (cf. vv. 7–9, ET 6–8), and Yahweh's throne was represented by the cherubim, which were closely associated with the Ark. Yet further support for this understanding is given by Psalm 68. Psalm 68.25 (ET 24) speaks of a procession into the Temple relating to Yahweh as king, and vv. 18–19 (ET 17–18) speaks explicitly of a divine ascent into the sanctuary, which reminds one of Psalm 47. It is therefore interesting that the very beginning of this psalm, Ps. 68.2 (ET 1), has more or less identical words to those used in connection with the Ark of the Covenant in Num. 10.35, 'Let God arise, let his enemies be scattered; let those who hate him flee before him!' This supports the view that the Ark was associated with Psalm 68. Quite apart from this, it should be noted that Psalm 68 contains a considerable number of textual obscurities suggestive of its antiquity. A further psalm that should be mentioned in connection with the Ark is Ps. 24.7–10. Here we find the well-known antiphonal liturgical interchange at the gates of the Temple:

> 'Lift up your heads, O gates!
> and be lifted up, O ancient doors!
> that the King of glory may come in.'
> 'Who is the King of glory?'
> 'The Lord, strong and mighty,
> the Lord, mighty in battle!'
> 'Lift up your heads, O gates!
> and be lifted up, O ancient doors!
> that the King of glory may come in.'
> 'Who is this King of glory?'
> 'The Lord of hosts,
> he is the King of glory!'

In this passage we clearly read of Yahweh's entrance into the Temple, and yet again this is associated with his kingship, as in Psalms 47 and 68. It is most natural to suppose that Yahweh is here again symbolized by the Ark. Such a supposition is further supported by the battle imagery ('The Lord, strong and mighty, the Lord mighty in battle!') and the reference to Yahweh as 'Lord of hosts', since the role of the Ark as a war palladium is well known and the term 'Lord of hosts' was associated with the Ark, as we know from 1 Sam. 4.4 and 2 Sam. 6.2. This psalm too, therefore, must be pre-exilic, though as Gunkel (1926: 104) and Kraus (1978, I: 344, ET 1988, I: 312) rightly note, the fact that the Temple's gates are described as 'ancient' suggests that the psalm dates from later rather than earlier within the pre-exilic period.

Psalms 24, 47 and 68 are all thematically related, each being associated with Yahweh's ascent into the Temple in connection with his kingship. Moreover, it has been shown above how in each of these psalms independent corroborative evidence supports the view that Yahweh's presence was symbolized by the Ark, a view that has gained quite wide support over the years (cf. fairly recently Jeremias 1987: 57–58, 60–62, 77). This indicates that the language of divine ascent is not merely metaphorical, which is how those who date these psalms to the post-exilic period must be constrained to interpret it. However, H. Niehr (1997: 86–87) has recently suggested an alternative non-metaphorical interpretation in which it is not the Ark but rather an image of Yahweh that is implied in these psalms. That there was an image of Yahweh in the Temple is, however, highly speculative and lacking clear supporting evidence, and in dismissing the Ark interpretation of these psalm passages Niehr fails to note the converging lines of evidence in its support to which I have drawn attention above.[12] But even on this unlikely hypothesis a pre-exilic date for Psalms 24, 47 and 68 would still be indicated, since however improbable it is that there was an image of Yahweh in the pre-exilic Temple, it would be even more implausible in the post-exilic Temple.

It is possible that there are also other allusions to the presence of the Ark in the Psalms. We know that the Ark could be referred to as God's 'power' ($^{c}\bar{o}z$) and 'splendour' (*tip'eret*), since these terms are used in Ps. 78.61 in connection with the loss of the Ark to the Philistines at the battle of Aphek/Ebenezer (cf. 1 Sam. 4.21–22, where the term *kābôd* 'glory' is similarly used in that connection). We have also already seen above the term $^{c}\bar{o}z$ used in association with the Ark in Ps. 132.8. Accordingly, it is possible that there are also references to the Ark in Ps. 63.3 (ET 2), where we read 'So I have looked upon you in the sanctuary, beholding your power ($^{c}\bar{o}z$) and glory (*kābôd*), and in Ps. 96.6, which similarly reads

12. Niehr states that the Ark did not have sufficient significance to denote Yahweh's presence, a strange assertion in the light of passages such as Num. 10.35–36. However, it is possible that he means that the Ark was not in existence when these psalms were composed, a view put forward by H. Spieckerman (1989: 93), which is included in the literature to which he refers. However, in claiming that the Ark was removed from the Temple not long after the end of the United Monarchy, Spieckermann fails to note the relevance of Jer. 3.16–17 and 1 Kgs 8.8, which imply the Ark was still in existence late in the monarchical period. On the question of the date of the disappearance of the Ark see Day 2005.

'power (ʿōz) and splendour (tip'eret) are in his sanctuary' (cf. Davies 1963).

1.4. *Enthronement Psalms*

The so-called Enthronement Psalms are Psalms 47, 93, 96–99, and their central theme is Yahweh's kingship, more precisely his enthronement as king. Scholars have disagreed as to whether they are all pre-exilic (e.g. Mowinckel 1922: 190–202; Johnson 1967: 60–61; Day 1990: 71–73; Willey 1997), all post-exilic (e.g. Snaith 1934: 66–69; Westermann 1961, ET 1966; Loretz 1988b; Gerstenberger 1988, 2001) or a mixture of both (e.g. Jeremias 1987). Those who claim that they are post-exilic tend to hold that they are dependent on Deutero-Isaiah, with which they have some striking verbal and thematic parallels.[13] Those, however, who claim that they are pre-exilic maintain that it is rather Deutero-Isaiah who is dependent on the Enthronement Psalms. Is there any way in which the matter can be decided?

In favour of the psalms being earlier than Deutero-Isaiah the following points should be noted. Whereas Deutero-Isaiah was an absolute monotheist, stating that no god existed apart from Yahweh (Isa. 44.6; 45.5, 14, 21; 46.9), the psalms maintain the earlier view that Yahweh was simply supreme over the other gods (Pss 96.4–5; 97.7, 9; cf. Ps. 95.3). This would be surprising if the psalms were as deeply indebted to Deutero-Isaiah as some scholars suppose, even granting that theological ideas do not always develop in straightforward evolutionary fashion. Again, some of Deutero-Isaiah's central themes are lacking in the psalms, which is odd if the psalms were dependent on his prophecy – for example, they are totally lacking in references to God as redeemer (gō'ēl) and the new Exodus, and they make no allusions to Babylon, the captivity there or the subsequent return from exile. Although Pss 96.1 and 98.1 and Deutero-Isaiah (Isa. 42.10) both declare 'Sing to the Lord a new song', the nature of the event that gives rise to the new song is not spelled out concretely in the psalms in terms of the deliverance from exile, such as we find in Deutero-Isaiah. Moreover, it is important to observe that the phrase 'sing to the Lord a new song' is characteristic of psalmody (besides Pss 96.1 and 98.1, cf. Pss 33.3; 40.4, ET 3; 144.9) but not of prophecy, suggesting that it has its origin in the Psalms and the appropriation of this phrase by the

---

13. For example, Yahweh as creator (Pss 93.1; 96.5, 10; cf. Isa. 40.12, 28), superior to other gods (Pss 96.4–5; 97.7, 9; cf. Isa. 45.21–22; 46.9), 'the Lord/God has become king' (Pss 47.8, ET 7; 93.1; 96.10; 97.1; 99.1; cf. Isa. 52.7), 'Sing to the Lord a new song' (Pss 96.1; 98.1; cf. Isa. 42.10), 'all the ends of the earth have seen (or shall see) the salvation of our God' (Ps. 98.3; cf. Isa. 52.10); 'his holy arm' (Ps. 98.1; cf. Isa. 52.10), 'in the sight of the heathen' (Ps. 98.2; cf. Isa. 52.10), 'clap their hands' (Ps. 98.8; cf. Isa. 55.12), 'from of old' (Ps. 93.2; cf. Isa. 44.8; 45.21; 48.3, 5, 7–8), and the appeal to nature to join in the song of praise to Yahweh (Ps. 96.11–12; cf. Isa. 44.23; 49.13).

prophet Deutero-Isaiah must therefore be secondary.[14] Moreover, there is ample evidence of Deutero-Isaiah's dependence on other psalmic forms throughout his prophecy, and P.T. Willey (1997: 98) has recently noted that passages in Deutero-Isaiah having parallels with Psalm 98 also show evidence of citation from other biblical passages.

With regard to the other Enthronement Psalms I have already noted that Ps. 47.6 (ET 5) presupposes the Ark, so must be pre-exilic. Furthermore, Psalm 99's declaration that Yahweh 'sits enthroned upon the cherubim' (v. 1) likewise implies a pre-exilic date, since there were no cherubim in the Second Temple.[15] Interestingly, Psalm 99 speaks of Yahweh's holiness three times (vv. 3, 5, 9); something akin to Psalm 99 presumably lies behind Isaiah 6's Temple vision of Yahweh as king, with its threefold 'holy, holy, holy', and the shaking of the foundations, all of which are paralleled in Psalm 99. Although R. Scoralick (1989) sees Psalm 99 rather as dependent on Isaiah 6, the fact that Isaiah's vision occurs in the Temple and clearly takes up Jerusalem cult traditions (e.g. the notion of Yahweh as king and the seraphim) makes it natural to suppose that the trisagion likewise reflects Jerusalem cultic tradition akin to Psalm 99.[16] Finally, Psalm 93 would also appear to be pre-exilic, standing close as it does to the underlying myth associating the divine kingship and conflict with the chaotic sea. Those such as Snaith, Westermann, Loretz and Gerstenberger who understand the Enthronement Psalms to be dependent

---

14. With regard to Isa. 42.10, the words subsequent to 'Sing to the Lord a new song, his praise from the end of the earth' are *yôrᵉdê hayyām ûmᵉlōʾô*, 'those who go down to the sea and all that fills it', which are widely accepted to be corrupt, since the context leads us to expect a jussive verb here (cf. the following lines). Many therefore follow the suggestion that we should read *yirʿam hayyām ûmᵉlōʾô*, 'let the sea roar and all that is in it', words found in Pss 96.11 and 98.7. If this proposal is correct we would then have a direct quotation from Ps. 96.1, 11 or 98.1, 7 in Isa. 42.10. The words *yôrᵉdê hayyām* have been appropriated from Ps. 107.23 (cf. L.C. Allen 1971: 146–47).

15. Those who take the psalm to be post-exilic are forced to conclude that the cherubim are the heavenly cherubim rather than those which had existed in the pre-exilic Temple. However, against this I would note: (i) the following verse (v. 2) states that 'The Lord is great in Zion', leading one most naturally to assume that the Lord is envisaged as enthroned in Jerusalem. (ii) All the other references to the Lord's being enthroned on the cherubim appear to relate to the pre-exilic situation. Thus, both 1 Sam. 4.4 and 2 Sam. 6.2 (the latter repeated in 1 Chron. 13.6) associate the expression with the Ark in the period prior to its taking up into Jerusalem, 2 Kgs 19.15 (repeated in Isa. 37.16) is part of Hezekiah's prayer in the Jerusalem Temple 'before the Lord' at a time when the physical cherubim still existed, and as for Ps. 80.2 (ET 1) it is widely accepted that this is part of a pre-exilic psalm. Although Yahweh rides on a heavenly cherub in Ps. 18.11 (ET 10), as part of a pre-exilic Royal Psalm this clearly dates from a time when the physical cherubim were still in existence in the Temple.

16. That there is, however, some post-exilic editing in Ps. 99 may be indicated by the reference to Aaron in v. 6 ('Moses and Aaron were among his priests'), since the post-exilic priesthood was Aaronite and pre-exilic references to Aaron tend to be negative.

on Deutero-Isaiah tend to interpret them simply as eschatological. If this were the case, however, one wonders why these psalmists could never bring themselves simply to say 'The Lord will be king' (*yahweh yimlōk*) rather than 'the Lord has become king' (*yahweh mālak*). This suggests that they are not simply eschatological.

In this connection one should also say something about Psalms 95 and 29, neither of which is an Enthronement psalm per se, but both of which are closely related in theme to them. Psalm 95.3 declares, 'For the Lord is a great God, and a great king above all gods'. This represents a more primitive theology than Deutero-Isaiah's statement that there is no god but Yahweh, so presumably is pre-exilic. Psalm 29 is remarkable for the way in which its depiction of Yahweh as a thundering storm god stands very close to the Ugaritic depiction of Baal, such that some scholars have proposed that a Canaanite psalm has simply been taken over with the substitution of the name Yahweh for that of Baal. Whilst I believe that is going too far (cf. Day 1985: 59–60), it cannot be denied that the depiction of Yahweh is very Baal-like. Psalm 29 is therefore likely to be an early psalm.

1.5. *Communal Laments Implying Israel has an Army*
Communal Laments in the nature of the case complain about major disasters that have come upon the nation. As we shall see below, some clearly relate to the time of the Babylonian exile, when Jerusalem and the Temple had been destroyed and some of the people were in exile. However, two of the Communal Laments which have occasionally been attributed to the exile are more likely pre-exilic, namely Psalms 44 and 60 (= 108 in part; Ps. 60.7–14, ET 5–12 = Ps. 108.7–14, ET 6–13). Neither makes specific mention of the destruction of Jerusalem or the Temple or laments the ending of the monarchy, the total absence of all three of these being surprising if the events of 586 BCE are in mind (contrast Pss 74; 79; 89). One of these, Ps. 60.10–11, ET 8–9 (= 108.10–11, ET 9–10) expresses hostility to Edom, a nation that appears to have given moral support to the Babylonians in 586 BCE (cf. Ps. 137.7; Lam. 4.21–22; Obadiah). However, the fact that this psalm also expresses hostility to Northern Israel, Moab and Philistia (Ps. 60.8–10, ET 6–8 = Ps. 108.8–10, ET 7–9) but completely fails to mention Babylon makes it difficult to believe that the events of 586 BCE are in view here. Psalm 44, on the other hand, makes no specific mention of any other nation by name at all. At the same time Psalms 44 and 60 (108) cannot be post-exilic, since both of them complain that Yahweh has not gone out with Israel's armies, which did not exist in the post-exilic period until we come to the time of the Maccabees. Thus, Ps. 44.10 (ET 9) declares, 'Yet you have...not gone out with our armies' and Ps. 60.12 (ET 10 = Ps. 108.12, ET 11) similarly complains, 'You do not go forth, O God, with our armies'. Accordingly, these psalms must be

pre-exilic, and those who would wish to see them as post-exilic have a real problem of interpretation here.[17] Since Ps. 44.18 (ET 17) uses the word 'covenant' one will doubtless be inclined to see this psalm as later rather than earlier in the pre-exilic period, though I have argued from the references in Hosea and Psalm 78 that the use of this term to describe Yahweh's relationship with Israel goes back at least to the eighth century BCE (Day 1986; cf. Nicholson 1986). G. Kwaakel (2002: 221–31) in a recent, thorough discussion of the date of Psalm 44 is inclined to place it in the context of Sennacherib's invasion of Judah in 701 BCE, which is not impossible. As Kwaakel 2002: 224, 227 notes, v. 12, ET 11 'You…have scattered us among the nations' need not refer to 586 BCE, since Sennacherib claims to have deported 200,150 people from Judah.

1.6. *Other Indicators of Pre-exilic Psalms*
There are a number of other psalms for which there are clear pre-exilic indicators but which are not covered by the criteria mentioned above. In the nature of things I cannot deal with all such possible psalms here but will concentrate on the following: Psalms 78, 104, 50 and 51.

Psalm 78 is a psalm on which a wide variety of dates have been proposed, with everything from the tenth century BCE to the post-exilic period being suggested. However, a pre-exilic date is clearly indicated by the fact that the Solomonic Temple is still standing and indeed is held to be inviolable: v. 69 states (in close connection with the election of David, v. 70), 'He built his sanctuary like the high heavens, like the earth which he has founded for ever'. Furthermore, the psalm contains no hint of the exile. Some of those who accept a pre-exilic date have seen it as reflecting Deuteronomistic influence, but against this stands the fact that this anti-Northern psalm makes no reference to the fall of the Northern Kingdom in 722 BCE, which for the Deuteronomists was the final and decisive sign of its rejection by God (cf. 2 Kings 17), mention of which would, moreover, have strengthened the psalmist's case that God had rejected the North. Rather, the decisive sign of the rejection of the North is the divine forsaking of the Shiloh sanctuary in c. 1050 BCE (v. 60), and the significant battle described in vv. 59–64 clearly mirrors that in 1 Samuel 4; compare not only the important role played by Shiloh in both, but also the loss of the Ark ('his power' and 'his splendour') in v. 61 (cf. 1 Sam. 4.21–22, where the Ark represents God's 'glory'), and the death of the priests in v. 64 (cf. Hophni and Phinehas in 1 Sam. 4.17). Interestingly, Psalm 78 knows precisely the seven Egyptian plagues of the J source, traditionally regarded as the earliest of the sources, in contrast to Psalm 105, a psalm which has sometimes been compared, but which also shows knowledge of

---

17. It does not seem plausible that a post-exilic author would imaginatively conjure up references to non-existent armies and complain that God had not gone out with them!

plagues unique to P and E.[18] A date prior to 722 BCE seems indicated for Psalm 78 (Day 1986; cf. too Stern 1995, who argues for a specifically eighth-century date).

Psalm 104 is remarkable for the way it concentrates on the theme of Creation from beginning to end, to an extent unparalleled elsewhere in the Psalter. Scholars have long noted the striking parallels between this psalm, specifically vv. 1–5, 10–26, and the fourteenth-century Pharaoh Akhenaten's hymn to Aton, the sun disc (cf. *ANET*, 369–71). Although the precise mode of transmission of Akhenaten's hymn is uncertain, the parallels are clear enough.[19] This suggests that many of the ideas behind the psalm are ancient. However, at the same time there are striking parallels between Psalm 104 and the Priestly account of Creation in Genesis 1.

Ps. 104.1–4	Creation of heaven and earth.	Cf. Gen. 1.1–5
Ps. 104.5–9	Waters pushed back	Cf. Gen. 1.6–10
Ps. 104.10–13	Waters put to beneficial use	Implicit in Gen. 1.6–10
Ps. 104.14–18	Creation of vegetation	Cf. Gen. 1.11–12
Ps. 104.19–23	Creation of heavenly luminaries	Cf. Gen. 1.14–18
Ps. 104.24–26	Creation of sea creatures	Cf. Gen. 1.20–22
Ps. 104.27–30	Creation of living creatures	Cf. Gen. 1.24–31

This close parallelism in order is clearly striking enough to suggest some connection between the two works. Moreover, there are also significant verbal parallels: the expression *l^{e}mô^{ca}dîm*, 'for seasons' (or 'to mark the seasons') is attested in the Old Testament only in Ps. 104.19 and Gen. 1.14, both times in connection with the heavenly luminaries, and the poetic form of the word for beasts, *ḥay^{e}tô*, appears in Ps. 104.11, 20 and Gen. 1.24, and elsewhere in the Old Testament only in other poetic texts. This suggests that Genesis 1 is dependent on a poetic text at this point, presumably Psalm 104. Sometimes it has been supposed that it is rather Psalm 104 that is dependent on Genesis 1 (e.g. Humbert 1935). However, it is much more likely that Psalm 104 is one of the sources lying behind Genesis 1 (cf. van der Voort 1951; Day 1985: 51–53). Thus, whereas in Genesis 1 God merely controls the cosmic waters, in Psalm 104 God engages in battle with them – Psalm 104 thus reflects the myth which it is generally recognized that Genesis 1 has demythologized, so is likely to be

---

18.   The description of the parting of the sea so that it stood up like a heap in Ps. 78.13 need not reflect P (Exod. 14.16, 21–22), since Exod. 15.8 already has the sea standing up like a heap, and Exod. 15 is widely agreed to be an old poem in view of its language (though not as old as some suppose, since it presupposes the Solomonic Temple in v. 17). Interestingly, Exod. 15 and Ps. 78 have often been compared in other ways, e.g. both present the election of Mt Zion as the climax of the *Heilsgeschichte*.

19.   R.J. Williams (1971: 286) interestingly points out that echoes of Akhenaten's hymn to the sun are likewise found centuries later in Egypt in text no. 60 from the tomb of Petosiris.

earlier. In this context, the words 'the *rûaḥ* of God was hovering over the face of the deep (*tᵉhôm*)' (Gen. 1.2) appear rather isolated and cryptic in the context of Genesis 1, but are immediately illuminated when seen against the background of Ps. 104.3, where we read that God rides on the wings of the wind (*rûaḥ*) in the context of the battle with the watery deep (*tᵉhôm*, Ps. 104.6–7; cf. too Ps. 18.11, ET 10). Similarly, whereas Gen. 1.21 speaks of 'great sea monsters', the corresponding place in Ps. 104.26 uses the more mythological term Leviathan.

Psalm 50 presents itself as a psalm of Covenant renewal. One pointer to its possibly being pre-exilic in origin is the apparent quotation from v. 2 of this psalm in Lam. 2.15, where we read, 'All who pass along the way clap their hands at you; they hiss and wag their heads at the daughter of Jerusalem; "Is this the city which was called the perfection of beauty, the joy of all the earth?"' As already noted above, the expression 'the joy of all the earth' is used of Jerusalem elsewhere only in Ps. 48.3 (ET 2), part of a psalm proclaiming Zion's inviolability, so its citation in Lam. 2.15 would be highly significant in the face of Zion's destruction. The other expression, 'the perfection of beauty' is used of Jerusalem in the Old Testament only in Ps. 50.2; if this is the source of the quotation, as seems plausible, it would prove Psalm 50's pre-exilic date.[20]

The argument for the pre-exilic date of Psalm 51 runs as follows. It is generally agreed that the ending of the psalm is a later addition; here the psalmist addresses God, saying 'Do good to Zion in your good pleasure; rebuild the walls of Jerusalem, then you will delight in right sacrifices, in burnt offerings and whole burnt offerings; then bulls will be offered on your altar' (vv. 20–21, ET 18–19). These words, which seem to miss the psalmist's profound point that no sacrifice was adequate to atone for his sin, appear to date from the exilic period when sacrifice was not possible because the Temple had been destroyed. Accordingly, the main body of the psalm, which precedes these words, must date from before then, and since it is clear from there that sacrifice was still being offered and was thus a spiritual rather than physical impossibility for the psalmist (cf. v. 18, ET 16), it presumably dates from the pre-exilic period. On this understanding we should therefore understand the words 'Do good to Zion in your good pleasure; rebuild the walls of Jerusalem' (v. 20, ET 18) as alluding to the restoration of Jerusalem generally and thereby implying

20. Cf. above n. 11. Very plausibly both Pss 48 and 50 had their setting in the pre-exilic feast of Tabernacles in Jerusalem. Pss 46 and 48 form a sandwich round Ps. 47, one of the Enthronement Psalms whose origin in the feast of Tabernacles is widely acknowledged (cf. Day 1990: 67–82 for a summary of the arguments). Interestingly, Zech. 14 combines references to the eschatological inviolability of Zion (vv. 1–5) alongside the future enthronement of Yahweh as king (vv. 9, 16–17) in connection with the feast of Tabernacles (vv. 16–17). The arguments for associating Covenant renewal (such as we find in Ps. 50) with Tabernacles are summarized in Day 1990: 82–85.

the rebuilding of the Temple. Although the main part of the psalm appears to be pre-exilic, it may well be from late within that period, as argued by E.R. Dalglish (1962: 223–32) in the only book-length study devoted to this psalm, who sees evidence of dependence on the prophetic tradition, as for example in its relativization of the importance of sacrifice.

2. *Evidence for Exilic Psalms*

There is a small number of psalms that may confidently be dated to the exile as well as a few other psalms that are possibly exilic. One such Psalm is Psalm 137, which begins 'By the waters of Babylon, there we sat down and wept...'. As noted earlier, whilst B. Duhm regarded this as the earliest psalm and I. Engnell held it to be the latest, both were agreed that it reflected the exilic experience! The concluding verses, with their curse on Babylon, suggest that Babylon has not yet fallen, so this psalm is more naturally exilic than post-exilic. Another psalm for which an excellent case can be made for regarding it as exilic is Psalm 74, which laments the destruction of the Jerusalem Temple. We know of no other destruction of the Temple in the Old Testament period except that of 586 BCE. (The supposition of Morgenstern 1956 that the Edomites devastated the Temple in c. 485 BCE, and that this could be referred to here, is widely rejected and totally without evidence.) Although it has sometimes been suggested in the past that Antiochus IV Epiphanes' violation of the Temple in 168 BCE is referred to here (cf. still Donner 1972), this is not possible, since Antiochus did not destroy the Temple (cf. v. 7) but only burned the gates of the Temple (cf. 1 Macc. 4.38; 2 Macc. 1.8; 8.33) and desecrated the sanctuary (1 Macc. 1.23, 39; 2 Macc. 6.5). The old view that Ps. 74.8's *môʿ ͨdê-ʾēl*, 'meeting places of God', must refer to synagogues, and so presuppose a later date, has been rightly rejected by Gelston (1984). Psalm 79 also appears to relate to the destruction of the Temple in 586 BCE (cf. v. 1, 'O God, the heathen have come into your inheritance; they have defiled your holy temple; they have laid Jerusalem in ruins'). Psalm 89 also most naturally dates to the exile, since it seems to lament the ending of the Davidic dynasty. Its sense of utter hopelessness fits this period better than any previous one.

3. *Evidence for Post-exilic Psalms*

3.1. *References to the Exile or Return from Exile*
The most obvious indication of a post-exilic date for psalms is their referring back to the exile or return from exile, such as we find in Pss 106.27, 47, 107.2–3 and 147.2. Psalm 106.47 prays, 'Save us, O Lord our

God, and gather us from among the nations...' (cf. v. 27), Ps. 107.2–3 declares, 'Let the redeemed of the Lord say so, whom he has redeemed from trouble and gathered in from the lands, from the east and from the west, from the north and from the south',[21] and Ps. 147.2 states, 'The Lord builds up Jerusalem; he gathers the outcasts of Israel'. Interestingly, all these psalms are in the last third of the Psalter.

A further psalm that refers to the return from exile is Psalm 126. This psalm seems to reflect the period after the return when the optimistic expectations raised by Deutero-Isaiah had not been realized (cf. Hag. 1). This is reflected in the contrast between vv. 1–3 and 4–6, 'When the Lord restored the fortunes of Zion, we were like those who dream...Restore our fortunes, O Lord, like the watercourses of the Negeb!' Finally, another psalm which seems to reflect this period is Psalm 85, where again we find expressed a tension between Yahweh's restoration of the nation (vv. 2–4, ET 1–3) and renewed lamentation (vv. 5–8, ET 4–7).

3.2. *References to the House of Aaron*

After the exile the Jerusalem priesthood was in the hands of a group known as 'the sons of Aaron', as we know, for example, from the books of Chronicles and the Priestly source. This was an élite group within the tribe of Levi, contrasting with the pre-exilic period, when the tribe of Levi as a whole were priests. It is therefore striking that we find references to 'the house of Aaron' in Pss 115.10, 12, 118.3 and 135.19, which most naturally refers to the post-exilic priesthood, and this constitutes an argument for the post-exilic date of these particular psalms. Interestingly, again, all these psalms are in the last part of the Psalter.

3.3. *Emphasis on the Law*

As is well known, post-exilic Judaism came to put extremely great emphasis on the meticulous keeping of the Law. This emphasis is particularly striking in Psalm 119. This psalm, the longest psalm by far in the entire Psalter, extols the psalmist's devotion to the Torah in verse after verse. Eight major terms for the Law are employed, and almost every verse in the psalm uses one of them. This clearly reflects post-exilic legal piety. The psalm also displays dependence on several other Old Testament books, including Deuteronomy, Proverbs and Jeremiah, again suggesting a post-exilic date. Another psalm reflecting the post-exilic Jewish emphasis on the Law is Psalm 1, which has been placed at the very beginning of the Psalter as a deliberate editorial device. Verse 2 refers to the righteous as one whose 'delight is in the law of the Lord, and on his law he meditates day and night' (cf. Josh. 1.8). A final psalm to be noted here is Ps. 19B (vv. 8–15, ET 7–14), which has in common with Psalm 119 not only a

---

21. Emending *yām*, 'west' to *yāmîn*, 'south' with most scholars, as the context requires.

striking emphasis on the Law but repeatedly refers to it under different terms, i.e. 'the law of the Lord', 'the testimony of the Lord', 'the precepts of the Lord', 'the commandment of the Lord', 'the fear of the Lord' and 'the ordinances of the Lord'. This too is surely post-exilic.

3.4. *Dependence on the Priestly Source*
Whereas Psalm 78 shows knowledge of the seven plagues of the Yahwist source (see above), Psalm 105's description of the plagues also shows knowledge of plagues distinctive of P and E (vv. 28–36). Since P is generally held to date from the sixth century BCE this psalm is likely to be no earlier than then. On the other hand, since part of Psalm 105 is quoted in 1 Chron. 16.8–22, the psalm should be no later than the fourth century BCE. We may therefore be pretty confident that Psalm 105 is an early post-exilic psalm.

3.5. *Positive References to Life after Death*
As a whole the Psalter shares the traditional belief in a shadowy Sheol as the destination of humans after death. Belief in a more blessed afterlife was slow in emerging in ancient Israel and developed in the post-exilic period, so any references to this in the Psalms must therefore date from that time. There are two probable examples of this belief, both in Wisdom Psalms, namely in Pss 49.16 (ET 15) and 73.24. In Psalm 49, after pondering in Job-like fashion the prosperity of the wicked and the suffering of the righteous, the psalmist declares in v. 16 (ET 15), 'But God will ransom my soul from the power of Sheol, for he will receive me'. Sometimes this has been taken as referring merely to the psalmist's temporary restoration to wellbeing in this world. However, vv. 14–15 (ET 13–14) state that Sheol will be the home of the wicked, and this is referred to as 'their end' (*'aḥ^{a}rîtām*). If the psalmist was merely expecting a temporary restoration in his world it could justly be claimed that Sheol would be his end too. There is also linguistic evidence supporting the post-exilic date of Psalm 49 (Schmitt 1973: 249–52). Interestingly, Ps. 49.16 (ET 15)'s use of the verb *lāqaḥ*, 'receive' is reminiscent of its use in connection with God's taking of Enoch and Elijah when they ascended into heaven (Gen. 5.24; 2 Kgs 2.3, 5, 9, 10). The same verb is used in Ps. 73.24, where the psalmist states, 'afterward you will receive me to glory'. Like Psalm 49 this too is a Job-like Wisdom Psalm contemplating the prosperity of the wicked and the suffering of the righteous. What exactly is meant by being received to glory depends on the meaning of 'afterward'. Probably the psalmist is expecting vindication in the afterlife. In support of this the verbal parallelism between the 'afterward' (*'aḥar*) of the psalmist's fate and the 'end' (*'aḥ^{a}rît*) of the wicked in Sheol (v. 17) may be noted. This contrast makes proper sense only if the ultimate end of the psalmist was not also to be in Sheol. As with Psalm 49, there is also

linguistic support for the post-exilic dating of Psalm 73 (cf. Schmitt 1973: 302–309).[22]

3.6. *Linguistic Evidence: Late Hebrew Forms and Aramaisms*

Another guide to dating can be the language employed in a psalm, reference to which has already been made in passing above. On this basis A. Hurvitz (1972; 1973) has identified eight psalms as indubitably post-exilic, all of them interestingly in the last third of the Psalter: Psalms 103, 117, 119, 124, 125, 133, 144:12–15 and 145. Clearly, the larger the number of late forms or Aramaisms that appear in a particular psalm, the stronger the case that can be made for such a psalm being late, but the apparent odd instance need not necessarily indicate such a thing, so caution is clearly necessary. An interesting example concerns the use of the Hebrew relative particle *še* instead of the normal classical Hebrew form *ʾᵃšer*. Whilst this can be early, as its presence in Judges 5 suggests (cf. v. 7), the fact that it became the regular relative particle in Mishnaic Hebrew proves that it could also be a late form, and such it surely is when it occurs in the Psalter. It appears there in some of the Psalms of Ascents or Steps (Pss 122.3, 4; 123.2; 124.1, 2, 6; 129.6, 7; 133.2, 3), as well as in Pss 135.2, 8, 10, 136.23, 137.8, 9 and 144.15. Of these Psalms 124, 133 and 144.12–15 already appear in Hurvitz's list of indubitably late psalms and Psalm 135 has been adjudged post-exilic above on the basis of its reference to the 'house of Aaron' in v. 19 (cf. Ps. 133.2), whilst Psalm 137 clearly reflects the experience of exile.[23] Add to this the observation that all the instances of *še* in Psalms occur in the last third of the Psalter, where cumulative evidence indicates that a large number of late psalms are concentrated, and the case becomes overwhelming that all the psalms containing *še* are no earlier than the exile, and apart from Psalm 137 are very likely post-exilic.

3.7. *Acrostics*

There are a number of psalms whose lines are arranged acrostically, that is according to the order of the letters of the alphabet; these are Psalms 9, 10, 25, 34, 37, 111, 112, 119 and 145. Although one cannot be dogmatic, the likelihood is that psalms with this form are at any rate not pre-exilic. First, outside the Psalter, the other acrostic passages are Lamentations 1–4, Prov. 31.10–31, Ecclus. 51.13–20, apocryphal Psalm 155, and Nah. 1.2–8. Of these Prov. 31.10–31, Ecclus. 51.13–20 and Psalm 155 are generally

---

22. For a more detailed defence of the afterlife interpretation of Pss 49.16 (ET 15) and 73.24 see Day 1996: 253–56.

23. The book of Lamentations also has several instances of *še* (Lam. 2.15, 16; 4.9; 5.18), which coheres with Ps. 137 in suggesting that the increase in the use of *še* was already beginning in the exile.

agreed to be post-exilic and Lamentations 1–4 is widely held to be exilic. Although for the most part the book of Nahum appears to be a late pre-exilic prophecy, focusing on the fall of Nineveh in 612 BCE, the acrostic introduction in Nah. 1.2–8 stands apart in many ways from the rest of the book and may be post-exilic; we should bear in mind that later additions often come at the beginning or end of works. Secondly, several of the acrostic psalms have other clear indications of a post-exilic date, e.g. Psalm 37 with its Job-like theme, Psalm 119 with its strong focus on the law, Psalm 145 with its late language (e.g. the use of the word *mal*^{e}*kût*, 'kingdom'), etc. Although it would be wrong to be dogmatic, it may be, therefore, that all the acrostic psalms noted above are post-exilic in origin.

4. *Conclusions*

It is not possible to know precisely how many pre-exilic psalms there are in the Psalter. However, as a result of the above study, it has been shown that a good case can be made that the following psalms are pre-exilic: the Royal Psalms, as well as other psalms which allude to the king, psalms which presuppose Zion's inviolability, psalms which imply the presence of the Ark, Enthronement Psalms, and Communal Laments which imply that Israel has an army. There are also certain other psalms with pre-exilic indicators not included under the above headings (though my consideration of these was not exhaustive). A few psalms have points indicating an exilic origin and a fair number have signs of post-exilic composition. Considerable evidence suggests that of those psalms for which it is possible to make a probable estimate of date, there are a higher number of pre-exilic Psalms in the first two-thirds of the Psalter and a higher number of post-exilic psalms in the last third. This coheres with the fact that at Qumran the Psalms in the earlier parts of the Psalter (books 1–3) have fixed order, whereas there is fluidity in the ordering of the psalms in the latter parts (books 4–5) suggesting that this was not yet fixed (unlike the Masoretic/LXX ordering, which had been fixed earlier) – which is more understandable if the psalms towards the end are mostly late. The fact that there is a fixed order in the earlier part of the Qumran Psalter, unlike the latter part, shows that the variation in order cannot simply be attributed to liturgical rearrangement (Flint 1997; cf. Sanders, 1965; 1967). But there are still many uncertainties, especially with regard to the Individual Psalms, especially the Individual Laments, which happen to be the most common type of psalm, most of which are in the first half of the Psalter. As has been seen above, some of these do have pre-exilic indicators (cf. Pss 28, 51, 61, 63), but for most of them we are somewhat in the dark. Arguably, since many of these Individual Laments are in the earlier part of the Psalter (which otherwise has a higher number of pre-exilic psalms) and were attributed to the 'Davidic Psalter' (suggesting they were believed to be ancient), there are likely to be a considerable number of pre-exilic psalms amongst them. It must be admitted, however, that even when we can assign a psalm to the pre- or post-exilic era, it is usually not possible to know the date more precisely within these periods. So far as post-exilic psalms are concerned, a good case can be made that no psalms are as late as the Maccabaean period, contrary to what was often imagined a hundred years ago. We actually possess late psalms in the form of the Psalms of Solomon and the Qumran Hodayoth (Thanksgiving Psalms), and these are quite different. As noted earlier, 1 Chron. 16.36 quotes Ps. 106.36, the concluding editorial doxology of this last psalm in book 4 of the Psalter, which strongly suggests that the editing of the Masoretic Psalter, at least up to this point, had been completed by the time of the Chronicler in the fourth century BCE.

Anyway, the view of such scholars as Gerstenberger, Loretz, Tournay and Treves who understand all or virtually all the Psalms to be late is certainly mistaken. Though many psalms are post-exilic (especially in the last third of the Psalter), there are also many pre-exilic psalms (especially in the first two-thirds of the Psalter).

Bibliography

Albrektson, B.

    1963   *Studies in the Text and Theology of the Book of Lamentations, with a Critical Edition of the Peshitta Text* (Studia Theologica Lundensia, 21; Lund: C.W.K. Gleerup).

Allen, L.C.

    1971   'Cuckoos in the Textual Nest at 2 Kings xx.13; Isa. xlii.10; xlix.24; Ps. xxii.17; 2 Chron. v.9', *JTS* NS 22: 143–50.

Astour, M.C.

    1992   'Melchizedek (person)', in *ABD*, IV: 684–86.

Barth, H.

    1977   *Die Jesaja-Worte in der Josiazeit: Israel und Assur als Thema einer produktiven Neuinterpretation der Jesajaüberlieferung* (WMANT, 48; Neukirchen–Vluyn: Neukirchener Verlag).

Becker, J.

    1977   *Messiaserwartung im Alten Testament* (SBS, 83; Stuttgart: Verlag Katholisches Bibelwerk). ET *Messianic Expectation in the Old Testament* (trans. David E. Green; Edinburgh: T. & T. Clark, 1980).

Birkeland, H.

    1933   *Die Feinde des Individuums in der israelitischen Psalmenliteratur* (Oslo: Grøndahl).

    1955   *The Evildoers in the Book of Psalms* (Oslo: Dybwad).

Bowker, J.W.

    1967   'Psalm cx', *VT* 17: 31–41.

Carroll, R.P.
  1981   *From Chaos to Covenant: Uses of Prophecy in the Book of Jeremiah* (London: SCM Press).
Clements, R.E.
  1980a   *Isaiah and the Deliverance of Jerusalem* (JSOTSup, 13; Sheffield: JSOT Press).
  1980b   *Isaiah 1–39* (NCB; Grand Rapids, MI: W.B. Eerdmans, and London: Marshall, Morgan & Scott).
Croft, S.J.L.
  1987   *The Identity of the Individual in the Psalms* (JSOTSup, 44; Sheffield: JSOT Press).
Dalglish, E.R.
  1962   *Psalm Fifty-One in the Light of Ancient Near Eastern Patternism* (Leiden: E.J. Brill).
Davies, G.H.
  1963   'The Ark in the Psalms', in F.F. Bruce (ed.), *Promise and Fulfilment: Essays Presented to Professor S.H. Hooke* (Edinburgh: T. & T. Clark).
Day, J.
  1981   'Shear-jashub (Isaiah vii 3) and "the Remnant of wrath" (Psalm lxxvi 11)', *VT* 31: 76–78.
  1985   *God's Conflict with the Dragon and the Sea: Echoes of a Canaanite Myth in the Old Testament* (UCOP, 35; Cambridge: Cambridge University Press).
  1986   'Pre-Deuteronomic Allusions to the Covenant in Hosea and Psalm lxxviii', *VT* 36: 1–12.
  1990   *Psalms* (OTG; Sheffield: JSOT Press).
  1996   'The Development of Belief in Life after Death in Ancient Israel', in J. Barton and D.J. Reimer (eds), *After the Exile: Essays in Honour of Rex Mason* (Macon, GA: Mercer University Press).
  2005   'Whatever happened to the Ark of the Covenant?', in J. Day (ed.), *Temple and Worship in Ancient Israel: Proceedings of the Oxford Old Testament Seminar* (JSOTSup; London and New York: T. & T. Clark International).
Donner, H.
  1972   'Argumente zur Datierung des 74. Psalms', in J. Schreiner (ed.), *Wort, Lied und Gottesspruch: Festschrift für Joseph Schreiner* (FzB, 1–2; 2 vols; Würzburg: Echter Verlag): II, 41–50.
  1991   'Der verläßliche Prophet: Betrachtungen zu 1 Makk 14,41ff und zu Ps 110', in R. Liwak and S. Wagner (eds), *Prophetie und geschichtliche Wirklichkeit in alten Israel: Festschrift für Siegfried Herrmann zum 65. Geburtstag* (Stuttgart: W. Kohlhammer): 89–98.
Duhm, B.
  1899   *Die Psalmen* (KHAT, 14; Freiburg i. B., Leipzig and Tübingen: J.C.B. Mohr [Paul Siebeck]), 2nd edn, Tübingen, 1922.
Eaton, J.H.
  1986   *Kingship and the Psalms* (The Biblical Seminar, 3; Sheffield: JSOT Press, 2nd edn). The 1st edn was published in 1976 by SCM Press (SBT, 2nd series, 32).
Emerton, J.A.
  1974   'A Neglected Solution of a Problem in Psalm lxxvi 11', *VT* 24: 136–46.

Engnell, I.
1943   *Studies in Divine Kingship in the Ancient Near East* (Uppsala: Almqvist and Wiksell), 2nd edn, Oxford: Basil Blackwell, 1967.
Flint, P.W.
1997   *The Dead Sea Psalms Scrolls and the Book of Psalms* (STDJ, 17; Leiden: E.J. Brill).
Gelston, A.
1984   'A Note on Psalm lxxiv 8', *VT* 34: 82–87.
Gerleman, G.
1981   'Psalm cx', *VT* 31: 1–19.
Gerstenberger, E.
1988   *Psalms, Part 1, With an Introduction to Cultic Poetry* (FOTL, 14; Grand Rapids, MI: W.B. Eerdmans).
2001   *Psalms, Part 2, and Lamentations* (FOTL, 15; Grand Rapids, MI, and Cambridge: W.B. Eerdmans).
Goulder, M.D.
1990   *The Prayers of David (Psalms 51–72): Studies in the Psalter, II* (JSOTSup, 102; Sheffield: JSOT Press).
Gunkel, H.
1926   *Die Psalmen* (HKAT, 2.2; Göttingen: Vandenhoeck & Ruprecht, 4th edn).
Gunkel, H., and J. Begrich
1928–33 *Einleitung in die Psalmen: die Gattungen der religiösen Lyrik Israels* (2 vols; HKAT, Ergänzungsbände; Göttingen: Vandenhoeck & Ruprecht). ET *Introduction to Psalms: The Genres of the Religious Lyric of Israel* (trans. James D. Nogalski; Macon, GA: Mercer University Press, 1998).
Hardy, E.R.
1945   'The Date of Psalm 110', *JBL* 64: 385–90.
Hayes, J.H.
1963   'The Tradition of Zion's Inviolability', *JBL* 82: 419–26.
Hossfeld, F.-L., and E. Zenger
1993, 2002 *Die Psalmen* (Die neue Echter Bibel; 2 vols [vol. 3 forthcoming]; Würzburg: Echter Verlag).
Houston, W.
1999   'The King's Preferential Option for the Poor: Rhetoric, Ideology and Ethics in Psalm 72', *BibInt* 7: 342–67.
Humbert, P.
1935   'La relation de Genèse 1 et du Psaume 104 avec la liturgie du Nouvel-An israélite', *RHPR* 15: 1–27.
Hurvitz, A.
1972   *Bên lāšōn lᵉlāšōn* (Jerusalem: Bialik).
1973   'Linguistic Criteria for Dating Problematic Hebrew Texts', *Hebrew Abstracts* 14: 73–79.
Jeremias, Jörg
1987   *Das Königtum Gottes in den Psalmen: Israels Begegnung mit dem kanaanäischen Mythos in den Jahwe-König-Psalmen* (FRLANT, 141; Göttingen: Vandenhoeck & Ruprecht).

Johnson, A.R.
    1967   *Sacral Kingship in Ancient Israel* (Cardiff: University of Wales Press, 2nd edn).
Kaiser, O.
    1981   'Klagelieder', in H. Ringgren and O. Kaiser, *Das Hohelied, Klagelieder, das Buch Esther* (ATD, 16.2; Göttingen: Vandenhoeck & Ruprecht, 3rd edn): 291–386.
Kirkpatrick, A.F.
    1902   *The Book of Psalms* (Cambridge Bible for Schools and Colleges; Cambridge: Cambridge University Press).
Kraus, H.-J.
    1978   *Psalmen* (BKAT, 15.1–2; 2 vols; Neukirchen–Vluyn: Neukirchener Verlag, 5th edn). ET *Psalms* (2 vols; Minneapolis: Augsburg, 1988–89).
Kwaakel, G.
    2002   *According to My Righteousness: Upright Behaviour as Grounds for Deliverance in Psalms 7, 17, 18, 26 and 44* (OTS, 46; Leiden: E.J. Brill).
Lindars, F.C. (B.)
    1967   'Is Psalm II an Acrostic Psalm?', *VT* 17: 60–67.
Loretz, O.
    1979   *Die Psalmen*, II (AOAT, 207.2; Neukirchen–Vluyn: Neukirchener Verlag, and Kevelaer: Butzon & Bercker).
    1988a   *Die Königspsalmen: die altorientalisch-kanaanäische Königstradition in jüdischer Sicht*, I: *Ps 20, 21, 72, 101 und 144* (UBL, 6; Münster: Ugarit-Verlag).
    1988b   *Ugarit-Texte und Thronbesteigungspsalmen: die Metamorphose des Regenspenders Baal-Jahwe (Ps 24, 7–10; 29; 47; 93; 95–100 sowie Ps 77, 17–20, 114)* (UBL, 7; Münster: Ugarit-Verlag)
Morgenstern, J.
    1956   'Jerusalem – 485 B.C.', *HUCA* 27: 101–79.
Mowinckel, S.
    1922   *Psalmenstudien*, II: *Das Thronbesteigungsfest Jahwäs und der Ursprung der Eschatologie* (Kristiania: Dybwad).
    1951   *Offersang og sangoffer* (Oslo: H. Aschehoug). ET *The Psalms in Israel's Worship* (trans. D.R. Ap-Thomas; 2 vols; Oxford: Basil Blackwell, 1962).
Nicholson, E.W.
    1986   *God and His People: Covenant and Theology in the Old Testament* (Oxford: Clarendon Press).
Niehr, H.
    1997   'In Search of YHWH's Cult Statue in the First Temple', in K. van der Toorn (ed.), *The Image and the Book* (Leuven: Peeters): 73–95.
Olley, J.W.
    1999   ' "Trust in the Lord": Hezekiah, Kings and Isaiah', *TynBul* 50: 59–77.
Provan, I.
    1991   *Lamentations* (NCB; Grand Rapids, MI: W.B. Eerdmans, and London: Marshall Pickering).

Roberts, J.J.M.
    1972   The Davidic Origin of the Zion Tradition', *JBL* 92: 329–44. Reprinted in *The Bible and the Ancient Near East: Collected Essays* (Winona Lake, IN: Eisenbrauns, 2002): 313–30.
Sanders, J.A.
    1965   *The Psalms Scroll of Qumrân Cave 11 (11QPs^a)* (DJD, 4; Oxford: Clarendon Press).
    1967   *The Dead Sea Psalms Scroll* (Ithaca, NY: Cornell University Press).
Schmitt, A.
    1973   *Entrückung, Aufnahme, Himmelfahrt: Untersuchungen zu ein Vorstellungsbereich im Alten Testament* (FzB, 10; Stuttgart: Katholisches Bibelwerk).
Schreiner, S.
    1977   'Psalm cx und die Investitur des Hohenpriesters', *VT* 27: 216–22.
Scoralick, R.
    1989   *Trishagion und Gottesherrschaft: Psalm 99 als Neuinterpretation von Tora und Propheten* (SBS, 138; Stuttgart: Katholisches Bibelwerk).
Seybold, K.
    1996   *Die Psalmen* (HAT, 1.15; Tübingen: J.C.B. Mohr [Paul Siebeck]).
Snaith, N.H.
    1934   *Studies in the Psalter* (London: Epworth Press).
Spieckermann, H.
    1989   *Heilsgegenwart: eine Theologie der Psalmen* (FRLANT, 148; Göttingen: Vandenhoeck & Ruprecht).
Stern, P.
    1995   'The Eighth Century Dating of Psalm 78 Re-argued', *HUCA* 66: 41–65.
Tournay, R.
    1988   *Voir et entendre Dieu avec les Psaumes* (Cahiers de la Revue Biblique, 24; Paris: J. Gabalda). ET *Seeing and Hearing God in the Psalms: The Prophetic Liturgy of the Second Temple in Jerusalem* (trans. J. Edward Crowley; JSOTSup, 118; Sheffield, JSOT Press, 1991).
Treves, M.
    1965   'Two Acrostic Psalms', *VT* 15: 81–90.
    1988   *The Dates of the Psalms: History and Poetry in Ancient Israel* (Pisa: Giardini).
Voort, A. van der
    1951   'Genèse I, 1 a II, 4^a et le Psaume 104', *RB* 58: 321–47.
Wanke, G.
    1966   *Die Zionstheologie der Korachiten* (BZAW, 97; Berlin: Alfred Töpelmann).
Westermann, C.
    1961   *Das Loben Gottes in den Psalmen* (Göttingen: Vandenhoeck & Ruprecht, 2nd edn). ET *The Praise of God in the Psalms* (trans. Keith R. Crim; London: Epworth Press, 1966).
    1993   *Die Klagelieder: Forschungsgeschichte und Auslegung* (Neukirchen–Vluyn: Neukirchener Verlag). ET *Lamentations: Issues and Interpretation* (trans. C. Muenchow; Edinburgh: T. & T. Clark).

Willey, P.T.

 1997   *Remember the Former Things: The Recollection of Previous Texts in Second Isaiah* (SBLDS, 161; Atlanta, GA: Scholars Press).

Williams, R.J.

 1971   'Egypt and Israel', in J.R. Harris (ed.), *The Legacy of Egypt* (Oxford: Clarendon Press): 257–90.

Chapter 12

HOW MUCH WISDOM LITERATURE HAS ITS ROOTS IN THE PRE-EXILIC PERIOD?

Katharine J. Dell

If much of recent scholarship on the wisdom literature is to be believed, virtually no final-form wisdom literature can be dated before the exile. In line with a general trend to date literature late, the production of wisdom literature is regarded as mainly a scribal function (e.g. Davies 1998;[1] Clements 1992[2]). Furthermore, the main period of wisdom's development is often regarded as being in the Persian period (e.g. Gese 1984) not just in terms of literary activity, but also in relation to the development of abstract theological ideas as found in Proverbs 1–9, notably in Proverbs 8. A distinction is usually made in regard to Proverbs between the oral stages of the material and the writing down process and some scholars would concede pre-exilic material, certainly oral, perhaps even some groupings of written source material, within a post-exilic literary production. However, a considerable body of scholarship sees the whole wisdom enterprise as having substantially arisen at or just after the exile, perhaps out of the institutional void that was left after the destruction of Temple and palace (e.g. Camp 1985; Clements 1992[3]). This is, in many ways, a return to older scholarly views that regarded the wisdom literature as so different from the rest of the Old Testament in its absence of concern with Israel and the Israelites and its more 'philosophical' character that it must have been post-exilic, at least in its final form, because it did not fit into

---

1. Davies acknowledges that whilst there might have been pockets of scribal activity and archiving in monarchical Judah, these groups were not extensive enough to have produced canonical literature. He writes, 'To assume that the canonized writings originate in the monarchic period, other than in the form of dimly recognized archived source material, is no more than a hunch' (Davies 1998: 87).

2. Clements, like Davies, is concerned with the period of the fixing of the material in literary form, but, more than this, considers that the period in which wisdom made most impression on the intellectual life of Israel.

3. Both Camp and Clements speak of a recontextualization of earlier material at the exile. Clements writes, 'wisdom became uniquely important to the development of a more universalist ethic and understanding of spirituality among Jews after 587 BCE' (1992: 38).

the developmental scheme able to be adduced from the prophets or Pentateuch (e.g. Toy 1899[4]). This view was only substantially changed by the publication in 1923 of Egyptian parallels to parts of Proverbs which suggested earlier roots,[5] although this discovery seemed to prove that the wisdom literature was a foreign import rather than home-grown on Israelite soil, which, in many scholarly circles, did little for its relevance in the discussion of Old Testament theology as a whole. We need to investigate why the wheel seems to have come full circle again (as much scholarship on the Old Testament is prone to do), although with many different nuances, not least appreciation of the Israelite nature of the wisdom literature. Proverbs, Job and Ecclesiastes, the main canonical wisdom books, are placed in a line of theological development that begins in Proverbs whenever we date it, and thus Proverbs is clearly the book on which we need to focus in our quest for pre-exilic wisdom material.

This picture of the wisdom literature as late and post-exilic supposes that the Solomonic attribution (in Prov. 1.1, 12; 10.1; 25.1) is a complete fiction in historical terms. There may have been canonical reasons for this attribution, but it is essentially imposed on the material by the post-exilic scribes, keen to give unity and credence to their collection.[6] It also supposes that the signs of wisdom influence in other parts of the Old Testament are largely editorial in relation to the books in which they are found. In other words, wisdom influence is not formative of the material, but a way of imposing editorial unity upon the material in a post-exilic milieu in which wisdom was of major concern.[7] Another presupposition of this picture is that the wisdom material in Proverbs, Job and Ecclesiastes is all post-exilic and whilst there may have been some theological development over time, this space of time was a short one, so that the doctrine of retribution upheld so strongly in Proverbs and then challenged so vehemently in Job did not require a long period of changing ideas with a catalyst such as the exile to cause it. Rather, the books are regarded as quite different in style, with Proverbs representing collective wisdom and Job an individual experience, and hence coming from different strands of

---

4.   Toy put 350 BCE as the date of the oldest part of Proverbs, thought to be a compilation of existing aphoristic material, and dated the completed book to 200 BCE.

5.   This refers to the publication by Budge (1922) of the Egyptian Instruction of Amenemope which was seen to have a direct relationship to Prov. 22.17–23.11 (extended by some to 24.22). This is still upheld by many scholars to this day, including Emerton (2001).

6.   E.g. Blenkinsopp (1995a: 3) writes, 'to attribute a book to Solomon, then, was a way of bringing it within the sapiential tradition and bestowing on it a special authority'.

7.   Whybray (1996) has an interesting chapter (2) on the Psalms and the possibility that signs of wisdom redaction may provide the key to the shaping of the Psalter. He decides against this possibility in favour of an eschatological redaction. The question of whether wisdom was a formative or an editorial influence upon the Psalms is a matter of debate; see discussion in Dell (forthcoming).

thought within the same post-exilic era. The prose tale of Job, which is also arguably pre-exilic (as is suggested by Ezek. 14.14, 20[8]) and is certainly set in patriarchal times, is seen entirely in a post-exilic context of the writing of the whole book by a post-exilic author[9] and the book of Ecclesiastes, despite the Solomonic attribution, is entirely placed in this period.[10]

It is the purpose of this paper to challenge this picture and present an alternative one of a vibrant and living wisdom tradition in the pre-exilic period. It is not easy to establish firm criteria for doing so and hence this is not an easy matter. I shall argue taking first a literary-historical approach, then a more theological one and finally I shall turn to a comparative method, referring to other parts of the Old Testament as well as considering the ancient Near Eastern parallels. I shall focus on the book of Proverbs and leave Job and Ecclesiastes mainly aside since it is arguments on the relative dating of parts of Proverbs that are of major concern as well as the wider issue of whether the thought-world of wisdom was in the consciousness of early Israelites.

Let us begin by supposing another scenario than the one painted above. Let us imagine the earliest tribes and clans of Israel in their everyday life, sharing experiences and passing them down from one generation to another in the form of short pithy sayings. Concerns were with human relationships, often against the backdrop of an agricultural setting (e.g. Prov. 10.5, 'A son who gathers in summer is prudent, but a son who sleeps in harvest brings shame'). Few were able to write and so a brief functional summary of the essence of an idea was all that it was practical to remember. There were statements of observation or experience (e.g. Prov. 27.19, 'As in water face answers to face, so the mind of man reflects the man'), often elaborated by interesting images or comparisons, and there were exhortations (e.g. 'Do not remove an ancient landmark or enter the fields of the fatherless', Prov. 23.10; cf. Prov. 22.22, 28). There may have

8.   The reference to Job, the character, alongside Noah and Daniel in Ezek. 14.14, 20 in the context of saving only his own life by his righteousness would suggest that Ezekiel was familiar with the story of Job as portrayed in the prose sections of the book and hence that the traditional tale about Job was pre-exilic.

9.   There is widespread consensus that the prose tale in some form was pre-exilic, but probably not as old as the patriarchal setting indicates. There is a possibility of two or more stages in its formulation. The use by the author of the prose dialogue of an older tale in order to say something more profound about the nature of suffering is a well-established scholarly position. The major formulation of Job in terms of prose, dialogue, speeches of God and Job's responses is usually dated to between the sixth and fourth centuries BCE. There may have been further additions of the hymn to wisdom in ch. 28 and the Elihu speeches in chs 32–37.

10.   Ecclesiastes is thought to come from around the third century BCE and Solomonic attribution is generally regarded as honorific. However, the link with Solomon may extend further with the royal testament form in Eccl. 1.12–2.26.

been a few elders or scribal families with the ability to write – in fact, for important occasions their skills might be sought. They might even have been interested in compiling some of the proverbs of the clan so that they were not lost as the centuries passed. As the nation grew and Israel had its own king with court and administration, the need for more educated men became greater and not just the copying of proverbs, but the copying of longer pieces of educational instruction became useful exercises in the attempt of those assigned a scribal/teacher function to train young men in the art of mastering the life-skills that they needed. The brevity of the short proverb did not allow more nuanced argument, which was increasingly desired, and the longer instruction form from Egypt provided an opportunity for a longer exploration of ideas. Mention of the king filtered through into some of the proverbial material (notably Prov. 16.10–15[11]). Instructional material from Egypt provided a useful model on which Israelite 'wise men', for such a group they were becoming, could base their own instruction in an educational context at court and even beyond. A traditional store of wise advice was also filtering down to them from largely oral tradition that they could build into a wider compendium of material that was not just for educational purposes, but which relayed the wisdom world-view that was about understanding human life and relationships and finding the hidden order in the world. And that meant emphasizing the role of God as creator of that order and as the beginning and end of wisdom and knowledge (e.g. Prov. 1.7; 9.10)

If this picture of the way wisdom grew up is at all plausible, and I will look at scholarly views of the likelihood of the various possibilities presented in a moment, the question remains as to whether wisdom literature was still largely a pre-exilic or a post-exilic phenomenon. For this we need to look at the historical possibilities for 'courtly wisdom', which would, it is generally assumed, be found in the pre-exilic period, either at the time of Solomon or of Hezekiah. The question of oral to literary still remains because one could with many recent scholars see much of the production of the actual literature as post-exilic and yet still incorporate a view of a pre-exilic thought-world for wisdom. However, the common acknowledgment is that such pre-exilic material is sporadic, disorganized and generally not cohesively formed in a literary manner, a process that only took place after the exile. The period of the coming together in final form of the wisdom literature, however, is not what I wish

---

11. See discussion of the sayings about the king in Dell (1998), in which it is argued that king sayings need not necessarily reflect a court setting or have been uttered by courtiers but may well have had a wider origin. Having said that, they are likely to reflect the pre-exilic situation when kings were active in Israel. Fox (1996) argues, on the contrary, for the transmission of some proverbs in royal circles, such as those mentioned in Prov. 25.1, the context probably being later than the Solomonic period itself.

to focus on here in that my remit is to see what of this material might belong in the pre-exilic period and I take that to mean 'finds its roots in' the pre-exilic period. However, this might also involve the production of material in written form, even if it is a long way from becoming canonized.

1. *A Literary-Historical Approach*

Let us begin with Solomon, who according to Jewish tradition wrote the Song of Songs in his youth, Proverbs in middle age and Ecclesiastes when he was old and presumably more cynical (*Baba Bathra* 15a). If only it were as simple as that! The whole book of Proverbs is ascribed to Solomon and it is made clear that King Solomon is meant by the additional identification of him as 'son of David, king of Israel' (Prov. 1.1). Those of the post-exilic persuasion argue, quite convincingly, that, as with the book of Ecclesiastes, the Solomonic attribution is a secondary editorial feature, included for reasons of ascribing authority to the book and even recognition for canonical purposes.[12] The argument is also made that we have evidence elsewhere that the beginnings and endings of books are often reworked in later circles (e.g. Camp 1985: ch. 6). It is interesting, however, that the ascription to Solomon is repeated in Prov. 10.1, often thought to be the beginning of another, older section of more traditional sayings. We then have a repeat mention of Solomon in Prov. 25.1 as well as a reference to Hezekiah, king of Judah, whose men copied Solomonic proverbs. Is this too an honorary ascription? If so, why include the detail about Hezekiah? Are these proverbs really to be ascribed to Hezekiah and later court circles around him (as argued by Scott 1955)? These collections were probably separate at some stage and in fact the Proverbs 25–29 group also reflect much that is traditional wisdom along the lines of Prov. 10.1–22.16, as I shall go on to discuss. Even if we consider Prov. 1.1 an editorial gloss, can we be so sure about the other references? Is there some historical basis to these claims or is it just the work of editors wishing us to believe that Solomon had a greater role than he in fact did? This is not in any way to deny that the real origin of many of the proverbs in these older collections is oral, family and tribe based. But it may be that they were collected together and written down in circles not so far from Solomon's court. There is the further issue of reputation. Solomon had a reputation for wisdom and 1 Kings 3 contains the famous story of his wise judgment in solving a dispute between two women over parentage. 1 Kings 5.9–14 (ET 4.29–34) describes his reputation for wisdom. In addition to riddling with the Queen of Sheba (1 Kgs 10), Solomon is also said to have had connections with Egypt, marrying a Pharaoh's daughter (1 Kgs 3),

---

12. See Dell (1993) where it is argued that the attribution to Solomon is not the chief factor in canonization of the book of Ecclesiastes.

providing a possible milieu for the borrowing of Egyptian instruction forms. Could this not mean that wisdom of some kind did flourish at his court and hence that we have evidence amongst these two collections at least of pre-exilic wisdom literature?

To state this is to hark back to the theory of a Solomonic enlightenment as proposed by scholars such as von Rad (1944, ET 1966; 1970, ET 1972)[13] and Heaton (1974) in the 1960s and 70s. This theory was largely based on Egyptian parallels in the wake of the discovery of the parallel of Prov. 22.17–23.11 (24.22) with the Instruction of Amenemope and has to a certain extent fallen from favour today, certainly in the terms in which scholars first proposed it.[14] Heaton's book pointed to the list of Solomon's officials in 1 Kgs 4.1–19 and posited that such detailed court structures very much paralleled the Egyptian system.[15] Scholars since have argued that Israel, a state on a much smaller scale, could not have supported such an elaborate court structure. In addition, Heaton argued for a court school at which education of administrators and courtiers took place, a school which used Egyptian instruction techniques. While we have no direct evidence for a 'school' structure at the time of Solomon, it might be at least plausible that some 'wise' at his court knew of Egyptian models and were able to train younger men in their arts.[16] It would be natural for literate men, who were few and far between, to cluster around the court and the king in order to find work.[17] Education and school structures may have been more widespread than simply at court[18] or we

13. Von Rad proposed that during the period of the early monarchy a move took place from a 'pan sacral' faith to a more experiential, critical engagement with the world and that contacts with neighbouring cultures were an important factor in this development. This change, he argued, is found not just in wisdom texts but in narrative texts such as the Succession Narrative (2 Sam. 9–1 Kgs 2) and the Joseph story in Gen. 37–50.

14. Weeks (1994) provides a strong critique of a whole range of accepted scholarly conclusions on these issues.

15. There have been weighty criticisms of the alleged Egyptian background of Israel's court officials in recent years, e.g. Weeks (1994: 115–31) and Day (1998: 88–90) who argue for a more local Canaanite background for the Israelite court.

16. Whether there was a class of 'the wise' or not is another debated issue amongst scholars, the most compelling evidence in favour being found in Isa. 5.21 and 29.14 and Jer. 8.8; 9.22 (ET 23) and 18.18.

17. Recently Hess (2002) discusses the extent of literacy in Israel and concludes, on the basis of extrabiblical parallels from Canaanite sources, that there were enough literate men to support some kind of court or administration. In fact he regards literacy as having been on quite a wide scale, not confined to palace scribes in Jerusalem.

18. Lemaire (1981; 1984) has argued consistently that schools existed throughout Israel. On the basis of archaeological evidence such as inscriptions, fragments of alphabets and ostraca which provide evidence of writing exercises as might have been done by schoolboys, Lemaire argues for the existence of schools even in villages. He also argues for a professional scribal school as the context for most biblical writings, but not necessarily of their oral antecedents.

may need to think more in terms of local elders.[19] The Solomonic enlightenment theory also suffered from the setback of being compared to the European enlightenment of the seventeenth century, which did the theory no favours. However, if we get away from the 'enlightenment' idea and simply see the court of Solomon (and possibly its beginnings under David[20]) as a place where educated wise men fulfilled various functions, possibly including an archival one in the preservation of the deeds of the king as well as preserving wisdom traditions and teaching, there may be some mileage in this less ambitious picture. There is a comparison to be made here with the ancient Near East and that is with the court of the king in ancient Sumer where there was an established *é-dub-ba* or tablet house in which educated men preserved traditions, wrote up court records, dealt with economic administration and even wrote poetry as well as teaching wisdom (Kramer 1958: 35–45).

If such a court tradition of wisdom and education was already established under Solomon, then by the time of Hezekiah it would be a part of the courtly set-up. There would be an increasing tendency to copy the wisdom of others rather than generate new ideas, wisdom being based on tradition and experience. This might then account for the use of the expression 'copied' in Prov. 25.1. However, some argue (e.g. Blenkinsopp 1995a) that archaeological evidence indicates that writing was more widespread in this later period of the eighth to early seventh century than it was in the ninth and indeed that this might well be the time of the first gathering together of these traditions in written form.[21] This is another possibility, although I would argue that many of the topics of Proverbs 25–29 have been found before, particularly in Prov. 10.1–22.16 (e.g. the nature of kingship, compare Prov. 25.5 with 16.12), or the importance of the spoken word (e.g. compare Prov. 25.11 with 15.23; 25.13 with 13.17), so this might suggest a time gap between the different collections, although the direction of dependence is not known. In the cases of

19. Crenshaw (1998), for example, prefers to speak of scribal apprenticeship within families rather than schools. He is against any widespread school system and concludes that there were probably guilds of scribes, as for other trades, some of whom were used in royal service, others of whom were employed in drawing up official documents and yet others of whom were employed in copying religious texts.

20. Brueggemann (1972) argued for the major development of the state under David, although he writes in a later work, in acknowledgment of von Rad's contribution to the debate, 'what von Rad has grasped…are the modifications in public life, political power, social organization, ideology, technology, and its management that accompanied, permitted and required a shift in intellectual perspective' (1990: 119).

21. Jamieson-Drake (1991) argues that the weight of archaeological evidence for written texts is from a slightly later period than that of Solomon. However, Davies (1995) criticizes him for not having taken proper account of earlier inscriptional evidence from the ninth century and earlier. Davies cautiously affirms the evidence for schools, probably just at administrative centres, but on a more limited scale until the eighth century.

Solomon and Hezekiah, both kings reigned in the pre-exilic period and so any attribution of material to either reign would be evidence of pre-exilic wisdom activity, possibly of the production of wisdom literature itself in its earliest stages.

The picture I painted above of an oral stage before the gathering of material by those who started to write it down needs some discussion. Oral material is notoriously difficult to pin down – proverbs might have circulated orally for thousands of years and it is arguable that they might have been written down at any time during the history of ancient Israel. Some scholars have argued that the proverbs are very literary construc-tions (e.g. McKane 1970), whilst others have seen them as more basic and primary. Eissfeldt (1913) put forward the view that short folk proverbs preceded more literary two-line sayings and were part of a development that saw a change in social setting from oral to more literary and learned. He argued that the meat of a proverb was often to be found in its first half, whilst the second half was not essential to its meaning (this is especially true of those proverbs that do not involve a contrast, e.g. Prov. 12.14; 20.27; 27.19, but it is arguable that many now parallel sayings originally consisted of an independent statement in the first line, e.g. Prov. 20.5[22]). Nel (1982) argues that both one and two-lined sayings could have an origin in a tribal context rather than in more educated circles, whilst Niditch (1996) has argued for an oral/literary continuum which does not allow one to be too prescriptive about an oral stage which developed into a more literary stage but, rather, such developments should be seen as piecemeal.

A closer look at the social context of what we might call primary sayings is of interest as are the indications of a predominantly agricultural setting for much of Prov. 10.1–22.16 (Whybray 1990; 1994a; Westermann 1990, ET 1995). The assumption is made that agricultural probably equals early, but this is accompanied by the argument that either short parallel or antithetical sayings were the staple diet of such settings (e.g. Prov. 10.5; 12.11; 16.26; 24.27; 28.19). Westermann argues that proverbs were essentially functional and only gradually gained more abstract qualities. There is also a point about traditional wisdom sayings found elsewhere in the Old Testament which, according to Westermann, 'confirm that there were, in fact, proverbs in the early part of Israel's history' (1990: 118, ET 1995: 104). He cites texts such as Judg. 8.21; 1 Sam. 10.12; 19.24; 28.13 and prophetic texts such as Hos. 8.7; Jer. 19.24; 23.28; 31.29 (cf. Fontaine 1982). If we are to posit that some collections of sayings may have been

---

22.   Westermann (1990: 18, ET 1995: 9) argues for Prov. 20.5a ('The purpose in a man's mind is like deep water, but a man of understanding will draw it out') having been an independent statement and compares it with a similar African proverb, 'The heart of a man is the sea'. He uses this method of comparative evidence to make this assertion.

made in written form before their incorporation into the final text of Proverbs as we have it today, we would perhaps need comparative evidence of other written texts that seem to predate their context (e.g. the Decalogue in Exod. 20 and Deut. 5). We might also need to look for evidence of a wisdom world-view in other parts of the Old Testament and this was found by those of the Solomonic persuasion in the Joseph narrative (von Rad 1953, ET 1966) and the Succession Narrative (Whybray 1968). If these texts can be shown to be pre-exilic and to have had a separate existence as texts and if they are clearly demonstrating a wisdom influence,[23] then that would be wider evidence of wisdom's presence in pre-exilic Israel.

When discussing the book of Proverbs so far I have been naturally dividing it up into sections and Whybray (1994a) stresses that this is the best approach in that each section seems to reflect a different social milieu and each has its own characteristics. Whilst I would support this approach, it must not be forgotten that there are many echoes of one part with another, repeats of proverbs and variations on specific ideas that overlap (as mentioned above in relation to Prov. 25–29 – and in fact most of ch. 29 repeats topics that have come up before. There are also actual repeats, e.g. in Prov. 26.7b and 9 the second line is identical; 28.6 has a first line that is identical with 19.1a and a second that is a variant of 19.1b). This suggests at least some unity of perspective, even if the book is not a literary unity. That the final form of the book may belong to the post-exilic period is a possibility, but in order to prove that there would need to be some fairly strong evidence of perspectives that could not belong in the pre-exilic period. This evidence has traditionally been sought in Proverbs 1–9, seen as the more theologically advanced section of the book on the presupposition that wisdom moved in that direction. This is by no means proven, although it is widely assumed. The personification of Wisdom features here, which does not appear in pre-exilic Old Testament thought in general[24] or in other parts of Proverbs, although we cannot say when it first arose as an idea. In fact, some scholars have sought a goddess figure behind this personification, which might suggest older roots for the

---

23.   This is by no means agreed by all scholars. One might note in particular the objections of Crenshaw to wisdom influence on both the Joseph Narrative and Succession Narrative (and Esther) (1969) and the comments of Weeks (1994: 92–109) on the Joseph Narrative which, he argues, is only connected to the wisdom literature by the appearance, in conjunction (which is striking but, he argues, not conclusive), of the expressions 'wise and discreet' and 'fear the Lord' in the same text.

24.   The divine quality of wisdom is attributed to God in Isa. 28.29; 31.2 and Jer. 10.12, which may be a forerunner of more developed ideas in Prov. 1–9 or might have been influenced by it. Cf. Kayatz (1966), who argued that close common features between Wisdom and Yahweh influenced the prophets.

concept.[25] Also the presence of instructions that appear to be based on Egyptian models is a well-established fact, and the argument that they probably had a separate existence before their placement in Proverbs 1–9 is widely accepted,[26] but the dating of these is difficult. Egyptian instructions were around from 2500 BCE onwards and Amenemope from c. 1200 BCE and so the influence upon Israelite wisdom may have come at any point, and more probably in the pre-exilic period as a formative influence (even if the final written text is later). This section and Prov. 22.17–23.11 (24.22) both show more evidence of Egyptian models and hence more concern with the process of education and the benefits it brings. However, Prov. 22.17–23.11 [24.22] is usually dated earlier than Proverbs 1–9 on the grounds of parallels with Amenemope and the lack of a final shaping by theological concerns, but the patterns of influence could well, it seems to me, be contemporaneous. Proverbs 1–9 is thought to indicate a city background (Whybray 1994a) which could indicate a later period than an agricultural one, but again does not provide firm evidence of dating. The omission of references to the king in this section is also a pertinent argument, although a general reference to kings does appear in Prov. 8.15.[27] However, arguments from omission are never that convincing. Perhaps the strongest argument for its lateness in relation to other parts of Proverbs is the theological one, which I will consider next.

2. *A Theological Approach*

The key factor in a theological approach to the issue is to accept the given of theological development over time (Dell 1997). Those of the post-exilic persuasion in dating these texts have tended to stress this factor less than previous generations and have, in fact, regarded parallel developments in thought as taking place. With the wisdom literature the key theological development is to see Job and Ecclesiastes as a reaction against the former wisdom world-view as represented in Proverbs. This would require some time difference between the books for that kind of change to come about – and it is something of a radical one with the 'black and white' retributive

---

25. Lang (1986) regards Wisdom as having originally been a goddess figure influenced by Canaanite models, a feature toned down by later Yahwistic monotheism. Day (1995: 69), however, finds not a scrap of evidence for such a Canaanite goddess. Kayatz (1966) considered the Israelite figure of Wisdom to possess features derived from the Egyptian figure of Ma'at and yet to have been essentially an Israelite concept.

26. Fox is against the quest for original instructions in the text by carving it up, but is also wary of overunification. He writes, 'The present essay argues that there is considerable cohesiveness in Prov 1–9, but it is not the result of single authorship. The authorship was, in a sense, collective, the work, perhaps, of several generations' (2000: 323).

27. This reference to 'kings' in the plural sounds universal and is unlikely to refer to the Israelite monarchy.

world-view of Proverbs being subject to severe scrutiny. If there were a historical catalyst for change, that would make it more plausible and, in this case, it can be arguably found at the exile with the change from a communal emphasis to a more individual one and with the recognition that catastrophe is able to strike even the righteous, even to the extent of the destruction of an entire nation. Some have seen the wisdom literature as somewhat outside these historical events and taking its own theological course, a view strengthened by the lack of mention in Proverbs of key characters and events in Israelite history. The just deserts theory is found again in the later wisdom of Ben Sira and so it does not appear to have been lost altogether. The theory of two co-existent strands is a possible one, although it is not the most widely accepted view. Perhaps a more fruitful approach is to look at the issue of theological development within Proverbs itself, since it is in this text that we are primarily looking for evidence of pre-exilic thought.

A whole wave of scholarship saw a development from a more secular type of wisdom to a more theological one which made it easy to assign non-theological proverbs to the pre-exilic period. McKane (1970) and Whybray (1965) particularly espoused such views, finding all references to Yahweh as secondary and editorial – a means by which the book was put into a later, more theological framework. This was achieved by the addition of Proverbs 1–9, which itself showed layers of editing with the theological as the last layer, to the older material which was itself subject to a few strokes with a theological brush. On this model, the quest for pre-exilic, secular wisdom would be made simple, but my view is that this is a misguided and oversimplified way of regarding the material.[28] The quest for editorial layers brings us back to a literary-historical approach, and in recent years that has been downplayed in favour of looking at the text more holistically. When one looks at Proverbs 1–9 one can see that the overall tenor of the section is more theological and indeed that earlier material may be contained within it, such as the instructions. However, as it stands as a unit it is hard to see it as ever having been carved up in quite such a clinical fashion.[29] In my view the injunctions to 'fear the Lord' are integral to the

28.   Weeks (1994: 57–73) argues that ancient Near Eastern parallels such as Amenemope contain religious elements from early times which would seem to reinforce the point that Israelite wisdom may well have done so (e.g. compare Amenemope 9.5 with Prov. 15.16–17 and Amenemope ch. 13 with Prov. 16.9; 19.21; 20.24 and 21.30–31).

29.   In fact, Fox (2000) is very critical of Whybray's method of cutting and pasting the texts, calling his method of identifying original instructions in Prov. 1–9 'procrustean', based on the mistaken assumption that the instructions were uniform to start with. In fact, Whybray himself modified his views somewhat in relation to his original work on the subject (1965), notably in the idea of a strict line of development from more secular material to more Yahwistic, although he still maintained in his 1994 commentary that there were two principal stages of editorial shaping in Prov. 1–9.

section and are often interchangeable with the role of Wisdom (e.g. in the first wisdom poem in Prov. 1.20–33, the fear of the Lord is mentioned in 1.29 in the context of Wisdom's prophetic-style call to those who reject her), rather than, as Whybray (1994b) argues, representing two layers of additions, the first equating the 'father's' words with that of the figure of Wisdom and the second aligning Wisdom with Yahweh. The more key question for this paper is where this material belongs – in the pre- or post-exilic era – and how it relates to the rest of Proverbs.

When one looks closely at Prov. 10.1–31.31 there are numerous references to Yahweh: he appears in nearly every chapter (four mentions in ch. 10; two in 11; two in 12; four in 14; eight in 15; ten in 16; two in 17; two in 18; five in 19; six in 20; five in 21; four in 22) and there are particular clusters in chs 15–16 at the centre of the collection. There are other proverbs that envisage God as behind the scenes judging behaviour, even if he is not explicitly mentioned.[30] This renders the description of Proverbs as 'secular' redundant in my view.[31] Whybray (1979) tried to show how these references are later additions because they are put in to recontextualize existing proverbs (e.g. Prov. 15.16 reinterprets 15.15, 17 and Prov. 18.10 contradicts 18.11). Links can be found with surrounding proverbs at times, although not systematically, and that is one of the problems with his theory. In fact, there is a tendency to appreciate more fully the links between clusters of proverbs in some recent scholarship, notably that of Heim (2001), who shows the integral nature of the Yahwistic sentiments, such that it is impossible to divorce the theological from the rest. Although, in my view, he slightly overstates the number of cohesive thematic clusters to be found in the book, he finds many more instances of theological consistency in Proverbs than hitherto believed. This would suggest that there were strong theological currents in Proverbs from earliest times – there was probably a complete mixture of theological and non-theological that was not even distinguished in the mass of traditional material being passed down in that faith in Yahweh was a key part of the wisdom world-view. Whybray (1994b) acknowledged that the frequency and primacy of the Yahwistic emphasis might suggest an origin for some Yahweh sayings in an oral tradition rather than in edited clusters. The reason for ultimately writing these proverbs down in clusters was, he argued, chiefly for instructional purposes. Once again we are brought back to distinguishing oral and written stages and different uses of material in different contexts for different purposes.

30. E.g. in Prov. 10.6a, 'Blessings are on the head of the righteous', it is arguable that the blessings have to come from somewhere and that they come from Yahweh. In fact the LXX adds 'of the Lord' to clarify the point.

31. Heim comments, 'the often assumed "secular" background of many sayings, including notions of theological "reinterpretation", should finally be put to rest' (2001: 316).

The question then remains whether Proverbs 1–9 takes a further theological step that renders the material later. In view of the greater number of references to the 'fear of the Lord' and in the link with personified Wisdom, that is possible to argue. Further theological developments in the direction of the identification of personified Wisdom with the law in Ben Sira and in the view of Wisdom as a hypostasis in the Wisdom of Solomon might be further evidence of a developing theological trend. However, scholars who find roots of a goddess figure in the personification of Wisdom, as mentioned above, might disagree and in fact these scholars place the roots of such ideas in the pre-exilic period. There is then the further dimension that even if we see Proverbs 1–9 as slightly more developed, the section still could belong to the pre-exilic period, depending on when we draw a line under the gathering together of the book, both in its oral and written stages. This is perhaps the hardest thing to do in that we have no internal dating scheme that will enable us to make such judgments. What we need to do is to look outside the wisdom literature itself to make comparisons with both other Old Testament material that we can more confidently date (although there is shifting sand in most areas of Old Testament study as to dating) and with comparative material from the ancient Near East.

3. *A Comparative Approach*

If we could establish wisdom influence in Old Testament books or segments of material that are fairly well-established as pre-exilic this might support the argument for the existence of a formative wisdom tradition from early times. Of course, this problem is avoided if we see wisdom influence as primarily a redaction rather than as a formative part of a text. Many wisdom features of texts have been regarded as later additions from the pen of scribes who shaped the text as it went into its final literary form. We cannot deny that this process may have occurred and where beginnings and endings of books have received this treatment the evidence is perhaps more compelling. However, what I am trying to isolate here is more than the addition of a few remarks about the paths of the righteous and the wicked (e.g. Ps. 1) or the occasional proverb (Ezek. 18.2). As well as the forms and content of wisdom, what I am looking for is evidence of the wisdom world-view, of its principles, outlook and theology.

The wisdom world-view is multifarious, but as it exists in Proverbs it has a number of features. It uses traditional material based on experience both to make comments about the world and about interrelationships – notably human relationships with each other, with the animal world and with God – largely for educational purposes. It presupposes that God is the creator of the world and sees God as behind the wisdom quest, directing it and providing the final answer to the mysteries of the universe. However, the emphasis is on what human beings can come to understand about 'life' and how each individual can maximize their chances of success. Wealth, health, offspring and longevity are particularly desired by the wisdom writers. The basic principle behind the rules of behaviour is the doctrine of just retribution, according to which the righteous are rewarded and the wicked punished. The wise person can walk the path of righteousness and hence receive the blessings due to such a person. There is particular interest in Proverbs in themes such as communication, and the method used is the contrasting of opposites such as the wise man and the fool, the righteous and the wicked.

There is a problem over the definition of 'wisdom' and how far wisdom influence extends. It is easy to designate a group of texts as 'wisdom books', since they show the forms, content and context of wisdom in large measure, but outside that is a grey area (Dell 2000: ch. 1). There was a phase of scholarship (see discussion in Morgan 1981) which sought wisdom in many books of the Old Testament and particularly in the prophets (Dell 2000: ch. 6). The eighth-century prophets were a particular goldmine for such findings and many argued that wisdom was one influence in their thought, alongside cultic and legal traditions. The amalgamation of such traditions was thought to have created the new genre of written prophecy that these prophets represent. Thus Amos as the first of such prophets was particularly interesting from this angle[32] and even more so since he seemed on occasion to subvert wisdom genres (Dell 1995). Hosea too could be regarded in this light in his use of everyday images (e.g. use of a proverb in Hos. 8.7) to convey God's message (Wolff 1965, ET 1974; Macintosh 1995) and to a lesser extent Micah (Wolff 1982, ET 1990) and Isaiah who appeared to be making use of the principle of natural law or retribution familiar from the proverbial material (Barton 1979) and was arguably educated amongst the wise (Whedbee 1971). Other scholars cast the net wider into the book of Deuteronomy with its emphasis on natural law and its didactic tone (Weinfeld 1972)[33] and into the Psalter (Perdue 1977; Dell 2000: ch. 5). There is perhaps some mileage

---

32.   A thorough study of wisdom influence on Amos was conducted by Wolff (1964, ET 1973; 1975, ET 1977). The numerical sequence of Amos 1–2 would seem to be a particularly good example (cf. Prov. 30.18–19). Not all scholars are in agreement that there is any definitive wisdom influence on Amos (notably Crenshaw 1967). Soggin (1995) airs the possibilities afresh, but is cautious of drawing far-reaching conclusions from uncertain materials.

33.   The idea of false weights and measures as an abomination to the deity is found in Deuteronomy (25.13–16); also in Proverbs (11.1; 16.11; 20.10) and in the Instruction of Amenemope, chs 16 and 17. It is likely that the direction of influence is Amenemope to Proverbs to Deuteronomy, thus indicating that this proverbial expression was one with pre-exilic roots.

in these comparative discussions, for which there is not adequate room here. Without wanting to water the distinctiveness of wisdom down too much, signs of its influence in texts widely agreed to be pre-exilic would certainly strengthen the argument for wisdom as a formative, pre-exilic influence.

Wisdom influence can be arguably regarded as a formative one and not just an editorial stage in regard to these comparative texts. The arguments are not absolutely conclusive, but they are probable when combined with the evidence from the proverbs themselves in relation to their content and possible social contexts. We need finally to turn to the ancient Near Eastern material, notably to the main parallel with Proverbs, the Instruction of Amenemope. I mentioned earlier the problem of dating ancient Near Eastern influence on Israelite material. However, it is likely that it was when Egypt was strong and powerful that such influence took place, which would be well before and during a period paralleling the pre-exilic period in Israel. We have early examples of Moses (Exodus 3) and of Joseph (Gen. 37–50) who both had experience of and were influenced by the Egyptian court. We read too in 1 Kings of Solomon's international contacts. This sets up a picture of influence in the pre-exilic period being rather more likely than in the post-exilic period when Israel was politically governed by foreign rulers and when Egypt was not as dominant as the empires of Babylon or Persia. The Instruction of Amenemope dates from c. 1200 BCE and there is evidence that it was used as a school text. If there were schools in Israel of a limited nature, perhaps just at the court, or else in a few urban areas, the kind of copying of a text that we know took place with Amenemope may well have occurred. We may have evidence in Proverbs 1–9 of such texts in the instructions, or we may wish to confine the evidence to Prov. 22.17–23.11 (24.22) which seems to form a close parallel to the Amenemope text.[34] The enigma seems to be, at least in relation to Proverbs 1–9, that this may be the latest part of Proverbs, and yet we may have evidence here of earlier educational material being put into a more theological context of poems about personified Wisdom. If the 'instruction' parts of Proverbs 1–9 are earlier this might ground the theological aspects more firmly in the early thought-world of wisdom. If there is a goddess figure behind Wisdom, even the Egyptian figure of Ma'at as Kayatz (1966) argued, we would have further evidence of pre-exilic thought in this section. One point to note in relation to 22.17–23.11 (24.22) and Proverbs 1–9 is that there are quite a few thematic links, as between Prov. 10.1–22.16 and 25–29. Proverbs 22.17–21 begins with an extended introduction comparable to 1.1–6 with close parallels between 22.17 and 4.20 and 22.18 and 5.2; Prov. 22.22 and 25 mention father and

---

34. The consensus of opinion is that this is a close parallel. This was challenged by Whybray (1994c), but maintained afresh by Emerton (2001).

mother in the same way as in 1.8 and 6.20. There are warnings against associating with criminals in Prov. 22.4–5; 23.17–18; 24.8–9 and 24.15–16 (cf. 1.18–19; 3.31; 4.14–19). This link has tended to be underplayed because of emphasis on ancient Near Eastern parallels, but might suggest a closer relationship between these sections of Proverbs and even a closer date of composition. One difference with Amenemope in Prov. 22.19 is the naming of Yahweh – is this an editorial afterthought or is trust in Yahweh the goal of the teaching as a whole? I would suggest that the latter is more plausible.

Some parallels have been found between small parts of Proverbs and the Wisdom of Ahiqar, an Aramaic text probably originating from the seventh century.[35] This is thought to be a work contemporary with Proverbs, unlike the Egyptian material, and so provides a close parallel in that sense. The most interesting aspect alongside the proverbial material is the possible personification of Wisdom in Ahiqar if 'it' is taken as 'she', 'Even to gods is it precious, to it forever belongs the kingdom, in heaven it is treasured up, for the lord of holiness has exalted it' (Ahiqar 95). It does not help the dating of wisdom much except to indicate a pre-exilic source for Proverbs. The closest parallels to the short proverbs in Prov. 10.1–22.16 are perhaps to be found in Sumerian proverbs, which represent some of the oldest proverbs in the world, reflecting an agricultural background and concern for family life. They might well have been oral at some stage but were used as part of the school curriculum later on and have been found on numerous tablets containing material of mixed type and language (Gordon 1959). 'A people without a king is like sheep without a shepherd' sounds as if it might be from Proverbs but it is from the Assyrian Collection of ancient Sumer. It is interesting that in the emergent Babylonian culture that took over Sumerian material there was a shift of interest from functional proverbs to more abstract questionings of the purpose of human life, a shift that appears to be represented in Israelite wisdom in the progression from Proverbs to Job.

4. *Conclusion*

There is a slight feeling of going around in circles with this argument, which does have elements of the chicken and egg situation about it. We are essentially looking at material that has a timeless and universal quality and attempting to date it early or late. In my view the best way of doing that is to compare it with other parts of the Old Testament which are

35. See Greenfield (1995); Day (1995: 62–65, 70). The most commonly cited parallel is between Prov. 23.13–14 and Ahiqar 81–82 which reads, 'Spare not your son from the rod; otherwise, can you save him [from wickedness]? If I beat you, my son, you will not die; but if I leave you alone, [you will not live].'

roughly datable as well as looking at historical and source-critical conclusions. This comparison raises the wider issue of wisdom's relationship with the more historical aspects of Israel's faith. There is a tendency to hive wisdom literature off into its own corner because it does not mention the salvation history and the great heroes of Israel's past.[36] However, there may be closer links than has sometimes been thought with mainstream Yahwism (as argued consistently by Murphy (1975; 1990; 2000), albeit that the emphasis here is on the creator God rather than the redeeming God of Israel (see Perdue 1994).[37] Furthermore, if the theological aspect of wisdom is more primary than has been often stated, then these parallel theological developments come more firmly into the frame in the discussion of the priority of ideas and their development.

Thus all we are left with is a 'balance of probability'. I remember coming across that phrase in relation to archaeology and the Bible (Bright 1960) – archaeology does not prove that events that are related in the Bible actually happened, but its findings confirm the wider context in which the events are plausible. It is somewhat the same with wisdom literature. We cannot prove that it had its roots in the pre-exilic era, but the balance of probability lies in favour of that on the grounds of the historical echoes of Kings Solomon and Hezekiah, the literary evidence of earlier and later sources and accompanying views on social context, the theological outlook found in Proverbs and the links of its wider worldview with other parts of the Old Testament and the development of its theological ideas, as well as with the ancient cultures of the Near East.

Bibliography

Barton, J.
  1979   'Natural Law and Poetic Justice in the Old Testament', *JTS* NS 30:1–14.
Blenkinsopp, J.
  1995a   *Wisdom and Law in the Old Testament: The Ordering of Life in Israel and Early Judaism* (Oxford: Oxford University Press, 2nd edn).
  1995b   *Sage, Priest, Prophet: Religious and Intellectual Leadership in Ancient Israel* (Louisville, KY: Westminster John Knox Press).
Bright, J.
  1960   *A History of Israel* (London: SCM Press).
Brueggemann, W.
  1972   *In Man We Trust* (Richmond, VA: John Knox Press).
  1990   'The Social Significance of Solomon as a Patron of Wisdom', in J.G. Gammie and L.G. Perdue (eds), *The Sage in Israel and in the Ancient Near East* (Winona Lake, IN: Eisenbrauns): 117–32.

---

36. G.E. Wright (1952), for example, could not fit wisdom literature into a model of God acting on the historical scene and hence marginalized this material.

37. Another fruitful text for comparison and for wisdom influence is Gen. 1–11.

Budge, E.A.W.
> 1922   *Second Series of Facsimiles of Egyptian Hieratic Papyri in the British Museum* (London: British Museum).

Camp, C.
> 1985   *Wisdom and the Feminine in the Book of Proverbs* (Sheffield: Almond Press).

Clements, R.E.
> 1992   *Wisdom in Theology* (Carlisle: Paternoster Press, and Grand Rapids, MI: W.B. Eerdmans).

Crenshaw, J.L.
> 1967   'The Influence of the Wise upon Amos', *ZAW* 79: 42–52.
> 1969   'Method in Determining Wisdom Influence upon "Historical" Literature', *JBL* 88: 129–42.
> 1998   *Education in Ancient Israel: Across the Deadening Silence* (New York: Doubleday).

Davies, G.I.
> 1995   'Were there Schools in Ancient Israel?', in J. Day, R.P. Gordon and H.G.M. Williamson (eds), *Wisdom in Ancient Israel: Essays in Honour of J.A. Emerton* (Cambridge: Cambridge University Press): 199–211.

Davies, P.R.
> 1998   *Scribes and Schools: The Canonization of the Hebrew Scriptures* (Louisville, KY: Westminster John Knox Press).

Day, J.
> 1995   'Foreign Semitic Influence on the Wisdom of Israel and its Appropriation in the Book of Proverbs', in J. Day, R.P. Gordon and H.G.M. Williamson (eds), *Wisdom in Ancient Israel: Essays in Honour of J.A. Emerton* (Cambridge: Cambridge University Press): 55–70.
> 1998   'The Canaanite Inheritance of the Israelite Monarchy', in J. Day (ed.), *King and Messiah in Israel and the Ancient Near East: Proceedings of the Oxford Old Testament Seminar* (JSOTSup, 270; Sheffield: Sheffield Academic Press): 72–90.

Dell, K.J.
> 1993   'Ecclesiastes as Wisdom: Consulting Early Interpreters', *VT* 44: 301–32.
> 1995   'The Misuse of Forms in Amos', *VT* 45: 45–61.
> 1997   'On the Development of Wisdom in Israel', in J.A. Emerton (ed.), *Congress Volume: Cambridge 1995* (VTSup, 66; Leiden: E.J. Brill): 135–51.
> 1998   'The King in the Wisdom Literature' in J. Day (ed.), *King and Messiah in Israel and the Ancient Near East: Proceedings of the Oxford Old Testament Seminar* (JSOTSup, 270; Sheffield: Sheffield Academic Press): 163–86.
> 2000   *'Get Wisdom, Get Insight': An Introduction to Israel's Wisdom Literature* (London: Darton, Longman & Todd).

forthcoming   '"I will Solve my Riddle to the Music of the Lyre" (Psalm 49.4 [5]): A Cultic Setting for Wisdom Psalms?', *VT*.

Eissfeldt, O.
> 1913   *Der Maschal im Alten Testament* (BZAW, 24; Berlin: W. de Gruyter).

Emerton, J.A.
> 2001   'The Teaching of Amenemope and Proverbs xxii 17-xxiv 22: Further Reflections on a Long-standing Problem', *VT* 51: 431–65.

Fontaine, C.R.
1982   *Traditional Sayings in the Old Testament: A Contextual Study* (Bible and Literature series 5; Sheffield: Almond Press).

Fox, M.
1996   'The Social Location of the Book of Proverbs', in M.V. Fox, V.(A.) Hurowitz, A. Hurvitz, M.L. Klein, B.J. Schwartz and N. Shupak (eds), *Texts, Temples, and Traditions: A Tribute to Manahem Haran* (Winona Lake, IN: Eisenbrauns, 1996): 227–39.
2000   *Proverbs 1–9* (AB, 18a; New York: Doubleday).

Gese, H.
1984   'Wisdom Literature in the Persian Period', in W.D. Davies and L. Finkelstein (eds), *The Cambridge History of Judaism*, I (Cambridge: Cambridge University Press).

Gordon, E.I.
1959   *Sumerian Proverbs: Glimpses of Everyday Life in Ancient Mesopotamia* (Philadelphia: University Museum, University of Pennsylvania).

Greenfield, J.C.
1995   'The Wisdom of Ahiqar', in J. Day, R.P. Gordon and H.G.M. Williamson (eds), *Wisdom in Ancient Israel: Essays in Honour of J.A. Emerton* (Cambridge: Cambridge University Press): 43–54.

Heaton, E.W.
1974   *Solomon's New Men* (London and New York: Pica Press).

Heim, K.M.
2001   *Like Grapes of Gold Set in Silver: An Interpretation of Proverbial Clusters in Proverbs 10.1–22.16* (BZAW, 273; Berlin and New York: W. de Gruyter).

Hess, R.S.
2002   'Literacy in Iron Age Israel', in V.P. Long, D.W. Baker and G.J. Wenham (eds), *Windows into Old Testament History: Evidence, Argument and the Crisis of Biblical Israel* (Grand Rapids, MI: W.B. Eerdmans): 82–102.

Jamieson-Drake, D.
1991   *Scribes and Schools in Monarchic Judah: A Socio-Archaeological Approach*, (JSOTSup, 109; Sheffield: Almond Press).

Kayatz, C.
1966   *Studien zu Proverbien 1–9: Eine form- und motivgeschichtliche Untersuchung unter Einbeziehung ägyptischen Vergleichmaterials* (WMANT, 22, Neukirchen–Vluyn: Neukirchener Verlag).

Kramer, S.N.
1958   *History Begins at Sumer* (London: Thames & Hudson).

Lang, B.
1986   *Wisdom and the Book of Proverbs: An Israelite Goddess Redefined* (New York: Pilgrim Press).

Lemaire, A.
1981   *Les écoles et la formation de la Bible dans l'ancien Israël* (OBO, 39; Fribourg, Switzerland: Editions Universitaires; Göttingen: Vandenhoeck & Ruprecht).
1984   'Sagesse et écoles', *VT* 34: 270–81.

Macintosh, A.A.
1995   'Hosea and the Wisdom Tradition: Dependence and Independence', in J. Day,

R.P. Gordon and H.G.M. Williamson (eds), *Wisdom in Ancient Israel: Essays in Honour of J.A. Emerton* (Cambridge: Cambridge University Press): 124–32.

McKane, W.
    1970   *Proverbs: A New Approach* (OTL; London: SCM Press).

Morgan, D.F.
    1981   *Wisdom in the Old Testament Traditions* (Atlanta, GA: John Knox Press).

Murphy, R.E.
    1975   'Wisdom and Yahwism', in J.W. Flanagan and A.W. Robinson (eds), *No Famine in the Land: Studies in Honor of John L. McKenzie* (Missoula, MT: Scholars Press): 117–26.
    1990   *The Tree of Life: An Exploration of Biblical Wisdom Literature* (New York: Doubleday).
    2000   'Wisdom and Yahwism Revisited', in D. Penchansky and P.L. Redditt (eds), *Shall not the Judge of all the Earth do what is Right? Studies on the Nature of God in Tribute to James L. Crenshaw* (Winona Lake, IN: Eisenbrauns): 191–200.

Nel, P.J.
    1982   *The Structure and Ethos of the Wisdom Admonitions in Proverbs* (BZAW, 158; Berlin: W. de Gruyter).

Niditch, S.
    1996   *Oral World and Written Word: Ancient Israelite Literature* (Louisville, KY: Westminster John Knox Press).

Perdue, L.G.
    1977   *Wisdom and Cult* (SBLDS, 30; Missoula, MT: Scholars Press).
    1994   *Wisdom and Creation* (Nashville: Abingdon Press).

Rad, G. von
    1944   'Der Anfang der Geschichtsschreibung im alten Israel', *Archiv für Kulturgeschichte* 32:1–42. ET 'The Beginnings of Historical Writing in Israel', in G. von Rad, *The Problem of the Hexateuch and Other Essays* (trans. E.W. Trueman Dicken; Edinburgh and London: Oliver & Boyd, 1966): 166–204.
    1953   'Josephsgeschichte und "altere Weisheit" ', in *Congress Volume: Copenhagen 1953* (VTSup, 1; Leiden: E.J. Brill). ET 'The Joseph Narrative and Ancient Wisdom', in G. von Rad, *The Problem of the Hexateuch and Other Essays* (trans. E.W. Trueman Dicken; Edinburgh and London: Oliver & Boyd, 1966): 292–300.
    1970   *Weisheit in Israel* (Neukirchen–Vluyn: Neukirchener Verlag). ET *Wisdom in Israel* (London: SCM Press, 1972).

Scott, R.B.Y.
    1955   'Solomon and the Beginnings of Wisdom in Israel', in M. Noth and D. Winton Thomas (eds), *Wisdom in Israel and in the Ancient Near East: Presented to Professor Harold Henry Rowley* (VTSup, 3; Leiden: E.J. Brill): 262–79.

Soggin, J.A.
    1995   'Amos and Wisdom', in J. Day, R.P. Gordon and H.G.M. Williamson (eds), *Wisdom in Ancient Israel: Essays in Honour of J.A. Emerton* (Cambridge: Cambridge University Press): 119–23

Toy, C.H.
    1899   *Proverbs* (ICC; Edinburgh: T. & T. Clark).
Weeks, S.
    1994   *Early Israelite Wisdom* (Oxford Theological Monographs; Oxford: Clarendon Press).
Weinfeld, M.
    1972   *Deuteronomy and the Deuteronomic School* (Oxford: Oxford University Press).
Westermann, C.
    1990   *Wurzeln der Weisheit: die ältesten Sprüche Israels und anderer Völker* (Göttingen: Vandenhoeck & Ruprecht). ET *Roots of Wisdom: The Oldest Proverbs of Israel and Other Peoples* (Louisville, KY: Westminster John Knox Press, 1995).
Whedbee, J.W.
    1971   *Isaiah and Wisdom* (New York: Abingdon Press).
Whybray, R.N.
    1965   *Wisdom in Proverbs* (SBT, 45; London: SCM Press).
    1968   *The Succession Narrative* (SBT, 9; London: SCM Press).
    1979   'Yahweh-sayings and their Contexts in Proverbs, 10,1–22,16', in M. Gilbert (ed.), *La sagesse de l'Ancien Testament* (Gembloux: Duculot, and Leuven: Leuven University Press): 153–65.
    1990   *Wealth and Poverty in the Book of Proverbs* (JSOTSup, 99; Sheffield: JSOT Press).
    1994a   *The Composition of the Book of Proverbs* (JSOTSup, 168; Sheffield: Sheffield Academic Press).
    1994b   *Proverbs* (NCB; London: Marshall Pickering, and Grand Rapids, MI: W.B. Eerdmans).
    1994c   'The Structure and Composition of Proverbs 22.17–24.22', in S.E. Porter, P. Joyce and D.E. Orton (eds), *Crossing the Boundaries: Essays in Biblical Interpretation in Honour of Michael D. Goulder* (Leiden: E.J. Brill): 83–96.
    1996   *Reading the Psalms as a Book* (JSOTSup, 222; Sheffield: Sheffield Academic Press).
Wolff, H.W.
    1964   *Amos' geistige Heimat* (WMANT, 18; Neukirchen–Vluyn: Neukirchener Verlag). ET *Amos the Prophet: The Man and His Background* (trans. Foster R. McCurley; Philadelphia: Fortress Press, 1973).
    1965   *Dodekapropheton, I: Hosea* (Neukirchen–Vluyn: Neukirchener Verlag). ET *Hosea* (trans. G. Stansell; Hermeneia; Philadelphia: Fortress Press, 1974).
    1975   *Dodekapropheton, II: Joel und Amos* (BKAT, 14.2; Neukirchen–Vluyn: Neukirchener Verlag, 2nd edn). ET *Joel and Amos* (trans. S. Waldemar Janzen, S. Dean McBride and Charles A. Muenchow; Hermeneia; Philadelphia: Fortress Press, 1977).
    1982   *Dodekapropheton. IV: Micha* (BKAT, 14.4; Neukirchen–Vluyn: Neukirchener Verlag). ET *Micah: A Commentary* (trans. G. Stansell; Minneapolis: Augsburg Fortress, 1990).
Wright, G.E.
    1952   *God Who Acts: Biblical Theology as Recital* (SBT, 8; London: SCM Press).

Chapter 13

IS THE COVENANT CODE AN EXILIC COMPOSITION?
A RESPONSE TO JOHN VAN SETERS

Bernard M. Levinson

Despite questions about its coherence, source-critical attribution, and precise textual delimitation, the Covenant Code has long been viewed as providing an important window into the pre-exilic history of ancient Israel. It has played a vital role in any reconstruction of Israel's cultus and sacrificial system, religious calendar, legal and ethical norms, and social structure. The development of the source-critical method could not have taken place without the successive attempts of eighteenth and nineteenth-century scholars to compare the laws of the Covenant Code with other biblical legislation and with the narratives of the historical books, so as to determine their relative sequence and priority. The 'New Documentary Hypothesis' worked from the conviction that the Covenant Code was pre-Deuteronomic in its fundamental orientation, based upon literary comparison of its altar law (Exod. 20.24) with that of Deuteronomy: 'Deut. 12 polemisirt gegen den durch Exod. 20,24 sanktionirten Zustand' (Wellhausen 1885: 203). On that basis, Deuteronomy presupposed the Covenant Code's prior existence and sought to challenge it: the innovation of centralization responded to a pre-existing religious, legal, and literary norm that assumed multiple altar sites as legitimate for the sacrificial worship of Yahweh. Comparison of other laws in the Covenant Code, such as the manumission laws (Exod. 21.2–11) and the festival calendar (Exod. 23.14–17), with those of Deuteronomy (Deut. 15.12–18; 16.1–17) yielded similar results, thereby corroborating the Covenant Code's literary-historical priority. With the core of the legal corpus of Deuteronomy associated with Josiah's centralization and purification of the cult (622 BCE), the Covenant Code's priority to Deuteronomy placed it solidly in the pre-exilic period.

Over the years, of course, there have been a number of questions about the neatness of this fit. Arguments for the Covenant Code's being extensively coloured by Deuteronomistic language, have frequently been seen as evidence for its later reworking at the hands of post-Deuteronomic editors during the exile. The final hands responsible for the creation of the

Sinai pericope (Exodus 19–24) and for the inclusion of the Decalogue in that unit have been seen to be Priestly and thus as exilic or post-exilic.[1] More recently, as part of the flux in contemporary Pentateuchal theory, a number of scholars have sought to invert the standard model by placing the Yahwist after Deuteronomy and the Deuteronomistic history.[2] From this revisionist perspective, 'the "golden age" of Israel's literature is no longer the beginning of the monarchy, but the exile' (Ska 2002: 20–21). Christoph Levin (1993), in particular, situates the Yahwistic narrative in the exilic or post-exilic period. He has begun to apply that model to the Covenant Code, which he does not see as an original part of the Yahwistic history. Instead, he sees it as having previously existed independently and as only subsequently inserted into the Sinai pericope.[3] On that basis, he accepts that some sections of the Covenant Code are pre-Deuteronomic and might have provided a literary source for Deuteronomy's laws of asylum and manumission (Levin 2000: 132–33). He sharply reverses the consensus view, however, with his claim that the altar law of the Covenant Code (Exod. 20.24) mounts a post-Deuteronomic polemic against centralization, seeking to relativize Jerusalem's special status.[4] In this view, the altar law finds its home in the exilic or post-exilic period and allegedly addresses the social conditions of the Diaspora. For the law that has long been the point of departure for understanding the social world of the Covenant Code, this marks a significant change.

More comprehensively, however, than Levin, John Van Seters (2003a) argues that the Covenant Code is a monument of Diaspora Judaism: that it is as an exilic composition without any pre-exilic content. If other scholars have proposed the imprint of the exile upon the Covenant Code, that imprint has been relatively minor and restricted to an overlay or to the stages of its final redaction, while allowing a substantial textual core that is pre-exilic. Not so for Van Seters, whose claims are maximal. He contends that the Sinai pericope as a whole, including the Covenant Code, belongs to a single compositional layer that represents the coherent work

---

1. The literature is of course immense; for a fine assessment of the most recent work, see Kratz (2002: 295–323).

2. For valuable contextualizations, see Nicholson (1998: 132–73) and Ska (2000: 195–207; 2002: 1–23).

3. 'Das Bundesbuch ist nicht Teil des jahwistischen Geschichtswerks gewesen, sondern nachträglich in die Sinaiperikope gelangt' (Levin 2000: 127). Similarly, earlier, Levin (1985: 180–81).

4. However there is scant evidence 'in der exilischen Diaspora' of any dispute about Jerusalem's status 'als einzigem legitimen Heiligtum'; thus astutely challenging Levin's hypothesis, see Hans-Christoph Schmitt (2003: 279). A different attempt to place the altar law in the exilic period is made by Wolfgang Oswald, who claims that 'die Pluralität der Kultorte' would have been self-evident in Judah during the exile (1998: 142–43). Schmitt correctly points out that there is no evidence to support such a premise (2003: 279).

of an exilic author, whom Van Seters identifies as the Yahwist. This distinctive rejection of the original redactional independence of the Covenant Code carries significant implications. Because he retains key components of the conventional model, Levin sees portions of the Covenant Code providing a source for Deuteronomy and therefore as pre-exilic. The analysis of Van Seters, which rejects redaction, denies that possibility. Far from representing the beginning of Israel's legal history, therefore, the Covenant Code would represent the conclusion of that history. This Yahwist, who is the author of the Covenant Code, now represents the latest literary source of the Pentateuch; he drew freely upon both Deuteronomy and the Holiness Code as literary and legal sources, responding to and adjusting their content to fit the situation of life in Babylonian exile (Van Seters 1996b: 546). Given his sustained argument, this discussion of whether there is pre-exilic law provides an extended analysis of the most forceful rejection of that possibility: *A Law Book for the Diaspora*, by John Van Seters (2003a).

Van Seters urges a profound reconfiguration of the existing model for any reconstruction of the history of Israelite religion. Without directly using the term, he calls for and proclaims a Copernican revolution: a fundamental reorientation of epistemology and hermeneutics. Like the series of studies that led up to it (1996a: 319–21; 1996b: 534–35), the rhetoric of the book suggests that it is only an arbitrary and entrenched bias of scholarship to view the Covenant Code and its laws as pre-Deuteronomic. The author promises to provide the first opportunity for scholars to read the Covenant Code on its own terms and to understand its relation to both Israelite and cuneiform law. The author makes repeated truth claims about his analysis in contrast to prevailing models. Curiously, even where possible connections might be made to the work of other scholars holding ostensibly similar positions, the connections are not made or simply overlooked.[5] This repeated claim to possess objectivity, which alleges that the broader scholarly world labours under long-standing epistemological error, merits a serious response.

By placing the composition of the Covenant Code in the Babylonian exile, Van Seters makes a substantial argument that there is no pre-exilic

---

5. For example, the earlier mentioned work of Christoph Levin on the Yahwist (1985; 1993; 2000) does not appear in this book's bibliography, despite their shared concern to redefine the corpus of the Yahwist, both narrative and legal, as post-Deuteronomic and therefore exilic. Given Levin's recent article (2000; note also 1993: 432–34) on the altar law of the Covenant Code, which plays such an important role in Van Seters's analysis (as will be discussed below), that omission is especially unfortunate. However, the non-dialogue between the two scholars is mutual. Levin's analysis of the altar law (2000) overlooks the study of the same text by Van Seters (1996a, published in an important series) as well as his related articles (1996b; 1997). The field would benefit if the two scholars engaged one another's work.

law except for the legal corpus of Deuteronomy, composed scant decades before the exile. Deuteronomy now stands at the beginning of Israel's legal tradition, not as the point of transition between earlier and later traditions of law.[6] Deuteronomy retains its role as the seventh-century 'Archimedean point' for the dating of Israelite literature (see Otto 1997); but, in the analysis of Van Seters, it now only establishes the pre-Deuteronomic legal and literary vacuum. The Covenant Code no longer serves as a pre-exilic literary source for Deuteronomy; rather, repositioned into the exile, it belongs to the reception history of Deuteronomy. To begin to do justice to these arguments requires selective focus on several key issues: (1) the author's hostility to redactional analysis; (2) the claim that correspondences of sequence and content between the Laws of Hammurabi and the Covenant Code point to the latter's composition in Babylon, during the exile; and (3) the argument that the altar law of the Covenant Code (Exod. 20.24) is a post-Deuteronomic affirmation of God's availability to the Judaean diaspora. In making each of these arguments, Van Seters provides lasting contributions to the field in the way that he challenges and rethinks existing models. At the same time, the alternatives that are set in place often seem vulnerable: driven more by theory than by full consideration of relevant textual, linguistic, or scholarly issues.[7]

1. *The Hostility to Redaction and the Model of Authorship*

Van Seters rejects the very notion that editors played any role in the composition of the Covenant Code. He dismisses redactional analysis as 'highly speculative' (2003a: 5). He stresses how 'revolutionary' is his finding that 'It is unnecessary to posit any redactors in the whole code!' (2003a: 173). This argument consists of two main claims. The first asserts the coherence of the Covenant Code (Exod. 21–23) as a unified literary composition. The formal and stylistic differences within it do not provide

---

6. That the argument here is made from literary and legal history only sharpens the point. Unlike the well-known 'minimalist' position (Lemche 1985; 1998; Thompson 1992), from which Van Seters correctly distinguishes himself (2003a: 172), the author does not deny the existence of a pre-exilic Israel more broadly. The motivation is not some cultural programme or ideology but a revisionist rethinking of conventional scholarly assumptions, something that has characterized his contributions from the beginning (1975). For a valuable assessment of the minimalist approach, see Brettler 2003.

7. Considerations of length led to the choice to address key issues of methodology and to provide an extended response to Van Seters's analysis of the altar law of the Covenant Code, given its importance to the history of scholarship. Similar issues apply in his approach to other laws, such as the manumission law (Exod. 21.2–6, 7–11), which he regards as post-Deuteronomic (Van Seters 1996b; 2003a: 118–19). For a response, see Levinson 2005.

evidence of its having a long compositional history (2003a: 21–29).[8] A single author is responsible for the composition of the whole, including: the prologue of the altar law in its narrative setting (Exod. 20.22–26); the casuistic laws (21.2–11, 13–14, 18–37; 22.1–16, ET 2–17); the participial prohibitions (21.12, 15–17; 22.17–19, ET 18–20); the apodictic commandments (22.20–30, ET 21–31; 23.1–9); the laws concerned with the religious calendar, including fallow year, Sabbath, and festivals (23.10–19); and the hortatory prologue (23.20–33).

The second claim is yet bolder: 'The whole of the law code, *along with its setting in the Sinai pericope*, is the work of a single author' (2003a: 45; emphasis added). The Covenant Code never existed, whether in whole or part, prior to or independent of the Sinai pericope:

> Without the assumption of the priority or of the Covenant Code's great antiquity, there is likewise no basis for the code's original independence from its narrative setting, and this has made it possible to relate the code of laws more closely within the literary work of the exilic Yahwist. All the strained arguments for maintaining its independence can be seen as special pleading for the code's antiquity. The code is the single unified work of the author J, which he calls "the Book of the Covenant" and which he makes the sole basis of the law given by Yahweh through Moses at Sinai. The scene on the mountain between Moses and the deity leads seamlessly into the opening laws… [T]his framework of the code shows unmistakable dependence upon the Deuteronomic tradition. (2003a: 172–73)

In terms of its literary history, the Sinai pericope thus represents an act of *creatio ex nihilo* that took place during the Babylonian exile. There never was a Covenant Code prior to the composition of the Sinai pericope; nor was there ever a Sinai pericope separate from the Covenant Code. With the sole exception of the Priestly material, the entire Sinai pericope (Exod. 19–24) represents the unified and original composition of a single author: Van Seters's exilic Yahwist (2003a: 53–54). To see any pre-history to this material is unjustified: 'Once the P supplements have been

---

8. Other scholars, of course, have adopted superficially similar positions based on their rejection of the source-critical method. However, for the coherence of the Covenant Code to be defended by someone with a very deep commitment to the source and literary criticism is unprecedented. Sprinkle (1994) rejects the validity of diachronic analysis and employs harmonistic legal exegesis to defend the coherence of the Covenant Code. The approach is not convincing. Westbrook (1994: 15–36) argued for the coherence of the casuistic portion of the Covenant Code, in effect thereby redefining and limiting its textual compass to Exod. 21.1–22.16 (ET 17). His arguments are based on the theory that there is no legal-historical development in either cuneiform or biblical law. For challenges to this approach, see Levinson (1994a; 1994b). See also Jackson (1995) and Van Seters (2003a: 38–44).

removed,[9] we are left with a text that presents a harmonious narrative sequence throughout. I have attributed this narrative to a single author, J, who is exilic in date and post-D' (2003a: 53).[10] The Sinai pericope represents a compositional unity, the work of a single author who drew freely upon a range of literary sources, both native (Deuteronomy and the Deuteronomistic history; the Holiness Code) and foreign (the Laws of Hammurabi).

Ironically, in order to defend his claim that the Sinai pericope represents the unified composition of an exilic Yahwist, Van Seters must deny the existence of the Covenant Code altogether as conventionally understood. As a discrete compositional unit, the Covenant Code has now been dissolved, since the formal criteria that define and delimit it no longer carry literary-critical or historical-critical significance. Although Van Seters continues to employ the conventional term, what he means by it is entirely different from what most scholars understand. The Covenant Code is now a section marker within the larger unit of the Sinai pericope, to which it has been subsumed.

Many of Van Seters's criticisms of scholarly assumptions about the redactional history of the Covenant Code are compelling. The way he has worked through the history of scholarship to challenge entrenched ways of approaching the text is engaging. Particularly impressive is his rejection of any simple one-to-one correlation between a particular legal or literary form and a reconstructed social or historical setting that is claimed as its *Sitz im Leben*, an approach that inevitably, then, requires the hypothesis of an editorial process for the literary integration of the various laws with their separate histories (Van Seters 2003a: 9–29). Rarely have the assumptions underlying this approach been so systematically thought through and challenged.

At the same time, the alternative model that is advanced is defended with arguments that, at key points, go beyond the evidence or overlook complicating material. Van Seters does not see himself as simply engaging in standard scholarly debate concerning the reconstructions of the compositional history of the Covenant Code as propounded by individual scholars like Albrecht Alt (1934, ET 1966), Martin Noth (1968), Brevard S. Childs (1974), Eckart Otto (1988; 1993; 1994), Ludger Schwienhorst-Schönberger (1990), Yuichi Osumi (1991), Frank Crüsemann (1992, ET

---

9.   Van Seters ascribes the following texts to P: Exod. 19.1, 12–13a, 20–25; 20.8–11; 24.1–2, 9–11, 15b–18a.

10.   Remarkably, Van Seters extends this argument to include Exod. 32–34 as well: 'The whole of non-P is indeed a unity' (2003a: 70). He thereby rejects (1999: 160–70) the classical position that the so-called 'cultic Decalogue' (Exod. 34.11–27) is ancient and Yahwistic, in contrast to the Elohist's 'ethical Decalogue' (Exod. 20). Similarly, he takes issue with recent work that regards Exod. 34 as an exilic revision of the Covenant Code and as therefore not on the same literary level with it (2003a: 69–70, rejecting Blum 1996).

1996), to name only a few of those engaged. Rather, he maintains that the very concept of redaction is inappropriate to both the Covenant Code and to the Sinai pericope. It represents a long-standing epistemological error that requires correction, in his view, just as he regards the assumption of Deuteronomy's priority to the Covenant Code as another arbitrary prejudice. Van Seters argues that his approach frees scholarship from anachronistic methodological assumptions.

Given the epistemological certainty attached to this claim, it is important to investigate whether viewing the Sinai pericope as a unified, post-Deuteronomic composition cogently accounts for the texts in question. Does the model, in other words, explain the text? Neither the argument for the synchronic coherence of the Sinai pericope nor that for the priority of Deuteronomy to the composition of the Sinai pericope can be defended in the light of the textual details. In both arguments, passages that offer important countervailing evidence need to be brought into the discussion, as does relevant comparative scholarship on the nature of textual composition in the ancient Near East. In this section, I shall attempt to show how the textual and comparative evidence requires an immanent model of redaction (one that differs from the form-critical model that Van Seters rejects). Attention to the text does not permit the Sinai pericope to be read as the cohesive product of a single, post-Deuteronomic author.

Van Seters's argument for the synchronic coherence of the Sinai pericope as the unified composition of the Yahwist presupposes a complex reconstruction of literary history.

1. '[T]he Deuteronomistic accounts of the Horeb events in Deut 4–5' provide the earliest account of the theophany, presenting the Decalogue as divine revelation (2003a: 54). In this original conception of the theophany, the Decalogue represents the direct address of Yahweh to the entire nation.

2. 'The exilic author J has simply made use of' that prior account in composing the Sinai pericope of Exodus 19–24 (ibid.). Nonetheless, the Yahwist introduces a series of changes into the earlier model. The most important of these is: 'In J there is no Decalogue spoken directly to the people' (ibid.). The Yahwist emphasizes and promotes the mediating role of Moses. The Yahwist's Sinai pericope, indeed, does not include a Decalogue; instead, the Covenant Code, alone, represents the Yahwist's conception of the content of the theophany, which is originally communicated directly to Moses upon Sinai and which Moses thereafter mediates to the people. The Sinaitic covenant is concluded solely on the basis of the Covenant Code.

3. In composing the Covenant Code, the Yahwist drew not only upon Deuteronomy and the Deuteronomistic history but also upon the

Holiness Code (Lev. 17–26) at multiple points, such as the manumission laws (2003a: 86, 88, 94–95; cf. 162; 172).

4. The Yahwist's distinctive notion of the Mosaic mediation of revelation (in the Sinai pericope) triggers subsequent Yahwistic glossing and correction of the Horeb narrative. Thus, the insistence by Moses that he stood between Israel and Yahweh to mediate the Decalogue (Deut. 5.5) – which contradicts the immediately preceding affirmation of direct divine revelation to the nation as a whole (Deut. 5.4) – is one of a series of 'other additions to Deuteronomy by J' (2003a: 55).

5. In a final stage, a significant interpolation disrupts the original design of the Yahwist. The Decalogue (Exod. 20.1–17), along with related material (19.20–25), represent a 'late P insertion into the text' (2003a: 48).

This reconstruction raises a series of methodological issues. Van Seters sharply rejects the very notion of Deuteronomistic redaction of the Sinai pericope (1999; 2003a: 21–29, 54, 174; 2003b). This emphatic denial of redaction in favour of the compositional coherence of the Sinai pericope requires, however, that redaction be retained. It is merely shifted elsewhere, and assigned a different siglum and date. The Yahwistic editing of Horeb replaces the Deuteronomistic redaction of Sinai.[11]

Given this reconstruction of literary history, the recovery of the Sinai pericope as the compositionally coherent creation of the Yahwist warrants closer attention. Table 1 shows how Van Seters reconstructs the Sinai pericope. Once the later interpolations attributed by Van Seters to the Priestly source are removed (2003a: 53), the Yahwist's coherent composition emerges:

Exodus	Original J verses **[later interpolations by P]**
19	**[1]**, 2–11, **[12–13a]**, 13b–19, **[20–25]**
20	**[1–17]**, 18–26
21–23	(entire unit is J)
24	**[1–2]**, 3–8, **[9–11]**, 12–15a, **[15b–18a]**, 18b

Table 1: The Yahwist's original Sinai pericope

11. There is another preliminary methodological issue. The premise that the Yahwist draws upon Deuteronomy, the Deuteronomistic history, and the Holiness Code, but undergoes later interpolation by the Priestly source, creates a source-critical sequence of: D, DtrH, H, J, P. The assumption that H precedes P, and that P is the final Pentateuchal redactor, is certainly defensible, per the classical model. But for the past several decades, a number of scholars on independent grounds have proposed that the Holiness School is later than P and edits it. Given the importance of this issue to Van Seters's reconstruction, one would wish for some acknowledgment that there is a debate concerning it (see Wright 2004).

It is difficult to see how this analysis of the original form of the Sinai pericope can be read as a synchronically coherent composition. At multiple points, the reconstruction does not read smoothly and logically on its own terms. There are far too many inconsistencies, repetitions, doublets, and aporia in the narrative.[12] The extent of them calls into question the

12. The following sample of the doublets, gaps, or inconsistencies in the reconstructed narrative suggests it cannot easily be read as coherent:

(1) The people's ready, unconditional willingness to heed the covenant (Exod. 19.8) makes it difficult to understand why, immediately thereafter, the concern exists to ensure that the people should heed and believe in Moses (19.9). The latter verse does not continue directly from 19.6–8 but more likely represents a doublet.

(2) Following God's command to Moses to report to the nation the divine announcement of Israel's election (19.6), the narrative continues logically with Moses reporting that speech to the nation, as commanded (19.7), securing the people's unconditional assent and then reporting that acceptance of the terms of national election back to the deity (19.8). In contrast, following the deity's announcement of a theophany so as to ensure the people's obedience to Moses (19.9), the continuation is unintelligible. Moses is said to report the people's words back to God even though the people have not said anything there, and he has not said anything to them of the divine plan to affirm him (19.9). Indeed, the note that Moses reports the speech back to the deity duplicates, but for a single word, the similar note in the previous verse: 'Moses reported (וישׁב) / told (ויגד) the words of the people to Yahweh' (19.8b/9b). In 19.8, the note logically follows the election formula; in 19.9, it lacks logical antecedent and hangs as a disconnected fragment. At issue in 19.9b seems to be a *Wiederaufnahme* or editorial doublet, marking the insertion of v. 9a.

(3) Van Seters seems to read 19.6–9 as a unified, coherent, prospective reference to the Sinai reference which is to follow, the goal of which is to affirm Mosaic mediation: 'Moses is to play a special role in this process [Yahweh's covenant with the people] because it is stressed that the words and commands will be mediated through Moses (19:6–9)' (2003a: 54). It is difficult to see how these verses constitute a single unit. More likely, 19.6–8 are one unit, since the people's asseveration of obedience in v. 8 directly alludes to v. 7. In contrast, v. 9 appears disjointed. The former unit refers to the nation's election and has v. 6 as antecedent; only v. 9 is prospective and validates Mosaic mediation. The summary by Van Seters, which sees vv. 6–9 as integrated and as jointly affirming Mosaic mediation, overlooks these distinctions.

(4) If the coherent narrative has Yahweh descend upon the peak of the mountain, with his presence marked by smoke, flame, and thunder, there to hold his colloquy with Moses (19.18), it becomes difficult to understand Yahweh's assertion, 'You have seen for yourselves that I spoke with you from heaven' (20.22). The two loci are mutually exclusive.

(5) The location of the people is difficult to understand. If they are to ascend the mountain (19.13b), and assembly at its base is only preparatory (19.17), one might have expected an initial ascent upon the mountain before the frightened people are said to withdraw (20.18). Nor is it clear how, once the people have withdrawn, leaving Moses alone on the mountain, they can nonetheless directly address him, so as to announce their fear (20.19). Moreover, having already withdrawn once (20.18), the reason for the repetition of that information, in nearly verbatim terms (20.21), is unclear. The unit cannot be compositionally coherent.

(6) The degree of correspondence between 19.7–8 and 24.3 (cf. v. 7), in both language

viability and intelligibility of the recovered text as compositionally coherent. Even more problematically, the very attempt to relegate the Decalogue to a subsidiary role in the composition of the Sinai pericope, by ascribing it to the interpolation of a late Priestly editor, also breaks down. As soon as one attempts a detailed analysis of the text, it becomes difficult to maintain Van Seters's model of a Sinai pericope oriented on the Covenant Code alone. Neither the language of the text nor the narrative line required by such a reconstruction support such a claim. In his account:

> The various laws that are contained in the Decalogue (the "ten words") are dispersed within the Covenant Code, beginning with a shortened version of the First and Second Commandments in 20:23. Thus, Moses receives all the laws, both the "words" (דברים) and the "command-ments" (משפטים), at the same time at Sinai, and these are all in "the Book of the Covenant," to which the people commit themselves. (2003a: 54)

With the reference to the 'words' and the 'commandments' received at Sinai, Van Seters clearly has in mind Exod. 24.3 (see below). In his reconstruction, that ostensibly coherent content of revelation is then inscribed in 'the Book of the Covenant', which, upon being read to the people, inspires their unconditional assent (Exod. 24.7).

The model proposed by Van Seters makes it difficult to understand the overall structure of the Sinai pericope. Claiming the originality of the Covenant Code alone, to the exclusion of the Decalogue, makes it very difficult to construe the text. In the Decalogue, God proclaims את כל הדברים האלה, 'all these words' (Exod. 20.1). That superscription provides the only logical antecedent to the narrator's account of the covenant ratification ceremony, whereby Moses came and recounted to the people: את כל דברי יהוה ואת כל המשפטים, 'all the words of Yahweh and all the ordinances' (Exod. 24.3a).[13] Immediately upon hearing them, the people agreed immediately to perform them: כל הדברים אשר דבר יהוה נעשה, 'all the words that Yahweh has spoken shall we perform' (Exod. 24.3b). Moses then hastens to transcribe the divine speech:

---

and sequence is so close as to go beyond what a single narrative line can easily sustain. It seems much more logical to regard the one as a doublet or imitation of the other: in the one case, affirming the nation's election by God; in the other, affirming the Decalogue as the basis of the nation's covenant with God.

13. Within the Sinai pericope (Exod. 19–24), the only other cases of the plural noun דברים, referencing divine legal proclamation, are Exod. 19.6, 7, 8 (all concerning the election formula, and with the oath of obedience already completed in v. 8); 19.9b (in which a sentence fragment seems to hang in the air; note that v. 19a is not apposite here, since the piel infinitive construct means 'when I speak'). On that basis, the superscription to the Decalogue (Exod. 20.1) – not some amorphous Decalogue commandments absorbed into the Covenant Code – makes most sense as the direct antecedent of Exod. 24.3a. Moreover, within the Covenant Code itself there is no appropriate self-stylization as the deity's 'word(s)'. In Exod. 22.9 and 23.7 the noun is singular. In both cases, as at 23.8 (where the

ויכתב משה את כל דברי יהוה, 'Moses wrote all the words of Yahweh' (Exod. 24.4a). Unaccounted for in these otherwise consistent references to the Decalogue as the 'words' of the deity (first proclaimed, then recapitulated, agreed to, and punctiliously transcribed) is the reference to כל המשפטים, 'all the ordinances' (Exod. 24.3a). No sooner is the unanticipated term introduced than it immediately disappears: it escapes both the people's eager oath of obedience (v. 3b) and the Mosaic transcription (v. 4a). Consequently, the present form of v. 3a makes the narrative incoherent. Ostensibly at the peak of their zealous piety, the people become curiously selective in what components of the divine speech they choose to heed. They deign to comply only with the divine 'words', to the exclusion of the 'ordinances' that Moses, apparently forgetting his own recitation, fails to transcribe. In the same way that the narrative line does not cohere, the syntax of the verse is equally problematic. The present formulation leaves ואת כל המשפטים, 'and all the ordinances', without explicit authorization as divine speech; the phrase follows and is external to the *nomen rectum* that defines את כל דברי יהוה as 'all the words of Yahweh'. This construction is syntactically anomalous.[14] Indeed, there is no other verse in the Hebrew Bible that coordinates the two plural nouns in question to designate, combined in this way, the divine revelation to Moses.[15]

---

noun is plural), the reference is consistently to human, not divine speech. Consequently, the most logical antecedent for 24.3 is the superscription to the Decalogue (20.1), contrary to the reconstruction proposed by Van Seters.

14. Since the same genitive cannot normally apply to two coordinated nouns, the second (or sometimes third) nomen 'regens must be added with a suffix referring [back] to the nomen rectum' (GKC § 128a). Accordingly, expected here would have been 'all the words of Yahweh and his ordinances'. That formulation, with the pronominal suffix on the second noun, would correspond to the norm attested in Gen. 41.8; Exod. 15.4; Judg. 8.14; 1 Kgs 8.28; 2 Kgs 2.12 (GKC § 128a for this list, adding Exod. 15.4). On this basis, I disagree with the contrary suggestion of Joüon/Muraoka (1996: § 129a) that allows בני דוד והבנות ('the sons of David and the daughters') as equally acceptable, if less common. The only example cited for that construction, however, is משקה מלך מצרים והאפה (Gen. 40.1), which Joüon/Muraoka translate as 'the cup-bearer and the baker of the king of Egypt'. That exception proves the rule. Despite the English translation provided, the Hebrew construct is objective genitive not subjective genitive. It employs the masculine singular active participle as nomen regens: 'the one who provides drink to the King of Egypt'. To have added a pronominal suffix to 'baker' in that context would have created an ambiguity about the intended antecedent.

15. The only other combination of the two nouns, in the plural, refers to the detailed requirements for the construction of the Temple (1 Kgs 6.38, with number variation in *qere/ kethibh* and the versions). Elsewhere, there is a telling distinction between the terminology used, in the plural, to designate the Mosaic law, as 'my statutes', 'my ordinances', and 'my commandments' (חקתי ... משפטי ... מצותי) on the one hand, and the use of the singular דברי on the other hand, to refer to the Davidic dynastic oracle (1 Kgs 6.12). In Ps. 119.43, the nouns once again have different referents: singular דבר refers to human speech. In Ps. 147.19, where three nouns are at issue, the singular דבר of the *kethibh* with the Septuagint, Samaritan, and Syriac, as in v. 18, seems more original than the plural *qere*.

If the Covenant Code were an original part of the Sinai pericope, to the exclusion of the Decalogue, this disruption of both narrative line and syntax would be unlikely. Classical source criticism provides the most elegant solution to this problem. The syntactically extrinsic term in Exod. 24.3a logically has the superscription to the Covenant Code as its antecedent: 'These are the ordinances (הַמִּשְׁפָּטִים) that you shall set before them' (Exod. 21.1). Even Van Seters's own model allows no alternative explanation. Other, potentially 'pre-Yahwistic' texts diverge from this verse either in syntax or in the terminology for Mosaically mediated divine law.[16] Accordingly, the phrase in Exod. 24.3a, which cannot be construed synchronically (whether in terms of narrative or syntax), points to a diachronic issue. The syntactical disturbance suggests that the Sinai pericope has a redactional history. The reference to 'the ordinances' is secondary; it reflects an *ex post facto* attempt to integrate an originally independent Covenant Code into the Sinai pericope as a supplement to the Decalogue.[17] Despite two references to Exod. 24.3 and a half dozen to the unit (Exod. 24.3–8) in Van Seters's book, the difficulties raised by the language and syntax of the verse are not discussed.[18] Textual specifics such as these call into question the author's claim to provide a more immanent reading of the Sinai pericope as the unified composition of a post-Deuteronomic author.

Just as the Exodus Decalogue still seems to cast its shadow in the reconstructed Sinai pericope, so also in the account of Horeb. According to the model, Deuteronomy 5 marks the beginning of the theophany tradition, which is then revised by the Yahwist in the Sinai pericope, who replaces direct divine revelation with Mosaic mediation of law. That model leaves a particular feature of the Horeb theophany without explanation. Immediately following his report of the Decalogue (Deut. 5.6–21 [18]), the Mosaic speaker continues. He begins with a *casus pendens* that emphasizes the uniqueness of the Decalogue as divine speech:

אֶת הַדְּבָרִים הָאֵלֶּה דִּבֶּר יְהוָה אֶל כָּל קְהַלְכֶם בָּהָר מִתּוֹךְ הָאֵשׁ הֶעָנָן
וְהָעֲרָפֶל קוֹל גָּדוֹל וְלֹא יָסָף וַיִּכְתְּבֵם עַל שְׁנֵי לֻחֹת אֲבָנִים וַיִּתְּנֵם אֵלָי

These words spoke Yahweh to your whole assembly, from the mountain, from the midst of the fire, the cloud, and the thick darkness, in a loud voice; *and he added no more*. Then he wrote them upon two stone tablets and gave them to me. (Deut. 5.22 [19])

16. While Deut 26.16 also employs the plural definite absolute ('the ordinances'), it does not refer to 'the words' but instead to 'these statutes'. Deut. 26.16 responds to the same kind of legal-historical issue discussed here (with much gratitude to Norbert Lohfink).

17. Following Eissfeldt 1956: 253, ET 1965: 213; and Levinson 1997: 152–53.

18. The narrative summary blends out the inconsistencies of language and syntax, in effect substituting harmonistic legal exegesis for the original narrative: 'After God declares all the laws to Moses, the latter repeats them to the people, who promise to keep them. They are then written in a "Book of the Covenant"...' (Van Seters 2003a: 54).

Van Seters cites this verse once while comparing several texts concerned with the writing of the law (2003a: 64). Nowhere discussed is the Mosaic speaker's insistence that it was the Decalogue alone that the deity first spoke from the mountain and that was then immediately transcribed. The speaker's strong denial calls attention to itself, since the necessity for it is unclear: it interrupts what otherwise seems to be a straightforward narrative. The sequence is also striking: the denial of further divine speech is found immediately after the recapitulation of that speech but before specifying the divine writing. What unprompted concern triggers the need to deny further divine speech at just this point? Even if the passage were discussed, it is not clear how Van Seters's model could account for it. Assuming the priority of Horeb to Sinai makes it impossible to understand the Mosaic speaker's insistence (Deut. 5.22) that nothing was spoken at Horeb other than the Decalogue.[19] More helpful in this context is the approach of Otto Eissfeldt (1956: 265, ET 1965: 222–23). In asserting that the divine speech 'did not continue' (Deut. 5.22) beyond the Decalogue, this text's Deuteronomistic author seeks to displace the divine speech of the Covenant Code and leave room for the Mosaic mediation of divine speech in the legal corpus of Deuteronomy. Deuteronomy's polemic rewrites literary history.[20] By circumscribing Sinai and silencing the Covenant Code, the redactors of Deuteronomy sought to clear a textual space for Moab as the authentic—and exclusive—supplement to the original revelation (Deut. 28.69, ET 29.1).

The argument that the entire Sinai pericope represents the unified composition of an exilic Yahwist is also defended on comparative grounds. After mounting strong arguments against Eckart Otto's analyses of the Covenant Code (Otto 1988; 1993; 1994), Van Seters moves to a larger rejection of the role of redaction as relevant for either biblical or cuneiform law:

---

19. The recognition that the Decalogue in Deut. 5 is Deuteronomistic, and presupposes the legal corpus of Deut. 12–26 (Van Seters 2003a: 54–55), does not circumvent this narrative issue. The narrator might still have continued to introduce the motif of the need for Mosaic mediation of the legal corpus without having to deny further speech.

20. That Deuteronomy 5 only makes sense as a response to the *prior* combination of the Decalogue and the Covenant Code is emphasized by Kratz (2000: 115):

> Die Einkleidung des dtn Gesetzes als Gesetzesproklamation vor dem Eintritt in das Land Kanaan, die dem Dtn auch an anderen Stellen eigen ist, wird so zur Promulgation des Gesetzes vom Sinai/Horeb, sprich: zur Promulgation des Bundesbuchs in seiner in Dtn vorliegenden, revidierten Ausgabe. Dtn 5 hat also den Zweck, das dtn Gesetz mit dem Bundesbuch, der litararischen Vorlage des Dtn, zu identifizieren. Die Identifizierung wäre nicht nötig und ergäbe keinen Sinn, hätte man Ex 19–24 nicht vor Augen.

> There is no need to call the compositional process that led to the formulation of the Hammurabi Code "redactional". That prejudices the whole point of the comparison. We simply do not know whether there were multiple editions behind this particular code and the extent to which this version "reformed" an earlier one. (2003a: 22)

This generalization finds support in a one-sentence observation that the redactional approach to cuneiform law was advocated by 'the legal historian P. Koschaker, but it is a viewpoint that is hotly disputed in current scholarship' (Van Seters 2003a: 180 n. 58). No actual scholarly literature on this matter is adduced. The initial agnosticism seems rapidly to become a normative claim. Just as redactional analysis is suspect in relation to the Laws of Hammurabi so is it for the composition of both the Covenant Code and the Sinai pericope, especially since the cuneiform text provided the Yahwist with a literary prototype for the composition of the Sinai pericope. At the same time, the concept of 'redaction' seems to be doubly restricted: first, to a process of legal-historical amendment and revision (as might be found in Roman legal history, which was the model employed by Koschaker); and, second, to questionable form-critical assumptions about the nature of textual growth (as Van Seters takes issue with the reconstruction of the Covenant Code by Eckart Otto in particular). However, neither of these theoretical models arose out of cuneiform literature: they are uncontrolled. The double restriction, without considering alternative models and without a direct discussion of the available scholarship, becomes a way to dismiss the very concept of redaction as meaningful for the analysis of either the Covenant Code or cuneiform literature.[21]

---

21. A related article carries these arguments further: the model of redaction is stigmatized as having an illegitimate intellectual pedigree in its application to the Pentateuch (Van Seters 2003b: 487–500). He argues that the very model of redaction criticism is self-contradictory: (1) because it was introduced via the back door from New Testament studies, especially Wellhausen's analysis of the formation of the synoptic tradition, and is therefore not an immanent development; and (2) because 'Wellhausen's redactor [as developed for New Testament scholarship] is being used [by Old Testament scholars] against Wellhausen's source criticism in an unconscious and ironic contradiction' (2003b: 499). Van Seters argues that many of the activities attributed to the redactor, when they involve fundamental structuring and ordering of a block of tradition in order to subordinate it to a single, overall ordering principle and ideology, are better described as the work of an author. He objects to 'the disappearance of the author who gives way to the redactor'. He advocates, therefore, the vision of the Deuteronomistic historian as described by Martin Noth (2003b: 498).

   Several issues arise here. First, the critique of the model of redaction addresses only the intellectual history of form-criticism, while using that restrictive model to dismiss redactional analysis altogether. The evidence of cuneiform literature, where meaningful controls exist, is still not brought into the discussion. Second, it seems unlikely that the history of scholarship permits things to be so neatly organized, with form criticism deriving so uni-directionally

In this conceptual slide from the specific to the general, Van Seters overlooks a more immanent model of redaction. The best analogy for the integration of the Covenant Code into the Sinai pericope is the process whereby the legal collection of the Laws of Hammurabi was joined to the literary frame of the prologue and epilogue.[22] The valuable monograph by Hurowitz (1994: 101) demonstrates how the literary frame of the Laws of Hammurabi includes extensive and at times verbatim 'borrowings from external texts', including royal hymns and inscriptions. These borrowings were marked by specific editorial devices and formal markers such as internal recapitulations that bracket the borrowed material[23] or reflect the sequence of the original text:

> The lexical identity combined with the significant structural relationship certainly indicates that the author of Codex Hammurabi was not merely drawing on stock phrases which were "in the air", but was actually citing specific literary compositions such as the royal inscriptions and hymns mentioned or other texts as yet unknown. As such, he has essentially written a literary pastiche or summary inscription, similar to later Assyrian inscriptions which cannibalize[24] annalistic accounts, rearranging and presenting events in geographical rather than chronological order. (Hurowitz 1994: 101)

This form of authorship breaks down the author–redactor dichotomy from which Van Seters, while mounting an important challenge to European form-critical assumptions, nevertheless himself fails to escape. The textual evidence does not support that binary model of textual composition. As Hurowitz (1994: 102) notes: 'The compiler of Codex Hammurabi may be characterized[25] as a combination scholar, editor, and

from New Testament scholarship. The *religionsgeschichtliche Schule*, with its creative work in Tübingen around 1890, included Old and New Testament scholars alike (such as Albert Eichhorn, Hermann Gunkel, Alfred Rahlfs, Ernst Troeltsch, William Wrede, and later, Rudolf Otto and Hugo Gressmann), who influenced one another extensively in both directions. Finally, the use of intellectual history to validate or invalidate the compositional model applied to the Pentateuch exposes Van Seters to a serious vulnerability. The model for authorship that he endorses (2003b: 498) is that of Martin Noth's description of the exilic Deuteronomistic historian, who, in the fundamental structuring of his materials, emerges as a *Verfasser*. Noth emphatically denied, however, the validity of this model for the Pentateuch (as Van Seters concedes). If the history of scholarship is to play a probative role in the argument, then Van Seters has placed himself in a serious 'ironic contradiction'.

22. Especially appropriate is Tigay's conclusion in his discussion of empirical models for biblical studies. He reminds us that, 'for the biblical critic, the discussion once again underlines the importance of considering the source criticism of ancient Near Eastern compositions *without assuming that they represent texts with no prehistory of hands and redactors*' (Tigay 1985c: 158; emphasis added).

23. This technique reflects the repetitive resumption or *Wiederaufnahme* (see Levinson 1997: 17–20).

24. This quotation corrects the typo in the original, 'canabalize'.

25. This quotation corrects the typo in the original, 'chacterized'.

author'. Indeed, many of the most important works of cuneiform literature similarly represent 'redactional compositions', whereby the author in fact is also an editor.[26] That applies particularly to the most famous work of cuneiform literature and the first ever to be published: 'The Babylonian Gilgamesh epic did not escape the attentions of a redactor' (George 1999: xxiv). The composition has a literary history. Its artistic and literary coherence is the accomplishment of a gifted redactor:

> The standard version uses and adapts some known Sumerian stories as well as others for which written forerunners are not known... But it also contains other material, particularly in the first part of the epic, which may never have existed independently. *With considerable skill a single work is created out of diverse elements.* The methods used to stitch the pieces together are several. (Dalley 1989: 46; emphasis added)

The creative genius of Sin-leqqi-unninni is that of an author who is also fully an editor: that is evident in the way that the standard edition combines material from the Old Babylonian versions, while reusing older language, rearranging material, dropping or adding lines, etc. (Tigay 1982: 129; 1985a: 40–41). His most brilliant compositional move was the redactional insertion of tablet XI of Gilgamesh, drawn from the *Epic of Atrahasis*, into the Old Babylonian material, to give rise to the standard edition of the Gilgamesh Epic (Tigay 1985c: 158–67).[27] The bracketing technique recalls that employed by the author–editor responsible for the Laws of Hammurabi.

The argument that Sinai is synchronically coherent and post-Deuteronomic provides, in the end, a coherent explanation neither of Sinai nor of Horeb. Too much of the text is left unaddressed or unexplained. The author–redactor dichotomy that Van Seters employs imposes an anachronistic notion of original authorship upon the literature of antiquity. Such a model reflects European Romanticism more than it does the complexity of textual composition in Israel or the ancient Near East. A more immanent reading of the legal-religious literature of the ancient Near East demands recognition of redaction as an essential

26. Note also the fine study by Eichler (1987), demonstrating the redactional logic involved in the expansion and reuse of legal sequences from the Laws of Eshnunna by the composers of the Laws of Hammurabi.

27. Major compositions of the Second Temple period equally reflect this model of redactional composition. That applies most notably to the Samaritan Pentateuch, whereby its version of the tenth commandment of the Decalogue embeds and conflates material from Deuteronomy 11 and 27, so as to legitimate Gerizim as the sanctuary elected by God (Tigay 1985b: 78–86). This kind of redactional conflation and re-sequencing is true more broadly for the presentation of the Sinai pericope in the Samaritan Pentateuch (Tigay 1995b: 68–78). One sees the same elsewhere as well. One major component of the originality of the Temple Scroll consists in its creative project of redaction—its conflation, expansion, and reordering of a wide range of biblical legal material (Levinson and Zahn 2002).

strategy of authorship. The Laws of Hammurabi, Van Seters's own paradigm for the composition of the Covenant Code, confirm the importance of redaction as a compositional technique. The Sinai pericope similarly makes most sense as a redactional composition. An immanent reading of the text suggests that the Covenant Code was secondarily added to the Sinai pericope rather than being composed by a single author simultaneously with it. On that basis, the Covenant Code has a literary history that is both independent of the Sinai pericope and, in at least one point, pre-Deuteronomic.

2. *The Context for the Influence of the Laws of Hammurabi upon the Covenant Code*

Classical source-criticism, since the time of Wellhausen, assumed that the legal collections of the Pentateuch related to the various narrative sources in a neat, one-to-one, correlation. On that basis, even if there were debates about the exact attribution of legal texts like the so-called Ritual Decalogue (Exod. 34), the Sinaitic Decalogue (Exod. 20), or the Covenant Code (Exod. 21–23), in effect, all these sources belonged to the monarchic history of pre-exilic Israel. The Covenant Code would regularly be dated sometime between the tenth and the eighth centuries BCE. This picture was complicated by two developments from the beginning of the twentieth century. First, *Gattungsgeschichte* attempted to move back behind the late dating of the Pentateuchal literary sources, so as to reach the older traditions that ostensibly lay behind these sources and that allegedly provided access to the pre-state period. Second, the discovery in 1901 and prompt publication of 'Codex Hammurabi' by Vincent Scheil (1902) forced the question of how to explain the analogies in legal form and content between it and the Covenant Code. Albrecht Alt's famous *Die Ursprünge des israelitischen Rechts* (1934, ET 1966) claimed that the 'casuistic' (third person, if-then) legal form reflected a common Near Eastern inheritance that Israel would have acquired in Canaan, during the settlement period. Subsequent scholarship (Greenberg 1960; Paul 1970; Finkelstein 1981), noting the absence of evidence for that alleged common legal heritage in Canaan, maintained a much closer connection between Mesopotamian legal collections and the Covenant Code. Common to all these approaches was the assumption that the similarity between the Covenant Code and the Laws of Hammurabi represents a phenomenon that goes back to the Late Bronze period of the second millennium.

It is to the lasting credit of Van Seters that this entire cluster of assumptions is systematically brought to the fore, critically investigated, and exposed as untenable. This section of his book reads less as a conventional review of the research than as an important exercise in intellectual history. It reflects upon the nature of the models that have been taken for granted for nearly the past century regarding both the composition of the Covenant Code and its connection to cuneiform legal traditions. More than with any other scholar, rather than simply rehearsing existing ways of thinking about the process of formation of the Covenant Code, he reflects upon the models that have been used to conceptualize that formation: what has been taken for granted and what has not yet been considered. His analysis deserves a brief review here as well as further reinforcement. He demonstrates that there is simply no meaningful way to account for a chain of transmission from second-millennium Mesopotamia to first-millennium Syro-Palestine. Rather, that impact should be understood as taking place only in the first millennium, during the Iron Age. Critical to this argument is his very systematic exploration of the model of oral tradition or some generalized cultural diffusion of legal forms or topoi as a way of explaining the close connections between the casuistic laws of the Covenant Code and the Laws of Hammurabi. Astutely drawing on the work of Meir Malul (1990), Van Seters sets up a clear set of criteria to distinguish the model of general cultural diffusion, on the one hand, and that of direct textual dependence and reuse, on the other. He makes a compelling case that the degree of correspondence between the two texts in terminology, literary form, legal topos, and sequence of laws, is explained most logically in terms of literary dependence and reuse. The correspondences he points to, and some additional ones, are depicted in Table 2 on the next page.[28]

The close connection between Hammurabi's Laws and the Covenant Code, which becomes especially evident upon detailed comparison of the goring ox laws in both cases (Laws of Hammurabi §§ 250–52; Exod. 21.28–32), cannot be explained in terms of some nebulous concept of general cultural diffusion or oral transmission.[29] The correspondence is

---

28. This table is a composite. Van Seters provides a valuable table showing correspondences of legal topos and sequence (2003a: 96–99). Wright expands upon that analysis, claiming connections between the casuistic laws of the Covenant Code and its literary frame, on the one hand, and the Laws of Hammurabi with the prologue and epilogue, on the other (Wright 2003: 72). For the convenience of the reader, I have attempted to provide a modest presentation of the correspondences based on Wright's work, but restricting the focus to the casuistic section of the Covenant Code (some of the connections in the apodictic material proposed by Wright are more open to discussion). Laws in the Covenant Code that do not exactly follow the sequence of the Laws of Hammurabi, although still close to it, are indicated with an asterisk.

29. The explanation of the wide diffusion of the Epic of Gilgamesh in terms of oral diffusion by a hypothetical 'musician-poet' attached to trading caravans or hired by a ship's captain for the entertainment of the crew, stresses the inevitable emergence of 'different versions ... [with] a variety of details' (Dalley 1989: 49). That model of oral diffusion therefore cannot account for the degree of detailed correspondence at issue here.

	Exodus	Legal Topos	Laws of Hammurabi §§
1.	21.2–11	Indenture	117, 119 (cf. 118, 175)
2.	21.10–11	Second wife + support	148–149, 178
*3.	21.12–14	Intentional death by striking	(206) 207
4.	21.15, 17	Child rebellion	192–193, 195
5.	21.18–19	Men fighting, injury, cure	206
6.	21.20–21	Negligent homicide of member of lower class	208 (cf. 196–205, 209–223)
7.	21.22–23	Miscarriage	209–214
8.	21.23–27	Talion laws, injury to slave	196–205, 229–240
9.	21.28–32	Goring ox	250–252
*10.	21.33–34	Negligence	229–240 (cf. 125)
11.	21.37 + 22.2b–3 (ET 3b–4)	Animal theft	253–265
12.	22.6–8, ET 7–9	'Safekeeping' of animals	265–266 (cf. 120, 124–125)
13.	22.9–12, ET 10–13	Injury and death of animals	266–267
14.	22.13–14, ET 14–15	Rented animals	268–271 (cf. 244–249)

Table 2: Correspondences between the Covenant Code
and the Laws of Hammurabi

best explained in terms of literary and textual dependence.[30] Such dependence is hard to imagine without the administrative structure, bureaucracy, scribal training, and complexity of society associated with the composition and redaction of a legal collection. That the correspondence makes most sense as a phenomenon of the first millennium rather than the second creates a new set of intellectual and analytical possibilities. Van Seters is among the first to have seen this issue and to have worked it through so carefully.[31] It is very hard to imagine that the older form-critical or traditio-historical models will withstand his thorough critique. He demonstrates the untenability of the attempt to see the Covenant Code as a window into the pre-monarchic history of Israel. By identifying the nostalgic or romantic view of history associated with that attempt, he accomplishes for biblical law the same kind of lasting epistemological clarification that he provided in his book on the patriarchal narratives (Van Seters 1975).

   In part, the proposal for literary transmission in the first millennium was anticipated by Rothenbusch (2000), whose extensive analysis is overlooked by Van Seters. Yet Rothenbusch still clings to the form-critical model. He assumes oral transmission of legal content from Mesopotamia to Israel, from second millennium to first millennium, from

---

30. See Finkelstein (1981: 19–20); Malul (1990: 113–52); Van Seters (2003a: 119–22); and Wright (2003: 24–25, 79).

31. Wright, however, clearly seems to have priority in recognizing the full extent of the sequential correspondences (on the history of this research, see Wright 2003: 13). Wright made available a lengthy preliminary manuscript of his work at the Annual Meeting of the Society of Biblical Literature (Nashville, November 2000).

Late Bronze to Iron Age (despite the cultural breaks between the two), while nonetheless locating the actual compilation and redaction of these laws in the monarchic period, during the Neo-Assyrian hegemony at the time of Ahaz (2000: 600). He believes the transmission to have taken place via Phoenicia during the early monarchy (2000: 511–13). The difficulty is that he still assumes a general Syro-Canaanite legal tradition as antecedent to the composition of the Covenant Code while separate from and independent of the specifically literary impact of cuneiform law. This 'missing link' represents a postulate necessary to retain the form-critical model (pre-monarchic origins of the legal tradition from the second millennium; general cultural diffusion) while attempting to maintain the connection between a casuistic legal collection and a royal bureaucracy, the essential nature of which he recognizes (2000: 600). In the end, Rothenbusch's approach attempts to have it both ways: to maintain pre-monarchic origins (positing a Syro-Palestinian casuistic legal tradition, the existence of which lacks evidence) alongside monarchic composition and compilation.[32] The hypothesis, which is based upon two mutually inconsistent models, lacks explanatory power.[33]

Van Seters should therefore be credited as the first to propose a consistent model for the composition of the Covenant Code under the influence of the Laws of Hammurabi as taking place in the first millennium. Nonetheless, once he cogently clears the ground for this model, he moves very quickly to delimit the possibilities:

> The belief in a vague transmission of the legal tradition from Mesopotamia to the Levant in the second millennium BCE, and hence from the "Canaanites" to the Israelites means that this comparativist method has nothing further to say about the problem of similarity between biblical codes. The simplest, most economic solution to the whole comparativist controversy is to admit that the casuistic laws of the Covenant Code were directly influenced on the literary level during

---

32. See Wright (2003: 12; 2004). Wright generously shared with me advance copies of both manuscripts.

33. Other scholars, too, recognizing that the literary legal collection in ancient Mesopotamia is invariably associated with an organized state and thus fits poorly into the pre-state period of ancient Israel, sometimes seek to have it both ways. Thus Eckart Otto (1993) argues that the legal content of the Covenant Code does not depend upon cuneiform law but rather represents part of the common heritage of the rural countryside, adjudicated by the elders at the village gate. Only the subsequent integration and redaction of these laws into a text bears the imprint of cuneiform law, and there in terms of the redactional techniques involved alone, mediated by Jerusalem schools of the eighth century. This attempt to rescue Alt's hypothesis only points to the incompatibility between *Gattungsgeschichte* and the literary history of cuneiform law. Van Seters offers an incisive critique of this approach (2003a: 110–12).

the Babylonian exile. That possibility has simply never been debated. (2003a: 45)

Elsewhere, too, after demonstrating a series of close parallels between the ideology of the larger Sinai pericope (Exod. 19–24) and that of the Laws of Hammurabi, Van Seters maintains:

> If one accepts the view that some of the casuistic laws are literarily dependent upon the Hammurabi Code, ... then this literary borrowing took place in Babylonia during the exile... Veneration of Babylonia's ancient past was at its height at this time [the Neo-Babylonian period] and almost certainly included the great law code. (2003a: 57)

Van Seters reasons that, in order to have the best chance of access to a literary exemplar of the Laws of Hammurabi, the author of the Covenant Code must have been

> an exile in Babylonia during the latter days of the Neo-Babylonian Empire... Therefore, it is not remarkable that he had direct access to some Babylonian law codes and could read and imitate them for his own code. There is clear attestation in surviving copies of the Hammurabi Code and other ancient laws that the ancient Babylonian legal tradition was known in the Neo-Babylonian period, and it is even likely that one of several copies of the original stele was still extant in Babylon in this period. (2003a: 173–74)

The repeated conjecture that the literary transmission of the Laws of Hammurabi to a first-millennium Judaean author would only occur in Babylon during the Neo-Babylonian period is open to question.[34] Both the chronological delimitation (the Neo-Babylonian period) and the geographical specification (an author living in exile in Babylon) are of course each possible. However, a possible context is not automatically a necessary context. The critical question is whether alternatives are considered before a conclusion is reached. In this case, the author's assumption of the Covenant Code's exilic authorship seems to control and delimit the hypothesis concerning the reception and reuse of cuneiform

---

34. Similarly: 'The point at which there would then be the greatest likelihood of direct cultural contact between Mesopotamia and Judah would be the exilic period in Babylonia itself' (Van Seters 2003a: 31). The discussion does not consider the possibility of such contact during the Neo-Assyrian period. Van Seters here seems not to distinguish between various forms of 'cultural contact': whether at the 'literary level' or at the 'reality level'. In dating the Covenant Code, he thus overlooks the crucial distinction between various means of 'historical connection', which he himself thoughtfully wields against those who deny the literary influence of Hammurabi's Laws upon the Covenant Code (2003a: 30; building on the work of Malul 1990: 93). The critical issue here is less that of 'direct cultural contact' than access to the scribal curriculum, and of defining the context or contexts when Old Babylonian texts were being copied and studied.

law. The prior assumption preempts due consideration of alternative historical or geographical contexts.

A fair examination of the evidence shows that the Neo-Babylonian period is not the most obvious one in which to posit greatest access to a manuscript of the laws. Table 3 below provides a comprehensive and up-to-date analysis of the distribution of the manuscripts of the Laws of Hammurabi, organized by historical period and provenance.[35] It confirms that, after the period of its composition (Old Babylonian), the greatest evidence of interest in the Laws of Hammurabi is in the Neo-Assyrian period (Wright 2003: 52). The degree of interest in the Neo-Assyrian period is more than twice as great as that in the Neo-Babylonian period, based upon manuscript evidence (nineteen, versus eight).[36] Indeed, there are nearly as many copies of the Laws extant from the Neo-Assyrian period (nineteen) as from the time of its promulgation (twenty).

Period	Copies	Tablets	Other Stele Fragments
OB	20	A, O, S, Y, X, p, q, r, t, u, w, y	K, M, Q, R, U, d, g, h
MB	4	I, V, a; N 5489	
MA	4	E, F, G, H	
NA	19	D, J, L, N, P, T, b, c, e, f, i, j, k, l, m, n, o, x; and 1 ms in Lambert 1992	
NB	8	B, C, W, Z, s, v; and 2 mss in Fadhil 1998	

Table 3: Extant copies of the Laws of Hammurabi

The predominance of the manuscripts of the Laws of Hammurabi in the Neo-Assyrian period creates a possibility never considered by Van Seters:

35.   This table should now provide the most up-to-date list of attested manuscripts of the Laws of Hammurabi available (the Louvre stele is not included). It was prepared drawing upon the analysis provided by Wright (2003: 67–71), while revising his ambiguous 'Late Babylonian' to the more standard term for the dialect, Neo-Babylonian. However, Wright bases his analysis exclusively upon Borger 1979: 1.2–5. Thereby overlooked are five additional manuscripts (u, v, w, x, y) provided in the more recent collation (Roth 1997: 251–53). Those manuscripts are included here. A number of additional manuscripts have been published since Roth's collation and are also included in the above table. They include two Neo-Babylonian manuscripts of the Prologue, discovered a decade ago at Sippar (Fadhil 1998); an additional Neo-Assyrian manuscript (Lambert 1992); and a Middle Babylonian exercise tablet with a copy of the Laws of Hammurabi § 1 (Veldhuis 2000: 71–72). Veldhuis (2000: 72) permits the correction of manuscript I (MAH 10828) from Old Babylonian (per the original publication) to Middle Babylonian (for this reference, I am grateful to Martha T. Roth). For discussion of the Sippar prologue tablets, see Hurowitz (2004).

36.   Van Seters notes in passing the existence of Neo-Assyrian tablets but does not compare the degree of manuscript attestation in the Neo-Assyrian or Neo-Babylonian periods; nor is the Neo-Assyrian period considered as an option for the author of the Covenant Code to gain access to the Laws of Hammurabi (2003a: 57). In fairness, the statistical issue may reflect less 'interest' than simple happenstance: in contrast to the situation for the Neo-Assyrian period, where we have discovered Ashurbanipal's library, no comparable Neo-Babylonian library has yet been recovered.

that the literary impact of the Laws of Hammurabi upon the Covenant Code may have taken place under Neo-Assyrian hegemony. Such a context would situate the composition and redaction of the Covenant Code in the pre-exilic period. Precisely this contextualization, with a very thorough assessment of the evidence, has been proposed by David Wright (2003: 47–67) in an extensive study of the composition of the Covenant Code, which makes a concerted argument for its literary dependence upon the Laws of Hammurabi.[37] Despite the contention of Van Seters, it is not clear that 'veneration of Babylonia's ancient past was at its height' during the Neo-Babylonian period (2003a: 57). Such a claim overlooks the extent to which Old Babylonian texts, often revised, collated, elaborated, and organized into standard editions by Middle Babylonian scholars in the last centuries of the second millennium, functioned as an important part of the scribal curriculum during the Neo-Assyrian period.[38] 'King Ashurbanipal's library, which was far bigger than any other, was the result of a deliberate programme of acquisition and copying. The purpose of this labour was to provide Ashurbanipal with the best possible expertise to govern in the manner that would please the gods' (George 1999: xxiv).

This Neo-Assyrian interest in the literary classics of second-millennium Babylon is also evident in the distribution of manuscripts of Gilgamesh. 'The standard version of the Babylonian epic is known from a total of 73 manuscripts extant: the 35 that have survived from the libraries of King Ashurbanipal at Nineveh, 8 more tablets and fragments from three other Assyrian cities (Ashur, Kalah, and Huzirina), and 30 from Babylonia, especially the cities of Babylon and Uruk' (George 1999: xxvii). Thus, in the context of the first millennium, Gilgamesh is better attested in Neo-

---

37. Wright (2003: 54) provides the most convincing argument for the composition of the Covenant Code in the last third of the eighth century in the context of Neo-Assyrian hegemony, with the author using the text of the Laws of Hammurabi as a literary model, while also reworking it to transform the royal speaker of the laws into Yahweh, as an anti-imperial strategy. While I find the arguments both for dependence and for historical context compelling, less certain are his arguments in favour of the coherence of the Covenant Code as a unified composition (thus, including both the casuistic and the apodictic material), with the literary imprint of Hammurabi evident throughout. His argument that the reuse of cuneiform literary tradition (in this case, primarily the Laws of Hammurabi) functions as a strategy of cultural subversion against the Neo-Assyrian suzerain thus posits for the Covenant Code the same kind of reception and reuse that has been posited for Deuteronomy, in its reuse of Neo-Assyrian loyalty oaths. For discussion and bibliography, see Otto (1996) and Levinson (1997: 134, 147; 2001: 237). Taken together, this raises the question of whether two legal texts that are diverse in cultic and social agenda (the Covenant Code and Deuteronomy) could each draw upon cuneiform traditions (the legal collection and the loyalty oath) during the Neo-Assyrian period with a single goal: to wield the expropriated literary model against the hegemony of Neo-Assyrian culture.

38. For a valuable study of the role of Kassite scholars in the transmission of Old Babylonian material to the first millennium, see Veldhuis (2000).

Assyria (43 manuscripts) than in Neo-Babylonia (30 manuscripts). Tablet XI was first discovered and published based in a fragment from Ashurbanipal's library. In the case of both Hammurabi and Gilgamesh, therefore, the period never considered by Van Seters provides the most evidence of official interest in commissioning scribes to recopy, preserve, and transmit the literary classics of the second millennium.

On other grounds, it is quite plausible that the imprint of the Laws of Hammurabi upon the Covenant Code points to the Neo-Assyrian rather than the Neo-Babylonian period. Of the cuneiform material found in first-millennium Canaan, by far the greatest proportion derives from the Neo-Assyrian period: sixteen inscriptions, versus one Neo-Babylonian or Late Babylonian, and four from the Persian period.[39] The composition of the Covenant Code does not require the Babylonian exile for cultural contact with Babylonian tradition to have been feasible. A Hebrew scribe need not necessarily have been 'an exile' (*pace* Van Seters 2003a: 173) to have had access, directly or indirectly, to cuneiform. Sargon II made it an important part of his foreign policy to indoctrinate foreigners with Assyrian culture, and established state officials in vassal states:

> Populations of the four world quarters with strange tongues and incompatible speech, dwellers of mountain and country, ...whom I had taken as booty at the command of Ashur my lord by the might of my sceptre, I caused to accept a single voice, and I caused native Assyrians who are all expert in all kinds of knowledge to dwell among them, and I sent overseers and officers with instructions to teach them to assimilate (?) [*sic*] and to respect god and king. (Dalley 1998: 27)

This desire for acculturation was reciprocal. 'Israelite charioteers from Samaria worked willingly for Sargon II, and many young men in search of fame and fortune came from Nubia, Palestine, Ionia, Urartu, and Elam as specialist mercenaries and returned home having gained prestige' (Dalley 1985; 1998: 26). A scribal school was established by the Neo-Assyrian empire in Syro-Palestine, at Huzirina, not far from Harran; Harran itself was the most important city of the Assyrian north-west, and was the city where the royal court was transferred after Nineveh and Kalhu were threatened by the Medes, Cimmerians, and Babylonians (Dalley 1998: 26–27). The penetration of the Neo-Assyrian vassal treaty into the Syro-Palestine realm is evident of course in the Aramaic treaties at Sefire. The

---

39. Of the approximately 89 cuneiform inscriptions found in Canaan, 40 date from the second millennium; many of these are lexical texts. Of the first-millennium material, 16 are from the Neo-Assyrian period. They include 4 steles, 3 administrative documents, 1 bulla, 1 judicial document, 3 cylinder seals (1 votive), 1 fragment, 2 land sale contracts, and 1 Lamaštu plaque. This analysis is based on Horowitz, Oshima and Sanders 2002. The reference here to 16 Neo-Assyrian finds is based on the actual count; contrast the authors' 'roughly fifteen' (2002: 754).

ability of Syro-Palestinian scribes to work in cuneiform is especially evident, of course, in the eighth-century bilingual inscription from Tell Fekherye in north-east Syria, with Neo-Assyrian on the front and Aramaic on the back (Abou-Assaf, Bordreuil and Millard 1982; Spycket 1985; and Sader 1987: 23–29). Such evidence makes plausible the existence of trained scribes in Syro-Palestine who could work with cuneiform documents during the Neo-Assyrian period.

Van Seters's argument that the first millennium rather than the second provides the most logical setting for the reception of cuneiform law into ancient Israel is compelling, as is his proposal for the literary influence of the Laws of Hammurabi upon the Covenant Code. However, the options within the first millennium are prematurely restricted to the Neo-Babylonian period and the Babylonian Diaspora as the only context for understanding that influence to operate. Moreover, the Covenant Code's non-mention of the monarch does not provide evidence for its composition as a work of the Babylonian exile, following the destruction of the Judaean state, as implied by Van Seters (2003a: 174). To the contrary, the non-mention of a monarch may simply reflect the literary model after which the casuistic laws of the Covenant Code are patterned, as well as the desire to present Yahweh as the divine monarch who proclaims law.[40] By not considering alternatives either of chronology or geography, Van Seters calls into question the objectivity of his analysis, as if the exilic period were not only a possible, but a necessary, historical context. The Neo-Assyrian period seems more likely, based upon the considerations above. Gathering an impressive amount of data, David Wright similarly makes a strong case for the Neo-Assyrian period, in either Judah (during the reigns of Ahaz [c. 742–727], Hezekiah [c. 727–698], or Manasseh [c. 697–642] or Israel (prior to its fall, or possibly just afterward) (Wright 2003: 52–54; cf. 58–67). Given the available evidence, it does not seem

---

40. Although Hammurabi is very powerfully introduced both in the literary frame of the law collection and in the dramatic presentation scene that dominates the stele, he is essentially invisible in the legal corpus itself. Within the 282 laws of Hammurabi, for example, the king (*šarrum*) is mentioned only once and there only incidentally: as a court of last appeal in the context of adultery. This single mention occurs in a law that lacks analogue in the Covenant Code, where the only consideration of sex and family law is the single law addressing rape of a virgin (Exod. 22.15–16, ET 16–17). In the context of Hammurabi, the legal collection represents, literally, his royal voice. It embodies his vision of justice and his divinely-sanctioned rule – even in the context of legal paragraphs where he passes almost entirely without mention. The monarch is similarly present in the Covenant Code as the voice of its promulgator. Distinctively in the case of Israel, the royal speaker of the law collection is its divine king, Yahweh, rather than a mortal king (Levinson 1997: 138; 2003: 12–14; and Wright 2003: 40–41, 51). The claim by Van Seters, 'For J, Moses is the Jewish Hammurabi' (2003a: 57) misconstrues this issue.

possible to assign a more specific date to the composition of the Covenant Code under the literary influence of cuneiform law.[41]

3. *The Question of Literary Context: An Immanent Reading of the Altar Law?*

In seeking to overturn Wellhausen and to provide a new model of the history of Israelite religion, Van Seters, like the author of the *Prolegomena*, begins with the history of sacrifice. His reason for doing so is clear: 'The law of the altar has been regarded by many scholars as the most important piece of evidence for establishing the Covenant Code as prior to that of Deuteronomy and its law of centralization in Deut 12' (2003a: 60).[42] Wellhausen argued that Deuteronomy's requirement for centralization and purification of the cult was a reaction against the *status quo* of Israelite religion, in which it was legitimate to worship God at multiple altar sites or sanctuaries throughout the land. The altar law of the Covenant Code is understood to represent that rejected norm of a non-centralized cultus. With this analysis, Wellhausen accounts for the divergence in rhetoric between the Covenant Code's prescription, in which 'a multiplicity of altars is not merely regarded as permissible, but assumed as a matter of course', and that of Deuteronomy 12, which 'is never weary of again and again' emphasizing that the requirement for centralization

---

41.   It does not seem possible to establish a clear fixed date for the Covenant Code or to connect it to something in the historiographic corpus that would provide an 'Archimedean point', as in the use of Josiah's reform (2 Kgs 22–23) for the dating of Deuteronomy. Accepting Deuteronomy's revision of key laws of the Covenant Code as a *terminus ante quem* still leaves open the question of an appropriate *terminus post quem*. Although it is tempting to propose that Amos (in 2.8a) might already be familiar with the Covenant Code's requirement for ethical conduct in pledges (Exod. 22.24–26, ET 25–27), that goes beyond the evidence. First, it overlooks the possibility that the prophet may be drawing on ethical guidelines found in wisdom literature (as in Job 22.6; 24.3–4, 9). Second, Amos's indictment does not seem a direct violation of the terms of the Covenant Code's law but, while moving in the semantic field of 'pledges', addresses a different wrongdoing. Finally, Amos does not directly invoke the language of the Covenant Code or allude to it to strengthen his social critique. Dion (1975) provides the most judicious assessment of whether (per his title): 'Le Message moral du prophète Amos s'inspirat-il du "droit de l'alliance"?' While Dion finds a number of affinities between the ethical demands of Amos and those of the Covenant Code, he finds no evidence of direct citation or dependence. Perhaps more important, he shows that the prophet evinces no concern to anchor his critique in a tradition of written law. (I am grateful to Professor Kevin Cathcart for drawing my attention to Dion's article.) On that basis, it would be impossible to use Amos as a means of dating the Covenant Code.

42.   Earlier Van Seters identifies the altar law and the festival calendar as the first of the 'four "pillars" ... used in earlier scholarship to support the literary precedence of the Covenant Code in relationship to the other law codes of the Pentateuch' (2003a: 8). He notes there how crucial these laws were to the formation of the New Documentary Hypothesis by Wellhausen.

marks a break with the legal and religious norms of the present and warns redundantly against that rejected present (Wellhausen 1883: 30, 34, ET 1885: 29, 33). To disprove the Wellhausian model, Van Seters must demonstrate that the altar law of the Covenant Code does not refer to multiple altar sites and that it presupposes cultic centralization.

But there is another issue as well. In Wellhausen's analysis of pre-Deuteronomic narrative and law, the local altar is not simply a place where sacrifice is performed but also a site of divine revelation. The connection between theophany and altar was already recognized by Wellhausen, for whom the altar memorializes a specific site of theophany: '[T]he altars, as a rule, are not built by the patriarchs according to their own private judgment wheresoever they please; on the contrary, theophany calls attention to, or at least afterwards confirms, the holiness of the place' (Wellhausen 1883: 32, ET 1885: 31). For Van Seters to overturn the standard model means that he must find a way also to deny theophany to the altar law of the Covenant Code. In order to demonstrate the falsity of 'the assumption of the Covenant Code's antiquity and priority to Deuteronomy' (2003a: 47), he must show how the altar law may be read as a post-Deuteronomic composition. He asserts that the conventional 'assumption of the Covenant Code's antiquity' obscures the evidence. His own analysis therefore seeks to recover the original meaning of this text, essentially for the first time in the history of modern biblical scholarship, as a reflection of the exile.

In order to give his arguments their full due, let us follow them closely, step-by-step, with particular attention to matters of reading, translation, and exposition. A perhaps unusual degree of detailed attention is warranted in this case, since the distinction between the eisegesis that Van Seters attributes to the consensus and the exegesis that he claims to provide is itself an important part of the argument. Van Seters offers the following translation of the most critical verse of the altar law (Exod. 20.24):

24a An altar of earth you are to make for me and sacrifice burnt offerings and thank offerings *from* your sheep or your cattle.
24b In every place where *you invoke* my name, I will come to you and bless you.[43]

Now here is the Hebrew for the same verse, accompanied by my own translation:

מזבח אדמה תעשה לי וזבחת עליו את עלתיך ואת שלמיך את צאנך ואת בקרך
בכל המקום אשר אזכיר את שמי אבוא אליך וברכתיך

24a An earthen altar shall you make for me and *upon it* you shall sacrifice

---

43. Van Seters 2003a: 61. For ease of reference, I have added the verse numbers, arranged the translation by line and colon, and added emphasis.

your burnt offerings and your well-being offerings, your sheep and
your cattle;
24b In every place that *I proclaim* my name, I will come to you and bless
you.

With regard to the Hebrew, which does not accompany the author's
translation, let us begin by reviewing Van Seters's rendering of Exod.
20.24a. One need not pay too much attention to the simple omission of the
prepositional phrase with the anaphoric pronoun, עליו, 'upon it'. More
interesting is the use of the partitive construction, *'from* your sheep or
your cattle', as if the phrase were introduced by מן, 'from'. The Hebrew,
in contrast, employs a double accusative construction, with the direct
object marker, את. The shift in construction does not seem to arise
naturally, since the first pair of direct objects is accurately rendered using
the accusative construction.[44] This realignment of syntax may find its
explanation in the history of interpretation. The centralization command
of Deuteronomy 12, in its requirements for sacrifice at the centralized
altar, at key points echoes the language of the altar law of Exodus.[45]
Strikingly, that law uses the same verb as well as the same two objects of
the verb, but employs a partitive rather than accusative construction:
וזבחת מבקרך ומצאנך, 'And you shall slaughter *from* your cattle and
from your sheep' (Deut. 12.21aβ). There is evidence that, already in
antiquity, the legal norm of Deuteronomy's centralization law affected the
translation and understanding of the Exodus altar law even at the level of
syntax. The Samaritan Pentateuch and Targum Pseudo-Jonathan both
embed Deuteronomy's partitive construction into their rendering of the
list of sacrificial animals in Exod. 20.24.[46] The translation provided by
Van Seters, employing 'from', is identical. In seeking to position the altar
law in a post-Deuteronomic context, is it possible that Van Seters
inadvertently proceeded as have these harmonistic ancient versions?
The commentary on Exod. 20.24a is significant. The indefinite
accusative (מזבח אדמה) placed in emphatic position before the verb is
understood to signify a singular number:

It is entirely possible, if not preferable, to interpret this whole law as
having reference to a single altar: "*An altar of earth* you may make . . .
but if you make an altar of stones. . . ." It is no more than guesswork to

---

44. The Hebrew of the original is not redundant. The second pair of accusatives glosses
the first; the phrase could therefore be rendered, 'namely, your sheep and your cattle'.

45. The extent of the linguistic overlap is denied by Van Seters (2003: 66), who references
my own work (Levinson 1997: 23–52) but overlooks a larger stream of discussion (Lohfink
1984; Smith 1987: 140).

46. For further discussion, see Levinson (1997: 36–38, 43). For the Targum text, see
Clarke (1984: 92).

suggest that the law applies to a number of altars. (Van Seters 2003a: 61;
emphasis added)

No footnote is provided in support of the assumption that the indefinite
singular has a restrictive function and means the numerical singular.
Given that the construct establishes a class, 'an earthen altar', one might
expect greater allowance for the syntax to have a distributive force. The
protasis of the manumission law, 'If you purchase a Hebrew slave' (Exod.
21.2), employs a similar construction, with an indefinite singular direct
object of the verb. That construction seeks to bring the entire class of
indentured servants under the guidelines of the law. The assumption is
that the law would apply to multiple such transactions, with multiple
indentured servants falling under consideration. The proposal that the
altar law of Exod. 20.22–26 intends but a single altar therefore seems
motivated less by the plain sense of the text than the desire to read it in a
post-centralization (and post-Deuteronomic) context.

If the proposal for the number reference intended by the law seems open
to question, so does the hypothesis for the most likely geographical and
chronological context in which the law might be found. Van Seters
suggests that it may not refer to an altar in the land of Canaan, as many
assume but rather to 'a temporary, rudimentary altar in the Babylonian
diaspora, corresponding to Ezekiel's "temporary sanctuary" (מקדש
מעט) in Ezek 11:16' (Van Seters 2003a: 61). There is a difficulty here.
The citation in question does not refer to a physical sanctuary at all,
provisional or otherwise. Rather, God here offers *himself* as a 'refuge' or
sanctuary to those Judaeans who were deported in 597 BCE and who are
taunted by the Jerusalem community. The poignant metaphor has been
taken completely out of context. This method of trying to recover the
alleged original meaning of the altar law, as an exilic composition that
presupposes centralization, comes dangerously close to eisegesis.

Turning to the next colon, Van Seters continues to establish the 'exilic
context' of the altar law (2003a: 61). His full discussion is significant:

> The most important argument for the antiquity of the Covenant Code
> and its priority rests upon the interpretation of verse 24b. The text of
> this verse is difficult to accept as it stands. The problem is in the first
> person of the verb אזכיר.[47] Since the most common meaning of the
> verb הזכיר is "to invoke," with the deity as object, it makes no sense
> for the deity to say, "I will invoke my name," and scholars have been
> ingenious in trying to invent other, more suitable meanings. It is most
> usual for humans to invoke a god or the name of a god in the context of
> worship or prayer.... Exod 20:24b would be the only instance where
> the god invokes his own name. Now within the Covenant Code we do

---

47. This corrects a typo in the Hebrew of the original of Van Seters.

have an instance of the usual idiom in 23:13 ("you are not to invoke
[תזכיר] the name of other gods"), which strongly suggests that the verb
in 20:24b should be *second*-person singular. Thus, I would reconstruct
the text: "In every place where you invoke my name, I will come to you
and bless you." (Van Seters 2003a: 62; emphasis in original)

The correction of the Hebrew text, from first to second person, was read
back into the author's original translation of the altar law on the previous
page (61), with the verb already changed to second person, but there
without a note to indicate the emendation (and without the Hebrew for
comparison). In a note that accompanies the excerpt provided above (185
n. 48), the author notes the congruence of his position with the variant
provided by the Syriac version and dismisses objections to the originality
of that reading as lacking support. That argument does not itself
investigate the text-critical issue: there is no discussion of any of the
versions nor of the Syriac itself, which is referred to in isolation from all
other versions, and with no discussion of the nature of the Peshiṭta as a
version.

The author's analysis raises a series of methodological difficulties. First,
the conceptual possibility of the deity proclaiming his own name is
dismissed out of hand with the assertion that 'it makes no sense'.[48]
Second, only one context is considered feasible for the divine name (שם)
to occur as the grammatical object of a verb of speech: 'in the context of
worship or prayer'. This analysis restricts the conceptual possibilities for
understanding the proclamation of the divine name to a single context:
that of human, not divine, speech.[49] Third, the defence of the emendation
of the verb to second person with reference to another law in the
Covenant Code, where 'the usual idiom' occurs (Exod. 23.13), is not
accompanied by any discussion. Whether the two texts correspond is
doubtful. Nonetheless, that view is widely held, especially by the very

---

48.   A century earlier, in nearly verbatim terms, Arnold B. Ehrlich (1899: 175) argued for
the same textual emendation and rejected the first person verb: לא יתכן שיאמר ה׳ אזכיר
שמי ('*It is incomprehensible* that the Lord could say, "I shall invoke my name"' (my
translation). Had this fascinating if eccentric commentary been taken into account by Van
Seters, it might have provided additional support. Ehrlich sees the 'corrected' version of the
altar law as most logical in a Diaspora context, one that he implicitly regards as post-Temple
in its religious sensibility and chronology.

49.   The same two assumptions govern Tigay's recent study, which makes the generalization: 'in the context of sacrifice and altars, it is always the worshipper, not God, who
invokes ... or calls upon ... God's name' (2004: 203; the author generously provided me with
an advance copy of his manuscript). Inevitably as a result, Tigay reaches the same conclusion
that Van Seters does and emends the MT to second person. Tigay reached his conclusions
independently (overlooking Toeg 1977: 88 n. 81; Van Seters 1996a, 2003a: 62; and Heger
1999: 29–30). Heger also advocates the emendation of the text and assumes prayer to be the
focus of the altar law. In doing so, he builds upon Van Seters 1996a, although taking the
arguments out of context and using them to defend the great antiquity of the altar law.

scholars whose redaction-historical conclusions, drawn from the alleged correspondence, Van Seters sharply opposes.[50] The claim for the equivalence of meaning based merely on the basis of the common verbal stem does not examine the semantic context and cannot be defended.[51] And fourth, a global generalization dismisses scholars holding an alternative position.

The conclusions are reached without a systematic analysis of the text-critical, lexicographical, or textual evidence. There is no study of the versional evidence.[52] The generalization about the scholars who attempt to make sense of the first-person reading as 'ingenious' in their inventions of meaning turns out to be quite limited in those taken into account: essentially only Edward Robertson's article (1948/49) and one by Eckart Otto (1994). Overlooked thereby are Johann Jakob Stamm's important study of the hiphil of root *zkr* (1945); relevant lexicography (Eising 1977, ET 1980; Schottroff 1967: 245–51); the seminal work of S. Dean McBride

---

50. More often, the observation leads to a redaction-historical conclusion that sees the two units (thus, Exod. 20.22–23, 24b; and 23.13) as belonging to the same post-exilic layer of the Covenant Code; so Otto (1988: 5–6); Schwienhorst-Schönberger (1990: 394–400); and, most recently, Schmitt (2003: 279–80).

51. The analogy proposed to the second-person prohibition against 'invoking' the name of other deities (Exod. 23.13) is cited in support of the hypothesis. That justification assumes that the latter law refers to prayer. That assumption needs to be defended and is not self-evident. The verse is less an independent law than a homiletical transition marker; it seems extraneous in its context. Note that in the Decalogue, the prohibition against use of the divine name in the context of oaths (Exod. 20.6) immediately precedes the Sabbath law (Exod. 20.7–10). Similarly, the command here not to invoke the names of foreign deities (Exod. 23.13) immediately follows the Sabbath law of the Covenant Code (Exod. 23.12). The association of the two laws in each case implies that the context for invoking the deity is judicial: an oath by the deity (*nīš ilim*), not a simple petitionary prayer. Note the similar construction, using *b-* (by) rather than an accusative: ובשם אלהיהם לא תזכירו ולא תשביעו ולא תעבדום ולא תשתחוו להם, '*Neither utter nor swear by the names of their gods*; do not serve them or bow down to them' (Josh. 23.7). There, the second-person hiphil of *zkr* occurs parallel to the verb for oath-taking; the two verbs are governed by the same complement (*šēm* + deity). The construction here clearly has the divine name invoked in the context of oaths or vows, rather than in prayer. Moreover, the next word pair contemplates only sacrificial worship, not prayer independent of an altar, as the context for gaining access to the deity.

52. Tigay (2004: 203–204) ostensibly goes further in defending the second person, noting its reflection not only in the Syriac, but also in several targumim and in mediaeval rabbinic exegesis. That approach does not constitute a meaningful text-critical analysis. It takes into account only secondary witnesses to the Hebrew text (nothing earlier than the Syriac). There is no discussion of the primary witnesses (LXX, Samaritan Pentateuch). The recourse to the Syriac and the targumic witnesses curiously fails to consider the extent to which both the Syriac and the targumim share a common exegetical tradition (see below). The relevant literature on these witnesses is not considered (Weitzman 1999; Maori 1995a; 1995b; 1998). As a result, the altar law is assimilated to an exegetical tradition that is presented as its original meaning.

(1969); de Boer's book (1962); and the important exposition of this text by Tryggve Mettinger (1982: 123–25). An entire stream of scholarly discussion on the altar law, its semantics, and its connections to the larger phenomenology of theophany in ancient Israel, does not come into play and is not cited in the book's bibliography.[53]

The author's preference for 'the more common' construction, with the divine name as object rather than as subject of speech, and with the speech thereby defined as human prayer, would, in most text-critical circles, immediately raise a red flag: it points to the phenomenon of levelling. When a distinctive use is assimilated to the more familiar one, the rule of *lectio difficilior praeferenda* normally applies. In this case, the opposite seems to be the case. The textual correction assumes that the distinctive reading is unintelligible and levels it to a more familiar idiom. Conversely, the process of textual corruption is left unexplained. What triggered the replacement of the 'common' and 'usual' meaning with such an anomalous first-person form, so that, allegedly, 'Exod 20:24b would be the only instance where the god invokes his own name'?[54]

This approach permits Van Seters to argue that the focus of v. 24b is prayer, not sacrifice. The deity's name is invoked in prayer by a human petitioner. It follows that the reference at the beginning of the colon to 'In every place' refers to the multiple locations from which Judaeans, exiled in the Diaspora, may pray toward the deity for succour:

> Since this activity of invoking the name of the deity is not necessarily bound to the existence of an altar, the suggested plurality of places in verse 24b cannot be used to argue for a plurality of altars. It is better to

53. Van Seters (2003a: 62–63) rules out the relevance of one of the texts discussed by Stamm (1945): the theophany tradition preserved in Gen. 28.10–22. This amounts to a circular argument: without engaging the relevant lexicographic literature, the claim is made that it is illogical for the deity to 'proclaim' his own name in a theophany because *zkr* in the *Hiphil* cannot have that meaning; therefore the altar law cannot refer to theophany and there is no analogy with the other contexts where the deity reveals himself in the context of an altar! Stamm's proposal to translate *zkr* in the hiphil in this context as *kundmachen* is compelling.

54. As noted in the incisive challenge to the earlier formulation (Van Seters: 1996a) by Ska (2000: 268–69). One such explanation had been proposed by Toeg, who also emends the verb to the second person. He thought that the first-person form might reflect an early 'nomistic' attempt to overcome the inconsistency between the altar law and the 'dominant law (characterized by cultic centralization)' (1977: 88 n. 89; my translation). The first person would then represent an accommodation to the Deuteronomic election formula, with its notion of Yahweh selecting the central sanctuary. Tigay independently offers a similar proposal (2004: 204 n. 29; 211 n. 52). This solution is not convincing. Given the strong connection between the words מקום, 'place', and 'altar' in the context of this law, even the hypothetical formulation, 'In/at any *place* that you proclaim my name', would still carry a cultic meaning (see further, below). The phrase would thereby denote plurality of altars and still conflict with the legal norm of centralization.

interpret verse 24b as an act of worship apart from the sacrificial cult. The deity declares that his blessing is not restricted to the reception of sacrifices at the one altar. (Van Seters 2003a: 62)

With this reading, the first half of the altar law (v. 24a) and the second half (v. 24b) are shorn apart. The focus of the first colon is sacrifice upon the [single] altar; that of the second colon, the accessibility of God in prayer, from multiple locations, completely independent of the sacrificial cultus. Without so much as an adversative *waw* or other conjunction to mark the contrast, the law's initial premise is undermined and rejected by its own continuation. Under normal circumstances, were two so incompatible positions to be found within the same verse, one might believe it to have suffered an editorial intervention. Here, the disjuncture is essential to the argument, for only so does it allow the law to be read, in effect, as a text that breathes the air of Second-Temple Judaism. Once this is accomplished, the altar functions similarly to the one memorialized in the late exilic insertion into Solomon's Temple Prayer (1 Kgs 8.46–53):

> It does not restrict worship to that place but allows for the possibility of invoking the deity and receiving a divine blessing everywhere, especially in the diaspora.... [It] ... envisages those in exile praying to the deity and receiving his mercy without the benefit of altar or sacrifice.... The law in Exod 20:24–26, especially verse 24b, may be seen as going beyond this specific act of repentance in a foreign land [envisioned in 1 Kgs 8.46–53] to invoking the deity in worship in a more general way and receiving his blessing. (Van Seters 2003a: 67; my insertion)

In this *tour de force* reading, the Exodus altar law gives birth to Second-Temple Judaism: it establishes prayer rather than sacrifice as the basis of the community's relation to God! Retroverted as Van Seters proposes, Exod. 20.24b offers a manifesto for the universal availability of God in prayer throughout the Diaspora. In fact, the colon launches a remarkable anti-altar polemic that is inconsistent in language and ideology with the unit in which it is found (Exod. 20.22–26), where the focus remains consistently upon the importance of the sacrificial worship that takes place at the altar. Table 4 (on the next page) illustrates Van Seters's reading of the altar law (and incorporates his emendation of the verb).

The argument that בכל המקום, 'in every place', refers to the dispersal of the Judaean population during the Babylonian exile, and the concomitant claim that the deity's name is invoked in prayer, create a sharp disjunction between v. 24b (with its focus upon prayer) and v. 24a (which requires construction of an altar for sacrificial worship). Were such a blatant inconsistency found in any other context, most biblical scholars would immediately identify this as an editorial interpolation. In fact, an entire stream of scholarship has long done just that: viewing v. 24b as Deuteronomistic and therefore eliminating it as 'ein literarischer Zusatz'

Verse	Key Text per Van Seters	Law's Focus and Content
20.24a	מזבח אדמה תעשה לי וזבחת עליו An earthen *altar* shall you make for me and upon it you shall sacrifice	*Altar-specific:* sacrifice
20.24b	בכל המקום אשר תזכיר את שמי In every place that you proclaim my name	Prayer, not sacrifice, as condition for divine relation
20.25	ואם מזבח אבנים תעשה לי If you make for me an *altar* of stones	*Altar-specific:* construction
20.26	ולא תעלה במעלת על מזבחי You shall not go up by steps to my *altar*	*Altar-specific:* respectful demeanour

Table 4: Van Seters's reading of the altar law (Exod. 20.24)

(Levin 2000: 124).[55] However, Van Seters permits no editors to play a role in the composition of the Covenant Code. Ironically, however, he succeeds in accomplishing the same results by less direct means. Verse 24b has in effect been completely severed from the literary unit and the cultural world of the altar law. It no longer deals with sacrifice. While denying editorial activity in the composition of the text, it becomes clear that such activity takes place now at another level, as suggested by the 'text-critical' emendation of the verb to second person, the claims about the meaning of the indefinite singular, the exposition of the kind of altar intended, etc. The adjustments of the altar law's number, grammar, syntax, and wording amount to *de facto* editorial reworking of the text, which accommodate it to a set of assumptions about what it must mean and say. It seems impossible to position the Exodus altar law as a post-Deuteronomic composition of the exile without eisegesis.

At a number of points, potential controls are not brought to bear even where they would seem relevant and called for. Even apart from the question of the textual emendation, other aspects of the wording of Exod. 20.24b provide information that could be helpful. Van Seters construes

55. Diethelm Conrad's study (1968) remains influential in rejecting Exod. 20.24b as secondary. It provides a point of departure for both Levin (2000: 124 n. 18) and Schmitt (2003: 269); indeed, the latter's article is published in a *Festschrift* for Conrad. The methodological assumptions of Conrad's approach are problematic. He simply assumes in his preface that second-person singular apodictic laws are directed against foreign cults. That presupposition, although nowhere justified on the basis of evidence, nonetheless drives his subsequent literary criticism. Those sections of Exod. 20.24–26 that fail to conform are dismissed as secondary accretions to the reconstructed original law that, formulated in the second person, constituted a polemic against foreign cults. The logic is water-tight – and circular. Conrad overlooks the evidence that the close literary connection assumed in Exod. 20.24 among (1) altar-building, (2) theophany, and (3) divine beneficence has parallels elsewhere in the Bible (see Gen. 12.7–8 and 1 Kgs 3.4–5). Indeed, the connection between a theophany and the divine's proclaiming his name in a cultic context was a convention within Israel and the ancient Near East (Mettinger 1982: 125–27). The question of theophany receives further attention later in this section.

the reference to בכל המקום, 'in every place', as a neutral term that designates the multiple locations from which the dispersed Judaean population, during the exile, might pray to God for support. While the noun can indeed have that kind of neutral meaning (as in Gen. 20.13; Deut. 11.24; Josh. 1.3), it is surprising that the well-known additional meaning attached to מקום, as specifically a cultic site, seems here to escape Van Seters's attention. In Hebrew, Phoenician, Aramaic, and Arabic, the word possesses the more technical meaning of a 'cult site' or, specifically, an 'altar'.[56] Since that use is also well attested biblically (note also Deut. 12.2), in both narrative and legal contexts, one might have expected it to be considered also in the context of a discussion of Exod. 20.24b. From this perspective, independent of the question of the textual emendation, independent criteria are at hand to help determine whether or not this section of the verse presupposes activity at an altar. This linguistic issue is not addressed by Van Seters.

This approach creates a serious vulnerability for Van Seters. If the verb of Exod. 20.24b remains first-person אזכיר, 'I proclaim', with the MT, then there can no longer be a question of the divine name being invoked in prayer by someone in the Diaspora. Instead, the divine name would be proclaimed by the deity himself. That, in turn, would require that the distributive plural formula, בכל המקום, 'in every place', would refer to the location of the deity, not to the Diaspora location of the one praying to God. In that case, the מקום, 'place', formula would legitimate multiple altar sites as possible locations for theophany; it would thereby not presuppose cultic centralization. The argument that the altar law of the Covenant Code is post-Deuteronomic hangs upon Van Seters's textual emendation. Without the second-person invocation of the divine name, there is neither prayer nor a diaspora-dating of the altar law.

The evidence, both text-critical and semantic, strongly favours the first-person verb of Exod. 20.24b MT. Once the evidence is adduced, it becomes clear that the deity proclaims his own name in a theophany that takes place in conjunction with sacrificial worship at an altar. The altar law itself emphasizes that a plurality of cult sites are presupposed as legitimate. Philology provides a series of controls that challenge the claims made by Van Seters and lend credence to the Wellhausian model that he rejects. To defend this position, I shall reverse Van Seters's procedure and turn first to the text-criticism and then to the intelligibility of the MT.

---

56. See *HALOT*, II: 627 (§ 6), 'sacred site'. S.R. Driver (1901: 139) adduces Gen. 12.6; 28.11; 1 Sam. 7.16; Jer. 7.12; and Arabic *maqām*, 'sacred place'. For valuable comparative evidence from Phoenician and Punic inscriptions, see Tomback (1978: 195–96). For inscriptional evidence, see Hoftijzer and Jongeling (1995: II, 680), *s.v. mqm*₁ (§ 1a). Note also Aramaic אתרא.

The primary textual witnesses uniformly attest the first-person verb as original:

MT
מזבח אדמה תעשה לי וזבחת עליו את עלתיך ואת שלמיך את צאנך ואת בקרך ^{24a}
בכל המקום אשר אזכיר את שמי אבוא אליך וברכתיך ^{24b}
^{24a} An earthen altar shall you make for me and upon it shall you sacrifice your burnt offerings and your well-being offerings, your sheep and your cattle;
^{24b} In every place that *I proclaim* my name I will come to you and bless you.[57]
LXX
²⁴ θυσιαστήριον ἐκ γῆς ποιήσετέ μοι, καὶ θύσετε ἐπ᾽αὐτοῦ τὰ ὁλοκαυτώματα καὶ τὰ σωτήρια ὑμῶν, τὰ πρόβατα καὶ τοὺς μόσχους ὑμῶν ἐν παντὶ τόπῳ, οὗ ἂν ἐπονομάσω τὸ ὄνομά μου ἐκεῖ, καὶ ἥξω πρὸς σὲ καὶ εὐλογήσω σε.
^{24a} ... and upon it you shall sacrifice your holocausts and your whole offerings, your sheep and your cattle, *in every place where I proclaim my name there,*
^{24b} and I will come to you and bless you.[58]
Samaritan Pentateuch
במקום אשר אזכרתי ⁵⁹
... in the place where *I proclaimed* [my name] ...
Targum Onqelos
בכל אתר דאשרי שכינתי לתמן אשלח ברכתי לך ואברכינך
In every place where <u>*I cause My Shekinah to dwell,*</u> there will I send My blessing to you and I shall bless you.[60]
Targum Pseudo-Jonathan
בכל אתרא דאשרי שכינתי ואנת פלח קדמי תמן אשלח ברכתי ואיבריכינך
In every place where <u>*I rest My Shekinah* and you worship before me,</u> there will I send upon you My blessing and I shall bless you.[61]

Table 5: The textual witnesses to Exodus 20.24b reflecting the verb in first person

The first person is consistently witnessed by the Septuagint, the Samaritan Pentateuch, Onqelos and Pseudo-Jonathan. The Septuagint warrants particular attention. While witnessing the originality of the first-person verb, this version parses the syntax of the underlying Hebrew text remarkably differently than does the MT. The latter regards בקרך, 'your cattle', as the end of the thought unit; it concludes the first half of the

57. All translations are mine, except as noted.

58. For the text, Wevers (1991: 246; my translation).

59. The Samaritan form is aphel perfect; the past tense refers back to the just preceding tenth commandment of the Decalogue, with the sectarian interpretation of the requirement to build a sanctuary on Mount Gerizim. Note that Samaritan Targum ms A reads the second-person imperfect. For a discussion, see Tal (1988: 189–216).

60. For the text, Sperber (1959: 122). My translation modifies both Drazin (1990: 206) and Grossfeld (1988: 57–58).

61. For the text, Clarke (1984: 92; my emphases and translation).

verse, or v. 24a (in the accentual system, this verse divider is marked with the disjunctive accent *'atnaḥ*). Consequently, the MT understands the key clause in question to begin a new thought unit, concerned with theophany and divine blessing: '*In every place that I proclaim my name* (בכל המקום אשר אזכיר את שמי), I will come to you and bless you' (v. 24b). For the LXX translator, however, the same prepositional phrase in the underlying Hebrew does not mark the beginning of a new thought unit (Le Boulluec and Sandevoir 1989: 213). Instead, the phrase is construed as a dependent relative clause. It continues from what precedes it, so as to define and restrict where the sacrificial activity of v. 24a may take place: not at any altar, completely randomly, but rather ἐν παντὶ τόπῳ, οὗ ἂν ἐπονομάσω τὸ ὄνομά μου ἐκεῖ, 'in every place where I proclaim my name there'. Only with that specification does the first part of the verse conclude. The new statement, whereby the deity affirms blessing, here becomes entirely independent of the requirement for altar construction and sacrifice. With the loss of the initial introduction to the final clause, it becomes necessary to add a coordinating conjunction so as to include the remaining phrase: καὶ ἥξω πρὸς σὲ καὶ εὐλογήσω σε, '*and* I will come to you and bless you'.

Several things come into play here. The most important is that the primary textual witnesses consistently reflect the first-person form of the verb. The fact that the Septuagint reflects the first person while nonetheless parsing the syntax of the verse so differently from *any other textual witness* increases its significance. The Septuagint reflects an understanding of the verse that is independent of the other textual witnesses (MT, Samaritan Pentateuch, Targum Onqelos, and Targum Pseudo-Jonathan), yet nonetheless testifies that its underlying Hebrew *Vorlage* contained the first person. In terms of text-critical methodology, it is hard to imagine a stronger corroboration of this reading as original. The Septuagint also points to several additional issues that should be kept in mind before proceeding to the other witnesses. The translator's parsing of the syntax of this verse seems less original than that of the MT: it reduces the formula for divine visitation and blessing to little more than an afterthought, loosely connected to the preceding. This rather forced rendering of the altar law is most logically understood as already beginning to respond to the strictures of Deuteronomy, which prohibit sacrifice at random locations: 'Take heed lest you offer your burnt offerings *in every place that you see* (בכל מקום אשר תראה)' (Deut. 12.13). On that basis, it seems that the Septuagint translator renders the Exodus altar law so as to preclude any such concerns. The translator in effect reads the requirement of Deuteronomy 12, that sacrifice should take place only 'in the place that Yahweh your God shall choose' (Deut. 12.13), back into the altar law of Exodus. Elsewhere, too, the Septuagint translator of Exodus adjusts his rendering in the light of

Deuteronomic norms.[62] The parsing of the syntax of the underlying Hebrew, in other words, is already coloured by harmonistic legal exegesis, even as the Septuagint translator remains true to the consonantal text of his underlying Hebrew *Vorlage*, with its first-person verb. Similar issues arise in Onqelos and Pseudo-Jonathan in terms of the choice of verbal stem, even as they retain the first-person verb.[63]

In contrast to the unanimity of the primary textual witnesses, the Aramaic exegetical tradition (the Peshiṭta and the Palestinian targumim) renders the verb in the second person (see Table 6 on the next page). In this view, the divine name is invoked in human prayer.

The additional changes that they introduce clarify what is at issue in their rendering.[64] The Hebrew text reflected by the MT emphasizes the immediacy of divine presence in a theophany by the altar, אבוא אליך, 'I shall come to you'. The manifestation of the deity in a theophany is here emphasized in association with the altar.[65] Yet the Aramaic targumim reject the physical theophany of the deity. They consistently reject the verb of motion – the verb that defines the deity's entry into space and time – and instead render it metaphorically, so as to preserve divine transcendence. Given their theological assumptions, the deity never makes himself immanent in a theophany. For the Fragment Targum and Neofiti, he does not 'come' but instead 'is revealed' by means of his name (*Memra*). Strikingly, for Onqelos and Pseudo-Jonathan, which reflect the first-person verb, the deity does not 'come' but instead 'sends' his blessing and will then (redundantly) 'bless you'.

---

62. Elsewhere too, even more explicitly, the Septuagint translator of Exodus levels 'the text not only within the immediate context but also within the context of the book and even of the Pentateuch as a whole' (Wevers 1992: 148). Wevers shows how the rendering of the 'list of nations occupying the land of promise' always includes the Girgashites, who are never part of the MT Exodus. 'This does not mean the parent text was longer; it simply reflects the translator's leveling with Deut 7₁' (ibid.). The translator also levels inconsistencies of verbal number, as discussed below.

63. The rendering of Onqelos (דאשרי שכינתי) and of Pseudo-Jonathan (דאשרי שכינתי) assumes a Hebrew *Vorlage* (שם) אשר אשים את שמי, rather than אשר אזכיר את שמי (MT Exod. 20.24). The rendering in both cases accommodates the Exodus lemma to the Deuteronomic election formula: לשום את שמי שם (Deut. 12.5), rendered by both Onqelos and Jonathan as לאשראה שכינתיה תמן. This exposition follows the valuable work of Prijs (1948: 96). Despite the accommodation of the translator to the model provided by Deuteronomy, the retention of the first person cannot be explained by the Deuteronomic model, which in both the Hebrew text and the targumic rendering involves an infinitive construct that is not inflected for person. The first person in both cases, which departs from the translation model, thus reflects the original Exodus text.

64. For a valuable overview of the dating and exegetical concerns of the Targums, see Alexander (1988).

65. Similarly, in the previous chapter, the deity promises to appear in a theophany to Moses, to affirm his authority: הנה אנכי בא אליך בעב הענן, 'I am about to come to you in a thick cloud' (Exod. 19.9).

Peshiṭta
ܬܕܒܚܐ ܕܐܪܥܐ ܐ ܬܥܒܕ ܠܝ. ܘܬܕܒܚ ܥܠܘܗܝ, ܥܠܘܬܟ ܘܩܘܪܒܢܝܟ. ܘܥܢܟ ܘܬܘܪܝܟ. ܒܟܠ ܐܬܪ ܕܬܕܟܪ ܫܡܝ ܐ ܬ ܠܘܬܟ ܘܐܒܪܟܟ.
mdbḥ' d'dmt' t'bd ly. wtdbḥ 'lwhy 'lwtk wqwrbnyk
w'nk wtwryk. bkl 'tr dtdkr' šmy 't' lwtk w'brkk.
An altar of earth you will make for me, and you will sacrifice upon it your burnt
offerings and your offerings, and your flocks and your bulls.
Wherever *you invoke* my name, I will come unto you and I will bless you.[66]
Fragment Targum
בכל אתר די תד[כ]רו ית שמי קדישא מימרי מתגלי עליכון ומברך יתכון
In every place that *you* [pl.] *invoke* my holy name, my Memra will be revealed unto you
and will bless you.[67]
Neofiti 1
בכל אתר די תדברון ית שמי בצלו אתגלי במימרה עליכון ומברך יתכון
In every place that *you* [pl.] *invoke* my name *in prayer*, I will be revealed to you by my
Memra and will bless you.[68]

Table 6: The textual witnesses to Exod. 20.24b reflecting the verb in second person

All the Aramaic targumim, whether or not they reflect the first-person verb, are consistent in removing any notion of divine immanence. They solve this problem in different ways: by transforming theophany into prayer; by transforming theophany into revelation merely of the name; or by replacing the idea of the deity's physically 'coming' in theophany in favour of his 'sending' non-corporal blessing. Even the targumim that reflect the first person reconfigure what is at stake. The name is no longer proclaimed directly by the deity who makes himself immanent in live, first-person speech and self-introduction. Instead, the deity affirms his transcendence while sanctioning his Shekinah, as hypostasis, to dwell in the sanctuary. The targumic tradition, *whether reflecting the first person or the second person of the verb*, uniformly subordinates the altar law of the Covenant Code (with its conception of theophany at the sacrificial altar) to the later theological norms of Deuteronomic Name theology (and the conception of the hypostasis). The Syriac falls neatly into place as part of this broader tradition. It therefore reflects exegesis.[69] It does

66.   For the text, Koster (1977: 164; my transcription and translation). I am grateful to Mr Robert R. Phenix for expert assistance in discussing the syntax of the Syriac.

67.   For the text, Klein (1980: I, 176). My translation modifies and corrects that provided by Klein (1980: II, 134).

68.   For the text, Díez Macho (1970; my translation).

69.   Already recognizing that the Syriac second-person rendering does not offer a true text-critical variant is the ground-breaking work of Heller (1911: 7–8; 1921: 23–24; and 1927–29: 2.97 n. 12). At the same time, however, his explanation of the exegetical issue involved (in terms of *atbash*) is untenable (Maori 1995b: 82). Krochmal ([1785–1840] 1961: 406) had also seen that the Syriac incorporates an exegetical tradition. I am grateful to Professor Maori for drawing my attention to the work of Heller and Krochmal.

not reflect a proper text-critical variant.[70] Elsewhere, too, in this verse it levels from specific to generic religious concepts.[71] The Peshiṭta translation arose in a community with scant interest in the cultus and its realia.[72] At issue, therefore, in the second-person rendering is not a textual variant but a tradition of exegesis that it shares with the other Aramaic targumim.[73] That exegetical tradition is unattested in the earliest textual witnesses.

As regards theology, terminology, and retention of number inconsistency (*Numeruswechsel*),[74] the text reflected by MT Exod. 20.24 is the one that most resists levelling:

---

70. Weitzman's posthumously published study (1999: 61; my emphasis) is incisive:

> If anything, past use of [the] P[eshiṭta] in the reconstruction of the Hebrew text has been excessive. The danger is that the translator [of the Syriac] has anticipated the modern critic: the very features sought by the critic in order to identify good readings may have been brought in long ago by the translator in order to foster smoothness and consistency in his version.
>
> Thus, in the area traditionally of greatest demand, namely the provision of variant Hebrew readings, P's role is modest. . . .
>
> The real interest of P lies elsewhere. *P shows in detail how – and to what degree – the Hebrew Bible was understood in a particular community in the earliest centuries of this era.*

71. For example, it levels שלמיך, 'your well-being offerings' (Exod. 20.24a) to the homogeneous *wqwrbnyk*, 'your offerings'. This contrasts with its normal rendering in the Syriac, 'whole-offering' (as at Lev. 3.1). This and similar confusions suggest that 'the translator had no prior halachic knowledge to prevent this confusion' or was indifferent to the distinction. See Weitzman (1999: 217).

72. 'The Judaism of P is non-rabbinic and indeed anti-ritual' (Weitzman 1999: 258).

73. For a valuable formulation of these issues, see Maori (1998: 67):

> The . . . Peshitta and the targums share a common exegetical tradition. Like the targums, the Peshitta drew upon the then-current exegetical tradition. The stylistic similarity between the Peshitta and the targums (as well as the stylistic similarity between the Peshitta and rabbinic literature) may be explained simply as the sharing of interpretations that were transmitted (not necessarily in writing) in set formulae.

74. The MT of the larger unit in which the altar law is found contains an unexplained shift from second-person plural used to address Israel (Exod. 20.22–23) to second-person singular in the altar law itself (20.24–26). Moderns see this inconsistency as evidence of separate literary strata (Schwienhorst-Schönberger 1990: 284–86; challenged by Van Seters 2003a: 61). The ancient witnesses were no less sensitive than modern critics to such inconsistencies and resolved them in the translation so as to produce a smoother text, free of the *Numeruswechsel*. Thus LXX employs second-person plural for v. 24a (Wevers 1992: 72, 111; cf. 148). This levels the public address in the altar law to the plural number of its narrative introduction (vv. 22–23). The same tendency is carried yet further by the Fragment Targum and Neofiti, both of which level the second-person plural through the altar law (22–26), making the entire unit (20.22–26) a consistent plural. The Syriac conforms to the number of the MT and does not level.

Witness	Rejection of cultic immanence as anthropomorphic	Second term in sacrifice list generalized and levelled	Levelling of Numeruswechsel of addressee (Exod. 20.22–26)
MT	–	–	–
LXX	+	–	+
SP[75]	–	–	–
Syriac	+	+	–
Onq	+	+	–
Ps-Jon	+	+	+
Fragment	+	+	+
Neofiti 1	+	+	+

Table 7: Textual phenomena subject to levelling (Exod. 20.24)

The primary textual witnesses thus support the first-person verb (as retained by MT Exod. 20.24b) as the original reading:

Witness	God proclaims own Name	Worshipper proclaims Divine Name in prayer
MT	+	
LXX	+	
SP	+	
Syriac		+
Onq	+	
Ps-Jon	+	+
Fragment		+
Neofiti 1		+

Table 8: Summary of evidence regarding the person of the verb

With the first-person verb defended text-critically, the question now arises as to its meaning. The dismissals of its meaningfulness by Van Seters and Tigay alike are difficult to understand, since they do not consider either the text-critical or the inner-biblical evidence. There is clear evidence for the deity's proclaiming his own name in a theophany:

Gen. 15.7   ויאמר אליו אני יהוה   And he said to him, 'I am Yahweh'
Gen. 17.1   ויאמר אליו אני אל שדי   And he said to him, 'I am El Shaddai'
Gen. 28.13   ויאמר אני יהוה   And he said, 'I am Yahweh'

75. On other grounds, of course, the Samaritan Pentateuch shows clear evidence of ideological intervention in the text of this verse (shift of the verb from future to past) and of the larger context; see n. 59 above.

In each of these cases, a theophany is marked by the deity's introducing himself by announcing his name.[76] In the latter case, that proclamation of the name in a theophany takes place specifically at a cultic 'place': the word מָקוֹם, 'place', recurs six times in the unit (Gen. 28.10–22).[77] That cult-site is, of course, Luz, renamed Bethel.[78] The connection between theophany and altar was already recognized by Wellhausen: '[T]he altars, as a rule, are not built by the patriarchs according to their own private judgment wheresoever they please; on the contrary, theophany calls attention to, or at least afterwards confirms, the holiness of the place' (Wellhausen 1883: 32, ET 1885: 31).

The deity's proclaiming his name in the context of a theophany remains an important motif throughout Exodus (see Table 9 on the next page).

The proclamation of the divine name in these cases is not merely the self-introduction of the deity to the addressee; rather, the proclamation of the name constitutes the revelation itself. It provides the means for the divine self-manifestation.[79] Van Seters (2003a: 63) argues that the 'expression (קָרָא בְשֵׁם) is the direct equivalent to invoking the name in Exod 20:24b in that it points to the activity of the worshipers and not the deity'. In making that generalization, Van Seters overlooks the contrary evidence of the literature concerned with the divine theophany at Sinai (Exod. 33.19; 34.5, 6).

The altar law of Exodus takes for granted that the deity makes himself present in a theophany by proclaiming his name. The deity 'comes to' (בָּא אֶל) the celebrant at the altar in the context of sacrifice, where he grants blessing. Priests play no role in this sacrifice, nor is there any other form of mediation. There is no notion of prayer, no human speech, petition, or invocation of the deity. In terms of the phenomenology of religion, the altar law of Exodus does not fit in the world of the exile. What is striking, however, is how inconsistent the altar law is with its context. In each of the other passages cited from Exodus, the theophany is independent of

76. Ironically, this close connection between altar building and theophany was essential to Van Seters's very compelling reconstruction of the compositional history of the birth story of Isaac. He reaffirms the old source-critical insight that the immediate literary antecedent of the theophany (Gen. 18.1) is Abraham's construction there of an altar (Gen. 13.18). 'The structure of the birth story (in [Gen.] 13:18; 18:1a, 10–14; 21:2, 6–7) is therefore fairly clear. Abraham builds an altar at Mamre and Yahweh appears to him there' (Van Seters 1975: 207).

77. Van Seters (2003a: 62–63) seems to overlook the significance of this word and its repetition in suggesting that the nexus between theophany and altar is here merely incidental and a later development.

78. Tigay's claim that 'in the context of sacrifice and altars, it is always the worshipper, not God, who invokes ... or calls upon ... God's name' (2004: 203) overlooks this evidence for the connection between theophany and altar.

79. In his valuable study of the 'Name theology', Mettinger (1982: 125) articulates this well and provides an extensive discussion of the relevant literature.

Exodus	Theophany		To Whom		Where		Time Reference	
	Divine self-introduction		Moses alone	Israel	Sinai/ Horeb	Altar	Once in distant past	Present
3.6, 15	ויאמר אנכי אלהי אביך He said, 'I am the God of your father' . . . . . . יהוה ... שלחני אליכם Yahweh … has sent me to you		+		+		+	
20.2	אנכי יהוה אלהיך I am Yahweh your God			+	+		+	
20.24	בכל המקום אשר אזכיר את שמי אבוא אליך וברכתיך In every place that I proclaim my name, I will come to you and bless you.			+		+		+
33.19	ויאמר אני אעביר כל טובי על פניך וקראתי בשם יהוה לפניך And he said, 'I will make all my goodness pass before you, and I will proclaim the name Yahweh before you'		+		+		+	
34.5	וירד יהוה בענן ויתיצב עמו שם ויקרא בשם יהוה Yahweh descended in the cloud, presenting himself to him there, and he proclaimed the name, 'Yahweh'.		+		+		+	
34.6	ויעבר יהוה על פניו ויקרא יהוה יהוה Yahweh passed before him, and proclaimed, 'Yahweh, Yahweh …'		+		+		+	

Table 9: Evidence for deity's proclaiming own name in a theophany

any altar but is rather associated with Sinai, as the mount of revelation. Moreover, in each of these cases, the theophany is a one-time event, as the deity discloses himself first to Moses, then to the entire nation, and then, after the incident of the golden calf, reaffirms the covenant by renewing the theophany to Moses.

That inconsistency may well explain the function of the altar law in the present context: it serves as a bridge between theophany as an inaccessible event of the past, situated at a no longer accessible sacred mountain found outside of the land, and the need to assure divine presence as something ongoing and accessible in the present.[80] The sacrificial cultus here channels theophany from the peak of Sinai into the daily life of the community, providing a transition from past to present, from one time event to an event that can be repeated and renewed. It ensures that the

80. With respect to the altar law (Exod. 20.22–26), Tigay describes this goal incisively: 'the coherence of the passage revolves around the means of securing God's presence' (2004: 196). I differ from him, however, in (1) not emending Exod. 20.24b to a notion of prayer and therefore as seeing sacrificial worship as essential to the conception of divine presence in this verse, since at issue is a theophany at an altar; (2) addressing the logic for the altar law's incorporation into its present context, and postulating its redactional coherence.

deity is accessible not only at the sacred mount of revelation but in the daily life of the people, in sacrifice. Such a conception is only conceivable in the pre-exilic period. Since the law, as Van Seters concedes, is a plural distributive ('in every place'), it envisions multiple altars as legitimate for sacrifice. On that basis, it is pre-Deuteronomic.

If this analysis is correct, it also suggests strongly that the insertion of the altar law in this context must be the work of a creative redactor. Table 10 indicates the redactional logic:

(Exod. 19.9)	ויאמר יהוה אל משה הנה אנכי בא אליך בעב הענן	A	*Theophany*
	Then Yahweh said to Moses, '*I am about to come to you in a dense cloud*'		
(Exod. 20.2)	אנכי יהוה אלהיך		B *Name*
	I am Yahweh, your God		
(Exod. 20.24b)	בכל המקום אשר אזכיר את שמי		B' *Name*
	In every place that I proclaim my name		
	אבוא אליך וברכתיך	A'	*Theophany*
	I will come to you and bless you.		

Table 10: The contextual logic of the altar as site for the renewal of theophany

By grafting together the two inconsistent conceptions of divine presence, he sought intentionally to assure the continuity of divine presence in the theophany, shifting its home from Sinai to the altar, the precursor of Zion. The redactor is here both author and theologian.

4. *Conclusions*

A Law Book for the Diaspora offers new ways for understanding key aspects of the Covenant Code: the extent of its relation to the Laws of Hammurabi, the first millennium as the most logical context for the reception and reuse of that text as a model for the drafter of the Covenant Code, and the importance of textual models in ancient Israel. In the process, basic assumptions of continental traditio-historical and form-critical methodology undergo an important critique. Any simplistic one-to-one correlation between specific literary form and a certain, discrete life-setting in which it allegedly arose, only then subsequently to be integrated by a redactor, will likely not survive the critique provided by this book. The issue is that the author goes so far in his opposition to the consensus that the arguments become extreme: 'not second millennium' too quickly translates into 'Neo-Babylonian' as if there were nothing in between. For Van Seters, 'no editor' (valuably rejecting the form-critical model of originally oral laws that arise from separate sociological contexts, which then require a compiler to integrate) too rapidly translates into a rejection of redaction altogether. Although the author claims that the model of editor currently used in the field is anachronistic (Van Seters

2003b), the alternative that he provides, which sees author and redactor as mutually exclusive concepts, seems to be a product of European Romanticism. This approach does not take cuneiform literature into account. In particular, it overlooks the evidence for the importance of redaction to the composition of the Laws of Hammurabi, the very text that allegedly served as the Covenant Code's literary exemplar. It also does not examine works like the Samaritan Pentateuch or the Temple Scroll, which might have offered additional controls concerning the nature of text composition in the Second-Temple period. In place of an editor he argues for an author, and for the compositional coherence, in synchronic terms, of the entire Sinai pericope, which he attributes to his exilic Yahwist.

While previous scholarship has not hesitated to regard the Sinai pericope in its final form as a work of the exilic or post-exilic period, Van Seters rejects any notion of separate literary strata and views the entire unit as exilic and as without any literary pre-history. On that basis, the exilic date for the composition of the Sinai pericope also attaches to the Covenant Code, as the latter is subsumed both chronologically and textually into the former. The resulting claim that the pre-exilic dating of the Covenant Code is simply an arbitrary prejudice of scholarship cannot be sustained. The textual analysis that reads the laws of the Covenant Code as responding to Deuteronomy requires extensive eisegesis; it also overlooks a series of text-critical and literary-critical issues. Similarly, the attempt to account for the impact of the Laws of Hammurabi upon the Covenant Code by explaining it as reflecting the Neo-Babylonian period, while possible in theoretical terms, overlooks a more compelling alternative: the Neo-Assyrian period, with its hegemony over Syro-Palestine.

The method used to remove the veil of misreading that has long plagued the text calls attention to itself for the frequency with which alternative models of explanation, complicating evidence (text-critical or Assyriological), and relevant scholarly discussions, are not brought to bear. In assuming the mantle of gadfly, the author does not sufficiently complicate his own assumptions. This occurs with sufficient frequency as to raise doubts in the reader's mind about the cogency of the book's larger claims. Critical evaluation of the book surely confirms the positions that it seeks to reject. First, the Sinai pericope is a redactional composition. It is the work of a brilliant author-redactor who, working in some ways like those responsible for Hammurabi and Gilgamesh, integrated diverse literary material into a new work, one that makes an original statement that goes beyond the original assumptions of its component parts. Among the component parts in question was, in whole or part, the pre-exilic Covenant Code. Second, the Neo-Assyrian period provides the most logical setting for a Judaean author to pattern the

Covenant Code after the Laws of Hammurabi. Third, and finally, the altar law of the Covenant Code is pre-Deuteronomic: in terms of syntax and meaning, the indefinite construct functions as a distributive plural. It assumes a plurality of cultic sites, not a single cult site. Consequently, the law cannot logically be construed as concerned with prayer. Instead, it affirms divine theophany as a consequence of the sacrificial worship of the deity. Sacrificial worship at an altar, not prayer, provides access to the deity; the altar permits the deity's immanence and assures his continued presence. This conception, like the Covenant Code prior to its redactional incorporation into the Sinai pericope, makes most sense in the pre-exilic, not the exilic, period.

Bibliography

Abou-Assaf, Ali, Pierre Bordreuil and A.R. Millard
  1982   *La Statue de Tell Fekherye et son inscription bilingue assyro-araméenne* (Cahier, 7; Paris: A.D.P.F.).

Alexander, Philip S.
  1988   'Jewish Aramaic Translations of Hebrew Scriptures', in Martin Jan Mulder (ed.), *Mikra: Text, Translation, Reading and Interpretation of the Hebrew Bible in Ancient Judaism and Early Christianity* (CRINT, 2.1; Assen and Maastricht: Van Gorcum; Minneapolis: Fortress Press): 217–53.

Alt, Albrecht
  1934   *Die Ursprünge des israelitischen Rechts* (Leipzig: S. Hirzel). Reprinted in *idem, Kleine Schriften zur Geschichte des Volkes Israel*, I (Munich: Beck, 1953), 278–332. ET 'The Origins of Israelite Law', in *idem, Essays on Old Testament History and Religion* (trans. R.A. Wilson; Oxford: Basil Blackwell, 1966): 79–132.

Blum, Erhard
  1996   'Das sog. "Privilegrecht" in Exodus 34,11–26: Ein Fixpunkt der Komposition des Exodusbuches?', in Marc Vervenne (ed.), *Studies in the Book of Exodus: Redaction – Reception – Interpretation* (BETL, 126; Leuven: Leuven University Press): 347–66.

Boer, Pieter Arie Hendrik de
  1962   *Gedenken und Gedächtnis in der Welt des Alten Testaments* (Franz Delitzsch Vorlesungen; Stuttgart: W. Kohlhammer).

Borger, Rykle
  1979   *Babylonisch-Assyrische Lesestücke* (AnOr, 54; 2 vols; Rome: Pontifical Biblical Institute, 2nd edn).

Brettler, Marc
  2003   'The Copenhagen School: The Historiographical Issues', *Association for Jewish Studies Review* 27: 1–21.

Childs, B.S.
  1974   *The Book of Exodus: A Critical, Theological Commentary* (OTL; Philadelphia: Westminster Press).

Clarke, E.G.

1984 *Targum Pseudo-Jonathan of the Pentateuch: Text and Concordance* (Hoboken, NJ: Ktav).

Conrad, Diethelm

1968 *Studien zum Altargesetz Ex 20:24–26: Inaugural-Dissertation* (Marburg: H. Kombächer).

Crüsemann, Frank

1992 *Die Tora: Theologie und Sozialgeschichte des alttestamentlichen Gesetzes* (Munich: Chr. Kaiser Verlag). ET *The Torah: Theology and Social History of Old Testament Law* (Minneapolis: Fortress Press, 1996).

Dalley, Stephanie

1985 'Foreign Chariotry and Cavalry in the Armies of Tiglath-Pileser and Sargon II', *Iraq* 47: 31–48.

1989 *Myths from Mesopotamia: Creation, The Flood, Gilgamesh, and Others* (Oxford and New York: Oxford University Press).

1998 'The Influence of Mesopotamia upon Israel and the Bible', in Stephanie Dalley (ed.), *The Legacy of Mesopotamia* (Oxford and New York: Oxford University Press): 57–83.

Díez Macho, Alejandro (ed.)

1970 *Neophyti 1*, vol. 2, *Éxodo* (Madrid: Consejo Superior de Investigaciones Científicas).

Dion, P.-E.

1975 'Le Message moral du prophète Amos s'inspirat-il du "droit de l'alliance"?', *Science et esprit* 27: 5–34.

Drazin, Israel

1990 *Targum Onkelos to Exodus* (Hoboken, NJ: Ktav).

Driver, G.R., and J.C. Miles

1952–55 *The Babylonian Laws* (2 vols; Oxford: Clarendon Press).

Driver, S.R.

1901 *Deuteronomy* (ICC; Edinburgh: T. & T. Clark, 3rd edn).

Ehrlich, Arnold B.

1899 *Mikrâ Ki-Pheschutô: Die Schrift nach ihrem Wortlaut*, I: *Der Pentateuch* (Berlin: M. Poppelauer). Reprinted in 3-vol. set with Prolegomenon by H.M. Orlinsky (Library of Biblical Studies; New York: Ktav, 1969) (Hebrew).

Eichler, Barry L.

1987 'Literary Structure in the Laws of Eshnunna', in F. Rochberg-Halton (ed.), *Language, Literature and History: Philological and Historical Studies Presented to Erica Reiner* (AOS, 67; New Haven: American Oriental Society): 71–84.

Eising, H.

1977 'זָכַר zākar', in *ThWAT*, II: cols 571–93. ET *TDOT*, IV (1980): 64–82.

Eissfeldt, Otto

1956 *Einleitung in das Alte Testament: Entstehungsgeschichte des Alten Testament* (Tübingen: J.C.B. Mohr [Paul Siebeck], 2nd edn). ET *The Old Testament: An Introduction* (trans. P.R. Ackroyd; Oxford: Basil Blackwell, 1965).

Fadhil, A.

1998 'Der Prolog des CODEX HAMMURAPI in einer Abschrift aus Sippar', in

XXXIVème Rencontre assyriologique internationale, 6–10/VII/1987 – Istanbul (Ankara: Türk Tarih Kurumu Basimevi): 717–29.

Finkelstein, Jacob J.
  1981   *The Ox That Gored* (Transactions of the American Philosophical Society, 71.2; Philadelphia: American Philosophical Society).

George, Andrew (trans.)
  1999   *The Epic of Gilgamesh: The Babylonian Epic Poem and Other Texts in Akkadian and Sumerian* (London: Penguin).

Greenberg, Moshe
  1960   'Some Postulates of Biblical Criminal Law', in Menahem Haran (ed.), *Yehezkel Kaufmann Jubilee Volume* (Jerusalem: Magnes Press): 5–28. Reprinted in *idem, Studies in the Bible and Jewish Thought* (Philadelphia: Jewish Publication Society of America, 1995): 25–50.

Grossfeld, Bernard
  1988   *The Targum Onqelos to Exodus: Translated, with Apparatus and Notes* (Aramaic Bible, 7; Wilmington, DE: Michael Glazier).

Heger, Paul
  1999   *The Three Biblical Altar Laws: Developments in the Sacrificial Cult in Practice and Theology; Political and Economic Background* (BZAW, 279; Berlin and New York: W. de Gruyter).

Heller, Chaim
  1911   *Untersuchung über die Peschîttâ zur gesamten hebräischen Bibel: Inaugural-Dissertation* (Berlin: H. Itzkowski).
  1921   *A Critical Essay on the Palestinian Targum to the Pentateuch* (New York: Alpha).
  1927–29 *Peshitta: In Hebrew Characters with Elucidatory Notes* (2 vols; Berlin: Gutenberg).

Hoftijzer, J., and K. Jongeling
  1995   *Dictionary of the North-West Semitic Inscriptions* (Handbuch der Orientalistik, 21; 2 vols; Leiden: E.J. Brill, 1995).

Horowitz, Wayne, Takayoshi Oshima and Seth Sanders
  2002   'A Bibliographical List of Cuneiform Inscriptions from Canaan, Palestine/ Philistia, and the Land of Israel', *JAOS* 122: 753–66.

Houtman, Cornelis
  1997   *Das Bundesbuch* (Documenta et Monumenta Orientis Antiqui, 24; Leiden: E.J. Brill).

Hurowitz, Victor Avigdor
  1994   '*Inu Anum ṣīrum*': Literary Structures in the Non-Juridical Sections of Codex Hammurabi* (Occasional Publications of the Samuel Noah Kramer Fund, 15; Philadelphia: University Museum).
  2004   'Hammurabi in Mesopotamian Tradition', in Pinḥas Artzi *et al.* (eds), *Yaakov Klein Jubilee Volume* (Bethesda, MD: CDL Press; in press).

Jackson, Bernard S.
  1995   'Modeling Biblical Law: The Covenant Code', *Chicago Kent Law Review* 70 (1995): 1745–1827.

Joüon, Paul, and T. Muraoka
  1996   *A Grammar of Biblical Hebrew* (trans. and rev. T. Muraoka; Subsidia Biblica,

14.1–2; Rome: Pontifical Biblical Institute, 2nd edn). Translation and revision of Paul Joüon, *Grammaire de l'Hébreu biblique* (Rome: Pontifical Biblical Institute, 1923).

Klein, Michael L.
1980   *The Fragment Targums of the Pentateuch According to their Extant Sources* (AnBib, 76; 2 vols; Rome: Pontifical Biblical Institute).

Koster, M.D.
1977   'Exodus', in Peshiṭta Institute (ed.), *The Old Testament in Syriac according to the Peshiṭta Version* (1.1; Leiden: E.J. Brill).

Kratz, Reinhard G.
2000   'Der literarische Ort des Deuteronomiums', in Reinhard G. Kratz and Hermann Spieckermann (eds), *Liebe und Gebot: Studien zum Deuteronomium: Festschrift zum 70. Geburtstag von Lothar Perlitt* (FRLANT, 190; Göttingen: Vanderhoeck & Ruprecht): 101–20.
2002   'Der vor- und der nachpriesterschriftliche Hexateuch', in Jan Christian Gertz, Konrad Schmid and Markus Witte (eds), *Abschied vom Jahwisten: Die Komposition des Hexateuch in der jüngsten Diskussion* (BZAW, 315; Berlin and New York: W. de Gruyter): 295–323.

Krochmal, Nachman [1785–1840]
1961   *The Writings of Nachman Krochmal* (ed. Simon Rawidowicz; London and Waltham, MA: Ararat Publishing Society Ltd, 2nd edn).

Lambert, W.G.
1992   Addenda et Corrigenda to W.G. Lambert, Cuneiform Tablets of the Kouyounjik Collection of the British Museum, Third Supplement (1992), in *Nouvelles Assyriologiques Brèves et Utilitaires* (December 1992): 4, No. 129.

Le Boulluec, Alain, and Pierre Sandevoir (eds)
1989   *L'Exode* (La Bible d'Alexandrie, 2; Paris: Cerf).

Lemche, Niels Peter
1985   *Early Israel* (VTSup, 37; Leiden: E.J. Brill).
1998   *The Israelites in History and Tradition* (London: SPCK, and Louisville, KY: Westminster John Knox).

Levin, Christoph
1985   'Der Dekalog am Sinai', *VT* 35: 165–91.
1993   *Der Jahwist* (FRLANT, 157; Göttingen: Vandenhoeck & Ruprecht).
2000   'Das Deuteronomium und der Jahwist', in Reinhard G. Kratz and Hermann Spieckermann (eds), *Liebe und Gebot: Studien zum Deuteronomium: Festschrift zum 70. Geburtstag von Lothar Perlitt* (FRLANT, 190; Göttingen: Vanderhoeck & Ruprecht): 121–36. Reprinted in Levin, *Fortschreibungen: Gesammelte Studien zum Alten Testament* (BZAW, 316; Berlin and New York: W. de Gruyter, 2003): 96–110.

Levinson, Bernard M.
1994a   Editor, *Theory and Method in Biblical and Cuneiform Law: Revision, Interpolation and Development* (JSOTSup, 181; Sheffield: Sheffield Academic Press).
1994b   'The Case for Revision and Interpolation within the Biblical Legal Corpora', in Bernard M. Levinson (ed.), *Theory and Method in Biblical and Cuneiform*

Law: Revision, Interpolation and Development (JSOTSup, 181; Sheffield: Sheffield Academic Press): 37–59.

1997   *Deuteronomy and the Hermeneutics of Legal Innovation* (Oxford and New York: Oxford University Press).

2001   'Textual Criticism, Assyriology, and the History of Interpretation: Deuteronomy 13:7a as a Test Case in Method', *JBL* 120: 211–43.

2003   ' "You Must Not Add Anything to What I Command You": Paradoxes of Canon and Authorship in Ancient Israel', *Numen: International Review for the History of Religions* 50: 1–51.

2005   *Rethinking Revelation and Redaction: Biblical Studies and Its Intellectual Models* (New York and Oxford: Oxford University Press).

Levinson, Bernard M., and Molly M. Zahn

2002   'Renewing Revelation: The Hermeneutics of ׳כ and כא in the Temple Scroll', *Dead Sea Discoveries* 9: 295–346.

Lohfink, Norbert

1984   'Zur deuteronomischen Zentralisationsformel', *Bib* 65: 297–328. Reprinted in *idem*, *Studien zum Deuteronomium und zur deuteronomistischen Literatur*, II (SBAB, 12; Stuttgart: Katholisches Bibelwerk, 1991): 125–42.

McBride, S. Dean

1969   'The Deuteronomic Name Theology' (PhD dissertation, Harvard University).

Malul, Meir

1990   *The Comparative Method in Ancient Near Eastern and Biblical Legal Studies* (AOAT, 227; Kevelaer: Butzon & Bercker, and Neukirchen–Vluyn: Neukirchener Verlag).

Maori, Yeshayahu

1995a   'Methodological Criteria for Distinguishing between Variant *Vorlage* and Exegesis in the Peshiṭta Pentateuch', in P.B. Dirksen and A. van der Kooij (eds), *The Peshiṭta as a Translation: Papers Read at the II Peshiṭta Symposium Held at Leiden 19–21 August 1993* (Monographs of the Peshiṭta Institute Leiden, 8; Leiden: E.J. Brill): 103–19, with discussion 121–27.

1995b   *The Peshiṭta Version of the Pentateuch and Early Jewish Exegesis* (Jerusalem: Magnes Press).

1998   'The Relationship between the Peshiṭta Pentateuch and the Pentateuchal Targums', in Paul V.M. Flesher (ed.), *Targum Studies*, II: *Targum and Peshiṭta* (South Florida Studies in the History of Judaism, 165; Atlanta, GA: Scholars Press): 57–73.

Mettinger, Tryggve N.D.

1982   *The Dethronement of Sabaoth: Studies in the Shem and Kabod Theologies* (trans. Frederick H. Cryer; Lund: CWK Gleerup).

Nicholson, Ernest W.

1998   *The Pentateuch in the Twentieth Century: The Legacy of Julius Wellhausen* (Oxford: Clarendon Press).

Noth, Martin

1968   *Das zweite Buch Moses: Exodus* (ATD, 5; Göttingen: Vandenhoeck & Ruprecht, 4th edn). ET *Exodus* (trans. J.S. Bowden; OTL; Philadelphia: Westminster Press).

Osumi, Yuichi

1991   *Die Kompositionsgeschichte des Bundesbuches Exodus 20,22b–23,33* (OBO, 105; Freiburg, Switzerland: Universitätsverlag, and Göttingen: Vandenhoeck & Ruprecht).

Oswald, Wolfgang

1998   *Israel am Gottesberg: Eine Untersuchung zur Literargeschichte der vorderen Sinaiperikope Ex 19–24 und deren historischen Hintergrund* (OBO, 159; Freiburg, Switzerland: Universitätsverlag, and Göttingen: Vandenhoeck & Ruprecht).

Otto, Eckart

1988   *Wandel der Rechtsbegründungen in der Gesellschaftsgeschichte des antiken Israel: Eine Rechtsgeschichte des 'Bundesbuches' Ex XX 22–XXIII 13* (StudBib, 3; Leiden: E.J. Brill).

1993   'Town and Rural Countryside in Ancient Israelite Law: Reception and Redaction in Cuneiform and Israelite Law', *JSOT* 57: 3–22.

1994   'Aspects of Legal Reforms and Reformulations in Ancient Cuneiform and Israelite Law', in Bernard M. Levinson (ed.), *Theory and Method in Biblical and Cuneiform Law: Revision, Interpolation and Development* (JSOTSup, 181; Sheffield: Sheffield Academic Press): 160–96.

1996   'Treueid und Gesetz: Die Ursprünge des Deuteronomiums im Horizont neuassyrischen Vertragsrechts', *Zeitschrift für altorientalische und biblische Rechtsgeschichte* 2: 1–52.

1997   'Das Deuteronomium als archimedischer Punkt der Pentateuchkritik: Auf dem Wege zu einer Neubegründung der de Wette'schen Hypothese', in Marc Vervenne and Johann Lust (eds), *Deuteronomy and Deuteronomic Literature: Festschrift C.H.W. Brekelmans* (BETL, 133; Leuven: University Press and Peeters): 321–39.

Paul, Shalom M.

1970   *Studies in the Book of the Covenant in the Light of Cuneiform and Biblical Law* (VTSup, 18; Leiden: E.J. Brill).

Prijs, Leo

1948   *Jüdische Tradition in der Septuaginta* (Leiden: E.J. Brill). Reprinted with *idem*, *Die grammatikalische Terminologie des Abraham Ibn Esra*, and an annotated bibliography by Eva Prijs (2 vols in 1; Hildesheim: Georg Olms, 1987).

Robertson, Edward

1948/49 'The Altar of Earth (Exodus xx, 24–26)', *JJS* 1: 12–21.

Roth, Martha T.

1997   *Law Collections from Mesopotamia and Asia Minor* (Society of Biblical Literature Writings from the Ancient World, 6; Atlanta, GA: Scholars Press, 2nd edn).

Rothenbusch, Ralf

2000   *Die kasuistische Rechtssammlung im 'Bundesbuch' (Ex 21,2–11.18–22,16) und ihr literarischer Kontext im Licht altorientalischer Parallelen* (AOAT, 259; Münster: Ugarit-Verlag).

Sader, Hélène S.

1987   *Les Etats araméens de Syrie depuis leur fondation jusqu'à leur transformation en provinces assyriennes* (Beiruter Texte und Studien, 36; Beirut: Orient-Institut der deutschen morgenländischen Gesellschaft).

Scheil, Vincent
    1902   *Code des lois (droit privé) de Hammurabi, roi de Babylone, vers l'an 2000 avant Jésus-Christ* (Délégation en Perse; Mémoires pub. sous la direction de M.J. de Morgan, délégué général; Paris, 1900– ; IV, Textes élamites-sémitiques; 2nd series): [11]–162; plates 3–15.

Schmitt, Hans-Christoph
    2003   'Das Altargesetz Ex 20,24–26 und seine redaktionsgeschichtlichen Bezüge', in Johannes F. Diehl, Reinhard Heitzenröder and Markus Witte (eds), '*Einen Altar von Erde mache mir ...': Festschrift für Diethelm Conrad zu seinem 70. Geburtstag* (Kleine Arbeiten zum Alten und Neuen Testament, 4/5; Waltrop, Germany: Spenner): 269–82.

Schottroff, Willy
    1967   '*Gedenken' im Alten Orient und im Alten Testament* (WMANT, 15; Neu-kirchen–Vluyn: Neukirchener Verlag, 2nd edn).

Schwienhorst-Schönberger, Ludger
    1990   *Das Bundesbuch (Ex 20,22–23,33): Studien zu seiner Entstehung und Theologie* (BZAW, 188; Berlin: W. de Gruyter).

Ska, Jean Louis
    2000   *Introduction à la lecture du Pentateuque: Clés pour l'interprétation des cinq premiers livres de la Bible* (trans. Frédéric Vermorel; Le livre et le rouleau, 5; Brussels: Lessius).
    2002   'The Yahwist, a Hero with a Thousand Faces: A Chapter in the History of Modern Exegesis', in Jan Christian Gertz, Konrad Schmid and Markus Witte (eds), *Abschied vom Jahwisten: Die Komposition des Hexateuch in der jüngsten Diskussion* (BZAW, 315; Berlin and New York: W. de Gruyter): 1–23.

Smith, Morton
    1987   *Palestinian Parties and Politics that Shaped the Old Testament* (London: SCM Press, 2nd edn).

Sperber, Alexander
    1959   *The Bible in Aramaic Based on Old Manuscripts and Printed Texts,* I: *The Pentateuch According to Targum Onkelos* (Leiden: E.J. Brill).

Sprinkle, Joe M.
    1994   *The Book of the Covenant: A Literary Approach* (JSOTSup, 174; Sheffield: JSOT Press).

Spycket, A.
    1985   'La Statue bilingue de Tell Fekheriyé', *RA* 79: 67–68.

Stamm, Johann Jakob
    1945   'Zum Altargesetz im Bundesbuch', *TZ* 1: 304–306.

Tal, Abraham
    1988   'The Samaritan Targum of the Pentateuch', in Martin Jan Mulder (ed.), *Mikra: Text, Translation, Reading and Interpretation of the Hebrew Bible in Ancient Judaism and Early Christianity* (CRINT, 2.1; Assen and Maastricht: Van Gorcum, and Minneapolis: Fortress Press): 189–216.

Thompson, Thomas L.
    1992   *Early History of the Israelite People from Written and Archaeological Sources* (SHANE, 4; Leiden: E.J. Brill).

Tigay, Jeffrey H.
    1982   *The Evolution of the Gilgamesh Epic* (Philadelphia: University of Pennsylvania
            Press).
    1985a   'The Evolution of the Pentateuchal Narratives in the Light of the Evolution of
            the *Gilgamesh Epic*', in Jeffrey H. Tigay (ed.), *Empirical Models for Biblical
            Criticism* (Philadelphia: University of Pennsylvania Press): 21–52.
    1985b   'Conflation as a Redactional Technique', in Jeffrey H. Tigay (ed.), *Empirical
            Models for Biblical Criticism* (Philadelphia: University of Pennsylvania Press):
            53–96.
    1985c   'The Stylistic Criterion of Source Criticism in the Light of Ancient Near
            Eastern and Postbiblical Literature', in Jeffrey H. Tigay (ed.), *Empirical
            Models for Biblical Criticism* (Philadelphia: University of Pennsylvania Press):
            149–74.
    2004   'The Presence of God and the Coherence of Exodus 20:22–26', in C. Cohen,
            A. Hurowitz and S.M. Paul (eds), *Sefer Moshe: The Moshe Weinfeld Jubilee
            Volume – Studies in the Bible and the Ancient Near East, Qumran, and Post-
            Biblical Judaism* (Winona Lake, IN: Eisenbrauns): 195–211.
Toeg, Arie
    1977   *Lawgiving at Sinai: The Course of Development of the Traditions Bearing on the
            Lawgiving at Sinai within the Pentateuch, with a Special Emphasis on the
            Emergence of the Literary Complex in Exodus xxi–xxiv* (Jerusalem: Magnes
            Press) (Hebrew).
Tomback, R.S.
    1978   *A Comparative Semitic Lexicon of the Phoenician and Punic Languages*
            (SBLDS, 32; Missoula, MT: Scholars Press).
Van Seters, John
    1975   *Abraham in History and Tradition* (New Haven: Yale University Press).
    1996a   'Cultic Laws in the Covenant Code and their Relationship to Deuteronomy
            and the Holiness Code', in Marc Vervenne (ed.), *Studies in the Book of
            Exodus: Redaction–Reception–Interpretation* (BETL, 126; Leuven: Leuven
            University Press): 319–45.
    1996b   'The Law of the Hebrew Slave', *ZAW* 108: 534–46.
    1997   'The Deuteronomistic Redaction of the Pentateuch: The Case against It', in
            M. Vervenne and J. Lust (eds), *Deuteronomy and Deuteronomic Literature:
            Festschrift C.H.W. Brekelmans* (BETL, 133; Leuven: Leuven University
            Press): 301–19.
    1999   'Is There Evidence of a Dtr Redaction in the Sinai Pericope (Exodus 19–24,
            32–34)?', in Linda S. Schearing and Steven L. McKenzie (eds), *Those Elusive
            Deuteronomists: The Phenomenon of Pan-Deuteronomism* (JSOTSup, 268;
            Sheffield: Sheffield Academic Press): 160–70.
    2003a   *A Law Book for the Diaspora: Revision in the Study of the Covenant Code*
            (Oxford and New York: Oxford University Press).
    2003b   'An Ironic Circle: Wellhausen and the Rise of Redaction Criticism', *ZAW* 115:
            487–500.
Veldhuis, Niek
    2000   'Kassite Exercises: Literary and Lexical Extracts', *JCS* 52: 67–94.

Weitzman, M.P.
　1999　*The Syriac Version of the Old Testament: An Introduction* (UCOP, 56; Cambridge: Cambridge University Press).

Wellhausen, Julius
　1883　*Prolegomena zur Geschichte Israels* (Berlin: Georg Reimer, 2nd edn). Reprinted from the 6th edn of 1927, with an index of scriptural citations (Berlin and New York: W. de Gruyter, 2001). ET *Prolegomena to the History of Israel* (trans. J.S. Black and A. Menzies; Edinburgh: A. & C. Black, 1885).
　1885　'Die Composition des Hexateuchs', *Jahrbücher für deutsche Theologie* 21 (1876): 392–450, 531–602; 22 (1877): 407–79. Subsequently published as *Die Composition des Hexateuchs und der historischen Bucher des Alten Testaments* (Berlin: W. de Gruyter, 1963, 4th edn).

Westbrook, Raymond
　1994　'What is the Covenant Code?', in Bernard M. Levinson (ed.), *Theory and Method in Biblical and Cuneiform Law: Revision, Interpolation and Development* (JSOTSup, 181; Sheffield: Sheffield Academic Press): 15–36.

Wevers, John William
　1991　*Exodus* (Septuaginta, 2.1; Göttingen: Vandenhoeck & Ruprecht).
　1992　*Text History of the Greek Exodus* (Mitteilungen des Septuaginta Unternehmens, 21; Göttingen: Vandenhoeck & Ruprecht).

Wright, David P.
　2003　'The Laws of Hammurabi as a Source for the Covenant Collection (Exodus 20:23–23:19)', *MAARAV* 10: 11–87.
　2004　Review of *A Law Book for the Diaspora: Revision in the Study of the Covenant Code*, by John Van Seters, *JAOS* 123 (in press).

Chapter 14

Yahweh's Asherah, Inclusive Monotheism and the Question of Dating

B.A. Mastin

It is desirable to tackle the revisionists on their own ground, and so extra-biblical evidence for religious ideas and practices in Palestine during the Iron Age (c. 1200–586 BCE) is of considerable importance. This essay will discuss the significance of inscriptions from Kuntillet ʿAjrud and Khirbet el-Qom which mention Yahweh 'and his asherah'. These texts will be studied, as far as possible, without reference to statements contained in the Old Testament, and it will be argued that, when account is taken of this information, a development which the revisionists put after the exile should be placed much earlier.

1. *The Texts*

Kuntillet ʿAjrud is in northern Sinai, and examination of the pottery from this site indicates that it was occupied 'between the end of the 9th century to the beginning of the 8th century B.C.E.' (Ayalon 1995: 198). Carbon-14 dating of samples of organic material points to the period 801–770 BCE (Carmi and Segal 1996), and Renz (1995: 51, 60 n. 7) holds on palaeographical grounds that the texts were written c. 800 BCE.

One inscription, which is on pithos A, includes the clause *brkt. ʾtkm. lyhwh. šmrn. wlʾšrth.*, 'I bless [or: have blessed] you by Yahweh of Samaria and by his asherah' (Davies 1991: 81 [§ 8.017.1–2]; Renz 1995: 61 [KAgr(9):8.1–2]), while another, which is on pithos B, contains the similar blessing *brktk. lyhwh tmn wlʾšrth.*, 'I bless [or: have blessed] you by Yahweh of Teman and by his asherah' (Davies 1991: 81 [§ 8.021.1]; cf. Renz 1995: 62 [KAgr(9):9.4–6]). A third inscription, which is also on pithos B, perhaps states *lyhwh. htmn. wlʾšrth.*, 'by Yahweh of the Teman and by his asherah' (Davies 1991: 80 [§ 8.016]; Renz 1995: 64 [KAgr(9):10.2]; but cf. Weippert 1997: 16 n.58 and Hadley 1987b: 187–88; 2000: 130 on *htmn*). In this case the phrase is not preceded by 'I bless you'. A fourth inscription (Davies 1991: 80 [§ 8.015]; Renz 1995: 58 [KAgr(9):6]), which was written on plaster on the wall, has been thought to refer to Yahweh and asherah. At the end of the first line Meshel (1992: 107; cf. 1993: 1462) reads *l[y]hwh [ ] tymn. wl[ ]ʾsrt[h]*, 'to [Y]ahweh of Teman and to [his] asherah', and he also restores *yhwh. hty[mn. wʾsrth...]*, 'Yahweh of Te[man and his asherah]', in the second line. Unfortunately the photograph which is provided by both Ahituv (1992: 159) and Meshel (1993: 1462) does not include the surviving parts of these scholars' identical reconstructions of the end of line 1. Zevit (2001: 373 n. 45) says that, in a personal communication dated 20 June 1999, S. Ahituv has informed him 'after a discussion with Meshel that the reconstruction is certain'. But Hadley (2000: 130–31, 133–35), who expresses the hope that the material will be published in full so that further study of it can be undertaken, gives convincing reasons for doubting the correctness of these restorations.

Thus at Kuntillet ʿAjrud there are two instances of a blessing by 'Yahweh and his asherah', and at least one other example of 'Yahweh and his asherah', though at present it would be unwise to rely on evidence supplied by an inscription on plaster as additional support for the association of Yahweh and asherah.

Inscription 3 from Tomb 2 at Khirbet el-Qom is also relevant here. Khirbet el-Qom is in the south of Palestine, between Hebron and Lachish, and the inscription is assigned to the middle of the eighth century BCE by Dever (1969–70: 165, 167) and Lemaire (1977: 603), to c. 725 BCE by Zevit (2001: 360), to the last quarter of the eighth century BCE by Renz (1995: 200, 203), and to '*ca.* 700 B.C. or perhaps slightly later' by Cross (in Dever 1969–70: 165 n.53).

Renz (1995: 207–11 [Kom(8):3]; cf. Davies 1991: 106 [§ 25.003]) transcribes it as follows:

> *ʾryhw. hʿsr. ktbh*
> *brk.ʾ ʾryhw. lyhwh*
> *wmṣryh. lʾsrth. hwsʿ lh*
> *lʾnyhw*
> *lʾsrth*
> *[..] wlʾ[s]rth*

Although Wiggins (1993: 171, 188) claims that the interpretation of this text is so uncertain that the information about Yahweh and his asherah which many scholars find in it should be disregarded, this is an unduly pessimistic judgment in the light of Hadley's careful examination of the evidence (1987a: 50–61; 2000: 84–102). Wiggins wrote some years before the publication of Hadley's book, but he used the thesis on which the book is based. Hadley (2000: 86) offers this translation:

> Uriyahu the rich wrote it.
> Blessed be Uriyahu by Yahweh
> for from his enemies by his (YHWH's) asherah he (YHWH) has saved him.

by Oniyahu
by his asherah
and by his a[she]rah

Her alternative rendering of line 3, '(and) by his asherah, for from his enemies he has saved him' (on which see Hadley 1987a: 56–57; 2000: 96), need not be considered here, since its adoption would not affect the argument of this essay.

Hadley's comprehensive treatment of the issues raised by the study of this text shows that there is a strong case for holding that Yahweh and his asherah are associated at Khirbet el-Qom. It is not clear, however, whether lines 5 and 6 form part of this inscription. They contain one, and perhaps two, further instances of 'by his asherah', but, if they once mentioned Yahweh, his name has not survived.

2. *The Meaning of* 'šrth *in these Texts*

The word 'šrth has been thought to be the name of a goddess, a title, or a term which describes a cultic object. Theories which have been advanced[1] have been discussed in detail by Emerton (1982: 13–18; 1999) and Hadley (2000: 4–11, 16–18, 46–47, 50–51, 98–99, 104–105), and it is unnecessary to cover this ground again. The word 'šrth may be analysed as the noun 'šrh + the third-person masculine singular pronominal suffix, which has the name Yahweh as its antecedent. Emerton (1982: 14–15, 18–19) notes that, while there are reasons for counselling caution 'in stating what was not possible in Hebrew ... nevertheless, the use of a suffix with a personal name is not in accordance with Hebrew idiom as far as we know it'. He argues that it would be 'unwise to interpret the newly-found inscriptions in such a way unless there is no satisfactory alternative', and he therefore prefers to understand the asherah of these inscriptions as 'the wooden symbol of the goddess' Asherah, a meaning which is amply attested in the Old Testament (e.g. Judg. 6.25, 26, 28, 30; 1 Kgs 14.15; 2 Kgs 17.10). Lemche (1998: 50–51) agrees that this 'seems obvious', even though, in accordance with his general approach to the Old Testament, he supposes that this is to rely on 'secondary evidence'. He also says, apparently inconsistently, that what an asherah was is 'so far unknown'.

The significance of the pronominal suffix 'his' will be discussed later in this essay.

---

1. But cf. also Zevit's recent defence (2001: 363–66) of his belief that 'šrth should be vocalized 'ašērātā(h) and Tropper's advocacy (2001: 100–102) of the form 'ašir(a)tā (the final ā being regarded as a case-ending), both of which are taken to be the name of the goddess who is known in the Old Testament as Asherah.

3. *The Goddess Athirat*

Epic texts from Ugarit which were written in the Late Bronze Age, but whose contents may be older than this, furnish information about the goddess Athirat (e.g. KTU^2 1.4.I.14; 1.6.I.40). The general consensus is that Athirat is to be identified with the goddess Asherah, who, according to the Old Testament, was worshipped in Palestine in the Iron Age (cf. Day 2000: 47). Lemche (1998: 50–51) agrees that the word 'asherah' at Kuntillet ʿAjrud and, if the reading is correct, at Khirbet el-Qom should be compared to both the name of the goddess Athirat and the name of a ruler of Amurru, ʿAbdi-Ashirta, 'the servant of Asherah', which is found in the Amarna letters (e.g. 60.2; 71.17). Attempts to dissociate Athirat and Asherah are reviewed by Hadley (2000: 8–11, 14) and Day (2000: 47–48), who find them unsatisfactory. A further theory, which was advanced by McCarter (1987: 146–49) and which is mentioned in passing by Hadley (2000: 137) but which is not discussed by Day (2000), will be examined below.

4. *What was the Social Context of these Texts?*

Meshel (1993: 1463–64) holds that Kuntillet ʿAjrud was 'a religious center' where 'a small group of priests' who 'provided cultic services for travelers' lived, though he concedes that 'the lack of objects related directly to cult, as well as the settlement's secular plan, indicate that the site was not a temple'. This hypothesis is reviewed by Hadley (1993; 2000: 106–20), together with the suggestions that at Kuntillet ʿAjrud there was either a scribal school (Lemaire 1981: 25–32; cf. Hadley 1993: 121–22; 2000: 114–15) or a shrine where prophets lived (Catastini 1982; cf. Hadley 1993: 120–21; 2000: 112–14). Hadley shows that these proposals are unconvincing and argues strongly (1993: 123; 2000: 120) that Kuntillet ʿAjrud was 'a desert way station, similar to the biblical *mālôn* [cf. Gen. 42.27; 43.21; Exod. 4.24; Jer. 9.1, ET 9.2], which could be used by anyone ... who sought food, water, and a safe place to spend the night while travelling'. But there is force in Zevit's contention (2001: 374–75 n. 47) that Hadley is wrong to hold that Kuntillet ʿAjrud must have been either a religious centre or a desert way station. A large inscribed stone bowl which is said to weigh around 200 kg was found there (Meshel 1978 and Illustration 10). It is a votive, and, whatever its exact weight, it is unquestionably heavy. Its presence at such a remote site is unlikely to be due to chance. Thus Kuntillet ʿAjrud appears to have had a religious dimension of some kind which goes beyond the 'religious ambience' detected by Hadley (2000: 108, 111; cf. 1993: 119). But it is unnecessary to claim with Zevit (2001: 374) that the site's '*raison d'être*' was cultic'. Just as religion was an integral part of life, so votives could have been deposited in part of a structure that was not primarily a religious centre.

Considerations of space make a full discussion of the origin of those who built and used the buildings at Kuntillet ʿAjrud impossible here. I hope to justify the conclusions in the next two paragraphs in Mastin (forthcoming).

Since 'no "Negeb-type pottery" supposedly associated with the nomadic inhabitants of the area' was found (Meshel 1992: 106), those who were in charge of the buildings presumably came from elsewhere. There are three texts written in a script which Renz (1995: 57–58) holds may be Phoenician, though Dijkstra (2001a: 22) may be right to think of a link with north Palestine rather than with Phoenicia. One of these texts is illegible, but the language of the other two is Hebrew. Hardly any Phoenician pottery was found. Phoenicians may have been among the artists who were responsible for the murals and the drawings on the pithoi (Keel and Uehlinger 1992: 244, ET 1998: 217), but, even if this is the case, there is no evidence that Phoenicians often travelled to Kuntillet ʿAjrud.

Names such as ʾAmaryau (ʾmryw) and Yoʿasah (ywʿśh), which mean respectively 'Yahweh has spoken' and 'Yahweh has made', together with six other names in texts from Kuntillet ʿAjrud which include the divine name Yahweh, all begin or end with the theophoric element spelt *yw* (Davies 1991: 80–81 [§§ 8.011–8.013, 8.017, 8.021]; Renz 1995: 56–57, 61–62 [KAgr(9):3–5, 8.1, 9.1]; Zevit 2001: 398). This is a north Palestinian spelling, though Zevit (2001: 381) correctly notes that it is 'uncommon but known in the south'. But Cross (1983: 57 = 2003: 108) states that it appears there during the eighth century BCE 'in a small group of seals', and none of the examples from Kuntillet ʿAjrud is on a seal. The absence of the south Palestinian spelling *yhw* at Kuntillet ʿAjrud and the presence of as many as eight examples of the spelling *yw* suggests strongly that these men were from north Palestine. Moreover, if a substantial number of travellers were from south Palestine, the only pottery they left behind which came from that area consisted of large vessels which seem to have contained supplies to be stored at Kuntillet ʿAjrud. It is more likely that the small vessels from north Palestine point to the identity of those who built Kuntillet ʿAjrud and used it on their journeys, and that the pithoi, many of the other storage vessels, and whatever they contained were acquired in the south and so were transported for as short a distance as possible. Finally, the invocation of 'Yahweh of Samaria' in the blessing on pithos A, if this is how *yhwh šmrn* should be understood,[2] is a further pointer to a link between Kuntillet ʿAjrud and north Palestine. Presumably this blessing was written by, or on behalf of, someone who worshipped Yahweh in Samaria (whether the city itself or the region

2. Cf. Renz 1995: 61 n.2.

surrounding it) and who thought it appropriate while he was travelling to call on Yahweh using the forms to which he was accustomed. Taken together, the names with a north Palestinian spelling, the pottery, and the worship of Yahweh of Samaria are evidence that Kuntillet ʿAjrud was built, manned, and used by those who lived in north Palestine.

The construction of the buildings at Kuntillet ʿAjrud in an inhospitable area would have required careful organization and considerable expenditure. Moreover, Keel and Uehlinger (1992: 278, ET 1998: 245) show that 'the official character of the site' is indicated by the wall paintings, which 'are intentionally there as a part of the architectural decor', and which include 'the portrayal of a (besieged?) city' and 'the representation of an enthroned prince with lotus blossom'. Thus, while allowing for the probability that the blessings on the pithoi reflect the outlook of those who used Kuntillet ʿAjrud rather than of those who built it, it would be unwise to assume that these texts are evidence for folk religion. Lemche (1998: 52–53) accepts the testimony of Assyrian inscriptions that there was a state in north Palestine from at least the middle of the ninth century BCE and that from at least the beginning of the eighth century BCE its capital was Samaria. In view of the links between Kuntillet ʿAjrud and north Palestine noted above, it is reasonable to suppose that this state was the authority which established the way station. If Yahweh is indeed called 'Yahweh of Samaria' in the blessing on pithos A, this is *prima facie* evidence for a temple of Yahweh at the capital Samaria, unless it be thought that Samaria is a region here, which would make Yahweh the god of the state in north Palestine (van der Toorn 1993: 533). In either case Yahweh would appear to have been a god of some importance, and, though this cannot be demonstrated, the information we have is consistent with the belief that Yahweh's asherah would have been regarded as a perfectly acceptable feature of his cult in north Palestine.

Not only is Khirbet el-Qom in south Palestine, but also both of the names in Inscription 3, Uriyahu (lines 1 and 2) and Oniyahu (line 4), end with the theophoric element spelt *yhw*, a form found exclusively in the south. Uriyahu is described as 'the rich' ($h^{\epsilon}\check{s}r$), and, though the correctness of this reading has been disputed, it is defended convincingly by Hadley (1987a: 53; 2000: 87–88), who adds, 'if Uriyahu were rich..., he could afford to have an inscription made for him'. The inscription is characterized by Dever (1969–70: 162) as 'more a graffito than a true lapidary inscription' and the craftsmanship is of poor quality, but the mere existence of a tomb inscription, if this is what it is, would support the belief that Uriyahu was well-to-do. Zevit (2001: 368, 370) holds that the tomb in which Uriyahu and others were buried 'was excavated at some significant expense'. It has, however, been claimed, most recently by Parker (2003: 278–82), that Uriyahu had used 'the tomb as a hiding place'. Parker supposes that the text is a copy of 'an inscription in a public place or sanctuary' which recorded Uriyahu's gratitude for his deliverance, put in the place where this happened. It could, however, have been incised while he was hiding there. Parker (2003: 261–78, 282), who adduces other inscriptions from southern Palestine which he thinks should be attributed to people hiding in a cave or a tomb, maintains that Uriyahu is one of several 'prominent members of Judean society temporarily in danger of their lives', who 'fled to hide in tombs'. Similarly, from a different perspective, Miller (2000a: 51, 236 n.15), who supposes that this is Uriyahu's tomb, concludes that he was 'probably a part of the upper class'. Thus not only is Yahweh associated with 'his asherah' in the giving of blessing in southern Palestine, but here too it was 'not just the general populace or common people' who 'regarded the asherah cult object as a legitimate part of Yahweh piety' (Miller 2000a: 52).

Further support for such a cult in southern Palestine may be provided by one, and perhaps two, inscriptions on pithos B at Kuntillet ʿAjrud which contain the phrase 'by Yahweh of (the) Teman and by his asherah', unless the hesitations of a few scholars about one or both of these readings and the identification of a place name in them are justified (cf. Conrad 1988: 563 n.5a; Scagliarini 1989: 207–209 and n.61; Ahituv 1992: 156; Renz 1995: 62 and n.5; Hadley 1987b: 187–88; 2000: 130). According to Hadley (1987b: 187; 2000: 130), Meshel says that three other texts from Kuntillet ʿAjrud mention Yahweh of Teman, but two of these are unpublished. The third text is the inscription on plaster which was discussed above, and, as was noted there, it would be unwise to rely on it as evidence until it is published in full. Despite the reservations of Conrad (1988: 563 n.5a), Scagliarini (1989: 207–208 and n.61), and Renz (1995: 62 and n.5), it is generally agreed both that *tmn* should be read in the longer text on pithos B (Davies 1991: 81 [§ 8.021.1]; cf. Renz 1995: 62 [KAgr(9): 9.5]), and that this is the place name Teman. The reading in the shorter text on pithos B (Davies 1991: 80 [§ 8.016]; Renz 1995: 64 [KAgr(9): 10.2]) is less certain (cf. Ahituv and Hadley). Some scholars believe that this shows that there was a cult of Yahweh and his asherah either in the south of Palestine or in Edom (cf. Hadley 1987b: 186; 2000: 127–29). But Emerton (1982: 9–10, 13, 19), who holds that Teman 'probably denotes a region of Edom', compares Hab. 3.3 and thinks it likely that the appeal is not to a god worshipped in Teman, but to a god who had come from Teman. Because of this 'the southern region…belongs in a special way to him', and so it was appropriate for ʾAmaryau 'to recall the one Yahweh's traditional connexion with Teman when he invoked a blessing on a friend'. If this is how the phrase 'Yahweh of Teman' should be understood, the inscription would not corroborate the evidence from Khirbet el-Qom, though, despite the circularity of the argument, it would indicate that the tradition attested in Hab. 3.3; Zech. 9.14 that Yahweh had come from the south was known at least as early as c. 800 BCE.

It is important not to claim too much on the basis of the limited amount we know. Dever (2001: 187) unwisely says 'that in *non*-biblical texts' mention of Yahweh's asherah 'was common, an acceptable expression of Israelite-Judean Yahwism throughout much of the Monarchy' (his italics). But the evidence is too sparse to show that mention of Yahweh's asherah was common, and it covers the period from c. 800 BCE to, at most, slightly over a hundred years later, not 'much of the Monarchy'. Yet the data from Kuntillet ʿAjrud and Khirbet el-Qom demonstrate that at least some in both north and south Palestine associated Yahweh and 'his asherah'. In addition, in both cases there are reasons for thinking that such a cult should not be dismissed as of marginal importance.

5. *Was the Goddess Asherah Worshipped in Palestine during the Iron Age?*

It is generally agreed that the word *ʾᵃšērâ* is normally used in the Old Testament to refer to a symbol of the goddess Asherah, and not to the goddess herself. Smith (1990: 17–18, 89) thinks that the phrase *šādayim wārāḥam* in Gen. 49.25, which, comparing Vawter (1955: 15–16), he translates 'Breasts-and-Womb', 'might be' the title of a goddess, whom he identifies as Asherah. Thus 'Asherah may have been the consort of El ... at some early point in Israelite religion'. But Smith (1990: 89–93) maintains that 'the evidence for Asherah as an Israelite goddess during the monarchy is minimal at best', and he finds only one 'clear reference' to her in the Old Testament, in a phrase in 1 Kgs 18.19, 'the four hundred prophets of Asherah' (*nᵉbîʾê hāʾᵃšērâ ʾarbaʿ mēʾôt*), which he regards as a gloss which 'perhaps belongs to the seventh or sixth century' BCE. This phrase is evidence that Asherah was thought to be a goddess, conceivably in the reign of Ahab in the mid-ninth century BCE, or perhaps, with Smith, late in the Iron Age, or even, with the revisionists, in the Persian or the Hellenistic period. It is reasonable to suppose that she is the same goddess who is called Athirat at Ugarit in the Late Bronze Age (see above), and there is a presumption that the later the phrase is dated, the longer it can be expected that the goddess will have been known.

Since there is one 'clear reference' to Asherah in the Old Testament, it would not be surprising if there were to be other references, but Smith (1990: 90–92) claims that Judg. 3.7; 2 Kgs 21.7; 23.4; Jer. 2.27, which are often thought to speak of the goddess, should not be taken in this way. Day (2000: 64–65, 43–45) agrees that this is so for Jer. 2.27, but argues strongly that in Judg. 3.7; 2 Kgs 21.7; 23.4, to which he adds 1 Kgs 15.13 (which Smith does not examine), the asherah is the goddess herself. Considerations of space make it impossible to discuss these verses here, but Smith seems unduly reluctant to allow that the goddess may be meant. It is of interest that Winter (1983: 558), one of the four scholars whose general position on this issue Smith (1990: 93) claims to share, says that 1 Kgs 15.13 and 2 Kgs 21.7 can be understood best if the asherah which they mention is the goddess.

Tigay (1986: 13, 71, 9; 1987: 163, 168, 161) observes that, 'with one or two exceptions (Isis and possibly ʾdt)', the second of which he thinks should be explained differently, 'no goddess appears' as an element in names of 'pre-exilic Israelites ... known from Hebrew inscriptions and foreign inscriptions referring to Israel'. He regards this as an indication that there was hardly any worship of goddesses in pre-exilic Israel or Judah. Yet, though Athirat was unquestionably worshipped at Ugarit (de Moor 1970: 191, 210), there are only three examples of a proper name which includes the theophorous element ʾatrt in texts found there (Gröndahl 1967: 316, cf. 103). Pardee (1988: 141) notes that 'there are many serious differences between the ritual texts taken as a whole, the mythological texts, and the theophoric elements of proper names' at Ugarit. This important point must be set against the absence of Asherah's name from the North-West Semitic inscriptions and onomastica from the period c. 1000–500 BCE which are surveyed by Lemaire, who discounts the evidence discussed in this essay and renders *lʾšrt*, found on a storage jar at Tel Miqne, 'for the sanctuary' (1994: 135, 146, 148). If Cross (1973: 28–35) is right to identify the Punic goddess Tannit with Asherah, this silence would be explained, at least in part. Moreover, an inscription indicates that Tannit was worshipped at Sarepta in Phoenicia in the seventh century BCE (Pritchard 1982: 84, 89, 91–92). But Barré (1983: 58–61, 169–72) and Day (1986: 388–89, 396–97) have shown that this identification is implausible, though Barré holds that 'it is entirely possible that certain traits of ʾAšerah were inherited by Tanit'.

Considerations of space make it impossible to do more than illustrate the problems involved in interpreting other relevant archaeological material. In 1968 a tenth-century cultic stand was discovered at Taanach (Lapp 1969: 42–44, including a photograph; for a drawing, see, e.g., Keel and Uehlinger 1992: 179, ET 1998: 159). I am grateful to Ms F.E. Fell for pointing out to me that it was found with other objects which could be cultic. In the lowest of its four registers a naked woman touches (?) the ears of two lions, while in the third register from the bottom two ibexes stand on their hind legs, one on each side of a sacred tree, and nibble the upper branches. It is generally agreed that the sacred tree is an asherah, a conclusion supported by the inscription 'An offering to my [Lad]y ʾElat' (*šy l[rb]ty ʾlt*) on a Late Bronze Age ewer found at Lachish (Cross 1954: 19–22 = 2003: 310–12; Hestrin 1987a: 74; 1987b: 212–14, 220; Hadley 2000: 156–60). 'ʾElat' is a name or title of Athirat at Ugarit (e.g. *KTU²* 1.3.V.37; 1.14.IV.35), and on the ewer this word is directly above a stylized tree flanked by two ibexes. It is also generally agreed that the naked woman in the lowest register of the cultic stand is a goddess.

Majority opinion holds that she is Asherah, perhaps largely because of a widespread belief that Asherah is the 'Lion Lady' (Cross 1973: 33–34), though this may well not be correct (Barré 1983: 69, 175; Wiggins 1991). By contrast, Beck (1994: 363, 368) says of this stand that 'the motif of a tree and goats has a long history in the ancient Near East, which goes back to the third millennium BCE.... It is generally interpreted as related to fertility, although there is no direct link to any specific deity', while 'the female figure ... is endowed with supernatural powers; she is possibly a goddess'. Despite this dissenting opinion, however, the scholarly consensus is that it remains probable that the stand is evidence for the worship of Asherah in a public cult in tenth-century Taanach.

The so-called Astarte plaques will not be discussed here, since the plaques 'which depict goddesses are not generally found in Palestine in levels dating from beyond the Late Bronze Age' (Hadley 2000: 194). There are, however, pillar figurines, most of which belong to the eighth and seventh centuries BCE, which have a pillar base that supports the upper body of a woman with prominent breasts (Keel and Uehlinger 1992: 373, ET 1998: 326). Kletter (1996: 73, 81) argues that, if all the Judaean pillar figurines 'represented one identical figure ... [and] had one basic function', which he thinks was probably to bestow '"plenty"', 'the simplest and most logical explanation' is that they represent Asherah, though this 'is not proven and should not be taken for granted'. It would be reasonable to understand pillar figurines from north Palestine in the same way. But other views are held. Thus, for example, Meyers (1988: 162) supposes that pillar figurines are votives 'expressing the quest for human fertility' and that they 'seem to depict human females rather than deific ones'. When Dever (2001: 197), who incautiously identifies Asherah with the Mother Goddess, asserts that 'we now know' (because it is supported by archaeological evidence) that Asherah 'enjoyed a vigorous life throughout the Monarchy', he puts the matter far too strongly.

Korpel (2001: 148) claims that, since 'no professionally executed graven image of the goddess Asherah has been found in Israel', 'if the figurines do represent goddesses, ... they nevertheless functioned only within the *family religion*, not within the official cult' (his italics). This is no doubt true as a statement about the figurines. But Hendel (1997: 212–18) lists some thirteen examples of representations of male gods from Iron Age Palestine which could be 'legitimate candidates for images of Yahweh'. Both because there are so few of these and because the sacred pole was Asherah's symbol, it would be unwise to suppose that failure to discover a 'professionally executed graven image' of Asherah means that she was not worshipped in the official cult. It should be noted that, though Uehlinger (1997: 102–39) assembles material which he thinks indicates that anthropomorphic cult statuary was well known in Palestine throughout the Iron Age, Na'aman (1999: 393–94) objects that the nature of the evidence is such that Uehlinger's case cannot succeed.

Lemche (1998: 51), like Smith, imagines that probably Asherah 'had lost her quality as a personalized deity' in the first millennium BCE in Palestine, though this position is not shared by all the revisionists. It is widely, though not universally, agreed that Asherah's name lies behind the word 'his asherah' in the inscriptions from Kuntillet ʿAjrud and Khirbet el-Qom (e.g. Day 2000: 47), and there is non-biblical evidence which is consistent with the theory that the worship of Asherah continued in Palestine during the Iron Age. There is also a small amount of biblical evidence that such worship persisted. The reasons given by Tigay for supposing that goddesses were hardly ever worshipped in pre-exilic Israel or Judah, and by Korpel for holding that Asherah was not worshipped as part of an official cult, are not persuasive. It is likely that the worship of Asherah was part of the religious scene when the inscriptions which are being discussed in this essay were composed.

6. *What was the Place of Yahweh's Asherah in the Cult?*

It is frequently said that the worship of Asherah was a domestic cult, patronized mainly by women, and popular in character. This, however, is to rely heavily on the evidence of the pillar figurines. Thus, for example, Kletter (1996: 61, 81) notes that Judaean pillar figurines are usually found in domestic contexts, though some are found in tombs. He observes that they 'were cheap, everyday objects, representing the goddess [Asherah] in private houses, in front of ordinary people (chiefly, though not only)'. Moreover, Dever (2001: 193), among others, under the influence of feminist ideology, claims that 'it would not be surprising if Yahweh ... seemed remote [to women], unconcerned with women's needs, or even hostile', so that 'women may have felt closer to a female deity'. It is highly probable that distinctive women's needs would have found distinctive religious expression, but Kletter (1996: 78) pertinently comments that 'if Judean women had no "feminist consciousness", possibly they would not have felt oppressed by the "official male religion", and would not turn to "female domestic cult"'. Professor G.I. Davies kindly points out to me that, as far as we know, all those mentioned in the texts from Kuntillet ʿAjrud and Khirbet el-Qom either as asking for blessing and help for others from Yahweh's asherah, or as actual or potential recipients of blessing and help, are men. Moreover, on one interpretation of the text from Khirbet el-Qom, 'for Uriyahu the inscribed thanksgiving attests his life-long experience of being sustained and kept by Yahweh (and his ʾ*ašērāh*)' (Miller 1981: 319 = 2000: 219). Too sharp a distinction should not be drawn between Yahweh as the god for men and Asherah as the goddess for women.

The term 'popular religion' often carries pejorative overtones, implying that other forms of religion are far superior. Dever (2001: 196), however, rightly gives a much more positive account of popular religion, and concludes by saying that 'it attempts to secure the same benefits as all religion, i.e., the individual's sense of integration with nature and society, of health and prosperity, and of ultimate well-being'. Kletter (1996: 81) suggests that 'the function of the Asherah figurines was possibly as a protecting figure in domestic houses, more likely a figure which bestowed "plenty", especially in the domain of female lives (but not necessarily used by women only)'. The blessing and protection bestowed through Yahweh's asherah according to the texts from Kuntillet ʿAjrud and Khirbet el-Qom may be compared. While it is important not to confuse information which these texts provide with theories about the possible significance of the pillar figurines, there are also similarities between the cult reflected in the texts and the cult which is assumed to have flourished in private houses.

In the decade after the publication of the texts from Kuntillet ʿAjrud it was not uncommon for the cult of Yahweh 'and his asherah' to be characterized as a form of highly syncretistic popular religion which flourished in a remote area and was protected by its isolation from interference by the proponents of a more orthodox Yahwism. Such views are rarer now, though Dijkstra (2001b: 120, cf. 97–98, 104) believes that 'veneration of YHWH and his Asherah … perhaps, occasionally, … had a place in the official cult'. Much more than this should be claimed. The mention of Yahweh and his asherah at Khirbet el-Qom shows that this cult was known in south Palestine, where, as has been noted above, it had as an adherent a man of some standing, while the invocation of 'Yahweh of Samaria and his asherah' at Kuntillet ʿAjrud should be seen in the light of the official state cult in north Palestine. It is self-evident that the Deuteronomic orthodoxy which dominates the Old Testament in its final form provides a quite different picture, but it has been recognized for a long while that this picture is not objective. For example, the Deuteronomistic history regularly condemns the kings of the northern kingdom of Israel for walking 'in all the way of Jeroboam the son of Nebat' (e.g. 1 Kgs 16.26), but modern scholarship wonders whether his sins are no more than the revival of authentic northern traditions (e.g. Cross 1973: 73–75, 198–99). Moreover, because the Old Testament in its canonical form is monotheistic in outlook, it is implied that true religion has always been monotheistic, though mainstream biblical scholarship finds the earliest expression of full monotheistic belief during the exile, in the oracles of Deutero-Isaiah. In addition, when the books of the Old Testament which purport to describe events before the exile are taken at face value, there are many gaps in our knowledge. Under these circumstances, it may be over-hasty to conclude that the association of

Yahweh and his asherah would necessarily have been heterodox. The possibility that the texts which refer to Yahweh's asherah provide an insight into normative religious attitudes in Palestine in the eighth century BCE should be taken seriously.

If, as has been claimed above, the asherah of the inscriptions is not the goddess herself, but her wooden symbol, this might seem to make little difference in practice, since the goddess and her symbol cannot be separated, and 'naming the cult symbol of the deity is synonymous with naming the deity herself' (Olyan 1988: 32). Similarly Hadley (2000: 207) holds that, if Asherah was still worshipped when Inscription 3 from Khirbet el-Qom was composed, this text 'would ... indicate a blessing by Yahweh and the representation of his consort which stood in the temple'. It must, however, be explained why the asherah is referred to as Yahweh's asherah. Emerton (1982: 15, 18) suggests that this is because it 'was sometimes associated with the altar or temple of Yahweh', and he notes both that 'Yahweh ... remains more important than the symbol of the goddess associated with him' and that the singling out of the asherah 'to be used alongside the name of Yahweh in blessings at Kuntillet ʿAjrud underlines its special importance in at least one form of popular Yahwism'. It is, however, strange that the cult symbol of a goddess should be spoken of as if it belonged to Yahweh, and a theory which associated the asherah more directly with Yahweh would be more satisfactory.

McCarter (1987: 149) argues that 'the asherah of Yahweh' 'means "the Trace [i.e., visible token] of Yahweh", that is, "the Sign/Mark of Yahweh" or perhaps even "the Effective/Active Presence of Yahweh"'. Thus 'in the cult Yahweh's *ʾăšērâ*, his trace, sign, or effective presence, was marked with an upright wooden pole, called an asherah'. The asherah was then personified, and came to be thought of as Yahweh's consort. This development took place within Yahwism, and so an Israelite goddess who originated independently of the Canaanite goddess Athirat came into existence. McCarter's theory depends on the etymology which he proposes for the word *ʾăšērâ*, but Smith (1990: 87–88, 109 n.65) demonstrates that this is not tenable and also offers further cogent criticisms of McCarter's position. Like McCarter, Miller (2000a: 35–36) believes that the asherah of the inscriptions is 'a cult object of Yahweh marking his presence' which possessed 'some kind of separate identity, related to Yahweh' but which 'does not have to be the goddess Asherah or even the goddess's cult symbol'. For Miller, too, there is movement towards creating an independent figure out of, in his opinion, 'the feminine dimension of deity'. But Miller's hypothesis can be maintained only if there is a persuasive case for identifying Yahweh's asherah as something other than the wooden cult object mentioned in the Old Testament. Several suggestions have been made, but, as has been noted above, serious objections can be raised to all of them. It is unsatisfactory for Miller to say that 'the term "asherah" does not have to be understood as referring to the cult symbol of the goddess Asherah' without providing an alternative explanation.

It has been argued above that the goddess Athirat is to be identified with Asherah, who was probably worshipped in Palestine during at least the first half of the Iron Age. This judgment is not shared by Miller (2000a: 35), but it is confirmed by the difficulty experienced in finding a suitable alternative meaning for the word $^{\prime a}\check{s}\bar{e}r\hat{a}$. It then becomes straightforward to suppose both that the goddess gave her name to the wooden pole which represented her, and that subsequently this pole became part of Yahweh's cult. This could have been facilitated by its presence in Yahweh's sanctuary. Both Smith (1990: 19, 94) and Lemche (1998: 51) think that, though the worship of the goddess herself died out in Palestine, according to Smith, 'perhaps as early as the period of the Judges', and, according to Lemche, probably before the first millennium BCE, what had been the goddess's symbol continued in use within Yahweh's cult. But if the worship of Asherah survived longer than this in Palestine, a similar development could equally well have occurred. It is unnecessary, and would probably be unwise, to suppose that identical religious beliefs were held throughout Palestine during even a part of the Iron Age. There is no reason to try to harmonize apparently conflicting religious views, provided there is evidence for a variety of outlook.

Miller (2000a: 35) cites with approval the claim made by Keel and Uehlinger (1992: 263–68, ET 1998: 232–36) that, in the ninth and eighth centuries BCE, the stylized tree, which is normally taken to be the symbol of a goddess, 'even more frequently represents a gender-neutral symbol of numinous power'. They maintain that this 'iconographically important evidence ... can best be understood if we interpret the Iron Age IIB *asherah* as a *mediating entity* associated with Yahweh, rather than as a personal, independently active, female deity' (their italics). If this theory is sound, it would be easier to explain how an asherah could come to be the channel of Yahweh's blessing. By contrast, Hadley (2000: 99, 105, 206–207) says it is possible 'that by the eighth century BCE Yahweh had begun to absorb the worship of Asherah into his cult', with the result that the asherah may have become the hypostasis 'of Yahweh's benevolence and succour', of his 'nurturing concern for his people', or of 'fertility aspects' which he took over as the worship of the goddess Asherah came to an end. Whichever of these positions is preferred, the difficulties encountered by other explanations of the phrase 'his asherah' are avoided.

Becking (2001: 191–92) describes inclusive monotheism as 'a form of religion that claims universal veneration of one deity by the community but does not charge others with this obligation', while in exclusive monotheism 'the veneration of one deity ... is presented as the only possibility for all human beings'. This is not how these terms are used in this essay. Exclusive monotheism is more accurately defined as the belief that one god, and only one god, exists, but without there necessarily being a requirement that all human beings should worship him. Inclusive monotheism involves the acquisition by one god of the spheres of activity of other gods and the absorption of their powers. Although the inscriptions from Kuntillet 'Ajrud and Khirbet el-Qom say nothing about other gods or goddesses, if Yahweh was absorbing the worship of Asherah into his cult, or if he had acquired a cultic symbol which had once belonged to her, this would represent a stage in the growth of inclusive monotheism.

7. *The Views of the Revisionists*

The revisionists constitute a school which shares a general approach, but whose members disagree among themselves on certain issues. From time to time views held by Lemche have been noted in this essay, but several of the revisionists, among whom are Garbini (1988: 59–60), Niehr (1990: 190), and Thompson (1999: 176), think that some or all of the inscriptions which speak of 'Yahweh and his asherah' refer to the goddess Asherah, who is to be understood as Yahweh's consort. This conclusion is also reached by a number of scholars who do not belong to the revisionist school. If they are right, the inscriptions are evidence for polytheism in Palestine in the eighth century BCE. It has, however, been claimed above that it is preferable to understand the asherahs of these inscriptions as wooden cultic symbols, and not as the goddess Asherah herself, and the question which will be addressed here is how far such an interpretation is consistent with the theories of the revisionists about the way in which religious belief developed in Palestine.

Attention will be concentrated on the views of Lemche and Thompson, whose contributions are central to the debate with the revisionists, together with Niehr's hypothesis about the development of Yahwism, since Lemche (1998: 185 n.74) and Davies (1995: 92 n.3) refer to it with approval, and Thompson (1999: e.g. 298, 383) has apparently been influenced by it.

As has already been indicated, Lemche (1998: 50–51) is in broad agreement with much of the argument of this essay. He concludes, however, that 'it is too early to speak about monotheism in any form' in Palestine during the Iron Age, though 'there is ... certainly a strong tendency toward a strengthening of the position of the chief god of the pantheon, to the cost of his minor colleagues, male as well as female deities'. But if, as Lemche believes, Asherah was probably no longer 'a personalized deity' in Palestine throughout the first millennium BCE, it is difficult to know how such a development can be detected, and it is also unclear where Lemche obtains information about any deity other than Asherah. He continues, 'this process towards monotheism was working in other places as well. It may even be possible to speak about a definite religious trend, which was in the Persian and Hellenistic-Roman period to develop into a monotheism of the kind understood by posterity as the belief in one god only. The decisive steps in that development have, however, not much to do with the Israelites and Judeans of the Iron Age'.

If the inscriptions which associate Yahweh and his asherah had belonged to the Persian or the Hellenistic period, Lemche might have been expected to cite them as examples of inclusive monotheism. He observes (1998: 74) that there is no 'solid evidence' (by which he means extra-biblical evidence) 'of a monotheistic Yahwism in, say, the twelfth to the eighth centuries B.C.E.', and contemporary mainstream biblical scholarship would, on the whole, agree that full monotheism cannot be identified until later than this. But the inscriptions which point to the existence of a different kind of monotheism in both the north and the south of Palestine in the eighth century BCE should be taken seriously as a sign that a significant development in the religion of Palestine had already begun. Lemche (1998: 165–66) distances 'the Israel found on the pages of the Old Testament' from 'the sociopolitical and religious realities of Palestine in the Iron Age', and he gives as an example of the difference the fact that Yahweh was 'related to the female deity Asherah in some way'. It is true that such a relationship would not have been tolerated by deuteronomic orthodoxy, but it has been argued above that the attestation of the worship of Asherah in the Old Testament is historically reliable. By combining this material with evidence provided by the inscriptions, a realistic account of the significance of Asherah in Palestine during the Iron Age can be given.

Thompson (1999) will be discussed here, since, as far as I know, he has not modified his views in any subsequent publication. He says that, although some 'traditions and fragments of traditions' which have been incorporated into the Old Testament 'have known roots even as early as the Assyrian period' (295), it was not until the middle of the second century BCE that there was 'the beginning of a comprehensive collection of the tradition', which led to the formation of the Old Testament (294). He considers that exclusive monotheism was a reaction to Seleucid attitudes, and 'became a rallying cry of traditionalists and nationalists against the empire' (296–97). By contrast, inclusive monotheism 'included many polytheistic traditions and metaphors for understanding the divine' (297). It 'was based on a reinterpretation of Palestine's religious past' (254). Everywhere in the ancient world, 'from at least the twilight of the Assyrian empire in the seventh century BCE ... [there was] a growing awareness of the patent irrelevance of tradition past' (298). It was recognized in Palestine 'that the world of gods was a world created by us'

(300, cf. 299, 382, 384), and so 'one of the central functions' of the Old Testament was the reinterpretation of 'no longer viable personal deities of Palestine's past in terms of a critical perception of both transcendent and ineffable truth' (388).

This approach, however, is too rationalistic and fails to understand how, apart from a few philosophers, people in the ancient Near East perceived the divine world. It was seen as parallel to the human world, and the one was assumed to reflect the other. Thus the conquest of southern Mesopotamia by Hammurabi (c. 1728–1686 BCE) was believed to be due to a decision taken by the leading gods to bestow a higher rank on Babylon's god Marduk (Jacobsen 1949: 207–208; cf. *ANET,* 164). What happened on earth was intimately connected with what happened in heaven, and the children of the Enlightenment should not underestimate the piety of earlier generations. Moreover, Thompson (92) maintains that, 'beginning first in the Assyrian period', there was a 'growing dominance of a more inclusive understanding of the divine as universal spirit'. As was noted above, Thompson thinks that the inscriptions which speak of Yahweh's asherah are evidence for polytheism, but if, as he says, the 'defining concept of inclusive monotheism finds its home in ongoing efforts to interpret polytheistic conceptions in universal and transcendent terms' (300), presumably in principle inclusive monotheism could be accommodated in Thompson's survey of the religious history of Palestine at a much earlier date than the one he selects.

Niehr (1990) supposes that the texts from Ugarit are not of primary importance for understanding the religion of Palestine in the Iron Age. He holds that the clue to the development of Yahwism before the exile lies in the recognition that Yahweh came to be identified with Baal of the Heavens, who, Niehr claims, was worshipped then as the supreme god in Syria and Phoenicia. But Engelken (1996) has shown that Niehr has exaggerated the rôle of Baal of the Heavens in this area, Röllig (1999: 151) observes that this god 'appears relatively late in the vicinity of Palestine', and Day (2000: 15 n. 11) argues convincingly for 'much greater continuity with the older Canaanite mythology from Ugarit' in Palestine than in Phoenicia and Syria. Niehr's hypothesis is unconvincing, but even so his reminder that there may have been influence on Palestinian religion from, in particular, Phoenicia, is timely.

To some extent the revisionists are trying to make bricks without straw when they attempt to describe possible developments in the religion of Iron Age Palestine, and Niehr's theory does not succeed in filling the gap caused by their rejection of the Old Testament as a source of reliable information about this period. The texts from Kuntillet ʿAjrud and Khirbet el-Qom may, however, reasonably be regarded as evidence for inclusive monotheism in Palestine in the eighth century BCE, several centuries before the revisionists identify it there.

8. Are there Analogies in Mesopotamian Religion?[3]

Miller (1973 [unavailable to me] = 2000: 383–87; 1986: 242–45 = 2000: 200–203; 2000a: 25–28, 30–31), following Riemann (1972), finds an analogy between the 'recognizable drive to see the forces that govern the cosmos as basically one and unified' in Mesopotamian religion (Jacobsen 1970: 21) and some aspects of Israelite religion. Jacobsen (1976: 233–34) tentatively suggests that behind this development may lie an understanding of 'the concept of king and ruler' in terms of absolute rule, so that there was 'an urge to sense, when the metaphor was applied to a deity, a concentration of power similar to that of the absolute monarch on earth'. If this is so, since there was no king with such extensive power in Palestine, any comparable development there must have had a different rationale.

At the end of the Epic of Creation Marduk's fifty names are pronounced. He has nine of these names already, and the other forty-one are names of other gods, whose powers are now delegated to him. The purpose of this, as of the fifty names which he has in the god list $AN = Anum$, is to show that he 'had taken over Enlil's powers and position' as head of the pantheon (Lambert 1984: 3–5; Foster 1996: 399 n. 4, cf. 357 n.1, and see 388–99 for a translation of this part of the Epic of Creation). Ashurbanipal's Hymn to Marduk, which is translated in Foster 1996: 704–709 and which contains the statement 'You bear the responsibilities of Anu, Enlil, and Ea', may be compared. Moreover, a god list (translated in full in Lambert 1975: 197–98) which identifies major gods with functions exercised by Marduk says, for example, 'Nergal (is) Marduk of battle.... Enlil (is) Marduk of lordship and consultations'. Lambert also refers to two hymns to Marduk, one of which begins 'Sin is your divinity, Anu your sovereignty' (see Foster 1996: 598–99 for a translation), while the other declares, for example, 'Your [...] is Šamaš, the light of heaven' (Lambert 1964: 5, 11–13). Lambert concluded (1964: 5) that Marduk's 'supremacy was verging on monotheism'. Subsequently he went further, and, with two qualifications, since the compiler of the god list might have allowed the existence of Marduk's wife Zarpānîtum, and also of demons (Lambert 1975: 198, but cf. Miller 1986: 244–45 = 2000: 203; 2000a: 30), he held that, because this compiler 'wished us to see Marduk as the sole possessor of power in the universe', the text has 'every claim to present Marduk as a monotheistic god'. Furthermore, in a Hymn to Ninurta (translated in Foster 1996: 619–20), important gods and goddesses are identified with parts of his body, so that Ninurta is told, for example, 'your face is Shamash..., Anu and Antum are your lips..., your neck is Marduk'. Albright (1957: 218) comments that 'this incorporation of all

---

3. I am grateful to Dr S.J. Sherwin for discussing this section of the essay with me, but he should not be held responsible for any errors in what I have written.

the gods and goddesses in one all-embracing deity is monotheistic to the extent that it deprives other deities of independent theological existence'.

It is, however, doubtful whether this trend in Mesopotamian religion should be called monotheistic. Foster (1996: 598, 619) holds that the Hymn to Marduk which he translates 'suggests henotheistic tendencies', and he describes the Hymn to Ninurta as 'henotheistic'. This understanding of the texts does not separate them so sharply from the polytheism which was universal in Mesopotamia, and, as Jacobsen (1976: 236) points out, 'nowhere else is there any indication that the gods here identified with aspects of Marduk or parts of Ninurta's body ceased to be depicted, described, addressed, or worshiped as anything other than themselves'. He thinks that there is in these texts 'a recognition of sameness of will and power in the bewildering variety of divine personalities', as well as, 'no doubt, a delight in voicing the versatility and many-faceted endowments of a favorite deity'. Moreover, Jacobsen notes 'the proclivity of Akkadian for using proper names metaphorically', so that to say of Marduk, 'your command is Anu' (e.g. the Epic of Creation 4.4.6), presumably implies that the response to Marduk's commands will be 'full, unconditional obedience', as if Anu had spoken. Maintaining 'that Ninurta's lips are Anu and Antum amounts to much the same thing'. If this interpretation is correct, polytheism is not so much rejected in these texts as viewed in a different way.

It should be added that, not only are goddesses as well as gods identified with parts of Ninurta's body, but also in the god list $AN = Anu \ \check{s}a \ am\bar{e}li$ 'the last name of Anu [the sky god] given there is Uraš "earth"', who is Anu's wife (Lambert 1975: 197). Thus in Mesopotamia a god might absorb a goddess.

Miller (2000a: 26, 30; cf. 1973 [unavailable to me] = 2000: 384–85; 1986: 243–45 = 2000: 201–203) correctly observes that 'one cannot transfer the process that led to this point in Babylonia and Assyria directly to Israel'. He thinks, however, that 'it may be that this integrative dimension, this drive to see the cosmic forces as unified, was reflected in Yahweh', and he claims that 'a number of Yahwistic factors [attested in the Old Testament] make sense on analogy with the Mesopotamian development'. One of these is 'an absorption [by Yahweh] of the feminine dimension in deity'.

For present purposes, what Miller says about material in the Old Testament must be put to one side. The speculations in the texts from Mesopotamia which have just been discussed have a polytheistic setting, but any move out of polytheism would necessarily have begun within it. If, however, Asherah's symbol became a hypostasis of some of Yahweh's qualities in Palestine, and no longer stood for a goddess, this would go beyond anything which is known to have happened in Mesopotamia. Moreover, while the texts from Mesopotamia seem to reflect the views of a small number of people, it has been argued above that the texts which refer to Yahweh's asherah may well be evidence for normative religious attitudes in Palestine in the eighth century BCE. The data from Mesopotamia provide a valuable insight into the thought-world of polytheism, and it is by no means impossible that there was a comparable 'drive to see the cosmic forces as unified' in Palestine, but developments in the worship actually offered in the cult there appear to have no parallel in Mesopotamia.

9. *Conclusion*

It has been argued in this essay that the texts from Kuntillet ʿAjrud and Khirbet el-Qom which mention Yahweh 'and his asherah' are evidence for a type of cult which was of more than marginal importance in both the north and the south of Palestine in the eighth century BCE. From the standpoint of Deuteronomic orthodoxy such a cult would have been syncretistic and heterodox, but the historian ought not see it in this way. The crucial issue for understanding the belief which is expressed in these texts is the meaning of 'his asherah'. If it be argued that a pronominal suffix can be added to a personal name, *ʾsrth* could signify either 'his Asherah' and refer to the goddess herself, or 'his asherah' and refer to the goddess's wooden symbol. If the rendering 'his Asherah' is correct, the texts would be evidence for polytheism, and Asherah would presumably have been Yahweh's consort. It is, however, more satisfactory to interpret the word in the light of known Hebrew usage, according to which a pronominal suffix is not added to a personal name. In that case the inscriptions refer to the goddess's wooden symbol.

The goddess Asherah should be identified with the goddess Athirat, who appears in texts from the Late Bronze Age found at Ugarit. A small number of biblical texts attest the worship of Asherah in Palestine in the Iron Age, and there is archaeological evidence which is consistent with this. But the existence of such worship is not decisive for the interpretation of the texts which mention Yahweh's asherah, since there is no reason why some people should not have continued worshipping Asherah while others understood the pole which had been her symbol in a different way. It must be explained why the asherah in these inscriptions is said to be Yahweh's asherah, and a theory which associates it directly with Yahweh would be more satisfactory than one that does not. If the goddess Asherah was being worshipped in Palestine, it is overwhelmingly probable that Yahweh's asherah was originally her symbol. Perhaps, as Keel and Uehlinger think, the stylized tree which is normally taken to be the symbol of a goddess had also become 'a gender-neutral symbol of numinous power' which was associated with Yahweh to mediate his blessing, or perhaps, as Hadley suggests, 'Yahweh had begun to absorb the worship of

Asherah into his cult'. Whatever the precise development, it should be classified as inclusive monotheism. Thus there is evidence from the eighth century BCE for a movement which the revisionists put much later. There appears to be no precise parallel in Mesopotamian religion to the cultic observance which is attested in the texts from Kuntillet 'Ajrud and Khirbet el-Qom, though there may well have been a 'drive to see the cosmic forces as unified' in Palestine as well as in Mesopotamia.

The references to Yahweh's asherah in these inscriptions are testimony to a movement away from polytheism towards monotheism. There is no extrabiblical evidence to show when it began, but in the eighth century BCE its influence can be seen in both the north and the south of Palestine, long before the Persian or the Hellenistic period, where the revisionists place it.

Bibliography

Ahituv, S.
1992   *Handbook of Ancient Hebrew Inscriptions* (in Hebrew; The Biblical Encyclopaedia Library, 7; Jerusalem: Bialik Institute).

Albright, W.F.
1957 [1940]   *From the Stone Age to Christianity: Monotheism and the Historical Process* (Garden City, NY: Doubleday, 2nd edn).

Ayalon, E.
1995   'The Iron Age II Pottery Assemblage from Horvat Teiman (Kuntillet 'Ajrud)', *Tel Aviv* 22: 141–205.

Barré, M.L.
1983   *The God-List in the Treaty between Hannibal and Philip V of Macedonia: A Study in Light of the Ancient Near Eastern Treaty Tradition* (Baltimore and London: The Johns Hopkins University Press).

Beck, P.
1994   'The Cult-Stands from Taanach: Aspects of the Iconographic Tradition of Early Iron Age Cult Objects in Palestine', in I. Finkelstein and N. Na'aman (eds), *From Nomadism to Monarchy: Archaeological and Historical Aspects of Early Israel* (Jerusalem: Yad Izhak Ben-Zvi and Israel Exploration Society; Washington: Biblical Archaeology Society): 352–81.

Becking, B.
2001   'Only One God: On Possible Implications for Biblical Theology', in B. Becking, M. Dijkstra, M.C.A. Korpel and K.J.H. Vriezen, *Only One God? Monotheism in Ancient Israel and the Veneration of the Goddess Asherah* (The Biblical Seminar, 77; London and New York: Sheffield Academic Press): 189–201.

Carmi, I., and D. Segal
1996   '[14]C Dating of an Israelite Biblical Site at Kuntillet Ajrud (Horvat Teman): Correction, Extension and Improved Age Estimate', *Radiocarbon* 38: 385–86.

Catastini, A.
1982   'Le iscrizioni di Kuntillet 'Ajrud e il profetismo', *AION* NS 42: 127–34.

Conrad, D.
1988 'Hebräische Bau-, Grab-, Votiv- und Siegelinschriften', in O. Kaiser (ed.), *Texte aus der Umwelt des Alten Testaments*, II.4: *Religiöse Texte: Grab-, Sarg-, Votiv- und Bauinschriften* (Gütersloh: Gütersloher Verlagshaus): 555–72.

Cross, F.M.
1954 'The Evolution of the Proto-Canaanite Alphabet', *BASOR* 134: 15–24. Reprinted in F.M. Cross, *Leaves from an Epigrapher's Notebook: Collected Papers in Hebrew and West Semitic Palaeography and Epigraphy* (HSS, 51; Winona Lake, IN: Eisenbrauns, 2003): 309–12.
1973 *Canaanite Myth and Hebrew Epic: Essays in the History of the Religion of Israel* (Cambridge, MA: Harvard University Press).
1983 'The Seal of Miqnêyaw, Servant of Yahweh', in L. Gorelick and E. Williams-Forte (eds), *Ancient Seals and the Bible* (Occasional Papers on the Near East, 2.1; Malibu, CA: Undena Publications): 55–63. Reprinted in F.M. Cross, *Leaves from an Epigrapher's Notebook: Collected Papers in Hebrew and West Semitic Palaeography and Epigraphy* (HSS, 51; Winona Lake, IN: Eisenbrauns, 2003): 107–13.

Davies, G.I.
1991 *Ancient Hebrew Inscriptions: Corpus and Concordance* (Cambridge, etc.: Cambridge University Press).

Davies, P.R.
1995 *In Search of 'Ancient Israel'* (JSOTSup, 148; Sheffield: Sheffield Academic Press, 2nd edn).

Day, J.
1986 'Asherah in the Hebrew Bible and Northwest Semitic Literature', *JBL* 105: 385–408.
2000 *Yahweh and the Gods and Goddesses of Canaan* (JSOTSup, 265; Sheffield: Sheffield Academic Press).

Dever, W.G.
1969–70 'Iron Age Epigraphic Material from the Area of Khirbet el-Kôm', *HUCA* 40–41: 139–204.
2001 *What did the Biblical Writers Know and When did they Know it? What Archaeology can Tell us about the Reality of Ancient Israel* (Grand Rapids, MI and Cambridge: W.B. Eerdmans).

Dijkstra, M.
2001a 'I have Blessed you by YHWH of Samaria and his Asherah: Texts with Religious Elements from the Soil Archive of Ancient Israel', in B. Becking, M. Dijkstra, M.C.A. Korpel and K.J.H. Vriezen, *Only One God? Monotheism in Ancient Israel and the Veneration of the Goddess Asherah* (The Biblical Seminar, 77; London and New York: Sheffield Academic Press): 17–44.
2001b 'El, the God of Israel – Israel, the people of YHWH: on the Origins of Ancient Israelite Yahwism', in B. Becking, M. Dijkstra, M.C.A. Korpel and K.J.H. Vriezen, *Only One God? Monotheism in Ancient Israel and the Veneration of the Goddess Asherah* (The Biblical Seminar, 77; London and New York: Sheffield Academic Press): 81–126.

Emerton, J.A.
    1982   'New Light on Israelite Religion: The Implications of the Inscriptions from
            Kuntillet ʿAjrud', *ZAW* 94: 2–20.
    1999   '"Yahweh and his Asherah": The Goddess or her Symbol?', *VT* 49: 315–37.
Engelken, K.
    1996   'BAʿALŠAMEM. Eine Auseinandersetzung mit der Monographie von H.
            Niehr', *ZAW* 108: 233–48, 391–407.
Foster, B.R.
    1996   *Before the Muses: An Anthology of Akkadian Literature* (2 vols; Bethesda,
            MD: CDL Press, 2nd edn).
Garbini, G.
    1988   *History and Ideology in Ancient Israel* (London: SCM Press).
Gröndahl, F.
    1967   *Die Personennamen der Texte aus Ugarit* (Studia Pohl, 1; Rome: Pontifical
            Biblical Institute).
Hadley, J.M.
    1987a   'The Khirbet el-Qom Inscription', *VT* 37: 50–62.
    1987b   'Some Drawings and Inscriptions on two Pithoi from Kuntillet ʿAjrud', *VT*
            37: 180–213.
    1993   'Kuntillet ʿAjrud: Religious Centre or Desert Way Station?', *PEQ* 125: 115–24.
    2000   *The Cult of Asherah in Ancient Israel and Judah: Evidence for a Hebrew
            Goddess* (UCOP, 57; Cambridge: Cambridge University Press).
Hendel, R.S.
    1997   'Aniconism and Anthropomorphism in Ancient Israel', in K. van der Toorn
            (ed.), *The Image and the Book: Iconic Cults, Aniconism, and the Rise of Book
            Religion in Israel and the Ancient Near East* (Leuven: Peeters): 205–28.
Hestrin, R.
    1987a   'The Cult Stand from Taʿanach and its Religious Background', in E. Lipiński
            (ed.), *Studia Phoenicia, V: Phoenicia and the East Mediterranean in the First
            Millennium B.C.* (Orientalia Lovaniensia Analecta, 22; Leuven: Peeters): 61–77.
    1987b   'The Lachish Ewer and the ʾAsherah', *IEJ* 37: 212–23.
Jacobsen, T.
    1949 [1946]   'Mesopotamia', in H. and H.A. Frankfort, J.A. Wilson and T. Jacobsen,
            Before Philosophy: The Intellectual Adventure of Ancient Man
            (Harmondsworth: Penguin Books): 135–234.
    1970   *Toward the Image of Tammuz and Other Essays on Mesopotamian History and
            Culture* (ed. W.L. Moran; Cambridge, MA: Harvard University Press).
    1976   *The Treasures of Darkness: A History of Mesopotamian Religion* (New Haven
            and London: Yale University Press).
Keel, O., and C. Uehlinger
    1992   *Göttinnen, Götter und Gottessymbole* (QD, 134; Freiburg im Breisgau: Herder).
            ET *Gods, Goddesses, and Images of God in Ancient Israel* (trans. Thomas H.
            Trapp; Edinburgh: T. & T. Clark, 1998).
Kletter, R.
    1996   *The Judean Pillar-Figurines and the Archaeology of Asherah* (British
            Archaeological Reports, International Series, 636; Oxford: Tempus
            Reparatum).

Korpel, M.C.A.
  2001   'Asherah outside Israel', in B. Becking, M. Dijkstra, M.C.A. Korpel and
          K.J.H. Vriezen, *Only One God? Monotheism in Ancient Israel and the
          Veneration of the Goddess Asherah* (The Biblical Seminar, 77; London and
          New York: Sheffield Academic Press): 127–50.

Lambert, W.G.
  1964   'The Reign of Nebuchadnezzar I: A Turning Point in the History of Ancient
          Mesopotamian Religion', in W.S. McCullough (ed.), *The Seed of Wisdom:
          Essays in Honour of T.J. Meek* (Toronto: University of Toronto Press): 3–13.
  1975   'The Historical Development of the Mesopotamian Pantheon: A Study in
          Sophisticated Polytheism', in H. Goedicke and J.J.M. Roberts (eds), *Unity and
          Diversity: Essays in the History, Literature, and Religion of the Ancient Near
          East* (Baltimore and London: The Johns Hopkins University Press): 191–200.
  1984   'Studies in Marduk', *BSOAS* 47: 1–9.

Lapp, P.W.
  1969   'The 1968 Excavations at Tell Ta'annek', *BASOR* 195: 2–49.

Lemaire, A.
  1977   'Les Inscriptions de Khirbet el-Qôm et l'Ashérah de YHWH', *RB* 84: 595–608.
  1981   *Les Ecoles et la Formation de la Bible dans l'Ancien Israël* (OBO, 39; Fribourg
          [Switzerland]: Editions Universitaires, and Göttingen: Vandenhoeck &
          Ruprecht).
  1994   'Déesses et Dieux de Syrie-Palestine d'après les Inscriptions (c. 1000–500 av.
          n. è.)', in W. Dietrich and M.A. Klopfenstein (eds), *Ein Gott allein? JHWH-
          Verehrung und biblischer Monotheismus im Kontext der israelitischen und
          altorientalischen Religionsgeschichte* (OBO, 139; Freiburg [Switzerland]:
          Universitätsverlag; Göttingen: Vandenhoeck & Ruprecht): 127–58.

Lemche, N.P.
  1998   *The Israelites in History and Tradition* (London: SPCK; Louisville, KY:
          Westminster John Knox Press).

McCarter, P.K.
  1987   'Aspects of the Religion of the Israelite Monarchy: Biblical and Epigraphic
          Data', in P.D. Miller, P.D. Hanson and S.D. McBride (eds), *Ancient Israelite
          Religion: Essays in Honor of Frank Moore Cross* (Philadelphia: Fortress
          Press): 137–55.

Mastin, B.A.
forthcoming 'Who Built and Who Used the Buildings at Kuntillet 'Ajrud?'

Meshel, Z.
  1978   *Kuntillet 'Ajrud: A Religious Centre from the time of the Judaean Monarchy on
          the Border of Sinai* (Catalogue no. 175; Jerusalem: The Israel Museum).
  1992   'Kuntillet 'Ajrud', *ABD*, IV: 103–109.
  1993   'Teman, Ḥorvat', *NEAEHL*, IV: 1458–64.

Meyers, C.
  1988   *Discovering Eve: Ancient Israelite Women in Context* (New York and Oxford:
          Oxford University Press).

Miller, P.D.
  1973   'God and the Gods: History of Religion as an Approach and Context for
          Bible and Theology', *Affirmation* 1: 37–62. Reprinted in P.D. Miller, *Israelite*

Religion and Biblical Theology: Collected Essays (JSOTSup, 267; Sheffield: Sheffield Academic Press, 2000): 365–96.

1981 'Psalms and Inscriptions', in J.A. Emerton (ed.), *Congress Volume: Vienna 1980* (VTSup, 32; Leiden: E.J. Brill): 311–32. Reprinted in P.D. Miller, *Israelite Religion and Biblical Theology: Collected Essays* (JSOTSup, 267; Sheffield: Sheffield Academic Press, 2000): 210–32.

1986 'The Absence of the Goddess in Israelite Religion', *HAR* 10: 239–48. Reprinted in P.D. Miller, *Israelite Religion and Biblical Theology: Collected Essays* (JSOTSup, 267; Sheffield: Sheffield Academic Press, 2000): 197–207.

2000a *The Religion of Ancient Israel* (London: SPCK; Louisville, KY: Westminster John Knox Press).

Moor, J.C. de

1970 'The Semitic Pantheon of Ugarit', *UF* 2: 187–228.

Na'aman, N.

1999 'No Anthropomorphic Graven Image. Notes on the Assumed Anthropomorphic Cult Statues in the Temples of *YHWH* in the Pre-Exilic Period', *UF* 31 (1999 but published in 2000): 391–415.

Niehr, H.

1990 *Der höchste Gott: Alttestamentlicher YHWH-Glaube im Kontext syrisch-kanaanäischer Religion des 1. Jahrtausends v. Chr.* (BZAW, 190; Berlin and New York: W. de Gruyter).

Olyan, S.M.

1988 *Asherah and the Cult of Yahweh in Israel* (SBLMS, 34; Atlanta, GA: Scholars Press).

Pardee, D.

1988 'An Evaluation of the Proper Names from Ebla from a West Semitic Perspective: Pantheon Distribution according to *Genre*', in A. Archi (ed.), *Eblaite Personal Names and Semitic Name-Giving* (Archivi Reali di Ebla. Studi, 1; Rome: Missione Archeologica Italiana in Siria): 119–51.

Parker, S.B.

2003 'Graves, Caves, and Refugees: An Essay in Microhistory', *JSOT* 27: 259–88.

Pritchard, J.B.

1982 'The Tanit Inscription from Sarepta', in H.G. Niemeyer (ed.), *Phönizier im Westen: Die Beiträge des Internationalen Symposiums über 'Die phönizische Expansion im westlichen Mittelmeerraum' in Köln vom 24. bis 27. April 1979* (Madrider Beiträge, 8; Mainz: Verlag Philipp von Zabern): 83–92.

Renz, J.

1995 *Die Althebräischen Inschriften, I: Text und Kommentar*, in J. Renz and W. Röllig (eds), *Handbuch der althebräischen Epigraphik*, I (Darmstadt: Wissenschaftliche Buchgesellschaft).

Riemann, P.

1972 An unpublished essay read to the Colloquium for Old Testament Research at Cambridge, MA.

Röllig, W.

1999 'Baal-Shamem *bʿl-šmyn, bʿl-šmm*', in *DDD* (2nd edn): 149–51.

Scagliarini, F.

1989 'Osservazioni sulle Iscrizioni di Kuntillet ʿAğrud', *RSO* 63: 199–212.

Smith, M.S.
1990   *The Early History of God: Yahweh and the Other Deities in Ancient Israel* (San Francisco: Harper & Row). It has not been possible to take account of the second edition of this book (2002), to which I had access only after this essay had been completed.

Thompson, T.L.
1999   *The Bible in History: How Writers Create a Past* (London: Jonathan Cape). Also published as *The Mythic Past: Biblical Archaeology and the Myth of Israel* (New York: Basic books).

Tigay, J.H.
1986   *You shall have no other Gods: Israelite Religion in the Light of Hebrew Inscriptions* (HSS, 31; Atlanta, GA: Scholars Press).
1987   'Israelite Religion: the Onomastic and Epigraphic Evidence', in P.D. Miller, P.D. Hanson and S.D. McBride (eds), *Ancient Israelite Religion: Essays in Honor of Frank Moore Cross* (Philadelphia: Fortress Press): 157–94.

Toorn, K. van der
1993   'Saul and the Rise of Israelite State Religion', *VT* 43: 519–42.

Tropper, J.
2001   'Der Gottesname *Yahwa*', *VT* 51: 81–106.

Uehlinger, C.
1997   'Anthropomorphic Cult Statuary in Iron Age Palestine and the Search for Yahweh's Cult Images', in K. van der Toorn (ed.), *The Image and the Book: Iconic Cults, Aniconism, and the Rise of Book Religion in Israel and the Ancient Near East* (Leuven: Peeters): 97–155.

Vawter, B.
1955   'The Canaanite Background of Genesis 49', *CBQ* 17: 1–18.

Weippert, M.
1997   'Synkretismus und Monotheismus: Religionsinterne Konfliktbewältigung im alten Israel', in his *Jahwe und die anderen Götter* (FAT, 18; Tübingen: Mohr Siebeck): 1–24. Reprinted from J. Assmann and D. Harth (eds), *Kultur und Konflikt* (Frankfurt: Suhrkamp Verlag, 1990), to which I have not had access.

Wiggins, S.A.
1991   'The Myth of Asherah: Lion Lady and Serpent Goddess', *UF* 23: 383–94.
1993   *A Reassessment of 'Asherah': A Study according to the Textual Sources of the First Two Millennia B.C.E.* (AOAT, 235; Kevelaer: Verlag Butzon & Bercker; Neukirchen–Vluyn: Neukirchener Verlag).

Winter, U.
1983   *Frau und Göttin: Exegetische und ikonographische Studien zum weiblichen Gottesbild im Alten Israel und in dessen Umwelt* (OBO, 53; Freiburg [Switzerland]: Universitätsverlag; Göttingen: Vandenhoeck & Ruprecht).

Zevit, Z.
2001   *The Religions of Ancient Israel: A Synthesis of Parallactic Approaches* (London and New York: Continuum).

Chapter 15

MESOPOTAMIAN SOURCES AND PRE-EXILIC ISRAEL

W.G. Lambert

'Israel' is used here meaning 'the kingdom of Israel' from King Saul to the division of the kingdom on Solomon's death, whereafter 'Israel' means the northern kingdom, and 'Judah' the southern kingdom. The question to be addressed is whether the historical material in the books of Samuel and Kings presents records from before the exile. Chronicles is of course excluded since its post-exilic origin is clear.

For many centuries Samuel and Kings stood virtually alone as a source for the early history of Israel and Judah. The only possible check came from extracts of Phoenician historians who wrote in Greek and were quoted by Christian writers. But these Phoenician sources were themselves often suspect and not independently verifiable. With the rise of archaeology in the nineteenth century documents contemporary with and relevant to Israel and Judah have come to light and offer solid evidence when critically handled. As it happens, little relevant has come from Egypt. The existence of Shishak, Tirhakah and Necho (II) has been confirmed by their own inscriptions, but almost no historical data have been communicated. From Palestine and Syria a few relevant inscriptions have been found, but only very few with important historical content, and these are dealt with in another chapter. The largest and historically most relevant body of material is Assyrian, though Assyria was geographically more remote from Israel than Egypt and Syria. The reasons for this are two: first the imperialistic character of the Assyrian state, and secondly the Assyrian custom of recording their conquests.

To the first: the Assyrians, from a very small homeland in the area around the modern Mosul, became an imperialistic military power apparently as a result of having been overrun by the Mitanni empire for a very short time in the middle of the second millennium BCE. A state ethic of military expansion developed and this was self-generating. Conquest of immediate neighbours brought in booty and regular tribute thereafter, but it also resulted in unhappy subjects and new neighbours apprehensive that their turn might come next. Hence plots and plans for anti-Assyrian action, which the Assyrians countered by further military expansion with subjugation of the new neighbours. This process was repeated from c. 1400 to 700 BCE, with one interruption about 1000 BCE, by which time the Assyrians were deeply involved in Egypt and central Anatolia as well as Babylonia, west Iran and Armenia. By this time Assyria was badly overstretched and this was a major factor in their quite sudden collapse as a superpower.

The kingdom of Israel arose during the pause in this Assyrian expansion, when, c. 1100–900 BCE, the Aramaeans flooded into Mesopotamia and north Syria in a massive migration, disrupting everything. When, in the ninth century BCE, the Assyrians had recovered enough, they began to expand once more. Their main direction was the same: westwards across the Tigris–Euphrates plain, terrain suitable for their military forces, unlike the mountains close to their east and north borders. Babylon, to their south-east, they treated with deference for religious and cultural reasons. The preferred westerly direction also led to Syria and Palestine, with their wealth in good times, and to possibilities of trade over the Mediterranean. Such economic factors are never explicitly mentioned in Assyrian sources, unless listing of booty seized and tribute exacted is so construed, but certainly this was one factor in their overall strategy.

By c. 850 BCE the Assyrians had again assumed control of the whole plain between Tigris and Euphrates upstream from about the modern Iraqi–Syrian border on the rivers. Then King Shalmaneser III (859–824 BCE) adopted a policy of rapid further westward expansion. This brought him first into conflict with north-Syrian states on the Euphrates, which resulted in turn in confronting Damascus. This was one of the new Aramaean states, situated at a key point on trading routes, and to further their central status they had a policy of organizing a coalition of neighbouring states to protect their common interests, by military action if necessary. A dozen or more small Syrian states and some larger ones saw the advantage and joined. At this time northern Israel was often in conflict with Damascus on the latter's southern borders, so as Assyria gradually increased pressure on the northern borders of the Damascene confederation it seemed that Israel had a potential ally in Assyria. This was a simplistic view, because as the power of Damascus gradually crumbled over some decades to Assyrian might Israel then became exposed to such attacks itself, to which it fell in 722 BCE. Judah experienced the same process, but a little later. Hezekiah was the king of Judah unfortunate enough to be on the throne at this moment, and though Sennacherib's siege of Jerusalem was (unusually for the Assyrians) called off, Judah was practically a vassal of Assyria until Nineveh fell in 612 BCE. At that time the Assyrians had their hands full with bigger problems than Judah, so payment of tribute from time to time allowed self-rule.

The Assyrian empire fell to the combined forces of Babylon and the Medes, but the former replaced Assyria as the superpower in the ancient Near East. This did not happen without effort. Smaller nations did not want the Assyrian yoke to be replaced by a Babylonian yoke, and in Palestine and Syria resistance was mustered, supported by the Egyptians, but in vain. Judah was caught up in this activity, but in 597 BCE Jerusalem fell to Nebuchadnezzar II and the Babylonian captivity began.

Study of Israelite history of this period must of course see it in the wider international context as just outlined. And non-Israelite sources must be used with full understanding of their original purpose and function. The relevant Assyrian documents are almost all royal inscriptions, composed in the court by royal scribes. In style they depend on a millennium-old tradition of tripartite royal inscriptions of dedicatory type:

(i)   For god so-and-so
(ii) King so-and-so
(iii) did this (e.g. gave a statue, built a temple)

The second part normally adds some title to the king, e.g. 'king of Babylon', but in Assyria this second part began to be expanded with allusions to the military campaigns ('conqueror of such-and-such lands'), and then formal narrative began to replace these descriptive phrases so that what had been a few epithets became the main part of the inscription. Its form was then:

(i)   God so-and-so (can be omitted)
(ii) Name of king with titles, epithets, short ancestry
(iii) Narrative of campaigns
(iv) Report of building activity

There was no fixed organization of part (iii). Most usefully for us some kings, including Shalmaneser III, give a record by numbered years of reign. Sennacherib in contrast gives only a numbered sequence of his campaigns not corresponding to his years of reign. When only summary accounts of conquests are given they may be presented in geographical organization rather than chronologically. Normally each campaign was written up by the scribes on its completion. In a few cases we know that such a detailed report was created in the form of a letter to Ashur, the Assyrian state god, and it is possible that this was regular practice. In any case the royal scribes were busy writing up reports of campaigns and building operations which were put in royal inscriptions with their master's titles. Some such inscriptions were put in hollows in walls of new or repaired buildings for future rulers to find. Other copies were engraved on stone and built into palace walls. Still other copies were put on bricks, if short, while longer ones on clay tablets would be kept in the royal archives. Due to the extreme rarity of literacy in Assyrian civilization there was no general circularization.

As a reign progressed the scribes began to combine the reports of the various campaigns into one inscription, and since the process would have resulted in massively long records for active kings, the scribes began to abbreviate the records for each year. Thus for kings who ruled for a fair time and were militarily active, and from whom we have abundant records in the form of royal inscriptions, we shall be well informed about the earlier years, but for the later years we shall have only very summary accounts of the campaigns. It may be that the later campaigns were written up as letters to Ashur in full detail, but very few of these have survived. In this editorial activity over a reign other changes could be made. Campaigns first recorded in chronological sequence, whether dated or not, might be moved around to geographical arrangement for simplicity of presentation, or for a more flattering narrative for posterity.

While these editorial processes impose some limitation on the historical value of the Assyrian royal inscriptions, there remains abundant value for two reasons. First, the royal inscriptions are contemporary with the king concerned. Very few copies indeed are known from after the king's death. Secondly, despite their being royal propaganda they are astonishingly factual and reliable. There is usually no difficulty in reading between the lines. When it is recorded that a king successfully attacked a certain city several years running until it fell, he clearly met stiff resistance. Sennacherib's account of the battle of Halulê in his eighth campaign draws on an epic to give a vivid literary portrait of a savage battle in which the blood flowed like a river. He claims victory, but a Babylonian chronicle states that he was forced to withdraw.

The reason for this relatively reliable material can be suggested. There was in Assyria a military aristocracy, which served as a counterbalance to the king. He had to justify himself to them, not formally, but practically by the extent he achieved what was expected. The letters to the state god were a kind of self-justification. Thus the aristocracy would know what had happened each year, and it would have been foolish to try and deceive them in the royal inscriptions.

A second source of major importance from Assyria is a reliable chronology of the period we are dealing with. Traditionally the Assyrians dated years by a *limu* officer, who held the post for one year, and it passed around the high officers of state, beginning with the king, who held it in his first (or perhaps second) year of reign. Lists of these officers were compiled and maintained for purely practical purposes, though one set adds a phrase or two for each year giving the great event of that year. One of these events is a solar eclipse, datable to 763 BCE, which ties down the whole sequence to modern time-reckoning. The odd scribal error, such as omission of one name, does occur, but at the most one or two years are involved. The list of officers' names ('Eponym Lists') are preserved for the years 910–649 BCE, and the lists with the extra phrases ('Eponym Chronicles') cover 840–727 and 719–700 BCE. The years to the fall of Assyria in 612 BCE are precisely known from an abundance of other evidence.

Assyrian records fail as the empire was collapsing, and of course after the fall, but appropriate Babylonian records survive. The Babylonians had no *limu* officers, but dated events by years of a king's reign. Thus king lists were compiled of royal names in sequence with years of reign given. The Assyrians also had such king lists, but for the period of concern here they have less importance, and they were probably extracted from the lists of *limus*.

Our aim now is to use this Mesopotamian material to ask how far the historical content of Samuel and Kings suggests pre-exilic origins. The question is pressing at the present time when such writers as T.L. Thompson, N.P. Lemche and P.R. Davies are claiming not only that Samuel and Kings are post-exilic in origin, but also that their authors had little or no pre-exilic sources available to them. We shall not take up all their arguments in detail since they can differ from each other in particular matters or offer somewhat different conclusions in various publications. So we shall refer in particular to P.R. Davies 1992 (*In Search of 'Ancient Israel'* [JSOTSup, 148; Sheffield: Sheffield Academic Press]) and N.P. Lemche 1998 (*The Israelites in History and Tradition* [Louisville, KY: Westminster John Knox Press, and London: SPCK]).

Before proceeding two preliminary matters must be dealt with. The fact that the text of the Old Testament was not firmly established before the first century CE does not in my judgment throw doubt on the historicity of the books concerned. In 1 Samuel 17–18 there are substantial omissions in the LXX as compared with the Masoretic Hebrew text, and a Dead Sea scroll has greater variation, with additional material. Similarly in Kings, the LXX has two substantial additions to 1 Kings 2. In ch. 12 it has both additions and omissions as compared with the Masoretic Hebrew, it puts ch. 21 after ch. 19, and transposes the reign of Jehoshaphat of Judah to before Ahab of Israel (after 16.28), from after Ahab (22.41–50). This last variation is due to the existence of two different chronological schemes for the two kingdoms, and the lesser known one has a single item in the Masoretic Hebrew, more attestation in the usually printed LXX text, but most attestation in the Lucianic manuscripts of the LXX. No one will doubt that some of this editorial activity was taking place after the exile, but its occurrence does nothing to prove post-exilic origin of the books.

The Hebrew historical books are often composite, having been compiled from pre-existing works by editors who selected and combined with their own contributions interwoven. In theory one might try to estimate the historical value of each source individually, but in practice this would be difficult since disentangling the books is not always certain and in our case it would not offer real help.

Secondly, concepts of history need attention. Many modern writers operate with two kinds of history: that of earlier ages and based on ideologies differing from their own, and their very own kind of history, which is strictly factual and impartial. In reality all historians select the material they present from a larger body of happenings, or depend on prior sources which made the selection. Too much happens in human society for everything to be recorded, and selections are made according to what the writer or story-teller considers important or interesting and so worthy of perpetuation. In the process of selection interpretation will come in, based on ideology, conscious or unconscious. We should not condemn as unhistorical ancient writers who had ideologies different from our own. One example has already been noted: historians from the ancient Near East do not normally allude to economic factors in their history. By chance there is one exception in Kings. 1 Kings 20.34 tells how a treaty between Ahab of Israel and Ben-Hadad (I) of Damascus allowed Ahab trading rights in Damascus as Ben-Hadad (I) had been granted in Samaria. Failure to refer to economic or other factors important to us does not necessarily indicate that ancient texts are not offering reliable history.

The following is a list of kings of Assyria with dates which cover the period when they came into contact with Israel and Judah. Following each relevant king's name are the names of the Hebrew kings mentioned in the royal inscriptions of the king of Assyria, and after the Israelite kings any other persons named in Kings and in the Assyrian materials are given in parentheses.

> Shalmaneser III 859–824
>> Ahab
>> Jehu
>> (Adad-idri = Ben-Hadad I)
>> (Hazael)
> Shamshi-Adad V 824–811
> Adad-nîrāri III 811–783
>> Joash of Samaria
> Shalmaneser IV 783–773
> Ashur-dan III 773–755
> Ashur-nîrāri V 755–745
> Tiglath-pileser III 745–727
>> Azariah of Judah (?)
>> (Jeho)ahaz of Judah
>> Menahem of Samaria
>> Pekah of Samaria
>> Hoshea of Samaria

(Rezin of Damascus)
Shalmaneser V 727–722
Sargon II 722–705
Sennacherib 705–681
    Hezekiah of Judah
    (Merodach-baladan)
Esarhaddon 681–669
    Manasseh of Judah
Ashurbanipal 669–627
    Manasseh of Judah

The above list is incomplete in that we list only names of kings, not mentions of campaigns naming the country only. Thus Sargon II mentions Samaria, House of Omri and Judah, but without naming the rulers. A detailed comparative study of Assyrian and Israelite history would be of book length, and cannot be done here. For further detailed material and studies there is plenty of literature. The relevant passages from the Assyrian royal inscriptions are all translated with brief notes in R. Borger 1984 ('Historische Texte in akkadischer Sprache aus Babylonien und Assyrien', in O. Kaiser [ed.], *Texte aus der Umwelt des Alten Testaments*, I.4: *Rechts- und Wirtschaftsurkunden: Historisch-chronologische Texte*, I [Gütersloh: Gütersloher Verlagshaus]: 354–410 [specifically 360–91]). A more recent edition of all Assyrian royal inscriptions from Shalmaneser III to Adad-nīrāri V, including some new ones is A.K. Grayson 1996 (*Assyrian Rulers of the Early First Millennium BC*, II *[858–745 BC]* [The Royal Inscriptions of Mesopotamia, Assyrian Periods, 3; Toronto: University of Toronto Press]). Full translations are given but no historical commentary. A more recent edition of all the royal inscriptions of Tiglath-pileser III is given by H. Tadmor 1994 (*The Inscriptions of Tiglath-pileser III King of Assyria* [Jerusalem: The Israel Academy of Sciences and Humanities]). This provides a vastly improved edition, with some major additions, and substantial discussions of historical matter. J.K. Kuan 1995 (*Neo-Assyrian Historical Inscriptions and Syria-Palestine*: *Israelite/Judean-Tyrian-Damascene Political and Commercial Relations in the Ninth–Eighth Centuries BCE* [Jian Diao Dissertation Series, 1; Bible and Literature, 1; Hong Kong: Alliance Bible Seminary]) deals with the kings Shalmaneser III to Shalmaneser V, giving text and translations of relevant texts, also gathering other evidence, with full discussion. A commentary on 2 Kings dealing particularly with the Assyrian evidence from original study is M. Cogan and H. Tadmor 1988 (*II Kings: A New Translation with Introduction and Commentary* [AB, 11; New York: Doubleday]). For the basis of the chronology of the period, see A.R. Millard 1994 (*The Eponyms of the Assyrian Empire 910–612 BC* (SAAS, 2; Helsinki: Neo-Assyrian Text Corpus Project]).

Conclusions

The first and obvious conclusion to draw from this material is that the books of Kings have the Israelite rulers in correct chronological sequence, not only judging from the succession of Assyrian kings, but even within one Assyrian reign: Ahab is mentioned in the sixth year of Shalmaneser III, and Jehu in his eighteenth year. (For a detailed discussion of the chronology of this period see Lambert 1994.) Unfortunately the annals of Tiglath-pileser III have survived in a very poor condition. The stone slabs were trimmed and reused in a later reign, and are mostly no longer existing, being known only from nineteenth-century CE copies, and some of those were made from squeezes which no longer exist. So the chronology of his reign has to be based mainly on the Eponym Chronicles. So the four or five Hebrew kings named in his inscriptions have no self-evident sequence in these sources.

A comparison of the contents of the Assyrian and Hebrew records is rewarding. Shalmaneser III notes that in his sixth year Ahab fought with the king of Damascus against Assyria, provided the largest contingent of chariots to the confederation and was defeated with big losses. There is no record of this in Kings. That Ahab should have joined Ben-Hadad (I) on one occasion is not implausible. He could easily have been convinced that Assyria was a threat to Israel and Damascus equally, and he would of course have preferred that Assyria was repulsed in the far north of Syria (Qarqar) before they could advance nearer to Israel. And if he lost most of his chariots in the battle, he might well have not seen eye to eye with Ben-Hadad (I) thereafter. Since the result was failure, it is quite likely that any official records of the northern kingdom would gloss over or omit any record of the event. Other Hebrew writing, from prophetic circles for example, might have recorded it as a warning not to trust in human diplomacy: we do not know, nor precisely how it came to be overlooked in Kings.

Jehu paid tribute to Shalmaneser III in the latter's eighteenth year according to the Assyrian annals. This too is not mentioned in Kings. It appears that Jehu was under no immediate threat from Assyria, his pressing problem was Damascus, which Assyria was menacing on its northern borders. Thus it was a politically wise move of Jehu to send a present to Shalmaneser III, which he interpreted as submission. Prophetic circles would of course condemn it as trusting in 'the arm of flesh', not in God. Thus court circles may well not have disclosed the gift but rather downplayed it. For whatever reason, it is not in Kings.

A statue inscription of Shalmaneser records the passing of Ben-Hadad (I) and the seizing of power by Hazael, a commoner. 1 Kings 8.7–15 records that Elisha, when Ben-Hadad (I) was ill, tipped off Hazael, who was acting as envoy for his king, that he would soon assume royal power.

So, the narrative continues, Hazael took the tip, suffocated his royal master and seized power. The narrative in Kings is taken from a religiously stimulated account of the doings of Elisha, which modern western minds tend to dismiss as fiction because of the miraculous content. But its record of the Damascene succession is basically sound. If Hazael did in fact murder Ben-Hadad (I) (we have no means of checking) then suffocating the king in a coma would be an obvious way to achieve the result.

Joash of Samaria has only a brief condemnatory treatment in 2 Kgs 13.10–13 with no mention of any dealings with Assyria, but the tribute exacted by Adad-nīrāri III is easily explained. According to Kings Joash had a war with Judah, and if so he would wish at all costs to escape hostile intentions of Assyria, and paying tribute was the obvious way.

Tiglath-pileser III mentions Menahem of Samaria and (Jeho)ahaz of Judah only as paying tribute. Kings, however, gives details of the events leading up to this payment: 2 Kgs 15.17–22 for Menahem, 2 Kgs 16.5–9 for (Jeho)ahaz. Two damaged inscriptions of Tiglath-pileser III record his invasion of Israel, the carrying off of something (now lost), the imposition of tribute, the death of Pekah and his appointing of Hoshea as king (Tadmor 1994: 140, 202). 2 Kings 15.29–30 allows one to suppose that people were carried off, but it adds that Pekah was conspired against by Hoshea and killed, so that Hoshea took the throne of Israel. Clearly Hoshea represented a pro-Assyrian faction in Israel since he was acceptable to Tiglath-pileser III. There is a certain contradiction between Kings and the Assyrian records. But Tiglath-pileser might have encouraged the revolt against Pekah, or when it had taken place he would no doubt have signalled somehow his approval. In either case he could claim to have been the king-maker. In both Assyrian and Hebrew records Rezin is a leader of opposition to Assyria in the area and in 2 Kgs 16.5–9 his defeat, the fall of Damascus and his death are reported. Tiglath-pileser III (Tadmor 1994: 78–83) gives the same general story, but after the siege of Damascus with Rezin inside, and its fall, nothing apparently is said of Rezin's fate.

Sennacherib's military campaigns are best known from an edition from later in his reign, recording eight campaigns the third of which is to the west, in the course of which he invaded Judah and besieged Jerusalem. This is certainly an abbreviation of an originally much longer and more detailed account, of which only one broken fragment remains (Naʾaman 1974), probably part of a letter to the god Ashur. There has been much discussion of campaigns of Sennacherib against Judah, and we do not wish to repeat such things (see, however, Cogan and Tadmor 1988: 246–51). Some points, however, must be made. First, the idea that there were two separate campaigns of Sennacherib against Judah seems to us to be based on a failure to accept fully the 'scissors and paste' method by which

2 Kings was compiled. Next, the apparent contradiction between the Hebrew implied claim of victory when the siege of Jerusalem was lifted and Sennacherib's claim of overall victory ignores what we stated above about reading between the lines in Assyrian royal inscriptions. The Assyrians were not only masters of military affairs, but also of psychological warfare. They knew that any military offensive begun but not achieved was an encouragement to their enemies to resist. Thus something must have happened to have caused the siege to be lifted, but that did not result in a total change in the balance of power. Assyria still had an unbeaten army. The mishap, whatever it was, is quietly passed over: very Assyrian! Two matters attest to historical veracity in the Hebrew version. First, the figures of tribute sent by Hezekiah to Sennacherib: 300 talents of silver and 30 talents of gold according to 2 Kgs 18.14, 800 talents of silver and 30 talents of gold according to Sennacherib. That the gold is the same cannot be a coincidence. The differing figures for silver no doubt result from scribal error. Secondly, the phenomenon of the Assyrian officer who harangued the people on the wall of Jerusalem with a propaganda speech during the siege of Jerusalem (2 Kgs 18.17–35) is paralleled in a letter from two Assyrian officers to Tiglath-pileser III. It comes from Babylonia which was in a state of revolt against Assyria in part and the city of Babylon was involved, but no Assyrian army was available to take immediate action. So the writers approached the city and engaged in exactly the same kind of verbal threats that are described in Kings as having happened at Jerusalem (see Saggs 2001: 20–21).

The account of Merodach-baladan's embassy to Hezekiah (2 Kgs 20.12–19) is much illuminated from extrabiblical knowledge. The envoys are said to have come to congratulate Hezekiah on his recovery from illness. But when the prophet Isaiah was unhappy with what took place and interrogated Hezekiah, of his two questions, 'What did these men say? Where did they come from', only the second was answered. Merodach-baladan, king of Babylon, tried to be a thorn in Assyria's side very regularly, but was a hopeless general who had more success as a diplomat. He persuaded others to join him in rebelling against Assyria. In principle he was right. The Assyrian empire was so far flung that it lacked adequate numbers of troops to control it effectively. So since Assyrian armies were often seen as invincible the only hope of defeating them was to instigate rebellions in different regions of the empire simultaneously. No doubt the congratulations on recovering from an illness were only the foil for a suggestion of rebellion. Isaiah would have known of Merodach-baladan's reputation and would easily have guessed the real purpose of the embassy. (For full details on this ancient Arafat see Baker 2001.)

So not only does Kings offer the Hebrew rulers in correct sequence, but many items it includes contain matter which depends on knowledge known to us from the Assyrian royal inscriptions. In post-exilic times most such records were no longer surviving. This of course does not prove the literal truth of every detail in Kings but it does point to pre-exilic origin. Assyrian royal inscriptions mostly perished with the fall of Assyria. Very few indeed have been recovered from Late Babylonian archives and libraries.

Now for P.R. Davies and N.P. Lemche. The present chapter is not the place for a full critical review of their various publications. Their ideology is redolent of postmodernism with a whiff of nihilism. They seem to be saying that the historicity of an ancient text has to be proved 100 per cent by irrefutable evidence, and that the historical books of the Old Testament are not history but 'literary constructs' with a bit of history in some of them. Historians generally operate with degrees of probability and exercise judgment in the case – most cases in fact – where absolute proof is lacking. If two capable and conscientious British historians were to write detailed accounts of the ejection of Mrs Thatcher from the leadership of the Conservative party they would almost certainly offer contradictory versions of some events, despite the availability of vast quantities of day-by-day evidence in print and in the minds of living participants. An ancient example is the fall of the First Dynasty of Babylon. The event took place c. 1600 BCE, or earlier by some chronologies, and modern historians unanimously ascribe the fall to the Hittite king Murshilish I. The evidence for this implausible march from central Anatolia to Babylon and back comes from a document of Telepinus, a Hittite king about a century later, and from a brief notice in a Babylonian chronicle copied out over a millennium or more after the claimed event. The chronicle does not name the king concerned.

The relationship of literary constructs to history can be illustrated by the conclusion of the biblical version of Sennacherib's invasion of Judah. After the angel of the Lord killed the Assyrian army besieging Jerusalem, Sennacherib withdrew and was murdered by two of his own sons (2 Kgs 19.35-37). The literary construct implies that the impious Assyrian who dared to threaten Jerusalem suffered divine justice for it. This is obviously the fiction of a pious Judahite author. But Sennacherib was in fact murdered by one of his sons: there is a contemporary Assyrian letter giving an account of events leading up to the crime (Parpola 1980). It gives the name of the son as Arda-Mullissi, corrupted in the Hebrew Bible to Adrammelech, the name of a god of Sepharvaim according to 2 Kgs 17.31. The reason for the plot and murder is nowhere communicated in Assyrian documents, but we have a shrewd suspicion. The Assyrians were divided about the chief Babylonian god Marduk. Some held him in deep respect, some wanted the chief Assyrian god Ashur to be put in his place, at the head of the pantheon. Sennacherib had campaigned against Babylon, sacked the city, and taken away the statue of Marduk virtually as a prisoner. In the atmosphere of the times this would have been construed as sacrilege by pro-Marduk Assyrians and they would fear divine retribution on the Assyrian state. To our knowledge this is the most likely reason for the plotting and murder, though it backfired on the conspirators.

In the book under consideration, P.R Davies (1992: 94) states:

> A certain amount of material, in the form of pieces of written or of oral literature – for example, stories about kings, warriors and holy men, songs cultic and non-cultic must have survived in Palestine [from pre-exilic times to the Persian period].

A few pages later this is summed up as 'relics from this earlier period' (Davies 1992: 99). But the evidence of the Neo-Assyrian royal inscriptions supports the sequence of kings of both kingdoms when they came into the purview of the Assyrian state, and it is a reasonable deduction that the other kings too, when no Assyrian invasion involved them, are equally historical figures, even back to Solomon. Kings has a certain unified style throughout and if Ahab was a real king is it reasonable to doubt the same for Solomon? Of course this does not commit us to the literal truth of every narrative, but it implies a connected written history from pre-exilic times, not only 'pieces' and 'relics'. The time of Solomon, if we accept him as a historic reality, would have been when Assyria was at its lowest ebb due to the Aramaean migrations into Mesopotamia and northern Syria, and that situation would have allowed a king of Jerusalem to build up some kind of empire.

Davies's extreme scepticism in dealing with the biblical narratives is matched by the opposite when using arguments to support his case. He refers to M. Noth as follows (Davies 1992: 99):

> ... surviving literature of the monarchic period, as Martin Noth quite correctly insisted, will surely have remained in Palestine, and not have been removed to Babylon. It is among those dismissed by the biblical narrative as the unworthy 'peoples of the land' who will have been responsible for preserving whatever was left to them ...

It sounds as though only one copy of the pre-exilic texts existed, which would either stay in Jerusalem or be taken to Babylon. The present writer assumes that some at least of the pious exiles would have owned scrolls of such texts and would have wished to take them along. We have no idea whether the Babylonian officers organizing the exile would regard such scrolls as seditious literature and try to confiscate and destroy them. Even if they did, pious Israelites would no doubt try to conceal the scrolls on their persons or in their baggage. We must not think of massive mediaeval synagogue Torah scrolls, but much smaller ones which private persons might own. The further assumption that 'the unworthy "people of the land"' were left with the responsibility of preserving Israel's heritage is taking 2 Kgs 25.12 too literally. It refers to the cleaning up operations in Jerusalem and area. The following narrative and related chapters of Jeremiah show that some of the Israelite aristocracy were not exiled because they were either out of Jerusalem when it fell, or they escaped as it fell. Some of them would surely have been concerned with their heritage. We know of Jeremiah and Baruch's continued presence in Palestine for a time. And the narratives we have are not of course comprehensive and exhaustive.

Lemche's treatment of the Neo-Assyrian evidence (1998: 51–55) is superficial and in one respect unexplained. He is preoccupied with the names of the two kingdoms. Judah is always called Judah, but Israel only very rarely bears that name, more often it is 'Samaria' or 'House of Omri'. The latter is declared to be 'the official name', though we have no official documents in contemporary copies to inform us. Use of the name of the capital town for the kingdom is paralleled in the name Babylon. It was the name of a town, but 'king of Babylon' refers to the kingdom. The author does not explain his recurring attention to the different names, but one suspects that the inference is to treat as historically suspect a country without a normal everywhere-used name. But the use of different names of places simultaneously is common in the ancient Near East and elsewhere. Tiglath-pileser III's royal inscriptions refer to the state of Damascus least as Dimashqi, a little more commonly as 'House of Hazael' and most commonly as Sha-imērishu (literally 'He of his donkey', a peculiarly Assyrian name of the place); see Tadmor 1994: 296–304. The Assyians called the ancient Armenian kingdom Urartu, the Babylonians Urashtu, the Israelites Ararat (vowels not guaranteed), but the people themselves Bianili. The terms 'House of Omri' and 'House of Hazael' permit the historical deduction that the two men had a big impact on their times, but the other various names offer no help whatsoever in assessing the historical value of the books of Kings.

Bibliography

Baker, H.D.
    2001   'Marduk-apla-idinna', in H.D. Baker (ed.), *The Prosopography of the Neo-Assyrian Empire* [editor-in-chief S. Parpola], II.2 (Helsinki: The Neo-Assyrian Text Corpus Project): 705–11.
Borger, R
    1984   'Historische Texte in akkadischer Sprache aus Babylonien und Assyrien', in O. Kaiser (ed.), *Texte aus der Umwelt des Alten Testaments*, I.4: *Rechts- und Wirtschaftsurkunden: Historisch-chronologische Texte*, I (Gütersloh: Gütersloher Verlagshaus): 354–410.
Cogan, M., and H. Tadmor
    1988   *II Kings: A New Translation with Introduction and Commentary* (AB, 11; New York: Doubleday).

Davies, P.R.
 1992 *In Search of 'Ancient Israel'* (JSOTSup, 148; Sheffield: Sheffield Academic Press).
Grayson, A.K
 1996 *Assyrian Rulers of the Early First Millennium* BC, II *(858–745 BC)* (The Royal Inscriptions of Mesopotamia, Assyrian Periods, 3; Toronto: University of Toronto Press).
Kuan, J.K.
 1995 *Neo-Assyrian Historical Inscriptions and Syria-Palestine: Israelite/Judean-Tyrian-Damascene Political and Commercial Relations in the Ninth–Eighth Centuries BCE* (Jian Dao Dissertation Series, 1; Bible and Literature, 1; Hong Kong: Alliance Bible Seminary).
Lambert, W.G.
 1994 'When did Jehu Pay Tribute?', in S.E. Porter, P. Joyce and D.E. Orton (eds), *Crossing the Boundaries: Essays in Biblical Interpretation in Honour of Michael D. Goulder* (Biblical Interpretation Series, 8; Leiden: E.J. Brill): 51–56.
Lemche, N.P.
 1998 *The Israelites in History and Tradition* (Louisville, KY: Westminster John Knox Press, and London: SPCK).
Millard, A.R.
 1994 *The Eponyms of the Assyrian Empire 910–612 BC* (SAAS, 2; Helsinki: The Neo-Assyrian Text Corpus Project).
Na²aman, N.
 1974 'Sennacherib's "Letter to God" on his Campaign to Judah', *BASOR* 214: 25–39.
Parpola, S.
 1980 'The Murderer of Sennacherib', in B. Alster (ed.), *Death in Mesopotamia: Papers read at the XXVIe Rencontre Assyriologique Internationale* (Mesopotamia: Copenhagen Studies in Assyriology, 8; Copenhagen: Akademisk Forlag): 171–82.
Saggs, H.W.F.
 2001 *The Nimrud Letters, 1952* (Cuneiform Texts from Nimrud, 5; London: British School of Archaeology in Iraq).
Tadmor, Hayim
 1994 *The Inscriptions of Tiglath-pileser III King of Assyria* (Jerusalem: The Israel Academy of Sciences and Humanities).

Chapter 16

HEBREW AND WEST SEMITIC INSCRIPTIONS AND PRE-EXILIC ISRAEL

André Lemaire

Like every historian, the historian of pre-exilic Israel must first assemble and then exploit the contemporary documentation concerning the society which he studies. Having worked for more than thirty years on pre-exilic palaeo-Hebrew epigraphy and more generally with North-West Semitic epigraphy from the same period, it is a pleasure for me to attempt to give an account of the contribution of West Semitic epigraphy to the history of Israel in the monarchical period, and in doing so, to clarify certain connections with the text of the Bible. Without claiming to be exhaustive this account will particularly emphasize the contribution of the last thirty years and will basically follow a chronological order.

If we consider the period from about 1200 till 587 BCE the West Semitic epigrapher may clearly distinguish two periods:

1. From the beginning of the Iron Age till about 830 BCE West Semitic inscriptions remain very rare and are mostly confined to Phoenicia, with more than fifty inscribed arrow heads (Deutsch and Heltzer 1999: 13–19; McCarter 1999; Puech 2000; Sader 2000), monumental inscriptions from Byblos (Gibson 1982: 9–24; *KAI* 1–3, vol. 1 of which has now appeared in a 5th edn [2002], which I cite here), and some inscriptions on bronze vases (Yardenna 2002). However, some inscriptions also attest the use of alphabetic writing in Palestine, both in central Cisjordan (Davies 1991: nos 21.001, 29.001, 35.001, 39.001, 40.001, 41.001; Bunimovitz and Lederman 2000: 107*; Mazar 2003) as well as in the Philistine plain. Some inscriptions, for example the ostracon from ʿIzbet Ṣarṭah (eleventh century BCE), the Gezer calendar (tenth century BCE) and the small inscriptions from Beth-shemesh and Tell Batash are probably on the borderline between Philistine and Israelite culture (Lemaire 2000), while the most ancient ostraca from Arad, in particular no. 76 (Aharoni 1981: 98–99), probably derive from this period. Written in ink, they directly testify to the presence of scribal activity.

2. Beginning at the end of the ninth century BCE, North-West Semitic inscriptions from the Near East become more numerous and appear over a broader area, including Egypt, southern Anatolia,

Transjordan, northern Mesopotamia and as far as Iranian Azerbaijan. Besides monumental inscriptions, often royal and perhaps stimulated by the Neo-Assyrian example (Na᾿aman 2000: 95), we increasingly encounter ostraca as well as inscribed seals and their derivative products: stamps, bullae and *cretulae* (i.e. pieces of clay sealing an object). Towards the end of this period we even possess three papyri, one in palaeo-Hebrew (Davies 1991: nos 33.001/2), one in Aramaic (Gibson 1975: 110–16; Porten 1981; *KAI* 266) and one perhaps in Phoenician (*KAI* 50). Moreover, in the seventh century BCE Upper Mesopotamia produces various Aramaic tablets, triangular or rectangular in shape, more than a hundred of which are now in the course of publication (Lemaire 2001a).

The inscriptions relating to the history of Israel that we shall now consider all belong to this second period, but the information they provide can sometimes indirectly shed light on the earlier period, and this is the case with the first three.

1. *The Tell Fekheryeh Inscription*

The Aramaean/Assyrian inscription from Tell Fekheryeh, discovered in 1979 at the source of the Khabur, is inscribed on a royal statue and probably dates from about 826–810 BCE (Abou-Assaf, Bordreuil and Millard 1982; Lipiński 1994: 19–81; *KAI* 309). The palaeography of this inscription, however, presents archaizing traits which would normally serve to date it to about 1000 BCE. This implies that this region employed Aramaic writing before the end of the second millennium and that the form of writing had not evolved much, probably because the region of the Khabur had been isolated from the heartland of Aramaean territory.

At least beginning in 894 BCE the king of Guzana, Abisalamu of Bit Bahiani, was compelled to pay tribute by Adad-nirāri II, putting an end to the Aramaean expansion in this region, which had reached its climax under Ashur-rabi (1012–972). This Aramaean expansion in Upper Mesopotamia probably corresponds to the biblical tradition of 2 Sam. 8.3, which reports that 'Hadadezer son of Rehob, king of Zobah' was active as far as the Euphrates at the time of King David prior to being conquered by him (Lemaire 2001c: 129, with bibliography). The connection with the history of Israel here is only indirect and, in part, conjectural. The situation is quite different with the following example.

2. *The Moabite Stone*

The Moabite stele of Mesha, king of Moab, discovered in 1868, is now in the Louvre. Unfortunately, it has never received an *editio princeps*. Since its discovery it has been emphasized that this stele explicitly mentions 'Israel' (*yśr'l*, lines 5, 7, 10–11, 14, 18), its God 'Yahweh' (*yhwh*, line 18), as well as its King 'Omri' (*'mry*, lines 4–5), 'his son' (*bnh*, line 6) and 'his house' (*bth*, line 7; cf. *bnh*, line 8). Moreover, certain biblical place names are also mentioned: Gad, Ataroth, Baal-meon, Kiriathaim, Nebo, Dibon, Aroer, Arnon, Bezer, Beth-diblathaim and Horonaim. The role of Kemosh in this inscription may also be compared with the Bible according to which Kemosh is 'the god of Moab' and Moab is 'the people of Kemosh', while we read in the Bible too that Mesha first paid tribute to Ahab but subsequently rebelled against Israel (2 Kgs 1.1; 3.4–27).

Most commentators have tried to correlate the conquests of Mesha with the account of the joint Israelite/Judaean campaign against Moab recounted in 2 Kgs 3.4–27, and have dated the inscription to about 850 or 840 BCE (Gibson 1971: 71–83; *KAI* 181) Well before the recent interpretation of T.L. Thompson (2000), which proposes to date the stele after the death of Mesha in order to affirm the fictitious character of the text – a theory which takes no account at all of the palaeography and of the literary genre (Emerton 2002) – we have had occasion to remark that the supposed agreement between the text of this inscription and the conquests of Mesha does not hold, for the stele probably dates from the end of the reign of Mesha about 810 BCE, as the expression 'Israel is destroyed for ever' (*yśr'l 'bd 'bd 'lm*, line 7) corresponds to Israel's situation in the reign of Jehoahaz (cf. 2 Kgs 13.7) (Lemaire 1987: 210–14; 1991b: 146–50).

Moreover, it should be emphasized that this stele recalls not only the past of the first half of the ninth century BCE – the reign of Omri (c. 885–874), king of Israel, and of Kemoshyat, Mesha's father – but also the even more distant past, going back at least to the tenth century BCE, since it recalls the fact that Gad had inhabited Ataroth for a long time (line 10) (Lemaire 1991b).

Furthermore, in studying this stele minutely I was able to propose reading in the damaged part at the end of line 31 the expression 'Beth-[Da]vid', designating the kingdom of Judah which controlled the city of Horonaim and a part of the territory to the south-east of the Dead Sea (Lemaire 1994a). This expression would naturally imply that David was considered the founder of the Judaean kingdom of Jerusalem and allows one to understand better the political evolution of the area south of the Dead Sea where Edom only asserted itself as an independent kingdom about 845 BCE (2 Kgs 8.22).

All in all, although the lower part of the stele is now lost, this inscription is a good example of West Semitic royal historiography of the ninth century, highlighting the chief acts of the king both in his great works and in war, in which he appears as the lieutenant of his national god Kemosh, carrying out the instructions of his oracles (lines 14, 32; Lemaire 2001b).

3. *The Aramaic Stele from Tel Dan*

The mention of 'Beth-David' in a damaged passage of the Moabite stele has been confirmed to some degree by the discovery of the first fragment of the Aramaic stele from Tel Dan, near the source of the river Jordan, on 21 July 1993 (Biran and Naveh 1993). In fact, we can clearly read the expression 'Beth-David' there in line 9. As this inscription was very fragmentary it was immediately the object of numerous articles proposing various historical interpretations with dates varying between c. 900 and c. 750 BCE. I myself proposed to connect it with the great Aramaean king of Damascus, Hazael, in the second half of the ninth century BCE (Lemaire 1994b).

One year later, in 1994, the discovery of two other fragments confirmed this historical interpretation with a clear reference to the *coup d'état* of Jehu in 841, recorded in 2 Kings 9–10, and mentioning the death of Jehoram, son of Ahab, king of Israel, and of Ahaziah, son of Jehoram, king of the 'house of David' (Biran and Naveh 1995). Even though the stele is still very fragmentary, this new fragment completely confirms the interpretation of 'Beth-David' as a designation of the kingdom of Judah (Lemaire 1998c; Ehrlich 2001; *pace* Gmirkin 2002; Athas 2003), the absence of the word divider between *byt* and *dwd* being easily explicable by the fact that the Aramaean scribe considered this expression as denoting a sole entity, Judah, parallel with Israel (line 8) (Rendsburg 1995; Couturier 2001).

The fact that the expression 'Beth-David' is attested in two steles of Israel's enemies shows that this expression formed part of the diplomatic language of the Levant and that, in line with other parallel terms for other kingdoms of the Levant, the kingdom of Jerusalem was reputed to have been founded by David.

It should be noted that the real historiographical problem posed by this stele is not the interpretation of the expression 'Beth-David' but the fact that the Aramaean king boasts of having killed the two kings of Israel and Judah, which seems to contradict the account of Jehu's *coup d'état* in 2 Kings 9–10, where the death of these kings is attributed rather to Jehu and his soldiers. Faced by these two diverging historiographical traditions N. Na'aman (1999: 115–16; 2000: 100–104; Naveh 1999; Irvine 2001: 113–17) claims that one should give preference a priori to the epigraphic version of the Aramaean king, but he forgets – something highlighted by current researches on Neo-Assyrian historiography – that royal inscriptions should also be interpreted critically and that we know of at least one parallel case in which an Assyrian king boasts of having killed another king (Michel 1954: 32–33), whereas in inscriptions nearer the events the death of this latter king is attributed to the local population (*ARAB*, I, § 563, 610). It seems to me that we have here a similar problem of interpretation, particularly if this inscription was written in the second half of the reign of Hazael, about 826–805/3 BCE (Schniedewind 1996: 84–85; Lemaire 1998c: 10–11).

On the other hand, a probable convergence with the Neo-Assyrian inscription of the monolith of Kurkh should be noted, which reports the battle of Qarqar in 853: in 841 at the time of the battle of Ramoth-Gilead, the army of the king of Israel and his vassal, the king of Judah, probably comprised 'two thousand chariots' (lines 6–7), as at Qarqar.

Although fragmentary the Tel Dan stele constitutes therefore important evidence not only for the history of the Aramaean kingdom of Damascus under King Hazael but also for the kingdoms of Israel and Judah, which in spite of the power of their army, suffered a grave defeat relating to a revolution.

Finally, both this Aramaic inscription and the Moabite stele reveal that royal historiography and propaganda were well developed among the neighbours of Israel and Judah during the second half of the ninth century and there is apparently no reason why it should not have been the same in the Hebrew kingdoms (Parker 1997: 74–75).

4. *The Stele of Zakkur*

The stele of Zakkur, king of Hamath and Lu'ash, said to come from Afis in northern Syria (Gibson 1975: 6–17; *KAI* 202), does not mention Israel but it does refer to king 'Barhadad son of Hazael, king of Aram' (lines 4–5), author of the preceding stele, and he is there at the head of a coalition of 'sixteen kings' of the Levant (Lemaire 1993). Like Hazael, this king of Damascus is well known from the Bible as an enemy of Israel, more precisely of King Joash who succeeded in liberating himself from his suzerainty (2 Kgs 6.24–7.20; cf. 1 Kgs 20, where Ahab has replaced an original reference to Joash).

This stele is also a fine example of North-West Semitic royal historiography highlighting building work and important deeds in war. Also the king refers explicitly to prophetic oracles of 'seers and spokesmen' (*ḥzyn*, *'ddn*), in his favour at the time of a particularly serious crisis (A, lines 11–17). The reference to the carrying out of prophetic oracles seems therefore quite normal in the royal historiography of the period and their presence in the books of Kings is not surprising (Lemaire 2001b: 93–96).

5. *The Aramaic Plaster Inscriptions from Deir 'Alla*

The relations between the Hebrews and Aramaeans were not limited to war. It is rather clear nowadays that Aramaean culture influenced Hebrew culture. The best example of this is provided by the plaster inscriptions from Deir 'Alla in the central Jordan valley (Lemaire 1991a; Weippert 1991; Lipiński 1994: 103–70; Segert 1995; Tropper 2001; *KAI* 312). We have here inscriptions in red and black ink from the first half of the eighth century BCE written on the plaster (or whitewashed surface) of a wall and which were collected at the foot of the wall. The minute work of restoration allows the fragmentary reading of seventeen lines which constitute the copy of a literary manuscript. I myself was able to restore the title in red ink: 'Book of [Ba]laam son of Beor, the man who saw the gods (*spr [b]l'm br b'r 'š hzh 'lhn*)' (Caquot and Lemaire 1977: 193–94).

We have here therefore the copy of an extract from the Aramaic book of the seer/prophet Balaam, son of Beor, already well known from the Bible in Numbers 22–24. This 'seer' of Aramaean origin was so famous that the Aramaeans of the kingdom of Damascus had written a book recounting stories about him. He was apparently also so famous that a Jerusalem scribe made him the chief character in Numbers 22–24 (Lemaire 1985), where he pronounces oracles in favour of Israel. The Balaam inscription also confirms the importance of prophecy in the West Semitic world, the importance of which was attested already as early as the Mari texts in the eighteenth century BCE (Lemaire 2001b: 96–101).

6. *Çineköy Bilingual Inscription*

The recent discovery in 1998 of a new bilingual Luwian-Phoenician inscription at Çineköy (Tekoğlu and Lemaire 2000), some 30 km south of Adana in Turkey does not reveal any direct connection with the history of Israel. However, its wording clarifies Israelite historiography a little on three points.

1. In line 2 Urikki, king of Que (Cilicia) in the second half of the eighth century BCE, proclaims himself to be 'of the line of Mopsos (*'šph mpš*)', which confirms the triple designation of the kingdom of Que as 'the house of Mopsos' in the Phoenician inscriptions from Karatepe (Bron 1979: 172–76; Röllig 1999). These expressions refer to the founder of the dynasty of Que who, if we believe a tradition recorded in the Chronicle of Eusebius of Caesarea (Helm 1984: 60b) and various Greek traditions (Vanschoonwinkel 1990), could have reigned from 1184 BCE, at the beginning of the Iron I period. The Phoenician expressions *'šph mpš* and *bt mpš* can be compared with the Hebrew expressions *bn dwd* and *byt dwd*.

2. In lines 7–10 Urikki recognizes that 'the king [of Ashur and] all the house of Ashur have been for me a father [and a] mother (*l'b [wl]'m*)' and that 'the Danunians and the Assyrians have become one house (*bt 'hd*)', expressions clearly alluding to a voluntary alliance/vassalage *vis-à-vis* Tiglath-pileser III and his successors. This voluntary attachment to the Assyrian suzerain, expressed in family terms, is parallel to the voluntary submission of King Ahaz

to the same Tiglath-pileser III, to whom he declares 'I am your servant and your son' (2 Kgs 16.7).

3. The Luwian term used to designate the kingdom of Que is *Hiyawa*. Leaving aside here the very interesting problem of the identification of *Hiyawa* with the *Ahhiyawa* of the Hittite texts, we may note that this term could explain the biblical ethnic term *ḥiwwî*/'Hivite' (cf. the suggestion of Mendenhall 1973: 154–56), which has usually been considered to be unexplained and enigmatic (de Vaux 1971: 134, ET 1978, I: 137–38).

7. *The Aramaic Stele from Bukân*

After the Deir ʿAlla inscription the connection between Hebrew literature and Aramaean culture is well illustrated by a recent publication in Persian (Kanzaq 1996): that of an Aramaic stele from the end of the eighth century found in the discoveries at Tapeh Qalaychi, near Bukân, south-east of Lake Urmia in Iranian Afghanistan, in a site which was probably the capital of the ancient Mannean kingdom (Lemaire 1998a and b; Ephʿal 1999; Sokoloff 1999; Lemaire 1999a; Kaufman 2002: 46–48; *KAI* 320).

The thirteen lines of the two fragments discovered constitute only the end of a monumental inscription, probably royal, with traditional curses against anyone who would damage the stele. Some of the curses are very close to the curses in the Aramaic inscriptions from Sefire as well as certain biblical formulations in Leviticus and Jeremiah. Thus, we read in lines 8–9: 'And may there disappear from his courts the smoke of fire and the sound of the two millstones'. This may be compared with Jer. 25.10b: 'And I will make disappear from them... the sound of the two millstones (*qôl rēḥayim*) and the light of the lamp', expressions which are taken up again in Rev. 18.22–23.

This new example illustrates well the closeness of the Aramaean and Hebrew cultures, even though the texts come from places several hundred km distant from each other.

8. *The Inscriptions from Kuntillet ʿAjrud*

The copy of a literary text on plaster (or the whitewashed surface) of a wall is found again from the same period as the Deir ʿAlla inscription (first half of the eighth century) in a kind of stopping off point or khan for caravans crossing the Sinai desert between Kadesh-Barnea and Eilat (Lemaire 1984). In 1975/76 texts were found in Phoenician script but Hebrew language written on the surface of a wall, as well as palaeo-Hebrew inscriptions with drawings, on fragments of large storage jars or pithoi (Meshel 1978; 1992). On one of them above a depiction we recognize a blessing formula: 'by Yahweh of Samaria and by his asherah (*lyhwh šmrn wl'šrth)'*. This formula has led to the spilling of much scholarly ink. In fact, the majority of commentators see here the Ugaritic goddess 'Asherah' who would have been the consort of Yahweh (Binger 1997; Hadley 2000 with nuances). However, other epigraphers, of whom I am one (Lemaire 2003: 73–82 with bibliography), note that for philological and historical reasons it is better to see in the Hebrew word *asherah* the designation of the sacred tree of the traditional Yahwistic sanctuaries.

9. *Khirbet el–Qom Inscription*

In fact, at about the same period, I also proposed reading a blessing formula associating 'Yahweh' and 'his *asherah*' in an inscription from Khirbet el–Qom, discovered in 1967 (Dever 1969/70: 163–65) in a tomb but very difficult to read as it was probably written as a graffito in semi-darkness (Lemaire 1977; Renz 1995: 202–11).

It must be emphasized that the inscriptions from Kuntillet ʿAjrud and Khirbet el–Qom are connected with northern Israelite and Judaean Hebrew respectively and that they both date from the first half or the middle of the eighth century. They are thus prior to the reigns of Hezekiah and Josiah and the religious reforms which biblical tradition attributes to them (Lemaire 2003: 103–21). In fact, the *asherah* is no longer attested in the blessing formulas or salutations at the beginning of epigraphic letters from the end of the monarchical period.

10. *Seals and Bullae Mentioning Kings of Israel and Judah*

Since we are now referring to palaeo-Hebrew inscriptions it is necessary to cite the references to the various kings of Israel and Judah of the eighth century who appear on seals or bullae. Already earlier four seals were known of servants/ministers of kings of Israel and Judah, those of 'Shema, servant of Jeroboam' (*WSS* 2), i.e. Jeroboam II king of Israel (c. 790–750), 'Shebanyaw' (*WSS* 3) and 'Abyaw' (*WSS* 4), servants of 'Uzziah', king of Judah (c. 776–739), and 'Ushna, servant of Ahaz' (*WSS* 5), king of Judah (c. 735–719). This last seal can be compared to a very recently published bulla with the inscriptions 'Ushna, servant of Hezekiah' (Deutsch 2003: no. 13a-c), probably meaning that the same person was minister under two successive kings.

In 1995 I myself published a magnificent seal, relating iconographically to the workshop of Samaria about 750–722, inscribed 'Belonging to Abdi, servant/minister of Hoshea' (Lemaire 1995), Hoshea being the last king of Israel, who reigned from 731 to 722 and is well known from the Bible and Neo-Assyrian texts. The Egyptianizing iconography and the setting in gold of the seal illustrate well Israel's culture and wealth at the end of the monarchical period (Lemaire 1997: 449–50; Deutsch and Lemaire 2000: 7).

However, it is not only seals of royal officials which have been found. Recently there have appeared two bullae of kings themselves belonging to the Moussaieff collection in London: an aniconic bulla in excellent condition with an inscription in three lines stating: 'Belonging to Ahaz, (son of) Jotham, king of Judah' (Deutsch 1999: XVIa-XVIIa) and a bulla blackened by fire with an inscription around a two-winged beetle stating, 'Belonging to Hezekiah, (son of) Ahaz, king of Judah' (Cross 1999a and b; Deutsch 1999: XVIb-XVIIb). Other bullae of King Hezekiah have been published very recently (Deutsch 2002). The authenticity of one of these latter bullae is assured by the fact that it had been made by the same seal as a bulla fragment published by Avigad in 1986 (no. 199) and which it had not been possible to identify because of its excessively fragmentary state. This latter seal impression formed part of a batch of several hundred bullae deriving from archives from the end of the Judaean monarchy, which shows that the document linked to this bulla had been preserved for more than a century.

11. *Philistine Inscription from Tell Miqne/Ekron*

During the summer of 1996, in the course of the last campaign of the joint American–Israeli excavations at Tell Miqne, ancient Ekron, which was one of the five Philistine cities and the one which was closest to the kingdom of Judah, a monumental inscription of five lines was discovered (Gitin, Dothan and Naveh 1997; Demsky 1997; *KAI* 286), a dedication of a temple giving the name of the governor/king of Ekron, as well as four of his ancestors: 'The temple which Akish/Akaious, son of Padi, son of Yasod, son of Ada, son of Ya'ir, governor of Ekron. . .'. Akish/Akaious, as well as his father Padi, were already known from Neo-Assyrian inscriptions. More particularly, Akish/Akaious seems to be a typically Philistine name, for it was already attested in the Bible as the name of the king of Gath in the time of Saul (1 Sam. 21.11–16; 27–29) and Solomon (1 Kgs 2.39–40). It probably means 'the Achaean', which sheds light on the origin of the Philistines, who were neighbours and sometimes enemies of Israel and Judah.

Furthermore a small inscription on jar (Gitin and Cogan 1999) reads: '(Belonging) to Baal and to Padi' and this association of god and king is also known from several passages in the Hebrew Bible: Exod. 22.27 (ET 28); 2 Sam. 15.21; 1 Kgs 21.13; Isa. 8.21; and Prov. 24.21 (Gitin and Cogan 1999: 198 n. 26; Williamson 2000).

12. *Bullae of Leading Judaean Officials*

During the last fifteen years the number of bullae inscribed in palaeo-Hebrew has grown from several dozen to about one thousand (Deutsch 2003), testifying to the development of the use of writing in the kingdom of

Judah from the second half of the eighth century BCE to the fall of Jerusalem in 587. These bullae sometimes bear a title that throws some light on the organization of the royal administration, and principally on the most important officials. Thus, the bulla of 'Mibtahiah, master of the palace (*"ser 'al habbayit*)' is an addition to the already rather long list of persons bearing this title, which apparently refers to the second in command in the state, next after the king, a sort of 'Prime Minister' (Deutsch 1999: no. 6; 2003: no. 36; cf. perhaps *WSS* 410: 'Mibtahiah, servant of the king').

Again, the bulla of 'Shemaiah, servant/minister of the king', published in 1994 (Deutsch and Heltzer: no. 12), bears a title which is rather frequent, probably referring to those who were the leading royal officials. In the eighth century, as we have seen above, the name of the king was explicitly indicated, while in the seventh century the name of the king is no longer given and one simply has the more general title 'servant of the king', a title which remains valid even if the king changes. This titulature could indicate a certain autonomy of these leading officials *vis-à-vis* the person of the king; however, it does impede us in dating these bullae more precisely. Finally, we should mention the bulla of the 'governor of the city', that is to say probably Jerusalem, the city par excellence, with symbolic iconography of military connotation, which no longer contains the name of the person but only the name of his office. Apparently the same seal could be used by several successive governors, which might testify to a certain autonomy of function with regard to the king on the part of those who assumed the title.

13. *Seals and Bullae Mentioning Non-Royal Persons in the Bible*

Besides kings, among the hundreds of seals and bullae from the end of the period of the Judaean monarchy we should reserve a place for those mentioning, in a more or less certain way, persons known from the Bible, in particular in the book of Jeremiah and the end of 2 Kings. According to whether the persons present two or three identical elements, the identification with the biblical homonym could be considered as possible, likely, probable or practically certain (Avigad 1987; Schneider 1991; Lemaire 1997; Mykytiuk 1998).

1. A seal presenting a galloping horse with the inscription, 'Belonging to Asaiah, servant of the king' (Deutsch and Heltzer 1994: no. 21). Identification is possible with 'Asaiah, servant of the king' in the reign of Josiah, mentioned in 2 Kgs 22.12, 14, alongside the scribe Shaphan and the priest Hilkiah.
2. A bulla discovered at the time of the excavations of the Ophel directed by Y. Shiloh, with fifty other bullae, in a room destroyed in 587 (Shiloh 1986; *WSS* 470), reading 'Belonging to Gemariah,

(so)n of Shaphan'. Identification is possible with 'Gemariah, son of Shaphan, the scribe' mentioned in Jer. 36.10–12, 25.

3.   A seal from about the middle of the seventh century, published in 1987 by N. Avigad (p. 237; *WSS* 90) reading 'Belonging to Azaliah, son of Meshullam'. According to Avigad identification is likely with the father of 'Shaphan, son of Azaliah, son of Meshullam, the scribe', mentioned in 2 Kgs 22.3. Together with the preceding bulla we are therefore in a position possibly to trace the family of Shaphan over four generations, a figure who played an important role at the time of the discovery of Deuteronomy.

4.   A seal of dark blue agate published by Josette Elayi in 1986, reading 'Belonging to Hanan, son of Hilkiah, the priest'. Identification is likely with a son of 'Hilkiah, the priest' mentioned in 2 Kgs 22.4–24 (Elayi 1987; 1992).

5.   A bulla discovered in the excavations on the Ophel, with the inscription 'Belonging to Azariah, son of Hilkiah' (*WSS* 596). Identification is possible with the brother of the preceding and with the priest 'Azariah, son of Hilkiah', a Zadokite ancestor of Ezra mentioned in Ezra 7.1 and 1 Chron. 5.39 (ET 6.13); 9.11 (Schneider 1988; 1991).

6.   A bulla coming from the excavations at Lachish, where we read, 'Belonging to Gedaliah, master of the palace' (Davies 1991: no. 100.149; *WSS* 405; cf. 409?). Following Roland de Vaux (1936) identification is possible with 'Gedaliah, son of Ahikam, son of Shaphan', whom Nebuchadnezzar established as governor of Judah after 587 (2 Kgs 25.22–25; Jer. 39.14; 40.7–16; 41.1–10, 18; 43.6).

7.   A bulla published in 1993 (Barkay 1993: 109–14) bears the inscription 'Belonging to Ishmael, son of the king'. Identification is possible with the murderer of Gedaliah, possible owner of the preceding bulla, referred to in the Bible as 'Ishmael, son of Netaniah, son of Elishama, of the royal family' (2 Kgs 25:23–25; Jer. 40.13–16; 41.1–18).

8.   A seal published in the last century bears the inscription 'Belonging to Elishama, son of the king' (*WSS* 11). Identification is possible with the grandfather of the possible owner of the preceding bulla (cf. 2 Kgs 25.25; Jer. 41.1).

9.   A bulla published by N. Avigad (1978: 53; *WSS* 414) reads, 'Jerahmeel, son of the king'. Identification is likely with 'Jerahmeel, son of the king', mentioned in Jer. 36.26 as a member of the royal court of Jehoiakim about 605/4.

10. A bulla from the Borowski collection reads, 'Belonging to Zedekiah, son of Hanani'. Identification is likely with 'Zedekiah, son of Hananiah', mentioned in Jer. 36.12 (Lemaire 1999b: 113*-14*).

11. A seal published by N. Avigad (1978: 56; *WSS* 390) reads,

'Belonging to Seraiah, (son of) Neriah'. Identification is possible with 'Seraiah, son of Neriah, son of Mahseiah...', the quartermaster (*śar m^{e}nûḥâ*) mentioned in Jer. 51.59 as sent to Babylon by king Zedekiah in 594/3.

12. A bulla attested in two examples made by the same seal reads, 'Berekiah, son of Neriah, the scribe'. Identification is practically certain with the scribe/secretary of Jeremiah, 'Baruch', mentioned in Jer. 32.12–16; 36.4–32; 43.3, 6; 45.1–2 (Avigad 1978: 53; *WSS* 417). We therefore very probably have two examples of the bulla which belonged to the early redactor of the book of Jeremiah, at least of the part edited in the lifetime of the prophet.

It will be noted that in these twelve possible, probable or practically certain cases of identification with persons mentioned in the Bible, four are mentioned in Jeremiah 36, three in 2 Kings 22 and three in 2 Kings 25 and Jeremiah 41. These four chapters reveal numerous names of leading royal officials under King Josiah, about 622, Jehoiakim, about 605 and after the fall of Jerusalem in 587. At the current rate of new seals and bullae becoming available (Deutsch 2003) it appears that we could soon make attempts at a study of certain families of leading Judaean officials and of their careers at the end of the monarchical period.

14. *Ostraca*

Our knowledge of the Judaean monarchy about 600 BCE is also illuminated by the well-known Lachish and Arad ostraca (Davies 1991: 1–38), as well as by ostraca which have recently appeared on the antiquities market and in private collections. Thus:

1. A first ostracon is a small accountancy text concerning flour dated to the 'seventh month of year six' (perhaps of King Zedekiah), and mention is made of the place name Maqqedah (Deutsch and Heltzer 1995: 81–83; Lemaire 1997: 457–58).
2. A second ostracon, a little more difficult to read as the ink is partly effaced (Lemaire 1977: 460–61), seems to constitute a kind of menu for a group of men on the 'Sabbath' (lines 8, 9) with 'bread (*lḥm*)', 'ripe olives (*grgrm*)', 'flat cakes (*ḥlt*)', 'vegetables (*yrq*)', 'date cakes (*'šprm*)' and 'wine (*yyn*)'.
3. A third presents an accounting list of proper names, here followed by a sum of silver (Deutsch and Heltzer 1995: 92–102; Lehman 1998). These lists constitute about half of these ostraca.
4. This same proportion is found again in groups of still unpublished ostraca.
5. These unpublished ostraca can also be messages in the style of the Lachish and Arad letters, such as an ostracon with a rather long initial polite formula and asking to come to the meeting of the

sender (front), and he specifies his name on the back, as one still does today on the back of an envelope containing a letter.

The publication of these unpublished ostraca on which I am currently working should throw light complementary to that furnished by the Lachish and Arad ostraca on the functioning of the Judaean administration on the eve of Nebuchadnezzar's second campaign in a region situated between Lachish and Hebron, as is implied by the mention of several place names: Maqqedah, Libnah and Ashan.

15. *Silver Amulets from Ketef Hinnom*

It is also about 600 BCE (*pace* Renz 1995: 447–56), but from the capital, Jerusalem, that we must date two silver amulets discovered in a tomb at Ketef Hinnom, south-west of the old city (Barkay 1986: 29–31; Yardeni 1991; Barkay 1992). Although they are very delicately engraved and damaged, we can read there the following blessing:

'May the Lord bless you and keep you (*ybrk yhwh wyšmrk*), may the Lord make his face shine upon you (*y'r yhwh pnyw 'lyk*), and may he give you peace! (*wyśm lk šlm*)'.

This wording here is practically identical to that of the Priestly blessing in Num. 6.24–26, but it is difficult to be precise about the exact connection between the two texts (*pace* Waaler 2002). Both could go back to a liturgical formula of the First Temple towards the end of the monarchical period.

16. *Conclusions*

Leaving aside numerous other inscriptions, in particular those relating to apprenticeship to writing linked with schools of the monarchical period, even if we think that it explains directly the birth of the biblical literary tradition, we must conclude this survey and emphasize that the relation of these inscriptions to the history of ancient Israel and to the understanding of the biblical text can take very different forms and the degree of directness can vary.

One thing, however, is clear: even if virtually all the papyri and all the parchments of the monarchical period no longer exist and have perhaps disappeared for ever, writing was well known in the kingdoms of Israel and Judah before 587. The attempt to redate some of these inscriptions to the Hellenistic period as was proposed lately about the Siloam Tunnel inscription (Rogerson and Davies 1996) is not serious from the point of view of epigraphy (Hendel 1996; Hackett, Cross, McCarter, Yardeni, Lemaire, Eshel and Hurvitz 1997) and archaeology (Frumkin, Shimron and Rosenbaum 2003).

In fact, Hebrew inscriptions were not unknown in the kingdoms of Israel and Judah before 587, any more than other West Semitic inscriptions were in the other kingdoms of the time in the Levant. Royal historiography and propaganda as well as prophetic literature are well attested in the neighbouring kingdoms and pre-exilic Israel, at least from the second half of the ninth century BCE.

Bibliography

Abou-Assaf, A., P. Bordreuil and A.R. Millard
    1982   *La statue de Tell Fekherye et son inscription bilingue assyro-araméenne* (Paris: Recherches sur les civilisations).

Aharoni, Y.
    1981   *Arad Inscriptions* (Jerusalem: Israel Exploration Society).

Athas, G.
    2003   *The Tel Dan Inscription: A Reappraisal and a New Interpretation* (JSOTSup, 360; Copenhagen International Seminar, 12; London and New York: Sheffield Academic Press).

Avigad, N.
    1978   'Baruch the Scribe and Jerahmeel the King's Son', *IEJ* 28: 52–56.
    1986   *Hebrew Bullae from the Time of Jeremiah* (Jerusalem: Israel Exploration Society).
    1987   'On the Identification of Persons Mentioned in Hebrew Epigraphic Sources', in D. Barag, G. Foerster and A. Negev (eds), *Michael Avi-Yonah Memorial Volume* (Eretz-Israel, 19; Jerusalem: Israel Exploration Society): 235–37.

Barkay, G.
    1986   *Ketef Hinnom: A Treasure Facing Jerusalem's Walls* (Israel Museum Catalogue, 274; Jerusalem).
    1992   'The Priestly Benediction on Silver Plaques from Ketef Hinnom in Jerusalem', *Tel Aviv* 19: 139–92.
    1993   'A Bulla of Ishmael, the King's Son', *BASOR* 290–91: 109–14.

Binger, T.
    1997   *Asherah in Ugarit, Israel and the Old Testament* (JSOTSup, 232; Copenhagen International Seminar, 2; Sheffield: Sheffield Academic Press).

Biran, A., and J. Naveh
    1993   'An Aramaic Stele Fragment from Tel Dan', *IEJ* 43: 81–98.
    1995   'The Tel Dan Inscription: A New Fragment', *IEJ* 45: 3–18

Bron, F.
    1979   *Recherches sur les inscriptions phéniciennes de Karatepe* (Hautes Etudes Orientales, 11; Geneva and Paris: Droz).

Bunimovitz, S., and Z. Lederman
    2000   'Tel Bet Shemesh – 1991–1996', *Excavations and Surveys in Israel* 20: 105*–108*.

Caquot, A., and A. Lemaire
    1977   'Les textes araméens de Deir ʿAlla', *Syria* 54: 189–208

Couturier, G.
	2001	'Quelques observations sur le *BYT DWD* de la stèle araméenne de Tel Dan', in
			P.M.M. Daviau, J.W. Wevers and M. Weigl (eds), *The World of the
			Aramaeans*, II: *Studies in History and Archaeology in Honour of Paul-Eugène
			Dion* (JSOTSup, 325; Sheffield: Sheffield Academic Press): 72–98.
Cross, F.M.
	1999a	'King Hezekiah's Seal Bears Phoenician Imagery', *BARev* 25.2: 42–45, 60.
	1999b	'A Bulla of Hezekiah, King of Judah', in P.H. Williams and T. Hiebert (eds),
			*Realia Dei: Essays in Archaeology and Biblical Interpretation in Honor of
			Edward F. Campbell* (Atlanta, GA: Scholars Press).
Davies, G.I.
	1991	*Ancient Hebrew Inscriptions, Corpus and Concordance* (Cambridge: Cambridge
			University Press).
Demsky, A.
	1997	'The Name of the Goddess of Ekron: A New Reading', *JANESCU* 25: 1–5.
Deutsch, R.
	1998	'First Impression. What We Learn from King Ahaz's Seal', *BARev* 24.3: 54–
			56, 62.
	1999	*Messages from the Past: Hebrew Bullae from the Time of Isaiah through the
			Destruction of the First Temple. Shlomo Moussaieff Collection and an Up to
			Date Corpus* (Tel Aviv: Archaeological Center Publications).
	2002	'"Lasting Impressions"'. New Bullae Reveal Egyptian-Style Emblems on
			Judah's Royal Seals', *BARev* 28.4: 42–51, 60–62.
	2003	*Biblical Period Hebrew Bullae: The Josef Chaim Kaufman Collection* (Tel Aviv:
			Archaeological Center Publications).
Deutsch, R., and M. Heltzer
	1994	*Forty New Ancient West Semitic Inscriptions* (Tel Aviv: Archaeological Center
			Publications).
	1995	*New Epigraphic Evidence from the Biblical Period* (Tel Aviv: Archaeological
			Center Publications).
	1999	*West Semitic Epigraphic News of the 1st Millenium BCE* (Tel Aviv:
			Archaeological Center Publications).
Deutsch, R., and A. Lemaire
	2000	*Biblical Period Personal Seals in the Shlomo Moussaieff Collection* (Tel Aviv:
			Archaeological Center Publications).
Dever, W.G.
	1969/70	'Iron Age Epigraphic Material from the Area of Khirbet el–Kôm', *HUCA* 40–
			41: 139–204.
Ehrlich, C.S.
	2001	'The *BYTDWD*-Inscription and Israelite Historiography: Taking Stock after
			Half a Decade of Research', in P.M.M. Daviau, J.W. Wevers and M. Weigl
			(eds), *The World of the Aramaeans*, II: *Studies in History and Archaeology in
			Honour of Paul-Eugène Dion* (JSOTSup, 325; Sheffield: Sheffield Academic
			Press): 57–71.
Elayi, J.
	1986	'Le sceau du prêtre Hanan fils de Hilqiyahu', *Sem* 36: 43–46.
	1987	'Name of Deuteronomy's Author Found on a Seal Ring', *BARev* 13.5: 54–56.

1992   'New Light on the Identification of the Seal of Priest Hanan Son of Hilqiyahu (2 Kings 22)', *BO* 49: cols 680–85.

Emerton, J.A.

2002   'The Value of the Moabite Stone as an Historical Source', *VT* 52: 483–92.

Eph'al, I.

1999   'The Bukân Aramaic Inscription: Historical Considerations', *IEJ* 49: 116–21.

Frumkin, A., A. Shimron and J. Rosenbaum

2003   'Radiometric dating of the Siloam Tunnel, Jerusalem', *Nature* 425 (11 Sept): 169–71.

Gibson, J.C.L.

1971   *Textbook of Syrian Semitic Inscriptions*, I: *Hebrew and Moabite Inscriptions* (Oxford: Clarendon Press).

1975   *Textbook of Syrian Semitic Inscriptions*, II: *Aramaic Inscriptions* (Oxford: Clarendon Press).

1982   *Textbook of Syrian Semitic Inscriptions*, III: *Phoenician Inscriptions* (Oxford: Clarendon Press).

Gitin, S., and M. Cogan

1999   'A New Type of Dedicatory Inscription from Ekron', *IEJ* 49: 193–202.

Gitin, S., T. Dothan and J. Naveh

1997   'A Royal Dedicatory Inscription from Ekron', *IEJ* 47: 1–16.

Gmirkin, R.

2002   'Tools Slippage and the Tel Dan Inscription', *SJOT* 16: 293–302.

Hackett, J.A., F.M. Cross, P.K. McCarter, A. Yardeni, A. Lemaire, E. Eshel and A. Hurvitz

1997   'Defusing Pseudo-Scholarship: The Siloam Inscription Ain't Hasmonean', *BARev* 23.2: 41–51.

Hadley, J.M.

2000   *The Cult of Asherah in Ancient Israel and Judah* (Cambridge: Cambridge University Press).

Helm, R.W.O. (ed.)

1984   *Eusebius Werke*, VII: *Die Chronik des Hieronymus* (Berlin: Academie-Verlag, 2nd edn).

Hendel, R.S.

1996   'The Date of the Siloam Inscription: A Rejoinder to Rogerson and Davies', *BA* 59: 233–37.

Irvine, S.A.

2001   'The Rise of the House of Jehu', in J.A. Dearman and M.P. Graham (eds), *The Land that I Will Show You: Essays on the History and Archaeology of the Ancient Near East in Honour of J. Maxwell Miller* (JSOTSup, 343; Sheffield: Sheffield Academic Press): 104–18.

Kanzaq, R.B.

1996   'Lecture complète de l'inscription de Bukân', in *Recueil d'articles du 1er colloque: Langues, inscriptions et textes anciens, Shiraz 12–14 Esfand (2–4 mars 1991)* (Teheran): 25–39 (in Persian).

Kaufman, S.A.

2002   'Recent Contributions of Aramaic Studies to Biblical Hebrew Philology and the Exegesis of the Hebrew Bible', in A. Lemaire (ed.), *Congress Volume: Basel 2001* (VTSup, 92; Leiden: E.J. Brill): 43–54.

Lehman, R.G.
1998   'Typologie und Signatur: Studien zu einem Listenostrakon aus der Sammlung Moussaieff', *UF* 30: 397–459.

Lemaire, A.
1977   'Les inscriptions de Khirbet el-Qôm et l'*ashérah* de Yhwh', *RB* 84: 595–608.
1984   'Date et origine des inscriptions paléo-hébraïques et phéniciennes de Kuntillet 'Ajrud', *SEL* 1: 131–44.
1985   'Les inscriptions de Deir ʿAlla et la literature araméenne', *CRAIBL*: 270–85.
1987   'Notes d'épigraphie nord-ouest sémitique', *Syria* 64: 205–16.
1991a   'Les inscriptions sur plâtre de Deir ʿAlla et leur signification historique et culturelle', in J. Hoftijzer and G. van der Kooij (eds), *The Balaam Text from Deir 'Alla Re-Evaluated* (Leiden: E.J. Brill): 33–57.
1991b   'La stèle de Mésha et l'histoire de l'ancien Israël', in D. Garrone and F. Israel (eds), *Storia e tradizioni di Israele: Scritti in onore di J. Alberto Soggin* (Brescia: Paideia): 143–69.
1993   'Joas de Samarie, Barhadad de Damas, Zakkur de Hamat. La Syrie-Palestine vers 800 av. J.-C.', in S. Ahituv and B.A. Levine (eds), *Avraham Malamat Volume* (Eretz-Israel, 24; Jerusalem: Israel Exploration Society): 148*–57*.
1994a   'La dynastie davidique (*byt dwd*) dans deux inscriptions ouest-sémitiques du IXᵉ s. av. J.-C.', *SEL* 11: 17–19.
1994b   'Epigraphie palestinienne: nouveaux documents. I. Fragment de stèle araméenne de Tell Dan (IXe s. av. J.-C.)', *Henoch* 16: 87–93.
1995   'Royal Signature: Name of Israel's Last King Surfaces in a Private Collection', *BARev* 21.6: 48–52.
1997   'Nouvelles données épigraphiques sur l'époque royale israélite', *REJ* 156: 445–61.
1998a   'Une inscription araméenne du VIIIᵉ s. av. J.-C. trouvée à Bukân', *Studia Iranica* 27: 15–30.
1998b   'L'inscription araméenne de Bukân et son intérêt historique', *CRAIBL* 1998: 293–99.
1998c   'The Tel Dan Stela as a Piece of Royal Historiography', *JSOT* 81, 3–14.
1999a   'La stèle araméenne de Bukân: mise au point épigraphique', *Notes Assyriologiques Brèves et Utilitaires* 1999.3: 57–58, § 57.
1999b   'Nouveaux sceaux et bulles paléo-hébraïques', in B.A. Levine, P.J. King, J. Naveh and E. Stern (eds), *Frank Moore Cross Volume* (Eretz-Israel, 26; Jerusalem: Israel Exploration Society): 123*–28*.
2000   'Phénicien et philistien: paléographie et dialectologie', in M.E. Aubet and M. Barthélemy (eds), *Actas del IV Congreso internacional de estudios fenicios y punicos, Cadiz, 2 al 6 de Octubre de 1995* (Cádiz: Universidad de Cádiz): 243–50.
2001a   *Nouvelles tablettes araméennes* (Hautes Etudes Orientales, 34; Geneva and Paris: Droz).
2001b   'Prophètes et rois dans les inscriptions ouest-sémitiques (IXᵉ-VIᵉ siècle av. J.-C.)', in A. Lemaire (ed.), *Prophètes et rois, Bible et Proche-Orient* (Lectio divina hors série; Paris: Cerf): 85–115.
2001c   'Les premiers rois araméens dans la tradition biblique', in P.M.M. Daviau, J.W. Wevers and M. Weigl (eds), *The World of the Aramaeans,* I: *Biblical*

Studies in Honour of Paul-Eugène Dion (JSOTSup, 324; Sheffield: Sheffield Academic Press): 113–43.

2003   *La naissance du monothéisme: Point de vue d'un historien* (Paris: Bayard).

Lipiński, E.
1994   *Studies in Aramaic Inscriptions and Onomastics*, II (OLA, 57; Leuven: Peeters).

McCarter, P.K.
1999   'Two Bronze Arrowheads with Archaic Alphabetic Inscriptions', in B.A. Levine, P.J. King, J. Naveh and E. Stern (eds), *Frank Moore Cross Volume* (Eretz-Israel, 26; Jerusalem: Israel Exploration Society): 123*–28*.

Mazar, A.
2003   'Three 10th–9th Century B.C.E. Inscriptions from Tel Rehov', in C.G. Den Hertog, U. Hübner and S. Münger (eds), *Saxa Loquentur: Studien zur Archäologie Palästinas/Israels. Festschrift für Volkmar Fritz* (AOAT, 302; Münster: Ugarit Verlag): 171–84.

Mendenhall, G.E.
1973   *The Tenth Generation* (Baltimore: The Johns Hopkins University Press).

Meshel, Z.
1978   *Kuntillet ʿAjrud: A Religious Centre from the Time of the Judaean Monarchy on the Border of Sinai* (Catalogue no. 175; Jerusalem: Israel Museum).
1992   'Kuntillet ʿAjrud', in *ABD*, IV: 103–109.

Michel, E.
1954   'Die Assur-Texte Salmanassars III. (858–824). 6. Fortsetzung', *WO* 2: 26–45.

Mykytiuk, L.J.
1998   'Did Bible Characters Really Exist? Part 1: An Annotated Bibliography on Methods of Evaluating Evidence in Hebrew Inscriptions', *Bulletin of Bibliography* 55.4: 243–49.

Naʾaman, N.
1999   'The Historical Background of the Aramaic Inscription from Tel Dan', in B.A. Levine, P.J. King, J. Naveh and E. Stern (eds), *Frank Moore Cross Volume* (Eretz-Israel, 26; Jerusalem: Israel Exploration Society): 112–18, 232*.
2000   'Three Notes on the Aramaic Inscription from Tel Dan', *IEJ* 50: 92–104.

Naveh, J.
1999   'Marginalia on the Inscriptions from Dan and Ekron', in B.A. Levine, P.J. King, J. Naveh and E. Stern (eds), *Frank Moore Cross Volume* (Eretz-Israel, 26; Jerusalem: Israel Exploration Society): 119–22, 232*.

Parker, S.B.
1997   *Stories in Scripture and Inscriptions* (New York and Oxford: Oxford University Press).

Porten, B.
1981   'The Identity of King Adon', *BA* 44.1: 36–52.

Puech, E.
2000   'Les pointes de flèches inscrites de la fin du IIe millénaire en Phénicie et Canaan', in M.E. Aubet and M. Barthélemy (eds), *Actas del IV congreso internacional de estudios fenicios y punicos, Cadiz, 2 al 6 de Octubre de 1995* (Cádiz: Universidad de Cádiz): 251–70.

Rendsburg, G.A.
    1995   'On the Writing *BYTDWD* in the Aramaic Inscription from Tel Dan', *IEJ* 45: 22–25.
Renz, J.
    1995   *Die althebräischen Inschriften*, I: *Text und Kommentar* (Handbuch der althebräischen Epigraphik; Darmstadt: Wissenschaftliche Buchgesellschaft).
Rogerson, J., and P.R. Davies
    1996   'Was the Siloam Tunnel Built by Hezekiah?', *BA* 59: 138–49.
Röllig, W.
    1999   'Appendix I – The Phoenician Inscriptions', in H. Çambel, *Corpus of Hieroglyphic Luwian Inscriptions*, II: *Karatepe-Aslantaş. The Inscriptions: Facsimile Edition* (Berlin and New York: W. de Gruyter): 50–81.
Sader, H.S.
    2000   'Une pointe de flèche phénicienne inédite du Musée National de Beyrouth', in M.E. Aubet and M. Barthélemy (eds), *Actas del IV Congresso internacional de estudios fenicios y punicos, Cadiz, 2 al 6 de Octubre de 1995* (Cádiz: Universidad de Cádiz): 271–80.
Schneider, T.
    1988   'Azariahu Son of Hilkiahu (High Priest?) on a City of David Bulla', *IEJ* 38: 139–41.
    1991   'Six Biblical Signatures', *BARev* 17.4: 26–33.
Schniedewind, W.M.
    1996   'Tel Dan Stela: New Light on Aramaic and Jehu's Revolt', *BASOR* 302: 75–90.
Segert, S.
    1995   'Bileam, der Sohn Beors', *ZAH* 8: 71–77.
Shiloh, Y.
    1986   'A Group of Hebrew Bullae from the City of David', *IEJ* 36: 16–38.
Sokoloff, M.
    1999   'The Old Aramaic Inscriptions from Bukân: A Revised Interpretation', *IEJ* 49: 105–15.
Tekoğlu, R., and A. Lemaire
    2000   'La bilingue royale louvito-phénicienne de Çineköy', *CRAIBL*: 961–1006.
Thompson, T.L
    2000   'Problems of Genre and Historicity with Palestine's Inscriptions', in A. Lemaire and M. Saebø (eds), *Congress Volume: Oslo 1998* (VTSup, 80; Leiden: E.J. Brill): 321–26.
Tropper, J.
    2001   'Dialektvielfalt und Sprachwandel im frühen Aramäischen: Soziolinguistische Überlegungen', in P.M.M. Daviau, J.M. Wevers and M. Weigl (eds), *The World of the Aramaeans*, III: *Biblical Studies in Honour of Paul-Eugène Dion* (JSOTSup, 326; Sheffield: Sheffield Academic Press): 213–22.
Vanschoonwinkel, J.
    1990   'Mopsos: légendes et réalités', *Hethitica* 10: 185–211.
Vaux, R. de
    1936   'Mélanges IV: le sceau de Godolias, maître du palais', *RB* 45: 96–102.
    1971   *Histoire ancienne d'Israël: Des origines à l'installation en Canaan* (Ebib; Paris:

J. Gabalda). ET *The Early History of Israel* (trans. David Smith; 2 vols; London: Darton, Longman & Todd).

Waaler, E.
2002   'A Revised Date for Pentateuchal Texts? Evidence from Ketef Hinnom', *TynBul* 53: 29–55.

Weippert, M.
1991   'The Balaam Text from Deir ʿAlla and the Study of the Old Testament', in J. Hoftijzer and G. van der Kooij (eds), *The Balaam Text from Deir ʿAlla Re-Evaluated* (Leiden: E.J. Brill): 151–84.

Williamson, H.G.M.
2000   'Isaiah 8:21 and a New Inscription from Ekron', *Bulletin of the Anglo-Israel Archaeological Society* 18: 51–55.

Yardeni, A.
1991   'Remarks on the Priestly Blessing on two Ancient Amulets from Jerusalem', *VT* 41: 176–85.

Yardenna, A.
2002   'A Fluted Bronze Bowl with a Canaanite–Early Phoenician Inscription from Kefar Veradim', in Z. Gal (ed.), *Eretz Zafon: Studies in Galilean Archaeology* (Jerusalem: Israel Authority Antiquities).

Chapter 17

Hebrew Poetic Structure as a Basis for Dating

Terry Fenton

1. *Introductory Remarks*

In seeking to establish the antiquity of biblical Hebrew literature – and of historical references contained within it – a comparative examination of its earliest poetic structures might seem a useful first step. Since the late nineteenth century, advanced Hebrew scholarship has usually held that the most ancient sections of the Hebrew Scriptures date from the latter half of the twelfth century BCE (the Song of Deborah is a favourite starting point and some of the poetry of the Pentateuch follows). With the discovery of the literature of ancient Ugarit this position seemed to be confirmed. Sceptical voices, however, denying the great affinity of certain biblical passages with Ugaritic texts, are often heard. Today one cannot descry widely accepted conclusions – possibly because the treatment of the new material was sometimes hasty rather than detailed and searching.[1] A decade ago (Fenton 1994) I attempted to engage this situation at specific points in the hope of achieving greater precision in assessing the significance of the 'new' sources but I cannot claim that my discussion has produced echoes. Recent references to, and surveys of, at least some of the material, have been vague or general, raising doubts and leaving open questions which I attempted to answer in detail. The former paper was designed to demonstrate affinity and draw conclusions for biblical thought (apart from linguistic and textual matters) from the way in which the Canaanite material was used. Here the emphasis must be on the dating of the biblical texts themselves and for this purpose structural detail, as I hope to show, is of the essence. Some of the same material is again relevant but a broader span of Ugaritic examples will be analysed in order to bring out the bounds of fixity and variability for

---

1. No criticism is implied. The impact of obvious and striking similarities was bound to elicit speedy announcements of discoveries. What is wondrous is the denial of the obvious by those who may contemplate it at leisure (some of the proposed parallels in the early years proved wrong but that is neither here nor there).

comparison with the biblical structures, and again, more of these will be treated. A new type of structure, hardly noticed and, to my knowledge, not yet laid under contribution for biblical comparison, will be introduced.

To return to our opening sentence, it is not *just* the demonstration that a given structure is 'ancient' which is significant: rather, the way in which an ancient structure is used and, in particular, the degree of its deviation from the ancient model, can shed light on the relative dating of the biblical passages in which it occurs. Beyond this, in a few instances, the suggested approach, combined with inner-biblical considerations, may enable us to distinguish between pre- or early monarchic as against later monarchic or exilic poetic layers; in one case I think, between pre-monarchic (?), exilic and post-exilic versions of the same verse. Despite the paucity of such material divined so far, it must, if our analysis is correct, be of consequence in the sense indicated – and may also provide a stepping-stone to further insights.

In the following discussion the terms 'Ugaritic' and 'Canaanite' will be used in different contexts for the pre-biblical poetry found at Ugarit. We take it for granted that Ugaritic poetry is Canaanite, whatever the ancient political use of this term and even though that poetry contains other elements. Its geographical references are not to the ambience of Ugarit itself but to Tyre and Sidon, Lebanon and Sirion, Ashtaroth and Edrei (*pace* other opinions), probably Lake Semechonitis and possibly other 'southerly' locations. It is also assumed that at its height Canaanite culture extended from the Taurus to the Sinai peninsula and from the Mediterranean littoral to the Syrian desert. At present the ancient Canaanite poetic tradition is known, with trifling exceptions, only from Ugarit and the Hebrew Scriptures, but Ugarit fell in ruins, never to rise again, just before the dawn of Hebrew poetic composition, if that was in the second half of the twelfth century. No Hebrew poet could ever have had contact with Ugarit itself – hence the need to refer to Canaanite poetry. This point is not merely academic. Some of those who reject suggested Ugaritic–biblical parallels ('exaggerated pan-Ugaritism') write as though parallels could be established only if the Hebrew poet were looking over the Ugaritic scribe's shoulder. In fact the two literary corpora arose from common sources, themselves, no doubt, diversified to a degree, and went their separate ways. What is of paramount importance for our enquiry is, initially, striking and detailed similarity, subsequently, notable, and then wild, divergence.

2. *'Climactic' or 'Staircase' Tricola*

It is not surprising that the descriptions of this structure and the terms used for it are hardly felicitous. Having a certain fixity in its earliest known Ugaritic forms, it also displays some highly flexible features and seems later to have undergone much change in the course of its Hebrew development. But for this development there would be no occasion for the following discussion. Partially discerned by mediaeval exegetes, the structure has been described as repetitive parallelism,[2] climactic or staircase parallelism and 'the expanded colon'. Repetition and parallelism, however, are essentially opposed features and the structure usually displays not climax but anticlimax, at least in its 'classical' form of the tricolon. If it takes a step up after its first colon it then remains on the same level at its third. As for S.E. Loewenstamm's 'expanded colon' (Loewenstamm 1969: 179–80 = 1980: 284–85), this term ignores the third colon, which I regard as originally an essential part of the structure, and the conception which the term embodies leads, in my view, to errors of analysis. Reflecting incomplete analyses, the notations used have not brought out the cohesion of the structure – or its appeal to our poetic sensibility.

The essential feature of this structure, in my view, is that it combines repetition with parallelism: this is what distinguishes it from the various more common types of parallelism in ancient Semitic poetry and invests it with its particular character. An appropriate designation would appear difficult to find. 'Repetitive-parallelistic tricolon' might be accurate but somewhat heavy; perhaps 'mixed tricolon' will serve in the course of discussion. These, of course, leave the problem of the related Hebrew repetitive bicolon without the third (parallel) colon. Pending a better idea, 'staircase bi/tricolon' might have to continue in service.

Although we shall not delve into the poetic origins or psychological effect of this usage (its 'processing' by hearer or reader) because these matters are not, I think, germane to the issue at hand, a word might be said on treatments of these matters, for one might well ask 'what is behind all this?' Loewenstamm thought that the figure arose from the expansion of a basic 'invitation' or statement into two parts and his very detailed and complicated article is concerned with the various patterns which this process produced. It is difficult to discern why, in his opinion, the poets were at pains to create such a structure.[3] It would seem that Loewenstamm's work contains much valuable observation of detail but his explanations do not always carry conviction. Particularly disturbing is his counting of words in each colon, whereas the significant units are those which constitute parallels or repetitions, irrespective of the number of

2.   Originally, apparently, by Robert Lowth in 1753, and again by W.F. Albright in 1950. There is a concise but comprehensive survey of study in S.E. Loewenstamm (1980 [1969]: 281–84).

3.   However, there are passages from which one may divine some of his basic notions (loc. cit. n. 2, 285–86, 306–308, 496).

words within them. I shall say no more on these points partly for the reason given above, partly because my treatment will show our differences plainly enough. E.L. Greenstein, on the other hand, in a most interesting 'interdisciplinary' paper, grounded in familiarity with modern developments in the fields of general linguistics, and especially, psycholinguistics, analysed the forms of this structure with regard to their impact on the hearer. His study results in the conclusion that some forms of 'climactic' parallelism compel the reader to suspend grammatical analysis until the second colon has been mentally 'processed', some compel reanalysis and some compel neither. Awareness of the processes enhances our appreciation of Canaanite poetics (Greenstein 1974). Greenstein, I think, has grasped the essence of this poetic figure more profoundly than Loewenstamm but I differ with respect to his syntactic analysis of those sentences which, in his view, compel reanalysis. For the reason given above I pursue this matter no further. As for the subsequent discussion between those scholars, in which both sides, especially Greenstein, make generous concessions on points of detail, that does not, I think, affect our argument (Loewenstamm 1975 = 1980: 496–502; Greenstein 1977).

In the following discussion transliterated Ugaritic and Hebrew quotations will be translated or rather, construed, in their original word order, so far as reasonable, in order to bring out the relationship of the various parts of the structure. Each semantic unit will be marked by a letter of the English alphabet according to its order of appearance. Repetitions (usually identical) are marked with the same letter which is used for the first occurrence of the unit. Parallel units receive a subscript numeral after the first unit, thus, a b c, a b d, d_2 b_2. Where a unit consists of more than one word the letter is placed under the middle of the unit. Nineteen certain examples of the 'mixed tricolon' are known to me in Ugaritic and some of the patterns they assume will now be illustrated. References are according to the first section of KTU^2 (Dietrich, Loretz and Sanmartín 1995), then text number, column and lines, e.g. KTU^2 1.2.IV.8–9. If the text has only one column the reference is given as e.g. KTU^2 1.100.70–74.

It will be noted that all the Ugaritic examples are of the form a b c, a b d in the first two cola. The element 'c' is either a deity or person addressed or the subject of the sentence[4] and it is never repeated or taken up by a parallel name or phrase. All cases save one have a third colon and in the one case the text may be suspected (KTU^2 1.10.II.10–12). This colon is normally parallel to the second but it may also contain a repetition, in which case a new element may be introduced and then there is no parallel! (There are two examples of the last case, obviously constructed on the

---

4. Except for KTU^2 1.161.20–22, in our only non-narrative context to date, but possibly, even here, a throne is addressed.

same model, KTU^2 1.10.II.13–15 and 26–28, in close proximity)[5]. These observations summarize both the stability and the flexibility of the structure, which will now be displayed.

A simple example is to be found in 'the offer of immortality' at KTU^2 1.17.VI.26–28:

irš	*ḥym*	*laqht*	*ġzr*	*irš*	*ḥym*	*watnk*	*blmt*	*wašlḥk*
a	b	c		a	b	d	b_2	d_2
Ask	life	O-Aqhat-hero,		ask	life	and-I'll-give-(it)-you,	non-death	and-I'll grant-(it)-you

A further example of this pattern may be found at KTU^2 1.16.VI. 54–57:

yṯbr	*ḥrn*	*ybn*	*yṯbr*	*ḥrn*	*rišk*	*ʿṯtrt šm bʿl*	*qdqdk*
a	b	c	a	b	d	b_2	d_2
May-Break	Horon	O-son,	may-break	Horon	your-head,	Ashtoreth-Name-of-Baal	your-pate

Here different grammatical structures have been accommodated to the same poetic pattern, in the second case with the assistance of 'gapping', the verb being deleted from the third colon but being 'understood' as present. A further example of the pattern may be found at KTU^2 1.100.71–72.

Sometimes the arrangement of the third colon is chiastic, d_2 b_2. This occurs in the famous lines KTU^2 1.2.IV.8–9, so illuminating for Ps. 92.10 (ET 9):

ht	*ibk*	*bʿlm*	*ht*	*ibk*	*tmḫṣ*	*ht*	*ṯṣmt*	*ṣrtk*
a	b	c	a	b	d	a	d_2	b_2
Lo	your-enemies	O-Baal,	lo	your-enemies	you-will-smite,	lo	you-will-destroy	your-foes

It will be noted that the a-element is repeated a third time in the final colon. This occurs in three other cases, in two of which the pattern is the same as here. I shall not dwell on these passages since, despite the fact that the pattern is unmistakable, lexical problems arise (KTU^2 1.17.I.6–8, the entire verse repeated at 9–11 and 11–13; KTU^2 1.17.I.13–15; 1.100.70–71). There are also two passages where the a-element is not repeated but paralleled, thus KTU^2 1.15.II.21–23:

att	*tqḥ*	*ykrt*	*att*	*tqḥ*	*btk*	*ġlmt*	*tšʿrb*	*ḥzrk*
a	b	c	a	b	d	a_2	b_2	d_2
(a) woman	you'll-take	O-Kirta,	(a) woman	you'll-take (to) your-home,		(a) girl	you'll-bring-into	your-court

---

5. Similar is the example in lines 21–23. All four of the last 'eccentric' examples are contained in the second column of tablet 10, which is not from the hand of Ilu-milku, who wrote the other tablets with which we are concerned: this may be significant.

The other passage, *KTU²* 1.6.IV.1–3, repeated in 12–14, has two words of which the translation is uncertain, including the 'a₂' word, which is unfortunate, for the pattern is clearly the same as in the passage quoted.

A chiastic third colon without an a-element is found, unfortunately with the final word(s) mostly illegible, at *KTU²* 1.16.VI.27–29:

lk	*labk*	*yṣb*	*lk*	*labk*	*wrgm*	*ṯny*	*l?*
a	b	c	a	b	d	d₂	b₂
Go	to-your-father	PN,	go	to-your-father	and-say,	recite	to?

Clearly the son of Kirta is addressed and the final word(s) must be addressed to Kirta himself, so the pattern of the third colon is d₂ b₂. The entire pattern found here occurs also at *KTU²* 1.100.73–74 (after necessary textual emendation).[6]

Finally one might adduce a passage where, uniquely (at present) the d-unit is neither repeated nor paralleled. The word itself is mostly illegible but the structure of the passage is clear. It is found at *KTU²* 1.2.I.36–37:

ʿbdk	*bʿl*	*yymm*	*ʿbdk*	*bʿl*	*--m*	*bn dgn*	*asrkm*
a	b	c	a	b	d	b₂	a₂
your-servant	(is) Baal	O-Sea	your-servant	(is) Baal	forever?	(the) son-of-Dagon	(is) your-captive

Armed with these examples[7] we can now examine some biblical passages. The first must be Ps. 92.10 (ET 9), alluded to above, for that is clearly a Hebrew version of the Canaanite verse which lies behind the Ugaritic text, as argued in the article noted. The Hebrew verse reads:

kî hinnēh	*ʾōyᵉbeykā*	*yhwh*	*kî-hinnēh*	*ʾōyᵉbeykā*	*yōʾbēdû*	*yitpārᵉdû*
for-behold	your-enemies	Yahweh,	for-behold	your-enemies	will-perish,	will-be-scattered
a	b	c	a	b	d	d₂

kol-pōʿᵃlê	*ʾāwen*
	b₂
all-evildoers	

---

6. The reconstruction of W.G.E. Watson seems to me the most convincing (Watson 1984a: 103) but if that of D.W. Young and, independently, D. Pardee is correct (Young 1977: 303; Pardee 1978: 100 n. 99; 1988: 222 n. 136) then the third colon will be of the pattern b₂ d₂ against my statement in the main text. Watson's version offers a better climax in the second colon.

7. Of the nineteen cases two have not yet been mentioned. The first, *KTU²* 1.3.V.19–21, has syntactic and other problems but the pattern seems clear a b c   a b d   d a₂ b₂, exhibiting again the fixity of the first two cola and the flexibility of the third. For convenience the final case will be included in the discussion of Ps. 77.17 (ET 16), below. (*KTU²* 1.2.IV.12–13, 19–20 may belong here but are more probably to be classified with the material in section 2.)

Beyond the demonstration that the verses are second cousins one notes the *almost* exact correspondence with the Ugaritic repetitive-parallelistic tricolon pattern, as noted above – abc abd ad$_2$ b$_2$. Apart from Ps. 29.1–2, to which I shall return, there would appear to be no example in the Hebrew Scriptures of the structure discussed with the a-element repeated exactly in all three cola.

Ever since the discovery of the similarity in language and structure of the Hebrew to the Ugaritic verse (Ginsberg 1936: 180–81; 1938: 7) scholars have disputed the detail and the significance of the alleged connection. Apart from what has been stated above and the reference to my previous study, I would indicate briefly what seem to be salient exegetical points in this matter. Psalm 92.2–6 and 13–16 (ET 1–5, 12–15) consist of bicola in 3:3 rhythm. The style is flowing, the parallelism exact, the handling of linguistic and poetic mechanisms adroit, the imagery rich and theme-enhancing. All this would point to an *ad quem* earlier than the change in poetic norms detectable at the end of the exilic period, but how much earlier is notoriously difficult to gauge. The theme is the well-being of the righteous under the aegis of a just deity. Into this atmosphere intrudes a darker theme, the apparent prosperity of the wicked, palpable from v. 7 (ET 6). In v. 8 (ET 7) we have a tricolon with a strange infinitive construction and then a monocolon (!) which seems to have the vaguest of connections with its context. Perhaps its function is to change the preceding tricolon into two bicola to fit the general form of the psalm – we shall find clear examples of this in the following discussion. Finally the old Canaanite verse appears, but now it refers not to the battle of a deity with his peers but to the fate of evil-doers. The enemies of the deity are now *pōʿᵃlê ʾāwen* as in v. 8 (ET 7), in accordance with the darker theme indicated. In such matters it is probably impossible to reconstruct the history of a text. It would seem, however, that the appearance here of an ancient verse in new garb is associated with an attempt to emphasize a theme which may well have been a part of the original composition (v. 7 (ET 6), though the *ʾet-zōʾt* seems suspicious).

Psalm 77 offers another clear example of the re-use of an ancient 'mixed tricolon' in a composition originally written in bicola. Verse 17 (ET 16) and the following three verses, which are tricola, belonged originally to a poem, in my opinion, on the ancient theme of the conflict between the Storm-god and the Sea-god (Fenton 1994: 80 n. 16; 1978: 358–60). These verses are inserted between two others which have a distinct style of their own and which refer to the redemption of 'thy people, the children of Jacob and Joseph' and the leading of 'thy people by the hand of Moses and Aaron'. This 'frame' is evidently designed to accommodate the notion of the Reed Sea crossing, between the Exodus and the Wandering in the Wilderness. The message is that the 'theomachy myth' is simply a poetic description of the division of the Reed Sea waters: the entire passage from

v. 16 (ET 15) to v. 21 (ET 20), with which the psalm abruptly breaks off, is a form of 'demythologization'. Verse 17 (ET 16) reads:

rāʾûkā	*mayim*	*ʾelōhîm*	*rāʾûkā*	*mayim*	*yāḥîlû*	*ʾap*	*yirgᵉzû*	*tᵉhōmôt*
a	b	c	a	b	d	e	d_2	b_2
Saw-you	(the) waters	God	saw-you	(the) waters	they-trembled	indeed	were convulsed	the-deeps

This displays the pattern abc abd ed$_2$b$_2$, which is exactly that of the Ugaritic verse *KTU^2* 1.14.I.21–23, 'Sees his progeny Kirta, sees his progeny ruined, very? his establishment?' Despite the question-marks, which indicate serious lexical and syntactical problems, the pattern is clear. The e word is *mid* = Heb. *mᵉʾōd* and corresponds to the word *ʾap* in the text discussed. Evidently short, emphatic words could be added to the four units (a b c d) which served as the base for repetition or the insertion of synonyms in 'mixed tricola'.

Recognition of the detailed affinity of the verse with a Ugaritic pattern illustrates the continuity of a clearly Hebrew literary tradition dating back at least to the early monarchy.

At least of equal antiquity is Psalm 93, almost in its entirety, or rather in what remains of it, for its four verses introduce a wealth of material in dramatic and highly skilled poetry but there is no continuation: one is left merely with introduction. Once again we have a truncated psalm (v. 5 with its totally different style, total lack of parallelism, use of *ʿēdâ* in the sense of law and so forth, is an addition, as often claimed, and I would say that the same process is at work here as at the end of Ps. 77). The main theme here is again the defeat of the Sea and, in this case, the resultant 'enthronement' of Yahweh. Every verse reflects Canaanite poetic structures, of which more will be said in the next section, and v. 3 contains both a 'staircase' and the *qtl-yqtl* variation of the same verb to report a past act (Fenton 1994: 74–75). The 'staircase' here presents the a-unit in all three cola, that is, the verb *nāśāʾ*, the form in the third colon being *yiśᵉʾû* as against *nāśᵉʾû* of the first two cola and therefore a$_2$. In this case then, the parallelism is grammatical and not lexical:

nāśᵉʾû	*nᵉhārôt*	*yhwh*	*nāśᵉʾû*	*nᵉhārôt*	*qôlām*	*yiśᵉʾû*	*nᵉhārôt*	*dokyām*
a	b	c	a	b	d	a_2	b	d_2
Lifted	(the) tides	Yahweh,	lifted	(the) tides	their-voice,	lifted	(the) tides	their-din?

Interestingly the b-unit, *nᵉhārôt*, also appears thrice: should the third occurrence have been *tᵉhōmôt*, or the like? If so, we should have had a further Ugaritic pattern (a$_2$ b$_2$ d$_2$) as above, *KTU^2* 1.15.II.21–23 and 1.6.IV.1–3.

In Psalm 93 we have a concentration of original ancient material in its pristine context. The 'staircases' in Psalms 92 and 77 were insertions. In

Psalm 94 we meet with a new procedure. The Psalm is composed of bicola but two tricola occur in disguise in vv. 1–4. The first is easy to identify:

ʾēl	nᵉqāmôt	yhwh	ʾēl	nᵉqāmôt	hôpîaʿ	hinnāśēʾ	šōpēṭ	hāʾāreṣ
a	b	c	a	b	d	d_2	a_2 -	b_2
God-of-	vengeance	Yahweh,	God-of-	vengeance	appear,	rise-up	Judge-of-	the-Earth

According to the rhythm of 'staircases', 'God' and 'vengeance' must be treated as two semantic units but 'Judge of the Earth' parallels them as a single concept. The verb *hôpîaʿ* must be pointed as an imperative and this was certainly the understanding of the writer, who inserted another sentence in the imperative. It seems clear that his intention was to turn a tricolon into two bicola. This is confirmed by the same treatment of a tricolon in vv. 3–4. The inserted words *hāšēb gᵉmûl ʿal-gēʾîm*, 'bring retribution on the proud' offer no fit parallel to the foregoing. 'Bring retribution' occurs at Ps. 28.4 and Lam. 3.64. In the following verses the addition is placed between the second and third cola of the tricolon which originally read:

ʿad-mātay	rᵉšāʿîm	yhwh	ʿad-mātay	rᵉšāʿîm	yaʿᵃlōzû	yitʾammᵉrû	kol-pōʿᵃlê ʾāwen
a	b	c	a	b	d	d_2	b_2
until-when	(the) evil	Yahweh,	until-when	(the) evil	will-scoff,	will-exalt- themselves	all evildoers

Here the inserted words *yabbîʿû yᵉdabbᵉrû ʿātāq*, 'they utter, they speak pride', are even less felicitous: they have probably been taken from the Song of Hannah, 1 Sam. 2.3, 'speak not so very high, (let not) pride go forth from your mouth'.

It would appear that the writer was attracted to the ancient tricola still available to his literary tradition but needed to adapt them to the bicolon form in order to use them in his composition. Those who 'edited' Psalms 92 and 77 felt less constraint. This is not surprising: it is clear that the course of biblical poetry reveals great attrition of once dominant modes of composition. The earlier the composition the more consistent – and creative – the parallelism, the later the laxer. Of tricola, we have seen that the repetitive-parallelistic form is a rarity, hardly preserved even in the earlier periods. Ordinary tricola seem not to survive the exilic period but by then the rhythmic consistency and balance of the bicolon is also in decline. The bicolon seems to be the preferred form until the destruction of the First Temple when it still flourishes, as in Psalms 74 and 89, composed shortly after that destruction (Fenton: 1994: 78–80).

The foregoing observations of reuse and modification of a Hebrew poetic structure which was originally derived from a Bronze Age Canaanite model, point to a long tradition which seems to have run its course, if not completely, by some time in the Persian period (where some would have it begin!). I hope to confirm the link with the most ancient Hebrew period in the next section, but what has been noted up to this point does, I claim, indicate different layers of composition even in the period of the monarchy, though my dating of these is only relative.

First, however, two passages seem to indicate developments which span the entire period. The much-discussed Psalm 29 opens with what appears to be a variant form of the structure. Instead of three there are four cola, of which the third is not parallel to the foregoing but is an almost exact repetition of it, including for a third time the opening a- and b- units. The fourth colon *does* parallel the second and herein lies the clue: the second and third cola are variants of each other which have both been included side by side in MT. If one is omitted we have the familiar structure:

hābû	lyhwh	b^enê-$^{\,}$ēlîm	hābû	lyhwh	kābôd wā$^{\,c}$ōz
a	b	c	a	b	d
ascribe	to-Yahweh	Divine family,	ascribe	to-Yahweh	honour-and-might

{hābû	lyhwh	k^ebôd $š^e$mô}	hištaḥ^{a}wû	lyhwh	b^ehad^{e}rat-qōdeš[8]
a	b	d	a_2	b_2	d_2
{ascribe	to-Yahweh	(the) honour-of-his-name}	bow-down	to-Yahweh	in-his-holy-spendour

Had the repetitive-parallelistic tricolon been carefully analysed and provided with appropriate notation, the presence of the doublet must have been speedily detected. The text, however, has been accepted as read and imaginative explanations provided (Loewenstamm 1969: 189 = 1980: 299). It is possible that Psalm 29 was originally composed in bicola (except for its opening) and that the 'doublet' was supplied for the same reason as in the last passages treated in Psalm 94. The fact that *kābôd* appears also in v. 3, where there is a superfluous colon, would seem to indicate associated textual disturbance.[9] However this may be, a later writer changed the offensive b^enê $^{\,}$ēlîm to mišp^{e}ḥôt $^{\,c}$ammîm, 'families of the peoples', added $š^{e\,}$û minḥâ ûbō$^{\,}$û l^ehaṣ^{e}rôtāyw, 'take an oblation and enter his courts' after the already existing doublet, and finally added ḥîlû mippānāyw kol-hā$^{\,}$āreṣ, 'tremble before him all the Earth', Ps. 96.7–9. As Loewenstamm says, the purpose of all this was to fit the text to later notions and prevent leaving the colon 'bow down etc.' in isolation (loc. cit.). In this process all resemblance to the ancient structure was obliterated. However, rephrasing Loewenstamm's words we can discern an effort to preserve the bicolon form of the poetry as explained above. Such an effort would not have been made, it seems to me, much later than

---

8. The Septuagint reading, with possessive pronoun suffix, is thought to reflect the original Hebrew.

9. M. Held has, I think, correctly reconstructed v. 3 as a bicolon (Held 1962).

the exilic period. The Chronicler's version, however, adds yet another colon (1 Chron. 16.30b) and MT adds this to the last colon of the Psalm 96 version, leaving a tricolon beforehand. Whatever we make of the Massoretic punctuation, it is clear from the way in which verses are assembled in this section of the chapter that there is no concern here for the preservation of bicola. Once again, from slight details we may trace changing stylistic preferences from (possibly) pre-monarchic times, through the monarchy to roughly exilic times and to the period of the Chronicler.

We might conclude this survey of mixed tricola with the wondrous example of Cant. 4.8:

'ittî	*mill^e bānôn*	*kallâ*	*'ittî*	*mill^e bānôn*	*tābô'î*
a	b	c	a	b	d
With-me[10]	from-Lebanon	bride,	with-me	from-Lebanon	come,

tāšûrî mērō'š	*'ā mānâ*	*mērō'š š^e nîr w^e hermôn*	*mimm^e 'ōnôt*	*'ā rāyôt*	*mēhar^e rê n^e mērîm*
d_2	b_2	(b_3)!	(b_4)!		(b_5)!
journey from(the) Head-of-Amana		from-(the)head-of-Senir-and-Hermon	from-the-lairs-of-lions		from-the-mountains-of-leopards

The first three cola, of course, constitute a fine example of the structure and seem to have pleased a later writer, but insufficiently. Accordingly he 'improved' the verse with three cola of his own, all 'parallel' with the third of the original. There is a certain gusto in the ring of the topographical and zoological evocations but some who appreciate poetry might be prepared to forgo them. The original tricolon is evidently ancient and the question as to its pristine context is intriguing, as is the question concerning the date of the addition. In the absence of answers it can be claimed only that here is a further illustration of development in Hebrew poetic composition and that its early stages reflect pre-monarchic models.

Various examples might be added, all of them illustrating or confirming the survival of the structure, all of them diverging to a greater or lesser degree from the Ugaritic examples and from those Hebrew examples which I have discussed, in their original forms. They cannot, it seems,

10. Repointing the verb to yield the sense 'come!', according to the Septuagint, depends on a view of the locations of the speaker and the addressee, which, without context, cannot be established. If, however, the tricolon is being used in accord with its pristine conception the translation 'come!' would be impossible, for that sense is synonymous with the verbs of the second and third cola, apart from its repetition in the second colon. Not only would the tricolon contain the inelegant and unimaginative fourfold expression of the notion 'come!' but its repetitive-parallelistic structure would be severely blemished. To use my notation, we would have the structure a b c   a b a_2 a_3 b_2!

increase our understanding of the developmental process. Without attempting to cover all instances one might list Exod. 15.11; Isa. 26.15; Hab. 3.8; Ps. 129.1–2; Prov. 31.4; Cant. 4.9, 10; 6.9. Not a few others which have been proposed may preserve some faint echo of the structure, but they cannot be classified with it. Neither formally nor in their poetic effect have they anything of its particular flavour.[11]

A similar situation obtains with respect to the 'staircase bicola'. As stated above, because they have but one dubious representative at Ugarit it would appear that they do not preserve the original structure from which the mixed tricolon developed. Nor do they conform very well, on the whole, to the abc abd structure. However, it seems difficult to maintain that there is no connection between them and the mixed tricola. It would seem, therefore, that they represent a truncated form of the latter and display increasing divergence in the course of time, in conformity with the process which has been posited. Examples are Exod. 15.6, 16; Judg. 5.7; Pss 67.4, 6 (ET 3, 5); 89.52 (ET 51); 124.1–2; Cant. 1.15; 4.12; 5.9; 6.1. A glance at these will show how some have remained simple, others have been expanded from simple models and some, just as the mixed tricola, have been integrated into larger structures, e.g. Ps. 124.1–5, in which, at an earlier stage, they would have had no place.

Finally, usually under the heading of 'expanded cola' or 'variations' of that structure (which allegedly, released it from the constraints of the 'rigid' Canaanite models) many passages have been associated with the material examined here, when all that they have in common is some form of repetition, often of one word (Loewenstamm 1969: 192–95 = 1980: 303–306; Avishur 1972: 7–10). This is to push the scope of 'variation' beyond the bounds of the meaningful. The repetitions referred to, moreover, are often of types distinctive enough to have been recognized in various literatures and to have their own descriptive terminology – anaphora, anadiplosis, sorites, etc. (Watson 1977: 284 n. 95; 1984b). As we have seen, the Canaanite models had the regularity required for successful poetic structures and sufficient flexibility to prevent that regularity from deteriorating into monotony. These are the qualities which have made it possible to distinguish between original and secondary and between early, late and later; that is, to trace the internal changes, or disintegration, of mixed tricola, and their insertion into later structures, from the end of the Bronze Age and through the Hebrew Scriptures up to the Persian period.

---

11.   The superb single-word-repetitive prose rhetoric of Eccl. 1.2 is not to be classified with poetic structures, superb though the poetry of Ecclesiastes himself undoubtedly is (Eccl. 1.4–9; 12.1–7, not 8).

3. *'Forked Parallelism'*

There exists another type of tricolon in Ugaritic which consists of a single-colon statement or command followed by two cola which explain, elaborate on or in some way continue the thought of the first, and are parallel to each other. The first is, so to say, the 'handle' from which 'fork out' two parallel 'prongs'. Hence, for want of a less figurative, or more elegant, term, I offer, provisionally at least, that in the heading for this section. First, an example from the 'Baal cycle', KTU^2 1.4.VII.49:

			lymru	*ilm*	*wnšm*
			that may grow fat	gods	and men,
aḥdy	*dymlk*	*ʿl*	*ilm*		
I alone	will rule	over	the gods,		
			dyšbʿ	*hmlt*	*arṣ*
			that may be full	the multitudes	of the Earth

Here the continuation states the alleged purpose of Baal's claiming the kingship and the two final clauses are parallel. Hoping that the notion has now been simply and clearly explained and illustrated, I now hasten to add that the phenomenon itself was first detected by Greenstein, at first in a footnote, and then as a 'side-issue', in the course of his main discussion with Loewenstamm referred to above (Greenstein 1974: 96 n. 47; 1977: 79).[12] He notes 'that there are in Ugaritic several tricola of a type in which the first line expresses a summary statement, which the second and third lines elaborate'. Six examples of this structure are mentioned (which we shall adduce immediately) and Greenstein insists, correctly, that they are not 'staircases'. Beyond this, however, he does not go. Parallelism is not mentioned and the structure, therefore, is not described in the terms used above. (No Hebrew connections are noted.) The following are the passages referred to by Greenstein: KTU^2 1.15.III.17–19

			tity	*ilm*	*lahlhm*
			proceeded	the gods	to their tents,
tbrk	*ilm*	*tity*			
Blessed	the gods	and proceeded,			
			dr	*il*	*lmšknthm*
			the generation	of El	to their dwellings

---

12. My own apprehension of the structure was achieved during an examination of monocola in Ugaritic within the framework of a larger interest – the existence of regularity alongside irregularity throughout ancient Semitic poetry, which I take to be *the* problem of that poetry (and to which much research has been devoted, though not in the terms here stated). Only when rereading, after some years, the debate on the staircase, for the purposes of this paper, did I realize that what Greenstein was talking about was the forked tricolon (in my terms) and that I had reassembled the passages (amongst a dozen or so more) that he had first noticed.

In our opening example above, the word *ilm* of the first colon was repeated in the second colon. Here the same word together with another is repeated chiastically. This sort of repetition often, but not always, occurs. *KTU²* 1.15.II.18–20

			ybrk	*il*	*krt*	*tʿ*
			blesses	El	Kirta the Noble,	
brkm	*ybrk*	*ʿbdh*				
He lavishes	blessing	on his servant,				
			ymrm	*nʿmn*	*ġlm*	*il*
			He grants benison to the pleasant servitor of El			

The reading of this disputed passage has been most professionally reconstructed by Pardee with the help of the parallel passage *KTU²* 1.17.I.34–36. In fact the two passages reconstruct each other (Pardee 1977: 52–56). The parallel 'prongs' merely elaborate on El's blessing of his servant, mainly by using Kirta's stock epithets. In the second passage the same formulaic language is applied to Dnil with his own stock epithets. *KTU²* 1.14.II.9–11

		rḥṣ	*ydk*	*amt*
		wash	your hands	to the elbow,
trtḥṣ	*wtadm*			
Wash yourself	and make yourself red,			
		uṣbʿtk	*ʿd*	*ṭkm*
		your fingers	to the	shoulder

Here the 'forking' proceeds merely from the general to the particular. *KTU²* 1.14.II.13–15

		imr	*dbḥ*	*bm*	*ymn*
		a lamb	of sacrifice	in (your) right hand	
qh	*imr*	*bydk*			
Take	a lamb	in your hand,			
		lla	*klatnm*		
		a lambkin	in both (hands).		

With the threefold specification of lambs and hands all cola here are parallel. The second two appear to define the type of lamb more closely (also which hand/s, hardly successfully) but in fact the variations have the purpose merely of producing a pleasing parallelistic structure. *KTU²* 1.114.2–4

tštn	*yn*	*ᶜd*	*šbᶜ*
drink	wine	to	satiety,

tlḥmn	*ilm*	*wtštn*
Eat	gods	and drink,

trṯ	*ᶜd*	*škr*
new wine	to	drunkenness

The invitation to feast is general but the parallel cola place the emphasis firmly on the bibation.

Further examples include:

KTU² 1.17.VI.16–19

lnpš	*kṯr*	*wḥss*
for the throat	of	Skilful-and-Expert,

ᶜdb	*imr*	*bpḫd*
Prepare	a lamb	from the flock,

lbrlt	*hyn*	*dḥrš*	*yd*
for the gullet	of Hyn	of the	forge

KTU² 1.3.III.18–20 (and in fragmentary remains *KTU²* 1.1.II.1–2, 21–23; 1.1.III.10–11; 1.1.IV.11–12)

ᶜmy	*pᶜnk*	*tlsmn*
to me	your feet	let run,

ḥšk	*ᶜṣk*	*ᶜbṣk*
Stay	your stave	and your staff,

ᶜmy	*twtḥ*	*išdk*
to me	let hasten	your legs

In this case I have attempted to imitate the assonance of the first colon. The 'stave' and 'staff' however are weapons, 'club' and 'mace' or the like, the addressee being enjoined to leave off fighting – and hasten to join the sender of the message in a peaceful venture. This is a particularly lively example of the structure, the 'handle' of the fork consisting of the urgent message 'desist' and the parallel 'prongs' then urging 'and hurry to me'.
KTU² 1.5.VI.25–26 (1.6.II.15–17 almost identical)

kl	*ġr*	*lkbd*	*arṣ*
every	mountain	to the bowels	of the Earth,

ap	*ᶜnt*	*ttlk*	*wtṣd*
indeed	Anat	went to and fro	and scoured,

kl	*gbᶜ*	*lkbd*	*šdm*
every	hill	to the depths	of the fields

Here both parallel cola are object-clauses to the first. The repetitions together with the parallels leave no doubt as to how the structure was perceived by the poet.

A veritable set of cutlery, if selective, is employed at *KTU*[2] 1.2.I.21–29, where six 'forks' constitute almost the entire narrative:

			tphn	*mlak*	*ym*
			they see	the messengers	of Yam,
hlm	*ilm*	*tphhm*			
Behold	the gods	see them,			
			t'dt	*tpt*	*nhr*
			The deputation	of	Chief Nahar
			lzr	*brkthm*	
			upon	their knees,	
tġly[13]	*ilm*	*risthm*			
Lowered	the gods	their heads,			

                                    wlkht   *zblhm*
                                    and to the thrones   of their princedom

(*bhm ygʿr bʿl* Baal rebuked them [saying,])

                              lzr   *brktkm*
                              upon   your knees,
lm   *ġltm*   *ilm*   *rištkm*
Why have you lowered, gods,   your heads,

                                    wln   *kht*   *zblkm*
                                    and to   the thrones   of your princedom

                              lht[14]   *mlak*   *ym*
                              to the mandate of the messengers of Yam,
ahd   *ilm*   *tʿny*
I see,   gods,   you submit,

                                    t'dt   *tpt*   *nhr*
                                    the deputation   of   Chief Nahar

                              lzr   *brktkm*
                              from upon   your knees,
šu   *ilm*   *raštkm*
Lift,   gods,   your heads,

                                    ln   *kht*   *zblkm*
                                    from   the thrones   of your princedom

---

13. This tricolon has been mentioned in connection with an Akkadian structure (with a very strict 3:2:2 word-count) which may, in the history of Semitic prosody, have had some remote connection with the structure under discussion (Watson 1975: 485).

14. The meaning of this word is guessed on the basis of the parallelism since former suggestions seem strained; see however N. Wyatt (1998: 60 n. 108). Perhaps a *l* has dropped out before the word *lht*, tablets ? that is, commission.

(*wank*   *ʿny mlak ym*   *tʿdt*   *ṭpṭ*   *nhr*
and *I* answer the messengers of Yam the deputation of Chief Nahar)

                         lẓr   *brktkm*
                         from upon your knees,

tšu   *ilm*   *rašthm*
Lift,   the gods,   their heads,

                         ln   *kḥt*   *zblhm*
                         from the thrones of their princedom

The concentration of instances of the structure stems, of course, from the staggered epic repetition which the poet has found appropriate for this episode in the narrative.

An interesting example appears to occur at KTU^2 1.3.IV.43–44:

               ṭl   *šmm*   *tskh*
               Dew   (which) the heavens dispensed

ṭl   *šmm*   *šmn* *arṣ*
Dew of heaven, oil of earth,

               rbb   *nskh*   *kbkbm*
               showers (which) dispensed   the stars.

At first glance this looks like a typical example, but the preceding line seems to form a couplet, or bicolon, with the first colon of our 'fork'. If this is the case the parallel cola could follow a bicolon instead of a single colon. The line in question reads *tḥspn mh wtrḥṣ* 'she pours water and washes' (in the dew, etc., quoted above). Thus understood, the structure would have a longer handle:

                     ṭl šmm tskh
tḥspn mh wtrḥṣ   *ṭl šmm šmn arṣ*
                     rbb nskh kbkbm.

However, there is a further possibility. The first two cola of the longer version are not really parallel – but if we dismiss the idea of a bicolon the preceding words will be left as a monocolon, which I find very unlikely for a colon of this type. Could it be that the bicolon I have suggested is another 'forked' tricolon?

                 ṭl   *šmm*
tḥspn   *mh*   *wtrḥṣ*
                 šmn   *arṣ.*

If this be the case the parallel cola are very short compared with all the examples quoted above (I am comparing the presumed number of stresses in a colon together with word length). This, however, may not be decisive, and if we do have a short tricolon this would result in the structure

2. *ṭl šmm*   4. *ṭl šmm tskh*

1. *thspn   mh   wtrḥṣ*

3. *šmn arṣ*   5. *rbb nskh kbkbn.*

There are then, so far, several alternatives, none of which seem to me impossible, even, in the worst case, a preceding monocolon. But if this were not enough there is a further complication: the same passage occurs at *KTU²* 1.3.II.38–41 with an extra colon before the final parallel cola: *rbb rkb ʿrpt* 'showers of the rider on the clouds'. The solution I offer, is that two alternative ancient (oral?) versions have been combined by a scribe, but a colon was lost in transmission in the shorter version. This would yield the two original variant versions:

	ṭl	*šmm*	*šmn*	*arṣ*			*ṭl šmm tskh*
1. *thspn mh wtrḥṣ*					2. *thspn mh wtrḥṣ*		
			rbb	*rkb*	*ʿrpt*		*rbb nskh kbkbm*

The intended combined version is that which appears at *KTU²* 1.3.II.38–41, to be understood as:

2. *ṭl šmm šmn arṣ*   4. *ṭl šmm tskh*

1. *thspn   mh   wtrḥṣ*

3. *rbb rkb ʿrpt*   5. *rbb nskh kbkbm.*

If correct, this disposes of the unusual monocolon and avoids the conjecture concerning two very short parallel cola to remedy a bicolon without parallelism. It will be noticed that the two final parallel cola contain the *yqtl-qtl* tense-variation of the same verb narrating a past action which was mentioned in the foregoing section.

Finally, a fork with three prongs, though the exact sense of the third escapes us:

KTU² 1.4.I.25–28

				ysq	*ksp*	*lalpm*
				casts	silver (objects)	by the thousand,
ysq	*ksp*	*yšlḥ*	*ḥrṣ*			
He casts	silver	chases	gold			
				ḥrṣ	*ysqm*	*lrbbt*
				gold (objects)	he casts by the ten thousand	
				ysq	*ḥym*	*wtbṯ*
				he casts	?	?

Similar to this example (with two repeated words in the first prong) are *KTU²* 1.2.IV.12–13 and 19–21, despite Loewenstamm and Greenstein (Greenstein 1977: 79).

The Ugaritic structure discussed is reflected in parts of the earliest poetry of the Hebrew Scriptures. An appropriate start may be made with the 'Blessing of Jacob' in Genesis 49. A simple example is the last verse of the 'Blessing', v. 27:

	babbōqer	*yōʾkal*	*ʿad*
	in the morning	he devours	(the) prey

binyāmîn   *zᵉʾēb*   *yiṭrāp*
Benjamin is a ravining wolf,

	wᵉlāʿereb	*yᵉhallēq*	*šālāl*
	and in the evening	he divides	(the) spoil

The general description is followed by two parallel elaborations.

Verses 3–4 concerning Reuben conform to the same model. It is sufficient, I deem, to display them in a construe only (and this I shall do in the following where possible but *BHS* should be at hand!).

my power and height of my potency,
Reuben you are my firstborn,
abundant in prowess, abundant in strength.

For you mounted your father's bed,
Wanton as water, you will not survive,
Then you defiled the couch you mounted.

The parallelism of v. 8, on Judah, does not follow the model so neatly for the praise/subservience of his brothers appears both in the first and third cola; however, submission seems to be the theme of the second and third:

Your hand on the neck of your foes,
Judah, you, will (?) your brothers praise,
The sons of your father will (?) bow down to you.

From the 'Blessing' as a whole it is not clear that the references here must be to the future (*vaticinia ex eventu*). Even the notorious 'Shiloh' verse need not necessarily imply monarchy, whatever may be made of its text. This subject cannot be dismissed with a word, but my sympathies are with those who do not find monarchy to be a palpable theme of the poem. Like the Benjamin verse, v. 8 might be a general statement. At any rate the ancient structures seem to reflect an ancient period especially since it would appear difficult to find them in any much later text, as will be noted. The four instances of forked parallelism here in only twenty-seven verses would appear significant. The inclusion of Judah then, in a verse structured in this way, is striking.

At Exod. 15.8 we have a fine example taken from the old theomachy myth (Fenton 1978: 362):

> The billows became motionless as a mound,
And by the wind of your nostrils the waters became a heap,
> The depths became solid on the sea bed.

The reference is to the drying up of the Sea-god by Baal, *KTU²* 1.2.IV.27, reflected also in texts such as Isa. 19.5; Nah. 1.4. Literal translation here would not convey the mythical conception, whether or not it has been used, as other verses, in support of the historical reconceptualization.

The song of Deborah has one clear example, Judg. 5.3:

> I to Yahweh, I shall sing,
Hearken kings, give ear princes,
> I shall chant to Yahweh, the God of Israel.

It is in the 'Blessing of Moses', however, that we first find some highly significant material. The verse Deut. 33.5 clearly celebrates the establishment of the monarchy and merits full quotation:

	bᵉhit'assēp	*rā'šê*	*ʿām*
	when assembled	the chiefs	of the people
wayᵉhî bîšurūn melek			
and there arose in Yeshurun a king			
	yaḥad	*šōpᵉṭê* (for *šibᵉṭê*)	*yiśrā'ēl*
	together	the leaders	of Israel.

In the first colon the fact is stated, in the two parallel cola the vital attendant circumstances are stressed. The ancient epithet Yeshurun, whatever its sense, is associated with the event. Since the structure appears to be confined to the most ancient layers of Hebrew poetic composition it seems that we have a tricolon composed close in time to the event narrated, whatever changes the surrounding material might have undergone and whatever later additions there may be to the poem as a whole. At any rate, verses such as this were not composed in the Persian period! A further example of the structure, again with the name Yeshurun, occurs at v. 26:

	rōkēb	*šāmayim*	*bᵉ'uzzô* (?)[15]
	riding	the heavens	in his strength (?)
'ên kᵉ'ēl[16] yᵉšurūn			
There is none like the God of Yeshurun			
	ûbᵉga'ᵃwātô		*šᵉḥāqîm*
	and in his majesty		the skies.

---

15. MT is unclear and the second person pronominal suffix does not fit the rest of the verse.

16. MT pointed with the definite article is clearly mistaken: it yields no satisfactory meaning.

These two verses frame those concerned with each of the individual tribes, the first immediately preceding the 'Reuben' verse and the second immediately following the 'Asher' verses, which conclude the 'tribal sayings'. Here then, is a true *inclusio*, which signifies that under the leadership of the monarchy and the protection of Yahweh all will be well with Yeshurun. Two of the four instances of this name then, are shared by two corresponding verses from each end of an *inclusio* and are cast in the form of a Bronze Age poetic structure no longer in use, apparently, after the initial period of the monarchy. My conclusion is that these verses are contemporary with that period and that their content, however circumscribed, is evidence for its events and thought. Again the mention of Judah within the framework may be significant. In this instance we have no poetic structure to suggest a dating for v. 7, which contains but a heading and two bicola. The MT is interesting, however, in that it implies an ambivalence in Judah's relationship with Israel, 'Hear, Yahweh, the voice of Judah and bring him to his people'. The Septuagint reading is different, and somewhat strange, but we cannot examine these matters here. Suffice to say that *should* the MT preserve a correct text and *should* that text be contemporary with the *inclusio*, or not much later, it would be inappropriate to the notion that Judah and Israel were totally different entities with no consciousness of a relationship in the eleventh century BCE. In their different ways the verses on Judah in the two Blessings seem to point in the same direction.

Despite textual difficulties v. 8 seems to furnish a further clear example. The first colon may have the general sense 'The Thummim and Urim are the privilege of those who proved loyal to you (i.e. the Levites)' and the following parallel cola read 'whom you tested at Massah, tried by the waters of Meribah', the text and meaning being guaranteed by the puns on the place names.

Verse 12 also appears to contain the structure, though the text is in a state of disorder and the exact sense unclear. On the other hand v. 13 provides an excellent instance:

> from the bounty of the heavens above
>
> Blessed of Yahweh is his land
>
> and from the deep crouching below.

The parallel 'above–below' (as Gen. 49.25) is obviously to be restored by the change of one letter and the strange description of subterranean water is a literary conceit which arises from the 'consubstantiality' of Tiamat, the underground sea and sea-monster.

These five instances of the forked tricolon in the 'Blessing of Moses', together with the four of the 'Blessing of Jacob', constitute by far the majority of clear Hebrew examples known to me. The pièce de résistance however, is contained in the 'Lament of David',

2 Sam. 1.22:

> qešet   yᵉhônātān   lōʾ   nāśôg ʾāhôr
> the bow   of Jonathan   did not turn back

middam   *ḥᵃlālîm*   *mēḥēleb*   *gibbôrîm*
From the blood of the slain, from the fat   of the warriors

> wᵉhereb   šāʾûl   lōʾ   tāšûb   rêqām
> and the sword of Saul did not return for nought.

To what has been written on the quality of this verse as poetry I would add only that much of it is due to the adroit handling of the forked parallelism. For our purpose the historical significance is of more concern. This, I believe, is the latest example of the structure which is clearly identifiable. It echoes the specific historical events and circumstances of its immediate and broader context. The structure then, indicates that the events and their background could not have been invented in a later age. They are the subject of poetry which employs a structure which hardly survived the end of the Bronze Age. There is a further example in v. 24:

> hammalbišᵉkem   šānî   ʿim   ʿᵃdānîm
> who clothed you in scarlet   with finery

bᵉnôt   *yiśrāʾēl*   *ʾel-šāʾûl*   *bᵉkeynâ*
Daughters of Israel   over Saul   weep,

> hammaʿᵃleh   ʿᵃdî   zāhāb   ʿal   lᵉbûšᵉken
> who put ornaments of gold on your raiment.

In this poem the style is so even and the subject-matter so concentrated that there is no reason to suspect layers or additions from different periods; and the piece is so clearly a response to recent tragedy that, apart from the question of dating, it constitutes historically reliable testimony to the events and to the circumstances which it depicts. This would extend also to the personalities concerned, even to the existence of a special friendship between Jonathan and David, and thereby, to confirmation of much of what is said elsewhere about David and the House of Saul. If tradition placed the lament on the lips of David, that would reflect, at least, a genuine historical situation.

A search for survivals and transformations of forked parallelism of the type so common in the case of mixed tricola and staircase bicola would appear to hold little prospect of success. One might mention Ps. 12.7 (ET 6), which appears to be a very ancient wisdom saying, despite some textual mishaps. There may be echoes in Pss 79.1-2, 13; 99.8; 143.5. One will notice a looseness of composition, lack of differentiation between 'handle' and 'prongs' in form or idea, or both; above all a lack of liveliness in conception and language. In fact tricola in the Psalms tend to be loosely put together and one might suspect that the resemblances to the structure arise from accident rather than from a linear tradition. But in one case one can reconstruct a genuine example, I believe, which, however, belongs to the most ancient period. The antiquity of Psalm 93 was stressed in the section on mixed tricola. A 'fork' may also be discerned in v. 1a. Lack of balance has always been noted here and the difficulty has been associated with the repetition of *lābēš*. The verb *'āzar* however is several times constructed with *ḥayil* as its object and if the words *yhwh ḥayil* are added the balance is restored, the result being a forked tricolon with 4:3:3 rhythm, as often:

				lābēš	*yhwh*	*'ōz*
				Is clothed	Yahweh	in strength
yhwh	*mālāk*		*gē'ût*	*lābēš*		
Yahweh	has become king,		he is	clothed in majesty		
				hit'azzēr	*yhwh*	*ḥāyil*
				has donned	Yahweh	might.

4. *Conclusion*

Comparison of Hebrew poetic structures with ancient Canaanite models establishes the antiquity of those structures and of historical material associated with them. Where the structure is reused in a context not original to it, interfered with, broken open or added to, in order to bring it into conformity with later literary preferences and religious ideas, it attests to continuous literary development. Details of content show that the time span of the biblical Hebrew literary tradition runs from at least the eleventh century BCE to the Persian period. Our structures fail to tell us anything beyond this point, for, to the extent that I have succeeded in checking, they have ceased to exist. But it is with the early periods that we have been concerned here.

Bibliography

Avishur, Y.
　　1972　　'Addenda to the Expanded Colon in Ugaritic and Biblical Verse', *UF* 4: 1–10.
Dietrich, M., O. Loretz and J. Sanmartín
　　1995　　*The Cuneiform Alphabetic Texts (KTU:* 2nd enlarged edn*)* (Münster: Ugarit-Verlag).
Fenton, T.L.
　　1978　　'Differing Approaches to the Theomachy Myth in Old Testament Writers', in Y. Avishur and J. Blau (eds), *Studies in Bible and the Ancient Near East Presented to Samuel E. Loewenstamm on his Seventieth Birthday* (2 vols.; Jerusalem: E. Rubinstein's Publishing House): 337–81 (Hebrew; summary in English vol.: 191–93).
　　1994　　'Nexus and Significance: is Greater Precision Possible?', in George J. Brooke,

Adrian H.W. Curtis and John F. Healey (eds), *Ugarit and the Bible* (UBL, 11; Münster: Ugarit-Verlag): 71–91.

Ginsberg, H.L.
1936   'The Rebellion and Death of Ba'lu', *Or* 5: 161–98.
1938   'Ba'l and 'Anat', *Or* 7: 1–11.

Greenstein, E.L.
1974   'Two Variations of Grammatical Parallelism in Canaanite Poetry and their Psycholinguistic Background', *JANESCU* 6: 87–105.
1977   'One More Step on the Staircase', *UF* 9: 77–86.

Held, M.
1962   'The YQTL-QTL (QTL-YQTL) Sequence of Identical Verbs in Biblical Hebrew and in Ugaritic', in M. Ben-Horin (ed.), *Studies in Honour of Abraham A. Neuman* (Leiden: E.J. Brill): 281–90.

Loewenstamm, S.E.
1969   'The Expanded Colon in Ugaritic and Biblical Verse', *JSS* 14: 176–96.
1975   'The Expanded Colon, Reconsidered', *UF* 7: 261–64.
1980   *Comparative Studies in Biblical and Ancient Oriental Literatures* (AOAT, 204; Neukirchen–Vluyn: Neukirchener Verlag).

Pardee, D.
1977   'An Emendation in the Ugaritic Aqht Text', *JNES* 36: 53–56.
1978   'A Philological and Prosodic Analysis of the Ugaritic Serpent Incantation UT 607', *JANESCU* 10: 73–108.
1988   *Les Textes Para-mythologiques de la 24e Campagne (1961)* (Ras Shamra-Ougarit, 4; Paris: Editions Recherche sur les Civilisations).

Watson, W.G.E.
1975   'Verse-Patterns in Ugaritic, Akkadian and Hebrew Poetry', *UF* 7: 483–92.
1977   'Ugaritic and Mesopotamian Literary Texts', *UF* 9: 273–84.
1984a   'Allusion, Irony and Wordplay in Micah 1, 7', *Bib* 65: 103–105.
1984b   *Classical Hebrew Poetry: A Guide to its Techniques* (JSOTSup, 26; Sheffield: Sheffield Academic Press).

Wyatt, N.
1998   *Religious Texts from Ugarit: The Words of Ilimilku and his Colleagues* (The Biblical Seminar, 53; Sheffield: Sheffield Academic Press).

Young, D.W.
1977   'With Snakes and Dates: A Sacred Marriage Drama at Ugarit', *UF* 9: 291–314.

INDEXES

INDEX OF REFERENCES

OLD TESTAMENT

Please note that where Hebrew and English verse numbers differ,
the Index refers to the Hebrew numbering

APOCRYPHA

NEW TESTAMENT

INDEX OF AUTHORS